Microsoft® Office Access 2010

A Lesson Approach, Complete

Microsoft® Office Access 2010
A Lesson Approach, Complete

Jon Juarez

John Carter

Connect
Learn
Succeed™

The McGraw-Hill Companies

Mc
Graw
Hill

Connect
Learn
Succeed™

MICROSOFT® OFFICE ACCESS® 2010: A LESSON APPROACH, COMPLETE

ISBN   978-0-07-733124-5
MHID   0-07-733124-9

Vice president/Editor in chief: *Elizabeth Haefele*
Vice president/Director of marketing: *John E. Biernat*
Executive editor: *Scott Davidson*
Developmental editor: *Alan Palmer*
Marketing manager: *Tiffany Wendt*
Lead digital product manager: *Damian Moshak*
Digital developmental editor: *Kevin White*
Director, Editing/Design/Production: *Jess Ann Kosic*
Lead project manager: *Rick Hecker*
Buyer II: *Sherry L. Kane*
Senior designer: *Marianna Kinigakis*
Media project manager: *Cathy L. Tepper*
Interior design: *Kay Lieberherr*
Typeface: *10.5/13 New Aster*
Compositor: *Aptara, Inc.*
Printer: *R. R. Donnelley*

Library of Congress Cataloging-in-Publication Data

Juarez, Jon.
  Microsoft Office Access 2010: a lesson approach, complete / Jon Juarez, John Carter.
    p. cm.
  Includes index.
  ISBN-13: 978-0-07-733124-5 (alk. paper)
  ISBN-10: 0-07-733124-9 (alk. paper)
  1. Microsoft Access. 2. Database management. I. Carter, John, 1949- II. Title.
QA76.9.D3J824 2011
005.75'65—dc22

                        2010028934

CONTENTS

ACCESS 2010

UNIT 1 Understanding Access Databases

UNIT 2 *Designing and Managing Database Objects*

Unit 3 *Integrating Database Objects*

Unit 4 *Using Advanced Database Features*

Microsoft Access 2010: A Lesson Approach is written to help you master Microsoft Access. The text guides you step by step through the Access features that you are likely to use in both your personal and business life.

Case Study

Learning the features of Access is one component of the text, and applying what you learn is another component. A case study has been created to offer an opportunity to learn Access in a realistic business context. Take the time to read the case study about EcoMed Services, Inc., a fictional business located in Kansas City, Missouri. All the documents for this course relate to EcoMed Services, Inc.

Organization of the Text

The text includes four units, and each unit is divided into lessons. There are fifteen lessons, each self-contained but building on previously learned skills. This building-block approach, together with the case study and the following features, enables you to maximize the learning process.

Features of the Text

- Objectives are listed for each lesson.
- The estimated time required to complete each lesson up to the Summary section is stated.
- Within a lesson, each heading corresponds to an objective.
- Easy-to-follow exercises emphasize learning by doing.
- Key terms are italicized and defined as they are encountered.
- Extensive graphics display screen contents.
- Ribbon commands and keyboard keys are shown in the text when used.
- Lessons contain important notes, useful tips, and helpful reviews.
- The Lesson Summary reviews the important concepts taught in the lesson.
- The Command Summary lists the commands taught in the lesson.
- Concepts Review includes true/false, short answer, and critical thinking questions that focus on lesson content.
- Skills Review provides skill reinforcement for each lesson.
- Lesson Applications ask you to apply your skills in a more challenging way.
- On Your Own exercises prompt you to apply your skills creatively.
- Unit Applications give you the opportunity to practice the skills you have learned throughout a unit.

- The text includes a glossary and an index. Appendixes include Leszynski naming conventions and systems analysis and design. An Appendix of Microsoft's Certification standards is also available on the Lesson Approach Web site at www.mhhe.com/lessonapproach2010.

Lesson Approach Web Site

Visit the Lesson Approach Web site at www.mhhe.com/lessonapproach2010 to access a wealth of additional materials.

Conventions Used in the Text

This text uses a number of conventions to help you learn the program and save your work.

- Text to be keyed appears either in **red** or as a separate figure.
- File names appear in **boldface**.
- Options that you choose from tabs and dialog boxes, but that aren't buttons, appear in green; for example, "Choose **Print** from the File tab."
- You are asked to save each document with your initials followed by the exercise name. For example, an exercise might end with this instruction: "Save the document as *[your initials]*4-12." Documents are saved in folders for each lesson.

If You Are Unfamiliar with Windows

If you are not familiar with Windows, review the next section, "Windows Tutorial," before beginning Lesson 1. This tutorial provides a basic overview of Microsoft's operating system and shows you how to use the mouse. You might also want to review "File Management" on the Lesson Approach Web site to get more comfortable with files and folders.

Screen Differences

As you practice each concept, illustrations of the screens help you follow the instructions. Don't worry if your screen is different from the illustration. These differences are due to variations in system and computer configurations.

You will need Microsoft Access 2010 to work through this textbook. Access 2010 needs to be installed on the computer's hard drive or on a network.

If you are not familiar with Windows, review this "Windows Tutorial" carefully. You will learn how to:

- Use a mouse.
- Start Windows and explore window features.
- Use the taskbar, menus, Ribbon, dialog boxes, and other important aspects of Windows.
- Practice using Search and Help.
- End a computer session.

If you are familiar with Windows but need help navigating Windows files and folders, refer to the "File Management" tutorial. There you will find information on how Windows stores information and how to use Windows Explorer, a tool for managing files and folders.

Computers differ in the ways they can be configured. In most cases, when you turn on your computer, Windows loads automatically and the Windows log-on screen appears. When you see the Windows log-on screen, you need to log on and key a password. In order to log on, you need to know how to use the mouse.

Using the Mouse

A *mouse* is a pointing device and is your access to the computer screen, allowing you to accomplish specific tasks. A mouse typically has two buttons—one on the left (primary) and one on the right (secondary). A mouse might also have a center button or a wheel. To use a mouse, place your right index finger over the left mouse button. Place your thumb on the left side of the mouse. (Left-handed users can switch mouse button functions by using the Control Panel.)

The mouse operates through a pointer, a screen object you use to point to objects on the computer screen. The normal shape for the mouse pointer is an arrow . To move the pointer arrow on the screen, you roll the mouse on any flat object, or on a mouse pad, which has a smooth surface designed for easy mouse rolling. Although you can use the keyboard with Windows, you will probably find yourself using the mouse most of the time.

To use the mouse to point to an object on the computer screen:

1. Turn on the computer (if it is not on already). Windows loads, and the log-on screen appears. The screen includes at least one log-on name and picture. If the computer has multiple users, you will see several names and pictures.

To log on, you need to move the mouse pointer to the log-on name that was assigned to you when your user account was created. The pointer on the computer screen mirrors the actions made by the mouse when you roll it. Place your hand over the mouse and roll it to the left. The pointer on the screen moves to the left.

NOTE

Laptop computers typically use a touch pad to select or move objects rather than a mouse.

NOTE

All examples in this tutorial refer specifically to Windows 7 using the Aero desktop feature. If you are using any other version of Windows, your screen might differ slightly from the images shown in this tutorial. However, because most basic features are common to all versions of Windows, this tutorial should be helpful to you no matter which version of Windows you use.

2. Roll the mouse to the right, and watch the pointer on the screen move to the right.

3. Practice rolling the mouse in all directions.

4. Roll your mouse to the edge of the pad, and then lift it up and place it back in the middle of the pad. When you feel that you can control the mouse position on the screen, roll the mouse to the name you have been assigned.

To log on, you will need to click the name to select it. Mouse clicks are covered in the next section; instructions for logging on to Windows 7 are covered in succeeding sections.

Clicks and Double-Clicks

Pointing is a mouse action used to position the mouse pointer at a specific screen location. The tip of the mouse pointer should be touching the object on the screen. You may see a ScreenTip when you point to an object. A *ScreenTip* identifies or describes the object or command.

Figure 1
ScreenTip

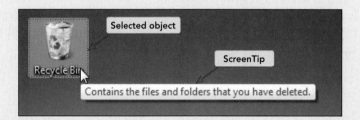

Single-click actions with the mouse are used to select objects or commands. To practice a single click:

1. Roll the mouse around on the mouse pad until the pointer on the screen is over the Recycle Bin icon. Remember that the direction in which you move the mouse on the pad represents the pointer's movement on the screen.

2. Press and release the left mouse button once. Pressing and releasing the mouse button is referred to as a *click*. The computer tells you that the action has been performed when the object you click is *highlighted* (typically, the color of the selected object changes) to indicate to you that it has been *selected*. In Windows, you often need to select an object before you can perform an action. For example, you usually need to select an object before you can copy it. Click a blank area of the computer screen to deselect the Recycle Bin icon.

Pressing and releasing the mouse button twice is referred to as a *double-click*. When you double-click an object on the screen, it is selected—the object is highlighted—and an action is performed. For example:

When you double-click a folder, it is highlighted and opens to a window showing the items the folder contains.

When you double-click a word in a text file, it is selected for a future action. In a text file, the pointer becomes an I-beam for selecting text in the document.

1. Point to and double-click the Recycle Bin icon. The Recycle Bin window displays.

Figure 2
Recycle Bin window

2. Locate and point to the red button in the upper-right corner of the Recycle Bin window. A ScreenTip identifies the Close button.
3. Click the Close button one time to close the Recycle Bin window.

NOTE

Whenever you are told to "click" or "double-click" an object on the computer screen, use the left mouse button. If you have difficulty double-clicking an object, adjust the double-click speed by opening the Mouse Properties dialog box. (Control Panel—Hardware and Sound—Mouse—Buttons tab)

Selecting and Highlighting

You can also select a larger object such as a picture or a block of text by using the mouse. Position the pointer on one side of the object, and hold down the left mouse button. Roll the mouse until the pointer reaches the other side of the object. Release the mouse button. The selected object is highlighted.

Drag and Drop—Moving an Object Using the Mouse

You can use the mouse to move an object on the screen to another screen location. In this operation, you select an object and drag the mouse to move the selected object, such as an icon. The operation is known as *drag and drop*. Follow the steps listed below to drag and drop objects.

1. Using the mouse, move the pointer over the object you want to drag.
2. Press the left mouse button but keep it pressed down. The selected object will be highlighted.
3. With the left mouse button still depressed, roll the mouse until the pointer and selected object are placed at the desired new location.
4. Release the mouse button to drop the object. The object is now positioned at the new location.

Using the Right Mouse Button

Pressing and quickly releasing the right mouse button is referred to as a *right-click*. Although the right mouse button is used less frequently, using it can be a real time-saver. When you right-click an icon, a *shortcut menu* appears with a list of commands. The list of commands displayed varies for each icon or object.

Figure 3
Shortcut menu

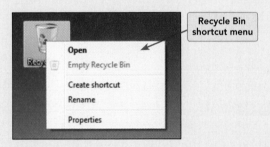

As you progress in this tutorial, you will become familiar with the terms in Table 1, describing the actions you can take with a mouse.

TABLE 1 Mouse Terms

TERM	DESCRIPTION
Point	Roll the mouse until the tip of the pointer is touching the desired object on the computer screen.
Click	Quickly press and release the left mouse button. Single-clicking selects objects.
Double-click	Quickly press and release the left mouse button twice. Double-clicking selects an object and performs an action such as opening a folder.
Drag	Point to an object on-screen, hold down the left mouse button, and roll the mouse until the pointer is in position. Then release the mouse button (drag and drop).
Right-click	Quickly press and release the right mouse button. A shortcut menu appears.
Select	When working in Windows, you must first select an object in order to work with it. Many objects are selected with a single click. However, depending on the size and type of object to be selected, you may need to roll the mouse to include an entire area: Holding down the left mouse button, roll the mouse so that the pointer moves from one side of an object to another. Then release the mouse button.

Pointer Shapes

As you perform actions on screen using the mouse, the mouse pointer changes its shape, depending on where it is located and what operation you are performing. Table 2 shows the most common types of mouse pointers.

TABLE 2 Frequently Used Mouse Pointers

SHAPE	NAME	DESCRIPTION
	Pointer	Used to point to objects.
	I-Beam	Used in keying text, inserting text, and selecting text.
	Two-headed arrow	Used to change the size of objects or windows.
	Four-headed arrow	Used to move objects.
	Busy	Indicates the computer is processing a command. While the busy or working in background pointer is displayed, it is best to wait rather than try to continue working. Note: Some of the working in background actions will not allow you to perform other procedures until processing is completed.
	Working in background	
	Link Select	Used to select a *link* in Windows' Help or other programs.

Starting Windows: The Log-on Screen

The Windows 7 log-on screen allows several people to use the same computer at different times. Each person is assigned a user account that determines which files and folders can be accessed and personal preferences, such as your desktop background. Each person's files are hidden from other users. However, users may share selected files using the Public folder. The log-on screen lists each user allocated to the computer by name.

If the administrator has added your name to a given computer, the log-on screen will include your name. If the computers are not assigned to specific individuals, you may find a box for Guest or for a generic user. If your computer is on a network, your instructor might need to provide you with special start-up instructions.

After you have logged on to Windows 7, the *desktop* is the first screen you will see. It is your on-screen work area. All the elements you need to start working with Windows appear on the desktop.

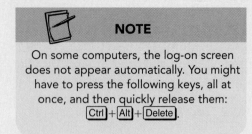

NOTE

On some computers, the log-on screen does not appear automatically. You might have to press the following keys, all at once, and then quickly release them: Ctrl + Alt + Delete .

1. If you have not already turned on the computer, do so now to begin the Windows 7 loading process. The Windows log-on screen appears.

2. Click your name to select it. The Password box appears with an I-beam in position ready for you to key your password.

3. Key your password.

4. Click the arrow icon to the right of the box. If you have entered the password correctly, the Windows desktop appears. If you made an error, the Password box returns for you to key the correct password.

The Windows Desktop

The Windows Desktop includes the Start button, taskbar, and Notification area. You may also see icons on the desktop that represent folders, programs, or other objects. You can add and delete icons from the desktop as well as change the desktop background. The Start button is your entry into Windows 7 functions.

Figure 4
Windows 7 Desktop

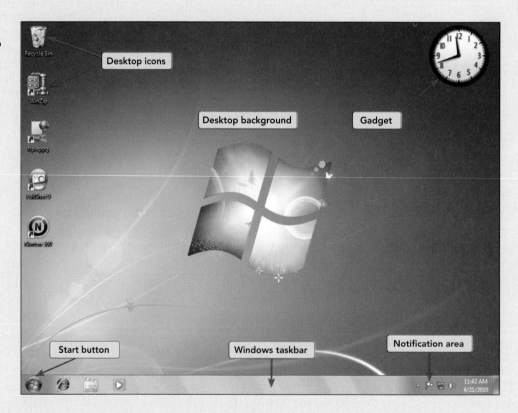

Using the Start Menu

Click the Start button 🌐 on the Windows taskbar to open the Start menu. You can also press the Windows logo key on the keyboard or press Ctrl + Esc to open the Start menu. Use the Start menu to launch programs, adjust computer settings, search for files and folders, and turn off the computer. If this is a computer assigned to you for log-on, your Start menu may contain items that differ from those of another user assigned to the same computer

1. To open and learn about the Start menu, first click the Start button on the Windows taskbar. The Start menu appears.

Figure 5
Start menu

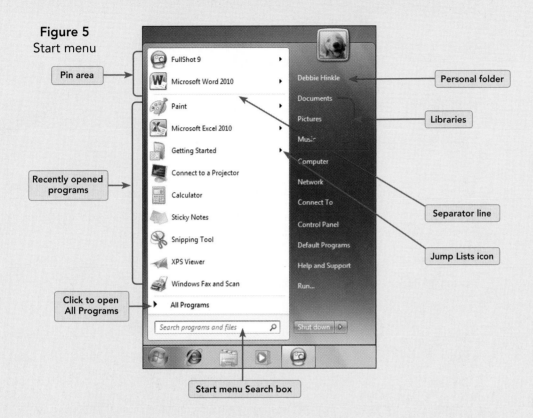

Pin area

Recently opened programs

Click to open All Programs

Personal folder

Libraries

Separator line

Jump Lists icon

Start menu Search box

The left pane consists of three sections divided by separator lines. The top section, called the *pin area*, lists programs that are always available for you to open. These programs can include your Internet browser, e-mail program, your word processor, and so forth. You can remove programs you do not want listed, rearrange them, and add those you prefer.

Below the separator line are shortcuts to programs you use most often, placed there automatically by Windows. You can remove programs you do not want listed, rearrange them, but not add any manually. The Recently opened programs list displays up to ten programs. Use the Jump Lists icon  for quick access to documents, files, or tasks. Simply click the Jump Lists icon ⏵, and a submenu appears to the right of the Start menu program. *All Programs* displays a list of programs on your computer and is used to launch programs not listed on the Start menu.

Below the left pane is the *Search box,* which is used to locate programs and files on your computer.

The right pane is also divided into three sections. It is used to select folders, files, and commands and to change settings. Use the Shut down button at the bottom of the right pane to end the computer session.

2. Close the Start menu by clicking a blank area of the desktop.

NOTE

The list of programs in your Start menu is dynamic. Installing new programs adds new items to the Start menu. Frequently used programs are placed in the left pane of the Start menu automatically.

Table 3 describes the typical components of the Start menu.

TABLE 3 Typical Components of the Start Menu

COMMAND	USE
Left Pane	
Pin area	Lists programs that are always available. You can add and delete items to the pin area.
Below the First Separator Line	
Programs	Lists programs that you use most often. You can add to and rearrange the programs listed.
Below the Second Separator Line	
All Programs	Click to display a list of programs in alphabetical order and a list of folders. Click to open a program.
Search	Use to search programs and folders. Key text and results appear.
Right Pane	
Personal folder	Opens the User folder.
Documents	Opens the Documents library.
Pictures	Opens the Pictures library.
Music	Opens the Music library.
Games	Opens the Games library.
Computer	Opens a window where you can access disk drives and other hardware devices.
Network	Opens the Network window where you can access computers and other devices on your network.
Connect To	Displays networks and other connections that you can access.
Control Panel	Opens the Control Panel.
Devices and Printers	Opens a window where you can view devices installed on your computer.
Default Programs	Opens the Default Programs window where you can define default programs and settings.
Help and Support	Opens the Windows Help and Support window. Help offers instructions on how to perform tasks in the Windows environment.
Run	Opens a program, folder, document, or Web site.
Shut down button	Turns off the computer.

Using the All Programs Command

Most programs on your computer can be started from the All Programs command on the Start menu. This is the easiest way to open a program not listed directly on the Start menu.

1. To open the All Programs menu, click the Start button 🖲. The Start menu appears.

2. Click **All Programs** or the triangle to the left near the bottom of the left pane. The All Programs menu appears, listing the programs installed on your computer. Every computer has a different list of programs. Notice that some menu entries have an icon to the left of the name and others display a folder. Click a folder, and a list of programs stored in that folder appears. Point to a program to see a short description of the program. Click a program to open it.

Figure 6
All Programs

Program icons

Folder containing programs

Click arrow to return to opening Start menu

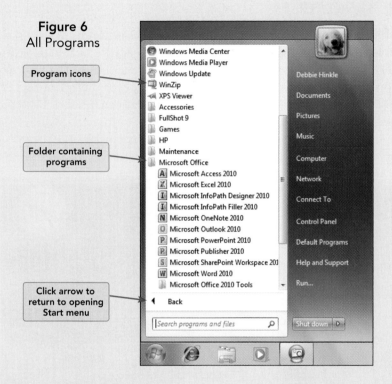

3. Click **Microsoft Office** to open a list of programs in the Microsoft Office folder. Click **Microsoft Word 2010**. (See Figure 6.) In a few seconds, the Word program you selected loads and the Word window appears. Notice that a button for the Word program 🗑 appears on the taskbar. Press Alt + F4 to close the window.

Customizing the Start Menu

Both the Start menu and the desktop can be customized. You can add shortcuts to the desktop if you prefer, and you can add and delete items from the Start menu. However, if your computer is used by others, the administrator may limit some customization functions.

To add a program to the pin area of the Start menu:

1. Point to the program you want to add to the pin list from the All Programs menu, and right-click it. A shortcut menu appears.

2. Click **Pin To Start Menu** on the shortcut menu. The program will be added to the pin list in the left pane above the first separator line.

To remove a program from the pin area of the Start menu:

1. Point to the program you want to remove from the pin list, and right-click. A shortcut menu appears.
2. Click Unpin From Start Menu. The program will be removed from the pin list.

To change the order in which programs are listed in the pin area:

1. Point to the program icon.
2. Drag the icon to the desired position.

Using the Taskbar

The taskbar at the bottom of your screen is one of the most important features in Windows 7. The taskbar is divided into several segments, each dedicated to a different use. The taskbar displays a button for launching Internet Explorer, Windows Explorer, and Windows Media Player, and each of these buttons is pinned to the taskbar. Point to each button to display a ScreenTip. The taskbar shows programs that are running, and you can use the taskbar to switch between open programs and between open documents within a program. A thumbnail preview appears when you move the mouse over a button on the taskbar.

Figure 7
The desktop and the taskbar

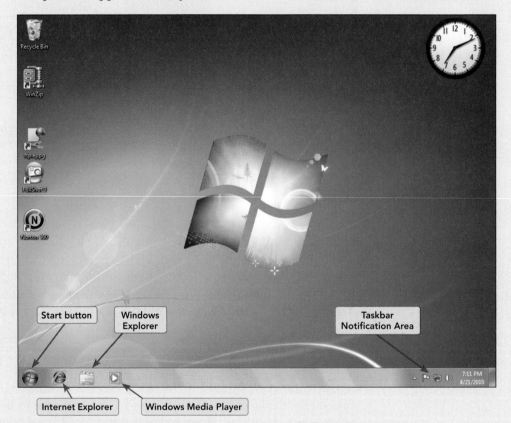

Taskbar Notification Area

The *notification area* is on the right side of the taskbar, where the current time is usually displayed. Along with displaying the time, tiny icons notify you as to the status of your browser connection, virus protection, and so forth. In the interest of removing clutter, the notification area hides most of the icons. Clicking the Show Hidden Icons button ▲ "hides" or "unhides" the icons in the tutorial notification area. Point to an icon to see a ScreenTip. Click an icon to open the control or program.

The Taskbar Notification area also includes the Show Desktop button ▌. The Show Desktop button appears at the right side of the taskbar. When you point to the Show Desktop button, the open program windows become transparent, and the desktop displays. The Show Desktop button is a toggle button. Click the Show Desktop button one time to minimize all open programs. Click again to display the programs. The *minimize* command temporarily removes a window from the desktop.

Figure 8
Taskbar Notification area

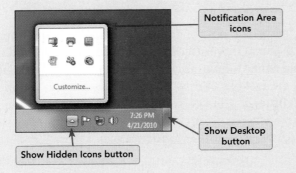

The Active Window

The window in which you are working is called the *active window*. The title bar for the active window is highlighted, and its taskbar button is also highlighted.

1. Click the **Start** button and then click **All Programs, Microsoft Office, Microsoft Word 2010** from the Start menu. The Word window displays.

2. Click the **Start** button and then click **All Programs, Microsoft Office, Microsoft Excel 2010** from the Start menu. The Excel window displays. Notice how the Excel window covers the Word window, indicating that the window containing Excel is now active. Notice, too, that a new button for Excel has been added to the taskbar ▣.

Figure 9
Excel (the active window) covering the Word window

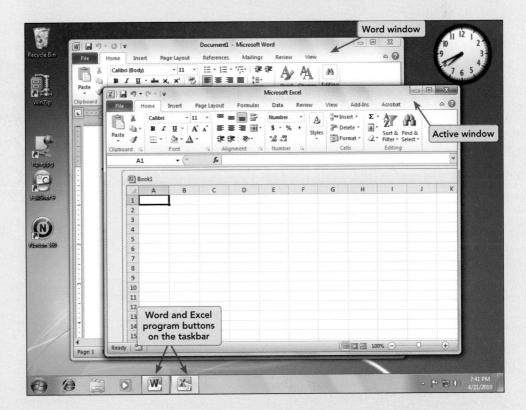

3. Click the button on the taskbar for Word, the first program you opened. Word reappears in front of Excel. Notice the change in the appearance of the title bar for each program.

4. Click the button on the taskbar for Excel. Notice that you switch back to Excel.

5. Click the Word button on the taskbar to return to Word.

Changing the Size of the Taskbar

You can change the size of the taskbar using your mouse if your toolbar is crowded. It is usually not necessary, because of the multiple document style buttons and other hide/unhide arrows on the taskbar. Before you can change the size of the taskbar, it may be necessary for you to unlock it. To unlock the taskbar, right-click an open area of the taskbar and click **Lock the Taskbar** to remove the checkmark. A checkmark is a toggle command. Click to turn it off, and click a second time to turn it on.

1. Move the pointer to the top edge of the taskbar until it changes from a pointer to a two-headed arrow ⭥. Using the two-headed arrow, you can change the size of the taskbar.

2. With the pointer displayed as a two-headed arrow, hold down the left mouse button and move the arrow up until the taskbar enlarges upward.

3. Move the pointer to the top edge of the taskbar once again until the two-headed arrow displays. Hold down the left mouse button, and move the arrow down to the bottom of the screen. The taskbar is restored to its original size.

4. Close the Word and Excel programs by clicking the Close button ⊠ for each program.

Parts of a Windows

Windows 7 displays programs and files in windows. When multiple windows display on the desktop, you will notice several common features in their appearance. Study the following windows and notice the similarities.

Figure 10
Notepad window

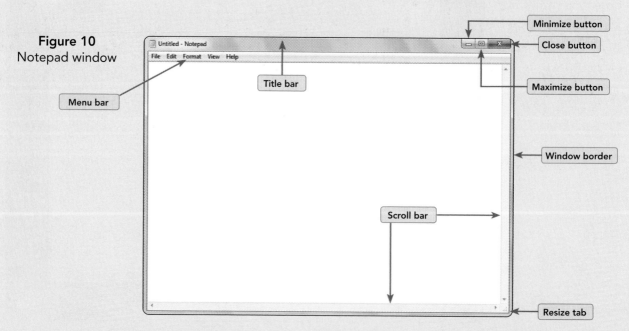

Figure 11
Microsoft Word
window

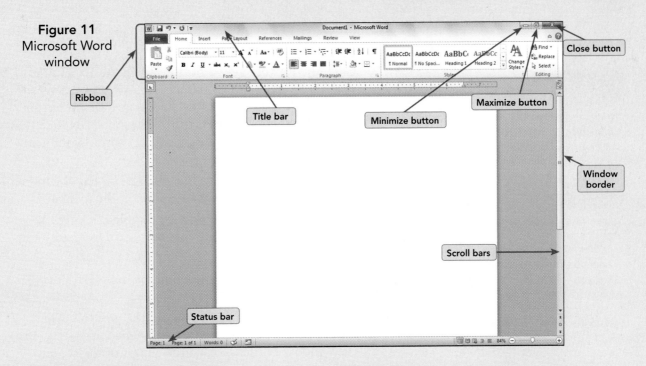

Ribbon

Title bar

Minimize button

Maximize button

Close button

Window
border

Scroll bars

Status bar

NOTE

Notice that the window occupies the entire desktop, and the Maximize button has changed to a Restore Down button. This type of function is known as a toggle: When a button representing one state (Maximize) is clicked, an action is performed, the button toggles to the alternate state, and the other button (Restore Down) appears. A number of actions in Windows operate this way.

Changing the Size of a Window

You can change the size of any window using either the mouse or the sizing buttons. Sizing buttons are the small buttons on the right side of the title bar that allow you to minimize or maximize the window (see Figures 10 and 11). This can be especially useful when you would like to display several open windows on your desktop and see them simultaneously.

1. Open the Word and Excel programs if necessary. Click the Maximize button on the Excel title bar if the Excel window does not fill the entire desktop.

Table 4 describes the sizing buttons.

TABLE 4 Sizing Buttons

BUTTON	USE
Minimize	Reduces the window to a button on the taskbar.
Maximize	Enlarges the window to fill the entire desktop (appears only when a window is reduced).
Restore Down	Returns the window to its previous size and desktop position (appears only when a window is maximized).

To practice changing the size of a window using the sizing buttons, follow these steps:

2. Click the **Restore Down** button on the Excel title bar. The Excel window reduces in size, and the Word window appears behind it. The Restore Down button has now changed to a Maximize button. Notice that the highlighted title bar of the Excel window indicates it is the active window.

3. Click the Excel **Minimize** button. The Excel window disappears, and its button appears on the taskbar.

4. Maximize the Word window by double-clicking the title bar. Double-click the title bar again to restore the window.

To practice resizing a window using the mouse, follow these steps:

5. Point to the lower right corner of the window. The mouse pointer changes to a two-headed arrow. Drag the window border toward the center of the screen. Drag the window border down and to the right to enlarge the window.

Figure 12
Sizing a window using the mouse

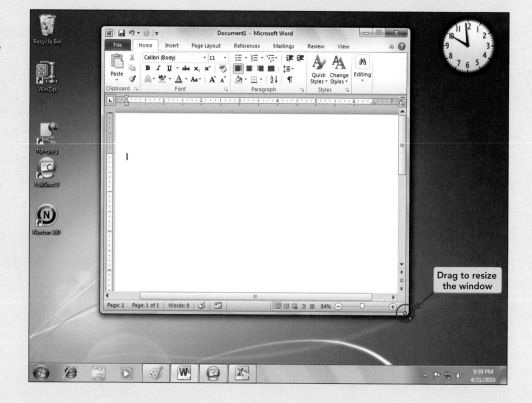

NOTE

You can place the pointer on any part of the window border to change its size. To change both the height and width of the window, move the pointer to the bottom right corner of the window. The double-headed arrow changes its orientation to a 45-degree angle (see Figure 12). Dragging this arrow resizes a window vertically and horizontally. Dragging a window border (top, bottom, left, or right) changes the vertical or horizontal size of the window. Sometimes the borders of a window can move off the computer screen. If you are having trouble with one border of a window, try another border or drag the entire window onto the screen by using the title bar.

6. Point to the top border of the window. Drag the border down to reduce the height of the window.

7. Point to the right border of the window. Drag the border to the left to reduce the width of the window.

8. Drag the window to the top of the screen. When the window outline expands to fill the screen, release the mouse.

Moving a Window

To move a window, point to the title bar and drag the window to a new location. You cannot move a maximized window.

1. Click the Word Restore Down button if necessary, and point to the Word title bar.

2. Drag the window to the lower left corner of the screen. Release the mouse.

Switch between Windows

When more than one program is open, you can switch between windows by using the sizing buttons or the taskbar. You can also press [Alt]+[Tab] to switch to the previous window.

1. If necessary, open Word and Excel, and maximize both windows.

2. Minimize the Excel window. The Word window displays.

3. Point to the Excel button [⊞] on the taskbar. A thumbnail preview of the Excel window displays. If you point to the thumbnail, the thumbnail enlarges so that you can preview the window. This feature is called *Aero Peek*.

Figure 13
Taskbar buttons and thumbnail preview

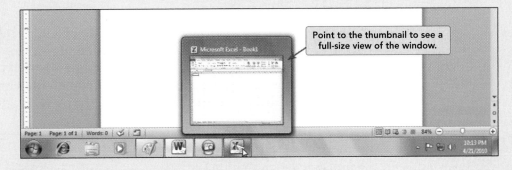

Point to the thumbnail to see a full-size view of the window.

NOTE

To display thumbnail preview, your computer must support the Windows Aero feature.

4. Click the Excel button to display the Excel window and to make it the active window.

5. Press [Alt]+[Tab] to switch to Word. You can switch to the previous window by pressing this shortcut, or you can continue to press [Tab] to switch to an open window on the desktop.

Display Two Program Windows Simultaneously

When multiple programs are open, you can arrange the windows using the following commands from the taskbar. You can also use the *Snap* feature to display two windows side by side on the desktop. To position two windows side by side, drag the title bar of one window to the left side of the screen until the window snaps to the left side. Release the mouse. Drag the second window to the right side of the screen until it snaps into place.

- Cascade windows
- Show windows stacked
- Show windows side-by-side
- Show the desktop

1. Open the Start menu, and display Excel and Word if necessary.
2. Right-click the taskbar, and click **Show windows side by side**. The windows display vertically.
3. Right-click the taskbar, and click **Cascade windows**. The windows display on top of each other. The title bar for each window is visible.
4. Click the Show Desktop button ▮ located on the right side of the taskbar to see the desktop. The Word and Excel programs are minimized.
5. Click the Show Desktop button ▮ again to restore the programs.
6. Right-click the taskbar, and click **Show windows stacked**. The windows are stacked vertically.
7. Click the **Close** button on the title bars of each of the two program windows to close them and to show the desktop.

Using Menus

When you open a window you may see a row of descriptive names just below the title bar. A menu bar contains a list of options for working with programs and documents. These operations are either mouse or keyboard driven. They are called commands because they "command" the computer to perform functions needed to complete the task you, the user, initiate at the menu level.

Executing a Command from a Menu

You open a menu by clicking the menu name listed in the menu bar. When a menu is opened, a list of command options appears. To execute a particular command from an open menu, press the left mouse button and then drag down and release the mouse (click and drag). You can also click the command once the menu is open.

Other Menu Symbols

Three dots following a menu option (an ellipsis . . .) indicate that a dialog box is displayed when that menu option is chosen. (Dialog boxes, discussed later, are small windows requesting and receiving input from a user.) Menus may also include a triangular arrow. Clicking the arrow displays a submenu with additional choices. If a menu command has a keyboard shortcut, the key or the combination of keys you press to activate the option appear on the right side of the menu. Commands that appear gray or dimmed are currently not available.

Figure 14
Notepad menu bar

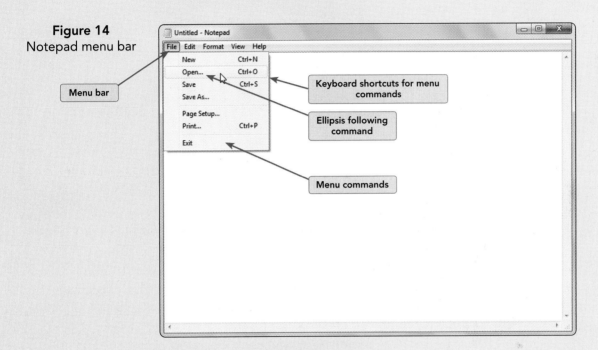

Perform the following steps for using menus:

1. Open the **Start menu**, click **All Programs**, and click the **Accessories** folder. Click **Notepad**. The Notepad program opens, and a button appears on the Windows taskbar.

2. Locate the menu bar, and click **File**. The File menu displays. Notice the keyboard shortcuts listed on the right side of the menu.

3. Locate the **Open** command and notice that three dots follow the command. Click the Open command. The Open dialog box displays. Click **Cancel** to close the Open dialog box.

4. Click **File** on the menu bar. Click **Exit** to close the Notepad window.

5. Click the Windows Explorer button ▦ on the taskbar. The Windows Explorer window displays.

6. Locate the Organize command [Organize ▾], and click the button. A menu of options appears below the command button.

Figure 15
Windows Explorer
window

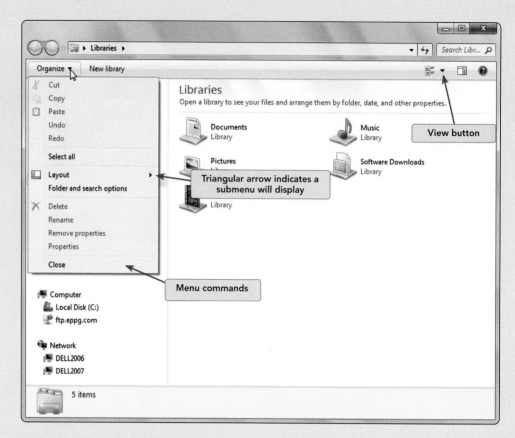

7. Click the **Layout** command, and a submenu displays with additional options. Notice that several of the options appear with a checkmark. The checkmark option ☑ indicates that the option is selected. Click the option again to turn off the checkmark.

8. Locate the View button ▦▾, and click the arrow beside the button. Drag the slider to **Medium Icons** and notice the change in the appearance of the icons in the Windows Explorer window.

9. Press the Alt key, and a traditional-looking menu bar appears. Press Alt again to hide the menu bar.

10. Press Alt+F4 to close the Windows Explorer window.

Displaying a Shortcut Menu

When the mouse pointer is on an object or an area of the Windows desktop and you right-click, a shortcut menu appears. A shortcut menu typically contains commands that are useful in working with the object or area of the desktop to which you are currently pointing.

1. Position the mouse pointer on a blank area of the desktop, and right-click. A shortcut menu appears with commands that relate to the desktop, including view and sort options.

2. Click outside the shortcut menu to close it.

3. Right-click the time in the bottom right corner of the taskbar. A shortcut menu appears.

Figure 16
Time shortcut menu

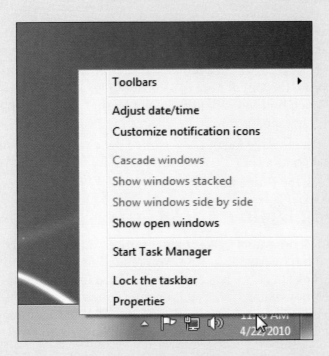

4. Click **Adjust date/time** on the shortcut menu. The Date and Time dialog box appears. You can use this dialog box to adjust your computer's date and time.

5. Click **Cancel**.

6. Right-click an icon on the desktop to display its shortcut menu, and then close the shortcut menu.

Using the Ribbon and Quick Access Toolbar

Microsoft Office 2010 applications include a Quick Access Toolbar and a Ribbon to access commands. The *Quick Access Toolbar* contains frequently used commands and is positioned above the Ribbon. The *Ribbon* consists of tabs, and each tab contains a group of related commands. The number of commands for each tab varies. A command can be one of several formats. The most popular formats include buttons and drop-down lists. The *File tab* displays a menu which lists the commands to create, open, save, and print a document.

1. Open the Word program. The Quick Access Toolbar arrow should point to the Save button.

Figure 17
Word window

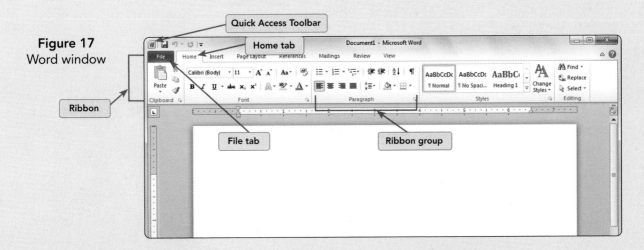

2. Point to and click the **File** tab. Notice the commands in the left pane.

3. Click the **Home** tab, and locate the groups of commands on the Home tab (Clipboard, Font, Paragraph, Styles, and Editing).

4. Locate the Quick Access Toolbar above the Ribbon. Point to each button to identify it. Notice that a keyboard shortcut displays beside each button.

5. Click the **Page Layout** tab. Notice the change in the number of groups and commands.

6. Click the **Home** tab.

Using Dialog Boxes

Windows programs make frequent use of dialog boxes. A *dialog box* is a window that requests input from you related to a command you have chosen. A dialog box appears when a command listed in a menu is followed by an ellipsis (. . .). Many dialog boxes contain tabs which resemble file folder tabs. Click a tab to select it and to display its options. All Windows programs use a common dialog box structure. Table 5 lists several options you will see in dialog boxes.

TABLE 5 Dialog Box Options

Check boxes are square in shape. Click a box to turn on (check) or turn off (uncheck) the option. You can select as many check box options as needed.	☑ Small caps ☐ All caps ☐ Hidden
A *Combo* or *List box* displays a list of choices. Use the scroll bar to display hidden choices. Use scroll arrows to move up or down in small increments. Drag the scroll box up or down to move quickly through the list of options. Click an item to select it, or key information in the text box.	Font: +Body +Body +Headings Agency FB Aharoni Albertus
Command buttons are rectangles with rounded corners, and they initiate an immediate action. If followed by an ellipsis (. . .) another dialog box opens.	OK Cancel Text Effects...
A *Drop-down list box* is rectangular in shape and displays the current selection in the rectangle. Click the arrow at the right of the box for a list of available options.	Font color:
Option buttons are round in shape. Only one option may be selected from within a group of options. If selected, the option contains a dot.	Alignment ◉ Left ○ Center ○ Right ○ Decimal ○ Bar
A *Slider* represents a range of values for a particular setting. Drag the slider left or right or click an arrow to change the current setting.	Brightness and Contrast Presets: ☼ ▼ Brightness: ——|—— 14% Contrast: ——|—— -34%

(continues)

TABLE 5 Dialog Box Options   (*continued*)

Spin Box/Spinner includes two arrows. Click the up arrow to increase value. Click the down arrow to decrease value. Changes usually occur in an increment of one. You can also select the current value, and key a new number.

Margins		
Top:	1"	▲▼
Left:	1"	▲▼
Gutter:	0"	▲▼

Text boxes are rectangular in shape and are used to enter data. An insertion point appears at the left side of the box, and text will be entered at the position of the insertion point. Press Delete or Backspace to delete or edit existing text. Double-click or drag over existing text to select it. Use the Home, End, or arrow keys to move the insertion point.

File name: ▢ ▼

Practice using dialog box options by completing the following instructions.

1. Open Word, if necessary, and click the **Home** tab.
2. Locate the **Font** group, and notice the arrow in the lower right corner ▫. Click the arrow (Font Dialog Box Launcher), and the Font dialog box displays.

Figure 18
Font dialog box

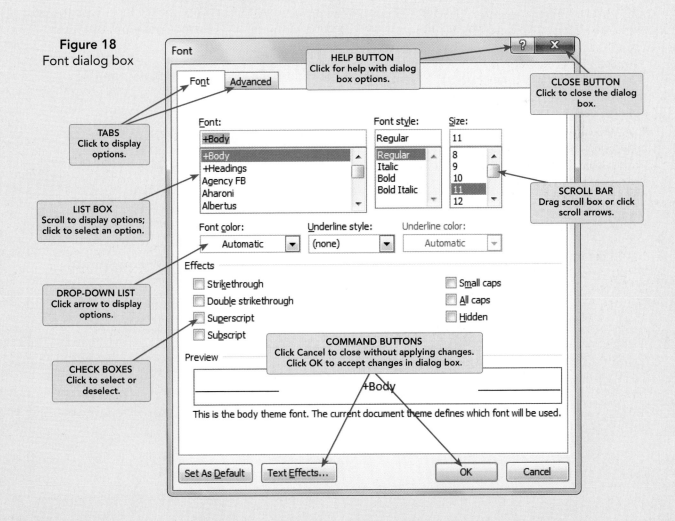

3. Click the Advanced tab, and notice the options in the dialog box. Click the Font tab.

4. Locate the Font group. The Font group displays a list box with several fonts available for formatting a document. Drag the scroll box to the bottom to view a list of available fonts. Click to select the Tahoma font. You can also click the up or down arrows to locate a font.

5. Locate the Font color group, and click the down arrow [▼] to the right of the box. Locate the Standard Colors, and point to the colors to view a ScreenTip. Click Blue. Notice the change in the Font color drop-down list.

6. Locate the Effects section. Click to select the check box for Small caps. A checkmark appears in the box.

7. Locate the command buttons at the bottom of the dialog box. Click Cancel [Cancel].

8. Close the Word program by clicking the Close button [X].

Changing the Desktop

Use the Control Panel to change the way Windows looks and works. Because your computer in school is used by other students, you should be very careful when changing settings. Others might expect Windows to look and work the standard way. Having Windows look or work in a nonstandard way could easily confuse other users. (Table 6 describes how to access other settings.) To change the appearance of your computer, follow these steps. Talk to your instructor first, however, before changing any settings on your computer.

1. Click the Start button on the taskbar.

2. Click Control Panel on the right pane. The Control Panel window displays.

Figure 19
Control Panel
window

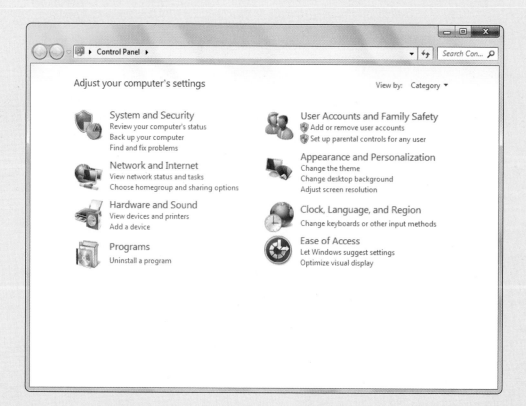

3. Click the Appearance and Personalization link. The Appearance and Personalization window displays.

4. Click Personalization and click the Window Color icon near the bottom of the window. Click a color from the color palette.

5. Click Save Changes.

6. Click the Desktop Background icon at the bottom of the Personalization window. Scroll through the list of pictures, and click to select a picture. Click Save Changes.

7. Close the Personalization window.

TABLE 6 Settings Options

OPTION	USE
Control Panel	Displays the Control Panel window, which lets you change background color, add or remove programs, change the date and time, and change other settings for your hardware and software. The items listed below are accessed from the Control Panel.
Network and Internet	Includes options to view the network status, connect to a network, set up file sharing, change Internet options, and so on.
Hardware and Sound	Includes options to add a printer, change default settings for AutoPlay, sound, mouse settings, keyboard, and so on.
Appearance and Personalization	Includes options to change the desktop background, adjust screen resolution, customize the Start menu and icons on the taskbar, and change sidebar properties.

Using the Search Command

If you do not know where a file or folder is located, you can use the Search command on the Start menu to help you find and open it. You can also use the Search box in Windows Explorer to locate an item.

1. Click the Start button on the taskbar. Notice the blinking insertion point in the Start Search box. You can start keying the name of a program, folder, or file immediately.

2. Key calculator. The Start menu is replaced with a list of options including programs, Control Panel items, files, and documents containing the characters you keyed in the Search box.

3. Click the Calculator option. The Calculator window displays.

4. Close the Calculator window.

5. Click the Windows Explorer button on the taskbar. The Windows Explorer window displays.

Figure 20
Windows Explorer
window

6. Locate the Search box in the upper right corner of the Windows Explorer window.

7. Click in the Search box, and key **penguins**. A picture of penguins appears in the window.

8. Close the Windows Explorer window.

Using the Run Command

Windows allows you to start a program by using the Run command and keying the program name. This command is often employed to run a "setup" or "install" program that installs a new program on your computer. It is best to use this command after you have become more familiar with Windows 7.

1. Click the Start button on the taskbar.

2. Click All Programs, and click the Accessories folder.

3. Click Run.

Figure 21
Run dialog box

4. If you know the name of a program you want to run, type the name in the **Open** text box. Often you will need to click **Browse** to open a drop-down list of the disk drives, folders, and files available to you.

5. Click **Cancel** to close the Run dialog box.

6. Open the **Start** menu, and locate the **Start Search** box.

7. Key **run**, and notice that the Run program displays under **Programs**.

8. Click the program name, and the Run dialog box displays.

9. Close the Run dialog box.

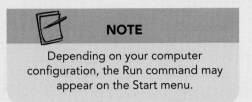

NOTE

Depending on your computer configuration, the Run command may appear on the Start menu.

Deleting Files Using the Recycle Bin

The *Recycle Bin* is the trash can icon on your desktop. To delete a file, click the file icon, and drag it to the Recycle Bin.

1. Double-click the **Recycle Bin** icon on the desktop. A window opens listing files you have deleted.

Figure 22
Recycle Bin window

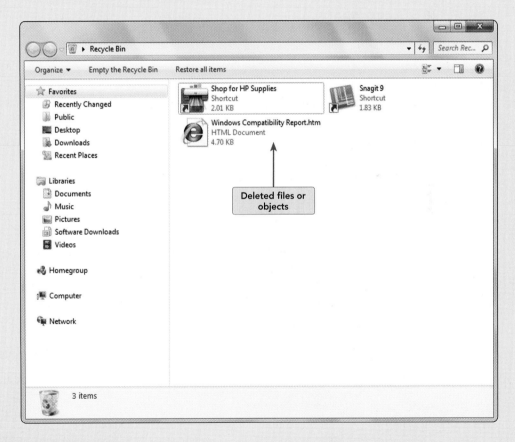

2. To undelete a file, merely drag it out of the Recycle Bin window and place it on the desktop or right-click the file and click Restore.

3. To empty the Recycle Bin and permanently delete files, click **Empty the Recycle Bin** in the Recycle Bin window, or right-click the Recycle Bin icon on the desktop. The shortcut menu appears. Click **Empty Recycle Bin**.

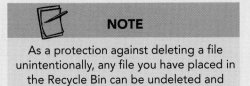

NOTE

As a protection against deleting a file unintentionally, any file you have placed in the Recycle Bin can be undeleted and used again.

Help and Support

Windows Help and Support is available to you as you work. Use the Help feature to answer questions, to provide instructions on how to do a procedure, or to troubleshoot problems you are experiencing.

1. Press the Windows logo key on the keyboard or click the Start button  to display the Start menu.
2. Locate the **Help and Support** feature on the right side of the Start menu, and click to open the Windows Help and Support window.

Figure 23
Windows Help and
Support Window

3. Key **gadget** in the Search Help text box, and press ⌷Enter⌷. A list of results for gadget appears in the Windows Help and Support window.

Figure 24
Search results for
gadget

4. Point to the topic entitled "**Desktop gadgets (overview)**." Notice the shape of the mouse pointer 🖑. Click the topic, and the Windows Help and Support window displays information about gadgets. Read the information on Desktop gadgets.

5. Click the Back button 🔙 located in the upper left corner. You return to the list of gadget topics. Notice that the "Desktop gadgets (overview)" topic is a different color. When you visit a topic, the color of the topic (link) changes.

6. Click the topic entitled "**Desktop gadgets: frequently asked questions**."

7. Locate the **Show all** link in the upper right corner of the window. Click **Show all** to expand the text.

8. Key the text keyboard shortcuts in the Search text box, and press ⌈Enter⌉. Click the link **Keyboard shortcuts**, then click the link **Windows logo key keyboard shortcuts**. Review the list. (You may want to print this list for future reference.)

9. Click the Browse Help button 📖 at the top of the Windows Help and Support window. Click the **All Help** link. A list of subject headings displays. Click a heading to view related categories.

10. Locate the Help button ❓ on the taskbar. Right-click the button, and choose Close window.

Exiting Windows

You should always exit any open programs and Windows before turning off the computer. This is the best way to be sure your work is saved. Windows also performs other "housekeeping" routines that ensure everything is ready for you when you next turn on your computer. Failure to shut down properly will often force Windows to perform time-consuming system checks the next time it is loaded. You can either log off the computer to make it available for another user, or shut it down entirely.

To Log Off

1. Click the Start button on the taskbar.
2. Click the arrow to the right of the Shut down button [Shut down ▷], and click Log Off.

To Shut Down

To exit Windows, use the Shut down command on the Start menu.

This command has two important shut-down options which are accessed by clicking the arrow beside the Shut down button.

- *Restart:* Restarts the computer without shutting off the power. This is sometimes necessary when you add new software.

- *Sleep:* Puts the computer in a low-activity state. It appears to be turned off but will restart when the mouse is moved. Press the computer power button to resume work.

To shut down completely, click the Shut down button [Shut down ▷]. *Shut down* closes all open programs and makes it safe to turn off the computer. Some computers will turn off the power automatically.

1. Click the Start button on the taskbar.
2. Click the Shut down button [Shut down ▷].
3. Windows prompts you to save changes in any open documents. It then prepares the computer to be shut down.

There is more to learning a database management program like Microsoft Access than simply pressing keys. Students need to know how to use Access in a real-world situation. That is why all the lessons in this book relate to everyday business tasks that a database manager would perform.

As students work through the lessons, they are guided through routine business tasks as if they are employed as interns for EcoMed Services, Inc., a fictional lighting company located in Kansas City, Missouri.

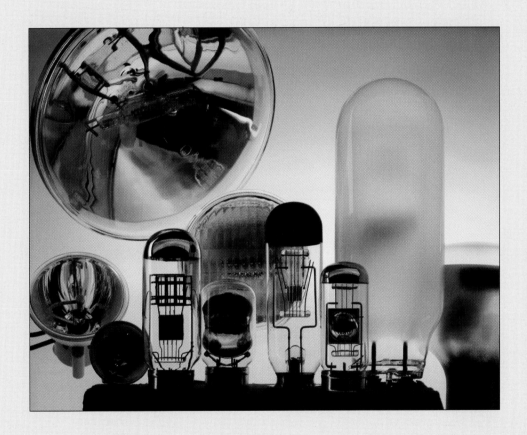

EcoMed Services, Inc.

EcoMed Services, Inc., is a leader in providing environmentally friendly lighting to medical facilities throughout the United States. The company's primary mission is to maximize effective, ecologically-minded solutions for medical clients without compromise. The company was founded in 1972, the year before the United States experienced its first energy crisis, and has steadily grown to partner with more than 150 medical facilities, ranging from small critical access clinics to large medical facilities with over 2000 patient beds.

The company stocks over 300 standard and specialized light bulbs, including diagnostic, surgical, utility-indoor, and utility-outdoor. Well-established business relationships with 29 vendors ensure that the company will have the type and shape of bulb that customers need. Currently EcoMed Services stocks 15 different common and specialized bulb shapes, including circuline, spiral, bayonet, canister, dish, mini-spiral, twin-tube, triple-tube, quadruple-tube, single-ended tube, and double-ended tube.

Ivon Gonzalez, the company's president and founder, promises that that the company's knowledgeable and professional employees will always meet or exceed its customers' expectations. Ms. Gonzalez has made it a company priority to invest in information management solutions, including improving the database functions that support the company's needs. The company recently started hiring interns to help manage and update the Access database that has been supporting its critical inventory, sales, and payroll functions.

Unit 1

UNDERSTANDING ACCESS DATABASES

Lesson 1
Getting Started with a Database

OBJECTIVES   *After completing this lesson, you will be able to:*

1. Identify basic database structure.

2. Work with a Microsoft Access database.

3. Identify components of Access.

4. Navigate Access recordsets.

5. Modify a datasheet's appearance.

6. Save and print a recordset.

7. Manage Access files.

Estimated Time: 1½ hours

Databases are part of everyday business. In this book, the database with which you will work involves a Case Study about EcoMed Services, Inc., a fictional company that sells illumination supplies to hospitals and medical centers. This book explains database usage and development as if you were a new student intern recently employed by the company.

EcoMed Services, Inc., uses several databases to take care of its business needs, such as payroll, shipping, and billing. Just like you, most student interns who work at EcoMed Services are somewhat familiar with databases through their school. You probably already know that your school uses databases to keep track of what courses you've taken, where you live, when you graduate, how to best contact you, and other important academic information. Just as you've learned to use your school's databases through your daily interactions, you will learn about EcoMed's business procedures and databases.

A *database* is a logically organized collection of data. The most common type of database in use today is relational. Other types of databases include flat, hierarchical, network, and dimensional. If you are familiar with spreadsheets such as Microsoft Excel, you have an understanding of a flat database. Excel has incorporated many simple database commands to be used in simple database structures. Microsoft Access creates relational databases that are much more complex than Excel spreadsheets.

Identifying Basic Database Structure

Microsoft Access follows the relational model for its design. Access databases are organized by major objects. In a relational database, all data are stored in tables. A *table* is the major database object that stores all data in a subject-based list of rows and columns. A database table can look similar to a table displayed in a spreadsheet program, or it can appear different.

Tables are made up of records and fields. A record is a complete set of related data about one entity or activity. A *record* is displayed as a row in a table. Examples of records include a phone directory listing, a sales transaction, or a bank deposit.

Figure 1-1
Data organization

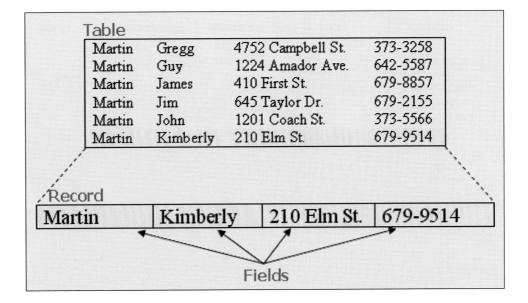

Records are composed of related fields. A *field* is the smallest storage element that contains an individual data element within a record. A field is displayed as a column in a table. A group of related fields make up a record. A group of related records make up a table, and a group of related tables make up a relational model database.

Figure 1-2
Data hierarchy

Although all data are stored in tables, often you use other objects to locate, organize, and modify recordsets. A recordset is a Microsoft object–oriented data structure consisting of grouped records. A *recordset* can be as small as a single field or as large as two or more combined tables.

Major objects in an Access database include the following:

- Tables store data about people, activities, items, and events. A table consists of records made up of fields. The information in a table appears in rows (records) and columns (fields), similar to an Excel worksheet.

- Queries display and organize data depending on the question being queried. You can specify criteria or conditions to show records and fields from one or more tables. You can also create queries to perform actions.

- Forms display data on a screen in user-friendly formats. Forms make data entry and editing simpler. With a form, you can view, add, and edit fields and records in a table.

- Reports organize and format data to be used as printable documents. Reports are professional looking, formal documents that display information, usually derived from database queries.

Figure 1-3
Major object
orientation

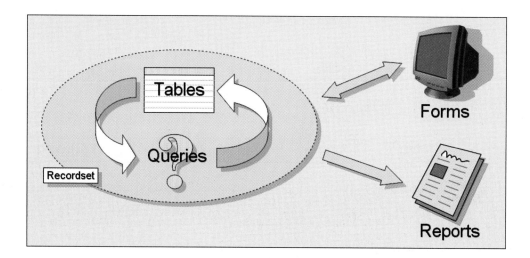

A recordset is most often displayed as either a form or a report. A form is a major database object used to display information in an attractive, easy-to-read screen format. Forms can be used to display, add, edit, or delete record-sets. A report is a major database object used to display information in a printable page format. Reports can only display recordsets.

Working with a Microsoft Access Database

Because of the complexity of a database, Access limits certain file operations that are available for other applications, such as Word or Excel. Access does not have the "Save As" file command. When a database is open, you cannot move or rename the file. Therefore, before you begin working with a database, you must place the file in a suitable storage location. The storage medium in which the database file is located (such as a USB flash drive) must provide enough space to allow the database to grow, and you must have rights to modify the file in that location. Some storage locations at your school or at EcoMed do not allow an average user to modify files. These locations can only be fully used by a person with administrative rights.

Exercise 1-1 MANAGE A DATABASE

At the beginning of each lesson, you will be required to copy the student lesson files onto a USB flash drive or a location where you have rights to copy, rename, and modify the database. The student lesson files are located online or are available from your instructor. The files you need for a lesson can be found in the folder that matches the lesson number. For example, in the first lesson, you will need the folder **Lesson 01**, which contains the database **EcoMed-01**. If you need help copying files to your computer, ask your instructor or lab manager for assistance.

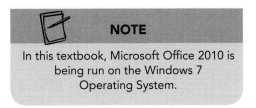

NOTE

In this textbook, Microsoft Office 2010 is being run on the Windows 7 Operating System.

1. Locate the **Lesson 01** folder.

2. Double-click the folder **Lesson 01** to see its content.

3. Right-click the file **EcoMed-01** and from the shortcut menu, and choose **Copy**.

4. Right-click an unused part of the folder and from the shortcut menu, choose **Paste**.

5. Right-click the new file and from the shortcut menu, choose **Rename**. Rename the file *[your initials]*-EcoMed-01.

6. Right-click *[your initials]*-EcoMed-01 and from the shortcut menu, choose **Properties**. Make certain that the **Read-only** attribute check box is not checked.

Figure 1-4
Properties dialog box

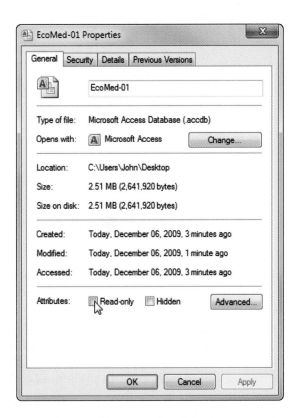

7. Click **OK** to close the dialog box. Close the Windows Explorer.

Exercise 1-2 START A DATABASE

The first screen that appears after starting Access is Getting Started with Microsoft Office Access. From this screen, you can create a new database, open an existing database, or view featured content from Microsoft Office Online.

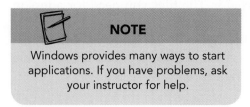

NOTE

Windows provides many ways to start applications. If you have problems, ask your instructor for help.

1. Click the **Start** button and choose **All Programs**.
2. Click on the **Microsoft Office** folder and choose **Microsoft Office Access 2010** to start Access in the Backstage.

Figure 1-5
Access Backstage

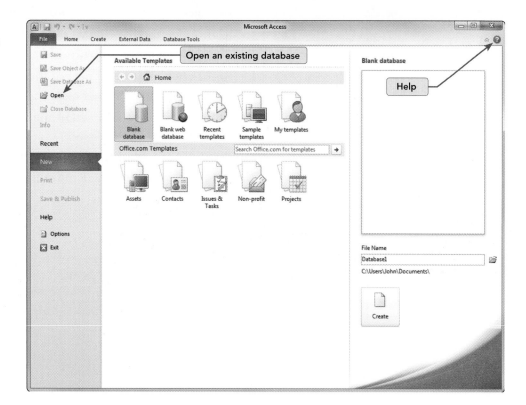

Exercise 1-3 OPEN A DATABASE

By double-clicking on the file icon of a database, you open it in the default mode. For most databases, the default mode is Shared. Shared mode is a method of opening a database in which multiple users may modify the file's data at the same time. In addition to Shared mode, Access databases can be opened in Read-only, Exclusive use, and Exclusive Read-only.

At most locations such as your school or EcoMed, each time you open a database, a security alert displays on the Message Bar. The Message Bar alerts you that the database may contain malicious code. Because all Access databases contain program code, this message normally displays. If you know that the database you are opening does not contain malicious code, enable the contents. After you enable the contents, you will be able to view and modify the contents of the database.

1. Click **Open** 📷 on the left of the screen.
2. Locate the folder **Lesson 01**. Select the file *[your initials]*-**EcoMed-01** and click **Open**.
3. In the Message Bar, a **Security Warning** message states that certain content is disabled. Click **Enable Content** to continue.

Identifying Components of Access

As with most Microsoft Office applications, in Access you will use Backstage View to print and manage most file operations. You will use command tabs and ribbons to complete specific tasks. The commands in each ribbon are organized by command groups. These groups are organized by command category.

In Access, you will use the Navigation Pane to control major database objects. The Navigation Pane is the rectangular area on the left side of the database window. The Navigation Pane organizes major database objects. When you become more familiar with general database functions, you will be able to use the Navigation Pane to organize database objects by business function such as payroll, inventory, or accounts receivable. All major database objects are accessed through the Navigation Pane.

Figure 1-6
Getting Started
window
EcoMed-01.accdb

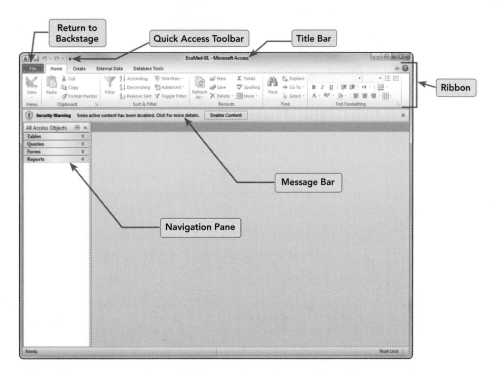

Exercise 1-4   MANIPULATE THE NAVIGATION PANE

The Navigation Pane displays the major database objects. Microsoft Access allows you to organize major objects by categories and groups. You can open an object by double-clicking on the object or by right-clicking on the object and selecting Open from the shortcut menu.

The EcoMed Services, Inc., database organizes objects by the category Object Type and grouped by All Tables. Access allows you to change the layout of the Navigation Pane.

1. In the **Navigation Pane**, click the **Tables** group to expand the group and show all the tables in this database.

Figure 1-7
Navigation Pane
EcoMed-01.accdb

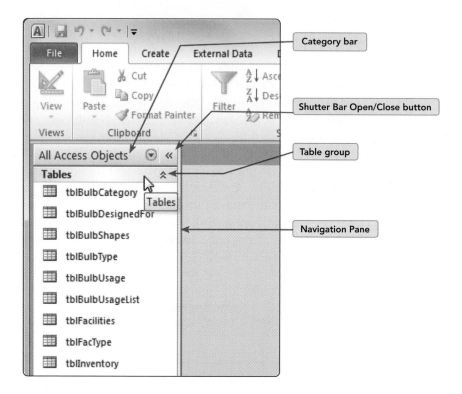

2. Click the **Tables** group again to collapse the group.
3. Click the **Reports** group to expand the group.
4. Click the **Forms** group. You can have multiple groups expanded at any time.
5. Click on the Category bar's drop-down arrow and select **Tables and Related Views**. Objects are now grouped by related major objects.

Figure 1-8
Navigation Pane
options
EcoMed-01.accdb

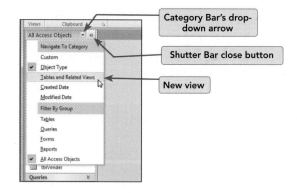

6. Click on the Category bar's drop-down arrow and select **Object Type** to return the **Navigation Pane** to its original layout.

7. Click the **Shutter Bar** button « to collapse the **Navigation Pane**. This action allows you to see more data on the screen.

8. Click the **Shutter Bar** button » to expand the **Navigation Pane**.

Exercise 1-5 EXPLORE TABS, RIBBONS AND GROUPS

Access uses tabs, ribbons, and groups, similar to other Microsoft Office applications. Some Access commands are the same as in Word and Excel. Other commands are unique to Access. Hovering over a command displays its ScreenTip. A *ScreenTip* is the name of or information regarding a specific object. This information can include images, shortcut keys, and descriptions.

When you click on a command tab, a unique set of command groups will appear in the ribbon. A *command group* is a collection of logically organized commands.

1. In the command tab **Home**, in the command group **Clipboard**, you will find the **Cut** button . Hover your mouse pointer over this command to display its ScreenTip.

Figure 1-9
Viewing ScreenTips
EcoMed-01.accdb

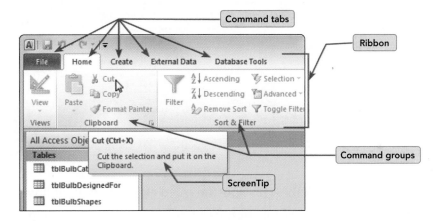

2. In the command tab **Create**, in the command group **Forms**, hover your mouse pointer over the **Form** button . Read the ScreenTip.

3. Click the **Home** command tab.

Exercise 1-6 OPEN AND CLOSE MAJOR OBJECTS

EcoMed Services, Inc., uses the internationally accepted Leszynski Naming Convention. The Leszynski Naming Convention is a method of naming objects that emphasizes the use of three-letter prefixes to identify the type of object. This naming convention does not allow the use of spaces or underscores. Although Access does not require the Leszynski Naming Convention to be applied, this convention is commonly used by software developers and programmers worldwide.

TABLE 1-1 Leszynski Naming Convention for Major Objects*

Prefix	Object Type	Example
tbl	Table	**tblBulbType**
qry	Query	**qryInvShort**
frm	Form	**frmInventory**
rpt	Report	**rptInvByVender**

*For a comprehensive list of control prefixes, see Appendix B-1.

1. In the **Navigation Pane**, verify the **Tables** group is expanded.
2. Double-click the table **tblInventory** to open it. The table that contains the inventory's information is now open.

Figure 1-10
Open a table
EcoMed-01.accdb
tblInventory

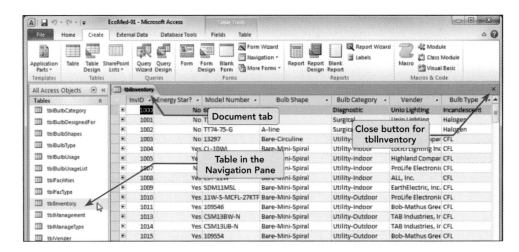

3. Click the **Close** button ⊠ to close the table **tblInventory**.
4. In the **Navigation Pane**, collapse the **Tables** group.
5. Expand the **Queries** group, right-click the query **qryManageType**, and select **Open** from the shortcut menu.
6. Right-click the document tab for **qryManageType**, then select **Close** ⊠ from the shortcut menu.

Exercise 1-7   EXPLORE DATASHEET AND DESIGN VIEWS

In Access, each major database object has multiple views. The view that allows you to see a recordset organized similarly to an Excel spreadsheet is called Datasheet View. A *Datasheet View* ▦ is a screen view used to display data in rows and columns. Records are displayed as rows, and fields are displayed as columns. Tables, queries, forms, and reports can be displayed in Datasheet View.

In addition to the Datasheet View, most major objects can be displayed in Design View. A *Design View* ◹ is a screen view used to modify the structure of a major object. Switching between different views can be completed by:

- Selecting, from the **Home** command tab, in the **Views** control group, the option arrow for the **View** button ⬛.
- Using the **View Shortcut** button (lower right corner of the screen).
- Right-clicking the object and selecting the view.

1. In the **Queries** group of the **Navigation Pane**, double-click **qryManageContacts** to open the query in **Datasheet View**.

2. On the command tab **Home**, in the command group **Views**, click the bottom half of the **View** split button ⬛ and select **Design View**. In this view, you can see the table that is used to create this query.

Figure 1-11
Switching views
**EcoMed-01.accdb
qryManageContacts**

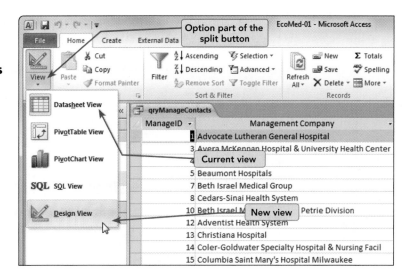

3. Right-click the document tab for the query, then select **Datasheet View**.

4. In the **Navigation Pane**, expand the **Tables** group.

5. Double-click **tblVender** to open the table in **Datasheet View**.

6. Right-click the document tab for the table, then select **Design View**. This view is where you define the structure of the table.

7. Right-click the document tab for the table, then select **Close All** 🗗. This action will close all open documents.

8. In the **Navigation Pane**, collapse both the **Tables** and **Queries** groups.

Navigating Access Recordsets

Now that you know how to navigate through the major objects in the **EcoMed-01** database, you now can learn how to navigate through records. Because most employees are familiar with Excel, you will first learn to edit data through Datasheet View.

Datasheet View has two modes: edit mode and navigation mode. *Edit Mode* is the mode in which changes to the content of a field can be made and the insertion point is visible. The insertion point looks like an I-beam. *Navigation Mode* is the mode in which an entire field is selected and the insertion point is not visible.

You will first learn to navigate around large datasheets by using the scroll bars, navigation buttons, and keyboard shortcuts. These procedures will be very similar to the procedures used in Excel.

Exercise 1-8   USE NAVIGATION BUTTONS IN A TABLE

In navigation mode, you can move between fields by using the keyboard shortcuts or record navigation buttons. A *Record navigation button* is an icon that moves the pointer within a recordset to the next, previous, first, or last record. The record navigation buttons are located on the navigation bar near the bottom of the window.

1. Expand the **Tables** group. Double-click the table **tblBulbUsageList** to open it. By default, the first record, first field, is selected.

Figure 1-12
Navigation buttons
EcoMed-01.accdb
tblBulbUsageList

2. In the Navigation Bar, click the Next Record button ▶ once. The **List ID** for the second record is highlighted.

3. Click the Previous Record button ◀ to return to the previous record.

4. Click the Last Record button ▶| to move to the last record in the table.

5. Click in the Current Record box. Delete the number in the box, key **75**, and press Enter. The pointer moves to the seventy-fifth record.

6. Right-click the document tab for the table, then select **Close**. Collapse the **Tables** group.

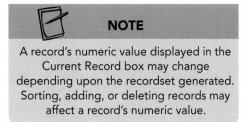

NOTE

A record's numeric value displayed in the Current Record box may change depending upon the recordset generated. Sorting, adding, or deleting records may affect a record's numeric value.

Exercise 1-9   USE NAVIGATION SHORTCUT KEYS IN A QUERY

Just as in a table's Datasheet View, you can use both the navigation buttons and keyboard shortcuts to navigate through a recordset. Often using the mouse seems the easiest for beginners. As you become more comfortable editing database information, using the keyboard shortcuts can be a faster method for entering and correcting data. You should use the method that works best for you.

1. Expand the **Queries** group. Double-click **qryManageContacts** to open it in **Datasheet View**.

2. Press Ctrl+End to move to the last field in the last record.

3. Press Home to move to the first field in the current record.

4. Press Ctrl+Home to move to the first field in the first record.

5. Press End to move to the last field in the current record.

6. Press ↓ to move to the last field of the second record.

7. Right-click the document tab for the table, then select **Close** and collapse the **Queries** group.

TABLE 1-2 Keyboard Shortcuts

Action	Shortcut
Move down one screen	PageDown
Move to the current field in the first record	Ctrl+↑
Move to the current field in the last record	Ctrl+↓
Move to the current field in the next record	↓
Move to the current field in the previous record	↑
Move to the first field in the current record	Home
Move to the first field in the first record	Ctrl+Home
Move to the last field in the current record	End
Move to the last field in the last record	Ctrl+End
Move to the next field	Tab or →
Move to the previous field	Shift+Tab or ←
Move up one screen	PageUp
Place the pointer in the Specific Record Box	F5
Save record changes	Shift+Enter

Modifying Datasheet Appearance

Not everyone likes seeing data in default view. Depending on the department at EcoMed, you may need to modify how the database looks. Although the data will remain the same, their appearance can be customized for each user. You can change the appearance of an Access datasheet very similarly to how you would change the appearance of an Excel worksheet. You can hide, display, and resize columns as well as rows.

You also can use formatting tools to change the appearance of text for the data displayed. Although the Datasheet View is similar in both Excel and

Access, in Access, format settings globally affect all text in every column and row. In Excel you can format individual cells, rows, and columns. Some commands, such as bold, underline, and italics, apply to the entire datasheet. Other commands, such as align left, center, and align right, can be applied to selected fields in the datasheet. Later you will learn to use Reports and Forms to better control the appearance of data.

Exercise 1-10   HIDE AND UNHIDE COLUMNS

EcoMed is a large company with large amounts of data. Some of the tables in its database contain many fields. When a table contains more fields than can be viewed on a single screen, you must scroll horizontally through the window to see all the information contained in a single record. To reduce the number of fields shown per record, you can hide columns within the datasheet.

1. Expand the **Tables** group. Double-click the table **tblFacilities** to open it. There are 17 fields in this table.

2. Click on the column header for the field **Facility Type** and drag through **Management Type**. The two selected columns are highlighted.

3. Right-click on the column header for the field **Management Type** and select **Hide Fields**.

Figure 1-13
Selecting multiple columns
EcoMed-01.accdb
tblFacilities

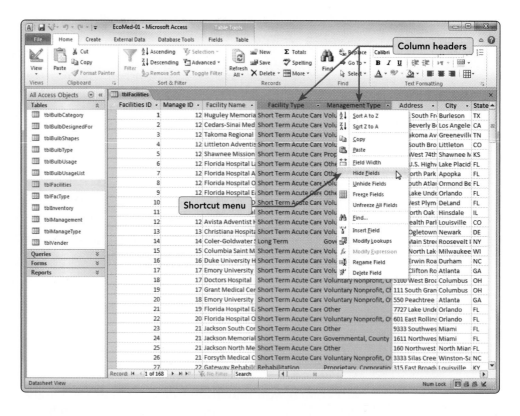

4. Right-click on the column header for the field **Facility Name** and select **Unhide Fields**.

5. Click the check boxes for the fields **Regions** and **Web Site** to remove their checkmarks. This dialog box can be used to hide and unhide fields.

NOTE

When you change the appearance or design of a major database object, Access prompts you to save the changes.

6. Click **Close**.

7. Right-click the document tab for the table, then select **Close**. A dialog box appears, prompting you to save the changes to the table. Click **Yes** to accept the changes.

Exercise 1-11   CHANGE COLUMN WIDTHS AND ROW HEIGHTS

By default, all columns in a datasheet are the same width. You can change the width of each column to optimize your view of the data in each field or to see the entire column title for each field. You also can make columns narrower if too much blank space is included.

Similarly to adjusting column widths, you can adjust row heights in Datasheet View. Although column widths can be set individually, row heights cannot. In Datasheet View, the row height is a global setting that applies to all rows in the entire datasheet.

1. Double-click the table **tblFacilities** to reopen it.

2. Place the pointer on the vertical border between column headers for **Facility Name** and **Address**. Notice that the pointer changes to a vertical bar between a two-headed arrow. This bar is the resize pointer.

Figure 1-14
Resize a column
EcoMed-01.accdb
tblFacilities

3. Drag the pointer to the right approximately three inches to allow enough space so the complete facility name is displayed for each record.

NOTE

The Best Fit command will widen a column based on the widest content visible but not the widest content in the column, like the same command in Excel.

TIP

You can save the changes to objects by using the keyboard shortcut, Quick Access toolbar, shortcut menu, or the Save dialog box.

4. Right-click the column header **Address**, and select **Field Width** 🔳 from the menu.

5. In the **Column Width** dialog box, click **Best Fit**.

6. Right-click on the record selector for the first row.

7. From the shortcut menu, select **Row Height**.

8. In the **Row Height** dialog box, key **30** and click **OK**. Notice that all rows are now taller.

9. Right-click on the record selector for any record and select **Row Height**.

10. Click the **Standard Height** check box and click **OK**.

11. Press Ctrl+S to save the changes to the table.

Exercise 1-12   USE THE FONT COMMAND GROUP

You can increase the readability of data by applying specific format commands from the Font command group. Font commands, such as bold, underline, and italics, apply to the entire datasheet. Other commands, such as align left, center, and align right, can be applied to selected fields in the datasheet.

EcoMed allows some latitude of individual choices when displaying data. However, certain standards are maintained to reduce clerical errors when entering or editing data. Decimal numbers are aligned right. Short whole numbers can be aligned either right or centered. Long text is aligned left. Short text such as a title can be aligned either right or centered.

1. In the command group **Text Formatting**, hover your mouse pointer over the word **Calibri**. The ScreenTip states that this is the Font command.

2. Click the Font drop-down arrow and select **Microsoft Sans Serif**. The font has been applied to the entire datasheet.

3. The command to the right of Font is Font Size. Change the Font Size to **10**.

4. Place the resize pointer on the vertical border between column header for **Facility Name** and **Address**.

5. Double-click to automatically adjust the column width of **Facility Name**.

6. Select the field **Manage ID** by clicking its column header. Click the Center button 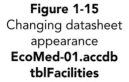. Only one field has been affected.

7. To the right of the command group **Text Formatting** is a button called Alternate Row Color ▦. Click its drop-down arrow to show the available colors.

8. In the **Standard Colors**, select **Medium Gray 2** (row 3, column 3) as the alternate color.

Figure 1-15
Changing datasheet appearance
EcoMed-01.accdb tblFacilities

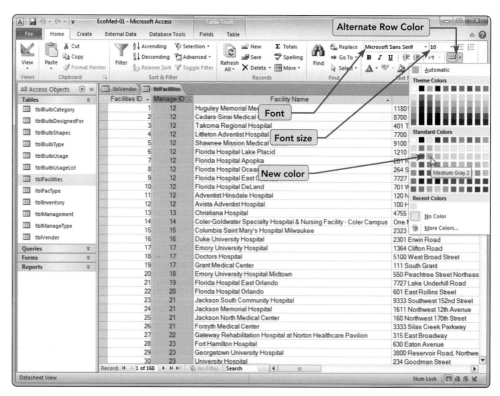

9. Right-click the document tab for the table **tblFacilities** and select **Save** 🖫.

10. Right-click the document tab for the table **tblFacilities** and select **Close** 🗙.

11. In the **Navigation Pane**, collapse the **Tables** group.

Saving and Printing a Recordset

To reduce paper waste, EcoMed has established best practices when printing. As an employee, you should follow these best practices. These practices include the following: (1) create electronic copies rather than paper copies, (2) preview all pages documents before printing, and (3) send documents as e-mail attachments. When possible, employees are asked to save electronic PDF or XPS files rather than printing to paper.

Any element in Access that can be printed can also be saved as a PDF or XPS file. *XPS* is the file extension used by a XML Paper Specification (XPS) file format that preserves document formatting and enables file sharing of printable documents. *PDF* is the file extension used by a Portable Document Format (PDF) for document exchange originally created by Adobe Systems in 1993 and released as an open standard in 2008.

The PDF or XPS format ensures that when the file is viewed online or is printed, it retains the original format without the viewer needing Access.

Exercise 1-13 PRINT A QUERY

If you are certain that you need to print an object, you have four methods of printing. These methods are:

- Click the **File** tab, from the **Print** option, choose **Quick Print** 🖨.
- Click the **File** tab, from the **Print** option, choose **Print** 🖨.
- Click the **File** tab, from the **Print** option, choose **Print Preview** 🔍. Click **Print** 🖨.
- Press Ctrl+P.

When you use the **Print** button 🖨 or the keyboard method, the **Print** dialog box displays to allow you to change print options. When you click the **Quick Print** button 🖨, Access sends the document directly to the default printer without allowing you to change print options.

1. Expand the **Queries** group. Double-click the table **qryManageContacts** to open it.

2. Press Ctrl+P to open the **Print** dialog box.

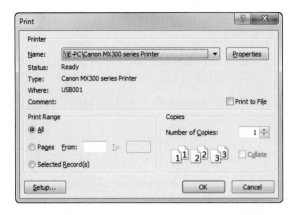

3. Depending on your class procedure, you can either print the table or cancel the print process. To cancel, click **Cancel**. To print the datasheet, click **OK**. If you are uncertain, ask your instructor.

4. To the far right of document tab for the query **qryManageContacts**, click **Close** ☒.

5. Collapse the **Queries** group.

Exercise 1-14 PRINT A TABLE

Before printing a datasheet, you can use Print Preview to determine whether to change the page orientation from portrait (vertical layout) to landscape (horizontal layout). Landscape is often the better option when a datasheet contains numerous fields or wide columns. Printing in landscape mode can reduce the number of pages required to print the information.

1. Expand the **Tables** group. Double-click the table **tblVender** to open it.

2. Click the **File** tab. From the **Print** tab, choose **Print Preview** 🔍.

3. Click the **Last Page** navigation button ▶| to display the last page.

4. From the **Print Preview** command tab, in the command group **Zoom**, click **Two Pages** 🔲 to view both pages.

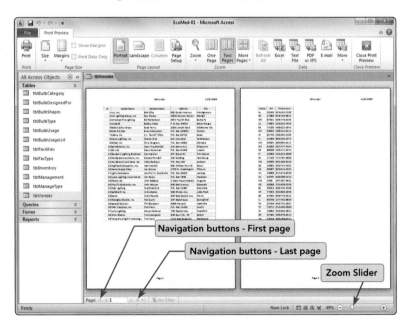

5. From the **Print Preview** command tab, in the command group **Page Layout**, click **Landscape** 📄 to reduce the total number of pages to print.

6. Based on your classroom procedure, you can either print the table or cancel the print process. If you are uncertain, ask your instructor.

7. From the **Print Preview** command tab, in the command group **Close Preview**, click **Close Print Preview** ⊠. This action will return you to the table's **Datasheet View**.

8. Close the table and collapse the **Tables** group.

Exercise 1-15 SAVE A TABLE TO AN EXTERNAL FILE

Rather than directly printing to paper, you should first create an electronic XPS or PDF file. The electronic file can be saved, printed, and e-mailed. Often, the electronic file can be used just as effectively as a paper copy. The XPS and PDF file formats preserve the formatting of the document. The file can be viewed on a screen or printed by anyone who has a copy of the file.

When creating a PDF file, you can save the document in reduced quality or high quality. Reduced quality is similar to draft quality printing. High quality produces a better printout but also increases the size of the file saved.

After creating an electronic file, you should check the size of the file to make certain that it is not too large for the company's e-mail. The EcoMed e-mail server does not allow file to be larger than two megabytes.

1. Expand the **Queries** group. Double-click **qrySurgicalBulbs** to open it.

2. Click the **File** tab and click on the **Save & Publish** tab. From here, you can save the database or a major database object.

3. In the **File Types** section, click **Save Object As** option, and choose **PDF or XPS** 📄 from the next level in the cascading menu.

Figure 1-18
Save database object as a file
EcoMed-01.accdb
qrySurgicalBulbs

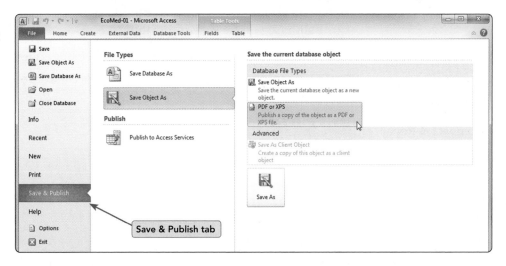

4. Change the location to the location where you will be storing your homework.

5. In the **File name** control, key *[your initials]*-01-15.

6. Click the **Save as type** option, and select **PDF**.

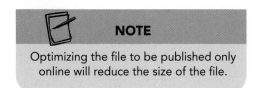

NOTE

Optimizing the file to be published only online will reduce the size of the file.

7. Make certain that the **Open file after publishing** check box is checked.

8. Click **Publish** to create the PDF file. Your file will open in a PDF Reader.

9. Depending upon your class procedure, you can print the PDF from the PDF Reader.

10. Close PDF Reader.

11. Right-click the **qrySurgicalBulbs** document tab and select **Close** .

12. Collapse the **Queries** group.

Managing Access Files

Access, similar to many database applications, is designed to display data quickly. To manipulate large amounts of data, space efficiency must be compromised. Normal database activities, such as adding, deleting, and moving data, can make the file unnecessarily large. After performing extensive work on a database, you should compact the data to save disk space. Depending on the type of work they do, employees at EcoMed are required to compact their databases periodically. Normally, databases are compacted at least once a week.

Regardless of how often employees compact their databases, all employees are required to back up their databases daily. A file can be backed up to the same location as the original file or to a new location.

Exercise 1-16   USE COMPACT AND REPAIR

The Compact and Repair Database command reclaims unused space and improves database efficiency. After compacting an inefficient database, many activities will perform quicker. Because you have only been looking at data rather than modifying data, compacting your current database may not change its size. Later, when you modify data and major objects, compacting your database will be very important.

1. Click the **File** tab to navigate to the Backstage View.

2. On the **Info** tab, click **Compact & Repair Database**.

Figure 1-19
Compact & Repair
EcoMed-01.accdb

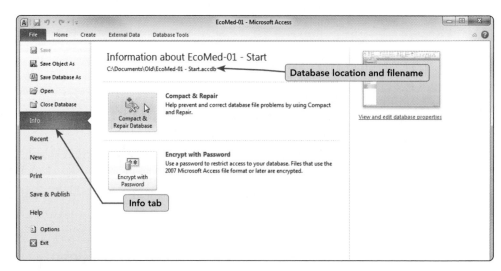

Exercise 1-17   BACK UP A DATABASE

You should get in the habit of backing up your database regularly. By default, the backup file is saved to the same location as the original file. The default name of your backup file is the current date and time appended to the end of the original file name. You can change both default values by typing in a new name.

1. Click the File tab to return to the Backstage.
2. From the list of commands on the left, click the Save Database As option to open the Save As dialog box.
3. In the dialog box's Navigation Pane (the left pane), select the location where you want to store your class work.
4. Press [Home] to move the cursor to the beginning of the filename in the File name control. Do not delete the current file name from the control.

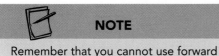

NOTE

Remember that you cannot use forward slash (/), semi-colon (;), or colon (:) symbols in filenames.

5. Key BK-*[mm]-[yy]-* (mm = current two-digit month, yy = current two-digit year.)
6. Click Save to close the old database and leave the backup copy of the database active.
7. In the Message Bar, click Enable Content.

Exercise 1-18   CLOSE A DATABASE

Now that you have compacted and backed up your database, you can close your database and exit Access.

You can use any of these methods:

- From the File command tab, choose Exit ⊠.
- In the upper right of the Access window, click the Close button ⊠ .
- From the File command tab, choose Close Database ⊡.
- Press [Alt]+[F4].

1. Click the File command tab.
2. From the list of command on the left, click the Exit button ⊠.

Lesson 1   Summary

- An Access database is relational, the most common type of database in use today.
- Major Access database objects include tables, queries, forms, and reports.
- A record is composed of related fields, a table is composed of related records, and a database is composed of related tables.

- A recordset is a Microsoft object–oriented data structure consisting of grouped records.
- A recordset is most often displayed as either a form or a report.
- An opened database cannot be moved or renamed.
- Shared mode is the default mode for most databases. This mode allows multiple users to use the database simultaneously.
- When opening a database for the first time in a location, a security warning displays on the Message Bar alerting you that the database may contain malicious code.
- In the Navigation Pane, major objects are organized by categories and groups.
- The Leszynski Naming Convention is a method of naming objects that emphasizes the use of three-letter prefixes to identify the type of object.
- Datasheet View and Design View are two methods of displaying each major object.
- Edit mode allows contents of fields to be changed.
- Navigation mode allows for movement among fields.
- The columns and rows of a datasheet can be hidden, displayed, or resized.
- Format changes to a datasheet affect all text in every column and row.
- In a datasheet, column widths can be changed individually; row heights must all be the same.
- In a datasheet, some format commands can be applied to individual fields; other commands apply to the entire datasheet.
- The Quick Print command sends a document directly to the default printer without allowing changes to print options.
- Documents can be printed or published in portrait or landscape orientation.
- A printable object can be saved as either an XPS or PDF file. The file preserves the document formatting in either reduced or high quality.
- Normal database activities such as adding, deleting, and moving data can unnecessarily increase the size of a database file.
- The Compact & Repair Database command reclaims unused space and improves database efficiency.

LESSON 1		Command Summary	
Feature	**Button**	**Task Path**	**Keyboard**
Close active object	✕ 🔲 🔲		Ctrl + W or Ctrl + F4
Close database	✕ 🔲 ✕	File, Exit	Alt + F4
Column width	↔	Shortcut menu, Column width	
Collapse Navigation Pane	«		
Compact database		File, Compact & Repair Database	
Database Properties		Shortcut menu, Properties	
Datasheet View	▦	Views, View, Datasheet View	
Design View	✎	Views, View, Design View	
Expand Navigation Pane	»		
Export Data	🗎	File, Share, Save Object As, PDF/XPS	
Font Face		Font, Font	
Font Size		Font, Font Size	
Hide Fields		Shortcut menu, Hide Fields	
Jump to next screen or record			Page Down
Jump to previous screen or record			Page Up
Move to beginning of field text			Home
Move to end of field text			End

continues

LESSON 1		Command Summary *continued*	
Feature	**Button**	**Task Path**	**Keyboard**
Move to first record	⏮		Ctrl + Home
Move to last record	⏭		Ctrl + End
Move to next field			Tab
Move to next record	▶		
Move to previous field			Shift + Tab
Move to previous record	◀		
Open database	📂	File, Open	Ctrl + O
Page Layout		Design View, Page Setup, Page Layout	
Print Preview	🔍	File, Print, Print Preview	
Print	🖨	File, Print	Ctrl + P
Row Height		Shortcut menu, Row Height	
Save	💾	File, Save	Ctrl + S
Save record changes			Shift + Enter
Unhide Fields		Shortcut menu, Unhide Fields	

Concepts Review

True/False Questions

Each of the following statements is either true or false. Indicate your choice by circling T or F.

T   F   1.   A record is the smallest storage element within a database.

T   F   2.   Through a form, you can edit fields in a recordset.

T   F   3.   In **Datasheet View**, each row can have a different height.

T   F   4.   You can use the navigation buttons to move to a specific record.

T   F   5.   A recordset cannot be more than a single field.

T   F   6.   In Access, the **Navigation Pane** organizes major database objects.

T   F   7.   The Leszynski Naming Convention emphasizes the use of spaces and underscores to identify types of objects.

T   F   8.   When you hide a column in **Datasheet View**, you are deleting the record from the table or query.

Short Answer Questions

Write the correct answer in the space provided.

1. What is the Leszynski Naming Convention prefix for table names?

_____

2. In **Datasheet View**, which buttons are used to move to different records?

_____

3. What is a collection of logically organized commands?

_____

4. What shortcut menu command displays a hidden column in **Datasheet View**?

_____

5. When you click the command tab **File**, what is the name of the resulting screen called?

_____

6. Which navigation button would move the insertion point from Record #3 if it is at Record #2?

_____

7. What format command allows alternating rows of a datasheet to display in different colors?

_____

8. Which database utility improves database efficiency and reduces storage requirements?

_____

Critical Thinking

Answer these questions on a separate page. There are no right or wrong answers. Support your answers with examples from your own experience, if possible.

1. Think of situations when it would be better to display a report as a PDF document rather than a printed paper. What best practice guidelines should your school implement to reduce the amount of paper used?

2. When establishing backup procedures, many companies make certain that daily copies are stored off site. Why would a company want to store copies of their data away from their offices? Where would you recommend that your school store backup copies of its databases? Where are you planning on storing copies of your homework or personal data?

Skills Review

Exercise 1-19

Database administrators often require databases to be documented. You have been asked to count the number tables and reports in the current database.

1. Locate and copy a database by following these steps:

   a. Locate and open the **Lesson 01** folder.

   b. If you already have a copy of *[your initials]*-**EcoMed-01**, skip to step 2.

   c. Right-click the file **EcoMed-01** and from the shortcut menu, choose **Copy**.

   d. Right-click an unused part of the folder. From the shortcut menu, choose **Paste**.

   e. Right-click the new file and from the shortcut menu, choose **Rename**. Rename the file *[your initials]*-EcoMed-01.

   f. Right-click *[your initials]*-**EcoMed-01** and from the shortcut menu, choose **Properties**. Make certain that the **Read-only** attribute check box is not checked. Click **OK**.

2. Open a database by following these steps:

    a. Double-click *[your initials]*-EcoMed-01.

    b. If the Message Bar's **Security Warning** appears, click the **Enable Content** button.

3. Create a Word document named *[your initials]*-01-19-A and record the answers to the following question:

    a. How many tables are in the database?

    b. Record your answer in the new Word file and place **Ex: 1-19 – Step 3a** next to your answer.

    c. How many reports are in the database?

    d. Record your answer in the same Word file as in step 3b and place **Ex: 1-19 – Step 3c** next to your answer.

    e. Add your name, class information, and today's date to the Word file.

01-19-A.docx
1 Page

Assessment

- According to your classroom procedure, turn in your database only when you have completed all assigned exercises.
- Depending on your class procedures, print or turn in the Word file.

-OR-

- Depending on your class procedures, print or turn in the Word file.

Exercise 1-20

You have been asked to create a PDF file of the Datasheet View of a table. First, you must resize the rows and columns.

1. The database *[your initials]*-EcoMed-01 is required to complete this exercise.

    a. If needed, double-click the database *[your initials]*-EcoMed-01.

    b. If the Message Bar's **Security Warning** appears, click the **Enable Content** button.

2. Navigate records in a table by following these steps:

    a. In the **Navigation Pane**, click the **Tables** group to expand the group.

    b. Double-click the table **tblFacType** to open it.

    c. In the Navigation bar, click the **Next Record** button ▶ twice to move to the third record.

    d. Press Tab to move to the second field.

    e. Press Ctrl+Home to move to the first field in the first record.

3. Resize rows and columns in **Datasheet View** by following these steps:

   a. Place the pointer on the vertical right edge of the column header for **Facility Type**.

   b. With the two-headed arrow showing, drag the pointer to the right until all the data in the field can be seen.

   c. Right-click on the record selector for the first row.

   d. In the **Row Height** dialog box, key **40** and click **OK**.

   e. Right-click the document tab for **tblFacType**, and choose **Save** 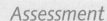.

4. View the **Datasheet View** of a table in **Print Preview** by following these step:

   a. Click the **File** tab.

   b. From the **Print** tab, choose **Print Preview** 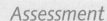.

5. Save the **Datasheet View** of the table by following these steps:

   a. In the **Data** command group, click **PDF or XPS** 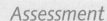 to save the printout as a file.

   b. Save the file with the following settings:

   - In the dialog box's **Navigation Pane**, select the location where you want to store your class work.
   - **File name** as *[your initials]*-01-20-A.
   - **Save as type** as PDF.
   - **Open file after publishing** should be checked.

   c. Click **Publish**. Close the PDF viewer and then close the **Export – PDF** window.

6. Close an object by following these steps:

   a. In the **Print Preview** tab, click **Close Print Preview** 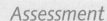.

   b. Right-click the **tblFacType** tab. From the shortcut menu, select **Close** 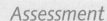.

   c. If Access asks you to save the changes, click **Yes**.

   d. In the **Navigation Pane**, collapse the **Tables** group.

7. Close an object by following these steps:

   a. In the **Print Preview** tab, click **Close Print Preview** 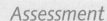.

   b. Right-click the **tblFacType** tab. From the shortcut menu, select **Close** 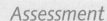.

   c. If Access asks you to save the changes, click **Yes**.

   d. In the **Navigation Pane**, collapse the **Tables** group.

01-20-A.pdf
1 Page

Assessment

- According to your classroom procedure, turn in your database only when you have completed all assigned exercises.
- Depending on your class procedures, print or turn in the PDF file.

-OR-

- Depending on your class procedures, print or turn in the PDF file.

Exercise 1-21

You have been asked to submit information located in the vender table to your supervisor. First, you must resize and hide columns.

1. The database *[your initials]*-**EcoMed-01** is required to complete this exercise.

    a. If needed, double-click the database *[your initials]*-**EcoMed-01**.

    b. If the Message Bar's Security Warning appears, click the Enable Content button.

2. Change the view by following these steps:

    a. In the Navigation Pane, expand the Tables group.

    b. In the Tables group of the Navigation Pane, double-click **tblVender**.

    c. In the command group Views, click the option arrow for the View button and select Design View.

    d. Right-click the document tab for the table, then select Datasheet View.

3. Hide and resize fields in a table by following these steps:

    a. Click on the column header for the field **PhoneNum** and drag through **FAX**.

    b. Right-click on the column header of a selected columns and select Hide Fields.

    c. Click on the column header for the field **VenderID** and drag through **ZIP**.

    d. Right-click on the column header of a selected columns and select Field Width.

    e. In the Column Width dialog box, click Best Fit.

    f. Right-click the document tab for **tblVender**, and choose Save.

4. View the Datasheet View of a table in Print Preview by following these step:

    a. Click the File tab.

    b. From the Print tab, choose Print Preview.

5. According to your classroom procedure, you can print the Datasheet View of a table or continue to one of the Assessment steps.

Assessment

- Close an object by following these steps:

    a. In the command group Close Preview, click Close Print Preview.

    b. Right-click the **tblVender** tab. From the shortcut menu, select Close.

    c. If Access asks you to save the changes, click Yes.

    d. In the Navigation Pane, collapse the Tables group.

- Turn in your database only when all assigned exercises have been completed, according to your classroom procedure.

-OR-

- Save the **Datasheet View** of the table by following these steps:

a. From the **Print Preview** tab, in the command group **Page Layout**, click **Landscape** .

b. In the **Data** command group, click **PDF or XPS** to save the printout as a file.

c. Save the file with the following settings:

   • In the dialog box's **Navigation Pane**, select the location where you want to store your class work.

   • **File name** as *[your initials]*-01-21-A.

   • **Save as type** as PDF.

   • **Open file after publishing** should be checked.

d. Click **Publish**. Close the PDF viewer and then the **Export – PDF** window.

e. Depending on your class procedures, print or turn in the PDF file.

- Close an object by following these steps:

a. In the command group **Close Preview**, click **Close Print Preview**.

b. Right-click the **tblVender** tab. From the shortcut menu, select **Close**.

c. If Access asks you to save the changes, click **Yes**.

d. In the **Navigation Pane**, collapse the **Tables** group.

01-21-A.pdf
1 Page

Exercise 1-22

You have been asked to submit to your supervisor information located in the query that counts bulb shapes. First, you must change the datasheet colors. You will also compact the database before closing it.

1. The database *[your initials]*-**EcoMed-01** is required to complete this exercise.

   a. If needed, double-click the database *[your initials]*-**EcoMed-01**.

   b. If the Message Bar's **Security Warning** appears, click the **Enable Content** button.

2. Change the view by following these steps:

   a. In the **Navigation Pane**, expand the **Queries** group.

   b. In the **Queries** group of the **Navigation Pane**, double-click **qryBulbShapeCount**.

   c. In the command group **Views**, click the option arrow for the View button and select **Design View**.

   d. Right-click the document tab for the queries, then select **Datasheet View**.

3. Change datasheet colors by following these steps:

   a. In the command group **Font**, click the down arrow for Alternate Row Color.

b. Of the **Standard Colors**, select **Maroon 2** (row 3, column 6) as the alternate color.

c. Press Ctrl+S to save the changes to the query.

Assessment

- Turn in your database only when all assigned exercises have been completed, according to your classroom procedure.

- Close an object by following these steps:

  a. Right-click **qryBulbShapeCount** document tab. From the shortcut menu select **Close**.

  b. If Access asks you to save the changes, click **Yes**.

  c. In the **Navigation Pane**, collapse the **Queries** group.

- Compact and close the database by following these steps:

  a. Click the **File** command tab.

  b. From the **Info** option, choose **Compact & Repair Database**.

  c. Click the **File** command tab and select **Exit** ⊠.

-OR-

- Save the **Datasheet View** of the table by following these steps:

  a. Click the **File** tab. From the **Print** option, choose **Print Preview** 🔍.

  b. In the **Data** command group, click **PDF or XPS** to save the printout as a file.

  c. Save the file with the following settings:

   • In the dialog box's **Navigation Pane**, select the location where you want to store your class work.

   • **File name** as *[your initials]*-01-22-A.

   • **Save as type** as PDF.

   • **Open file after publishing** should be checked.

  d. Click **Publish**. Close the PDF viewer and then the **Export – PDF** window.

  e. Depending on your class procedures, print or turn in the PDF file.

- Close an object by following these steps:

  a. Right-click the **qryBulbShapeCount** document tab. From the shortcut menu, select **Close**.

  b. If Access asks you to save the changes, click **Yes**.

  c. In the **Navigation Pane**, collapse the **Queries** group.

- Compact and close the database by following these steps:

  a. Click the **File** command tab.

  b. From the **Info** option, choose **Compact & Repair Database**.

  c. Click the **File** command tab and select **Exit** ⊠.

01-22-A.pdf
1 Page

Lesson Applications

Exercise 1-23

You have been asked to modify the Datasheet View of the query that counts the number of facilities per state.

1. Using the database *[your initials]*-EcoMed-01, make sure that all content is enabled.

2. Open **qryFacStateCount** in Datasheet View.

3. Change the Font Size to **14** and apply the italic font style.

4. Size each column to fit its longest data and column title.

5. Save the changes to the query.

Assessment

- Close all objects and collapse all groups in the Navigation Pane.
- Turn in your database only when all assigned exercises have been completed, according to your classroom procedure.

-OR-

- Save as a PDF file named *[your initials]*-01-23-A.
- According to your class procedures, print or turn in the PDF file.
- Close all objects and collapse all groups in the Navigation Pane.

01-23-A.pdf
1 Page

Exercise 1-24

You have been asked to change the appearance and font selection of the Datasheet View of a table. You have also been asked to change the orientation of the datasheet to landscape orientation.

1. With database *[your initials]*-EcoMed-01, open **tblBulbShapes** in Datasheet View.

2. Apply the Alternate Row Color 🔲 to the standard color Green 3 (row 4, column 7).

3. Change the Font to Courier New and the Font Size to 16.

4. Size each column to fit its longest data and column title. All the data should fit on one page.

5. Change the orientation to Landscape 🔲.

Assessment

- Close all objects and collapse all groups in the Navigation Pane.
- Close the query, save changes to the datasheet, and collapse the query group in the Navigation Pane.
- Turn in your database only when all assigned exercises have been completed, according to your classroom procedure.

-OR-

- Save as a PDF file named *[your initials]*-01-24-A.
- According to your class procedures, print or turn in the PDF file.
- Close the query, save changes to the datasheet, and collapse the query group in the Navigation Pane.

01-24-A.pdf
1 Page

Exercise 1-25

You have been asked to create a simple PDF file showing facility IDs, facility names, and phone number for facilities in Texas.

1. Using the database *[your initials]*-**EcoMed-01**, make sure that all content is enabled.

2. Open **qryFac-TX** in Datasheet View.

3. Hide all columns except **Facilities ID**, **Facility Name**, and **Phone Number**.

4. Resize the row height to **20**.

5. Size each column to fit its longest data and column title.

6. Set the orientation of the printout to Portrait 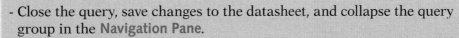.

7. Save the Datasheet as a PDF file named *[your initials]*-01-25-A.

01-25-A.pdf
1 Page

Assessment

- Close the query, save changes to the datasheet, and collapse the query group in the Navigation Pane.
- Turn in your database only when all assigned exercises have been completed, according to your classroom procedure.

-OR-

- According to your class procedures, print or turn in the PDF file.
- Close the table, save changes to the datasheet, and collapse the table group in the Navigation Pane.

UNIT 1 LESSON 1

Exercise 1-26 ◆ Challenge Yourself

You have been asked to document specific aspects of the database.

1. Using the database *[your initials]*-**EcoMed-01**, make sure that all content is enabled.

2. Expand the Tables group and Query group in the **Navigation Pane**.

3. Create a Word document called *[your initials]*-**01-26-A** and record the answers to the following questions.

4. Which query has the most records?

5. Which table has the fewest records?

6. How many queries are in this database?

7. Include your name, class information, and today's date on your answer sheet.

01-26-A.docx
1 Page

Assessment

- Close all objects and collapse all groups in the **Navigation Pane**.
- Turn in your database only when all assigned exercises have been completed, according to your classroom procedure.
- According to your class procedures, print or turn in the Word document.

-OR-

- According to your class procedures, print or turn in the Word document.
- Close all objects and collapse all groups in the **Navigation Pane**.

On Your Own

In these exercises, you work on your own, as you would in a real-life work environment. Use the skills you've learned to accomplish the task—and be creative.

NOTE

The "On Your Own" exercises in this text are all related. They form a single project. To complete the project, you must do all the "On Your Own" exercises in each lesson.

Exercise 1-27

Assume that you are forming a new club or professional association. Begin analyzing your needs on paper. Decide the name of your organization. Write one or two paragraphs describing the mission or purpose of your group. After you have completed this exercise, continue to the next exercise.

Exercise 1-28

Now think about the specific type of information your club or association will need to track its membership. Write a bulleted list of information you want to collect for each member (e.g., first name, e-mail address). You should have no fewer than seven items. Continue to the next exercise.

Exercise 1-29

Using the list you created in Exercise 1-28, gather information on five potential members. On a single sheet of paper, record the data you collected. Submit your work for Exercises 1-27 through 1-29 to your instructor.

Lesson 2
Viewing and Modifying Records

OBJECTIVES   *After completing this lesson, you will be able to:*

1. Modify recordsets in a table.

2. Modify recordsets through a query.

3. Use Office edit tools.

4. View and modifying recordsets through a form.

5. Manage attachments.

6. Preview, print and save data through a report.

Estimated Time: 1½ hours

In Lesson 1, you learned general information about the database environment, including how to identify major objects in the EcoMed database such as tables, queries, forms, and reports. In this lesson, you will learn to add, edit, delete, and print data. You also will learn how to use time-saving edit commands like duplicate, copy, and paste. Finally, you will learn how to attach images to a record in tables.

As a student intern for EcoMed Services, Inc., you will work directly with data in tables or as a recordset through a query, form, or report. Although you can modify data through a table in Datasheet View, more often it is easier to use a query and form to limit the amount of data viewed at one time.

Modifying Recordsets in a Table

Records are routinely added to databases. For example, whenever a new student enrolls at your school, several records regarding the new student are added to your school's database. Whenever EcoMed Services, Inc., gets a new customer, you will need to add the customer's information to the database.

On other occasions, a record might be deleted if the information will no longer be used. However, not all databases allow records to be deleted. For example, when a bank customer closes an account, all records are not deleted. The account is moved to an inactivate status and is no longer accessible for use, but all information is retained indefinitely.

Exercise 2-1 OPEN A DATABASE

In a real company, you would be working with only one primary database. However, for the purposes of this textbook, you will use a new database for each lesson. For Lesson 2, the database and related files are located in the **Lesson 02** folder provided with the book. At the beginning of each lesson, you will use the appropriate database needed for the lesson. Before working with the file, you must copy and rename the file.

1. Open the folder **Lesson 02**.

2. Right-click the file **EcoMed-02** and from the shortcut menu, choose Copy.

3. Right-click the file **EcoMed-02** and from the shortcut menu, choose Rename. On your keyboard, press Home to move to the beginning of the file name. Key your initials and then a hyphen. Press Enter to accept the new name.

TIP

If a Read-Only message appears in the Message Bar, you will need to close the database, deselect the Read-only property, and reopen the file.

4. Right-click *[your initials]*-**EcoMed-02** and from the shortcut menu, choose Properties. Make certain that the Read-only attribute check box is not checked. Click OK.

5. Double-click *[your initials]*-**EcoMed-02** to open the database.

6. If the Message Bar's Security Warning appears, click the Enable Content button.

Exercise 2-2 EDIT FIELDS IN A TABLE

You do not need to "save" when you make changes to data in a record. Access automatically saves your changes as soon as you move the insertion point from the modified record to any other record.

You can determine if a record was saved by the shape of pointer in the *Record Selector*. If a shape does not appear in the record selector, then the record has already been saved. Two shapes can appear in the record selector:

*   A pencil icon appears while you are adding or editing text. This shape indicates the record changes have not been saved.

*   An asterisk marks a new record that does not have data in any field.

1. In the Navigation Pane, expand the Tables group and double-click **tblManagement** to open it in Datasheet View.

2. Locate the **ManageID** 3 and click in the second field **Management Company**. This action places the insertion point in the field.

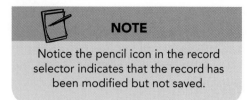

NOTE

Notice the pencil icon in the record selector indicates that the record has been modified but not saved.

3. Press End to move the insertion point to end of the data in the field.

4. Press Ctrl + Backspace to delete the word to the right of the insertion point, "Center."

Figure 2-1
Modifying a record
EcoMed-02.accdb
tblManagement

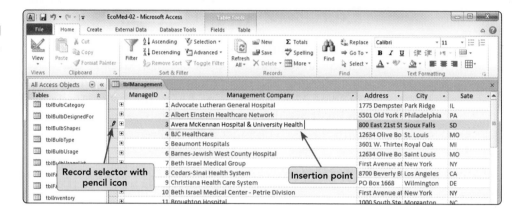

5. Key **Complex**.

6. Press ↓. Notice that the pencil icon has disappeared from the record selector, which indicates that the changes to the record have been saved.

7. Press ↑. The whole field is selected without an insertion point. Press End to move to the last field in the record.

TIP

Keys like End behave differently when the insertion point is present.

8. Press Shift + Tab to move to the previous field.

9. Key **Butler** to change the last name.

10. Press Tab to move to the next field.

11. Press the space bar to delete the selected data.

12. Press Esc to undo the deletion of the **ContractEnds** data.

NOTE

Esc acts as an undo but only for the changes in the current field.

13. Press ↓ to save the changes to the record.

Exercise 2-3 ADD A RECORD IN A TABLE

For a person familiar with spreadsheets, the simplest way to add records to a table is in Datasheet View. Datasheet View looks very similar to a worksheet. You add new records to the last row of the table. The last row of the table is marked by an asterisk in the record selector. You move to the new record row using any of the following steps:

• Right-click a record selector and on the shortcut menu, select **New Record** .

• From the Navigation buttons, click the New Record button .

• From the **Home** tab, in the command group **Records**, select **New** .

• Ctrl + +.

TIP

When a new record is being added to a table, a star icon will appear in the record selector of the new record.

NOTE

The first column lists field names. The second column contains data to be entered along with special characters and instructions. Red text is entered exactly as shown. Black symbols (such as in the phone number) automatically appear and do not need to be keyed. *Orange italic* indicates specific instructions for the field.

1. From the command tab Home, in the command group Records, click New ⬜. This action moves the insertion point to the empty record at the bottom of the table.

2. Key the information below to create a new record. Press [Tab] to move from one field to the next.

ManagementID:	*Press* [Tab]
Management Company:	Rhode Island Hospital
Address:	593 Eddy Street
City:	Providence
State:	RI
ZIP:	02903
Phone Number:	(401) 444-4000
Contact First Name:	Kenneth
Contact Last Name:	Hammond
ContractEnds:	*Press* [Ctrl]+[;]

3. Press [Shift]+[Enter] to save the changes without leaving the new record.

4. Press [Ctrl]+[PageUp] to return to the first field in the record.

Exercise 2-4 DELETE A RECORD IN A TABLE

There are times when you find that records are no longer needed and should be removed from a table. An example might be that you find a record that was entered into the wrong table.

To delete one or more records, you must first select the record(s) that you intend to delete. After selecting the record(s) you can use one of four methods:

- Select a record and press [Delete].
- Right-click a selected record and on the shortcut menu, select Delete Record.
- From the command tab Home, in the command group Records, select Delete ✕.
- [Ctrl]+[-].

REVIEW

The record selector is the narrow gray column to the left of the first field in the Datasheet View of a table or query.

1. In the Datasheet View of the table tblManagement, click in the record selector to select the record for "High Country Hospital" (ManageID 111).

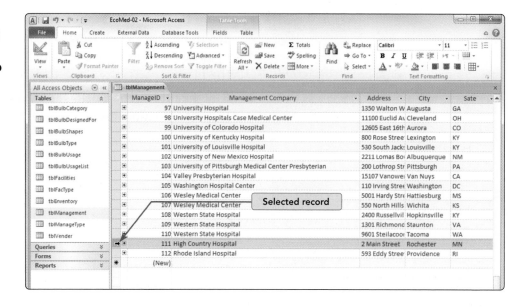

2. Press Delete. The record disappears, and a dialog box opens asking you to confirm the deletion.

3. Click **Yes**. Access deletes the record.
4. Click in the record selector to select the record for "Western State Hospital" (**ManageID** 110).
5. Press Ctrl + - and then click **No** to decline the deletion.
6. In the **Navigation Pane**, collapse the **Tables** group. Do not close the table.

Modifying Recordsets through a Query

Modifying data through a table is not always practical. If the table is large, you will spend excessive time moving around the table. To be more efficient, you should use a query instead of a table. When you use a query to make changes to data, you are making changes to the recordset. Although the records display in the query, the data are actually stored in a table.

An advantage to editing through a query over a table is that the recordset of a query does not have to display all the records or fields in the table. Using a query allows you to view only the relevant fields and records. When you edit a record in a query, the data in the underlying table are changed automatically.

Exercise 2-5 EDIT FIELDS THROUGH A QUERY

When editing a record, you can insert text or use the Overtype mode to key over existing text. Use [Insert] to switch between Insert and Overtype modes.

1. In the **Queries** group of the **Navigation Pane**, double-click the **qryManageUniv**. Notice that there are only 22 records. This query is showing only management companies that are universities.

2. In the record for "Temple University Hospital," in the field **Contact Last Name**, click to the right of "-" in "Salamanca-Riba."

3. Press [Insert] to switch to **Overtype** mode. When you are in **Overtype** mode, "Overtype" appears on the status bar, and the insertion point becomes a block.

Figure 2-4
Overtype mode
EcoMed-02.accdb
qryManageUniv

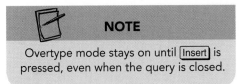

Methodist University Hospital	Wei	(901) 516-7000
North Shore University Hospital	Monagle	(516) 562-0100
Ohio State University Hospital	Jiang	(614) 293-8000
Robert Wood Johnson University Hospital	Kissiah	(732) 828-3000
Robert Wood Johnson University Hospital at Rahway	Ashigh	(732) 381-4200
Robert Wood Johnson University Hospital Hamilton	Fetterolf	(609) 586-7900
Shands at the University of Florida	Herd	(352) 265-8000
Temple University Hospital	Salamanca-Riba	(215) 707-2000	Insertion point becomes a block
Thomas Jefferson University Hospital	Shukla	(215) 955-6000
University Hospital	Conlee	(513) 584-1000

NOTE

Overtype mode stays on until [Insert] is pressed, even when the query is closed.

4. Key **Simm**.

5. Press [Insert] to return to **Insert** mode. The block returns to an insertion point.

6. Press [Ctrl]+[S] to save the record while leaving the insertion point in the field.

7. Click the document tab for **tblManagement** and click in the **ManageID** 87.

8. Press [Tab], then [End] to move to the last field in this record. The changes that you made to the last name in the query are saved in the table.

Exercise 2-6 ADD A RECORD THROUGH A QUERY

The additions made in a query's recordset are simultaneously made to the underlying table. In the EcoMed database, additions made through qryManageUniv are actually stored in tblManagement. The corresponding fields in the table are updated through a query, even though the query's recordset does not display all the fields in the source table.

1. Click on the document tab for **qryManageUniv** and press [Ctrl]+[+] to move to a new record.

2. Key the customer information below to create a new record. Press [Tab] to move from one field to the next.

Management Company: University Hospital
Contact Last Name: *Key [your full name]*
Phone Number: (555) 555-1800

NOTE

In this text, to help identify your work, you often are asked to key an identifier such as your name or initials.

NOTE

The **ManageID** field has been set to assign a unique sequential number automatically. This unique number helps identify individual records.

3. From the command tab **Home**, in the command group **Records**, click **Save** to save the record.

4. Click the **tblManagement** tab and, using the record navigation button Last record , move to the last record.

5. From the command tab **Home**, in the command group **Records**, click **Refresh All**. This action forces the table to update changes to the record.

6. You should now see the record that you just created. Because the query did not display all the fields in the table, the newly created record is incomplete.

Exercise 2-7   DELETE A RECORD THROUGH A QUERY

Similar to adding a record through a query, you can delete a record through a query. The record will be removed from both the query (qryManageUniv) and the underlying table (tblManagement).

1. Click the document tab for **qryManageUniv** and click the record selector for the last record. This record should be the record for "University Hospital" that you entered earlier.

NOTE

When you deleted the record while in the query **qryManageUniv**, Access automatically refreshed the query. By selecting Refresh All, you force Access to refresh the data being displayed in all open objects.

2. Right-click the selected record. From the shortcut menu, select **Delete Record** . Click **Yes** to confirm the deletion.

3. Click the document tab for **tblManagement**. Notice that the record you deleted has "#Deleted" in each cell.

4. From the command tab **Home**, in the command group **Records**, click **Refresh All** .

5. Press Ctrl + End and then Home . Notice that the record with your name has now been deleted.

6. Right-click the **tblManagement** tab. From the shortcut menu, select **Close All** .

7. In the **Navigation Pane**, collapse the **Queries** group.

Using Office Editing Tools

Similar to Word and Excel, Access uses AutoCorrect. *AutoCorrect* is an application feature that automatically corrects commonly misspelled words. The AutoCorrect Options button appears next to text being automatically corrected. Choices within the button allow you to customize the correction process. You can undo the correction, cancel future automatic corrections for this error, or turn off the AutoCorrect option completely.

The Office Clipboard is a feature available in Microsoft Word, Excel, PowerPoint, Access, and Outlook. You can use this clipboard to collect and paste multiple items. You can copy items from any program that provides copy and cut functionality, but you can only paste items into a Microsoft Office application. If you have multiple Office programs running, the contents of the Office Clipboard are deleted after you close the last Office program.

Exercise 2-8　USE AUTOCORRECT

Text edit commands are used to make changes to the data within a record. AutoCorrect corrects commonly misspelled words as you key the text. For example, if you type "hte," AutoCorrect will change it to "the." AutoCorrect fixes many capitalization errors.

1. Click the **File** tab, and then click **Options** .
2. In the left pane, click **Proofing**.
3. In the right pane, click the **AutoCorrect Options** button to open the **AutoCorrect** dialog box.

Figure 2-5
AutoCorrect dialog box
EcoMed-02.accdb

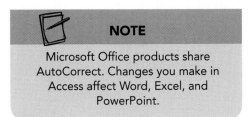

NOTE

Microsoft Office products share AutoCorrect. Changes you make in Access affect Word, Excel, and PowerPoint.

4. Make sure all checkboxes are checked. These are the automatic actions that AutoCorrect will perform during data entry.
5. Scroll down the list of entries to see which words are in the AutoCorrect dictionary.

TABLE 2-1 AutoCorrect Options

Options	Description
Show AutoCorrect option buttons	Option button appears after a word was automatically corrected.
Correct TWo INitial CApitals	Corrects words keyed with two initial capital letters, such as "THis."
Capitalize first letter of sentences	Capitalizes the first letter in a sentence.
Capitalize names of days	Capitalizes days of the week and months.
Correct accidental use of cAPS LOCK key	Corrects words keyed with Caps Lock on but [Shift] key pressed, such as cAPS.
Replace text as you type	Makes corrections as you work.

6. Click **OK** to close the **AutoCorrect** dialog box.

7. Click **OK** to close the **Access Options** dialog box.

8. In the **Tables** group of the **Navigation Pane**, double-click the table **tblVender**.

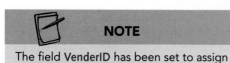

NOTE

The field **VenderID** has been set to assign a unique sequential number automatically.

9. Press [Ctrl]+[+] to add a new record.

10. Press [Tab] to move to the **VenderName** field.

11. Key **ACN**.

12. Press the space bar. Notice that "ACN" changed to "CAN".

13. Place your pointer over the corrected word. Click the **AutoCorrect Options** icon ⓩ. When it appears, select **Change back to "ACN"**.

14. Key **Inc.** to complete the field.

15. Press [Tab] to move to the **ContactName** field.

16. Key **TOm Heart**. Notice that AutoCorrect corrected the name to "Tom Heart."

17. Press [Tab] to move to the next field.

Exercise 2-9 USE COPY, PASTE, AND THE OFFICE CLIPBOARD

You can copy a block of text from one part of a table to another. There are three ways to copy and paste text:

- From the ribbon, click **Copy** 🗎, then click **Paste** 📋.
- Press [Ctrl]+[C] (copy), then [Ctrl]+[V] (paste).
- Right-click and from the shortcut menu, choose **Copy**, then **Paste**.

When you copy the second text block, the Office Clipboard pane opens. You can use the Office Clipboard to paste multiple blocks of text. From that pane, you can select the item you want to paste.

You can use the duplicate command to copy one field at a time. You can duplicate the data from a field in the previous record to the same field in the current record by pressing Ctrl+' (apostrophe).

You can also paste an entire record from one location to another by using the Paste Append command. To use this command you must match all fields in both records.

1. From the command tab **Home**, in the right lower corner of the command group **Clipboard**, click the dialog box launcher ⌐ to open the **Clipboard** pane.

2. Find the record for **VenderID** 27 and click to the left of the "C" in "Capitol." Press Shift+End to select all text to the right of the insertion point.

3. Press Ctrl+C to copy. Notice that the selected text has been added to the **Clipboard**.

4. Hover your mouse over the copied text in the **Clipboard** pane. An option arrow appears to the right of the copied text.

Figure 2-6
Clipboard pane
EcoMed-02.accdb
tblVender

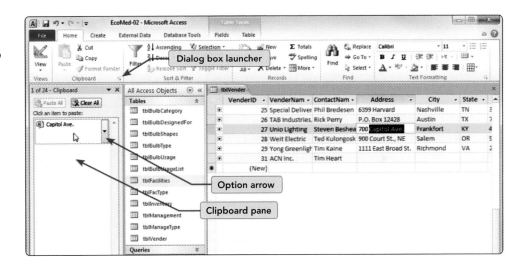

5. Press Tab to move to the **City** field.

6. Right-click the selected text and choose **Copy** from the shortcut menu. This text has been added to the **Clipboard** pane.

7. Press Tab to move to the **State** field.

8. From the command tab **Home**, in the command group **Clipboard**, click **Copy** 📋. You now have three items in the **Clipboard** pane.

9. Click in the **Address** field for **VenderName** "ACN Inc." and key **2800**.

10. Press the space bar.

11. In the **Clipboard** pane, click the option arrow for "Capitol Ave." and select **Paste** from the menu. The copied text has been added to the field you were editing.

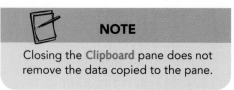

NOTE

Closing the **Clipboard** pane does not remove the data copied to the pane.

12. Press Tab. From the **Clipboard** pane, click "Frankfort."

13. Press Tab. From the **Clipboard** pane, click "KY."

14. Press Shift + Enter to save the changes to the record.

15. In the upper right of the **Clipboard** pane, click **Close** ✕.

Exercise 2-10   USE UNDO

In a previous exercise you used Esc to cancel changes in a field. You will now use the Undo button ↶, which can affect fields, records, or even major objects.

Access remembers changes to the record and lets you undo most edits. If you accidentally delete text in a field, you can use the Undo command to reverse the action. One exception is if you delete a record, which cannot be undone. There are two ways to undo an action:

• On the Quick Access Toolbar click Undo ↶.

• Press Ctrl + Z.

1. Press Tab. Press Ctrl + ' to copy the data from the field above into the current record. This number is not the correct ZIP for this record, but the point here is to show the keystroke shortcut.

2. In the Quick Access Toolbar, click Undo ↶. All unsaved changes to the record are removed.

Figure 2-7
Undo changes to a record
**EcoMed-02.accdb
tblVender**

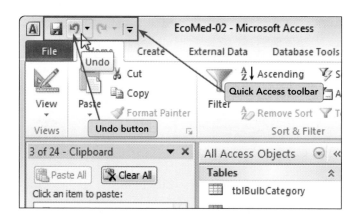

3. Click the Record Selector for vender "ACN Inc." and press Delete.

4. Read the dialog box and then click **Yes** to confirm the deletion.

5. Press Ctrl + Z to attempt to undo the deletion. Nothing happens because once a record is deleted, it cannot be undone.

6. Right-click the document tab for **tblVender**. From the shortcut menu, select **Close** ◳.

7. In the **Navigation Pane**, right-click the table **tblVender**, and from the shortcut menu, choose **Delete**.

8. In the dialog box, click **Yes**. The table is deleted.

9. Press Ctrl+Z to undo the deletion of the table.

10. In the **Navigation Pane**, collapse the **Tables** group.

Viewing and Modifying Recordsets through a Form

A form is a major Access object. A form is designed to be used on a computer screen. Through a form, you can enter, view, sort, edit, and print data. Most often when making changes to records, it is easier to use a form rather than a table. A form uses the same navigation buttons, scroll bars, and text editing features as a table.

Exercise 2-11 NAVIGATE THROUGH FORMS

A form is linked to a recordset. The fields displayed through a form are the same as in the table or query from which they originate.

1. In the **Forms** group of the **Navigation Pane**, double-click the form **frmVender**. This form is using the Single Form view.

2. In the **Forms** group of the **Navigation Pane**, double-click the form **frmVenderList**. This form is using the Multiple Items Form view to display data.

3. In the **Forms** group of the **Navigation Pane**, double-click the form **frmVenderSplit**. This form is using the Split Form view.

Figure 2-8
Multiple open documents
EcoMed-02.accdb frmVenderSplit

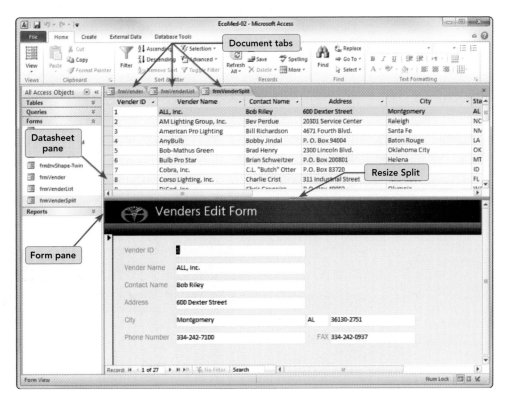

4. Click the document tab for **frmVenderList**.

5. Press Tab to move the cursor to the second field (**Vender Name**) in the first record.

6. Press Ctrl+PageDown to move to the second record in the same field.

7. Press Ctrl+End to move to the last field in the last record.

8. Click the document tab for the form **frmVender**.

9. Press Tab seven times. Notice the selected field order is not always left to right or top down.

10. Press PageDown to move to the next record. Notice that the field **State** is still selected.

11. In the record navigation tool, click the **Last Record** button ⏭. The record for vender 27 is now visible.

12. Click the document tab for **frmVenderSplit**.

13. Press Tab to move through the first record. Notice that the fields in the form are not in the same order as in the datasheet.

14. Press PageDown to move to the next record. Notice that the information in the selected record and the form are the same.

Exercise 2-12   EDIT FIELDS THROUGH A FORM

You can edit data in a form with the same shortcuts you use in a table or a query. For example, Backspace deletes a single character, and the keyboard combination Ctrl+Delete deletes everything to the right of the insertion point.

The data displayed in each field of a form is stored in a table. By using Datasheet View, you can also delete text from a form in the same way you can delete text from a table.

1. Click the document tab for the form **frmVenderList**.

2. Press Ctrl+Home to move to the first record.

3. Press Tab three times to move to the **Address** field.

4. Press F2 to place the insertion point into the field.

5. Press Ctrl+Backspace to delete one word to the left of the insertion point.

6. Key **Blvd.** Notice the pencil icon in the record selector.

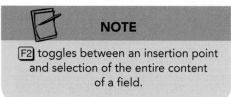

NOTE

F2 toggles between an insertion point and selection of the entire content of a field.

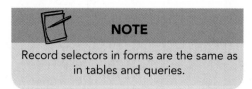

NOTE

Record selectors in forms are the same as in tables and queries.

Figure 2-9
Edit data in a form
**EcoMed-02.accdb
frmVenderList**

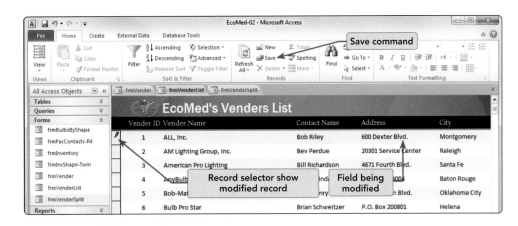

7. From the command tab **Home**, in the command group **Records**, click **Save** ▣.

8. Click the document tab for **frmVenderSplit**.

9. In the datasheet at the top of the form, click in the **Address** field for vender 8.

10. In the field, double-click the word Street and key **Blvd.**.

11. Press [Shift]+[Enter] to save the changes. Notice that the data in the **Address** field has not changed in the lower part of the form.

12. Press [↓] and then [↑]. The changes now appear in the form.

13. Click in any field in the form (lower half.)

Exercise 2-13 ADD RECORDS THROUGH A FORM

A form can make it easier for you to add records. A well-designed form utilizes field placement to improve the efficiency of data entry. Forms in the EcoMed database are designed for effective and efficient data entry.

1. From the command tab **Home**, in the command group **Records**, click **New** ▣. The record selector will display an asterisk until you key new data.

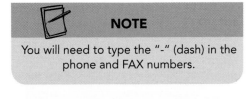
NOTE
You will need to type the "-" (dash) in the phone and FAX numbers.

2. Key the following new record, pressing [Tab] between entries:

Vender ID:	*Press* [Tab]
Vender Name:	*Key [your school's name]*
Contact Name:	*Key [your full name]*
Address:	825 Canal Street
City:	Cary
State:	NC
ZIP:	27513
Phone:	919-555-1601
FAX:	919-555-1602

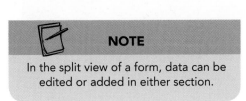
NOTE
In the split view of a form, data can be edited or added in either section.

Figure 2-10
Adding a new record
**EcoMed-02.accdb
frmVenderSplit**

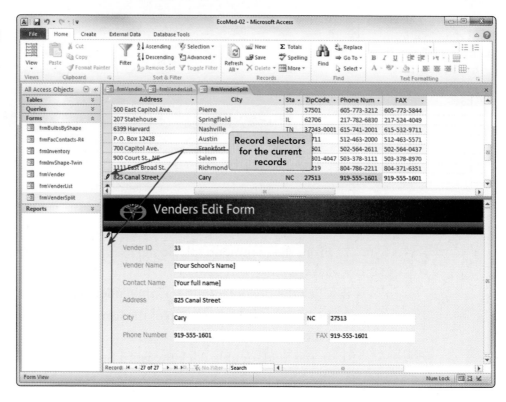

3.   Press Ctrl+S to save the new record.

Exercise 2-14   DELETE RECORDS THROUGH A FORM

You can delete the current record by using all the same methods you used when deleting a record in a table. The records will disappear from the form and the underlying table.

1.   Click the document tab for **frmVenderList**.

2.   Click in any field for the vender "EarthElectric, Inc." (**Vender ID** 10).

3.   From the command tab **Home**, in the command group **Records**, click the **Delete** option arrow ☒ and choose **Delete Record** 📄.

Figure 2-11
Delete options
**EcoMed-02.accdb
frmVenderList**

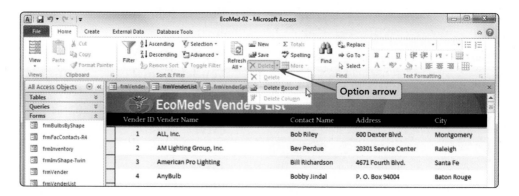

4.   Click **Yes** to confirm the deletion.

5.   Click the document tab for the form **frmVenderSplit**. Navigate to where vender 10 should be. Notice that there is a row with "#Deleted" in each field.

6. From the command tab **Home**, in the command group **Records**, click **Refresh All** 🔄.

7. Right-click the **frmVenderSplit** tab. From the shortcut menu, select **Close All**.

8. In the **Navigation Pane**, collapse the **Forms** group.

Managing Attachments

Some tables include an image with each record. The Inventory table and the Bulb Shapes table include a field with an image of the product. The attached images can be any type of image file including jpg, gif, or tiff.

In addition to images, you can attach certain types of data files such as documents, worksheets, or text files. The Attachments window allows you to add, remove, open, or save an attachment. Attached files cannot be larger than 256 megabytes or be non-data files such as programs, system files, or batch files.

Exercise 2-15   ATTACH AN IMAGE

When attaching an image, you must know the location of the file and in which record the file will be stored.

1. In the **Tables** group of the **Navigation Pane**, double-click the table **tblInventory**.

2. Click anywhere in the record for **InvID** 5.

3. Press F2 and then End to move to the last field in this record.

4. Press Shift+Tab. Double-click in the attachment field for the selected record. The **Attachments** dialog box appears.

Figure 2-12
Adding an attachment
EcoMed-02.accdb
tblInventory

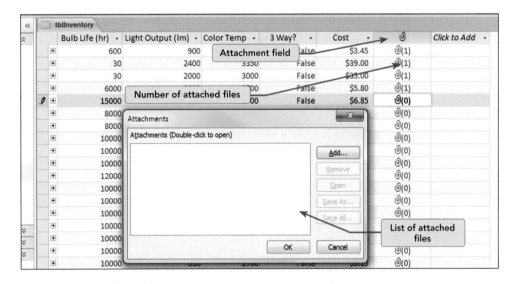

5. Any names of attached field will appear in this dialog box. Click **Add**.

6. In the **Lesson 02** folder, double-click the file **CL-10WL.jpg**.

7. Click **OK** to close the **Attachment** dialog box.

8. Press Ctrl+S to save the changes for the record.

9. Right-click the table's document tab, and choose **Close** from the shortcut menu.

10. In the **Navigation Pane**, collapse the **Tables** group.

11. In the **Forms** group of the **Navigation Pane**, double-click the form **frmInventory**.

12. Press PageDown until you get to **InvID** 5's record.

13. Click the picture. A mini toolbar appears above the image.

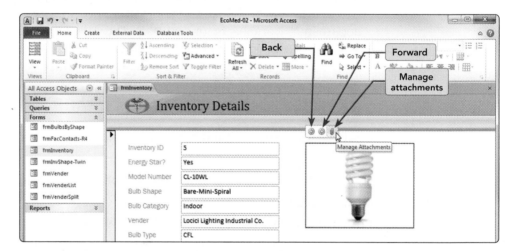

14. On the mini toolbar, click the Manage Attachments button 🔗.

15. In the **Attachments** dialog box, click **Add**.

16. In the **Lesson 02** folder, double-click the file **CL-10WLc.jpg**. You now have two files attached to this record.

17. Click **OK** to close the **Attachment** dialog box.

18. On the mini toolbar, click the **Forward** button ◉ to see the second file.

Exercise 2-16　EXTRACT AN IMAGE FROM THE DATABASE

Extracting is different than removing an image. When you remove an image, you delete that image from the record. When you extract an image, you save a copy of the image as a file that can be stored outside the database. Extracting a file does not affect the original image stored in the database.

1. Press PageUp until the data for **Inventory ID** 4 are displayed in the form.

2. Double-click the image of the product to open the **Attachment** dialog box.

3. Click **Save As**.

4. In the **Save Attachment** dialog box, change the **File name** to **Circuline.jpg**.

5. Check the file path in the location bar. Change if needed.

6. Click **Save** to save a copy of the image outside of the database.

REVIEW

If you close a major object after modifying or adding a record, Access will save the changes without prompting the user.

7. Click **OK** to close the **Attachment** dialog box.

8. Close the form by right-clicking the form's document tab and choosing **Close**.

9. In the **Navigation Pane**, collapse the **Forms** group.

Previewing, Printing, and Exporting Data through a Report

Just as forms are designed to view data on a screen, reports are designed to view data on paper. Forms are designed to fit on a standard computer screen, while reports are designed to fit on sheets of paper. From the Print dialog box, you can set a print range or change the page orientation.

Exercise 2-17   PREVIEW A REPORT

Print Preview shows you how the selected report prints on paper. *Print Preview* is a method for displaying on the screen how an object will appear if printed on paper.

TIP

To use the Print Preview ribbon for tables, queries, and forms, you must click the **File** tab and select the **Print** option.

1. In the **Reports** group of the **Navigation Pane**, double-click the report **rptInvShort**.

2. Right-click the report's document tab and choose **Print Preview** 🔍.

3. From the command tab **Print Preview**, in the command group **Page Layout**, click **Portrait** 📄.

Figure 2-14
Print Preview
EcoMed-02.accdb
rptInvShort

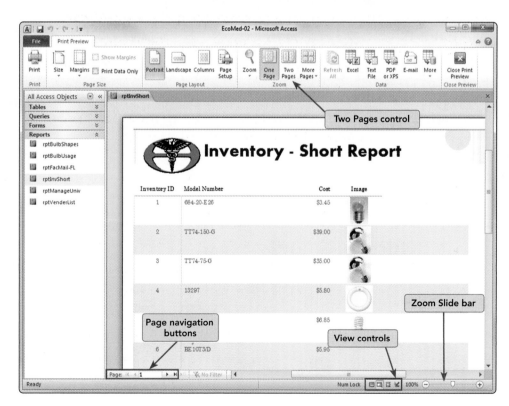

4. From the command tab **Print Preview**, in the command group **Zoom**, click **One Page** . Even though this command was already selected, clicking it again will resize the report so that the first page will fit fully on the screen.

5. In the Page navigation control located in the lower left corner of the **Print Preview** window, click Last Page ⏮. This report is 22 pages long.

6. Right-click the report's document tab and choose **Close** ⬛.

Exercise 2-18   PRINT A REPORT

Depending on the size of the report, you may need to change the page orientation, margins, or both. You can set the print orientation to either portrait or landscape depending on the data being printed.

1. In the **Reports** group of the **Navigation Pane**, double-click the report **rptVenderList**.

2. In the right end of the status bar are the change view buttons. Click **Print Preview** ⬛.

NOTE

Most printers cannot print all the way to the edge of a page. Each printer may have a slightly different margin setting. Reports can act differently depending on your printer. If you do not get exactly the same results as depicted in this exercise, you may need to modify the report.

3. A warning dialog box appears. This report has a problem with its width. Click **OK**.

4. From the command tab **Print Preview**, in the command group **Zoom**, click **Two Pages** ⬛. Notice that this report has overflowed onto a blank page.

5. From the command tab **Print Preview**, in the command group **Page Size**, click the **Margins** option arrow ⬛ and select **Narrow**.

Figure 2-15
Changing margin settings
EcoMed-02.accdb
rptVenderList

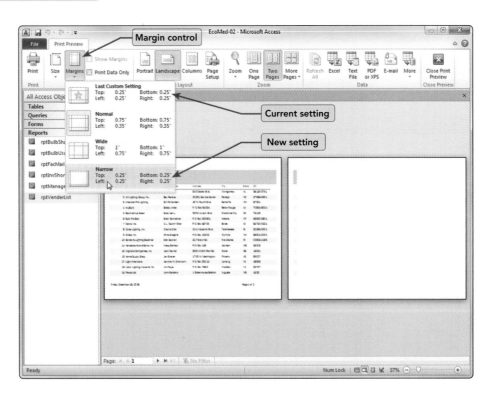

6. From the command tab **Print Preview**, in the command group **Print**, click **Print** 🖶. The **Print** dialog box opens.

7. Based on your classroom procedure, you can either print the report or cancel the print process. To cancel, click **Cancel**. To print the report, click **OK**. If you are uncertain, ask your instructor.

Exercise 2-19   SAVE A REPORT

You can save a report as an electronic XPS file. A saved report can be viewed or printed through XPS viewer, which is a standard Microsoft report format. Beginning with Office 2007, PDF is also a standard report format used by Microsoft.

1. From the command tab **Print Preview**, in the command group **Data**, click **PDF or XPS** 📄.

2. Change the location to the location where you will be storing your homework.

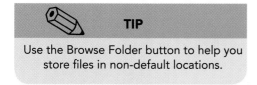

TIP

Use the Browse Folder button to help you store files in non-default locations.

3. In the **File name** control, type *[your initials]*-02-19.

4. Click the **Save as type** control, and select **XPS Document**.

5. Verify that the **Open file after publishing** check box is checked.

Figure 2-16
Save a report to a file
EcoMed-02.accdb
rptVenderList

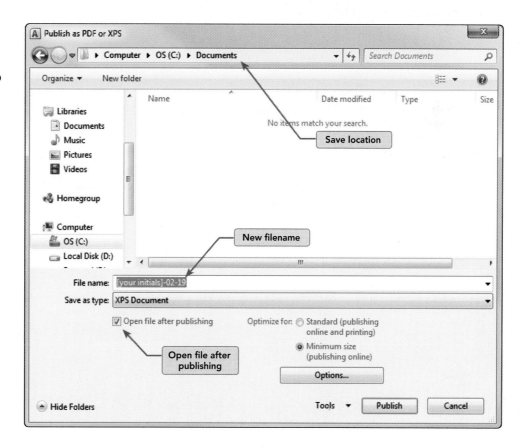

REVIEW

Optimizing the file for online exporting and printing increases the size of the file.

6. Click **Publish** to create the XPS file. Your file opens in Internet Explorer.
7. Close Internet Explorer. Click the **Close** button for the **Export-XPS** dialog box.
8. Right-click the **rptVenderList** tab. From the shortcut menu, select **Close**.
9. In the **Navigation Pane**, collapse the **Reports** group.
10. Click Close to close the database.

Lesson 2 Summary

- Access automatically saves changes to a record when you move the insertion point to another record.
- Records are stored in tables.
- Records can be added, edited, and deleted in a table, through a query, or through a form.
- You can delete records from a table by clicking on the Record Selector and pressing the delete key Delete.
- When editing a record, you can insert text or use the Overtype mode to key over existing text.
- AutoCorrect corrects commonly misspelled words.
- Press Ctrl+' to duplicate the contents in the field from the previous record.
- Press Ctrl+; to enter the current system date into a field.
- Press Ctrl+C to copy and Ctrl+V to paste text.
- Click Undo to restore previously deleted text.
- You can attach an image or document file to a record.
- Print Preview displays on screen how an object will appear when printed.
- An exported object can be viewed or printed at a later time.

LESSON 2		Command Summary	
Feature	**Button**	**Task Path**	**Keyboard**
Add record		Home, Records, New	Ctrl + +
Attachment			
Copy		Home, Clipboard, Copy	Ctrl + C
Date, Current			Ctrl + ;
Delete record		Home, Records, Delete	Ctrl + −
Duplicate field			Ctrl + '
Export		MS Office, Print Preview, Data, XPS	
Margins		Print Preview, Page Size, Margins	
Paste		Home, Clipboard, Paste	Ctrl + V
Refresh All		Home, Records, Refresh All	
Save record		Home, Records, Save	Ctrl + Enter
Undo		Edit, Undo	Ctrl + Z

Concepts Review

True/False Questions

Each of the following statements is either true or false. Indicate your choice by circling T or F.

T F 1. The pencil icon appears in the Record Selector after the data is saved.

T F 2. You can use the Undo button ↶ to restore up to 24 deleted records.

T F 3. When you enter or edit data through a form, you automatically update data in the underlying table.

T F 4. You can duplicate the data from a field in the previous record to the same field in the next record by pressing the keyboard shortcut Ctrl + D.

T F 5. Forms can be designed to show more than one record per screen.

T F 6. You can add records in a table, through a query, or through a form.

T F 7. Reports are designed to view data on paper.

T F 8. Only one image can be attached to each table.

Short Answer Questions

Write the correct answer in the space provided.

1. From which command group can you delete a record?

_____

2. In a table, where is a new record added?

_____

3. What is the keyboard shortcut to delete a record in a table or form?

_____

4. What Office feature automatically capitalizes days of the week?

_____

5. After copying text to the clipboard, what keyboard shortcut can be used to paste the text to a new location?

_____

6. In **Datasheet View**, what is the keyboard shortcut to move to the first record?

_____

7. What happens when you click the Quick Print button 🖨?

_____

8. Which command is carried out by pressing Ctrl+Z?

_____

Critical Thinking

Answer these questions on a separate page. There are no right or wrong answers. Support your answers with examples from your own experience, if possible.

1. In addition to images, you can attach various types of files to a record. However, certain files, such as those used by the operating system, cannot be attached. Think about standard file extensions and create a list of file extensions that cannot be used as attachments.

2. Access database files cannot exceed 2 gigabytes in size. Each time you add an image to a database, you increase the size of the database. Discuss what kind of restrictions a company should impose on the use of images in a database to avoid exceeding the maximum file size.

Skills Review

Exercise 2-20

Now that you are familiar with changing data within a table, you have been asked to update data in the bulb category table.

1. Locate and copy a database by following these steps:
   a. Locate and open the **Lesson 02** folder.
   b. If you already have a copy of *[your initials]*-EcoMed-02, skip to step 2.
   c. Right-click the file **EcoMed-02** and from the shortcut menu, choose Copy.
   d. Right-click an unused part of the folder. From the shortcut menu, choose Paste.
   e. Right-click the new file and from the shortcut menu, choose Rename. Rename the file *[your initials]*-EcoMed-02.
   f. Right-click *[your initials]*-**EcoMed-02** and from the shortcut menu, choose Properties. Make certain that the Read-only attribute check box is not checked. Click OK.

2. Open a database by following these steps:
   a. Double-click *[your initials]*-**EcoMed-02**.
   b. If the Message Bar's Security Warning appears, click the Enable Content button.

3. Edit a record by following these steps:

   a. In the **Navigation Pane**, expand the **Tables** group and double-click **tblBulbCategory**.

   b. Click anywhere in the **Bulb Category** field for the third record.

   c. Press Home to move to beginning of the field.

   d. Key **Utility-**.

   e. Press Shift+Enter to save the record.

4. Add a new record by following these steps:

   a. Click the **New Record** button ▸ navigation button.

   b. Press Tab.

   c. Press Ctrl+' to copy the text from the field above.

   d. Place the insertion point to the right of the dash (-).

   e. Press Ctrl+Delete to delete all text to the right of the insertion point.

   f. Key **Outdoor**.

   g. Press Tab and key *[your full name]*.

   h. Click the command tab **Home**. In the command group **Records**, click **Save** 🖫.

Assessment

- Close an object by following these steps:

  a. Right-click the document tab **tblBulbCategory**. From the shortcut menu, select **Close** ⌧.

  b. In the **Navigation Pane**, collapse the **Tables** group.

- According to your classroom procedure, turn in your database only when you have completed all assigned exercises.

-OR-

- Save a datasheet by following these steps:

  a. Click the **File** tab. From the **Print** option, choose **Print Preview** 🔍.

  b. In the **Data** command group, click the **PDF or XPS** button 🖺 to save the printout as a file.

  c. Save the file with the following settings:

     • In the dialog box's **Navigation Pane**, select the location where you want to store your class work.

     • **Save as type** as PDF.

     • **File name** as *[your initials]*-02-20-A.

     • **Open file after publishing** should be checked.

  d. Close the **Export–PDF** window.

  e. Depending on your class procedures, print or turn in the PDF file.

02-20-A.pdf
1 Page

   REVIEW

Check with your instructor on how he or she wants your homework delivered.

- Close an object by following these steps:

a. Right-click the document tab **tblBulbCategory**. From the shortcut menu, select **Close** 🗅.

b. In the **Navigation Pane**, collapse the **Tables** group.

Exercise 2-21

Sometimes it is more efficient to use a query to locate the specific records that you need to modify. You now will use a query to edit and add records. Although you will be using qryInvShape-Twin, the record source is the inventory table.

1. The database *[your initials]*-**EcoMed-02** is required to complete this exercise.

   a. If needed, double-click the database *[your initials]*-**EcoMed-02**.

   b. If the Message Bar's **Security Warning** appears, click the **Enable Content** button.

2. Edit text by following these steps:

   a. In the **Navigation Pane**, expand the **Queries** group and double-click **qryInvShape-Twin**.

   b. From the command tab **Home**, in the lower-right corner of the command group **Clipboard**, click the dialog box launcher to open the **Clipboard** pane.

   c. Click in the **Model Number** field for the second record and press F2 to select all the content in the field.

   d. Press Ctrl+C to copy the selected data.

   e. Press F2 and then End. Key **-13w**.

   f. Press the ↓. From the **Clipboard** pane, click the option arrow for the copied text "C2U" and select **Paste** 🗐.

   g. Key **-14w**.

   h. Press Ctrl+S to save the record.

3. Add a new record by following these steps:

   a. From the command tab **Home**, in the command group **Records**, click **New** 🗅.

   b. Key the following to add a new record:

InvID:	*Press* Tab
Model Number:	*Key [your full name]*
Wattage:	18
Bulb Life:	*Press* Ctrl+'
Light Output	980
Color Temp:	*Press* Ctrl+'
Cost:	68.50
Bulb Shape:	*Press* Ctrl+'

   c. From the Quick Access toolbar, click Save 🖫.

TIP

Data entry goes much faster if you press Tab between fields.

Assessment

- Close an object by following these steps:

   a. Right-click the document tab **qryInvShape-Twin**. From the shortcut menu, select **Close** .

   b. In the **Navigation Pane**, collapse the **Queries** group.

   c. Close the **Clipboard** pane.

- Turn in your database only when all assigned exercises have been completed, according to your classroom procedure.

-OR-

- Save a datasheet by following these steps:

   a. Click the command tab **File**. From the **Print** option, choose **Print Preview** ▣.

   b. From the command tab **Print Preview**, in the command group **Page Layout**, click **Landscape** ▣.

   c. From the command tab **Print Preview**, in the command group **Page Size**, click **Margins** and choose **Normal**.

   d. In the **Data** command group, click **PDF or XPS** ▣ to save the printout as a file.

   e. Save the file with the following settings:

     • In the dialog box's **Navigation Pane**, select the location where you want to store your class work.

     • **Save as type** as PDF.

     • **File name** as *[your initials]*-02-21-A.

     • **Open file after publishing** should be checked.

   f. Close the **Export–PDF** window and **Clipboard** pane.

   g. Depending on your class procedures, print or turn in the PDF file.

- Close an object by following these steps:

   a. Right-click the document tab **qryInvShape-Twin**. From the shortcut menu, select **Close** .

   b. In the **Navigation Pane**, collapse the **Queries** group.

   c. Close the **Clipboard** pane.

02-21-A.pdf
1 Page

Exercise 2-22

As an intern in the IT department, you can modify data either directly in the table or through a query. However, most employees of EcoMed can only use forms. You now will use the inventory form to edit and add records.

1. The database *[your initials]*-EcoMed-02 is required to complete this exercise.

   a. If needed, open the database *[your initials]*-EcoMed-02.

   b. If the Message Bar's **Security Warning** appears, click **Enable Content**.

2. Add records by following these steps:

  a. In the Navigation Pane, expand the Forms group and double-click **frmInventory**.

  b. From the command tab Home, in the command group Records, click New ⬚.

  c. Key the following fields into a new record (skip fields that are not listed):

Inventory ID:	*Press* Tab
Model Number:	C2U-20-*[your full name]*
Bulb Shape:	Bare-Twin Tube
Wattage:	20
Bulb Life:	8000
Light Output:	1050
Color Temp:	2700
3 Way?:	False
Cost:	72.50

  d. Right-click the document tab **frmInventory**. From the shortcut menu, select Close ⬚.

3. Delete a record by following these steps:

  a. In the Navigation Pane, double-click **frmInvShape-Twin**.

  b. The first record in the form is for **Inventory ID** 202. Click anywhere in this record.

  c. Press Ctrl+- to delete the current record.

  d. Click Yes to verify the deletion.

  e. Right-click the document tab **frmInvShape-Twin**. From the shortcut menu, select Close ⬚.

  f. In the Navigation Pane, collapse the Forms group.

4. Open a query in Datasheet View by following these steps:

  a. In the Navigation Pane, expand the Queries group and double-click **qryInvShape-Twin**.

  b. Click and drag the bottom of the Record Selector for the first record and double the height of the row.

  c. Resize the each field until all data can be seen.

  d. Press Ctrl+S to save the changes.

Assessment

- Close an object by following these steps:

  a. Right-click the **qryInvShape-Twin** tab. From the shortcut menu, select Close All.

  b. In the Navigation Pane, collapse the Queries group.

- Turn in your database only when all assigned exercises have been completed, according to your classroom procedure.

-OR-

- Save a datasheet by following these steps:

a. Click the **File** tab. From the **Print** option, choose **Print Preview** .

b. From the command tab **Print Preview**, in the command group **Page Layout**, click **Landscape** 🖻.

c. From the command tab **Print Preview**, in the command group **Page Size**, click **Margins** and choose **Normal**.

d. In the **Data** command group, click **PDF or XPS** 🖳 to save the printout as a file.

e. Save the file with the following settings:

- In the dialog box's **Navigation Pane**, select the location where you want to store your class work.
- **Save as type** as PDF.
- **File name** as *[your initials]*-**02-22-A**.
- **Open file after publishing** should be checked.

f. Close the **Export–PDF** window.

g. Depending on your class procedures, print or turn in the PDF file.

- Close an object by following these steps:

a. Right-click the **qryInvShape-Twin** tab. From the shortcut menu, select **Close All**.

b. In the **Navigation Pane**, collapse the **Print** group.

02-22-A.pdf
1 Page

NOTE

Check to see if all 8 fields fit on one page. If not, you should either repeat step 4 or change the margins so that the printout is only one page.

Exercise 2-23

You now are being asked to attach an image of a light bulb to a specific record. You will use frmBulbsByShape to attach and view the image. You will then print rptBulbShapes to verify your work.

1. The database *[your initials]*-**EcoMed-02** is required to complete this exercise.

a. If needed, open the database *[your initials]*-**EcoMed-02**.

b. If the Message Bar's **Security Warning** appears, click **Enable Content**.

2. Attach a file by following these steps:

   a. In the Navigation Pane, expand the Forms group and double-click **frmBulbsByShape**.

   b. The first record has a picture in an attachment control.

   c. Press ⌈PageDown⌉ until you find the record for Bare-Triple Tube.

   d. Double-click the attachment control. In the Attachment dialog box, click Add.

   e. In the folder **Lesson 02**, double-click the file **Triple-tube.gif**.

   f. Click OK.

   g. Close the form and collapse the Forms group.

Assessment

- See new image in a report by following these steps:

  a. Double-click the report **rptBulbShapes**.

  b. Verify that the new image is visible in the report.

  c. Right-click the **rptBulbShapes** tab. From the shortcut menu, select Close.

  d. In the Navigation Pane, collapse the Reports group.

- Turn in your database only when all assigned exercises have been completed, according to your classroom procedure.

-OR-

- Save a report by following these steps:

  a. Double-click the report **rptBulbShapes**.

  b. Right-click the document tab for **rptBulbShapes**. From the shortcut menu, select Print Preview.

  c. In the Data command group, click PDF or XPS 🔽 to save the printout as a file.

  d. Save the file with the following settings:

  • In the dialog box's Navigation Pane, select the location where you want to store your class work.

  • Save as type as PDF.

  • File name as *[your initials]*-02-23-A.

  • Open file after publishing should be checked.

  e. Close the Export–PDF window.

  f. Depending on your class procedures, print or turn in the PDF file.

- Close an object by following these steps:

  a. Right-click the **rptBulbShapes** tab. From the shortcut menu, select Close.

  b. In the Navigation Pane, collapse the Reports group.

02-23-A.pdf
1 Page

Lesson Applications

Exercise 2-24

Using a form, you now will add a new record. You will verify your work by printing the Datasheet View of query. To see the complete records, you will need to print the datasheet in landscape orientation.

1. Using the database *[your initials]*-**EcoMed-02**, make sure that all content is enabled.

2. In the form **frmFacContacts-R4**, add the following new facility:

Facilities ID:	*Press* Tab
Facility Name:	*Key [your school's name]*
Contact First Name:	*Key [your first name]*
Last Name:	*Key [your last name]*
Phone Number:	(555) 444-1234

3. Open the query **qryFacContacts-R4**. Resize each field so that all data can be seen.

4. Change the query's **Page Layout** to **Landscape** with **Wide Margins**.

Assessment

- Close the form and query.
- Turn in your database only when all assigned exercises have been completed, according to your classroom procedure.

-OR-

- Save the query's **Datasheet View** as a PDF file named *[your initials]*-**02-24-A**.
- According to your class procedures, print or turn in the PDF file.
- Close the form and query.

02-24-A.pdf
1 Page

Exercise 2-25

The sales representative for region five has identified several records in the facilities table that are incomplete or incorrect. You now need to use the qryFacContacts-R5 to modify the appropriate records.

1. Using the database *[your initials]*-**EcoMed-02**, make sure that all content is enabled.

2. Open **qryFacContacts-R5** in **Datasheet View**.

3. Delete the facility Clarian Arnett Hospital (**Facility ID** 50).

4. Hide the field **Phone Number**.

5. Using the data in Figure 2-17, modify each record to include all the changes indicated in red.

Figure 2-17

Facilities ID	Facility Name	First Name	Last Name
19	Grant Medical Center	Jeanette	Stone
80	Beaumont Hospital, **Grosse Pointe**	Sonja	**Chung**
81	Beaumont Hospital, **Troy**	Louise	Thomas
114	Mount Sinai Hospital	Cheryl	**Rodriguez**

6. In the first record, change the fields **First Name** and **Last Name** to your name.

7. Resize fields so that all data can be seen on one page.

8. Set the **Page Layout** to **Portrait** and the margin to normal.

Assessment

- Save and close the query.
- Turn in your database only when all assigned exercises have been completed, according to your classroom procedure.

-OR-

- Save as a PDF file named *[your initials]*-02-25-A.
- According to your class procedures, print or turn in the PDF file.
- Save and close the query.

02-25-A.pdf
1 Page

Exercise 2-26

You have been asked to print the report that displays the mailing addresses for the facilities. Before you can print the report, you will need to correct errors in the source recordset.

1. Using the database *[your initials]*-**EcoMed-02**, make sure that all content is enabled.

2. Open **qryFacMail-FL** in Datasheet View.

3. Use the Office Clipboard and navigation commands to find the records to be changed.

4. In the field **Address**, change all occurrences of "Street" to St..

5. In the field **Address**, change all occurrences of "Avenue" to Ave..

6. In the first record, replace the **Address** data with your full name.

UNIT 1 LESSON 2

7. Open the **rptFacMail-FL** in **Print Preview View** and set the **Page Layout** to **Landscape** .

Assessment

- Close the query and report.
- Turn in your database only when all assigned exercises have been completed, according to your classroom procedure.

-OR-

02-26-A.pdf
1 Page

- Save as a PDF file named *[your initials]*-02-26-A.
- According to your class procedures, print or turn in the PDF file.
- Close the query and report.

Exercise 2-27 ◆ Challenge Yourself

You now are being asked to use just a table to attach an image of a light bulb to a specific record. You will then print rptBulbUsage to verify your work.

1. Using the database *[your initials]*-EcoMed-02, make sure that all content is enabled.

2. Open **tblBulbUsage**.

TIP

Try to find an image that is less than 100kb in size. This size will keep your database from getting too large.

---

3. Use the Internet to locate and save an image of a decorative light bulb.

4. For the **Usage ID** 2, attach the image you found on the Internet.

5. Add the **Hanging Pendant.jpg** image found in the **Lesson 02** folder to the **Usage ID** 5's record.

6. In the record for **Usage ID** 4, add your last name after the word "Fan."

7. Open **rptBulbUsage** in **Print Preview View** and set the **Page Layout** to **Portrait** .

02-27-A.pdf
1 Page

Assessment

- Close the table and report. Exit the database.
- Turn in your database only when all assigned exercises have been completed, according to your classroom procedure.

-OR-

- Save as a PDF file named *[your initials]*-02-27-A.
- According to your class procedures, print or turn in the PDF file.
- Close the table and report. Exit the database.

On Your Own

In these exercises, you work on your own, as you would in a real-life work environment. Use the skills you've learned to accomplish the task—and be creative.

Exercise 2-28

Search the Web for companies that would sell products of interest to members of the club you formed in Lesson 1. If you are unable to locate any companies, search the Web for companies selling clothing that appeals to you. Write down at least five URLs (Web page addresses). Continue to the next exercise.

Exercise 2-29

On each of the five Web sites, determine what information the company asks a person when that person places an order or requests a catalog. On the same sheet of paper where you wrote down the five URLs, organize and write a bulleted list of customer information collected by the companies (e.g., first name, e-mail). Continue to the next exercise.

Exercise 2-30

On a second sheet of paper, create a new field list by combining the list you created in Exercise 1-28 (in Lesson 1) with the list you created in Exercise 2-28. On a third sheet of paper, organize the items from your new list to sketch a form layout. Submit your work for Exercises 2-28 through 2-30 to your instructor.

Lesson 3
Finding, Filtering, Sorting, and Summarizing Data

OBJECTIVES   *After completing this lesson, you will be able to:*

1. Find and replace data.
2. Use wildcards.
3. Sort records.
4. Add and modify the totals row in datasheets.
5. Use filters.
6. Use the database documenter.

Estimated Time: 1½ hours

The main purpose of the EcoMed database is to turn raw data into useful information. The data stored are too complex to find specific information easily, such as the total number of halogen bulbs currently in stock. To locate specific information, you can use standard Access tools to search, find, sort, and filter records. By applying the proper combinations of tools, the cumbersome data become useful information.

EcoMed Services, Inc., sells 316 different types of lighting devices that are divided into three different categories and five different bulb types. If you want to know which items are the most expensive for each category, you would sort the inventory by cost in descending order and filter by each category. You will often use a combination of tools to display specific information.

Finding and Replacing Data

Finding information can be time consuming if you have to scroll through several thousand records. Searches can be conducted quicker when fields contain unique data. For example, if you know the phone number of a particular facility, you can find that company quickly because no two companies share the same phone number. However, if you only know the company's area code, then the search can take quite a bit longer, because your database may contain numerous facilities that share the same area code.

Although most often you change single records, on occasion, you will find it necessary to update the same data listed in multiple records. Customers at EcoMed Services are classified by management type. If the management type for a group of customers changes, then these changes need to be reflected throughout the entire database. To make these changes, you will need to find the original management classifications and replace them with the new classifications.

Exercise 3-1 USE THE SEARCH TOOL

Using the Search tool is a quick way to find data in a recordset. The Search tool begins its search at the first field of the first record and stops at the first match. If the recordset contains more than one match, only the first match is found. Because of this limitation, the Search tool is best used when searching for unique data, such as a phone numbers or specific names. The Search tool can be used in tables, queries, and forms.

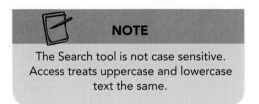

NOTE

The Search tool is not case sensitive. Access treats uppercase and lowercase text the same.

1. Locate and open the **Lesson 03** folder.

2. Make a copy of **EcoMed-03** and rename it *[your initials]*-EcoMed-03.

3. Open and enable content for *[your initials]*-**EcoMed-03**.

4. From the **Navigation Pane**, open the table **tblFacilities** in **Datasheet View**.

Figure 3-1
Search tool
**EcoMed-03.accdb
tblFacilities**

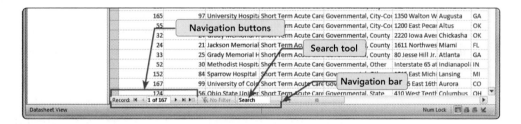

5. In the Navigation bar, click in the **Search** tool.

6. Key **h**. Starting from the upper left, the first "h" is selected.

7. Key **o**. Starting from the upper left, the first "ho" is selected.

8. Key **u**. The selection has moved to the 37th record (Facilities ID 38).

9. Press Backspace three times to remove the content of the **Search** tool.

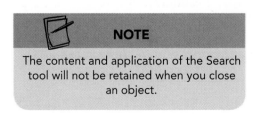

NOTE

The content and application of the Search tool will not be retained when you close an object.

10. Key **chic**. The selection has moved to the **City** field of the 32nd record.

11. Clear the content of the **Search** tool.

12. Key **303**. The selection has moved to the **Phone Number** field of the 4th record.

13. Clear the content of the **Search** tool.

Exercise 3-2 USE THE FIND COMMAND

Similar to the Search tool, the Find and Replace dialog box finds matches in a recordset. However, there are two major differences. First, the Find and Replace command begins a search at the insertion point, and second, this command includes options for fine-tuning how the text is matched.

TABLE 3-1 Find and Replace Dialog Box Options

Option	Description
Look In	Sets the search for the current field or the entire table.
Match: Any Part of Field	Finds records with matching characters anywhere in the field.
Match: Whole Field	Finds records in which an entire field matches the value in the Find What text box.
Match: Start of Field	Finds records in which the beginning of a field matches the Find What entry.
Search: All	Searches forward to the end of the table and wraps back to the beginning.
Search: Up	Searches in the Up (backward) direction only.
Search: Down	Searches in the Down (forward) direction only.
Match Case	Finds exact uppercase and lowercase matches.
Search Fields As Formatted	Enables you to key data in its display format. To find a date that is stored as 1/25/01, you can key 25-Jan-01. This is the slowest search.

There are two ways of opening the Find and Replace dialog box using the Find tab:

- From the Home tab, in the Find group, click Find 🔍.
- Press Ctrl+F.

1. Click anywhere in the table. Press F2 and then Ctrl+Home to move to the top of the table **tblFacilities**.
2. From the Home tab, in the Find group, click Find 🔍.
3. In the Find What control, key jack.
4. Click the drop-down arrow for the Look In control and choose **Current Document**.
5. Click the drop-down arrow for the Match control and choose **Any Part of Field**.

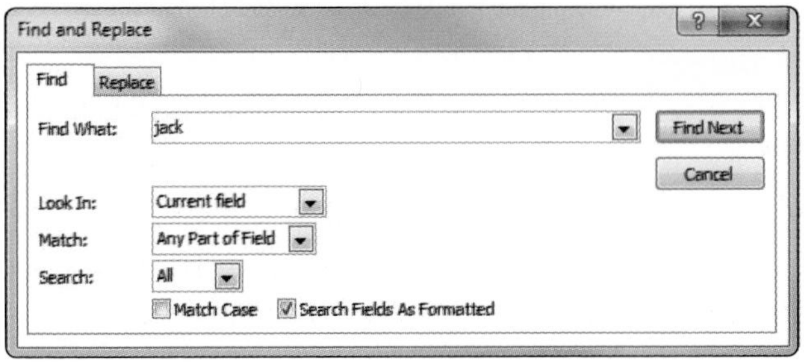

Figure 3-2
Find option of the Find and Replace dialog box
EcoMed-03.accdb tblFacilities

NOTE

To see the results of a search, you can drag the Find and Replace dialog box by its title bar to a location on the screen that does not conceal the results of the search.

6. Click **Find Next**. The first occurrence of "jack" is located in the field **Facility Name**. To search in only one field, you must click in that field before starting the search.

7. Click in the **Contact First Name** field of the first record. You do not need to close the **Find and Replace** dialog box to interact with the underlying table.

8. Click the drop-down arrow for the **Look In** control and choose **Current field** and set the **Match** control to **Whole Field**.

9. Click **Find Next** to find "jack" in record 44.

10. Click **Find Next** to find the next occurrence, and continue until you reach the end of the table.

11. Read the message box and click **OK**.

12. Click **Cancel** to close the **Find and Replace** dialog box.

Exercise 3-3 USE THE REPLACE COMMAND

The Replace tab finds matches in the same way as the Find tab. With Replace, you not only find the match, but you can also replace each matched value with a new value. You can replace either a single occurrence or every occurrence of the value.

When using the Replace All option, you must be careful that all occurrences in the recordset are values that you plan to replace. Sometimes, unanticipated errors can occur. For example, if you try to replace the word "form" with "report," then a field containing the word "information" will become "inreportation."

There are two ways of opening the Find and Replace dialog box using the Replace tab:

• From the **Home** tab, in the **Find** group, click **Replace** .

• Press Ctrl+H.

1. In **tblFacilities**, widen the field **Facility Name** so that you can see all of the data.

2. Click in the field **Facility Name** for the first record.

3. Press Ctrl+H to open the **Find and Replace** dialog box.

4. In the **Find What** control, key **university**.

TIP

Make sure that you have keyed the period after "Univ.".

5. In the **Replace With** control, key **Univ.**.

6. Verify that the **Look In** control is set to **Current field**.

7. Click **Find Next**. A dialog box appears to tell you that this text string was not found. Click **OK**.

8. Click the drop-down arrow for the **Match** control and choose **Any Part of Field**.

9. Click **Find Next**. The first occurrence after the insertion point is selected.

10. Click **Replace** to replace the first occurrence of "university" with "Univ." and to find the next occurrence of "university."

11. Click **Find Next** to skip this occurrence of "university" and move to the next.

12. Click **Replace All**.

13. Read the message box about not being able to undo this operation and click **Yes**.

14. Click **Cancel** to close the dialog box.

Using Wildcards

Up to this point, you have used exact text when finding text. On occasion, you may not know the exact value you want to match. For example, you might need to find a particular facility but not know its exact name. You may know part of the name such as "Regional." Since you only know part of the name, you would need to search the name field using a wildcard. A *wildcard* is a character or group of characters used to represent one or more alphabetical or numerical characters.

Exercise 3-4   FIND DATA USING AN ASTERISK "*"

The asterisk (*) is a wildcard that represents one or more characters. If you search for "Mar*" as a name, you will match names such as "Mar," "Mart," "Martin," "Marigold," or "Marblestone." All fields matched will begin with "Mar" regardless of the remaining characters in the field.

1. In the table **tblFacilities**, click Ctrl+↑ to move to first record in the **Facility Name** field.

2. Press Ctrl+F to open the **Find and Replace** dialog box.

3. Click the drop-down arrow for the **Match** control and choose **Whole Field**.

4. In the **Find What** control, key univ*.

5. Click **Find Next**. The "Univ. Hospital" is selected in record 30.

6. Click in the table and scroll down to "Indiana Univ. Hospital," **Manage ID** 47. This record was skipped by the **Find** utility because the **Facility Name** did not start with "Univ.".

7. Click **Cancel** to close the dialog box.

Exercise 3-5   FIND DATA USING A QUESTION MARK "?"

The question mark (?) is a wildcard that represents a single character. If you search for "Mar?" as a first name, you will find names such as "Mari," "Mark," "Marv," or "Mary." All fields containing only four characters and starting with "Mar" will be matched. Fields containing more than four characters or not beginning with "Mar" will not be matched.

1. In the table **tblFacilities**, click Ctrl+↑ to move to the first record in the **Facility Name** field.

2. From the **Home** tab, in the **Find** group, click **Find** 🔍.

3. In the **Find What** control, key o??o.

4. In the **Look In** control, select **Current field**.

5. In the **Match** control, select **Any Part of Field**.

6. Click **Find Next** to find the first occurrence of any field's content that has two charters between two "o." The first match is in the word "D<u>oct</u>ors."

7. Click **Find Next** a few more times to see the different words that can be found.

8. Click **Cancel**.

Sorting Records

In a table, records are displayed in the order in which they were entered. For example, whenever a new facility is added, its name is added to the end of a table. Most often though, this order is not useful when trying to find a specific record.

You can change the sort order of the recordset depending on the information you need. When creating a facilities phone list, you would sort the recordset by the facility name.

Exercise 3-6 SORT RECORDS IN DATASHEET VIEW

You can sort data in three ways:

TIP

A small up or down arrow appears on the column header of a sorted column. This sort order arrow appears to the right of the column header's drop-down arrow.

- From the **Home** tab, in the **Sort & Filter** group, choose **Ascending** or **Descending**.

- On a column selector, click the option arrow and select the **Sort A to Z** or **Sort Z to A**.

- In a field, right-click and select the **Sort A to Z** or **Sort Z to A**.

1. In the table **tblFacilities**, in the **Facility Name** field, click the option arrow on the column header, and choose **Sort A to Z**.

Figure 3-3
Apply Sort to a column
EcoMed-03.accdb tblFacilities

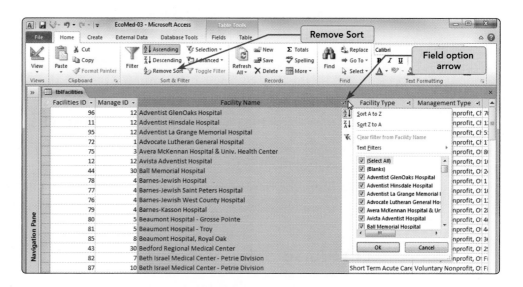

2. From the **Home** tab, in the **Sort & Filter** group, click **Remove Sort** ⚋. Notice that the sort order arrow no longer displays in the column header.

3. Select both the **Contact First Name** and **Contact Last Name** fields.

4. Right-click the selected column headers and choose **Sort Z to A** ⚥. The table is now sorted in descending order by first name and then by last name.

5. In the **Navigation Pane**, open the query **qryFacContacts** in **Datasheet View**. This query gets its data from **tblFacilities**.

6. Notice that the query is not sorted by contact names. Click on the document tab for **tblFacilities**.

7. Click in the **Revenue** field, click the option arrow on the column header, and choose **Sort Largest to Smallest** ⚥.

8. Right-click the table's document tab and choose **Save** 🖫.

9. Right-click any document tab and choose **Close All** 🗗.

Exercise 3-7 SORT RECORDS IN A FORM

A form can be set to view a single record at one time or multiple records at once. All forms can be sorted. When multiple records are displayed in a form, the sort order is observable. To see the results of a sort to a single record form, you will need to navigate through the recordset one screen at a time.

1. From the **Navigation Pane**, open the form **frmFacContacts** in **Form View**.

2. Click in the **Facility Name** field for the first record.

3. From the **Home** tab, in the **Sort & Filter** group, click **Ascending** ⚥. A different record is now displayed.

4. Press PageDown to move through all the records to see that the form is indeed sorted by **Facility Name**.

5. Click in the **Last Name** field.

6. From the **Home** tab, in the **Sort & Filter** group, click **Ascending** ⚥.

7. Use the Record Navigation buttons to move through the records and see the change.

8. Right-click the form's tab and choose **Close All** 🗗.

9. From the **Navigation Pane**, open the form **frmFacContacts** in **Form View**. Notice that the form retained the last sort order.

10. From the **Home** tab, in the **Sort & Filter** group, click **Remove Sorts** ⚋.

11. Right-click the form's tab and choose **Close** ⚟.

Exercise 3-8 SORT RECORDS IN A REPORT

The recordset displayed in Layout View of a report can be sorted similarly to a recordset in Form View of a form. Layout View of a report allows you to fine-tune the display of data, including sorting fields and adjusting column widths.

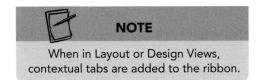

NOTE

When in Layout or Design Views, contextual tabs are added to the ribbon.

1. From the Navigation Pane, open the report **rptVenderList** in Report View. This report is sorted by Vender ID.

2. From the Home tab, in the Views group, click View and choose Layout View.

3. Click the column heading **Contact Name** to select the entire column of data.

4. From the Home tab, in the Sort & Filter group, choose Descending.

Figure 3-4
Sort in a report
**EcoMed-03.accdb
rptVenderList**

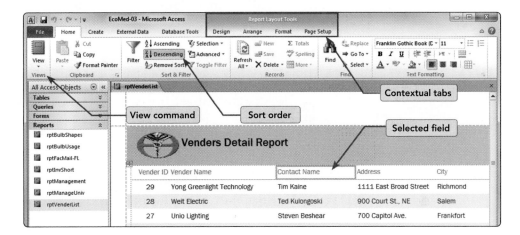

5. From the Home tab, in the Views group, click View and choose Report View.

6. Right-click the report's tab and choose Close.

7. Click Yes to save the changes.

Adding and Modifying the Totals Row in Datasheets

The Totals row is a feature that you can use to summarize data quickly. For example, if you need to know the total annual revenue of your customers, you would need to create a sum total for the revenue field in the facilities table. In addition to being able to total a field, you can determine the average, count, maximum value, minimum value, standard deviation, and variance of the values.

Exercise 3-9 ADD A TOTALS ROW TO A QUERY

The Totals row uses an aggregate function to summarize a field. An *aggregate function* is a dynamic mathematical calculation that displays a single value for a specific field. Any change to a recordset automatically triggers recalculations of the aggregate functions located in the Totals row.

TABLE 3-2 Totals Row Aggregate Functions

Function	Description
Average	Calculates the average value for a column containing numeric, currency, or date/time data.
Count	Counts the number of items in a column.
Maximum	Returns the item with the highest value. For text data, the highest value is the last alphabetic value.
Minimum	Returns the item with the lowest value. For text data, the lowest value is the first alphabetic value.
Standard Deviation	Measures how widely values are dispersed from an average value.
Sum	Adds the items in a column containing numeric or currency data.
Variance	Measures the statistical variance of all values in the column containing numeric or currency data.

1. From the **Navigation Pane**, open the query **qryFacStats** in **Datasheet View**.

2. From the **Home** tab, in the **Records** group, click **Totals** Σ to add a **Totals** row at the bottom of the **Datasheet View**.

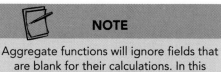

NOTE

Aggregate functions will ignore fields that are blank for their calculations. In this case, every record has a **Regions** value so the result of the **Count** function equals the number of records in the recordset.

3. In the **Totals** row, click in the **Regions** field. A drop-down arrow appears on the left of the field.

4. Click the drop-down arrow to show the list of available functions.

5. Choose **Count** from the list. There are 167 records with **Regions** data.

Figure 3-5
Adding Totals row
to a datasheet
**EcoMed-03.accdb
qryFacStats**

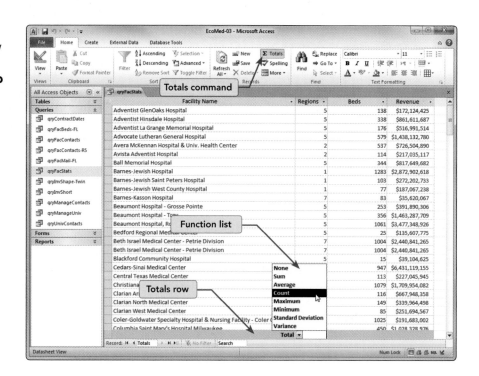

Exercise 3-10   MODIFY A TOTALS ROW IN A QUERY

A Totals row is always present. Once you've created a Totals row in a datasheet, you can never truly delete it. You either modify it with a new function or hide it. Each time you display the Totals row, the functions that you last saved will appear.

TIP

When you see "#####" in a field, it indicates that a number is in the field but is too large to be seen in its entirety with the current column width. To view the number, resize the column to make it wider.

1. In the query **qryFacStats**, click in the Totals row for the **Beds** field.

2. Click the drop-down arrow and choose the function **Average**. The average number of beds is shown.

3. In the Totals row, click in **Revenue**.

4. Click the drop-down arrow and choose **Maximum**. The largest yearly gross revenue of our client facilities appears.

5. From the **Home** tab, in the **Records** group, click Totals **Σ** to remove the Totals row.

6. Click **Close** ✕ to close the query.

7. Click **Yes** to save the changes.

8. Reopen the query **qryFacStats**.

9. From the **Home** tab, in the **Records** group, click Totals **Σ** to add the Totals row. Notice that the functions you added have been saved.

10. Click **Close** ✕ and then click **Yes** to save the changes.

Using Filters

A *filter* is a database feature that limits the number of records displayed. A filter uses a criterion to determine which records will be displayed. A *criterion* is a rule or test placed upon a field. When the tested field in a record matches the filter criterion, then the record is displayed. If the tested field does not match the filter criterion, then the record is not displayed.

Once you define a filter, you can toggle to either apply or remove it. When applied, a filter displays only matching records. When removed, the entire recordset displays. Whether applied or removed, the actual number of records in the underlying recordset remains constant.

Exercise 3-11   CREATE AND APPLY A FILTER BY SELECTION

Filter By Selection is a filter applied to a single field. The filter can be created to match the entire field or a portion of a field. The selection will be compared to field values in the recordset based upon a comparison option selected from a contextual menu. A contextual menu is a varying list of options based upon an item selected.

The filter options displayed depend upon the type of field and data selected. Options displayed for a date field differ from options displayed for a text field. Some options, such as "Begins With" or "Ends With," display only when the beginning portion or the ending portion of a text field is selected.

When filtering with more than one field, only records that match all filters will display. For example, if you need to list all nonprofit client facilities, you will need to create criteria for the management field. Only records that match "Voluntary Nonprofit, Other" will appear.

TABLE 3-3 Common Contextual Filter Options

Field Type	Filter Option
Date	Equals Does Not Equal On or Before On or After
Numeric	Equals Does Not Equal Less Than or Equal To Greater Than or Equal To Between
Text	Equals Does Not Equal Contains Does Not Contain Begins With Does Not Begin With Ends With Does Not End With

1. From the **Navigation Pane**, open the table **tblFacilities** in **Datasheet View**.

2. In the table **tblFacilities**, in the **Facility Name** field, click the option arrow on the column header, and choose **Sort A to Z** ⬇.

3. Click the **Search** tool and key **hos**. The Search tool finds the first case of hospital in the first record.

4. Double-click the word "hospital" to select the whole word.

5. From the **Home** tab, in the **Sort & Filter** group, click **Selection** ⚡.

6. From the menu, choose **Contains "Hospital"**. There are 142 records that contain "hospital" in their name. Notice that the word hospital can appear in any part of the facility name.

Figure 3-6
Creating a Filter By Selection
EcoMed-03.accdb
tblFacilities

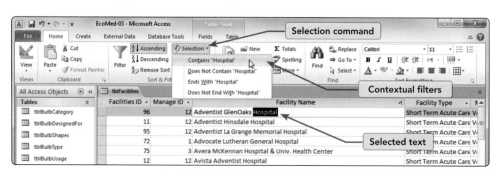

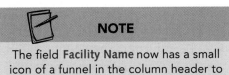

NOTE

The field **Facility Name** now has a small icon of a funnel in the column header to indicate the table has a filter by this field enabled.

7. From the **Home** tab, in the **Sort & Filter** group, click **Toggle Filter** to turn off the filter.

8. Press Tab to move to the **Facility Type** field.

9. From the **Home** tab, in the **Sort & Filter** group, click **Selection** and choose **Does Not Equal "Short Term Acute Care"**. You find 17 client facilities that are not a Short-Term Acute Care facility.

10. From the Navigation bar, click **Toggle Filter** to disable the filter.

11. Press Tab to move to the **Management Type** field.

12. Click the **Search** tool and delete the previous text.

TIP

When the insertion point is in a field with no characters selected, Filter By Selection assumes the whole field is selected.

13. In the **Search** tool, key **, s**. The search tool finds the **Management Type** "Governmental, State" in the 55th record.

14. Click in the selected field so that no text is selected and the insertion point is located between any two characters in the field.

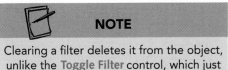

NOTE

Clearing a filter deletes it from the object, unlike the **Toggle Filter** control, which just turns the filter on and off.

15. From the **Home** tab, in the **Sort & Filter** group, click **Selection** and choose **Equals "Governmental, State"**. Ten facilities have this type of management.

16. Click the drop-down arrow next to the funnel icon in the column heading for the **Management Type** field and choose **Clear filter from Management Type**.

Figure 3-7
Clear a filter
**EcoMed-03.accdb
tblFacilities**

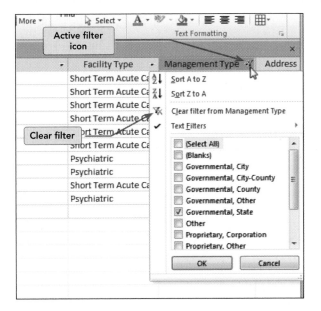

Exercise 3-12　FILTER FOR A SPECIFIC VALUE

When filtering for a specific value, you select one or more values from a predefined criteria list. Each item on a list can be "selected for" or "omitted from" the filter condition. When two or more criteria are selected, either criterion must match for the record to display. For example, assume you select "NY" and "CA" for the state; then, all records from New York as well as all records from California would display.

The criteria list is dynamically created based upon the unique values found in the field. The first two items in every criteria list will be "Select All" and "Blanks." "Select All" toggles between selecting and omitting all values. Selecting "Blanks" includes records for which the criterion field is left empty.

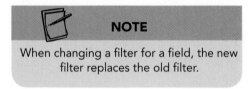

NOTE

When changing a filter for a field, the new filter replaces the old filter.

1. With the table **tblFacilities** open, verify that the focus (column header is yellow) is on the **Management Type** field.

2. From the **Home** tab, in the **Sort & Filter** group, click **Filter** 🔽.

3. In the menu, click the check box **(Select All)** to remove all checkmarks.

4. Click the check boxes for **Governmental, City** and **Governmental, State**. All records for both customers display.

5. Click **OK**. All records for both types of customers are displayed.

Figure 3-8
Filter logic: Specific value
EcoMed-03.accdb

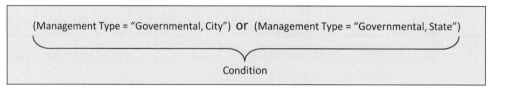

6. From the **Home** tab, in the **Sort & Filter** group, click **Filter** 🔽. From the menu, choose **Clear filter from Management Type**.

7. Press [Tab] until you are at the **Beds** field.

8. From the **Home** tab, in the **Sort & Filter** group, click **Filter** 🔽.

9. In the menu, click the check box **(Select All)** and then click the check box for **(Blanks)**.

10. Click **OK** to apply the filter. Only records that do not have data in the **Beds** field are shown.

11. Click the drop-down arrow for **Beds**. From the menu, choose **Clear filter from Beds**.

12. Click the **Close** button ⊠ and then click **Yes** to save the changes.

Exercise 3-13 FILTER FOR A RANGE OF VALUES

Other contextual filter options, such as calendar filters, have even more options. If you filter on a date field, you can select to filter dates by days, weeks, months, quarters, or years. The options available will vary depending on the date selected and the current date. For example, if the date selected is within the current year, then "This Year" becomes an available filter option.

1. From the **Navigation Pane**, open the report **rptManagement**.

2. From the **Home** tab, in the **Views** group, click **View** and click **Layout View** 📄.

3. Press Shift + Tab to move to the last field header, **Contract Ends**. Right-click this header and from the menu click Date Filters. From the menu choose Between....

4. In the Between Dates dialog box, click in the Oldest control.

5. Key 1/1/2015 and press Tab.

6. Press the Calendar button 🗐 for the Newest control.

7. Use the arrows to move through the calendar until you get to December 2015. Click the 31st to add the date to the Newest control.

Figure 3-9
Calendar control
EcoMed-03.accdb
rptManagement

8. Click OK. The report now only shows details of the management companies whose contracts expire in 2015.

Figure 3-10
Filter logic: Range
of values
EcoMed-03.accdb

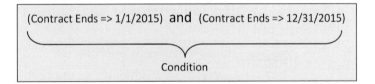

9. From the Home tab, in the Sort & Filter group, click Toggle Filter ▼.

10. Right-click the report's tab and choose Close ✕.

Exercise 3-14 CREATE AND APPLY A FILTER BY FORM

Filter By Form allows you to define a collection of criteria for one or more fields using a template. When using Filter By Form in a form, the template appears as a blank form. Alternatively, when using Filter By Form in a datasheet, the template appears as a blank datasheet.

Collections in Filter By Form are organized by tabs. The first tab is called "Look for" and is located in the lower left-hand corner of the template. In a tab, all conditions must be met for a record to be displayed. For example, in the "Look for" tab, if you defined the criterion "NY" for the state and the criterion "Albany" for the city, then only records from "Albany, NY" would be included in the active recordset.

1. From the Navigation Pane, open the form **frmFacContacts** in Form View.

2. From the Home tab, in the Sort & Filter group, click Advanced 🗐 and choose Filter By Form 🗐.

3. Click the drop-down arrow for the **Region** and choose **2**.

Figure 3-11
Filter By Form
**EcoMed-03.accdb
frmFacContacts**

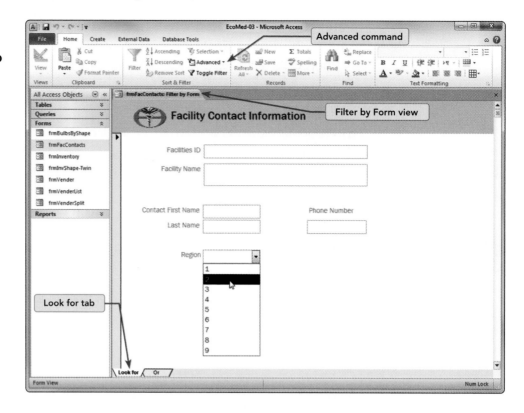

Figure 3-11
Filter By Form
**EcoMed-03.accdb
frmFacContacts**

4. From the **Home** tab, in the **Sort & Filter** group, click **Toggle Filter** ⊽. This action returns you to the form and enables the filter, which 10 records match.

5. Press ⌷PageDown⌷ to move through the records.

6. From the **Home** tab, in the **Sort & Filter** group, click **Advanced** 🗐 and choose **Filter By Form** 🗐. The last setting for **Region** is still present.

7. Click in the **Facility Name** field, and key ***center***.

8. From the **Home** tab, in the **Sort & Filter** group, click **Toggle Filter** ⊽. Only four records display.

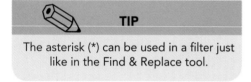

TIP

The asterisk (*) can be used in a filter just like in the Find & Replace tool.

Figure 3-12
Filter logic: Filter By Form
EcoMed-03.accdb

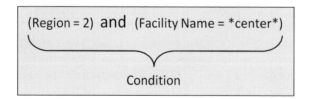

(Region = 2) **and** (Facility Name = *center*)

Condition

9. Press ⌷PageDown⌷ to move through the records.

Exercise 3-15 USE FILTER BY FORM OR OPTION

In the previous exercise, you used Filter By Form to create a set of filters in a single tab. There are times that you may need to create a more complex filter using multiple tabs. The Filter By Form has the ability to add alternate sets of filters. Alternative collections of filters are located on the "Or" tab. When using multiple tabs, displayed records must match all conditions on the first tab or all conditions on the additional "Or" tabs.

Suppose that you need to display a list of client facilities in Kansas and Missouri. Although you might say "Kansas and Missouri," this request is actually an OR condition. You really want to display all the records that are in the state "KS" or the state "MO." Because both values are applied to the same field, you must place the first filter on the "Look for" tab and the second on the "Or" tab.

1. From the Home tab, in the Sort & Filter group, click Advanced 🔁 and choose Filter By Form 🔁. The filter is set to find facilities that are in Region 2 and are "Centers."

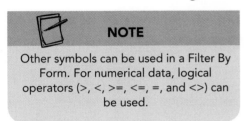

NOTE

Other symbols can be used in a Filter By Form. For numerical data, logical operators (>, <, >=, <=, =, and <>) can be used.

2. Click the Or tab next to the Look for tab to open an alternative collection of fields.

3. Click the drop-down arrow for the **Region** and choose **3**.

4. Click in the **Facility Name** field, and key *center*.

Figure 3-13
Filter logic: Filter By Form with Or
EcoMed-03.accdb

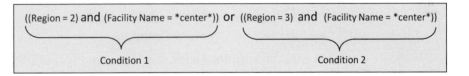

((Region = 2) and (Facility Name = *center*)) or ((Region = 3) and (Facility Name = *center*))

Condition 1   Condition 2

5. From the Home tab, in the Sort & Filter group, click Toggle Filter ▼. There are eight records that match both conditions.

6. From the Home tab, in the Sort & Filter group, choose Toggle Filter to disable the filter.

7. Click the Close button ⊠ to close the form.

Using the Database Documenter

External documentation helps EcoMed's IT department document changes to its database. An easy way to document the structure of the database is to create a report using the Database Documenter. The *Database Documenter* is an Access tool that lists the indexes, properties, relationships, parameters, and permissions of major database objects.

Exercise 3-16   SAVE A REPORT FOR A TABLE

When documenting a single object, you often need to include details for fields and indexes. By default, the Database Documenter does not include fields or indexes in its report. It is always a good idea to check which options are selected before printing a report.

1. From the Database Tools tab, in the Analyze group, click Database Documenter 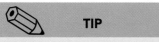.

2. In the Documenter dialog box, on the Tables tab, click the check box for **tblFacilities**.

Figure 3-14
Database
Documenter
EcoMed-03.accdb

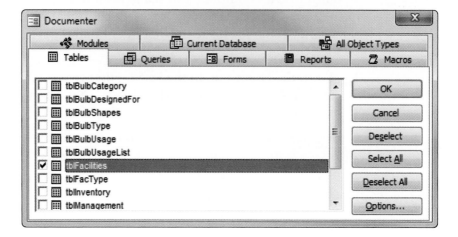

3. Click Options to open the Print Table Definition dialog box.

4. For the Include for Table section, check Properties, Relationships, and Permissions by User and Group.

5. For the Include for Fields section, select Names, Data Types, Sizes, and Properties (third option).

6. For the Include for Indexes section, select Names, Fields, and Properties (third option).

7. Click OK to accept the changes and close the dialog box.

8. Click OK to view the report.

TIP

In this book, you will be asked to generate a Documenter report when the structure of an object has been modified. To reduce the number of pages in the report, you will be asked to apply specific option settings.

9. From the Print Preview tab, in the Zoom group, click More Pages ⊞ and choose Twelve Pages from the menu. This nine-page report contains all the available information on the design of this table.

10. Click the Close Print Preview button ⊠.

11. From Database Tools tab, in the Analyze group, click Database Documenter 🖹.

12. In the Documenter dialog box, on the Tables tab, click the check box for **tblFacilities**.

13. Click Options to open the Print Table Definition dialog box.

14. For the Include for Table section, only check Properties and Relationships.

15. For the Include for Fields section, select Names, Data Types, and Sizes (second option).

16. For the **Include for Indexes** section, select **Nothing** (first option).

Figure 3-15
Print Table Definition
options
EcoMed-03.accdb

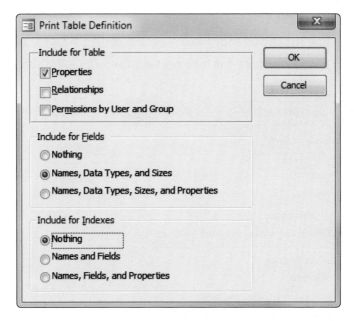

17. Click **OK** to accept the changes and close the dialog box.

18. Click **OK** to view the report. This version of the report is only one page.

19. From the command tab **Print Preview**, in the command group **Data**, click **PDF or XPS** 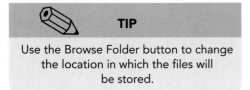.

20. Change the location to the location where you will be storing your work.

TIP

Use the Browse Folder button to change the location in which the files will be stored.

21. In the **File name** control, type *[your initials]*-03-16.

22. Click the **Save as type** control, and select **PDF**.

23. Verify the **Open file after publishing** check box is checked.

24. Click **Publish** to create the PDF file.

25. Close the PDF viewer. Click the **Close** button for the **Export-XPS** dialog box.

26. Click **Close Print Preview** ⊠.

Exercise 3-17   SAVE REPORT FOR OTHER OBJECTS

The documentable properties of a query are different than the properties of a table. Because a query has criteria, it also has an SQL statement. The SQL statement is a text representation of the query's criteria.

1. From **Database Tools** tab, in the **Analyze** group, click **Database Documenter** 📄.

2. In the **Documenter** dialog box, on the **Queries** tab, click the check box for **qryFacMail-FL**.

3. Click **Options** to open the **Print Query Definition** dialog box.

4. For the **Include for Query** section, only check the check boxes for **Properties** and **SQL**.

5. For the **Include for Fields** section, select **Names, Data Types, and Sizes**.

6. For the **Include for Indexes** section, select **Nothing**.

Figure 3-16
Print Query
Definition options
EcoMed-03.accdb

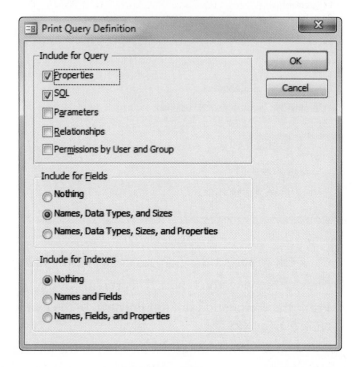

7. Click **OK** to accept the changes and close the dialog box.

8. Click **OK** to view the report. Notice that the information for the query fits on one page.

9. From the **Print Preview** tab, in the group **Data**, click **PDF or XPS** .

10. Change the location to the location where you will be storing your homework.

11. In the **File name** control, type *[your initials]*-03-17.

12. Click the **Save As type** control, and select **PDF**.

13. Verify that the **Open file after Exporting** check box is checked.

14. Click **Publish** to create the PDF file. This report is only one page.

15. Review the PDF file in the PDF reader, then close the file and the **Export-XPS** dialog box.

16. In Access, click the **Close** button to close the database.

Lesson 3   Summary

- To locate specific information, you can use Access tools to search, find, sort, and filter.

- You can improve search speeds by specifying unique data.

- The Search tool begins its search at the first field of the first record and stops at the first match.

- The Find and Replace command begins a search at the insertion point and includes options for fine-tuning how text is matched.

- A wildcard is a character or group of characters used to represent one or more alphabetical or numerical characters.

- The Totals row is a feature that you can use to calculate aggregate functions quickly.

- Each time you display the Totals row, the functions that you last saved will appear.

- A filter is a database feature that limits the number of records displayed.

- When applying a filter to a recordset, only records matching the criterion will display.

- The Filter By Selection options displayed depend upon the type of field and data selected.

- When filtering for a specific value, you select one or more values from a dynamically created list.

- The date filter options available vary depending on the date selected and the current date.

- Filter By Form allows you to define a collection of criteria for one or more fields using a template.

- Filter By Form has the ability to add alternate sets of filters located on the "Or" tab.

- The Database Documenter is an Access tool that lists the indexes, properties, relationships, parameters, and permissions of major database objects.

LESSON 3		Command Summary	
Feature	**Button**	**Task Path**	**Keyboard**
Database Documenter		Database Tools, Analyze, Database Documenter	
Filter by Form		Home, Sort & Filter, Advanced, Filter By Form	
Filter Range of Values		Home, Sort & Filter, (data type) Filters	
Filter Selection		Home, Sort & Filter, Selection	
Filter Specific Value		Home, Sort & Filter, Filter	
Find		Home, Find, Find	Ctrl + F
Replace		Home, Find, Replace	Ctrl + H
Sort Ascending		Home, Sort & Filter, Ascending	
Sort Descending		Home, Sort & Filter, Descending	
Sort Remove		Home, Sort & Filter, Clear All Sorts	
Totals Rows	Σ	Home, Records, Totals	
Layout View		Home, Views, Layout View	
Report View		Home, Views, Report View	

Concepts Review

True/False Questions

Each of the following statements is either true or false. Indicate your choice by circling T or F.

T F 1. The Search tool is case sensitive and treats uppercase and lowercase text differently.

T F 2. Press Ctrl+H to open the **Find and Replace** dialog box with a focus on the **Replace** tab.

T F 3. The asterisk (*) is a wildcard that represents one or more characters.

T F 4. The aggregate function average calculates values for columns containing text, numeric, currency, and date/time data.

T F 5. When applied, a filter hides all matching records.

T F 6. When the insertion point is in a field with no characters selected, Filter By Selection assumes the whole field is selected.

T F 7. The options available for the calendar filter will vary depending on the date selected and the current date.

T F 8. The documentable properties of a query are the same as those of a table.

Short Answer Questions

Write the correct answer in the space provided.

1. What shortcut keys open the **Find and Replace** dialog box with focus on the **Find** tab?

2. When using the Search tool, if a recordset contains more than one match, which match will be found?

3. What is a group of characters used to represent one or more alphabetical or numerical characters called?

4. In **Filter By Form**, what is the name of the first tab?

5. When using **Filter By Form** in a form, how will the template appear?

6. What action automatically triggers recalculations of the aggregate functions located in the **Totals** row?

7. What Find and Replace option finds records in which an entire field matches the value in the Find What text box?

8. What is a rule or test placed upon a field?

Critical Thinking

Answer these questions on a separate page. There are no right or wrong answers. Support your answers with examples from your own experience, if possible.

1. In addition to by month and by year, Access can filter data by quarters. Why do many businesses display financial information by calendar quarters?

2. Businesses and schools often sort information for specific needs. In addition to sorting information by student names, how might your school sort student information?

Skills Review

Exercise 3-18

EcoMed will be sending out new billing procedures to all venders. Before creating the mailer, you have been directed to correct mailing addresses. You will need to hide several columns in the datasheet view of the table to create a printout to verify the changes.

1. Locate and copy a database by following these steps:

   a. Locate and open the **Lesson 03** folder.

   b. If you already have a copy of *[your initials]*-**EcoMed-02**, skip to step 2.

   c. Right-click the file **EcoMed-03** and from the shortcut menu, choose Copy.

   d. Right-click an unused part of the folder and from the shortcut menu, choose Paste.

e. Right-click the new file and from the shortcut menu, choose Rename. Rename the file to *[your initials]*-EcoMed-03.

f. Right-click *[your initials]*-**EcoMed-03** and from the shortcut menu, choose Properties. Make certain that the Read-only attribute check box is not checked. Click OK.

2. Open a database by following these steps:

   a. Double-click *[your initials]*-**EcoMed-03**.

   b. If the Message Bar's Security Warning appears, click the Enable Content button.

3. Replace data by following these steps:

   a. In the Navigation Pane, open the table **tblVender** in Datasheet View.

   b. Press ⌈Ctrl⌉+⌈H⌉ to open the Find and Replace dialog box.

   c. In the Find What control, key **street**.

   d. In the Replace With control, key **St.**.

   e. Click the drop-down arrow for the Look In control and choose Current document.

   f. Click the drop-down arrow for the Match control and choose Any Part of Field.

   g. Click the drop-down arrow for the Search control and choose All.

   h. Click Replace All and click Yes to the message box.

   i. Click Cancel to close the dialog box.

   j. Click in the first record's **ContactName** field. Replace the current name with your full name.

4. Hide columns in a Datasheet View by following these steps:

   a. Click and drag over the column headers for **PhoneNum** and **FAX**.

   b. Right-click the column headers and choose Hide Fields from the menu.

Assessment

- Close an object by following these steps:

   a. Right-click the **tblVender** tab. From the shortcut menu select Close ⌷.

   b. Click Yes when asked to save the changes.

- According to your classroom procedure, turn in your database only when you have completed all assigned exercises.

-OR-

- Save a datasheet in landscape orientation by following these steps:

   a. Click the File tab and from the Print option, click Print Preview ⌷.

   b. From the Print Preview tab, in the Page Layout group, click Landscape ⌷ to save the printout as a file.

   c. From the Print Preview tab, in the Data group, click PDF or XPS ⌷ to save the printout as a file.

03-18-A.pdf
1 Page

d. Save the file with the following settings:

- In the dialog box's **Navigation Pane**, select the location where you want to store your class work.
- **Save as type** as PDF.
- **File name** as *[your initials]*-03-18-A.
- **Open file after publishing** should be checked.

e. Close the **Export – PDF** window.

f. Depending on your class procedures print or turn in the PDF file.

g. Right-click the **tblVender** tab. From the shortcut menu, select **Close** .

h. Click **Yes** when asked to save the changes.

Exercise 3-19

Many times before sending out a mailer, EcoMed sorts the addresses by state or city. You will be modifying the report for facilities in Florida to sort all records by the city in which the facility is located.

1. The database *[your initials]*-**EcoMed-03** is required to complete this exercise.

   a. Double-click the database *[your initials]*-**EcoMed-03**.

   b. If the Message Bar's **Security Warning** appears, click the **Enable Content** button.

2. Sort data by following these steps:

   a. In the **Navigation Pane**, open the report **rptFacMail-FL**.

   b. From the **Home** tab, in the **Views** group, click **Layout** .

   c. From the **Page Setup** tab, in the **Page Layout** group, click **Landscape** .

   d. Right-click the column headers for **City** and choose **Sort A to Z** .

3. Change the print settings for a report by following these steps:

   a. From the **Home** tab, in the **Views** group, click **Print Preview** .

   b. In the **Page Layout** group, click **Margins** option arrow and choose **Narrow**.

   c. In the **Zoom** group, click **Two Pages** . The report should fit on one page.

Assessment

- Close an object by following these steps:

  a. Right-click the **rptFacMail-FL** tab. From the shortcut menu, select **Close** .

  b. Click **Yes** to save the changes.

- According to your classroom procedure, turn in your database only when you have completed all assigned exercises.

-OR-

- Save a report in landscape orientation by following these steps:

   a. From the **Print Preview** tab, in the **Data** group, click **PDF or XPS** to save the printout as a file.

   b. Save the file with the following settings:

   - In the dialog box's **Navigation Pane**, select the location where you want to store your class work.
   - **Save as type** as PDF.
   - **File name** as *[your initials]*-03-19-A.
   - **Open file after publishing** should be checked.

   c. Close the **Export – PDF** window.

   d. Depending on your class procedures print or turn in the PDF file.

- Close an object by following these steps:

03-19-A.pdf
1 Page

   a. Right-click the **rptFacMail-FL** tab. From the shortcut menu select **Close** .

   b. Click **Yes** to save the changes.

Exercise 3-20

The sales department would like to know the number of beds for each facility in Florida. Modify qryFacBeds-FL to calculate the total beds.

1. The database *[your initials]*-**EcoMed-03** is required to complete this exercise.

   a. Double-click the database *[your initials]*-**EcoMed-03**.

   b. If the Message Bar's **Security Warning** appears, click the **Enable Content** button.

2. Add a Totals row by following these steps:

   a. In the **Navigation Pane**, open the query **qryFacBeds-FL** in **Datasheet View**.

   b. From the **Home** tab, in the **Records** group, click **Totals** Σ.

   c. In the **Totals** row, click the drop-down arrow in the **Beds** field.

   d. Choose **Average** from the list.

Assessment

- Close an object by following these steps:

   a. Right-click the **qryFacBeds-FL** tab. From the shortcut menu select **Close** .

   b. Click **Yes** to save the changes.

- According to your classroom procedure, turn in your database only when you have completed all assigned exercises.

-OR-

- Save a report by following these steps:

  a. Click the File tab. From the Print option, choose Print Preview .

  b. From the Print Preview tab, in the Data group, click PDF or XPS 📄 to save the printout as a file.

  c. Save the file with the following settings:

  - In the dialog box's Navigation Pane, select the location where you want to store your class work.
  - Save as type as PDF.
  - File name as *[your initials]*-03-20-A.
  - Open file after publishing should be checked.

  d. Close the Export – PDF window.

  e. Depending on your class procedures print or turn in the PDF file.

- Close an object by following these steps:

  a. Right-click the **qryFacBeds-FL** tab. From the shortcut menu, select Close ⬜.

  b. Click Yes to save the changes.

03-20-A.pdf
1 Page

Exercise 3-21

EcoMed maintains contracts with its clients. You will need to modify the query that tracks the ending dates of each contract. You will display only the contracts that end during the first quarter of the year. Records will be sorted by state.

1. The database *[your initials]*-EcoMed-03 is required to complete this exercise.

   a. Double-click the database *[your initials]*-EcoMed-03.

   b. If the Message Bar's Security Warning appears, click the Enable Content button.

2. Filter a query by following these steps:

   a. In the Navigation Pane, open the query **qryContractDates** in Datasheet View.

   b. Click anywhere in the **Contract Ends** field.

   c. From the Home tab, in the Sort & Filter group, choose Filter 🔽.

   d. In the menu, choose Date Filters. In the next menu, choose All Dates in Period, then Quarter 1.

3. Sort data by following these steps:

   a. Click anywhere in the field **State**.

   b. From the Home tab, in the Sort & Filter group, click Ascending 🔼.

4. Close an object by following these steps:

   a. Right-click the **qryContractDates** tab. From the shortcut menu, select Close ⬜.

   b. Click Yes to save the changes.

Assessment

 - According to your classroom procedure, turn in your database only when you have completed all assigned exercises.

-OR-

 - Create a Database Documenter reports by following these steps:

a. From the Database Tools tab, in the Analyze group, choose Database Documenter.

b. In the Documenter dialog box, on the Queries tab, click the check box for **qryContractDates**.

c. Click Options to open the Print Query Definition dialog box.

d. For the Include for Query section, check Properties and SQL.

e. For the Include for Fields section, select Nothing.

f. For the Include for Indexes section, select Nothing.

g. Click OK to close the Print Table Definition dialog box.

h. Click OK to create the document report.

- Save a Database Documenter report by following these steps:

a. Click the File tab. From the Print option, choose Print Preview.

b. From the Print Preview tab, in the Data group, click PDF or XPS to save the printout as a file.

c. Save the file with the following settings:

   • In the dialog box's Navigation Pane, select the location where you want to store your class work.

   • Save as type as PDF.

   • File name as *[your initials]*-03-21-A.

   • Open file after publishing should be checked.

d. Close the Export – PDF window.

e. Depending on your class procedures, print or turn in the PDF file.

f. From the Print Preview tab, in the Close Preview group, click Close Print Preview.

03-21-A.pdf
1 Page

Lesson Applications

Exercise 3-22

You have been directed to modify records in the inventory table. Use the replace command to change the records. Then apply an appropriate filter to only the fields that you need to display to verify your work.

1. Using the database *[your initials]*-EcoMed-03, make sure that all content is enabled.

2. Open the form **tblInventory** in Datasheet View.

3. Find all the occurrences of "Other" in the **Bulb Category** field and replace them with Outdoor.

4. Filter the datasheet to only show records that have **Bulb Category** "Outdoor" and the **Bulb Shape** "A-line."

5. Hide the fields **Vender** through **Image**.

6. Widen each column so that all data can be seen.

7. Sort the table in ascending order by **InvID**.

8. Add a Totals row that will **Count** the **Model Number** field.

Assessment

- Close the table and save the changes.
- According to your classroom procedure, turn in your database only when you have completed all assigned exercises.

-OR-

- Save the table **tblInventory** as a PDF file named *[your initials]*-03-22-A.
- According to your class procedures, print or turn in the PDF file.
- Close the table and save the changes.

03-22-A.pdf
1 Page

Exercise 3-23

The director of IT department has directed you to modify the structure of a query. After making the appropriate changes, you will need to verify your work by creating a Database Documenter report.

1. Using the database *[your initials]*-EcoMed-03, make sure that all content is enabled.

2. Open the query **qryInvShape-Twin** in Datasheet View.

3. Sort the **Cost** field in ascending order.

4. Close the query and save the changes.

5. Create a **Database Documenter** report for **qryInvShape-Twin** using the following settings:

   • Include for Query: **Properties** and **SQL**

   • Include for Fields: **Names, Data Types, and Size**

   • Include for Indexes: **Nothing**

6. Save the **Documenter** report as a PDF file named *[your initials]*-03-23-A.

7. Close the **Export – PDF** window and the query.

03-23-A.pdf
1 Page

Assessment

- According to your classroom procedure, turn in your database only when you have completed all assigned exercises.
- Depending on your class procedures, print or turn in the PDF file.

-OR-

- According to your class procedures, print or turn in the PDF file.

Exercise 3-24

The table that stores the information regarding the corporate management for each client has address errors. You have been directed to modify the data and print the datasheet view of the table in landscape orientation.

1. Using the database *[your initials]*-**EcoMed-03**, make sure that all content is enabled.

2. Open the table **tblManagement** in **Datasheet View**.

3. Clear all filters and/or sorts.

4. Filter the datasheet to only show companies who have the area code "212."

5. Find all the occurrences of "Street" and replace the text with **St.**.

6. Hide all fields except **Management Company**, **Address**, and **Phone Number**.

7. Sort the table in descending order by **Management Company**.

8. Add your full name to the end of the first **Management Company**.

9. Widen each column so that all data can be seen.

10. Set the **Page Layout** to **Landscape**.

Assessment

- According to your classroom procedure, turn in your database only when you have completed all assigned exercises.

-OR-

- Save the table's **Datasheet View** as a PDF file named *[your initials]*-03-24-A.
- According to your class procedures, print or turn in the PDF file.
- Close the **Export – PDF** window. Close the table while saving the changes.

03-24-A.pdf
1 Page

Exercise 3-25 ◆ Challenge Yourself

You have been asked to calculate statistical values for some inventory items. You are directed to use a query to determine average, maximum, and minimum values for the inventory costs. You will need to record the values in a Word document.

1. Using the database *[your initials]*-**EcoMed-03**, make sure that all content is enabled.

2. Open the query **qryInvShort**.

3. Create a Word document called *[your initials]*-**03-25-A** and record the answers to the following questions.

4. Filter the query to only show records that have a **Bulb Shape** of Bare-Mini-Spiral and are 13 watt.

5. Record the average, maximum, and minimum **Cost** for these bulbs.

6. Include your name, class information, and date.

7. Save the Word file *[your initials]*-**03-25-A**.

03-25-A.docx
1 Page

Assessment

- According to your classroom procedure, turn in your database only when you have completed all assigned exercises.
- Depending on your class procedures, print or turn in the Word file.

-OR-

- Depending on your class procedures, print or turn in the Word file.

On Your Own

In these exercises, you work on your own, as you would in a real-life work environment. Use the skills you've learned to accomplish the task—and be creative.

Exercise 3-26

Review the Web sites you located in Exercises 2-28 and 2-29. Of companies that sell products of interest to members of the organization you formed, determine which companies allow products to be sorted or displayed by different conditions. On a sheet of paper, write down the fields that can be sorted or selected. Continue to the next exercise.

Exercise 3-27

For one of the Web sites, print three lists of products sorted or filtered by various methods. Write a brief description of the sort or filter being applied on each of the three printouts. Continue to the next exercise.

Exercise 3-28

Refer to the form you created in Exercise 2-30. Write down the fields that can be used to sort or filter the information displayed on the form. Sketch two new forms based on your sorting and filtering parameters. Submit your work for Exercises 3-26 through 3-28 to your instructor.

Lesson 4
Creating New Databases and Tables

OBJECTIVES *After completing this lesson, you will be able to:*

1. Create a database.
2. Create a table.
3. Manage external data.
4. Control field appearance.
5. Control data integrity.
6. Add and delete fields in a table.

Estimated Time: 2 hours

EcoMed Services, Inc., maintains a database that tracks customer information, including contact names, facilities, addresses, and phone numbers. The database also tracks product information, including model numbers, product types, pricing, and technical specifications. All of these data are vital information necessary to operate a company on a day-to-day basis.

As the company grows, EcoMed's day-to-day activities may change. New procedures or new departments may need to be implemented. To meet the changing requirements, new data may need to be tracked and managed. Sometimes an entirely new database will be created. Other times, only a new table will be added.

The structure of a database is critical for a company's ability to convert data into useful information. A database must be both efficient and effective. It must be designed to improve data management and protect the integrity of the data.

Creating Databases

The president of EcoMed Services, Inc., has decided that the company should begin keeping up with technological advances in energy management. The sales department has been given the new tasks of attending energy conferences and tracking new contacts they make at the conferences. You have been directed to create two new databases to track the conferences and the contacts.

There are two methods for creating a new database. One method uses templates to create a structured database containing major objects (tables, queries, forms, or reports). The second method creates a blank database without any objects.

Exercise 4-1 CREATE A DATABASE USING A TEMPLATE

When creating a new database, you sometimes can find a database template on which to base your preliminary design. A *database template* is a ready-to-use database containing all the tables, queries, forms, and reports needed to perform a specific task.

For example, Access includes an events template designed for tracking events, which includes the event name, start time, end time, description, and location. The events template also includes two forms and five reports that can display the events by start time or event type. Creating this template will be useful for developing a functional conference database.

1. Click the **Start** button  on the Windows taskbar and point to **All Programs**.

2. Click **Microsoft Office Access 2007** to start Access. (You might have to first point to a program group, such as Microsoft Office).

3. Access opens to the **Backstage** with the **New** tab selected.

4. In the **Available Templates** section, click **Sample templates**.

5. Click the **Contacts Web Database** template.

Figure 4-1
Events database templates

6. Click the **File New Database** button.

7. In the **File New Database** dialog box, navigate to the location where you want to store your class work. Change the **File name** to *[your initials]-Contacts*. Click **OK**.

8. Click **Create** to launch the template. The new database opens with a form already open.

9. In the **Security Warning** message, click **Enable Content** to continue.

10. Click the **Shutter Bar Open/Close** button ⟩ to expand the **Navigation Pane**.

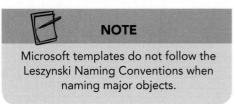

NOTE

Microsoft templates do not follow the Leszynski Naming Conventions when naming major objects.

11. This database has two tables, one query, 13 forms, and six reports. Open a few forms and reports to see the layouts of the objects.

12. Open the table **Contacts**. Review the types of data that can be stored. Many of these fields are not needed for our company.

13. Right-click the document tab for the table **Contacts** and choose **Close**.

Exercise 4-2   SET DATABASE PROPERTIES

Database properties do not change the functionality of the database. They only provide useful information to help identify the file. Adding properties to a database can help you and other database managers identify the purpose of the database. Some database properties, such as the title, author, and company, are defined automatically when the database is created. The information automatically entered comes from the identification settings of the workstation on which the database is created.

When creating a new database, you should change the properties to reflect the purpose for which the database was created. Some properties, such as Compact on close, help keep the size of the database manageable.

1. Click the **File** tab. In the Backstage View, the **Info** option is selected. At the far right of the screen, click **View and edit database properties**.

2. Click in the textbox for the **Title** property and key the name of your class.

3. Change the value for **Author** to *[your full name]*.

4. In the property **Comments**, key **This database was created using Microsoft Contacts template on** *[today's date]*.

5. Click **OK** to close the dialog box.

6. While in the Backstage View, click the **Options** button.

7. In the left pane, click the **Current Database** category. Locate the **Compact on Close** property and click the check box to add a checkmark.

Figure 4-2
Changing properties

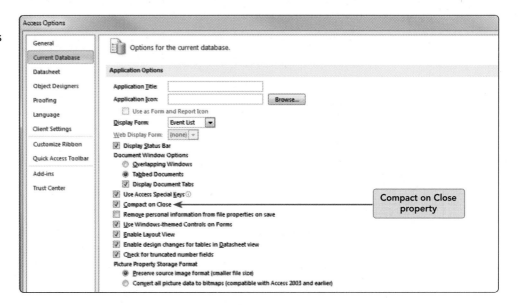

8. Click **OK** to close the **Access Option** dialog box.

9. A warning dialog box appears to inform you that the database must be restarted before your changes will be implemented. Click **OK**.

10. Click the **File** tab. Click **Close Database** 📁 to close the active database without closing Access.

Exercise 4-3 CREATE A BLANK DATABASE

If you cannot find a database template to meet your needs, you must create a blank database from scratch. The process requires you to name the database and specify the location in which it will be saved. Once the database is created, you will be able to add other major objects, such as tables, queries, reports, and forms.

1. In the **New** option tab, click **Blank database** 📄.

2. Click the **File New Database** button 📂.

3. In the **File New Database** dialog box, navigate to the location where you want to store your class work. Change the **File name** to *[your initials]*-EcoMed-Contacts. Click **OK**.

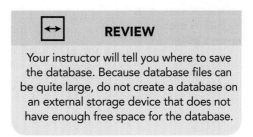

↔ REVIEW

Your instructor will tell you where to save the database. Because database files can be quite large, do not create a database on an external storage device that does not have enough free space for the database.

Figure 4-3
Create a blank
database

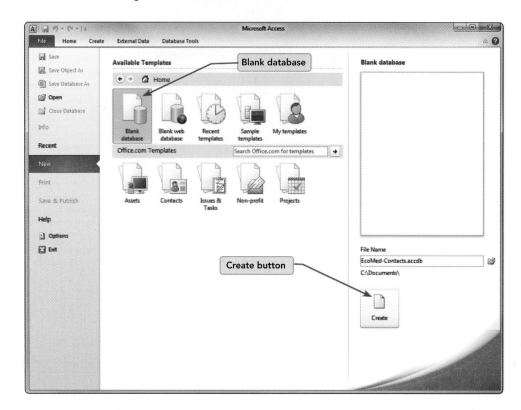

4. Click **Create** 🗋. A new table opens in **Datasheet View**.

5. Click the **Close** button ⊠ for the table. Notice that because the table does not contain fields, it is not listed in the Navigation Pane.

Creating a Table

The company president wants EcoMed Services, Inc., to begin developing sales leads. You have been directed to create a table to store contact information for potential customers. In a well-designed database, each table should store data for a unique purpose. The new table that you create will store only new sales lead contacts.

Exercise 4-4   CREATE A TABLE IN DESIGN VIEW

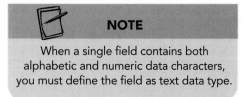

NOTE

When a single field contains both alphabetic and numeric data characters, you must define the field as text data type.

Design View offers you the greatest flexibility when defining field names, types, and properties. The order and type of field defined depends on the data that will be stored. When defining new fields, you will need to determine the field name, size, and type. For example, prices should be stored as currency, names as text, and images as attachments.

TABLE 4-1 Access Data Types

Setting	Type of Data
Text	Alphanumeric characters. A text field can be a maximum of 255 characters long. Use Text as the Data Type for numbers that are not used in calculations, such as addresses or phone numbers.
Memo	Descriptive text such as sentences and paragraphs used for text greater than 255 characters in length or for text that uses rich text formatting.
Number	Numbers (integer or real). Data in a number field can be used in arithmetic calculations. Use Number as the Data Type when values will used in calculations.
Date/Time	Formatted dates or times used in date and time calculations. Each value stored includes both a date component and a time component.
Currency	Money values used for storing monetary values (currency). Values can be used in arithmetic calculations and can display a currency symbol.
AutoNumber	A unique numeric value automatically created by Access when a record is added. Use AutoNumber Data Type for generating unique values that can be used as a primary key.
Yes/No	Boolean value displayed as check boxes. Use Yes/No Data Type for True/False fields that can hold one of two possible values.
Attachment	Pictures, images, binary files, or Office files. Preferred data type for storing digital images and any type of binary file.
Hyperlink	Navigation element for an Internet site, e-mail address, or file pathname. Use Hyperlink Data Type for storing hyperlinks to provide single-click access to Web pages through a URL (Uniform Resource Locator) or files through a name in UNC (universal naming convention) format.

1. From the **Create** tab, in the **Tables** group, click **Table** ⊞. A new table is created, and the ribbon now shows the contextual tabs **Fields** and **Table**.

2. From the **Fields** contextual tab, in the **Views** group, click the top part of the split button ⬓ to switch to **Design View**.

3. In the **Save As** dialog box, key **tblContacts** and click **OK**. The table is now in **Design View**.

Figure 4-4
Design View of
a table
**EcoMed-Contacts.
accdb
tblContacts**

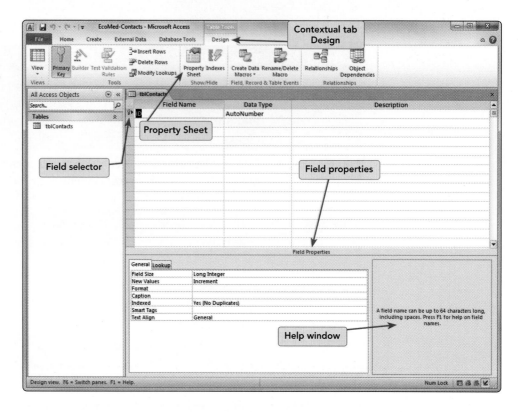

4. In the first row, in the **Field Name** column, key **ContactID**.

5. Press Tab to move to the **Data Type** column. The default **Data Type** for the first field in a new table is **AutoNumber**.

6. Press Tab to move to the **Description** column. Key **Contact identification number**.

7. Press Tab to move to the second field in the **Field Name** column. Key **LastName**.

8. Press Tab to move to the **Data Type** column. The default data type is **Text**.

9. Press Tab and key **Last name of contact**.

10. Enter the following fields:

Field Name	Data Type	Description
FirstName	Text	First name of contact
Company	Text	Contact's company
EmailAddr	Hyperlink	Contact's company Email
PhoneNum	Text	Office phone number
Fax_Num	Text	Office FAX number
FirstContact	Date/Time	Date that first contact was made
Notes	Memo	Comments about the contact

11. Click the **Close** button ⊠ for the table.

Figure 4-5
Structure changes to
a table
**EcoMed-Contacts.
accdb
tblContacts**

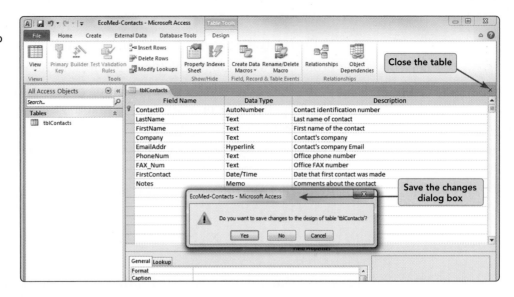

12. Click **Yes** to save the changes to the design of the table.

Exercise 4-5   MODIFY TABLE PROPERTIES

Table properties do not change the functionality of the table. They only provide useful information to help identify the object. Some properties, such as owner or date/time modified, are automatically updated according to the workstation settings.

1. In the **Navigation Pane**, right-click the table **tblContacts**, and choose **Table Properties**.

2. In the Description textbox, key **This table stores the information for EcoMed's contacts**.

Figure 4-6
Table Properties
**EcoMed-Contacts.
accdb
tblContacts**

tblContacts Properties

General

tblContacts

Type: Table
Description: This table stores the information for EcoMed's contacts

Created: 12/20/2009 7:03:59 PM
Modified: 12/20/2009 7:27:02 PM
Owner: Admin

Attributes: ☐ Hidden

OK   Cancel   Apply

3. Click **OK**.

4. In the **Navigation Pane**, double-click the table **tblContacts**.

5. From the **Home** tab, in the **Views** group, choose **View** ⬛.

6. From the **Design** tab, in the **Show/Hide** group, click **Property Sheet** 🖻. The **Property Sheet** appears. Notice that the **Description** property contains the text from Step 2.

7. From the **Design** tab, in the **Show/Hide** group, click **Property Sheet** 🖻 to close the **Property Sheet**.

8. Right-click the **tblContacts** document tab and choose **Close** ◳.

Managing External Data

EcoMed Services, Inc., uses electronic data interchange whenever possible. *Electronic data interchange* (EDI) is the transfer of electronic data from one computer system to another. EDI transfers data from one system to another without re-entering or re-keying data. Importing data electronically prevents errors that may occur when data is re-keyed incorrectly.

Each time you import data, you duplicate the original data. The original data remain in the source application while you work with a copy of the data in your database.

Exercise 4-6 COPY TABLE STRUCTURE FROM AN EXTERNAL TABLE

When copying a table, you have three options: You can select to include only the structure, the structure and data, or only the data. When you copy only the structure, you create an empty table without any records. You can add records at a later time.

1. From the **External Data** tab, in the **Import & Link** group, click **Access** 🖾.

2. In the **Get External Data** dialog box, click **Browse**.

3. In the **File Open** dialog box, locate the **Lesson 04** folder and select the file **EcoMed-04**. Click **Open**.

4. Back in the **Get External Data** dialog box, make sure that the **Import table, queries, forms, reports, ...** option is selected. Click **OK**.

5. In the **Import Objects** dialog box, click the **Options** button.

6. Remove the checkmark from **Relationships**.

7. In the **Import Tables** section, select **Definition Only**.

8. Select the table **tblManagement** from the list of tables.

Figure 4-7
Import table options
**EcoMed- Contacts.
accdb
tblManagement**

9. Click OK. Close the Get External Data dialog box.

10. In the Navigation Pane, double-click **tblManagement**. This table has no records. Only the table structure was copied.

11. Right-click the **tblManagement** document tab and choose Close ⊠.

12. Click the File tab. Click Exit ⊠.

Exercise 4-7 EXPORT A TABLE TO ACCESS

You can export an Access table directly to another Microsoft application, such as Word or Excel. Access tables can also be exported directly to non-Microsoft applications such as dBASE and Paradox. For applications not supported by Access, you can export a table using a file format such as text, XML, or HTML. When exporting a table, you can save the steps used in the export operation. Saving the steps can greatly decrease the time it takes to export the same table next time.

1. Locate and open the **Lesson 04** folder.

2. Make a copy of **EcoMed-04** and rename it *[your initials]*-EcoMed-04.

3. Open and enable content for *[your initials]*-EcoMed-04.

4. Right-click the table **tblVender** in the Navigation Pane and choose Export, then Access ⒶⱩ.

Figure 4-8
Export a table
EcoMed-04.accdb
tblVender

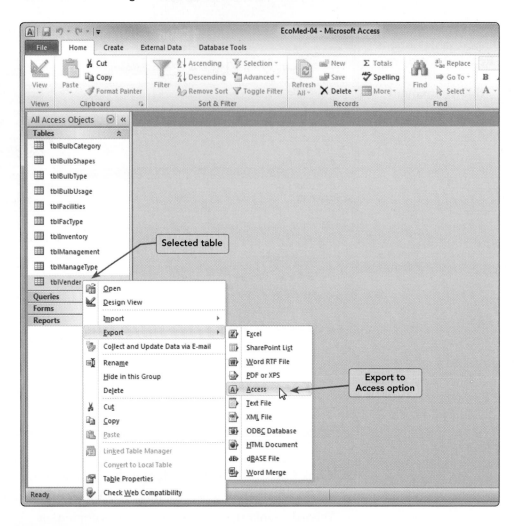

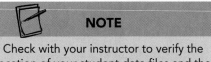

NOTE

Check with your instructor to verify the location of your student data files and the location in which you will be working. The folder "Documents" is often the default folder when you create or store files.

5. In the **Export – Access Database** dialog box, click **Browse**.

6. In the **File Save** dialog box, locate and click *[your initials]*-**EcoMed-Contacts**, which you created earlier in this lesson. Click **Save**.

7. Click **OK** to close the **Export – Access Database** dialog box.

Figure 4-9
Export dialog box
EcoMed-04.accdb
tblVender

Export

Export tblVender to:

| tblVender |

in EcoMed-Contacts.accdb

Export Tables

◉ Definition and Data

○ Definition Only

[OK]   [Cancel]

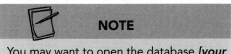

NOTE

You may want to open the database *[your initials]*-EcoMed-Contacts to verify that the table was exported.

8. Click OK to export the table **tblVender** with its data and structure.

9. In the Export – Access Database dialog box, click Close.

Exercise 4-8 EXPORT DATA TO WORD

You can export a table, query, form, or report to Microsoft Word using the Access Export Wizard. A copy of the object's data will be stored as a Rich Text Format (rtf) file. For tables, queries, and forms, the visible fields and records appear as a table in the Word document. Hidden or filtered columns and records are not exported.

1. In the Navigation Pane, select the query **qryUnivContacts**.
2. From the External Data tab, in the Export group, click More 🔩 and then select Word 🔳.
3. In the Export – RTF File dialog box, delete "qry" from the file name.
4. Click the check box Open the destination file after the export operation is complete. Click OK.
5. View the table in Word, then close the application Word.
6. In the Export – RTF File dialog box, click Close.

Exercise 4-9 IMPORT DATA FROM EXCEL

For most non-Access applications, a wizard steps you through the import process. When importing from an Excel workbook, you may select all columns and rows from a worksheet or just a range of cells. The ease of importing data greatly depends upon how the information is stored in the source spreadsheet.

1. In the Navigation Pane, double-click the table **tblManagement**. Notice that there are 107 companies in this table.
2. Close the table.
3. From the External Data tab, in the Import & Link group, click Excel 📑.
4. In the Get External Data – Excel Spreadsheet dialog box, click Browse.
5. In the File Open dialog box, locate the folder **Lesson 04**, and select the Excel file **New Management**.
6. Click Open.
7. Select the option Append a copy of the records to the table:, click the drop-down arrow, and select **tblManagement**.

Figure 4-10
Import data from
Excel
EcoMed-04.accdb
tblManagement

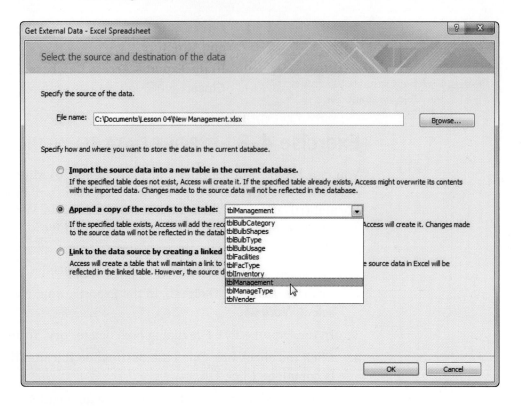

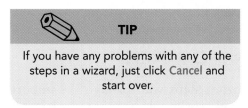
TIP

If you have any problems with any of the steps in a wizard, just click Cancel and start over.

8. Click **OK** to start the **Import Spreadsheet Wizard**.

9. In the first step of the **Import Spreadsheet Wizard**, you see the data from the Excel file. Click **Next**.

10. Access has identified the information in the first row as header information. These headers will be treated as field names. Click **Next**.

11. Click **Finish**. In the **Get External Data – Excel Spreadsheet** dialog box, click **Close**.

12. Open **tblManagement** in **Datasheet View**. There are now 110 records. Three records were imported. Close the table.

Adding and Deleting Fields in a Table

Although infrequent, sometimes the changes needed by EcoMed Services, Inc., require that a table be modified. Adding and deleting require a different level of care.

Before adding a field to a table, you first should make certain that it does not duplicate an existing field's data. Adding a new field in one table to store data that is already in another table creates an inefficient data design and can lead to data entry errors.

Deleting a field can be much more dangerous than adding one. Before deleting a field from a table, make certain that the data in the field will never be needed in the future. Many database administrators would rather move data to an archive table than delete historical information.

Exercise 4-10   ADD AND DELETE FIELDS IN DATASHEET VIEW

You also can insert and delete fields in Datasheet View. When inserting a text field in a datasheet, the default width of the field is 255 spaces. Each field will be named Field*n*, where n is a sequential number starting with one (1). Although the task of deleting a field from datasheet may appear similar to hiding the field, deleting a field is a permanent action that cannot be undone.

1. In the **Navigation Pane**, double-click the table **tblManagement**.

2. From the **Home** tab, in the **Records** group, click **More** and click **Unhide Fields** from the menu.

3. In the **Unhide Fields** dialog box, click the check box for **Click to Add**. Click **Close**.

4. Press End to move to the last field in the table.

5. Right-click the field header **Click to Add** and choose **Yes/No** from the shortcut menu. The field is now called **Field1**, and a new **Click to Add** column has been added.

6. Key **NonProfit** and press ↓. Check boxes appear in the new field. A checkmark equals "Yes," "True," or "On."

7. Press End and Shift+Tab to return to the last field.

> **TIP**
>
> In field names, using symbols other than dashes (-) or underscores (_) can cause problems. There are no such problems with captions.

8. From the **Fields** tab, in the **Properties** group, click **Name & Caption** .

9. Press Tab to move to the **Caption** textbox. Key **NonProfit?**.

10. Press Tab to move to the **Description** textbox. Key **A checkmark indicates that a company is a NonProfit organization**. Click **OK**.

11. Notice that the **Caption** setting is what you see as the field header. Also the **Description** now appears in the status bar.

12. Click on the column header for the **CEO**.

13. From the **Fields** tab, in the **Add & Delete** group, click **Delete**. Click **Yes** to confirm the deletion.

Exercise 4-11   ADD AND DELETE FIELDS IN DESIGN VIEW

Adding fields through Design View is more flexible than through Datasheet View. In addition to text, numeric, and date fields, you can define and size all field types.

> **NOTE**
>
> When you insert a field, the new row is placed in the row selected, and all fields below are moved down.

1. From the **Fields** tab, in the **Views** group, click **View** to switch to **Design View**.

2. Click on the field selector for **PhoneNum**.

3. From the **Design** tab, in the **Tools** group, click **Insert Rows** .

Figure 4-11
Inserting a row
EcoMed-04.accdb
tblManagement

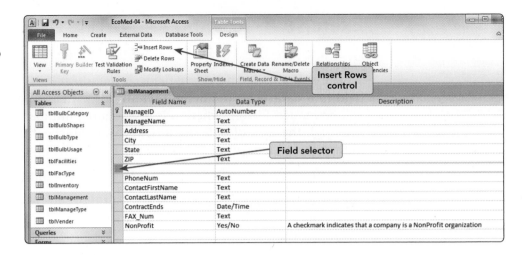

4. Click in the **Field Name** for the blank row and key **CellNum**.
5. Press Tab. The default **Data Type** is **Text**. Press Tab.
6. In the **Description** for **CellNum** key **Contact's work cell number**.
7. From the **Design** tab, in the **Views** group, click **View** ▦ to switch to **Datasheet View**.
8. Click **Yes** to save the changes to the table's structure.

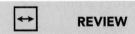

REVIEW

Changes to field data are saved automatically; however, you must save design changes to the table.

9. From the **Home** tab, in the **Views** group, click **View** ◣ to switch to **Design View**.
10. Select the field selector for **FAX_Num**.
11. From the **Design** tab, in the **Tools** group, click **Delete Rows** ⇥. Click **Yes** to confirm the deletion.
12. From the Quick Access Toolbar, click **Save** 🖫.

Controlling Field Appearance

Certain field properties control how a field appears to database users. A change to one of these properties only affects the field's appearance without changing the underlying structure or size of the field.

Changing a field's appearance may be necessary for functional reasons, not merely cosmetic ones. For example, when most records use the same area code, you may change the default value for the phone number. This simple change may improve the speed, accuracy, and consistency of your data entry.

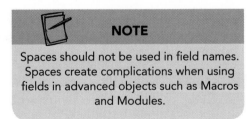

NOTE

Spaces should not be used in field names. Spaces create complications when using fields in advanced objects such as Macros and Modules.

TABLE 4-2 Text Field Properties

Property	Purpose
Field Size	Controls the size of a text field and can be up to 255 characters.
Format	Defines the appearance of data. Custom formatting changes the appearance of the data without changing the underlying record.
Input Mask	Displays a pattern for entering the data. Examples are the use of parentheses around an area code or hyphens in a social security number.
Caption	Sets a label or title for the field. The Caption replaces the field name as the column title in a datasheet and as the control label in forms and reports.
Default Value	Specifies the value that automatically appears in a field when creating a new record. The value can be accepted or changed.
Validation Rule	Condition specifying criteria for entering data into an individual field. A Validation Rule of ">100" requires values to be larger than 100.
Validation Text	Error message that appears when a value prohibited by the validation rule is entered. For the Validation Rule ">100," the Validation Text might be "You must enter a value greater than 100."
Required	Requires entry of a value in the field when set to "Yes."

Exercise 4-12 CHANGE FIELD PROPERTY CAPTION

When no caption is defined, the name of the field displays as its column heading on a datasheet or as its control label in a form or report. When a field caption is defined, the caption will be used instead.

1. In the **Design View** of **tblManagement**, double-click the field **ManageID** to select the **Field Name**. Press Ctrl+C.

2. In the **Field Properties** section, click in the **Caption** property.

3. Press Ctrl+V. Add a space between "Manage" and "ID".

4. Press ← and key **ment**.

Figure 4-12
Change the caption
property
EcoMed-04.accdb
tblManagement

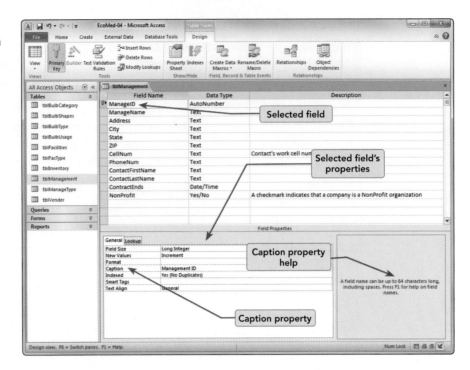

5. Double-click the **Field Name PhoneNum** and press Ctrl + C.

6. Press F6 to move to the **Field Properties** section.

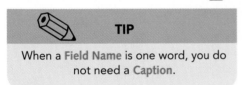

TIP

When a **Field Name** is one word, you do not need a **Caption**.

7. Press Tab three times to move to the **Caption** property.

8. Press Ctrl + V. Add a space between "Phone" and "Num."

9. Press End and key **ber**.

10. Press Ctrl + S to save the changes to the table structure.

Exercise 4-13 CHANGE FIELD PROPERTY DEFAULT VALUE

Setting a default value is useful when a significant number of records contain the same field value. For example, if the majority of your employees live in the same state, you might choose to set a default value for the state field. All new records will display the default value, and previously entered records will not be changed. Whenever a record contains a different value for the field, the user can key a new value to replace the default value.

1. In the **Design View** of **tblManagement**, click the field selector for **NonProfit** and press F6.

2. Press Tab until you reach the **Default Value** property.

3. This property is set to "0," which represents the cleared check box.

4. Change the zero to a **-1**. The -1 value represents the checked check box.

5. From the **Home** tab, in the **Views** group, click **View** 🔲 to switch to **Datasheet View**. Click **Yes** to save the changes.

6. Press Ctrl + End to move to the last record. Notice that the record selector with the asterisk (*) has a checked check box. This row is the new record row.

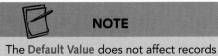

NOTE

The Default Value does not affect records that have already been added to the table. Only new records will have this value if no other value is given to that field.

7. From the **Home** tab, in the **Views** group, click **View** 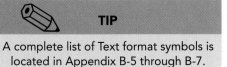 to switch to **Design View**.

8. Key **0** to change the **Default Value** property for **NonProfit** back to "0".

9. Press Ctrl+S to save the changes to the table structure.

Exercise 4-14 CHANGE FIELD PROPERTY FORMAT

You can improve data entry by specifying formats. For example, you can set the format for a date to display the name of the month, set the format for currency to show dollar signs, or set the format for text to display as uppercase letters. For some data types, you can select from predefined formats. For others, you can enter a custom format.

1. In the **Design View** of **tblManagement**, click the field selector for **ContractEnds**, and press F6.

2. In the **Format** property, click the drop-down arrow and select **Medium Date**.

Figure 4-13
Setting Format property
EcoMed-04.accdb
tblManagement

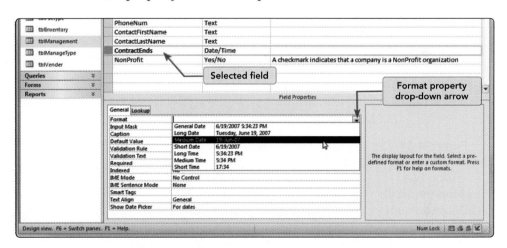

3. From the **Design** tab, in the **Views** group, click **View** to switch to **Datasheet View**. Save your changes.

4. Press Tab until you see the **ContractEnds** field. The appearance of the dates has changed.

5. From the **Home** tab, in the **Views** group, click **View** to switch to **Design View**.

6. Click the field selector for **State** and press F6.

7. In the **Format** property, key **>**. This will visually make the content of this field appear in upper case.

8. From the **Design** tab, in the **Views** group, click **View** to switch to **Datasheet View**. Save your changes.

TIP

A complete list of Text format symbols is located in Appendix B-5 through B-7.

9. In the **State** field for **Management ID** 1, key **il**. Press Tab. The data display as upper-case characters.

10. From the **Home** tab, in the **Views** group, click **View** to switch to **Design View**.

Exercise 4-15 CHANGE FIELD PROPERTY INPUT MASK

An input mask is used to format the display of data and control the format in which values can be entered. Input masks can be used for text or numeric data types. You can use the Input Mask Wizard for common formats, such as telephone numbers and social security numbers.

TABLE 4-3 Input Masks

Character	Description
0	Digit (0 through 9, entry required; plus <+> and minus <–> signs not allowed).
9	Digit or space (entry not required; plus and minus signs not allowed).
#	Digit or space (entry not required; blank positions converted to spaces, plus and minus signs allowed).
L	Letter (A through Z, entry required).
?	Letter (A through Z, entry optional).

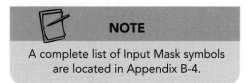

NOTE

A complete list of Input Mask symbols are located in Appendix B-4.

1. In the **Design View** of **tblManagement**, click the field selector for **PhoneNum** and press F6.
2. Click the **Input Mask** property row.
3. From the **Design** tab, in the **Tools** group, click **Builder**.

Figure 4-14
Input Mask Wizard dialog box
**EcoMed-04.accdb
tblManagement**

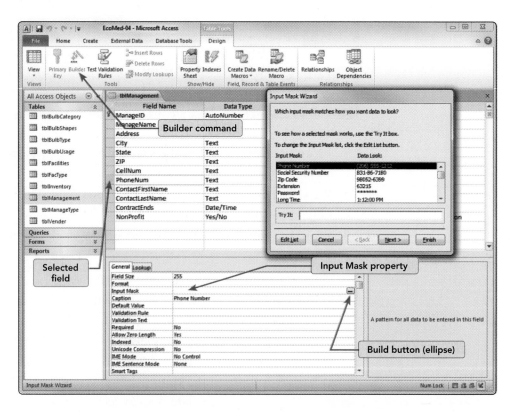

4. The **Input Mask Wizard** lists several common masks and shows how the data are displayed. Select the **Phone Number** mask.

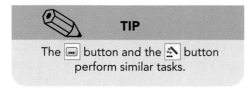

TIP

The ⊟ button and the ⬉ button perform similar tasks.

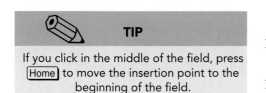

TIP

If you click in the middle of the field, press Home to move the insertion point to the beginning of the field.

5. Click **Next**. The wizard asks if you want to change the input mask. Click in the **Try It** entry box.

6. Press Home. Key your phone number.

7. Click **Next**. The wizard asks how you want to store the data. Select **With the symbols in the mask, like this:**.

8. Click **Next**. Read the final message and click **Finish**.

9. From the **Design** tab, in the **Views** group, click **View** ▦ to switch to **Datasheet View**. Save your changes.

10. For the first record, press Tab until you reach the **Phone Number** field and try entering your phone number.

11. From the **Home** tab, in the **Views** group, click **View** ⬟ to switch to **Design View**.

Exercise 4-16   CHANGE FIELD PROPERTY DATE PICKER

Depending on the workstation's language settings, the date picker displays either to the right or left sides of a Date/Time field. Clicking the date picker launches a calendar control from which you can select a date. If the field is empty, the Date Picker will default to the current date.

1. In the **Design View** of **tblManagement**, click the field selector for **ContractEnds** and press F6.

2. Move to the **Show Date Picker** property, click the drop-down arrow, and select **For dates**.

3. From the **Design** tab, in the **Views** group, click **View** ▦ to switch to **Datasheet View**. Save your changes.

4. Click in the first record's **ContractEnds** and click the Date Picker ▦.

Figure 4-15
Date Picker
EcoMed-04.accdb
tblManagement

ber ▾	ContactFirstName ▾	ContactLastN ▾	ContractEnds ▾	NonProfit? ▾
10	Paola	Bandini	30-Apr-16	☐
90	Antonio	Lara		☐
00	Deanna	Zitterk		☐
00	John	Lovela		☐
	Sharon	MacKe		☐
10	Janie	Ward		☐
00	Joydeep	Mitra		☐
	Sandra	Hambr		☐
	Robert	Czerni		☐
00	John	Leyba	31-Aug-16	☐
11	Mildred	Latini	31-Dec-15	☐
	Roberta	Himebrook	30-Apr-16	☐
00	Roberto	Apodaca	31-Jul-16	☐
00	Anil	Runasingha	30-Nov-15	☐

Date Picker — April, 2016

Su	Mo	Tu	We	Th	Fr	Sa
27	28	29	30	31	1	2
3	4	5	6	7	8	9
10	11	12	13	14	15	16
17	18	19	20	21	22	23
24	25	26	27	28	29	30
1	2	3	4	5	6	7

Today

5. Press Esc to exit the field without saving any changes.

6. Click the **Close** button ✕ for the table.

Controlling Data Integrity

EcoMed Services, Inc., requires certain procedures to increase data efficiency but also to ensure data integrity. *Data integrity* is the condition through which data can be assumed to be accurate. One way of improving data integrity is by defining the field properties for tables.

Certain field properties restrict values stored in a field. A change to one of these properties can affect both the structure and the size of the field. Because these changes might alter your data, it is best to make them before adding records to a table. If a table already contains data and you are uncertain if your data will be affected, back up your database before making changes to field properties.

Exercise 4-17   SET THE PRIMARY KEY

Most tables contain a primary key. A *primary key* is a field or set of fields in a table that provide a unique identifier for every record. Each record must store a unique value in a primary key field. Most often primary keys are numeric data types; however, other data types can be used.

1. In the **Navigation Pane**, double-click the table **tblBulbType**.

2. From the **Home** tab, in the **Views** group, click **View** ⬘ to switch to **Design View**.

3. From the **Design** tab, in the **Tools** group, click **Insert Rows** ⦿.

4. Key **BulbTypeID** and press ⎀Tab⎀.

5. In the **Data Type** column, key **a**. **AutoNumber** is the only data type on the list that starts with an "A."

6. From the **Design** tab, in the **Tools** group, click **Primary Key** ⬚.

Figure 4-16
Set a Primary Key
EcoMed-04.accdb
tblBulbType

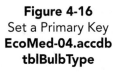

7. From the **Design** tab, in the **Views** group, click **View** ▦ to switch to **Datasheet View**. Save your changes.

8. The field **BulbTypeID** has now been populated with a unique number.

Exercise 4-18 SET THE FIELD PROPERTY FIELD SIZE

Changing the field size alters the space available to store data. The numeric value defined in the Field Size property is the maximum number of characters allowed for storage of data. Changing the field size in Design View is different than changing the column width in Datasheet View.

1. From the **Home** tab, in the **Views** group, click **View** ⬖ to switch to **Design View**.

2. In the **Design View** of **tblBulbType**, click the field selector for **BulbType** and press F6.

3. In the **Field Size** property, change 255 to **15**.

TIP

Text fields should be wide enough to hold most data but not so unnecessarily wide that they waste storage space.

4. From the **Design** tab, in the **Views** group, click **View** ▦ to switch to **Datasheet View**.

5. Read the message dialog box. Click **Yes**. If any record stores more than 15 characters in the **BulbType** field, all characters beyond the first 15 characters will be deleted.

6. Right-click any document tab and choose **Close** ⬛.

Exercise 4-19 SET THE FIELD PROPERTY VALIDATION TEXT AND RULES

A *Validation Rule* is a condition specifying criteria for entering data into an individual field. You define a validation rule to control what values can be entered into a field. You also can enter an optional validation text to match your rule. *Validation text* is an error message that appears when a value prohibited by the validation rule is entered.

For example, you could define the validation expression ">=100" for a quantity field to prevent a user from entering values less than 100. For the corresponding validation expression, you could enter "You must enter a number equal to or greater than 100."

When you set a validation rule for a field that contains data, Access will ask if you want to apply the new rule to the existing data. If you answer yes, Access evaluates the rule against the existing data in the table. If any record violates the validation rule, you will be notified that the data must be corrected before the rule can be applied.

The Test Validation Rules button checks the current data in the field to see if it matches the Validation Rule. If it does not, Access displays an error message alerting you to the conflict.

1. In the **Navigation Pane**, double-click the table **tblManagement**.

2. From the **Home** tab, in the **Views** group, click **View** ⬖ to switch to **Design View**.

3. Click the field selector for **ContractEnds** and press F6.

4. Tab to the **Validation Rule** property and key >=1/1/2015. This rule restricts users to enter a date before January 1, 2015.

5. Press Enter to move to the **Validation Text** property.

6. Key **All new contracts must terminate after or on 1/1/2015.**.

7. Press Ctrl+S to save the changes to the table. A data integrity dialog box appears asking if you want to test the current data with the new rules. Click **Yes**.

8. From the **Design** tab, in the **Tools** group, click **Test Validation Rules**. Click **Yes** in the dialog box.

9. The next dialog box tells you that all the data in this table pass the validation rule you just created. Click **OK**.

10. From the **Design** tab, in the **Views** group, click **View** to switch to **Datasheet View**.

11. Press Tab until you reach the **ContractEnds** field.

12. Key **1/1/2011** and press Enter.

Figure 4-17
Validation Text
dialog box
EcoMed-04.accdb
tblBulbType

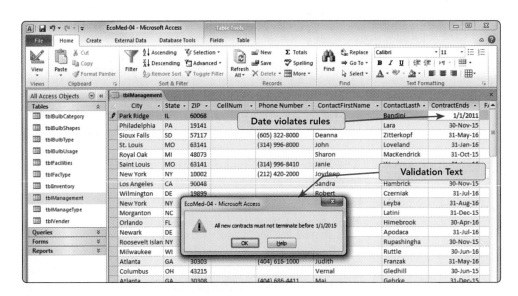

13. Click **OK** to close the dialog box. Press Esc until the original data reappear in the field.

14. Close the table. Compact and close the database.

Lesson 4 $\quad$ Summary

- The two methods for creating a new database are using a template or creating a blank database.

- A database template is a ready-to-use database containing all the tables, queries, forms, and reports needed to perform a specific task.

- A new database created as a blank database does not contain objects or data.

- Some database properties come from the operating system of the workstation on which the database is created.

- The two methods for creating a new table are using a template and creating a blank table.

- Table templates provide a quick and easy method to produce a table containing commonly used fields based on a specific need.

- When a single field contains both alphabetic and numeric data characters, you must define the field as text data type.

- When copying a table, you can select to include only the structure, the structure and data, or only the data.

- Before adding any field to a table, you first should make certain that it does not duplicate an existing field's data.

- When tables are created using Datasheet View, Access evaluates the data entered to determine the data type for the field to create.

- A Caption is a field property that displays as a column heading in Datasheet View or as a control label in a form or report.

- Spaces should not be used in field names. Spaces create additional requirements when using fields in advanced objects, such as macros and modules.

- An input mask is used to format the display of data and control the format in which values can be entered.

- Depending on the workstation's language settings, the date picker displays either to the right or left side of a Date/Time field.

- A primary key is a field or set of fields in a table that provide a unique identifier for every record.

- Changing the field size in Design View is different than changing the column width in Datasheet View.

- The data contained in a field defined as the primary key of a table must be unique.

- A Validation Rule is a condition specifying criteria for entering data into an individual field.

- Validation text is an error message that appears when a value prohibited by the validation rule is entered.

- Importing data prevents errors that may occur when re-keying data.

- Data can be exported to another Microsoft application such as Word or Excel or non-Microsoft applications such as dBASE and Paradox.
- Data imported from another Access database, a non-Access database, or a non-database application can be added to an existing table or used to create a new table.

LESSON 4		Command Summary	
Feature	**Button**	**Task Path**	**Keyboard**
Application Parts		Create, Templates	
Change field name		Fields, Properties, Name & Caption	
Database, blank		New, Blank database	
Database, new		File, New	
Delete column		Fields, Add & Delete, Delete	
Delete rows		Design, Tools, Delete Rows	
Export, Word		External Data, Export, More, Word	
Field, properties		Home, Views, Design View	
Field, properties, toggle			F6
Import, Excel		External Data, Import & Link, Excel	
Insert rows		Design, Tools, Insert Rows	
Paste		Home, Clipboard, Paste	Ctrl + V
Primary key		Design, Tools, Primary Key	
Table, create		Create, Tables, Table	
Table, properties		Right click object, properties	

Concepts Review

True/False Questions

Each of the following statements is either true or false. Indicate your choice by circling T or F.

T F 1. After you create a table using a template, you can rename fields and change the data type of fields in Design View.

T F 2. A database template is a ready-to-use database containing only tables but lacking the queries, forms, and reports needed to perform specific tasks.

T F 3. Data integrity is the condition through which data can transferred from one computer system to another.

T F 4. The primary key field of a table must contain unique data.

T F 5. Fields can be deleted only through Design View.

T F 6. When applying a validation rule to a field that contains data, Access asks if you want to apply the new rule to the existing data.

T F 7. In Datasheet View, the Description property of a field displays as the column header.

T F 8. When exporting a table to Microsoft Word using the Access Export Wizard, a copy of the object's data will be stored as a Rich Text Format (rtf) file.

Short Answer Questions

Write the correct answer in the space provided.

1. When must you create a blank database from scratch?

_____

2. When using the Leszynski Naming Conventions, what would you rename a table called Food Costs?

_____

3. Name the four ways to add/create a table to a database.

_____

4. What kind of data type does a template use for a street address?

_____

5. What field data type can store more than 255 characters?

_____

6. In what view can you change the data type or description of a field?

_____

7. In **Design View**, which function key toggles the insertion point between the lower and upper panes?

_____

8. What kind of field must store unique or different data for each record?

_____

Critical Thinking

Answer these questions on a separate page. There are no right or wrong answers. Support your answers with examples from your own experience, if possible.

1. Access Templates use field names such as StateOrProvince and PostalCode instead of State or ZIPCode. Why do you think Access does this? Give an example when using the default field names might not be appropriate.

2. Many businesses find it necessary to import tables into Access. Give an example when a business might need to import data.

Skills Review

Exercise 4-20

You have been asked to create a new database to help track tasks for company employees. You create a new database to manage these tasks.

1. Create a new database by following these steps:
   a. With Access running and no database open, click **Sample templates** and choose **Tasks**.
   b. In the **File Name** textbox, key *[your initials]*-EcoMed-Tasks.
   c. Verify the save location.
   d. Click **Create** ☐.

2. Change the appearance of the **Navigation Pane** by following these steps:
   a. Click **Enable Content**.
   b. Expand the **Navigation Pane**, click the **Task Navigation** bar, and choose **Object Type**.
   c. Close the form **Task List**.
   d. Double-click the table **Tasks**.

3. Delete fields in **Datasheet View** by following these steps:

    a. Click on the column header for the **Description**.

    b. From the **Fields** tab, in the **Add & Delete** group, click **Delete** 🗡.

4. Delete fields in **Design View**, by following these steps:

    a. From the **Home** tab, in the **Views** group, click **View** 🔽 to switch to **Design View**.

    b. Click on the field selector for **Attachments**.

    c. From the **Design** tab, in the **Tools** group, choose **Delete Rows** 🖹.

    d. Press [Ctrl]+[S] to save the changes.

5. Change field properties by following these steps:

    a. Click on the field selector for **Title**.

    b. In the property **Field Size**, key 200.

    c. Press [Ctrl]+[S] to save the changes.

6. Close an object by following these steps:

    a. Right-click the **Tasks** tab. From the shortcut menu, select **Close** 🗙.

Assessment

- Close the database.
- According to your classroom procedure, turn in your database only when you have completed all assigned exercises.

-OR-

- Create a Database Documenter report by following these steps:

    a. From the **Database Tools** tab, in the **Analyze** group, choose **Database Documenter** 🖹.

    b. In the **Documenter** dialog box, on the **Tables** tab, click the check box for **Tasks**.

    c. Click **Options** to open the **Print Table Definition** dialog box.

    d. For the **Include for Table** section, check **Properties**.

    e. For the **Include for Fields** section, select **Names, Date Types, and Size**.

    f. For the **Include for Indexes** section, select **Nothing**.

    g. Click **OK** to close the **Print Table Definition** dialog box.

    h. Click **OK** to create the document report.

- Save a Database Documenter report by following these steps:

    a. From the **Print Preview** tab, in the **Data** group, click **PDF or XPS** 🖹 to save the printout as a file.

    b. Save the file with the following settings:

      • In the dialog box's **Navigation Pane**, select the location where you want to store your class work.

      • **Save as type** as PDF.

      • **File name** as *[your initials]*-04-20-A.

      • **Open file after publishing** should be checked.

04-20-A.pdf
1 Page

c. Close the **Export – PDF** window.

d. Depending on your class procedures, print or turn in the PDF file.

e. From the **Print Preview** tab, in the **Close Preview** group, click **Close Print Preview** ⊠.

f. Close the database.

Exercise 4-21

The structure for the table inventory needs to be modified. Using Design View, modify the structure and then verify your work by saving a documenter report.

1. Locate and copy a database by following these steps:

   a. Locate and open the **Lesson 04** folder.

   b. If you already have a copy of *[your initials]*-**EcoMed-04**, skip to step 2.

   c. Right-click the file **EcoMed-04** and from the shortcut menu, choose **Copy**.

   d. Right-click an unused part of the folder. From the shortcut menu, choose **Paste**.

   e. Right-click the new file and from the shortcut menu, choose **Rename**. Rename the file to *[your initials]*-EcoMed-04.

   f. Right-click *[your initials]*-**EcoMed-04** and from the shortcut menu, choose **Properties**. Make certain that the **Read-only** attribute check box is not checked. Click **OK**.

2. Change the design of a table by following these steps:

   a. Open **tblInventory**. Switch to **Design View**.

   b. In the top pane, click in the **BulbShapes** row and press F6.

   c. In the **Field Size**, key 20.

   d. In the top pane, click in the **BulbCategory** row and press F6.

   e. In the **Field Size**, key 15.

   f. In the top pane, click in the **3Way**.

   g. From the **Design** tab, in the **Tools** group, click **Delete Rows** ⇥×. Click **Yes** to confirm the deletion.

   h. In the top pane, click in the **EnergyStar**.

   i. From the **Design** tab, in the **Tools** group, click **Insert Rows** ⋛.

   j. Key **Available** as the new **Field Name**.

   k. Press Tab and choose **Yes/No** as the new **Data Type**.

3. Close an object by following these steps:

   a. Right-click the **tblInventory** tab. From the shortcut menu select **Close** ⌐.

   b. Save the changes to the table and click **Yes** when warned that some data might be lost.

Assessment

- According to your classroom procedure, turn in your database only when you have completed all assigned exercises.

-OR-

- Create a Database Documenter report by following these steps:

  a. From the Database Tools tab, in the Analyze group, click Database Documenter 📄.

  b. In the Documenter dialog box, on the Tables tab, click the check box for **tblInventory**.

  c. Click Options to open the Print Table Definition dialog box.

  d. For the Include for Table section, check Properties only.

  e. For the Include for Fields section, select Names, Data Types, and Size.

  f. For the Include for Indexes section, select Nothing.

  g. Click OK to close the Print Table Definition dialog box.

  h. Click OK to create the document report.

- Save a Database Documenter report by following these steps:

  a. Click the File tab. From the Print option, choose Print Preview 🔍.

  b. From the Print Preview tab, in the Data group, click PDF or XPS 📄 to save the printout as a file.

  c. Save the file with the following settings:

    • In the dialog box's Navigation Pane, select the location where you want to store your class work.

    • Save as type as PDF.

    • File name as *[your initials]*-04-21-A.

    • Open file after publishing should be checked.

  d. Close the Export – PDF window.

  e. Depending on your class procedures, print or turn in the PDF file.

  f. From the Print Preview tab, in the Close Preview group, click Close Print Preview ✖.

04-21-A.pdf
1 Page

Exercise 4-22

The structure for the table bulb shapes needs to be modified. Using Design View, modify the structure, then verify your work by saving a documenter report.

1. The database *[your initials]*-**EcoMed-04** is required to complete this exercise.

    a. Double-click the database *[your initials]*-**EcoMed-04**.

    b. If the Message Bar's Security Warning appears, click the Enable Content button.

2. Add fields by following these steps:

    a. Open **tblBulbShapes**. Switch to Design View.

    b. In the top pane, click in the **BulbShape** row.

    c. From the Design tab, in the Tools group, select Insert Row ⌗.

    d. For the Field Name key **BulbShapeID**.

    e. For the Data Type select AutoNumber.

3. Change a field's properties by following these steps:

    a. From the Design tab, in the Tools group, select Primary Key 🔑.

    b. Double-click to select the field name **BulbShape**. Press Ctrl + C.

    c. Press F6. Change the Field Size to 30.

    d. In the Format property, key >.

    e. Press ↓ until you reach the Caption property. Press Ctrl + V.

    f. Add a space between the words "Bulb" and "Shape."

4. Close an object by following these steps:

    a. Right-click the **tblBulbShapes** tab. From the shortcut menu, select Close ⌧.

    b. Save the changes to the table and click Yes when warned that some data might be lost.

Assessment

- According to your classroom procedure, turn in your database only when you have completed all assigned exercises.

-OR-

- Create a Database Documenter report by following these steps:

    a. From the Database Tools tab, in the Analyze group, choose Database Documenter 📑.

    b. In the Documenter dialog box, on the Tables tab, click the check box for **tblBulbShapes**.

    c. Click Options to open the Print Table Definition dialog box.

    d. For the Include for Table section, check Properties.

    e. For the Include for Fields section, select Names, Data Types, Size, and Properties.

    f. For the Include for Indexes section, select Nothing.

    g. Click OK to close the Print Table Definition dialog box.

    h. Click OK to create the document report.

- Save a Database Documenter report by following these steps:

    a. Click the File tab. From the Print option, choose Print Preview 🔍.

    b. From the Print Preview tab, in the Data group, click PDF or XPS 📥 to save the printout as a file.

c. Save the file with the following settings:

- In the dialog box's Navigation Pane, select the location where you want to store your class work.
- Save as type as PDF.
- File name as *[your initials]*-04-22-A.
- Open file after publishing should be checked.

d. Close the Export – PDF window.

e. Depending on your class procedures, print or turn in the PDF file.

f. From the Print Preview tab, in the Close Preview group, click Close Print Preview ⊠.

04-22-A.pdf
2 Pages

Exercise 4-23

New bulbs to be added to the inventory table have been entered into an Excel spreadsheet. Rather than retype the information, you have been instructed to import the records from the spreadsheet and append these records into the inventory table.

1. The database *[your initials]*-EcoMed-04 is required to complete this exercise.

    a. Double-click the database *[your initials]*-EcoMed-04.

    b. If the Message Bar's Security Warning appears, click the Enable Content button.

2. Import Excel data by following these steps:

    a. From the External Data tab, in the Import & Link group, click Excel 📷.

    b. In the Get External Data dialog box, click Browse.

    c. Locate the **Lesson 04** folder and select **New Bulbs**. Click Open.

    d. Select the Append a copy of the records to the table: option. Select the table **tblInventory**. Click OK.

    e. Click Finish.

    f. The message box tells you that the table has been imported. Click Close.

    g. Open **tblInventory** in Datasheet View.

3. Filter the table by following these steps:

    a. Click anywhere in the **BulbShapes** field.

    b. From the Home tab, in the Sort & Filter group, click Filter ▼.

    c. Click the (Select All) check box to remove the checkmark.

    d. Scroll down the list and click on **Other**. Click OK.

    e. Resize each column to show all the data.

4. Hide fields in a table by following these steps:

    a. Select the field header **Available**.

    b. From the Home tab, in the Records group, click More and choose **Hide Fields**.

    c. Select the field header **Wattage** through **Color Temp**.

    d. From the Home tab, in the Records group, click More and choose **Hide Fields**.

    e. Save the changes to the table.

5. Change the print settings for a datasheet by following these steps:

    a. Click the **File** tab. From the Print option, choose **Print Preview** 🔍.

    b. From the tab **Print Preview**, in the **Page Layout** group, click **Landscape** 📄.

Assessment

🗄️ DB

- Close an object by following these steps:

    a. Right-click the **tblInventory** tab. From the shortcut menu, select **Close** 🗙.
    b. Compact and close the database.

- According to your classroom procedure, turn in your database only when you have completed all assigned exercises.

-OR-

📄 PDF

- Save datasheet for a table by following these steps:

    a. From the **Print Preview** tab, in the **Data** group, click **PDF or XPS** 📥 to save the printout as a file.

    b. Save the file with the following settings:

    - In the dialog box's **Navigation Pane**, select the location where you want to store your class work.
    - **Save as type** as PDF.
    - **File name** as *[your initials]*-04-23-A.
    - **Open file after publishing** should be checked.

    c. Close the **Export – PDF** window.
    d. Depending on your class procedures, print or turn in the PDF file.

- Close an object by following these steps:

    a. Right-click the **tblInventory** tab. From the shortcut menu, select **Close** 🗙.
    b. Compact and close the database.

04-23-A.pdf
1 Page

Lesson Applications

Exercise 4-24

The sales department needs to send marketing literature to the Chief Executive Officers (CEOs) of all client facilities. Rather than have the sales department work with the full database, you have been asked to create a temporary facilities database. You will import the facilities table from the EcoMed database and add a CEO field to the table.

1. Create a blank database named *[your initials]*-EcoMed-Facility.

2. Import **tblFacilities** from *[your initials]*-EcoMed-04.

3. Rename the table **tblFacility**.

4. Add a text field named **CEO** as the last field of the table.

5. Set the field size to **50**.

Assessment

- Close and save the table, then compact and close the database.
- According to your classroom procedure, turn in your database only when you have completed all assigned exercises.

-OR-

- Create a **Database Documenter** report for **tblFacility** using the following settings:
  - Include for Table: **Properties** only
  - Include for Fields: **Names, Data Types, and Size**
  - Include for Indexes: **Nothing**
- Save the **Documenter** report as a PDF file named *[your initials]*-04-24-A.
- According to your class procedures, print or turn in the PDF file.
- Close the **Export – PDF** window.
- Close and save the table, then compact and close the database.

04-24-A.pdf
1 Page

Exercise 4-25

The sales department has determined that the company now needs to track sales events. You have been asked to add a new table to the existing database.

1. Use the database *[your initials]*-EcoMed-04 database.

2. Create a new table named **tblSalesEvent**.

3. Open the table in Design View. Add the following fields to the table.

Field	Data Type	Caption
SalesRep	Text	Sales Representative
StartDate	Date/Time	Start Date
EndDate	Date/Time	End Date

4. Change the Format to Short Date for the StartDate and EndDate fields.

5. Add Short Date Input Mask for both dates.

6. Change the Field Size property for Sales Rep to 35.

7. Rename the field ID to SaleEventID.

Assessment

- Close and save the table, then compact and close the database.
- According to your classroom procedure, turn in your database only when you have completed all assigned exercises.

-OR-

- Create a Database Documenter report for tblSalesEvent using the following settings:
  • Include for Table: Nothing
  • Include for Fields: Names, Data Types, Size, and Properties
  • Include for Indexes: Nothing
- Save the Documenter report as a PDF file named *[your initials]*-04-25-A.
- According to your class procedures, print or turn in the PDF file.
- Close and save the table, then compact and close the database.

04-25-A.pdf
2 Pages

Exercise 4-26

On occasion, employees purchase supplies for the company. These expenses need to be tracked. Create a new table to track employee expenses.

1. Using the database *[your initials]*-EcoMed-04 database, create a new blank table.

2. In Datasheet View, add the following record:

ID:	*Press* Tab
Column 2:	464-4824
Column 3:	Supplies
Column 4:	10/15/11
Column 5:	$14.85
Column 6:	Cleaning Supplies
Column 7:	Trash Bags, Soap, and Paper Towels

TIP

To add a new field in Datasheet View, you must click in the Click to Add column.

3. Save the table as **tblEmpExp-**_[your initials]_.

4. Set **Field1** as the primary key and delete the **ID** field.

5. Rename the field names to the following:

Field1:	**EmpID**
Field2:	**ExpenseType**
Field3:	**DatePurchased**
Field4:	**AmountSpent**
Field5:	**Purpose**
Field6:	**Description**

6. Set the **Caption** for **EmpID** to **Employee ID**.

7. Create appropriate captions, by adding a space, for the fields **ExpenseType**, **DatePurchased**, and **AmountSpent**.

8. Enter the following record:

Employee ID:	**234-7890**
Expense Type:	**Supplies**
Date Purchased:	**10/22/11**
Amount Spent:	**$25.34**
Purpose:	**Office Supplies**
Description:	_Key [your full name]_

9. Resize columns so all data is visible.

Assessment

- Close and save the table, then compact and close the database.
- According to your classroom procedure, turn in your database only when you have completed all assigned exercises.

-OR-

- Save the table **tblEmpExp** as a PDF file named _[your initials]_**-04-26-A**, in landscape orientation.
- According to your class procedures, print or turn in the PDF file.
- Close and save the table, then compact and close the database.

04-26-A.pdf
1 Page

Exercise 4-27 ◆ Challenge Yourself

Normally, EcoMed payments are tracked by the accounting department through a separate application. The director of the IT department would like to test tracking expenses through the current access database. Create a new database and add the appropriate table.

1. Create a blank database and name it *[your initials]*-Application-04.

2. Create a new table named tblPayments-*[your initials]*, and use Design View to add the following fields:

Field Name	Data Type	Field Size
PaymentID	AutoNumber	
CustomerID	Number	Integer
OrderID	Number	Integer
PaymentAmount	Currency	
PaymentDate	Date/Time	
Description	Text	40

3. Delete the Field ID.

4. Set PaymentID as the primary key.

Assessment

- Close and save the table, then compact and close the database.
- According to your classroom procedure, turn in your database only when you have completed all assigned exercises.

-OR-

- Create a Database Documenter report for **tblPayments** using the following settings:

  • Include for Table: Properties only

  • Include for Fields: Names, Data Types, and Size

  • Include for Indexes: Nothing

- Save the Documenter report as a PDF file named *[your initials]*-04-27-A.

- According to your class procedures, print or turn in the PDF file.

- Close and save the table, then compact and close the database.

04-27-A.pdf
1 Page

On Your Own

In these exercises you work on your own, as you would in a real-life work environment. Use the skills you've learned to accomplish the task—and be creative.

Exercise 4-28

Using the Contact Template, create a new database to store the member information you collected and organized for the On Your Own exercises of Lessons 1 through 3. Enter the member information. Print the datasheet view of the table. On the first sheet of your printout, write your name and class information. Continue to Exercise 4-29.

Exercise 4-29

Review the structure of the main table in the database you created in Exercise 4-28. On a blank sheet of paper, list the fields, data types, and field sizes from the table that are most appropriate for your organization's needs. Add any additional fields that would improve the usability of the table. Without using a database template, create a blank database. Create a table to store the data. Enter the member information. Print properties for the table. Continue to Exercise 4-30.

Exercise 4-30

Search the Templates section of the Microsoft Office home page. Locate a template that will enhance the database you created in the previous exercise. Using the template you located on the Internet, create a new database. Enter appropriate data for at least five records. Print the table. Submit to your instructor the printouts from Exercises 4-28 through 4-30 along with your field list from 4-30. Make sure your name, the date, and your class information is written on the printouts. Keep a copy of the three databases you created in Exercises 4-28 through 4-30. They may be used in subsequent lessons.

Unit 1 Applications

Unit Application 1-1

Data in the management table needs to be update. Using the Datasheet View for the table, modify the data and print the recordset as directed.

1. Locate and open the **Unit 1** folder.

2. Make a copy of **EcoMed-U1** and rename it to *[your initials]* -EcoMed-U1.

3. Open and enable content for *[your initials]*-EcoMed-U1.

4. Open **tblManagement**. Change the font of the datasheet to Arial Narrow.

5. Hide the columns **Contact First Name**, **Contact Last Name**, and **Contract Ends**.

6. Make the changes shown in Figure U1-1.

Figure U1-1
Editing
tblManagement

Manage ID	Management Company	ZIP	Phone Number
9	Christiana Health Care System	19899-**1668**	(302) 568-6544
17	Ohio Health Corporate Office	43215	(614) 585-4777
23	Health Alliance — *[your full name]*	45209	(513) 619-5522
30	Clarian Health — Administration Offices	46206-**1367**	(317) 916-3525

7. Add the following new record:

Manage ID:	*Press* Tab
Management Company:	*Key [your full name]*
Address:	522 Bend Ave.
City:	Dayton
State:	OH
ZIP:	45390
Phone Number:	(555) 222-6464

8. Delete the record for **Manage ID** 96.

9. Apply a filter to only show management companies from **DE**, **IN**, and **OH**.

10. Size all columns wide enough to show the longest text or column heading for each field.

11. Sort the table in ascending order by **Management Company**.

12. Make sure that all data fit on one page in **Landscape** orientation.

Assessment

- Save and close **tblManagement**. Compact and close the database.
- According to your classroom procedure, turn in your database only when you have completed all assigned exercises.

-OR-

- Save the table datasheet as a PDF named *[your initials]*-U1-01-A.
- Depending on your class procedures, print or turn in the PDF file.
- Save and close **tblManagement**.
- Compact and close the database.

U1-01-A.pdf
1 Page

Unit Application 1-2

The descriptions of the bulb shapes need to be updated. Rather than describe them as "can," the data need to read "Canister." In addition, several records need to be updated. Make the appropriate changes and verify your work by printing the inventory report.

1. Open *[your initials]*-**EcoMed-U1** and enable its content.

2. Open **tblInventory** in **Datasheet View**.

3. Find all bulb shapes that are "can" and replace the text with **Canister**.

4. Add the following new record, leaving fields blank as shown.

Inv ID:	*Press* Tab
Energy Star:	No
Model Number:	CN157-990-IG
Bulb shape:	Canister
Image:	*Attach* **CN157-990-IG.jpg**

5. Open **frmInventory**.

6. For the **Model Number** FL450-175-BF, change the **Vender** to *[your full name]*.

7. For the **Model Number** FL450-300-BF, change the **Bulb Type** to **Halogen**.

8. Open **rptInventory**.

9. Sort records by **Model Number** in **Ascending** order.

10. Filter the report to only show the **Bulb Shape** canister.

> **NOTE**
>
> The image file can be found in the **Unit 01** folder.

Assessment

- Save and close all objects.
- Compact and close the database.
- According to your classroom procedure, turn in your database only when you have completed all assigned exercises.

-OR-

- Save the report as a PDF named *[your initials]*-U1-02-A.
- Depending on your class procedures, print or turn in the PDF file.
- Save and close all objects.
- Compact and close the database.

U1-02-A.pdf
1 Page

Unit Application 1-3

To track procedural issues, you have been directed to create a new table. This table will need to be able to track issues by date and key words. Each event should also be able to include an attachment, such as a memo typed in Microsoft Word. Create the table and document your work by printing the Database Documenter report for the table.

1. Open *[your initials]*-EcoMed-U1 and enable its content.

2. Create a new table. Name the table **tblIssues**.

3. Add the following fields:

Field Name	Data Type	Format	Field Size	Caption
IssueID	AutoNumber			
Summary	Memo			
OpenedDate	Date/Time	Short Date		Opened Date
DueDate	Date/Time	Short Date		Due Date
KeyWords	Text		100	
Resolution	Text		100	
Attachments	Attachment			
ReportedBy	Text		30	

4. Add your full name as the Description for the field **ReportedBy**.

5. Make the **IssueID** the Primary Key.

6. For the field **OpenedDate**, add a Validation Rule of >=1/1/1900.

7. Add the Validation Text Value must be greater than 1/1/1900.

Assessment

- Save and close all objects.
- Compact and close the database.
- According to your classroom procedure, turn in your database only when you have completed all assigned exercises.

-OR-

- Create a Database Documenter report for **tblIssues** using the following settings:

  • Include for Table: Properties only
  • Include for Fields: Names, Data Types, Size, and Properties
  • Include for Indexes: Nothing

- Save the Documenter report as a PDF file named *[your initials]*-U1-03-A.
- According to your class procedures, print or turn in the PDF file.
- Close and save the table.
- Compact and close the database.

U1-03-A.pdf
4 Pages

Unit Application 1-4 ◆ Using the Internet

You have been asked to research possible lighting venders. Using an Internet search, locate a vender, and enter the contact information included on the Web site. Print the vender table in landscape orientation.

1. Using the Internet search engine of your choice, locate a company that sells light bulbs. Find the company (vender) name, address, city, state, ZIP, and FAX number.

2. Open *[your initials]*-**EcoMed-U1** and enable its content. Open **tblVender** in Datasheet View.

3. Hide the **ContactName**, **Phone Number**, and **FAX** field.

4. Add a new Hyperlink field to the table called URL.

5. Key the new company's information into the table.

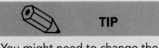

TIP

You might need to change the margins to get all the data on one page.

6. Enter the Web address for the company you located into the **URL** field.

7. Size all columns appropriately.

8. Make sure that all data fit on one page in Landscape orientation.

Assessment

- Save and close all objects.
- Compact and close the database.
- According to your classroom procedure, turn in your database only when you have completed all assigned exercises.

-OR-

U1-04-A.pdf
1 Page

- Save the table datasheet as a PDF named *[your initials]*-U1-04-A.
- Depending on your class procedures, print or turn in the PDF file.
- Save and close all objects.
- Compact and close your database.

Unit 2

DESIGNING AND MANAGING DATABASE OBJECTS

Lesson 5
Managing Data Integrity

OBJECTIVES   *After completing this lesson, you will be able to:*

1. Create relationships between tables.
2. Work with referential integrity.
3. Work with subdatasheets.
4. Use the Lookup Wizard.
5. Use Analyze tools.
6. Track object dependency.

Estimated Time: 1½ hours

A major advantage of a database over a spreadsheet is the ability to create relationships. A *relationship* is a link or connection of a common field between two tables, two queries, or a table and a query. Relationships change a flat data structure that contains isolated data into a linked data structure. For tables to be related, they must share common data and have a common field.

Relationships must be planned; they do not just happen. Understanding them—and how to set them—takes time and practice. As you work more extensively with databases, you will learn more about creating and maintaining relationships.

The EcoMed Services, Inc., database stores customer information in two tables. The facilities table stores the names and addresses of the medical facilities to which products are shipped. The management table stores the name and address of the parent organization to which invoices are shipped.

If each parent company managed only one facility, then a flat relational structure could work. However, each management company can have more than one facility associated to it. Therefore, a relational structure is required to link the two tables. After you create a relationship between the facilities table and the management table, you will be able to create forms and reports that can identify which management organization is responsible for which medical facility.

Creating Relationships between Tables

Relational database management systems, such as Microsoft Access, are the predominant structure used for business applications. In a relational database, related tables are connected by a join line. A *join line* is a graphical representation of the relationship created between two recordsets that are connected by common fields. In Access, the common fields must be the same data type and size; however, they do not need to use the same name.

When you select a primary key in both related tables, you create a One-To-One relationship. A *One-To-One relationship* is a relationship that occurs when the common field is a primary key in the first table and a primary key field in the second. This status means one record in the first table can relate to only one record in the second table.

When you select a primary key in only one field, you create a One-To-Many relationship. A *One-To-Many relationship* is a relationship that occurs when the common field is a primary key in the first table and not a primary key field in the second. This status means one record in the first table can relate to one or more records in the second table.

When you do not select a primary key in either table, you create an Indeterminate relationship. An *Indeterminate relationship* is a relationship that occurs when Access does not have enough information to determine the relationship between the two tables. An Indeterminate relationship occurs when the common fields in the first and the second table are not primary key fields.

Exercise 5-1   LOOK AT AN EXISTING RELATIONSHIP

The EcoMed database links or relates the Vender table to the Inventory table. You can see this link in the Relationships window. The *Relationships window* is a visual interface that displays, creates, destroys, or documents relationships between tables, queries, or both.

One or more relationships can be displayed at any time. When more than two tables are displayed, you should arrange and resize the table list boxes to allow optimum viewing of field names and join lines. You now will use the Relationships window to examine the relationship between the tables Vender and Inventory.

1. Locate and open the **Lesson 05** folder.

2. Make a copy of **EcoMed-05** and rename it *[your initials]*-EcoMed-05.

3. Open and enable content for *[your initials]*-**EcoMed-05**.

4. From the **Database Tools** tab, in the **Relationships** group, click **Relationships** ⊞ to opens the Relationships window.

TIP

To resize a list box, you can use the left, right, and bottom borders. Clicking and dragging the top area (title bar) will move the list box.

5. From the **Design** tab, in the **Relationships** group, click **All Relationships** ▦. All tables that have a relationship with other tables will open. The line connecting two tables represents the relationship between the tables.

6. Click and drag the bottom and right edges of the **tblVender** Field List until all field names are visible.

Figure 5-1
Relationships window with Field Lists rearranged
EcoMed-05.accdb Relationships window

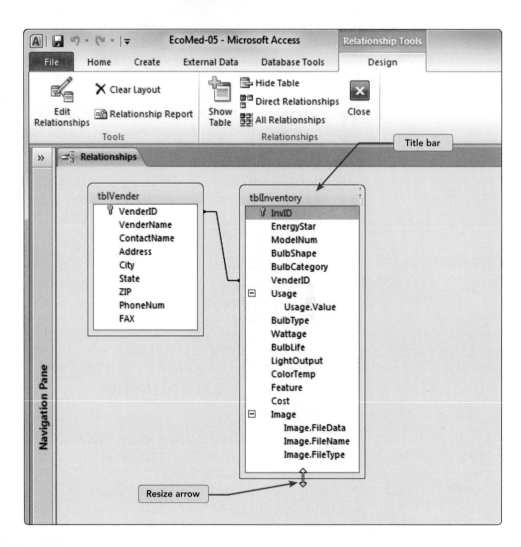

7. Resize the field list for **tblInventory** until all its fields are visible.

8. Right-click the sloping part of the join line between **tblVender** and **tblInventory** to open the shortcut menu for a join line.

TIP

Make certain that you open the shortcut menu for the join line. The menu enables you to edit the relationship or delete the join line. If you accidentally open the shortcut menu for the Relationships window or for a Field List, the menu displayed will not offer the option to edit relationships or delete the join line.

Figure 5-2
Shortcut menu
**EcoMed-05.accdb
Relationships
window**

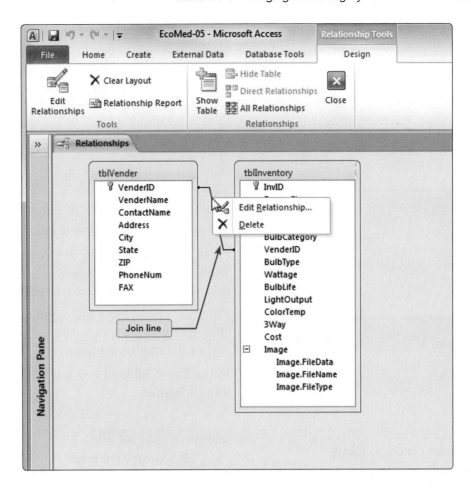

9. Choose **Edit Relationship** 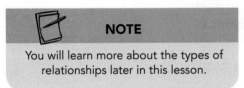. Notice that these two tables have a One-To-Many relationship using the common field **VenderID**.

> **NOTE**
>
> You will learn more about the types of relationships later in this lesson.

Figure 5-3
Edit Relationships
dialog box
**EcoMed-05.accdb
Relationships
window**

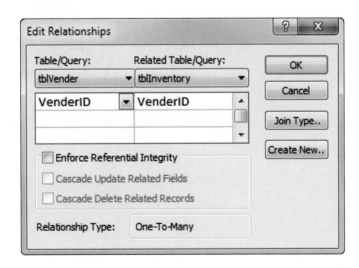

10. You will not be making changes to this dialog box, so click **Cancel**.

Exercise 5-2   CREATE A RELATIONSHIP IN THE RELATIONSHIPS WINDOW

You can create different types of relationships depending on whether you chose a primary key as a common field. When a primary key in one table links to a common field in another table, the common field becomes a foreign key. A *foreign key* is a common field that links to a primary key field in a related table.

You will now create a relationship between the tables Inventory and Bulb Shapes. You will use the bulb shape field. The field bulb shape is a key field in tblBulbShape and a common field in tblInventory.

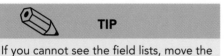

NOTE

The Show Table dialog box sometimes opens automatically when no relationships are present in the database.

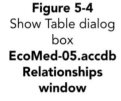

TIP

If you cannot see the field lists, move the Show Table dialog box by its title bar.

1. From the **Design** tab, in the **Relationships** group, click **Show Table** 🖼. The **Show Table** dialog box lists the tables and queries that are in the database.

2. From the **Show Table** dialog box, in the **Tables** tab, click **tblInventory**. Click **Add** to add the table's Field List to the Relationships window.

3. In the **Show Table** dialog box, double-click **tblBulbShapes**.

Figure 5-4
Show Table dialog box
EcoMed-05.accdb Relationships window

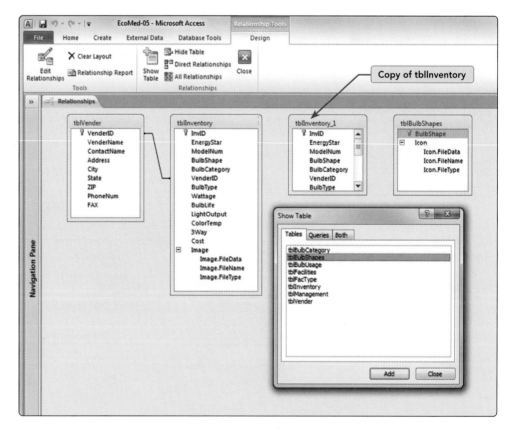

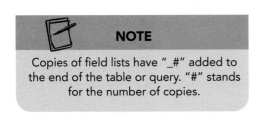

NOTE

Copies of field lists have "_#" added to the end of the table or query. "#" stands for the number of copies.

 REVIEW

The Primary Key indicates that this field contains a unique identifier for each record.

4. In the Show Table dialog box, click Close.

5. The table **tblInventory** has been entered twice. Click on the field list **tblInventory_1** and press Delete to remove this copy.

6. In the **tblBulbShapes** Field List, click the **BulbShape** field. The field name has a key symbol because it is the primary key in this table.

7. Click and drag the **BulbShape** field from the **tblBulbShapes** Field List to the **BulbShape** field in the **tblInventory** Field List.

8. The Edit Relationships dialog box opens. The Relationship Type is One-To-Many because the common field **BulbShape** (primary key) appears only once in the table **tblBulbShapes**, but the **BulbShape** (foreign key) can appear many times in the table **tblInventory**.

9. Click Create. A join line links the common field names.

10. Resize and move each Field List to appear as shown in Figure 5-5.

Figure 5-5
Show Table dialog box
EcoMed-05.accdb Relationships window

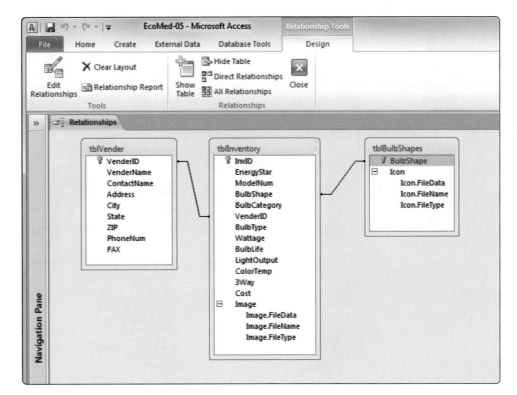

11. From the Design tab, in the Tools group, click Clear Layout 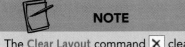.

12. Click Yes to clear the layout.

13. From the Design tab, in the Relationships group, click All Relationships.

NOTE

The Clear Layout command X clears the way tables are arranged in the Relationships window but does not affect relationships.

14. Resize each of the field lists so that all their fields are visible.

15. From the **Design** tab, in the **Relationships** group, click **Close** ⊠. Click **Yes** to verify the changes to the layout of the Relationships window.

Exercise 5-3   SAVE RELATIONSHIPS

Generating a Relationship Report helps a database administrator document and manages data integrity. A *Relationship Report* is a graphical report displaying one or more relationships. Each Relationship Report you create must have a unique name.

1. From the **Database Tools** tab, in the **Relationships** group, click **Relationships** 📇.

2. From the **Design** tab, in the **Tools** group, click **Relationship Report** 🖼.

3. From the Quick Access toolbar, click **Save** 🖫.

4. In the **Save As** dialog box, key **rptRelInventory-Shape** and press **OK**. This saved report can opened or printed at any time.

Figure 5-6
Save a Relationship
Report
**EcoMed-05.accdb
rptRelInventory-
Shape**

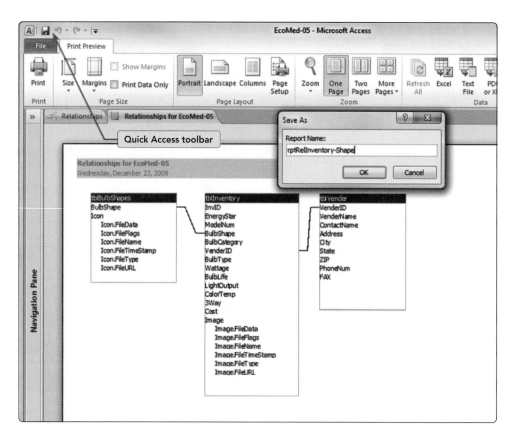

5. Right-click the **Relationships** document tab, and choose **Close All** 🖼.

Working with Referential Integrity

The use of referential integrity helps reduce human error through accidental deletions or other common errors. *Referential integrity* is a set of database rules for checking, validating, and tracking data entry changes in related tables. Enforcing referential integrity in two or more tables ensures that values stored in each table are consistent throughout the entire database.

For example, if you enforce referential integrity between the management table and the facilities table, then you can prevent someone from entering a new record for a medical facility without creating corresponding management information. This restriction would prevent shipping product to a company for which we do not have a billing address. The enforced integrity also would prevent someone from deleting a record for a management company without first deleting the associated facilities.

Exercise 5-4   ENFORCE REFERENTIAL INTEGRITY

You can enforce referential integrity between tables in a One-To-Many relationship. When referential integrity is enforced, the join line between the tables displays a 1 for the "one" side of the relationship and an infinity symbol (∞) for the "many" side. Referential integrity cannot be set for indeterminate relationships.

You can set referential integrity when the following conditions are met:

- The linking field from the main table is a primary key.

- The linked fields have the same data type.

- Both tables belong to the same Microsoft Access database.

1. Open **tblInventory**. In the first record (InvID #1), change the **Bulb Shape** to **Flood**. Press Ctrl+S to save the record.

2. Open **tblBulbShapes**. Notice that "Flood" is not listed as a **Bulb Shape**. Remember that the purpose of the "One" side of the relationship is to store a unique list of items to be used in the "Many" side of the relationship.

3. Close both tables.

NOTE

Before Access applies referential integrity rules to a relationship, the data in the two tables must pass the rules created. In this case, data exist in the "Many" side of the relationship that does not exist in the "One" side. The Bulb Shape "Flood" in tblInventory does not pass the rules.

4. From the Database Tools tab, in the Relationships group, click Relationships.

5. Double-click the sloping part of the join line between **tblInventory** and **tblBulbShapes**. The Relationship Type is One-To-Many.

6. Click the check box to select Enforce Referential Integrity and click OK.

7. Read the error message and click OK.

Figure 5-7
Enforcing referential
integrity
**EcoMed-05.accdb
Relationships
window**

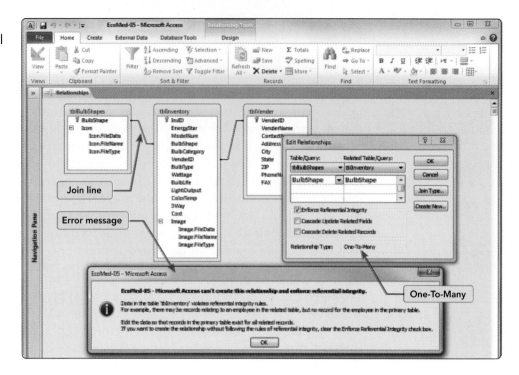

8. Click **Cancel** to close the **Edit Relationships** dialog box without saving the changes.

9. Open **tblInventory**. In the first record (InvID #1), change the **Bulb Shape** to **A-line**.

10. Close **tblInventory**.

11. In the document tab **Relationships**, double-click the sloping part of the join line between **tblInventory** and **tblBulbShapes**.

12. Click the check box to select **Enforce Referential Integrity** and click **OK**. This time, the changes were accepted, and the symbols "1" and "∞" have been added to the join line.

Figure 5-8
One-To-Many
relationship
**EcoMed-05.accdb
Relationships
window**

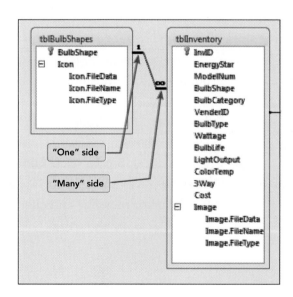

13. From the **Design** tab, in the **Relationships** group, click **Close** ⊠.

14. Open **tblInventory**. In the first record (InvID #1), change the **Bulb Shape** to **Flood** and press ⬇.

15. A message box alerts you to a problem.

Figure 5-9
Referential Integrity
finds an error
**EcoMed-05.accdb
Relationships
window**

16. Click **OK**. Press [Esc] to reject the changes to the record.

17. Close the table.

Exercise 5-5 REMOVE REFERENTIAL INTEGRITY

Referential integrity is a property of a relationship. When you remove referential integrity from a relationship, you merely remove the validation rules while preserving the original relationship between the tables. Removing Referential Integrity does not destroy the relationship.

1. From the **Database Tools** tab, in the **Relationships** group, click the **Relationships** button ☷.

2. Right-click the sloping part of the join line between **tblInventory** and **tblBulbShapes**.

3. Choose **Edit Relationship** from the shortcut menu.

4. In the **Edit Relationship** dialog box, remove the checkmark from **Enforce Referential Integrity**. Click **OK**.

5. From the **Design** tab, in the **Relationships** group, click **Close** ⊠.

Working with Subdatasheets

A table on the "One" side of a One-To-Many relationship, by default, has a subdatasheet. A *subdatasheet* is a datasheet linked within another datasheet. A subdatasheet contains data related to the first datasheet. The common field linking the two datasheets is the primary key field in the main datasheet and the foreign key field in the linked datasheet.

You can insert a subdatasheet into a main datasheet even when a relationship does not exist between the two objects. When a relationship does not exist, Access will automatically create one. You can insert a subdatasheet into any major object that has a Datasheet View such as a table, query, or form.

Exercise 5-6 INSERT A SUBDATASHEET

You can insert a subdatasheet into a main datasheet even when a relationship does not exist between the two objects. When you insert a subdatasheet, you must identify the table that will be used as the subdatasheet, the Link Child Fields, and the Link Master Fields. The child field is the linked field in the subdatasheet and the master field is the linked field in the master or source recordset.

When a relationship does not exist between the child and master, Access will automatically create one. You can insert a subdatasheet into any major object that has a Datasheet View such as a table, query, or form. You will now insert the inventory table as a subdatasheet for the table Bulb Shapes.

NOTE

In tables that have a relationship with the table to be used as a subdatasheet, the common field will be selected from the fields used in the relationship. If there is no relationship between the two tables, you can fill the properties Link Child Field and Link Master Fields by hand.

NOTE

You can expand or collapse all subdatasheets by using the Expand All or Collapse All commands found on the Home tab; in the Records group, click More, and choose Subdatasheet menu.

1. Open **tblBulbShapes** in Design View.

2. From the Design tab, in the Show/Hide group, click Property Sheet.

3. In the Property Sheet, the property Subdatasheet Name is set to [None]. Click on this property. Click the drop-down arrow and choose Table.tblInventory. Notice that Access has selected the field **BulbShape** as the common field and placed this field into the Link Child Fields and Link Master Fields.

4. From the Design tab, in the Show/Hide group, click Property Sheet to close the Property Sheet.

5. Switch to Datasheet View and save the changes to the table.

6. Notice that the beginning of each record now has an Expand icon ⊞ symbol. Click the Expand icon ⊞ for the **BulbShape** "Bare-Triple Tube." There are five bulbs in our inventory that have the shape Bare-Triple Tube.

Figure 5-10
Expanding a subdatasheet
EcoMed-05.accdb
tblBulbShapes

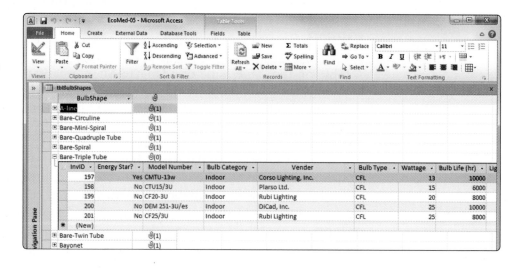

7. Click in the subdatasheet's first record. The Record Navigation buttons are now set to the subdatasheet.

8. Close and save the changes to **tblBulbShapes**.

Exercise 5-7   REMOVE A SUBDATASHEET

Not all subdatasheets need to be displayed in the master recordset. If most database users do not need to use the subdatasheet, you can remove it from the main datasheet.

1. From the **Navigation Pane**, open **tblVender** in **Datasheet View**.

2. Click the **Expand** icon ⊞ for the **VenderID** "AnyBulb." There are 15 bulbs that we buy from this vender.

3. From the **Home** tab, in the **Records** group, click **More** 🖩, and choose **Subdatasheet**, then **Subdatasheet** 🖾, from the menu. The common field is **VenderID**.

Figure 5-11
Viewing a subdatasheet's settings
EcoMed-05.accdb tblVender

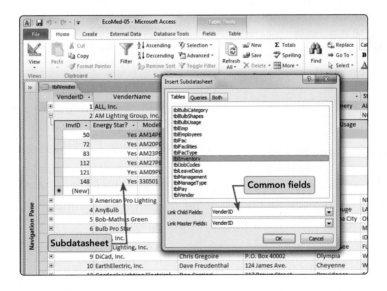

4. Click **Cancel** to close the **Insert Subdatasheet** dialog box.

5. From the **Home** tab, in the **Records** group, click **More** 🖩, and choose **Subdatasheet**, then **Remove**, from the menu. The symbols are gone, but the relationship between this table and **tblInventory** is still present.

6. Close the table. You are asked if you want to save the changes. Adding and removing a subdatasheet counts as a structure change for the table. Click **Yes**.

Using the Lookup Wizard

A *Lookup field* is a field property that displays input choices from another table and allows these choices to be selected from a list. Lookup fields are used often when a company uses specialized codes within their databases. An example of a specialized code is the two-letter abbreviation for a state. Prior to the adoption of the two letter codes by the United States Postal Service in 1949, states were only identified by their complete name.

Codes use less space than lengthy text describing the record. Some codes are readily understandable, such as standardized abbreviations for common names such as NASA. Other codes are less obvious and need a Lookup field for a data entry operator to use.

In addition to reducing the amount of data stored in a table, a Lookup field can improve the efficiency and consistency of data entry. The best fields to convert to a Lookup value are those that contain a finite number of values. Lookup fields use list boxes to display a list of possible values.

Exercise 5-8 CREATE A LOOKUP FIELD

In Microsoft Access, you can add a field to a table to look up information in another table. You typically use this technique when you use a numeric code as a common field to relate the two tables. In the EcoMed database, we'll use a numeric value to identify the bulb category. By using this technique, we can reduce the storage size of the records in the inventory table.

NOTE

Lookup fields can use text or numerical data to link two tables. The numerical option takes up less space in the database.

1. Open **tblBulbCategory** in Datasheet View. There are four categories: Diagnostic, Surgical, Indoor, and Outdoor, each with a **BulbCategoryID** 1 through 4.

2. Open **tblInventory** in Datasheet View.

3. Click the field option arrow for the field **Bulb Category**. This field lists the four common categories contained in **tblBulbCategory**. Click Cancel.

4. While the **Bulb Category** field is selected, press Ctrl+H. Key Diagnostic in the Find What control and 1 in the Replace With control. Click Replace All and click Yes to confirm the replacements.

5. Repeat step 4 for the following data:

Find What	Replace With
Surgical	2
Indoor	3
Outdoor	4

6. Close the Find and Replace dialog box. Click the field option arrow for the field **Bulb Category**. This field should now only contain the numbers 1–4. Click Cancel.

7. From the Home tab, in the Views group, click View to switch to Design View.

NOTE

Lookups create relationships, and just like other relationships, the fields used in a relationship must be the same Data Type.

TIP

Always save the changes to your table before starting the Lookup Wizard.

8. The field **BulbCategory** has the Data Type of Text. Change the Data Type to Number. Notice that the field's Field Size property is now Long Integer.

9. Press Ctrl+S to save the changes. The warning message warns that some data may be lost. Click Yes.

10. Click the option arrow for the **BulbCategory** Data Type and choose Lookup Wizard.

11. The Lookup Wizard dialog box appears. Verify that **I want the lookup field to get the values from another table or query.** is selected. Click Next.

12. From the list of tables, choose Table: **tblBulbCategory** and click **Next**.

13. Click the Add All button >> to move both fields from the **Available Fields** to the **Selected Fields** area.

14. Click **Next**. Click the first drop-down arrow and choose **BulbCategory** as the sort order field.

15. Click **Next**. Double-click the right edge of the column header to resize the column to fit the widest data.

16. Click to remove the checkmark from the **Hide key column** control. The **BulbCategoryID** field is displayed.

Figure 5-12
Choose the value from the Lookup column.
EcoMed-05.accdb
tblInventory

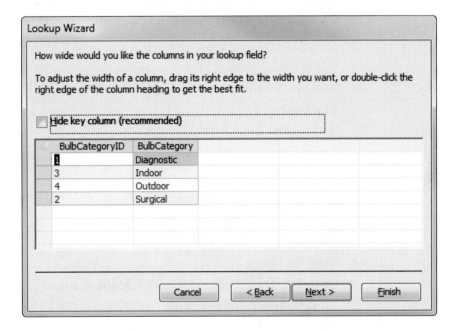

17. Click to add the checkmark to the **Hide key column** control. The ID will be stored in the field and the text will be seen in **Datasheet View**.

18. Click **Next**. Accept the default field name and click **Finish**.

19. Click **Yes** to save the table and return to **Datasheet View**.

Exercise 5-9 ADD DATA WITH A LOOKUP FIELD

In addition to reducing the size of records in the inventory table, adding data through a Lookup field reduces the number of keystrokes necessary to enter a value. Because values in a Lookup field are listed alphabetically in ascending order, you only need to type the first letter of the bulb category to display the corresponding category. You will now test the Lookup field you just created.

1. Click in the first record's **InvID** field and press ⟨Tab⟩ until you reach the **Bulb Category** field and key **s**. The combo box will display **Surgical** because only one option from the list starts with the letter "s."

Figure 5-13
Choose the value
from the Lookup
column.
**EcoMed-05.accdb
tblInventory**

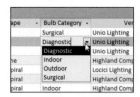

2. Press ⬇ to move to the next record.

3. Click the drop-down arrow to the right of the field to display the list of categories and choose **Diagnostic**. You no longer have to worry about a typographical error in this field.

Exercise 5-10 CREATE A LIST LOOKUP FIELD

You will now use the Lookup Wizard to modify the field named 3-Way. Currently the field is a Text. We now want to use the field to identify the bulb as capable of being used in a 3-Way or Dimmer fixture. You rename the field from 3-Way to Features and then change the field type to Lookup.

1. Switch to **Design View** and select the field **3-Way**. This is a **Text** field.

2. For the field **3Way**, click the option arrow for its **Data Type** and choose **Lookup Wizard**.

3. The **Lookup Wizard** dialog box appears. Select **I will type in the values that I want**. Click **Next**.

4. In the first cell under **Col1** type **3-Way**. Press ⬇.

5. Key **Dimmer**.

6. Double-click the right edge of the column header to resize the column to fit the widest data. Click **Next**.

7. You are asked to change the label. Key **Feature**.

8. Click **Finish**.

9. Switch to **Datasheet View** and save the changes.

10. Press Tab until you reach the field **Feature**. Click the drop-down arrow to see the choices.

11. Press Esc and return to **Design View**.

Exercise 5-11 MODIFY A LOOKUP FIELD

The list of values displayed in a Lookup field can be limited or editable. When you set the Limit To List value to yes, only the database designer can add new values to the list. When you set the Limit To List value to no, you allow the user to enter new values.

1. Click the field **Feature**.

2. In the properties section, click the **Lookup** tab.

3. Click the **Limit To List** property. Read the description in the Help window.

4. Change this properties value to **Yes**.

5. Double-click the property **Allow Value List Edits** to change the value from "No" to "Yes."

Figure 5-14
Change Lookup
properties
**EcoMed-05.accdb
tblInventory**

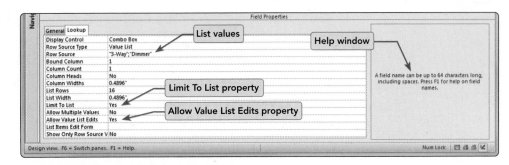

6. Read the Help window on this property. Save the table and switch to
   Datasheet View.

7. In the first record, click in the field **Feature** and click the drop-down
   arrow. A small icon appears below the expanded list.

8. Click the Edit List icon 📝. The **Edit List Items** dialog box opens.

9. Key **None**.

10. In the **Default Value** control, select **None** from the list.

Figure 5-15
Edit a Lookup
field list
**EcoMed-05.accdb
tblInventory**

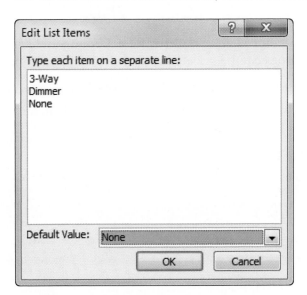

11. Click **OK** to close the dialog box.

12. Click the drop-down arrow for the field **Feature**. You now have
    three options.

Exercise 5-12   CREATE A MULTI-VALUED LOOKUP FIELD

A Lookup field can be set to be a multi-valued Lookup field. A multi-valued
Lookup field is a Lookup field that can store more than one value per record.
This type of field is very useful when it is possible for a single field to have
multiple values. You will now create a multi-valued Lookup field for the bulb
usage field.

1. Switch to **Design View**.

2. Click on the **Field Name BulbType**.

3. From the **Design** tab, in the **Tools** group, click **Modify Lookups** 🔲.
   A new field has been added, and the **Lookup Wizard** dialog box opens.

4. Verify that **I want the lookup field to get the values from another table or query.** is selected. Click **Next**.

5. From the list of tables, choose **Table: tblBulbUsage** and click **Next**.

6. Click the **Add All** button >> to move both fields from the **Available Fields** to the **Selected Fields** area.

7. Click **Next**. Click the first drop-down arrow and choose **Usage**.

8. Click **Next**. Double-click the right edge of the column header to resize the column to fit the widest data. Click **Next**.

9. Name the field **Usage**.

10. For the control **Allow Multiple Values**, click the check box.

11. Click **Finish**. Click **Yes** to save the changes.

12. Switch to **Datasheet View**.

Exercise 5-13   ADD DATA WITH A MULTI-VALUED LOOKUP FIELD

Each value stored in a multi-valued Lookup field is linked to the source record. Values can be selected or de-selected for any record.

1. For the fourth record, click the drop-down arrow for the field **Usage**.

2. Click the Check boxes for **Ceiling Mount**, **Fan**, and **Table Lamp**.

Figure 5-16
Multiple Values
Lookup field
**EcoMed-05.accdb
tblInventory**

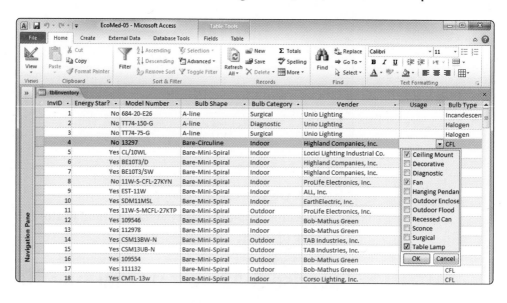

3. Close **OK**. Resize the column so you can see all the data. Each value is stored separated by a comma.

4. Switch to **Design View**.

5. Click in the **Usage** field. Notice the **Data Type** is **Number**. Only the **UsageID** is being stored in this field.

6. In the properties section, click the **Lookup** tab. The **Allow Multiple Values** property is set to **Yes**.

7. Save and close all tables.

Exercise 5-14 VIEW RELATIONSHIPS CREATED BY LOOKUP FIELDS

A Lookup field creates a relationship between the main table and the linked table. The relationship uses the Lookup field as the common field. This relationship can be displayed and documented in the Relationships window.

1. From the Database Tools tab, in the Relationships group, click Relationships.

2. From the Design tab, in the Tools group, click Clear Layout ⊠. Click Yes to clear the layout.

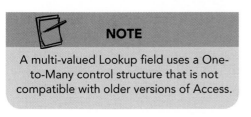

NOTE

A multi-valued Lookup field uses a One-to-Many control structure that is not compatible with older versions of Access.

3. From the Navigation Pane, drag **tblInventory** and **tblBulbUsage** to the Relationships window. A join line appears between the two tables. Creating the Lookup from one table to the other has created this relationship.

4. Arrange the field lists so you can clearly see all fields and relationships.

5. Double-click the join line between **tblInventory** and **tblBulbUsage** to open the Edit Relationships dialog box. This is a One-To-Many relationship. The main table is **tblBulbUsage**; it has the primary key. Click OK.

Figure 5-17
Relationships created by Lookups
EcoMed-05.accdb Relationships window

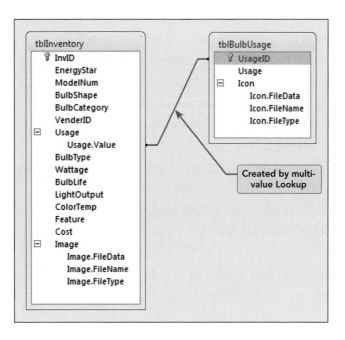

6. Close the Relationships window. A message box asks if you want to save the changes to the layout. Click Yes.

Using Analyzing Tools

The Table Analyzer Wizard is a tool that analyzes a database and recommends changes for normalization. *Normalization* is the process of restructuring a relational database for the purposes of organizing data efficiently, eliminating field redundancy, and improving data consistency.

The wizard analyzes table structures and field values. When the wizard identifies duplicated data or improper table structures, you are given the option to allow the wizard to make changes to your database automatically or for you to make changes manually. This type of analysis tool is used most often when designing a database or creating new structures.

Exercise 5-15   ANALYZE A TABLE

When the Table Analyzer identifies a significant number of records that contain repeating field values, the Analyzer will recommend that you split the table into two new tables. If you split the table, the structure and contents of the original table will be preserved.

1. Open **tblInventory** in **Datasheet View**. You can see there is redundancy in the **Bulb Type** information.

2. Close the table.

3. From the **Database Tools** tab, in the **Analyze** group, click **Analyze Table** 📇.

4. In the **Table Analyzer Wizard** dialog box, read the description of the problems that this wizard will try to address.

5. Click **Next**. Read the description of how the wizard will try to fix the problem.

6. Click **Next**. From the list of **Tables**, select **tblInventory**.

7. Click **Next**. Select **Yes, let the wizard decide**.

8. Click **Next**. Resize the Fields Lists so that you can see all the fields.

9. Double-click the **Table1** Field List header. Rename this table **tblInv**. This table will contain the main data for the inventory.

10. Double-click the **Table2** Field List header. Rename this table **tblBulbType**. This table will contain the unique data for the bulb types.

11. Notice that the wizard has selected both the **BulbShape** and **BulbType**. In the Field List **tblBulbType**, drag **BulbShape** back to the **tblInv** Field List under **VenderID**.

Figure 5-18
Table Analyzer
Wizard
EcoMed-05.accdb
Table Analyzer
Wizard

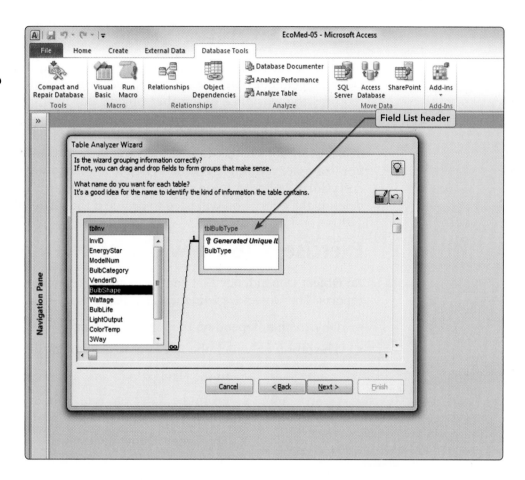

12. Click Next. In the field list **tblInv**, click InvID and click the Set Unique Identifier button ▯ to make this field the Primary Key for the table.

13. Click Next. The wizard thinks that there might be some typographical errors in your data and gives you an opportunity to correct these errors.

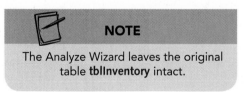

NOTE

The Analyze Wizard leaves the original table **tblInventory** intact.

14. The data shown are correct. Click Next and Yes to move to the next step. In the last step, select No, don't create the query option.

15. Click Finish. If the Access Help window appears, close it. You now have two new tables, **tblInv** and **tblBulbType**.

16. Click the **tblInv** tab. Press End. The wizard has placed the new Lookup field at the end of the table.

17. Click in the **Lookup to tblBulbType** field.

18. From the Fields tab, in the Properties group, click Name & Caption ▯.

19. Change the **Name** property to **BulbType** and the **Caption** to **Bulb Type**. Click **OK**.

20. Close and save both tables.

Tracking Object Dependency

Access provides a database tool to display information regarding dependencies among major objects. *Object dependency* is a condition in which an object requires the existence of another object. For example, the inventory form depends upon the inventory table.

Understanding dependencies helps maintain database integrity. Before deleting an object, you first should track the dependencies for that object. For example, you might decide to delete a query, only to discover that a data entry form is based upon that query rather than the source table. Before deleting the query, you will need to decide if the form will need to be changed.

Exercise 5-16   VIEW OBJECT DEPENDENCY

An Object Dependency List can be generated for tables, queries, forms, and reports. The Object Dependency List displays:

- Objects that depend on the selected object.
- The object on which the selected object depends.

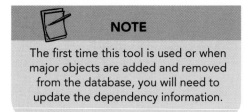

NOTE

The first time this tool is used or when major objects are added and removed from the database, you will need to update the dependency information.

1. In the **Navigation Pane**, select **qryManageUniv**.

2. From the **Database Tools** tab, in the **Relationships** group, click **Object Dependencies** 🖼.

3. The **Object Dependencies** pane appears on the right side of your window. In the dialog box, click **OK** so the Access can update the dependencies.

Figure 5-19
Object
Dependencies task
pane
EcoMed-05.accdb
Object
Dependencies Task
Pane

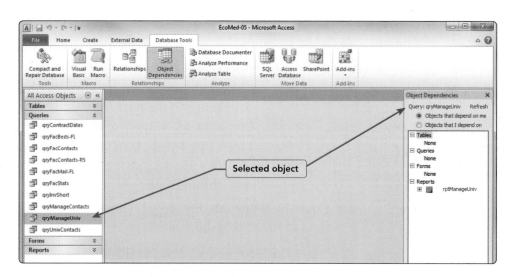

4. The first view is Objects that depend on me, and it shows that the report **rptManageUniv** depends on the query **qryManageUniv**.

5. Click **rptManageUniv** in the pane. The report opens in Design View.

6. From the Design tab, in the Tools group, click Property Sheet . In the Property Sheet, click the Data tab. Notice that the Record Source property is set to **qryManageUniv**.

7. Close the Property Sheet and the report.

8. In the Object Dependencies pane, click Objects that I depend on. This result shows that the query **qryManageUniv** depends on the table **tblManagement**.

9. Click **tblManagement** to open the table in Design View.

10. Close the table.

Exercise 5-17 VIEW A MISSING DEPENDENCY

If a database object is not functioning properly, you should look at its dependency list. For example, if a form does not display data, the record source upon which it depends might be missing. Viewing "Objects that I depend on" identifies the source recordset for that object.

1. In the Navigation Pane, select **qryFacMail-FL**.

2. In the Object Dependencies pane, click Refresh. Notice that this object needs the table **tblFacilities**.

3. Click Objects that depend on me. Notice that this query is needed by the report **rptFacMail-FL**.

4. In the Navigation Pane, right-click **qryFacMail-FL** and choose Delete from the menu. Click Yes to confirm the deletion.

5. In the Navigation Pane, select **rptFacMail-FL**.

> **REVIEW**
>
> Remember to backup your database!

6. In the Object Dependencies pane, click Objects that I depend on. Click Refresh. If a dialog box appears, click OK.

7. You can see that **qryFacMail-FL** is now missing. For the report to work, a new query would need to be created.

8. Close the Object Dependencies pane.

9. Compact and repair the database, and then close it.

Lesson 5   Summary

- Relationships between tables change a flat database, containing isolated data, into a relational database, containing linked data.

- Graphical relationships between tables can be viewed in the Relationships window.

- Related fields must be of the same data type and size but do not need to be named the same.

- A One-To-One relationship occurs when the common field is a primary key in the first table and a primary key field in the second.

- A One-to-Many relationship occurs when the common field is a primary key in the first table and not a primary key field in the second.

- An Indeterminate relationship occurs when Access does not have enough information to determine the relationship between the two tables.

- One or more relationships can be displayed in the Relationships window.

- When a common field is a primary key in the first table, it becomes a foreign key in the second table.

- A Relationship Report is a graphical report showing related tables.

- Referential integrity is a set of database rules for checking, validating, and keeping track of data entry changes in related tables.

- A subdatasheet is a datasheet linked within another datasheet containing related data.

- A Lookup field is a field property that displays input choices from another table and allows these choices to be selected from a list.

- A multi-valued Lookup field is a Lookup field that can store more than one value per record.

- The Table Analyzer Wizard displays options for improving table structures of your database based upon field types and the values stored.

- Object dependency is a condition in which an object requiring the existence of another object.

LESSON 5		Command Summary	
Feature	**Button**	**Task Path**	**Keyboard**
Collapse Subdatasheet	⊟		
Expand Subdatasheet	⊞		
Layout, Clear	✕	Database Tools, Relationships, Relationships, Tools, Clear Layout	
Lookup field, Create		Design, Tools, Modify Lookups	
Lookup field, Limit To List		Design View, Lookup, Limit To List	
Lookup field, Multi-valued, Create		Design View, Lookup, Allow Multiple Values	
Object Dependency		Database Tools, Relationships, Object Dependencies	
Primary Key, Set			
Referential Integrity, Enforce		Database Tools, Relationships, Edit Relationship, Enforce Referential Integrity	
Relationship Report, Create		Database Tools, Relationships, Relationships, Design Tools, Relationship Report	
Relationships, Show All		Database Tools, Relationships, Relationships, Design, Relationships All Relationships	
Relationships, Table, Show		Database Tools, Relationships, Relationships, Design, Relationships Show Table	
Relationships, View		Database Tools, Relationships, Relationships	
Subdatasheet, Insert		Design, Show/Hide, Property Sheet	
Subdatasheet, Remove		Home, Records, More, Subdatasheet, Remove	
Table, Analyze		Database Tools, Analyze, Analyze Table	

Concepts Review

True/False Questions

Each of the following statements is either true or false. Indicate your choice by circling T or F.

T F 1. A Lookup field lets you select a value from a list instead of keying the value.

T F 2. When you clear the Relationships window, you also delete the relationships.

T F 3. The set of database rules for relationships is known as validating norms.

T F 4. A. subdatasheet is a datasheet linked within another datasheet containing related data.

T F 5. Values in a Lookup field are always listed in ascending order.

T F 6. Deleting the join line between two field lists in the Relationships window deletes the corresponding common fields in each of the two tables.

T F 7. The Relationships window can display more than one relationship at a time.

T F 8. Normalization is the process of restructuring a relational database for the purposes of organizing data efficiently, eliminating field redundancy, and improving data consistency.

Short Answer Questions

Write the correct answer in the space provided.

1. What graphic represents the relationship between two tables in the Relationships window?

_____

2. How do you delete a relationship in the Relationships window?

_____

3. When the common field is a primary key in one table, what does it become in the other table?

_____

4. In a One-To-Many relationship with referential integrity, how can you identify the table on the "many" side of the relationship?

_____

5. Referential integrity cannot be set for what type of relationship?

_____

6. What type of Lookup field can store more than one value per record?

_____

7. What analyzing tool provides recommendations for restructuring a
    relational database for the purposes of organizing data efficiently,
    eliminating field redundancy, and improving data consistency?

_____

8. What is an association placed on an object that requires the existence of
    another object known as?

_____

Critical Thinking

**Answer these questions on a separate page. There are no right or wrong
answers. Support your answers with examples from your own experience,
if possible.**

1. The One-To-Many relationship is the most commonly used relationship
    in business databases. Why do you think this is true?

2. Multi-valued Lookup fields can be very useful for most types of data;
    however, some fields should not have more than one value. What type of
    examples can you think of that should never contain more than one value?

Skills Review

Exercise 5-18

**The IT director has noticed that a relationship needs to be created
between the facilities and the facilities type tables. You are directed to
create the relationship and document your work.**

1. Open a database by following these steps:
    a. Locate and open the **Lesson 05** folder.
    b. If you already have a copy of *[your initials]*-**EcoMed-05**, skip to
        step 1d.
    c. Make a copy of **EcoMed-05** and rename it *[your initials]*-
        EcoMed-05.
    d. Open and enable content for *[your initials]*-**EcoMed-05**.

2. Create a relationship by following these steps:

    a. From the **Database Tools** tab, in the **Relationships** group, click **Relationships** .

    b. From the **Design** tab, in the **Tools** group, click **Clear Layout** ☒. Click **Yes** to clear the layout.

    c. From the **Design** tab, in the **Relationships** group, click **Show Table** 🖼.

    d. From the **Show Table** dialog box, double-click **tblFacilities** and **tblFacType**.

    e. Click **Close**.

    f. Resize the Field Lists so you can see every field.

    g. From the **tblFacilities** field list, click and drag the **FacType** field to the **FacType** field in the **tblFacType** field list.

    h. In the **Edit Relationship** dialog box, click **Create**.

3. Create a Relationship Report by following these steps:

    a. From the **Design** tab, in the **Tools** group, click **Relationship Report** 🖼.

    b. Save the report as **rptRelFac-Type** and click **OK**.

Assessment

- Right-click the **rptRelFac-Type** tab, and choose **Close All**.

- According to your classroom procedure, turn in your database only when you have completed all assigned exercises.

-OR-

05-18-A.pdf
1 Page

- Save a Relationship Report by following these steps:

    a. Click the **File** tab and from the **Print** option, click **Print Preview** 🔍.

    b. From the **Print Preview** tab, in the **Data** group, click **PDF or XPS** 🗔 to save the printout as a file.

    c. Save the file as a PDF and name the file *[your initials]*-05-18-A.

    d. Depending on your class procedures, print or turn in the PDF file.

Exercise 5-19

Now that a relationship has been created between two tables, insert a subdatasheet into the facilities type table using the appropriate field as the link.

1. The database *[your initials]*-**EcoMed-05** is required to complete this exercise.

    a. Open and enable content for *[your initials]*-**EcoMed-05**.

2. Insert a subdatasheet by following these steps:

    a. Open **tblFacType** in Datasheet View.

    b. From the Home tab, in the Records group, click the More button and choose Subdatasheet, then Subdatasheet, from the menu.

    c. From the list, select **tblFacilities** with the Child and Master fields **FacType**. Click OK.

    d. Close the table and save the changes.

3. Set Enforce Referential Integrity by following these steps:

    a. From the Database Tools tab, in the Relationships group, click Relationships.

    b. Right-click the sloping part of the join line between **tblFacilities** and **tblFacType**, and choose Edit Relationship.

    c. Click the check box to select Enforce Referential Integrity and click OK.

    d. From the Quick Access toolbar, click Save.

    e. Close the Relationship window.

Assessment

- According to your classroom procedure, turn in your database only when you have completed all assigned exercises.

-OR-

- Create a Database Documenter report by following these steps:

    a. From the Database Tools tab, in the Analyze group, click Database Documenter.

    b. From the Documenter dialog box, click the **tblFacType** check box.

    c. Click Options.

    d. For Table, include Properties and Relationships.

    e. From the Include for Fields section, choose Nothing.

    f. From the Include for Indexes section, choose Nothing.

    g. Click OK twice to go to Print Preview.

- Save a Database Documenter report by following these steps:

    a. From the Print Preview tab, in the Data group, click PDF or XPS to save the printout as a file.

    b. Save the file as a PDF and name the file *[your initials]*-05-19-A.

    c. Depending on your class procedures, print or turn in the PDF file.

    d. From the Print Preview tab, in the Close Preview group, click Close Print Preview.

05-19-A.pdf
1 Page

Exercise 5-20

The client facility information stored in the facilities table includes a field to identify the corresponding information for the client's corporate (management) information. Create a Lookup field to allow a user to select the management location by the name of the company.

1. The database *[your initials]*-EcoMed-05 is required to complete this exercise.

   a. Open and enable content for *[your initials]*-EcoMed-05.

2. Create a Lookup field by following these steps:

   a. Open **tblFacilities** in Design View and select the field **ManageID**.

   b. Click the down-arrow for the **ManageID**'s Data Type and select Lookup Wizard.

   c. In the Lookup Wizard dialog box, click Next.

   d. From the list of tables, select Table: tblManagement and click Next.

   e. In the Available Fields area, double-click ManageID and ManageName. Click Next.

   f. Click the drop-down arrow and choose ManageName. Click Next.

   g. Resize the ManageName column so all data can be seen. Click Next.

   h. Name the field Management. Click Finish.

   i. Save the table and switch to Datasheet View.

   j. Close the table.

3. Identify Object Dependency by following these steps:

   a. Create a Word document called *[your initials]*-05-20-A and record the answers to the following questions.

   b. Select **tblFacilities**.

   c. From the Database Tools tab, in the Relationships group, click Object Dependencies.

   d. Select Objects that depend on me. What objects depend on **tblFacilities**?

   e. Select Objects that I depend on. What objects does **tblFacilities** depend on?

   f. Include your name, class information, and today's date on your answer sheet.

   g. Close the Object Dependency pane.

05-20-A.pdf
1 Page

Assessment

- According to your classroom procedure, turn in your database only when you have completed all assigned exercises.
- Depending on your class procedures, print or turn in the Word file.

-OR-

05-20-B.pdf
2 Pages

- Create a Database Documenter report by following these steps:
    a. From the Database Tools tab, in the Analyze group, click Database Documenter .
    b. From the Documenter dialog box, click **tblFacilities** check box.
    c. Click Options.
    d. For Table, include Properties and Relationships.
    e. For Fields, select the option Names, Data Types, and Sizes.
    f. For Indexes, select the option to Nothing.
    g. Click OK twice to go to Print Preview.
- Save a Database Documenter report by following these steps:
    a. From the Print Preview tab, in the Data group, click PDF or XPS to save the printout as a file.
    b. Save the file as a PDF and name the file *[your initials]*-05-20-B.
    c. Depending on your class procedures, print or turn in the PDF file.
    d. Close Print Preview.
- Depending on your class procedures, print or turn in the Word file.

Exercise 5-21

As you learned before, using the Table Analyze Wizard can help identify how best to change your table structure. Use the analyzer and make any appropriate changes to the database. Document any changes that you make.

1. The database *[your initials]*EcoMed-05 is required to complete this exercise.
    a. Open and enable content for *[your initials]*-EcoMed-05.

2. Create a Lookup field by following these steps:
    a. From the Database Tools tab, in the Analyze group, click the Analyze Table .
    b. In the Table Analyze Wizard, click Next twice.
    c. From the list of Tables, select **tblFacilities**. Click Next.
    d. Verify that the option Yes, let wizard decide is selected. Click Next.

UNIT 2 LESSON 5

e. In Table3, click and drag the field **FacType** back into Table1 under the field **FacName**.

f. Double-click Table1 and name the table **tblFac**.

g. Double-click Table2 and name the table **tblManageType**. Click Next.

h. In the table **tblFac**, select the field **FacilitiesID**. In the upper right corner click the Primary key button . Click Next.

i. No corrections are needed. Click Next. Click Yes.

j. Verify that the option **No, don't create a query**. Click Finish.

3. Rename a column in Datasheet View by following these steps:

a. Close the table **tblManageType**.

b. Open **tblFac** in Datasheet View.

c. Select the column header for the field **Lookup to tblManageType**.

d. From the Fields tab, in the Properties group, click Name & Caption .

e. Rename the Name to ManageTypeID and the Caption to Manage Type.

f. Save and close the table.

Assessment

- According to your classroom procedure, turn in your database only when you have completed all assigned exercises.

-OR-

- Create a Database Documenter report by following these steps:

a. From the Database Tools tab, in the Analyze group, click Database Documenter.

b. From the Documenter dialog box, click **tblFac** check box.

c. Click Options.

d. For Table, include Properties and Relationships.

e. For Fields, select the option Names, Data Types, and Sizes.

f. For Indexes, select the option Nothing.

g. Click OK twice to go to Print Preview.

- Save a Database Documenter report by following these steps:

05-21-A.pdf
1 Page

a. From the Print Preview tab, in the Data group, click PDF or XPS to save the printout as a file.

b. Save the file as a PDF and name the file *[your initials]*-05-21-A.

c. Depending on your class procedures, print or turn in the PDF file.

d. Close Print Preview.

Lesson Applications

Exercise 5-22

EcoMed employees take days off from work as both vacation and sick days. To display the days taken when the employee uses leave, you will need to link the table storing the employee information to the table storing the leave days. Create a relationship and document any changes that you make.

1. Using the database, *[your initials]*-**EcoMed-05**, make sure that all content is enabled.

2. Open the Relationships window and clear the layout.

3. Add **tblEmployees** and **tblLeaveDays** to the window. Size the Field Lists so that all fields are visible, and identify the common field.

4. Create a One-To-Many relationship with referential integrity between the tables. Save and close the layout.

5. Create a Relationship Report for these two tables.

6. Save the report as rptRelEmpLeave.

Assessment

 - According to your classroom procedure, turn in your database only when you have completed all assigned exercises.

-OR-

 - Save the Relationship Report as a PDF file named *[your initials]*-05-22-A.
- Depending on your class procedures, print or turn in the PDF file.
- Close Print Preview.

05-22-A.pdf
1 Page

Exercise 5-23

Now that a relationship has been created between two tables, insert a subdatasheet into the employees table using the appropriate field as the link. After creating the subdatasheet, identify the dependencies for the table.

1. Using the database *[your initials]*-**EcoMed-05**, make sure that all content is enabled.

2. Open **tblEmployees** in Design View.

05-23-A.pdf
1 Page

3. Create a subdatasheet to **tblLeaveDays**.

4. Create a Word document called *[your initials]*-05-23-A and record the answers to the following questions:

5. What queries, forms, and reports depend on **tblEmployees**?

6. On what queries, forms, and reports does **tblEmployees** depend?

7. Include your name, class information, and date.

Assessment

- According to your classroom procedure, turn in your database only when you have completed all assigned exercises.
- According to your class procedures, print or turn in the Word file.

-OR-

- Create a Database Documenter report for **tblEmployees** using the following settings:
  - Include for Table: Properties, Relationships only
  - Include for Fields: Nothing
  - Include for Indexes: Nothing
- Save the Documenter report as a PDF file named *[your initials]*-05-23-B.
- Depending on your class procedures, print or turn in the Word file *[your initials]*-**05-23-A**.
- Depending on your class procedures, print or turn in the PDF file *[your initials]*-**05-23-B**.

05-23-B.pdf
1 Page

Exercise 5-24

EcoMed employees are classified as either salaried or hourly employees. You have been directed to modify the pay table to have a Lookup field for these two pay classifications.

1. Using the database *[your initials]*-**EcoMed-05**, make sure that all content is enabled.

2. In **tblPay**, add a Lookup field to the end of the table.

3. In the Lookup wizard, you will type the values **Hourly** and **Salary**.

4. Limit entries to the list.

5. Name the new field **PayType**.

6. Do not allow users to edit the list.

7. Change the **PayType**'s field size to **6**.

8. The values in the field **PayClass** are "1" and "2." The "1" represents salary, and the "2" represents hourly. Add values to the new field **PayType**. In each record where the **PayClass** is "1", enter **Salary** for the **PayType** field. In each record where the **PayClass** is "2", enter **Hourly** for the **PayType** field.

9. Delete the field **PayClass** and sort the table in ascending order by **Employee ID**.

Assessment

- According to your classroom procedure, turn in your database only when you have completed all assigned exercises.

-OR-

- Create a Database Documenter report for **tblPay** using the following settings:

  - Include for Table: None
  - Include for Fields: Names, Data Types, Sizes, and Properties
  - Include for Indexes: Nothing

- Save the Documenter report as a PDF file named *[your initials]*-05-24-A.
- According to your class procedures, print or turn in the PDF file.
- Save the Datasheet View of **tblPay** in portrait layout as a PDF. Name the file *[your initials]*-05-24-B.
- According to your class procedures, print or turn in the PDF file.

05-24-A.pdf
2 Pages

Exercise 5-25 ◆ **Challenge Yourself**

As you learned before, using the Table Analyze Wizard can help identify how to best change your table structure. Use the analyzer on the employees table and make any appropriate changes to the database. Document any changes that you make.

05-24-B.pdf
1 Page

1. Using the database *[your initials]*-**EcoMed-05**, make sure that all content is enabled.

2. Using the Table Analyzer Wizard, select **tblEmployees** but do not let the wizard decide which fields are to be used.

3. Create a new table named **tblJobCodes** by dragging the **JobCode** field out of **Table1**.

UNIT 2 LESSON 5

TIP

The Wizard doesn't always pick the field you want, so you can always drag the unwanted field back to the main table and drag out of the main table the field that you do want.

4. Rename Table1 to **tblEmp**.

5. In **tblEmp**, rename the new Lookup field JobCodeID and its Caption Job Code.

6. In **tblJobCodes**, set the ID field's Caption property to Job Code ID.

Assessment

- According to your classroom procedure, turn in your database only when you have completed all assigned exercises.

-OR-

- Create a Database Documenter report for **tblEmp** using the following settings:

  • Include for Table: Properties, Relationships only

  • Include for Fields: Names, Data Types and Sizes

  • Include for Indexes: Nothing

- Save the Documenter report as a PDF file named *[your initials]*-05-25-A.

- According to your class procedures, print or turn in the PDF file.

05-25-A.pdf
1 Page

On Your Own

In these exercises you work on your own, as you would in a real-life work environment. Use the skills you've learned to accomplish the task—and be creative.

Exercise 5-26

Review the designs for the three databases you created in Exercises 4-29 through 4-31. Select one of the three databases to continue developing. Identify two additional tables you might need to make your database designs more useful. The relationships between the main table and the two additional tables should be One-To-Many. On a blank sheet of paper, list the field names, data types, field sizes, and attributes for the two new tables. Identify the common fields among the three tables. Continue to Exercise 5-27.

Exercise 5-27

Create the two tables you designed in Exercise 5-26. Add appropriate field properties to each table to make your design more useful. Create One-To-Many relationships with referential integrity between the tables. Test the referential integrity of the tables. Add at least five records to each empty table. Print the datasheet and a database documenter report each table. Continue to Exercise 5-28.

Exercise 5-28

Search the Internet for images or graphics you might wish to use in your database. Design and create a new table to store the images. Create an appropriate relationship between this new table and the main table. Insert the images into the new table. Print a Relationship Report displaying all four tables. Submit to your instructor the printouts from Exercises 5-27 through 5-28, along with your field list from 5-26. Keep a copy of the database you modified in this exercise. You will use it for the On Your Own exercises in subsequent lessons.

Lesson 6
Designing Queries

OBJECTIVES *After completing this lesson, you will be able to:*

1. Create and modify select queries.
2. Add criteria and operators to queries.
3. Apply logical operators.
4. Modify query properties.
5. Add calculations to queries.
6. Create queries with wizards.
7. Apply PivotChart/PivotTable Views.

Estimated Time: 1½ hours

In most relational databases, queries locate, add, modify, and delete records. The effectiveness and efficiency of a query depends on its ability to access information quickly. A query is designed by selecting the appropriate fields, specifying appropriate criteria, and sorting recordsets.

Queries make data more manageable and often are the record source for reports and forms. For example, a report based on an employee table with 1,000 employees would show all 1,000 records. A report based on a query might show only a manageable subset of the entire table. The query might specify information, such as who is eligible for retirement, who is on vacation this week, or who has worked for the company for less than five years.

As with any computer application, executing a complex query takes processing resources. For a large database executing a very complicated query, the processing time might be extensive. To create effective queries, a skilled database administrator must be knowledgeable about the numerous types of queries available. In this lesson, you will learn to use common Access queries.

 REVIEW

A query is similar to a filter in some respects. However, a table can have only one filter but multiple queries.

Creating and Modifying Select Queries

In business situations, the most common type of query is a select query. A select query functions like a question that returns a different answer each time it is executed. For example, if you create a query to display names of employees who are over the age of 40 years, the results would be different depending on the day you executed the query and the employees who currently work for the company.

A select query locates data from one or more tables and displays the results as a datasheet. These results can be grouped, filtered, and sorted. In addition, a select query can calculate sums, averages, standard deviations, and other types of statistical functions.

In addition to Datasheet View and Design View, a query can be displayed in SQL View. SQL (*Structured Query Language*) is a computer language designed to manipulate data in relational databases. SQL was developed in the early 1970s, specifically designed to manipulate data in IBM's original relational database. In 1986 SQL was adopted as a standard by the American National Standards Institute.

Exercise 6-1 VIEW A SELECT QUERY AND ITS REPORT

You most often use the Query Design window to create and modify a query. The Query Design window has an upper and lower pane. The upper pane is the field list pane in which you choose the data source from one or more field lists. The lower pane is the design grid in which you specify criteria. The lower pane is also known as the QBE (Query by Example) grid.

The Design View of a query is the visual interface for the SQL statement. The Datasheet View displays the results of the SQL question asked of Access. The SQL statement is the actual code stored in an Access database.

1. Locate and open the **Lesson 06** folder.
2. Make a copy of **EcoMed-06** and rename it *[your initials]* **-EcoMed-06**.
3. Open and enable content for *[your initials]***-EcoMed-06**.
4. Open **qryEmpPhone** in **Design View**. This query uses four fields from the table **tblEmployees**.

Figure 6-1
Query design
window
EcoMed-06.accdb
qryEmpPhone

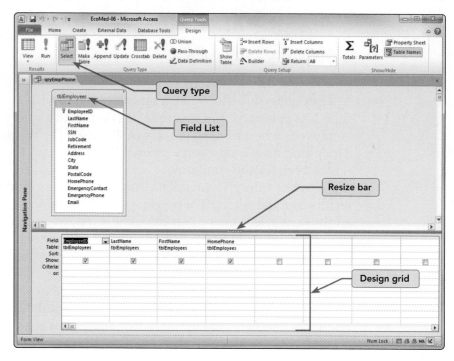

5. Right-click the document tab for **qryEmpPhone** and choose **SQL View** 🔲.

Figure 6-2
SQL statement
EcoMed-06.accdb
qryEmpPhone

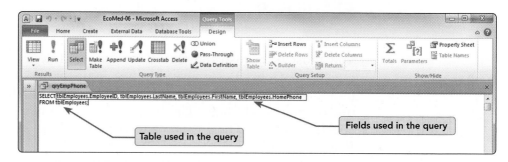

6. Open **rptEmpPhone** in **Design View**.

7. From the **Design** tab, in the **Tools** group, click **Property Sheet** 🔲.

8. In the **Property Sheet**, click the **Data** tab. The **Record Source** property shows that this report is based on **qryEmpPhone**.

Figure 6-3
Report's property
sheet
EcoMed-06.accdb
rptEmpPhone

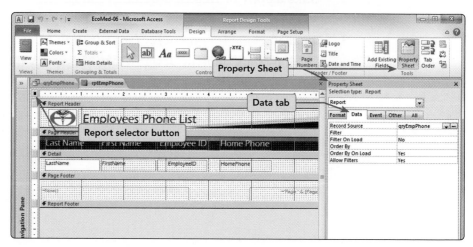

9. Right-click the document tab for **rptEmpPhone** and choose **Close All** 🔲.

Exercise 6-2 CREATE A SELECT QUERY BASED ON A SINGLE TABLE

You will now create a query to display bulb prices. Rather than display all fields and records from the Inventory table, you will define appropriate criteria. You will define criteria and field lists in the Design View of a query. You then will display the resulting recordset through the datasheet of the query.

When you view the results, only the fields and records that you specified will display. The fields and records that you specify in the design grid create a dynaset. A *dynaset* is dynamic recordset that automatically reflects changes to its underlying data source.

1. From the Create tab, in the Queries group, click Query Design 🔲.

2. In the Show Table dialog box, double-click **tblInventory**. The **tblInventory** Field List appears in the upper pane of the Query Design window.

Figure 6-4
Show Table dialog box
EcoMed-06.accdb
QryBuldPrices

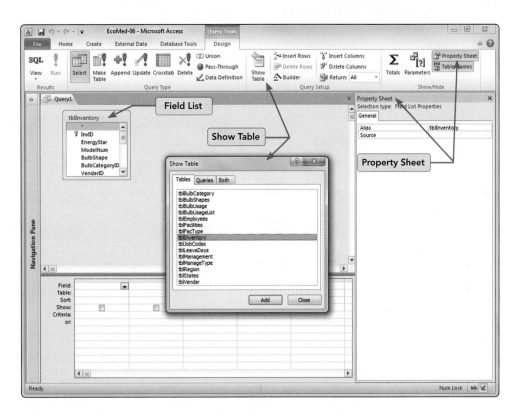

3. Click Close in the Show Table dialog box.

⟷ **REVIEW**

If you accidentally open two copies of the same Field List, right-click the second list and select Remove Table. You can also click the title bar of the Field List window and press ⌷Delete⌷ to remove the second copy.

4. Resize the Field List so all fields can be seen.

5. If the Property Sheet is not open, click Property Sheet 📋.

6. Click the **tblInventory** Field List. The Property Sheet is now showing the properties of the table.

7. Click the blank area to the right of the Field List. The Property Sheet is now showing the properties of the query.

8. From the Quick Access toolbar, click Save 🔲.

9. In the Save As dialog box, key **qryBulbPrices** and click OK.

Exercise 6-3   ADD FIELDS TO A QUERY

You can add fields to the design grid of a query by any of the three following ways:

- Double-click the field name in the Field List.
- Drag the field from the Field List to a Field row in the design grid.
- Click the Field row in the design grid and select a field name from the drop-down list.

1. From the Field List, double-click **ModelNum**. The field appears as the first field in the Field row in the design grid at the bottom of the screen.

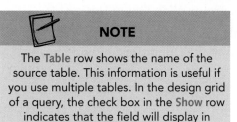

NOTE

The Table row shows the name of the source table. This information is useful if you use multiple tables. In the design grid of a query, the check box in the Show row indicates that the field will display in Datasheet View.

2. The Property Sheet now shows the properties of the field. Click Property Sheet to hide the Property Sheet.

3. Drag the **BulbShape** field from the Field List to the Field row, second column.

4. In the third column, click the Field row, then click its drop-down arrow. Choose **Cost** from the list of field names.

Figure 6-5
Adding fields to the design grid
**EcoMed-06.accdb
qryBulbPrices**

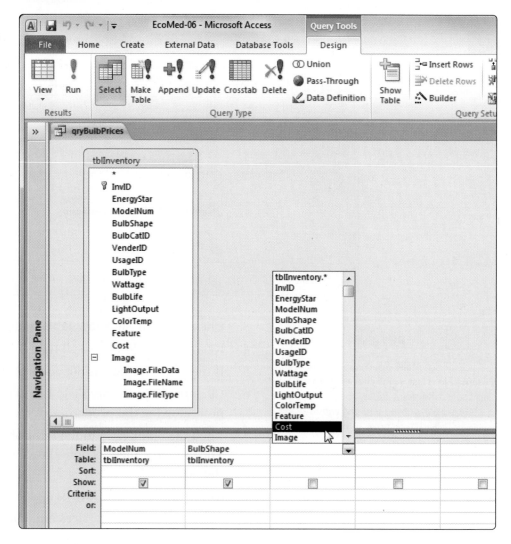

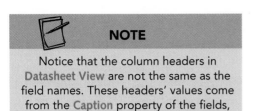

NOTE

Notice that the column headers in Datasheet View are not the same as the field names. These headers' values come from the Caption property of the fields, just like the Datasheet View of a table.

5. From the Design tab, in the Results group, click Datasheet View ▦. Only the three fields that you selected are shown.

6. Save and close the query.

Exercise 6-4 CREATE A SELECT QUERY BASED ON TWO TABLES

A query is based on one or more field list. Each Field List is a recordset created by a table or query. When you use two or more Field Lists, you must link the Field Lists through a common field. This link will combine the matching records between the two tables. The link must be established through a field common to both tables.

1. From the Create tab, in the Queries group, click Query Design ▦.

2. From the Show Table dialog box, double-click **tblInventory** and **tblBulbCategory**.

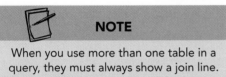

NOTE

When you use more than one table in a query, they must always show a join line.

3. Double-click **tblBulbCategory** again to add a second copy. Click Close.

4. The second copy of **tblBulbCategory** ends with "_1".

5. Resize and move the Field Lists so all fields can be seen.

6. From the **tblInventory** Field List, double-click **InvID** and **ModelNum**.

7. From the **tblBulbCategory** Field List, double-click **BulbCategory**.

NOTE

In a select query, the Run command ▮ and Datasheet View command ▦ produce the same results.

8. From the Design tab, in the Results group, click Run ▮.

9. This query resulted in a dynaset of 1,240 records. Notice the many copies of the **Model Number**. Switch to Design View.

10. Right-click the **tblBulbCategory_1** Field List and choose Remove Table.

11. From the Design tab, in the Results group, click Run ▮.

12. The dynaset now contains only 310 records. The extra records came from having a copy of a table in the query.

13. Save the query as **qryBulbList**.

14. From the Home tab, in the Views group, click the bottom half of the Design View ▨ and choose SQL View ▣. This SQL statement shows the tables used in the query and their relationship.

Figure 6-6
SQL statement for two-table query
EcoMed-06.accdb
qryBulbList

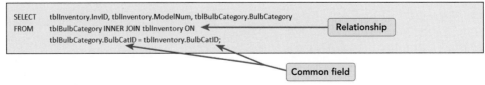

15. Close the query.

Adding Criteria and Operators to a Query

Adding criteria to a query is similar to adding criteria to a filter. One major difference is that more than one condition can be placed on multiple fields. When the query is executed, each condition placed as a criterion must be evaluated against field values for each record in the dynaset. The combination of conditions and operators is evaluated as a single criterion statement.

An *operator* is a word or symbol that indicates a specific arithmetic or logical relationship between the elements of an expression. Operators are used to create conditions. Operators can include arithmetic operators, such as the plus sign (+); comparison operators, such as the equals sign (=); logical operators, such as the word "And"; concatenation operators, such as & and +; and special operators, such as "Like," "Between," or "In."

In addition to operators, a condition can include one or more functions. A *function* is a procedure used in an expression. Most functions include multiple arguments. An *argument* is a reference in a function assigned as a single variable. Some functions such as "Date" do not require arguments. Other functions such as "DateDiff" contain both required arguments and optional arguments.

TABLE 6-1 Types of Operators

Type	Definition	Examples
Arithmetic operator	A word or symbol that calculates a value from two or more numbers.	+, −, *, /, \, ^
Comparison operator	A symbol or combination of symbols that specifies a comparison between two values. A comparison operator is also referred to as a relational operator.	=, <>, <, <=, >, >=
Logical operator	A symbol, word, group of symbols, or group of words used to construct an expression with multiple conditions.	And, Or, Eqv, Not, Xor
Concatenation operator	A symbol, word, group of symbols, or group of words used to combine two text values into a single text value.	&, +
Special operators		Like, Between, In, True, False

Exercise 6-5   USE A SINGLE CRITERION

Text, numbers, or expressions can be used as criteria. When you create criteria using text values, you must include leading and closing quotation marks around the text. Criteria using date values include leading and closing pound signs (#). Numbers and expressions do not require leading or closing symbols. You will now create a select query using a single criterion.

1. Open **qryBulbPrices** in Design View.

2. Click the Criteria row for **BulbShape**. Key **canister**.

Figure 6-7
Entering criteria
EcoMed-06.accdb
qryBulbPrices

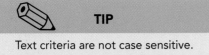

Field:	ModelNum	BulbShape	Cost	
Table:	tblInventory	tblInventory	tblInventory	
Sort:				
Show:	☑	☑	☑	☐
Criteria:		canister		
or:				

TIP

Text criteria are not case sensitive.

TIP

After you run a query, Access places leading and closing quotation marks around the text used as the criterion.

NOTE

This query has reduced the dynaset from 310 records to 6 records.

3. From the Design tab, in the Results group, click Datasheet View ▦. Only those products of **Bulb Shape** "canister" are shown.

4. Switch to Design View.

5. Click in the Criteria row for **BulbShape** and press F2 to select the criterion. Press Delete.

6. In the Criteria row for **BulbShape**, key **dish**.

7. From the Design tab, in the Results group, click View ▦. Only those products of **Bulb Shape** "dish" are shown.

8. From the Home tab, in the Views group, click the bottom half of the Design View ▼ and choose SQL View ▧. This SQL statement now shows the criteria.

Figure 6-8
SQL statement:
criteria
EcoMed-06.accdb
qryBulbPrices

```
SELECT    tblInventory.ModelNum, tblInventory.BulbShape, tblInventory.Cost
FROM      tblInventory
WHERE     (((tblInventory.BulbShape)="dish"));  ◄──────────  Criteria
```

9. Switch to Design View.

10. Click in the **Criteria** row for **BulbShape** and press [F2]. Press [Delete] to remove the criteria.

11. Save and close the query.

Exercise 6-6   USE COMPARISON OPERATORS

Queries often use comparison operators to evaluate data. Comparison operators allow you to evaluate numbers, text, and dates. For example, the expression ">10/17/11" would display all records with a date after October 17, 2011. The expression ">=10/17/11" would display all records with a date on or after October 17, 2011.

When comparing text, fields are evaluated alphabetically. The expression <"smith" would display all records that appear in a dictionary before the word "smith".

TABLE 6-2 Comparison Operators

Operator	Meaning
=	Equal
<>	Not equal
<	Less than
<=	Less than or equal to
>	Greater than
>=	Greater than or equal to

1. Open **qryEmpLeave** in **Datasheet View** and notice that the dynaset is sorted by **Leave Date**.

2. Switch to **Design View**. Click in the **Criteria** row for **LeaveDate**.

3. Key **<=3/31/10** and press [↓]. Access adds "#" around the date criteria.

4. Switch to **Datasheet View**. Records for which the **Leave Date** is on or before March 31, 2010, display (50 records).

5. From the **Home** tab, in the **Views** group, click the bottom half of the **Design View** ☒ and choose **SQL View** [SQL]. This SQL statement now shows the criteria and sort order.

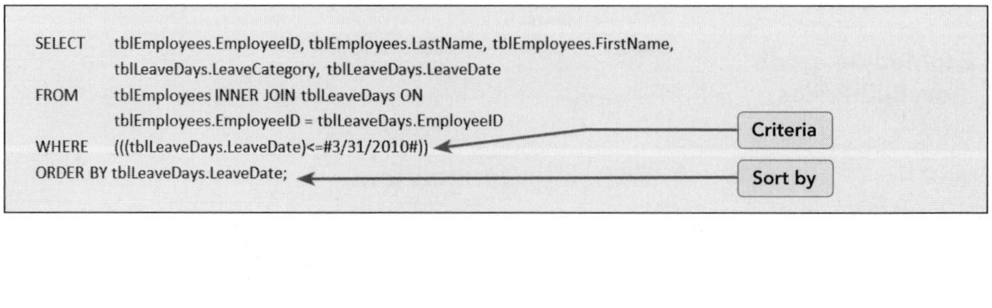

Figure 6-9
SQL statement:
criteria and sort
**EcoMed-06.accdb
qryEmpLeave**

```
SELECT    tblEmployees.EmployeeID, tblEmployees.LastName, tblEmployees.FirstName,
          tblLeaveDays.LeaveCategory, tblLeaveDays.LeaveDate
FROM      tblEmployees INNER JOIN tblLeaveDays ON
          tblEmployees.EmployeeID = tblLeaveDays.EmployeeID              ← Criteria
WHERE     (((tblLeaveDays.LeaveDate)<=#3/31/2010#)) ←
ORDER BY tblLeaveDays.LeaveDate; ←                                       ← Sort by
```

6. Switch to **Design View** and delete the criteria for **LeaveDate**.
7. Save and close the query.

Exercise 6-7 USE WILDCARDS IN CRITERIA

In much the same way you would use wildcards in the Find command, you can use wildcards in a query. When using a wildcard in the Criteria row of a query, the Like operator compares the criterion condition to each record.

For example, in the first name field, the criterion Like "Joa" would display records that contain fields such as "Joan", "Joann", and "Joaquin." When using a wild card, Access automatically adds the keyword "Like."

> ↔ **REVIEW**
>
> The wildcard * represents any number of characters. Thus, the criteria "f*" specifies the letter "f" followed by any number of characters.

You will now modify an existing query to display all facilities with the word "Hospital" in its name.

1. Open **qryFacDetails** in **Design View**.
2. In the **Criteria** row for **FacName**, key **f***.

Figure 6-10
Using the * wildcard
EcoMed-06.accdb
qryFacDetails

Field:	FacilitiesID	FacName	ManageTypeID	MedicareID	Revenue
Table:	tblFacilities	tblFacilities	tblFacilities	tblFacilities	tblFacilities
Sort:		Ascending			
Show:	☑	☑	☑	☑	☑
Criteria:		*f			
or:					

3. From the **Design** tab, in the **Results** group, click **Run** [!]. Records in which the **Facility Name** starts with "f" are displayed.
4. Switch to **Design View**. Access inserts the keyword **Like** and formats the text with quotes.
5. Press [F2] and [Delete] to delete the criteria.
6. In the **Criteria** row for **FacName**, key ***hospital***.
7. Switch to view the dynaset. Records where the **Facility Name** contains "hospital" are displayed.
8. Switch to **Design View**. Delete the criteria.
9. In the **MedicareNum Criteria** row, key **"??2*"**. This criterion will look at the third number in the **Medicare Number**, which indicates the type of facility. In this case, "2" refers to Long-Term facilities.
10. Press [↓].

> ✎ **NOTE**
>
> When using the "?" wildcard, you must place the quotation marks around your criteria. Otherwise Access will tell you that you have a syntax error.

Figure 6-11
Using the * and ? wildcards
EcoMed-06.accdb
qryFacDetails

Field:	FacilitiesID	FacName	ManageTypeID	MedicareNum	Revenue
Table:	tblFacilities	tblFacilities	tblFacilities	tblFacilities	tblFacilities
Sort:		Ascending			
Show:	☑	☑	☑	☑	☑
Criteria:				Like "??2*"	
or:					

11. View the dynaset. Three records are displayed.

12. Return to **Design View** and delete the criteria.

Exercise 6-8   USE KEYWORDS IN CRITERIA

Only the keyword "Like" is automatically added to a criterion. All other keywords must be specified. Criteria expressions can be viewed in the Zoom box. You can open the Zoom box by pressing Shift + F2.

TABLE 6-3 Criteria Keywords

Keyword	Returns records where the field ...
Is Null	has no data, is "blank," or is "empty."
Between	value is between two numbers.
Like	value equals a defined text.
Not	value does not match the defined value.

1. In the **Design View** of **qryFacDetails**, in the **Criteria** row for **MedicareNum**, key null and press ↓. Access has inserts the keyword "Is" to the criteria and capitalized "Null."

2. View the dynaset. There are 18 facilities that don't have **Medicare Numbers**.

3. Return to **Design View**.

4. Edit the **MedicareNum** criteria to show is not null.

5. View the dynaset. There are 146 facilities that do have **Medicare Numbers**.

6. Return to **Design View** and delete the criteria.

7. From the Fields List, add the field **Beds**.

8. Right-click in the **Criteria** row for **Beds** and choose **Zoom** 🔍.

9. In the **Zoom** dialog box, key is between 100 and 300 and click **OK**.

10. View the dynaset. There are 38 facilities with between 100 and 300 beds.

11. Switch to **Design View**.

12. In the **Show** row, click to remove the checkmark for **Beds**.

13. View the dynaset. The numbers of beds are no longer showing, but the field is still being used for the criteria.

14. Switch to **SQL View**.

Figure 6-12
SQL statement:
Between keyword
EcoMed-06.accdb
qryFacDetails

```
SELECT   tblFacilities.FacilitiesID, tblFacilities.FacName, tblFacilities.ManageTypeID,
         tblFacilities.MedicareNum, tblFacilities.Revenue
FROM     tblFacilities
WHERE    (((tblFacilities.Beds) Between 100 And 300))
ORDER BY tblFacilities.FacName;
```

Criteria using
key word

15. Return to **Design View** and delete the criteria.

16. Close the query and save the changes.

Applying Logical Operators

An AND criterion or an OR criterion compares two conditions in a single statement. You use AND criteria when two conditions must occur simultaneously for the statement to be true. You use OR criteria when either condition must occur for the statement to be true.

The design grid of a query allows for AND and OR statements without using AND or OR as keywords. When you create an AND criteria, you enter all conditions on the same Criteria row of the design grid. When you create an OR criteria, you enter the conditions on different Criteria rows of the design grid.

Exercise 6-9 USE AND CRITERIA

An AND condition can be created for a single field or multiple fields. When an AND condition is placed on a single field, the keyword AND must be placed between the two conditions. When an AND condition is placed on multiple fields, the keyword is not entered. When more than one field contains a condition on the same Criteria row, then an AND condition is created automatically by Access.

You will now create a query that uses the AND condition. You will search for all facilities that are in the state of Florida and in the city of Miami.

1. From the **Create** tab, in the **Queries** group, click **Query Design** .

2. From the **Show Table** dialog box, double-click **tblFacilities** and click **Close**.

3. Resize the Field List so all field names can be seen.

4. Add the following fields to the query design grid: **FacName**, **Address**, **City**, **State**, **ZIP**.

5. In the **FacName** column, click the drop-down arrow in the **Sort** row and choose **Ascending**.

6. Switch to **Datasheet View** to see the results. Resize the columns so all data are visible.

7. Right-click the document tab for the query and choose **Save** . Key **qryFacAddress** and click **OK**.

8. Switch to **Design View**.

9. In the **State** column, key **fl** in the **Criteria** row.

10. Switch to **Datasheet View** to see how many facilities are in Florida. Return to **Design View**.

11. In the **City** column, key **miami** in the same **Criteria** row.

Figure 6-13
AND criteria on the same row in the design grid
EcoMed-06.accdb
qryFacAddress

Field:	FacName	Address	City	State	ZIP
Table:	tblFacilities	tblFacilities	tblFacilities	tblFacilities	tblFacilities
Sort:	Ascending				
Show:	☑	☑	☑	☑	☑
Criteria:			miami	"fl"	
or:					

12. Switch to **Datasheet View**. Only records that matched both the state and city criteria are shown. Return to **Design View**.

13. Click in the **Criteria** row for the **City** field. From the **Design** tab, in the **Query Setup** group, click **Delete Rows** ⬚.

14. Click in the **Criteria** row for the **State** field. Key **tn and nc**.

15. Switch to **Datasheet View**. No records match the criteria because no facility's state can be both TN and NC.

Exercise 6-10   USE OR CRITERIA

An OR condition can be created for a single field or multiple fields. When an OR condition is placed on a single field, the keyword OR must be placed between the two conditions. When an OR condition is placed on two or more fields, the keyword is not entered. When multiple conditions are placed on multiple Criteria rows, then an OR condition is automatically created by Access.

You will now create a query that creates an OR condition. You will search for all facilities that are in the state of Tennessee or the state of North Carolina.

1. Switch to **Design View**. Point to the right of the word "Criteria" in the **Criteria** row to display a black arrow pointing right. Click to select the **Criteria** row and press ⌈Delete⌋.

Figure 6-14
Selecting a Criteria row
EcoMed-06.accdb
qryFacAddress

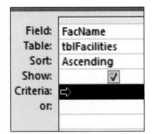

2. Click in the **Criteria** row for the **State** field, and key **tn**. View the dynaset to see nine matching records. Return to **Design View**.

3. Key **nc** in the row below "tn" to enter a second condition. The first **or** row is directly below the **Criteria** row.

Figure 6-15
OR criteria on separate rows in the design grid
EcoMed-06.accdb
qryFacAddress

Field:	FacName	Address	City	State	ZIP
Table:	tblFacilities	tblFacilities	tblFacilities	tblFacilities	tblFacilities
Sort:	Ascending				
Show:	☑	☑	☑	☑	☑
Criteria:				"tn"	
or:				nc	

4. View the dynaset. Each record meets one of the "OR" conditions. Return to **Design View**.

5. Save and close the query.

6. Open **qryFacAddress** in **Design View**. Notice that Access has combined the two criteria to one row using the "OR" keyword.

7. Switch to **SQL View**.

Figure 6-16
SQL statement: Or criteria
EcoMed-06.accdb
qryFacAddress

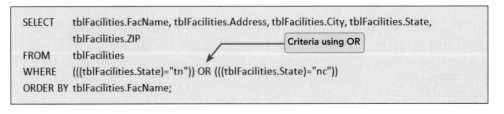

```
SELECT    tblFacilities.FacName, tblFacilities.Address, tblFacilities.City, tblFacilities.State,
          tblFacilities.ZIP                          ⟵ Criteria using OR
FROM      tblFacilities
WHERE     (((tblFacilities.State)="tn")) OR (((tblFacilities.State)="nc"))
ORDER BY  tblFacilities.FacName;
```

8. Switch to **Design View** and delete the criteria.

9. Save and close the query.

Modifying Query Properties

Queries display specific data and sorted data. By setting specific properties on a query, you can display top values and subdatasheets. For example, if you need to list the five facilities with the highest revenue, you would sort the facilities table by revenue in descending order and apply the Top Value property. The original query, including its criteria, would remain the same. You would only modify its properties to display the top values.

The Top Values property displays either a static number of records (such as the top 5) or a percentage of all records in the dynaset (such as the top 5 percent). Depending on the sort order, Top Values can display either the highest (top) or lowest (bottom) values. For example, when you sort a numeric field in ascending order, the "top" of the list will be the lowest numbers. When you sort a numeric field in descending order, the "top" values are the largest numbers.

Exercise 6-11 FIND THE TOP AND BOTTOM VALUES

When using the Top Values property, Access displays records based on the defined sort order. If a query is sorted by a numeric value, then the top values will be based on the sorted numeric field. If a query is sorted by a text field, then the top values will be based on the sorted text field.

To find the top 5 percent of the facilities that have the greatest annual revenue, you will apply the appropriate property to the FacDetails query. You must first sort the dynaset and then apply the top 5 percent property.

1. Open **qryFacDetails**.

2. Switch to **Design View**. Click in the **Sort** row for the **FacName** field. Click the drop-down arrow and choose **(not sorted)**.

3. Click in the **Sort** row for the **Revenue** field. Click the drop-down arrow and choose **Descending**.

4. Switch to **Datasheet View**. The facilities are sorted in descending order, starting with the facilities with the greatest annual revenue.

5. Switch to **Design View**.

6. From the **Design** tab, in the **Show/Hide** group, click **Property Sheet** .

7. Click anywhere to the right of the **tblFacilities** Field List to make the **Property Sheet** display the **Query Properties**.

8. Click the property **Top Values** and the drop-down arrow. Choose **5**.

Figure 6-17
Top Values property
**EcoMed-06.accdb
qryFacDetails**

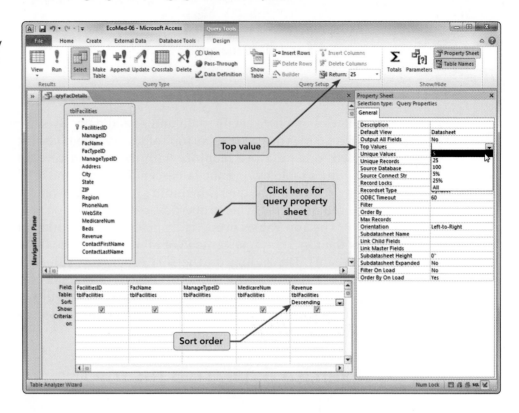

9. Switch to **Datasheet View**. Because the field **Revenue** is sorted in descending order, the five greatest revenues are shown.

10. Switch to **Design View**. From the **Design** tab, in the **Query Setup** group, click the **Return** list box 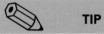 and select **5%**.

TIP

The Top Values property also can be changed in the Return list box found on the Design tab, Query Setup group.

11. Switch to **Datasheet View**. The top 5 percent of facilities according to their revenues equals 9 records that are displayed.

12. Switch to **SQL View**.

Figure 6-18
SQL statement:
Top 5 Percent
**EcoMed-06.accdb
qryFacDetails**

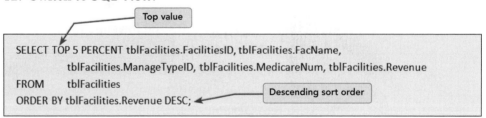

13. Switch to **Design View** and reset the **Return** list box to **All**.

14. Close and save the query.

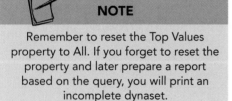

NOTE

Remember to reset the Top Values property to All. If you forget to reset the property and later prepare a report based on the query, you will print an incomplete dynaset.

Exercise 6-12   CREATE A QUERY WITH A SUBDATASHEET

Just as a table can display a related table as a subdatasheet, a query can also contain a subdatasheet. A subdatasheet is created by defining a Subdatasheet Name as a query property. The sheets must be linked by a common field. You will now modify qryMgtContacts by linking the ManageID field between the tables management and facilities.

1. Open **qryMgtContacts**.

2. Switch to **Design View**. Open the **Property Sheet** if it is not already visible.

3. Click in the open space next to the Field List to select the query properties and not the field properties.

4. In the **Property Sheet** for the query, click the property **Subdatasheet Name** and click the drop-down arrow. Choose **Table.tblFacilities** from the list.

> **NOTE**
>
> If the **Property Sheet** shows "Field Properties," click again in the top pane. You may also need to resize the **Property Sheet** to see all values.

5. Click the **Link Child Fields** property and key **MgtID**.

6. Click the **Link Master Fields** property and key **MgtID**.

7. Close the **Property Sheet** and switch to **Datasheet View**.

8. Click the **Expand** button ⊞ for any record to see which facilities are managed by each company.

9. Collapse the subdatasheet.

10. Close the query and save the changes.

Adding Calculations to a Query

The queries you have created so far have been select queries. Select queries display the resulting dynaset as individual records, similar to a datasheet of a table. In addition to selecting fields and records to display, a select query can display results of calculations.

To display a calculation in a query, you use an aggregate function. An *aggregate function* is a sum, average, maximum, minimum, or count for a group of records. For example, you can create a query to display the total bed count for all facilities associated with a single management organization.

A select query also can have a calculated field. A *calculated field* is a field that uses an expression or formula as its data source. After creating a calculated field in a query, you can add those fields to forms and reports. In later lessons, you will learn to add calculated fields directly to the forms and reports.

A calculated field does not store data in the source dynaset. The value of a calculated field is generated each time you run the query. Only the definition and properties of the calculated field are stored in the query object, not the field values.

Because a calculated field is not part of the source dynaset, each calculated field must have a unique name. When a field does not have a name, Access assigns an alias name. The alias name for a calculated field displays as text followed by a colon, in front of the calculation.

Exercise 6-13 USE A FORMULA IN A CALCULATED FIELD

You will learn to create a calculated field by constructing an equation to calculate the sales price of inventory items. EcoMed marks up its inventory by 48 percent. The sales price is calculated by using the formula of cost times 1.48. That means an item that costs $1.00 will sell for $1.48, and an item that costs $2.00 will sell for $2.96.

Calculated fields can be entered directly into the design grid or can be entered using the Expression Builder. The *Expression Builder* is an interface used to create a function, calculation, or expressions.

TABLE 6-4 Expression Builder Components

Component	Description
Expression box	White area at the top of the window that shows the formula as you build it. (Also called the preview area.)
Expression Elements	List of elements available to build an expression.
Expression Categories	Subset of the elements found in the Expression Elements panel.
Expression Values	Subset of the categories found in the Expression Categories panel.

1. Open **qryInvShort** in **Design View**.
2. Click the empty **Field** row in the fifth column.
3. From the **Design** tab, in the **Query Setup** group, click **Builder** 🔧.

Figure 6-19
Building an expression for the query
EcoMed-06.accdb
qryInvShort

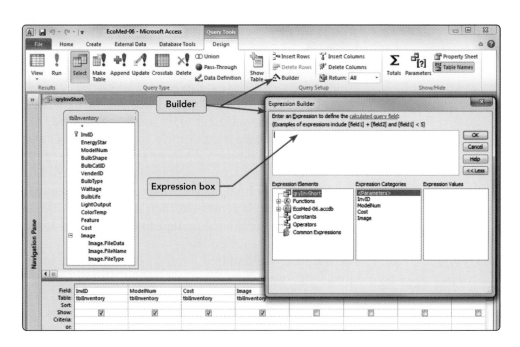

4. The current query is at the top of the **Expression Elements** panel. In the **Expression Categories** panel, click the field **Cost**.

5. In the **Expression Values** panel, double-click <Value> to paste the value of the **Cost** field to the Expression box.

6. In the **Expression Elements** panel, click **Operators**.

7. In the **Expression Values** panel, double-click * (the asterisk) which acts as a multiplication operator.

8. In the Expression box, key **1.48** as the numerical equivalent of a 48 percent markup.

9. Click **OK** to close the **Expression Builder**.

10. Switch to **Datasheet View**. Notice that the last column shows the markup cost of each item in the inventory.

11. Access has given the calculated field a label (or alias) of "Expr1." Switch to **Design View**.

12. Replace "Expr1" with **Retail**. Be certain to leave the colon between the label and the expression.

13. From the **Design** tab, in the **Show/Hide** group, click **Property Sheet** .

14. In the property **Format**, click the drop-down arrow and choose **Currency**.

15. Close the **Property Sheet**.

16. Switch to **Datasheet View**. The calculated field is now formatted.

17. Save and close the query.

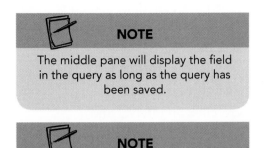

NOTE

The middle pane will display the field in the query as long as the query has been saved.

NOTE

Square brackets are used to surround field names.

Figure 6-20
Building a formula
EcoMed-06.accdb
qryInvShort

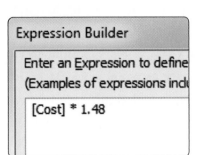

Expression Builder

Enter an Expression to define
(Examples of expressions incl

[Cost] * 1.48

REVIEW

To see the calculation more easily, you can open the Zoom window by using Shift + F2.

Exercise 6-14　USE A FUNCTION IN A CALCULATED FIELD

In addition to constructing a calculated field directly, you can use the Expression Builder to look up and insert arguments and operators for a predefined function. For this exercise, you will use the DateDiff and Now functions to calculate the difference between two dates. The two dates that you will use are the employee's date of birth and today's date. The resulting difference will be the age of the employee.

1. Open **qryEmpDates** in **Design View**.

2. Click the empty **Field** row in the fifth column.

3. From the **Design** tab, in the **Query Setup** group, click **Builder** 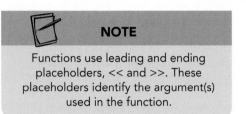.

4. In the **Expression Elements** panel, double-click **Functions** and click **Built-In Functions**.

5. In the **Expression Categories** panel, click **Date/Time**.

6. In the **Expression Values** panel, double-click **DateDiff**. This function has five parameters or values. We need to fill three of them.

7. In the Expression box, click on **interval** and key **"yyyy"**.

8. In the Expression box, click on **<<date1>>** to select the placeholder.

9. In the **Expression Elements** panel, click **qryEmpDates**. In the **Expression Categories** panel, double-click **DOB** to add the date of birth field to the expression.

> **NOTE**
>
> Functions use leading and ending placeholders, << and >>. These placeholders identify the argument(s) used in the function.

10. In the Expression box, click on **<<date2>>**.

11. In the **Expression Elements** panel, click **Built-In Functions**.

12. In the **Expression Categories** panel, click **Date/Time**.

13. In the **Expression Values** panel, double-click **Now**. This function has no parameters but still needs to have its parentheses.

14. Press ⌈Delete⌉ until you have deleted the remaining commas and placeholders. Do not delete the right parenthesis.

Figure 6-21
Building a function
**EcoMed-06.accdb
qryEmpDates**

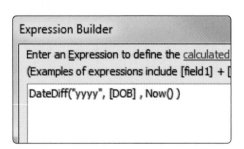

15. Click **OK**. Press ⌈↓⌉. Access has added the alias "Expr1".

16. Replace the alias with **Age**.

17. From the **Design** tab, in the **Show/Hide** group, click the **Property Sheet** . In the **Age Property Sheet**, click in the **Format** property and key **#" years"**. There is a space before the "y" in years.

18. Switch to **Datasheet View**. The newly calculated field shows the employee's age plus a text string.

19. Return to **Design View** and close the **Property Sheet**.

20. Save the query.

Exercise 6-15 USE A CONCATENATION EXPRESSION IN A CALCULATED FIELD

In addition to mathematical, date, and statistical functions, Access also includes text functions. Text functions allow you to extract or combine text. In this lesson, you will concatenate text. *Concatenate* is the operation of joining two or more character strings end to end. For example, the two text strings "twenty" and "three" can be concatenated with the symbol "-" to produce the single string "twenty-three".

1. Click the empty **Field** row in the sixth column.
2. From the **Design** tab, in the **Query Setup** group, click **Builder** 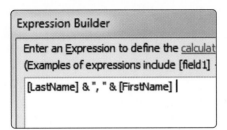.
3. In the **Expression Categories** panel, double-click **LastName**.
4. In the **Expression Elements** panel, click **Operators**.
5. In the **Expression Categories** panel, click **String**. There is only one string operator.
6. In the **Expression Values** panel, double-click the **&** (ampersand).
7. Click in the Expression box and key **", "** (double quotation, comma, space, double quotation).
8. Press [Spacebar] and key **&**.
9. In the **Expression Elements** panel, click **qryEmpDates**.
10. In the **Expression Categories** panel, double-click **FirstName**. Click **OK**.

Figure 6-22
Concatenation expression
**EcoMed-06.accdb
qryEmpDates**

> **Expression Builder**
>
> Enter an Expression to define the <u>calculat</u>
> (Examples of expressions include [field1]
>
> [LastName] & ", " & [FirstName] |

11. Edit the alias "Expr1" to **FullName**.
12. Switch to **Datasheet View**. The newly calculated field shows the last and first names of employees in one field.
13. For the first record, change the **Last Name** from "Abdone" to **Smith**.
14. Press [↓]. Notice the **FullName** value has changed to show the new last name of the employee.
15. Switch to **SQL View**.

Figure 6-23
SQL statement: calculated fields
**EcoMed-06.accdb
qryEmpDates**

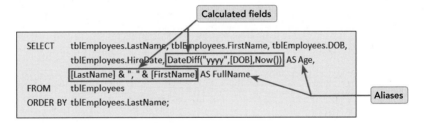

16. Save and close the query.

Creating Queries with Wizards

Relationships and referential integrity prevent data duplication or unmatched relationships. However, when using data from other sources, such as an on-line Web site, the table you create might not follow your relationship rules. Access provides two queries that assist you in verifying the accuracy of your data.

You use the Query Wizard to create the Find Unmatched Records Query and the Find Duplicate Records Query. The Query Wizard can also be used to create a Crosstab query.

Exercise 6-16 USE THE SIMPLE QUERY WIZARD

You have been asked to create a query that will display the name of the vender, the inventory model number, the shape of the bulb, and the image of the bulb. Because these four fields do not exist in a single table, you will need to create a query and link the appropriate fields. You can use the Query Wizard to create this query.

When creating a query using a wizard, you must select the record source and the associated fields. The record source can be one or more related tables or queries. The dynaset will generate on the basis of the relationship between the three tables.

1. From the **Create** tab, in the **Queries** group, click **Query Wizard** 📧.

Figure 6-24
New Query Wizard
EcoMed-06.accdb

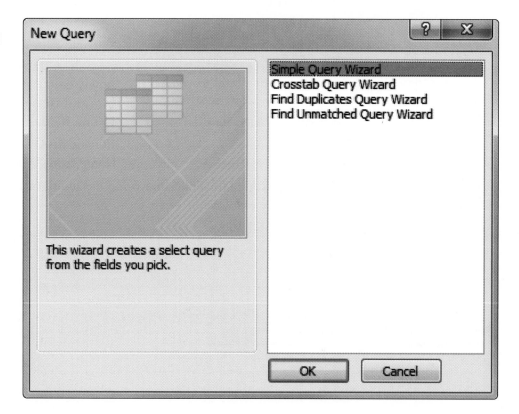

2. In the **New Query** dialog box, double-click **Simple Query Wizard**.
3. From the **Tables/Queries** list box, choose **Table: tblVender**.
4. In the **Available Fields** list, double-click **VenderName**.
5. From the **Tables/Queries** list box, choose **Table: tblInventory**.
6. In the **Available Fields** list, double-click **ModelNum** and **BulbShape**.
7. From the **Tables/Queries** list box, choose **Table: tblBulbShapes**.
8. In the **Available Fields** list, double-click **Icon**.
9. Click **Next**. The default type of select query is **Detail**. Click **Next**.
10. Delete the suggested title and key **qryVenInv&Shape**.

11. Click **Finish**. This dynaset lists the venders, inventory, and shape of each bulb.

12. Switch to **Design View**. Resize and move each Field List to match Figure 6-25.

Figure 6-25
Query created by the Simple Query Wizard
EcoMed-06.accdb
qryVenInv&Shape

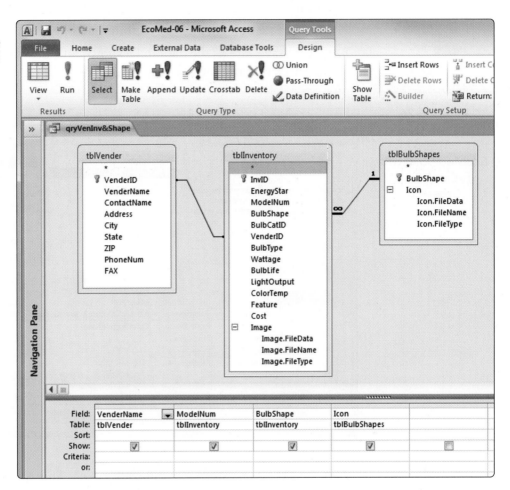

13. Notice that the tables are linked to one another with join lines. Close and save the query.

Exercise 6-17   USE THE CROSSTAB QUERY WIZARD

A crosstab query displays information similar to that in a spreadsheet. The Total row calculates sum, average, count, or other totals. The Crosstab row defines the fields used for the data, column headings, and row headings. Data are grouped by two fields, one listed on the left and the other listed across the top.

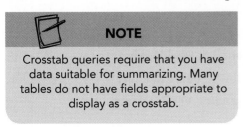

NOTE

Crosstab queries require that you have data suitable for summarizing. Many tables do not have fields appropriate to display as a crosstab.

1. Open **qryEmpLeave** in **Datasheet View** and sort by **Last Name** in ascending order.

2. Notice that each employee has taken multiple sick and vacation days. Close the query without saving.

3. From the **Create** tab, in the **Queries** group, click **Query Wizard**.

4. In the New Query dialog box, double-click Crosstab Query Wizard.

5. In the View control, click Queries. From the list, select Query: qryEmpLeave. Click Next.

6. From the Available Fields, double-click **LastName** and **FirstName** as the row headings. Click Next.

7. Select **LeaveCategory** as the column heading and click Next.

8. Select **LeaveDate** as the data to be shown and Count as the function. Click the check box Yes, include row sums to deselect the control. Click Next.

Figure 6-26
Crosstab Query
Wizard
**EcoMed-06.accdb
qryEmpLeave_
Crosstab**

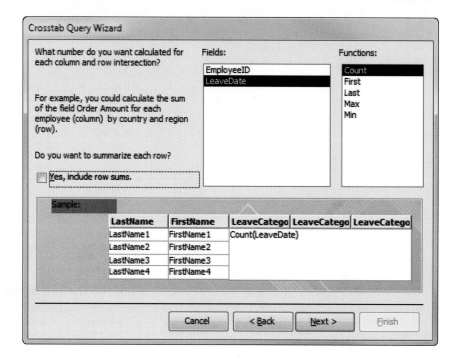

9. Accept the suggested title and click Finish. This query counts each sick and vacation day for each employee.

10. Switch to Design View. Two new rows were added to the design grid by the wizard: Total and Crosstab.

11. Close and save the query.

Exercise 6-18   USE THE FIND DUPLICATE QUERY WIZARD

The Find Duplicates Query Wizard analyzes a table for duplicate data. If duplicates are identified, you decide what action to take, including deleting or editing the records.

1. From the Create tab, in the Queries group, click Query Wizard 🖾.

2. In the New Query dialog box, double-click Find Duplicates Query Wizard.

3. From the list of table, select Table: tblVender. Click Next.

4. From the Available fields list, double-click **VenderName**.

Figure 6-27
Choose the field that
might have
duplicates.
EcoMed-06.accdb
qryVenDuplicates

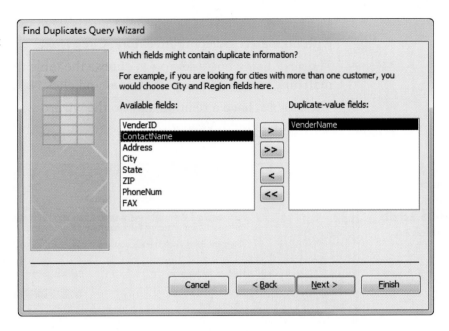

5. Click **Next**. Click the **Add All** button >> to show all fields in the resulting dynaset. Click **Next**.

6. Delete the suggested title and key **qryVenDuplicates** and click **Finish**. The query shows the two duplicate records.

7. From the **Home** tab, in the **Records** group, click **More** ▦ and choose **Subdatasheet**, then **Subdatasheet** ▦ from the menu.

8. In the **Insert Subdatasheet** dialog box, on the **Tables** tab, select **tblInventory**.

9. Using the drop-down arrows, set the **Linked Child Fields** and **Linked Master Fields** fields to the common field, **VenderID**. Click **OK**.

10. Expand both subdatasheets. Notice that **VenderID** 31 does not have any inventory related to it, so it is safe to delete this record.

11. Select the record for **VenderID** 31.

12. From the **Home** tab, in the **Records** group, click the **Delete** option arrow and choose **Delete Record** ▧. Click **Yes** to verify the deletion.

13. From the **Home** tab, in the **Records** group, click **Refresh All** ▨. The query is run again, but this time there are no duplicates.

14. Close and save any changes to the query.

Exercise 6-19 USE THE FIND UNMATCHED QUERY WIZARD

The Find Unmatched Query Wizard finds unmatched, or orphaned, records. Orphaned records occur when referential integrity has not been enforced. When working on a database designed by someone else, it is can be beneficial to check if there are unmatched records.

1. From the **Create** tab, in the **Queries** group, click **Query Wizard** ▧.

2. In the **New Query** dialog box, double-click **Find Unmatched Query Wizard**.

3. The first dialog box asks you to choose a table that might have records with no match. Select **tblInventory**. Click **Next**.

4. The next dialog box asks you to choose the table that should have the matching records. Choose **tblVender** and click **Next**.

5. These tables have a relationship, so the wizard was able to determine the common field, **VenderID**.

Figure 6-28
Match the common field.
EcoMed-06.accdb
qryInvNoVen

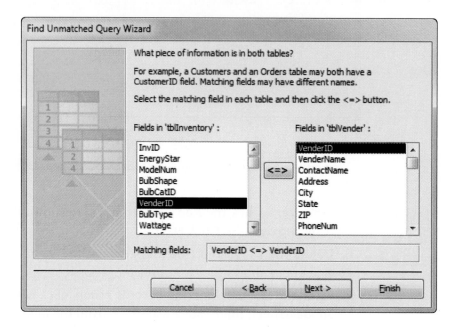

6. Click **Next**. In the **Available fields**, double-click **InvID**, **ModelNum**, and **VenderID**. Click **Next**.

7. Delete the suggested title, key **qryInvNoVen**, and click **Finish**. The query shows there are 15 bulbs in the inventory table without a vender. We will not be fixing this error at this time.

8. Close the query.

Applying PivotChart/PivotTable Views

PivotTables and PivotCharts are methods of viewing complex information in summarized formats. PivotTables and PivotCharts can automatically sort, count, and total data in a summarized format. You can change the summary's structure by dragging and dropping fields using a graphical interface.

You use PivotTables and PivotCharts to analyze related totals or to compare related information from a large data set. In a PivotTable or PivotChart, each column or field in your source data becomes a PivotTable field that summarizes multiple rows of information. When you rearrange the fields in a PivotTable, the changes appear as changes to columns in the related Pivot-Chart. You can save changes to and print PivotTables and PivotCharts.

Exercise 6-20   USE PIVOTTABLE VIEW

A *pivot table* is an interactive table that combines and compares data in a summarized view. You create a pivot table by using a graphical interface to drag and drop fields into appropriate column, row, and data locations.

1. Open **qryInvCostByVen**.

2. From the Home tab, in the Views group, click the bottom half of the View button and choose PivotTable View 🗗.

3. To open the PivotTable Field List, click the Design tab, and in the Show/ Hide group, click Field List.

4. From the PivotTable Field List, select **VenderName**. Click the drop-down arrow in the lower right corner. It contains a list of all drop zones in the table. Choose Row Area. Click Add to.

Figure 6-29
Adding a field to a
PivotTable.
**EcoMed-06.accdb
qryInvCostByVen**

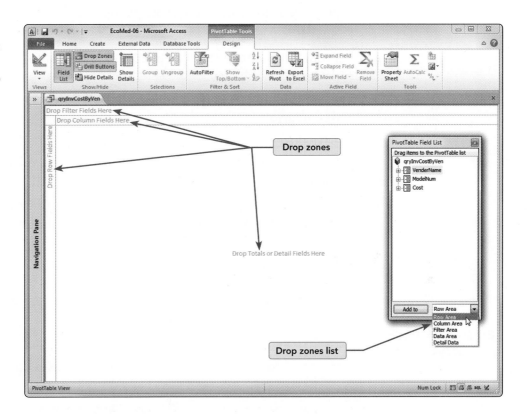

5. Drag the **ModelNum** field from the PivotTable Field List into the Drop Totals or Detail Fields Here zone of the PivotTable.

6. In the PivotTable Field List, select **Cost**. In the drop-down list at the bottom of the list, choose Detail Data drop zone. Click Add to.

7. From the Design tab, in the Show/Hide group, click the Field List 🗐 to close the Field List.

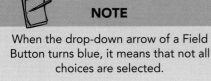

NOTE

When the drop-down arrow of a Field Button turns blue, it means that not all choices are selected.

8. In the PivotTable, click the **VenderName** button's drop-down arrow. Remove the checkmark for All. Add a checkmark to "Cobra, Inc." and click OK. This action adds a filter to the PivotTable.

9. Click the **VenderName** button's drop-down arrow. Add the checkmark for **All** and click **OK**.

10. Close and save the query.

Exercise 6-21   USE PIVOTCHART VIEW

A PivotChart View displays the same information as a crosstab query, including counts and sums of numeric fields. A *PivotChart View* is an interactive graphical representation of data displayed in a PivotTable.

A PivotChart displays field values that can be switched or pivoted to display different views of the same data. You set different levels of detail by dragging fields and items or by showing and hiding items in the field drop-down lists.

1. From the **Create** tab, in the **Queries** group, click **Query Design**.

2. Double-click **tblInventory** and **tblBulbCategory** to add the tables to the grid, then close the **Show Table** dialog box.

3. Size the Field Lists.

4. From **tblInventory**, double-click **InvID** and **Cost** to add them to the design grid.

5. From **tblBulbCategory**, double-click **BulbCategory** to add it to the design grid.

6. Save the query as **qryCostByCategory**.

7. From the **Design** tab, in the **Results** group, click the bottom half of the **View** button and choose **PivotChart View**.

8. Select **BulbCategory** from the **Chart Field List**. Click the drop-down arrow in the lower right corner. It contains a list of all drop zones in the chart. Choose **Category Area**.

9. Click **Add to**.

Figure 6-30
PivotChart
EcoMed-06.accdb
qryCostByCategory

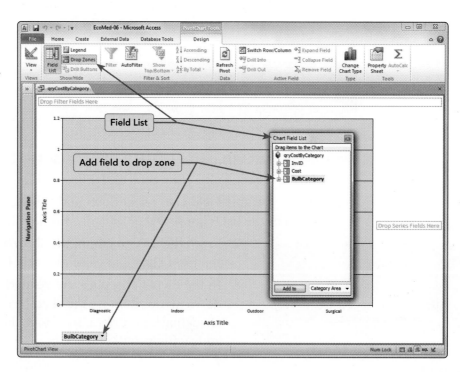

NOTE

The Chart Field List displays a field name in a bold font whenever the field is used in the chart.

TIP

When dragging a field to a drop zone, make sure that the drop zone "lights up" before you release the field. In the case of the Data Area, a blue box will appear above the chart.

10. Drag the **Cost** from the **Chart Field List** into the center of the PivotChart. The data is added to the chart, and the **Sum of Cost** field button is added to the top of the chart.

11. Right-click the **Category Axis Title** at the bottom of the chart. Choose **Properties**. Click the **Format** tab. In the **Caption** control, key **Bulb Categories**.

12. Click the **Value Axis Title** to the left of the chart. Clicking on a new object automatically switches the property sheet to that new object. Key **Base Cost** as the new **Caption**. Close the **Properties** sheet.

13. From the **Design** tab, in the **Show/Hide** group, click **Field List** 🔲 to remove the **Chart Field List**.

14. From the **Design** tab, in the **Show/Hide** group, click **Drop Zones** 🔳 to remove the unused drop zones.

Figure 6-31
Finished PivotChart
EcoMed-06.accdb
qryCostByCategory

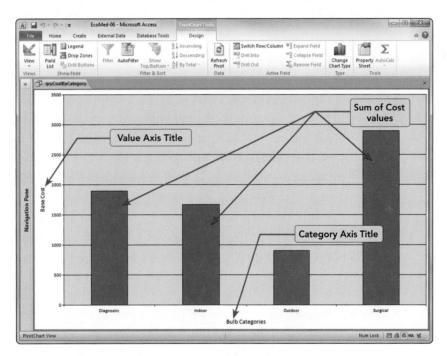

15. Switch to **Datasheet View**. Notice that making changes to the query's PivotChart has no effect on the dynaset. The **PivotChart View** is just another way of viewing the data.

16. Save and close the query.

17. Compact and close the database.

Lesson 6   Summary

- Queries make data more manageable and often are the record source for reports and forms.

- In addition to Datasheet View and Design View, a query can be displayed in SQL View.

- A select query, the most common type of query, locates data from one or more tables and displays the results as a datasheet.

- The Query Design window has an upper and lower pane. The upper pane is the Field List pane in which you choose the data source from one or more Field Lists. The lower pane is the design grid in which you specify criteria.

- A dynaset is dynamic recordset that automatically reflects changes to its underlying data source.

- In the design grid of a query, the check box in the Show row indicates that the field will display in the Datasheet View.

- When you use two or more tables in a query, the tables must be linked through a common field.

- In a query, more than one criterion can be placed on a single or multiple fields.

- When the query is executed, each condition placed as a criterion must be evaluated against field values for each record in the dynaset.

- An operator is a word or symbol that indicates a specific arithmetic or logical relationship between the elements of an expression.

- Operators can include arithmetic operators, comparison operators, logical operators, concatenation operators, and special operators.

- A function is a procedure used in an expression.

- An argument is a reference in a function assigned as a single variable.

- Criteria using text values include leading and closing quotation marks. Criteria using date values include leading and closing pound signs (#). Numbers and expressions do not require leading or closing symbols.

- When using a wildcard in the Criteria row of a query, the Like operator compares the criterion condition to each record.

- Only the keyword "Like" is automatically added to a criterion. All other keywords must be specified.

- Criterion expressions can be viewed in the Zoom box. You can open the Zoom box by pressing Shift + F2.

- An AND criteria exists when two conditions must occur simultaneously for the statement to be true.

- An OR criteria exists when one of two conditions must occur for the statement to be true.

- When using the Top Values property, Access displays records based on the defined sort order.

- The Top Values property displays either a static number of records (such as the top 5) or a percentage of all records in the dynaset (such as the top 5 percent).
- A calculated field is a field that uses an expression or formula as its data source.
- When a field does not have a name, Access assigns an alias name. The alias name for a calculated field displays as text followed by a colon.
- Calculated fields can be entered directly into the design grid or can be entered using the Expression Builder. The Expression Builder is an interface used to create a function, calculation, or expressions.
- Concatenate is the operation of joining two or more character strings end to end.
- A crosstab query displays information similar to that in a spreadsheet. Crosstab queries require that you have data suitable for summarizing. Many tables do not have fields appropriate to display as a crosstab.
- The Find Duplicates Query Wizard analyzes a table for duplicate data.
- The Find Unmatched Query Wizard finds unmatched, or orphaned, records.
- A PivotTable is an interactive table that combines and compares data in a summarized view.
- A PivotChart is an interactive graphical representation of data displayed in a PivotTable.

LESSON 6		Command Summary	
Feature	**Button**	**Path**	**Keyboard**
SQL View	SQL	Home, Views, SQL View	
Open Zoom dialog box			
Query, Add Top feature		Design, Query Setup, Return	
Create, Query wizard		Create, Macros & Code, Query Wizard	
PivotTable View		Home, Views, PivotTable View	
Open PivotTable Field pane		Design, Show/Hide, Field List	
PivotChart View		Home, Views, PivotChart View	
View, Toggles Drop Zones		Design, Show/Hide, Drop Zone	

Concepts Review

True/False Questions

Each of the following statements is either true or false. Indicate your choice by circling T or F.

T F 1. A dynamic recordset automatically changes its underlying data source.

T F 2. You can build criteria by using logical and relational operators.

T F 3. You cannot use a query as the source of records for another query.

T F 4. You can add a field to a query in Design View by double-clicking the field name in the Field List window.

T F 5. Count and Sum are types of aggregate functions.

T F 6. Before using the Top Values property, you must sort a dynaset by its primary key.

T F 7. In the design grid, OR criteria are entered in the same row.

T F 8. The criteria "is not null" finds records with a blank or empty field.

Short Answer Questions

Write the correct answer in the space provided.

1. What is the grid name of the lower pane of a query in which you sort data and enter criteria?

2. In what view do you see the dynaset of a query?

3. What property displays the highest or lowest values?

4. What type of criteria do you use when you want two conditions to be true at the same time?

5. What is the operation of joining two or more character strings end to end?

6. In Access, what keyword(s) means is "blank" or is "empty"?

7. When you key a wildcard in a query, what operator does Access use to compare your criteria with each record?

_____

8. What symbol represents "not equal"?

_____

Critical Thinking

Answer these questions on a separate page. There are no right or wrong answers. Support your answers with examples from your own experience, if possible.

1. When an expression has two or more math operators, the Expression Builder follows the mathematical order of operations rules. List these rules and the symbols used with them, and give examples of their use.

2. AND and OR criteria are common to database, programming, and spreadsheets. You can build a logic table to help you visualize what happens with two criteria in these situations. Complete Figure 6-32 (on a separate sheet of paper) to show if the result is True or False (a match or no match).

Figure 6-32
Logic table

AND				OR		
First Criterion	**Second Criterion**		**Answer ? (T/F)**	**First Criterion**	**Second Criterion**	**Answer ? (T/F)**
T	AND T	=		T	OR T	=
T	AND F	=		T	OR F	=
F	AND T	=		F	OR T	=
F	AND F	=		F	OR F	=

Skills Review

Exercise 6-22

You have been asked to create a query to display the names of employees for a specific job code. Follow these steps to create the query.

1. Open a database by following these steps:
    a. Locate and open the **Lesson 06** folder.
    b. If you already have a copy of *[your initials]*-EcoMed-06, skip to step 1d.
    c. Make a copy of **EcoMed-06** and rename it *[your initials]*-EcoMed-06.
    d. Open and enable content for *[your initials]*-EcoMed-06.

2. Use the Simple Query Wizard by following these steps:

   a. From the **Create** tab, in the **Queries** group, click **Query Wizard** .

   b. In the **New Query** dialog box, double-click **Simple Query Wizard**.

   c. From the **Tables/Queries** list box, choose **Table: tblEmployees**.

   d. In the **Available Fields** list, double-click **LastName**, **FirstName**, and **JobCode**.

   e. From the **Tables/Queries** list box, choose **Table: tblJobCodes**.

   f. In the **Available Fields** list, double-click **JobTitle**.

   g. From the **Tables/Queries** list box, choose **Table: tblPay**.

   h. In the **Available Fields** list, double-click **EmpPay**.

   i. Click **Next**. The default type of select query is **Detail**. Click **Next**.

   j. Delete the suggested title and key **qryEmpPay**. Click **Finish**.

3. Add criteria to fields by following these steps:

   a. Switch to **Design View**.

   b. In the **Criteria** row for **JobCode**, key **mf03**, press ⬇, and key **mf04**.

   c. From the **Design** tab, in the **Results** group, click **Run** .

   d. Switch to **Design View**.

4. Sort and hide a field by following these steps:

   a. In the **Sort** row for **JobTitle**, click the drop-down arrow and choose **Ascending**.

   b. In the **Show** row for **JobCode**, remove the checkmark. This field is only needed for criteria, so there is no need to include it in the final dynaset.

   c. Switch to **Datasheet View**.

   d. Save and close the query.

Assessment

- According to your classroom procedure, turn in your database only when you have completed all assigned exercises.

-OR-

- Create a **Database Documenter** report for **qryEmpPay** following these steps:

   a. From the **Database Tools** tab, in the **Analyze** group, click **Database Documenter**.

   b. In the **Documenter** dialog box, click the **Queries** tab, and select **qryEmpPay**. Click **Options**.

   c. For **Query**, include **Properties** and **SQL**.

   d. From the **Include for Fields** section, choose **Nothing**.

   e. From the **Include for Indexes** section, choose **Nothing**.

   f. Click **OK** twice to go to **Print Preview**.

06-22-A.pdf
1 Page

- Save a **Documenter** report by following these steps:

a. From the **Print Preview** tab, in the **Data** group, click **PDF or XPS** to save the printout as a file.

b. Save the file as a PDF and name the file *[your initials]*-06-22-A.

c. Depending on your class procedures, print or turn in the PDF file.

d. Close **Print Preview** and the query.

Exercise 6-23

Create a query to display the names of all the interns. Include the names of the intern identification number and concatenate the first and last names together.

1.   The database *[your initials]*-EcoMed-06 is required to complete this exercise.

a. Open and enable content for *[your initials]*-EcoMed-06.

2.   Create the query by following these steps:

a. From the **Create** tab, in the **Queries** group, click **Query Design**.

b. In the **Show Table** dialog box, double-click **tblInterns** and click **Close**.

c. Resize the Field List so all fields can be seen.

d. From the **tblInterns** Field List, double-click **InternID**, **LastName**, and **FirstName**.

e. From the Quick Access toolbar, click **Save**. Name the query **qryIntern**.

3.   Add a calculated field to a query by following these steps:

a. In the design grid, click in the fourth column in the **Field** row.

b. From the **Design** tab, in the **Query Setup** group, click **Builder**.

c. In the **Expression Categories** panel, double-click **LastName**.

d. In the Expression box after [LastName], key & ", " &.

e. In the **Expression Categories** panel, double-click **FirstName**. Click **OK**.

> **NOTE**
>
> Make sure that you add a space after the comma inside of the quotes.

f. In the calculated field, modify the alias by replacing "Expr1" with **Full Name**.

4.   Sort and delete fields by following these steps:

a. In the **Sort** row for **Full Name**, click the drop-down arrow and choose **Ascending**.

b. In the design grid, select both **LastName** and **FirstName** fields. Press Delete to remove the fields from the design grid.

c. From the Quick Access toolbar, click **Save**.

d. From the **Design** tab, in the **Results** group, click **Run**.

e. Save and close the query.

Assessment

- According to your classroom procedure, turn in your database only when you have completed all assigned exercises.

-OR-

- Create a **Database Documenter** report for **qryIntern** following these steps:

  a. From the **Database Tools** tab, in the **Analyze** group, click **Database Documenter**.

  b. In the **Documenter** dialog box, click the **Queries** tab and select **qryIntern**. Click **Options**.

  c. For **Query**, include **Properties** and **SQL**.

  d. From the **Include for Fields** section, choose **Nothing**.

  e. From the **Include for Indexes** section, choose **Nothing**.

  f. Click **OK** twice to go to **Print Preview**.

- Save a **Database Documenter** report by following these steps:

  a. From the **Print Preview** tab, in the **Data** group, click **PDF or XPS**  to save the printout as a file.

  b. Save the file as a PDF and name the file *[your initials]*-06-23-A.

  c. Depending on your class procedures, print or turn in the PDF file.

  d. Close **Print Preview**.

06-23-A.pdf
1 Page

Exercise 6-24

You have been asked to create a query to display the number of beds per facility, but only for nonprofit facilities.

1. The database *[your initials]*-**EcoMed-06** is required to complete this exercise.

   a. Open and enable content for *[your initials]*-**EcoMed-06**.

2. Create a query in **Design View** by following these steps:

   a. From the **Create** tab, in the **Queries** group, click **Query Design**.

   b. In the **Show Table** dialog box, double-click **tblFacilities** and **tblManageType**. Click **Close**.

   c. Resize the Field List so all fields can be seen.

   d. From the **tblFacilities** Field List, double-click **FacName** and **Beds**.

   e. From the **tblManageType** Field List, double-click **ManageType**.

   f. From the Quick Access toolbar, click **Save**. Name the query **qryNonProfitBeds**.

3. Add a criterion to a field by following these steps:

   a. In the **Criteria** row for **ManageType**, key *nonprofit*.

4. Sort and show the top 5 percent of records by following these steps:

   a. In the **Sort** row for **Beds**, click the drop-down arrow and choose **Descending**.

   b. From the **Design** tab, in the **Query Setup** group, click **Return** and then choose **5%**.

   c. Switch to **Datasheet View** to the see the resulting 6 records.

   d. Save and close the query.

Assessment

- According to your classroom procedure, turn in your database only when you have completed all assigned exercises.

-OR-

- Create a **Database Documenter** report for **qryNonProfitBeds** following these steps:

   a. From the **Database Tools** tab, in the **Analyze** group, click **Database Documenter**.

   b. In the **Documenter** dialog box, click the **Queries** tab and select **qryNonProfitBeds**. Click **Options**.

   c. For **Query**, include **Properties** and **SQL**.

   d. From the **Include for Fields** section, choose **Nothing**.

   e. From the **Include for Indexes** section, choose **Nothing**.

   f. Click **OK** twice to go to **Print Preview**.

- Save a **Database Documenter** report by following these steps:

   a. From the **Print Preview** tab, in the **Data** group, click **PDF or XPS**  to save the printout as a file.

   b. Save the file as a PDF and name the file *[your initials]*-06-24-A.

   c. Depending on your class procedures, print or turn in the PDF file.

   d. Close **Print Preview**.

06-24-A.pdf
1 Page

Exercise 6-25

Create a PivotChart to display the number of leave dates taken by employees.

1. The database *[your initials]*-**EcoMed-06** is required to complete this exercise.

   a. Open and enable content for *[your initials]*-**EcoMed-06**.

2. Create a query in **Design View** by following these steps:

   a. From the **Create** tab, in the **Queries** group, click **Query Design** .

   b. In the **Show Table** dialog box, double-click **tblEmployees** and **tblLeaveDays**. Click **Close**.

c. Resize the Field List so all fields can be seen.

d. From the **tblEmployees** Field List, double-click **JobCode**.

e. From the **tblLeaveDays** Field List, double-click **LeaveDate** and **LeaveCategory**.

f. From the Quick Access toolbar, click **Save** 🔲. Name the query **qryEmpLeaveChart**.

3. Add a criterion by following these steps:

a. In the **Criteria** row for **JobCode**, key m*.

4. Modify a PivotChart view by following these steps:

a. Switch to **PivotChart View**. From the **Chart Field List**, click the Expand button for **LeaveDate By Month**. Drag the **Months** into the **Drop Category Fields Here** zone (bottom of the chart) of the PivotChart.

b. From the **Chart Field List**, drag the **LeaveCategory** into the **Drop Series Fields Here** zone (right of the chart) of the PivotChart.

c. From the **Chart Field List**, drag the **LeaveCategory** into the **Drop Data Fields Here** zone (middle of the chart) of the PivotChart. The default function for this data type is **Count**.

d. Close the **Chart Field List**. From the **Design** tab, in the **Tools** group, click **Property Sheet** 🔳.

e. On the PivotChart, click the Value Axis Title (left of the chart). In the **Properties** dialog box, click the **Format** tab. Change the **Caption** property to **Number of Days**.

f. On the PivotChart, click the Category Axis Title (bottom of the chart). In the **Properties** dialog box, change the **Caption** property to **Year to Date**. Close the **Properties** dialog box.

g. From the **Design** tab, in the **Show/Hide** group, click **Drop Zone** 🔳 to remove the zone markers.

h. From the **Design** tab, in the **Show/Hide** group, click **Legend** 🔳 to add the **Legend** to the PivotChart.

i. Save the query.

Assessment

- According to your classroom procedure, turn in your database only when you have completed all assigned exercises.

-OR-

- Save a query's **PivotChart View** by following these steps:

a. Click the **File** tab. From the **Print** option, choose **Print Preview** 🔍.

b. From the **Print Preview** tab, in the **Page Layout** group, click **Landscape** 🔳.

c. From the **Print Preview** tab, in the **Data** group, click **PDF or XPS** 🔳 to save the printout as a file.

d. Save the file as a PDF and name the file *[your initials]*-06-25-A.

e. Depending on your class procedures, print or turn in the PDF file.

f. Close **Print Preview** and the query.

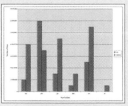

06-25-A.pdf
1 Page

- Create a **Database Documenter** report for **qryEmpLeaveChart** following these steps:

   a. From the **Database Tools** tab, in the **Analyze** group, click **Database Documenter**.

   b. In the **Documenter** dialog box, click the **Queries** tab and select **qryIntern**. Click **Options**.

   c. For **Query**, include **Properties** and **SQL**.

   d. From the **Include for Fields** section, choose **Nothing**.

   e. From the **Include for Indexes** section, choose **Nothing**.

   f. Click **OK** twice to go to **Print Preview**.

- Save a **Database Documenter** report by following these steps:

   a. From the **Print Preview** tab, in the **Data** group, click **PDF or XPS** 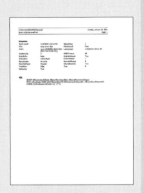 to save the printout as a file.

   b. Save the file as a PDF and name the file *[your initials]*-06-25-B.

   c. Depending on your class procedures, print or turn in the PDF file.

   d. Close **Print Preview**.

06-25-B.pdf
1 Page

Lesson Applications

Exercise 6-26

Create a query to display the name of the management company, the name of the facility, and the state in which the facility is located. Display only records from region 2.

1. Open and enable *[your initials]*-EcoMed-06.
2. Launch the Simple Query Wizard.
3. From **tblManagement** use the fields **ManageName**.
4. From **tblFacilities** use the fields **FacName**, **State**, and **Region**.
5. Save the query as **qryRegion2**.
6. Sort the dynaset in ascending order by **ManageName**.
7. Only show records that are from **Region** 2.
8. Review the 9 records. Save and close the query.

Assessment

- According to your classroom procedure, turn in your database only when you have completed all assigned exercises.

-OR-

- Create a **Database Documenter** report for **qryRegion2** using the following settings:
  - Include for Query: **Properties**, **SQL**
  - Include for Fields: **Nothing**
  - Include for Indexes: **Nothing**
- Save the **Documenter** report as a PDF file named *[your initials]*-06-26-A.
- According to your class procedures, print or turn in the PDF file.

06-26-A.pdf
1 Page

Exercise 6-27

Create a query to display the names and addresses of your employees. Display the city, state, and zip code of the employees in a format that can be used on mailing labels.

1. Using *[your initials]*-EcoMed-06, create a new query in Design View.
2. From **tblEmployees**, add the fields **FirstName**, **LastName**, **Address**, **City**, **State**, and **PostalCode**.
3. Save the query as **qryEmpAddress**.
4. Create a calculated field that will concatenate **FirstName** and **LastName** with a space between the fields.

5. Change the alias of the first calculated field to FullName.

6. Create a calculated field that will concatenate **City**, **State**, and **PostalCode** using ", " between **City** and **State** and two spaces between **State** and **PostalCode**.

7. Change the alias of the second calculated field to Address2.

8. Sort the dynaset in descending order by **LastName**.

9. Display only the fields **FullName**, **Address**, and **Address2** in this order.

Assessment

- According to your classroom procedure, turn in your database only when you have completed all assigned exercises.

-OR-

- Create a Database Documenter report for **qryEmpAddress** using the following settings:

- Include for Query: Properties, SQL
- Include for Fields: Nothing
- Include for Indexes: Nothing

- Save the Documenter report as a PDF file named *[your initials]*-06-27-A.
- According to your class procedures, print or turn in the PDF file.

06-27-A.pdf
1 Page

Exercise 6-28

Create a query to display names and job codes of employees. Also include the leave categories and leave dates. Convert the query to a PivotChart.

1. Using *[your initials]*-EcoMed-06, create a new query in Design View.

2. Include **tblEmployees** and **tblLeaveDays**.

3. From **tblEmployees**, add **LastName**, **FirstName**, and **JobCode**.

4. From **tblLeaveDays**, add **LeaveCategory** and **LeaveDate**.

5. Name the query qryLeaveByJob.

6. Create a PivotChart, using the following settings:

- Add **JobCode** to the x-axis.
- Add **LeaveCategory** to the Legend. Add the Legend to the chart.
- Add **LeaveDate** to the Data area of the chart with a default function of Count.
- Rename the x-axis Job Codes-*[your full name]*.
- Rename the y-axis to Count.
- Remove the drop zones.

Assessment

- According to your classroom procedure, turn in your database only when you have completed all assigned exercises.

-OR-

- Save the **PivotChart View** in Landscape as a PDF. Name the file *[your initials]*-06-28-A.
- According to your class procedures, print or turn in the PDF file.

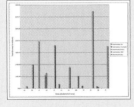

06-28-A.pdf
1 Page

Exercise 6-29 ◆ Challenge Yourself

Create a PivotChart to the revenue of facilities in relationship to the type of management structure to which the facility reports.

1. Using *[your initials]*-EcoMed-06, create a new query in **Design View**.
2. Include **tblManagement**, **tblFacilities**, and **tblManageType**.
3. From **tblManagement**, add **ManageName**.
4. From **tblManageType**, add **ManageType**.
5. From **tblFacilities**, add **FacName**, **State**, and **Revenue**.
6. Only show records that have any governmental **ManageType**.
7. Save the query as **qryGovRevChart**.
8. Add a calculated field named **Rev** that will divide the **Revenue** by 1 million (1,000,000).
9. Create a PivotChart, using the following settings:

   - Add **State** to the x-axis.
   - Add **ManageType** to the **Legend**. Add the **Legend** to the chart.
   - Add **Rev** to the **Data** area with a default function of **SUM**.
   - Rename the x-axis to **States-***[your full name]*.
   - Rename the y-axis to **Total Revenue (In Millions)**.
   - Remove the drop zones.

06-29-A.pdf
1 Page

Assessment

- Save and close the query.
- According to your classroom procedure, turn in your database only when you have completed all assigned exercises.

-OR-

- Save the **PivotChart View** in Landscape as a PDF. Name the file *[your initials]*-06-29-A.
- According to your class procedures, print or turn in the PDF file.

06-29-B.pdf
1 Page

- Save and close the query.
- Create a Database Documenter report for **qryGovRevChart** using the following settings:

  • Include for Query: Properties, SQL
  • Include for Fields: Nothing
  • Include for Indexes: Nothing

- Save the Documenter report as a PDF file named *[your initials]* **-06-29-B**.
- According to your class procedures, print or turn in the PDF file.

On Your Own

In these exercises you work on your own, as you would in a real-life work environment. Use the skills you've learned to accomplish the task—and be creative.

Exercise 6-30

Review the design of the database that you modified in Exercise 5-28. On a sheet of paper, list information that a user of your database might need. Design three queries that might provide the information needed. Use a variety of query types. Write your name and Exercise 6-30. Before proceeding to the next exercise, have your instructor approve your database design and intentions. Continue to the next exercise.

Exercise 6-31

Create the queries you designed in Exercise 6-30. Enter at least five additional records into each table of the database. Print the tables. Review the design of the database. On a sheet of paper, design a dynaset that incorporates data from two or more tables. Identify the type of query needed to create the dynaset. On the same sheet of paper, list all fields to be used in the query. For each field, include the name of the table from which the field originates. Identify the key fields and any foreign fields. Write down the criteria that would be required for the query. Name the query appropriately. Write your name and Exercise 6-31 on each sketch. Continue to the next exercise.

Exercise 6-32

Based on the designs that you created in Exercises 6-30 and 6-31, create the queries. Print the definitions for each query. Print a copy of the dynaset for each query. Submit to your instructor the designs and printouts that you created for Exercises 6-30 through 6-32. Keep a copy of the database you modified in this exercise. You will use it for the On Your Own exercises in subsequent lessons.

Lesson 7
Adding and Modifying Forms

OBJECTIVES   *After completing this lesson, you will be able to:*

1. Generate forms quickly.

2. Modify controls in Layout View

3. Work with form sections.

4. Modify controls in Design View.

5. Add calculated controls to a form.

6. Print/save forms.

Estimated Time: 2 hours

Although you can enter, edit, and delete data directly in the datasheet of a query or table, most often database operators will use forms to perform these activities. When you use the Datasheet View of a table or a query, the dynaset can display only in columns and rows. In Datasheet View, when each record of the dynaset contains numerous fields, the entire record cannot be seen on one screen.

The limitations of a datasheet emphasize the need for forms. A form can be designed to view an entire record on a single screen. Other advantages of forms include:

- You can arrange data in an attractive format that may include special fonts, colors, shading, and images.

- You can design a form to match a paper source document.

- You can include calculations, functions, and totals in the form.

- You can display data from more than one table.

Generating Forms Quickly

The quickest way to create a form is to use the Form Wizard or use a tool in the Forms Group. When using the Form Wizard, select the source dynaset(s), fields, layout, and style. The fields may be from multiple tables or queries, as long as a relationship exists between the recordsets.

When using a tool, all fields from the source dynaset are automatically placed on the form. You can use the new form immediately, or you can modify the form in Layout View or Design View. Database designers often use either the Wizard or a tool in the Forms group to create a beginning form that they can later modify and enhance.

Exercise 7-1   CREATE A FORM WITH A WIZARD

The Form Wizard lets you select fields, a layout, and a style. The layout determines whether the records are arranged in columns, rows, or a hybrid of columns and rows. The style automatically sets the colors, background, and fonts used for the form.

You will now create a form based on the facility beds query. The form will include all fields in the query except for the Web site hyperlink.

1. Locate and open the **Lesson 07** folder.

2. Make a copy of **EcoMed-07** and rename it *[your initials]*-**EcoMed-07**.

3. Open and enable content for *[your initials]*-**EcoMed-07**.

4. From the **Create** tab, in the **Forms** group, click **Form Wizard** 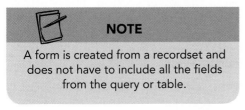.

NOTE

A form is created from a recordset and does not have to include all the fields from the query or table.

Figure 7-1
Form Wizard dialog box
EcoMed-07.accdb

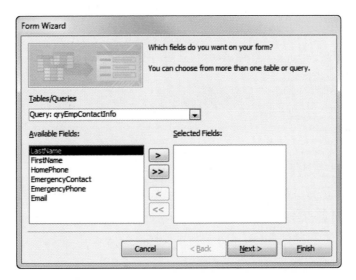

5. In the **Tables/Queries** drop-down box choose **Query: qryFacBeds**.

6. The dialog box asks which fields to use on the form. Click the Add All button [>>] to choose all fields.

7. In the **Selected Fields** list, click **WebSite**. Click the Remove One button 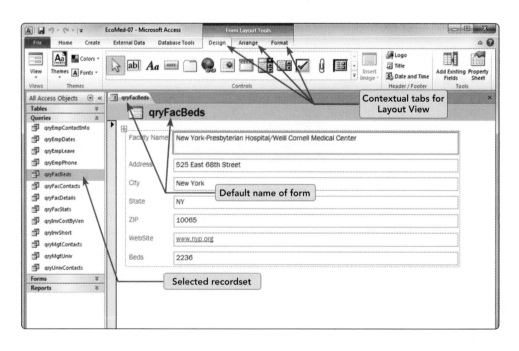 to move it back to the list on the left.

8. Click **Next**. The dialog box asks you to choose a layout. Click each layout to see a preview. Select **Tabular**.

9. Click **Next**. The dialog box asks for a title for the form. This title is used both as a title and as the name of the form. Key **frmFacBeds**.

10. Select **Open the form to view or enter information** and then click **Finish**.

11. The form shows all 164 records, each on one row. Close the form.

Exercise 7-2   GENERATE A FORM WITH ONE CLICK

When using the Forms tool, you can create a Simple Form, Split Form, or Multiple Items Form by selecting the appropriate command button located in the Forms group. Each command uses all the fields in the source recordset to create a predetermined form.

The Simple Form tool creates a form for entering one record at a time. The Split Form tool creates a form that shows the datasheet of the source recordset in the upper section and a form in the lower section. The Multiple Items tool creates a form that shows multiple items in a datasheet, with one record per row.

1. In the **Navigation Pane**, select **qryFacBeds**.

2. From the **Create** tab, in the **Forms** group, click **Form** 📇. The new form is now in **Layout View**, showing only one record.

Figure 7-2
New form in
Layout View
**EcoMed-07.accdb
frmFacBeds**

REVIEW

When creating a new form, you should use the Leszynski Naming Conventions. This method means forms are preceded by the prefix "frm," and the first letter of main words are capitalized with no spaces between words.

3. Right-click the new form's document tab and choose **Save**. The default name is the name of the recordset used to create the form.

4. In the **Save As** dialog box, key **frmFacBedsOne** and click **OK**.

5. In the **Navigation Pane**, select **qryFacBeds** again.

6. From the **Create** tab, in the **Forms** group, click **More Forms** 📇 and choose **Split Form** ▦. The new form is now in **Layout View**, showing one record at the top and the recordset at the bottom.

7. From the Quick Access toolbar, click **Save** 🖫 to save the new form.

8. In the **Save As** dialog box, key **frmFacBedsSplit** and click **OK**.

9. In the **Navigation Pane**, select **qryFacBeds** again.

10. From the **Create** tab, in the **Forms** group, click **More Forms** 📇 and choose **Multiple Items Form** ▦. The new form is now in **Layout View**, showing all records.

11. Press `Ctrl`+`S` to save the new form.

12. In the **Save As** dialog box, key **frmFacBedsList** and click **OK**.

13. In the **Navigation Pane**, select **qryFacBeds** again.

14. From the **Create** tab, in the **Forms** group, click **More Forms** 📇 and choose **Datasheet** ▦. The new form is now in **Datasheet View** showing all records. Even though this form looks like the **Datasheet View** of a table, it does not store data.

15. Press `Ctrl`+`S` to save the new form.

16. In the **Save As** dialog box, key **frmFacBedsData** and click **OK**.

17. Right-click any document tab and choose **Close All**.

Modifying Controls in Layout View

A *control* is a database object that displays data, performs actions, and allows you view and work with information. A control enhances the visual appearance of the interface, such as labels and images. Controls can be bound, unbound, or calculated.

A *bound control* is a control whose data source is a field in a table or query. You use bound controls to display values from the source recordset. The values can be text, dates, numbers, Yes/No values, pictures, and even graphs. An *unbound control* is a control without a source recordset. You use unbound controls to insert lines, symbols, or static pictures onto the form. A *calculated control* is a control whose data source is an expression rather than a field.

Exercise 7-3   MODIFY A CONTROL LAYOUT

Access uses a control layout function to group controls together. A control layout assists you to horizontally and vertically align grouped controls within a form. A control layout is similar to a table in which each cell is a control. A control layout has two controllable features: padding and a margin. *Control padding* is the space between the gridline of the form and the control. A *control margin* is the specified location of information inside a control.

1. From the **Navigation Pane**, right-click **frmFacilities** and choose **Layout View** . The layout of the controls is known as **Stacked**.

Figure 7-3
Form Layout View
**EcoMed-07.accdb
frmFacilities**

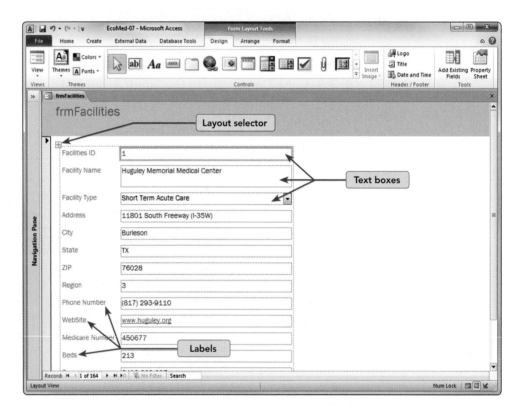

2. Click the **Layout Selector** to select the entire control layout.
3. From the **Arrange** tab, in the **Position** group, click **Control Padding** and choose **Narrow** . The space between all controls has been reduced.
4. From the **Arrange** tab, in the **Position** group, click **Control Padding** and choose **Medium** . The space between controls has increased.

Exercise 7-4   RESIZE AND MOVE CONTROL LAYOUTS

Whenever you are in the Layout View of an object, you can easily see how resizing or moving controls within a form will affect the visibility of the data.

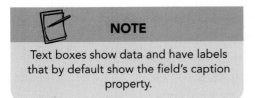

NOTE

Text boxes show data and have labels that by default show the field's caption property.

While viewing the source data on the form, you can rearrange the controls and adjust their sizes to improve the form's appearance and functionality.

1. Click the **Facility Name** text box. An orange box indicates the control is selected.

2. Place your mouse pointer on the right edge of the select text box. When you see the resize pointer, drag the control to make it smaller, but make sure all data can still be seen.

Figure 7-4
Resize a text box in Layout View
EcoMed-07.accdb frmFacilities

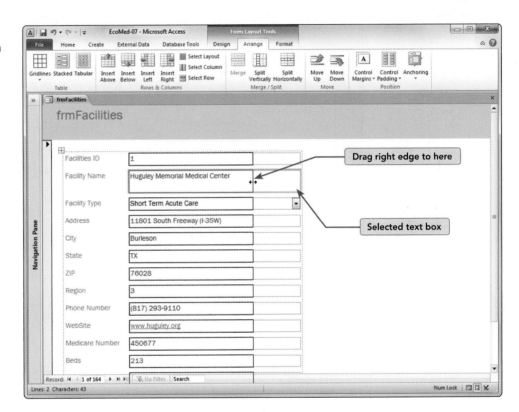

3. Click the **WebSite** label.

4. From the **Arrange** tab, in the **Rows & Columns** group, click **Select Row** to select both controls in the row.

5. While pressing Ctrl, click the labels for **Medicare Number**, **Beds**, **Revenue**, **Contact First Name**, and **Contact Last Name**.

6. From the **Arrange** tab, in the **Rows & Columns** group, click **Select Row** to select the six text boxes and their labels.

7. From the **Arrange** tab, in the **Table** group, click **Stacked** [icon]. The six controls have created their own control layout.

8. Click the **Layout Selector** [icon] for the new control layout and drag it to the right of the other control layout so that the top **Facilities ID** and **Website** controls are aligned.

Figure 7-5
Moving a control
layout
EcoMed-07.accdb
frmFacilities

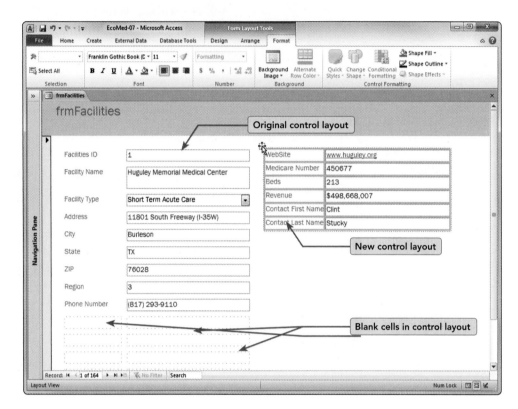

9. From the **Arrange** tab, in the **Position** group, click **Control Padding** [icon] and choose **Medium** [icon].

10. Save the form.

Exercise 7-5 ADD CELLS TO A CONTROL LAYOUT

Control layouts are like tables in Word and PowerPoint. In addition to inserting columns, you can also split and merge cells.

1. Click the **City** text box.
2. From the **Arrange** tab, in the **Merge/Split** group, click **Split Horizontally** ⊞. The **City** text box is now not as wide.
3. Click the blank cell to the right of the **City** text box.
4. From the **Arrange** tab, in the **Merge/Split** group, click **Split Horizontally** ⊞.

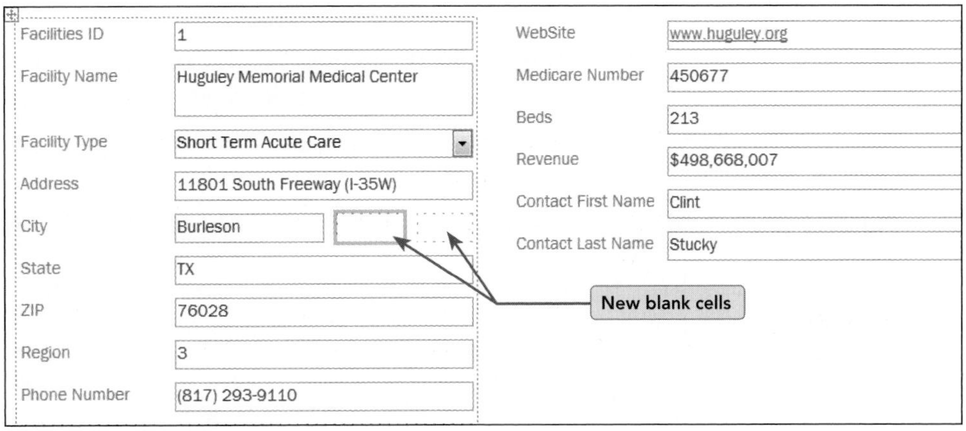

Figure 7-6
Adding cells to a control layout
EcoMed-07.accdb
frmFacilities

5. Click the **State** text box.
6. Left-click and drag the **State** text box to the blank cell to the right of the **City** text box. When the blank cell turns orange, release the mouse button.
7. Click the **ZIP** text box.
8. Left-click and drag the **ZIP** text box to the blank cell to the right of the **State** text box.
9. Click the **State** label and press [Delete].
10. Click the **ZIP** label and press [Delete].
11. Click the **City** label and press [Delete].
12. Save the form.

Exercise 7-6 ADD, DELETE, AND MOVE CONTROLS IN A CONTROL LAYOUT

A single form can have multiple control layouts. For example, you might have a tabular layout to create a row of data for each record, and then one or more stacked layouts underneath, containing more data from the same record.

In tabular control layouts, controls are arranged in rows and columns like a spreadsheet, with labels across the top. Tabular control layouts always span two sections of a form; whichever section the controls are in, the labels are in the section above.

In stacked layouts, controls are arranged vertically like you might see on a paper form, with a label to the left of each control. Stacked layouts are always contained within a single form section.

1. Click the **Region** label.

2. From the **Arrange** tab, in the **Rows & Columns** group, click **Select Row** ▦.

3. Press Delete to delete both controls from the layout.

4. Click the **WebSite** label. From the **Arrange** tab, in the **Rows & Columns** group, click **Select Row** ▦.

5. Drag the selected control to the blank cells above the **Phone Number** label.

6. Click the **Medicare Number** label. From the **Arrange** tab, in the **Rows & Columns** group, click **Select Row** ▦.

7. From the **Arrange** tab, in the **Move** group, click **Move Up** ⇗.

Figure 7-7
Move a control in a control layout
EcoMed-07.accdb
frmFacilities

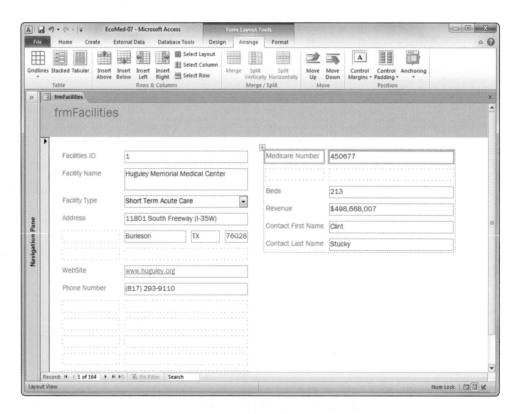

8. From the **Design** tab, in the **Tools** group, click **Add Existing Fields** ▦. The top panel contains the recordset (**tblFacilities**) on which this form is based and its fields.

9. From the top panel of the **Field List**, click and drag **MgtTypeID** between the **Revenue** and **Contact First Name** text boxes until you see an insertion point between the two controls.

Figure 7-8
Use the Field List to
add a field
**EcoMed-07.accdb
frmFacilities**

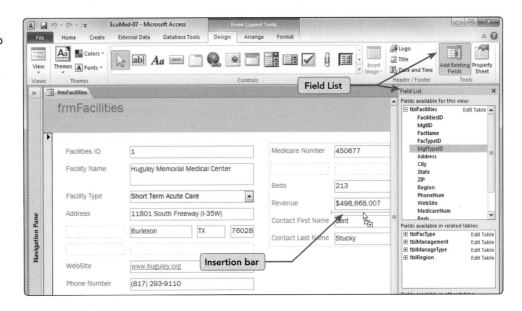

10. From the **Design** tab, in the **Tools** group, click **Add Existing Fields** to close the **Field List**.

11. From the **Arrange** tab, in the **Rows & Columns** group, click **Insert Below** to add a blank row in the control layout.

12. From the **Arrange** tab, in the **Rows & Columns** group, click **Insert Below** to insert a second blank row.

13. From the **Design** tab, in the **Header/Footer** group, click **Date and Time**.

Figure 7-9
Adding a Date and
Time control
**EcoMed-07.accdb
frmFacilities**

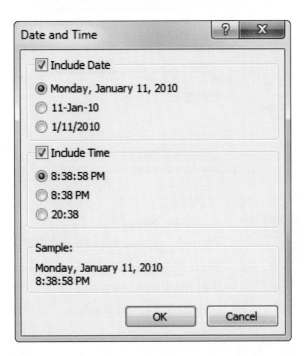

14. Click **OK**. The data and time control is added to the header of the form.

15. Save the form.

Exercise 7-7 SET TAB ORDER

Tab order is a form setting that determines the movement of the insertion point through a form. The tab order determines the order in which the insertion point moves from control to control. The usual tab order is top-to-bottom, left-to-right; however, you can change the order based on the layout of the form.

1. From the **Design** tab, in the **Views** group, choose **Form View** 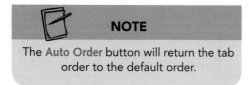.
2. Press [Home] to move the pointer to the first field. Press [Tab] to move through all the controls on the form. This order is the default tab order.
3. From the **Home** tab, in the **Views** group, choose **Design View** .
4. From the **Design** tab, in the **Tools** group, click **Tab Order** .
5. Click and drag the field selectors for **WebSite** through **PhoneNum**. Drag the two fields below **MgtTypeID**.

Figure 7-10
Tab Order dialog box
EcoMed-07.accdb
frmFacilities

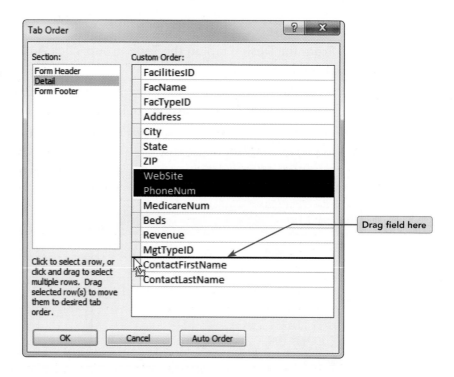

6. Click **OK**.
7. From the **Design** tab, in the **Views** group, click **Form View** to switch to **Form View**.

NOTE

The **Auto Order** button will return the tab order to the default order.

8. Press [Tab] to move from text box to text box. Notice that **Medicare Number** is now after **ZIP** in the tab order.
9. Switch to **Layout View**.

Exercise 7-8 FORMAT A FORM IN LAYOUT VIEW

You can easily refine the placement and size of controls through the Layout View. Layout View allows you to modify the properties of controls by viewing the source data in each control. In Layout View, you can navigate through the dynaset to determine the best layout for the controls.

1. Click below the label that contains the name of the form, "frmFacilities" and press Delete. The header of the form (purple background) reduces in height.
2. From the **Design** tab, in the **Header/Footer** group, click **Title** 🗐.
3. Key **Facility Information**. Press Enter.
4. Double-click the right edge of the title label to auto-size the label.

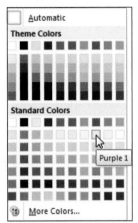

Figure 7-11
Selecting a standard color
EcoMed-07.accdb
frmFacilities

5. From the **Format** tab, in the **Font** group, click Font Color 🅰 and choose **Automatic**.
6. Click in the blank area below the **Contact Last Name** the controls.
7. From the **Format** tab, in the **Font** group, click Background Color 🎨.
8. From the **Standard Colors**, choose **Purple 1** (eighth column, second row).
9. Switch to **Form View**.
10. Save and close the form.

Working with Form Sections

A basic form contains controls only in a single detail section. Advanced forms use multiple sections. Some sections display on every screen or on every page if the form is printed. Other sections display only at specific times. The five form sections are:

- The Detail Section is part of a form or report that displays data once for every row in the record source. This section makes up the main body of the form or report.

- The Form Header Section is a section of a form that displays once at the beginning of a form. This section often is used to display objects that would appear on a cover page, such as a logo, title, or date.

- The Form Footer Section is a section of a form that appears once at the end of a form. This section often is used to display summary information such as totals.

- The Page Header Section is a section of a form that displays at the top of each printed page. This section often is used to display title information or page numbers to be repeated on each page.

- The Page Footer Section is a section of a form that displays at the bottom of each printed page. This section often is used to display title information or page numbers to be repeated on each page.

The Page Header Section and Page Footer Section can only be seen in Print Preview or when the form is printed. The sections that initially appear in a form depend on the type of form originally created.

Exercise 7-9   OPEN AND SIZE FORM SECTIONS

When you scroll through a form, the Form Header always displays at the top of the screen. The Form Footer always appears at the bottom of the screen. The values in the detail section will change based on the values in the recordset.

1. From the **Navigation Pane**, right-click **frmFacContacts** and choose **Design View** ☑. This form is using two sections: **Form Header** and **Detail**.

2. Place the mouse pointer on the top of the **Form Footer** section bars. When the pointer changes to a two-headed arrow, click and drag up to the 3-inch mark on the vertical ruler. You have resized the **Detail** section of the form.

3. Place the mouse pointer on the bottom of the **Form Footer** section bars. When the pointer changes to a two-headed arrow, click and drag down ½ inch.

Figure 7-12
Open a form section
EcoMed-07.accdb
frmFacContacts

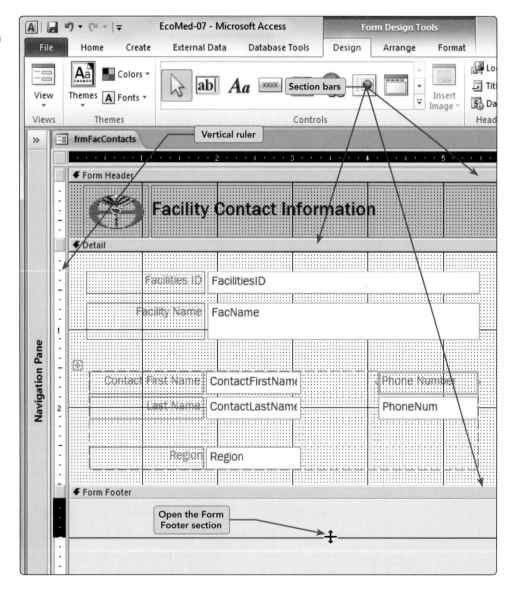

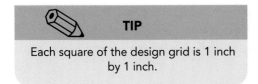

TIP

Each square of the design grid is 1 inch by 1 inch.

4. Right-click the **Detail** section bar and choose **Page Header/Footer** . This command adds two more sections.

Figure 7-13
All form sections expanded
**EcoMed-07.accdb
frmFacContacts**

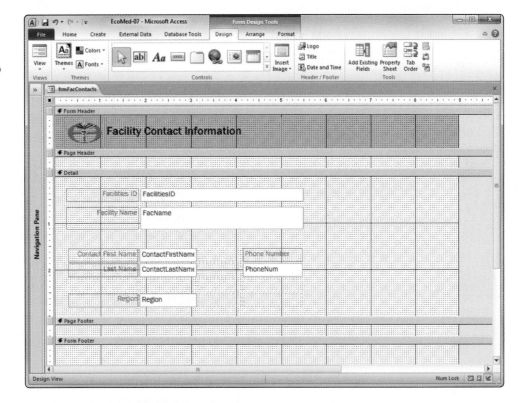

5. The width of the form is 9-inches. Click and drag the right edge of the form to the 7.5 inch mark.

6. Save the form.

Exercise 7-10 ADD LABELS AND VIEW FORM SECTIONS

The Label tool in the Toolbox is used to enter text or titles in a form. The text displayed in a label is independent of the recordset and does not change when a new record is displayed.

When you select a label or any other object, selection handles appear around the object. Selection handles are eight small rectangles around an active object. The top left selection handle is known as the Moving handle and is used to move the object without resizing it. The other seven handles are known as sizing handles. Sizing handles are any selection handles on a control except the top left one, used to adjust the height and width of the object.

1. From the **Design** tab, in the **Controls** group, click Label . The pointer changes to a crosshair mouse pointer with the letter A.

2. Place the pointer in the **Form Header** section at the 6-inch mark. Click and drag down and to the right to draw a box about 1.5 inches wide and around 5 dots tall. When you release the mouse button, you see the box with a text insertion point.

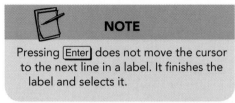

NOTE

Pressing Enter does not move the cursor to the next line in a label. It finishes the label and selects it.

3. Key **Form Header** and press Enter. The label box is selected and displays the eight selection handles around its edges.

Figure 7-14
Adding a label to the Form Header
EcoMed-07.accdb frmFacContacts

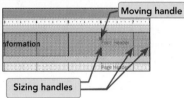

4. In the **Page Header** section, add a Label that is the same size as the one in the **Form Header** section. Key **Page Header** in the label.

5. In the **Page Footer** section, add a Label that is the same size as the one in the **Form Header** section. Key **Page Footer** in the label.

6. In the **Form Footer** section, add a Label that is the same size as the one in the **Form Header** section. Key **Form Footer** in the label.

7. Switch to **Form View**. The "Form Header" and "Form Footer" labels are visible.

8. Press PageDown to move to the next record. There is no change in the **Form Header** and **Form Footer** sections of the form.

9. Press Ctrl+End to move to the last record. There is no sign of the "Page Header" and "Page Footer."

10. Click the **File** tab, and from the **Print** option, click **Print Preview** 🔍. Click near the top of the preview to zoom in. You can see the "Form Header" and "Page Header" labels at the top of the first page.

11. Scroll down to see the "Page Footer" label at the bottom of the page.

12. In the **Page** navigation controls, click the **Last Record** button ⏭. After the last record, you can see the "Form Footer" label appear.

13. From the **Print Preview** tab, in the **Close Preview** group, click **Close Print Preview** ✖.

14. Close the form and save the changes.

Modifying Controls in Design View

NOTE

A form inherits the field properties of the table. Changes to the form's properties do not affect the table's properties.

Certain actions cannot be completed in Layout View. To perform these tasks, you will need to switch to Design View. Design View provides a different and more detailed view of the form's structure. In Design View, you can view the Header, Detail, and Footer sections. Unlike Layout View, when the form is in Design View, the form does not display the recordset data in each control.

Exercise 7-11   FORMAT A FORM IN DESIGN VIEW

When using Design View to modify the format of a form, you can often begin by selecting a predefined format.

1. From the **Navigation Pane**, right-click **frmInventory** and choose **Design View** .

2. Double-click the **Form Header** bar to open the **Property Sheet** for this section.

3. In the **Property Sheet**, on the **Format** tab, click the **Back Color** property. An drop-down arrow appears to the right of the property.

4. Click the drop-down arrow and choose **Access Theme 5**.

Figure 7-15
Assigning a theme
**EcoMed-07.accdb
frmInventory**

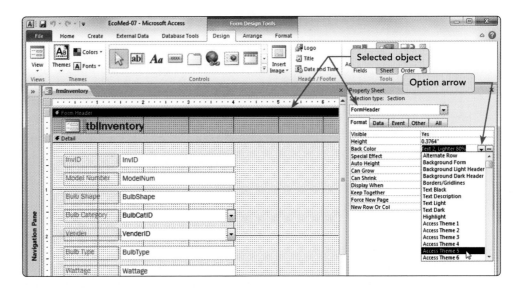

5. Click the **Detail** section bar. The **Property Sheet** now shows this object's properties.

6. In the **Property Sheet**, on the **Format** tab, click the **Back Color** property. Click the drop-down arrow and choose **Access Theme 2**.

7. Place your mouse pointer over the top edge of **InvID** text box. When a small black down arrow appears, click. All controls below the arrow are now selected.

Figure 7-16
Selecting multiple objects
**EcoMed-07.accdb
frmInventory**

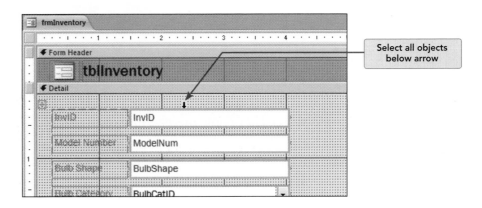

8. While pressing Ctrl, click the **Image** control to remove it from the selection.

9. Right-click the selected objects. From the pop-up menu, select **Special Effect** and choose Special Effects: Shadowed .

10. Click the **Detail** section to deselect the text box controls.

11. From the **Design** tab, in the **Header/Footer** group, click **Title** and key **Inventory Details**. Press Enter.

12. Right-click the **Title** label and select **Size** and choose **To Fit** .

13. From the **Design** tab, in the **Tools** group, click **Property Sheet** to close the **Property Sheet**.

14. Save the form.

Exercise 7-12   RESIZE AND MOVE CONTROLS

When resizing and moving controls, you can use the gridline marks in Design View. You can use the vertical and horizontal rulers to position the edges of each control. You will now add an image control to the form.

REVIEW

If you make an error deleting, sizing, or moving a control, click the Undo button and try again.

1. Click the **InvID** text box.

2. From the **Arrange** tab, in the **Rows & Columns** group, click **Insert Right** twice. This action creates two new columns of blank cells.

3. Click the **Image** control. Drag the **Image** control to the upper-right-most blank cell.

Figure 7-17
Moving a control
EcoMed-07.accdb
frmInventory

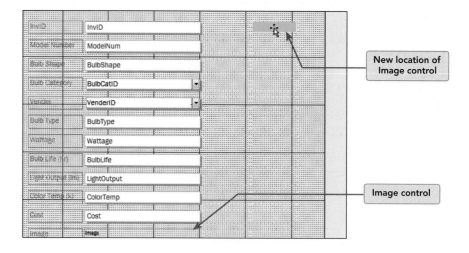

4. While pressing the Ctrl key, click the five blank cells just below the **Image** control.

5. From the **Arrange** tab, in the **Merge/Split** group, click **Merge** . The six selected cells are now merged into one cell.

6. Click any blank cell to the left of the **Image** control. Drag the right edge of the control left to the 4.5-inch mark on the horizontal ruler. This action reduces the width of the blank column.

Figure 7-18
Resizing a column
**EcoMed-07.accdb
frmInventory**

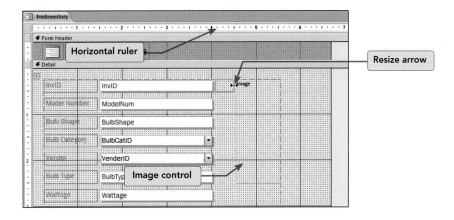

7. Click the **Image** control. Drag the right edge of the control right to the 6.75-inch mark on the horizontal ruler to widen the **Image** control and the column.

8. Click the **Image** control's label and press Delete. This action deletes the label but not the cell.

9. Click the blank cell where the **Image** label was located and press Delete. Because none of the cells in that row were being used, the whole row of blank cells was deleted.

10. Click the blank cell below the **Image** control. From the Arrange tab, in the Merge/Split group, click Split Horizontally .

11. Click the label and text box for the **Cost** control. Drag both controls to the right-most blank cell from the step above.

12. Click the **Wattage** text box. From the Arrange tab, in the Rows & Columns group, click Insert Above .

13. Switch to Form View.

Figure 7-19
New layout
**EcoMed-07.accdb
frmInventory**

14. Save the form.

Exercise 7-13   MODIFY PROPERTY SETTINGS

Every control has property settings. The property settings allow you to modify a control more precisely. For example, through the property settings, you can modify how an image will appear. The Picture Size Mode settings for an image include the following:

- Clip Mode sizes an image to its original size.
- Stretch Mode sizes an image to fit the control without regard to the proportions of the original image.
- Zoom mode sizes an image to fit the control while maintaining the proportions of the original image.

1. Switch to **Layout View** and click the **Image** control.
2. From the **Design** tab, in the **Tools** group, click **Property Sheet** 📇.
3. On the **Format** tab, click the **Picture Size Mode**. Click the drop-down arrow and choose **Clip**. This mode shows the image at normal size.
4. Change the **Picture Size Mode** to **Stretch**. This mode changes the shape of the image to make it fit the width and height of the control.
5. Change the **Picture Size Mode** to **Zoom**. This mode changes the size of the image until the image's width or height is the same as the controls.
6. In the **Property Sheet** for the **Image** control, click the **Picture Alignment** property.
7. Click the drop-down arrow and choose **Center**.
8. In the **Width** property, key **2.2**. This entry changes the width for all the cells in this column.
9. In the **Special Effect** property, choose **Shadowed**.
10. Switch to **Form View**. The image control now has the same effect as the other controls.
11. Switch to **Design View** and save the form.

Exercise 7-14   ADD A LABEL

Adding a label to a form helps identify the entire form or aspects of the form. For example, you might add a label to identify the department for which the form was created or a date on which the form was last modified.

1. Drag the bottom of the **Form Footer** section down ½ inch.
2. From the **Design** tab, in the **Controls** group, click Label **Aa**.
3. Place the pointer in the **Form Footer** section around the ¼-inch mark on the horizontal ruler. Click and key **Prepared by:** *[your full name]*.
4. Click the **Form Footer** bar. In the **Property Sheet**, change the property **Back Color** to **Access Theme 2**.
5. Close the **Property Sheet**.
6. Switch to **Form View** to see your new label.
7. Save the form.

Adding Calculated Controls to a Form

Access allows you to use a standardized format using a theme. A *theme* is a set of unified design elements and color schemes for bullets, fonts, horizontal lines, background images, and other elements of a database object. Using themes helps you create professional and consistent forms and reports.

Exercise 7-15 ADD UNBOUND TEXT BOXES

Although any control that has a Control Source property can be used as a calculated control, an unbound text box is the easiest control to change into a calculated control. You will now create a calculated control to calculate the retail price of items. First you must add an unbound text box to the form.

1. Switch to **Layout View** for **frmInventory**.

2. Click in the blank cell under the **Cost** control.

3. From the **Arrange** tab, in the **Merge/Split** group, click **Split Horizontally** ▦. The size of the new cells match the **Cost** controls.

4. From the **Design** tab, in the **Controls** group, click **Text Box** 🔲. The pointer changes to a crosshair mouse pointer with the letters "ab."

5. Hover your mouse over blank cells in the layout. An orange box appears in the potential location of the new control. Click the blank cell below the **Cost** text box control.

6. Adding an unbound text box also means that you receive a label to the left of the text box. Double-click the new label and replace the text with **Retail**.

Figure 7-20
New unbound text box added
EcoMed-07.accdb frmInventory

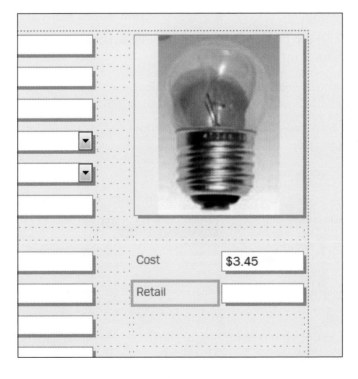

7. Save the form.

Exercise 7-16   ADD A CALCULATED CONTROL

You can use a calculated control to display the solution to a calculation. The calculation can be an expression or a function. For example, if you have a form displaying the number of items sold and the unit price for each item, you can add a calculated control to multiply the two fields and display a total price. In this example, you calculate the retail price of items. The retail price is 48 percent above the unit cost or 1.48 times the unit cost.

1. Switch to **Design View**.

2. Double-click the unbound text box to display its **Property Sheet**. Click the **Data** tab.

3. Click the **Control Source** property; read the description of this property in the status bar.

4. To the right of the control source property, you can see the Build button. The Build button appears as an ellipsis. Click the Build button ⊡ to open the **Expression Builder** dialog box.

5. In the **Expression Elements** panel, your **frmInventory** form is shown as the current object at the top of the list.

6. The object **frmInventory** is selected in the **Expression Elements** panel. In the **Expression Categories** panel, click the field **<Field List>**.

REVIEW

Square brackets are used to surround field names.

7. In the **Expression Values** panel is a list of fields from this form's recordset. Double-click **Cost** to paste the value of the **Cost** field to the Expression box.

8. In the **Expression Elements** panel, click **Operators**.

9. In the **Expression Values** panel, double-click "*" (asterisk).

10. In the Expression box, key **1.48** as the numerical equivalent for a markup of 48 percent.

Figure 7-21
Expression Builder with an expression **EcoMed-07.accdb frmInventory**

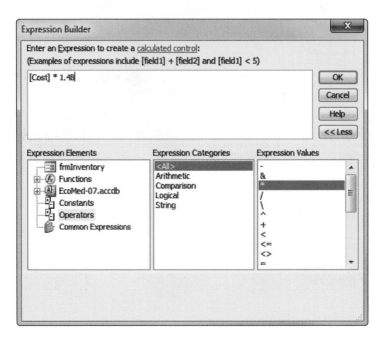

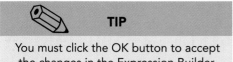

TIP

You must click the OK button to accept the changes in the Expression Builder.

11. Click **OK** to close the **Expression Builder**. The equation appears in the unbound text box.

12. Click the **Format** tab in the **Property Sheet**. Click the **Format** property and its drop-down arrow. Choose **Currency**.

13. Click the **Text Align** property. Click the option arrow and choose **Right**.

14. Click the **Cost** text box. Change its **Text Align** property to **Right**.

15. Close the **Property Sheet** and switch to **Form View**.

16. Press ⌈PageDown⌋ to view a few records.

Figure 7-22
Completed form
EcoMed-07.accdb
frmInventory

frmInventory		

Inventory Details

InvID	2	
Model Number	TT74-150-G	
Bulb Shape	A-line	
Bulb Category	Diagnostic	
Vender	Unio Lighting	
Bulb Type	Halogen	

Wattage	150	Cost	$39.00
Bulb Life (hr)	30	Retail	$57.72
Light Output (lm)	2400		
Color Temp (k)	3350		

Prepared by: [Student's full name]

17. Save and close the form.

Printing/Saving Forms

Although forms are designed to view data on a screen, on occasion you may need to print a form. If you choose to print the entire form, all records will display. Each record may display on a single page, on multiple pages, or on a portion of a page, depending on the size of the form and the size of the paper on which you print.

When printing a form, the Page Header section and Page Footer section will print on each vertical page. If a form is wider than the paper width, a single page of the form may print on two or more pages of paper. You can change the width of the form and the margins of the page to optimize the print quality of a form.

Prior to printing, you can select a single record. When you select a single record, you cannot use Print Preview. With forms, Print Preview can only be used when printing or saving all records or a range of printable pages.

Exercise 7-17   PRINT SPECIFIC PAGES

As with other Office applications, such as Word, you can print a specific page or range of pages. When printing a specific range of pages, you must enter a single page number, a list of page numbers separated by commas, or a page range including the first page through the last page.

1. From the Navigation Pane, double-click **frmVenderList**.

2. Click the File tab and from the Print option, click Print Preview 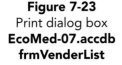.

3. From the Print Preview tab, in the Zoom group, click Two Pages. This form shows all records on two pages.

4. From the Print Preview tab, in the Print group, click Print.

5. In the Print dialog box, in the Print Range section, choose Pages.

6. In the From control, key 1. The To control is now active.

Figure 7-23
Print dialog box
EcoMed-07.accdb
frmVenderList

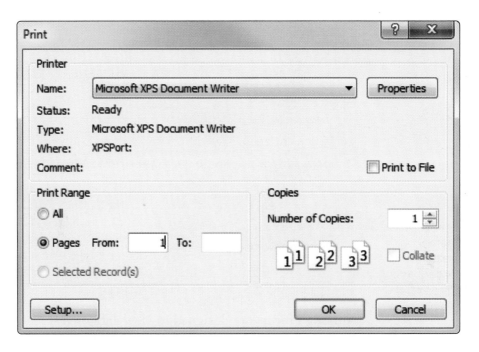

7. Click the To control and key 1.

8. Based on your classroom procedure, you can either print the form or cancel the print process. To cancel, click Cancel. To print the form, click OK. If you are uncertain, ask your instructor.

9. From the Print Preview tab, in the Close Preview group, click Close Print Preview.

10. Save the form.

Exercise 7-18 PRINT ONE RECORD

When printing a single record, you must first select the record through the form. You cannot select to print a single record through the Options in the Print or Print Preview commands.

1. In the **Form View** of **frmVender**, press PageDown until you reach the record for the vender "AnyBulb."

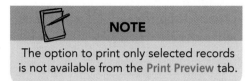

NOTE

The option to print only selected records is not available from the **Print Preview** tab.

2. Click the record selector on the left side of the form. The record selector is very tall in this form because the form is set to only show one record at one time.

3. Click the **File** tab and from the **Print** option, click **Print** 🖶.

4. In the **Print** dialog box, in the **Print Range** section, choose **Selected Record(s)**.

5. Based on your classroom procedure, you can either print the form or cancel the print process. To cancel, click **Cancel**. To print the form, click **OK**. If you are uncertain, ask your instructor.

Exercise 7-19 PRINT MULTIPLE RECORDS

Similar to printing a single record, you can print a contiguous range of records. The order in which the multiple records will print depends on how the dynaset is sorted.

1. Switch to **frmVenderList** in **Form View**.

2. Click the record selectors for **Vender ID** 1.

3. Drag down to **Vender ID** 4. These are all the venders whose names start with "A."

Figure 7-24
Multiple records selected
EcoMed-07.accdb
frmVenderList

4. Click the **File** tab and from the **Print** option, click **Print** 🖶.

5. In the **Print** dialog box, in the **Print Range** section, choose **Selected Record(s)**.

6. Based on your classroom procedure, you can either print the form or cancel the print process. To cancel, click **Cancel**. To print the form, click **OK**. If you are uncertain, ask your instructor.

Exercise 7-20   SAVE A RECORD

Just as with other major objects, a form can be saved as a PDF or XPS file. To save a single record or range of records through a form, the record or records first must be selected. The process for saving a single record is the same process that you would use for saving a range of records.

1. Switch to the form **frmVender**.
2. Press PageDown until you reach the vender "Cobra."
3. Click the record selector on the left side of the form.
4. Click the **File** tab and from the **Save & Publish** option, click **Save Object As** 🖺.
5. In the **Database File Types** section, double-click **PDF or XPS**.
6. In the **Publish as PDF or XPS** dialog box, click the **Options** button
7. In the **Options** dialog box, in the **Range** section, click **Selected records** and click **OK**.

Figure 7-25
Saving selected records as a PDF
EcoMed-07.accdb
frmVender

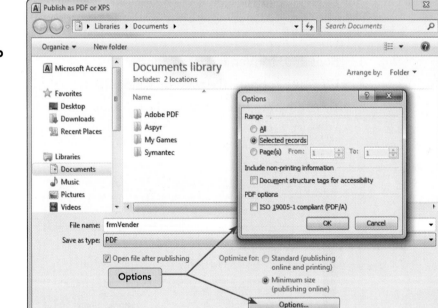

8. Change the location to match where you will be storing your work.
9. Name the file **07-20-10**.
10. Verify that the file type is **PDF** and click **Publish**.
11. Close both forms.
12. Compact and close the database.

Lesson 7   Summary

- A form can be designed to view an entire record on a single screen.
- A form can include calculations, functions, and totals.
- The quickest way to create a form is to use the Form Wizard or a tool in the Forms group.
- The Form Wizard lets you select fields, a layout, and a style.
- When using the Forms tool, you can create a Simple Form, Split Form or Multiple Items Form by selecting the appropriate command button located in the Forms group.
- A control is a database object that displays data, performs actions, or controls user interface information, such as labels and images. Controls can be bound, unbound, or calculated.
- A control layout assists you to horizontally and vertically align the controls within a form. A single form can have multiple control layouts.
- In Layout View of a form, you can rearrange and adjust the size of controls to improve the form's appearance and functionality.
- In Layout View, you can navigate through the dynaset to determine the best layout for the controls.
- Aligning a control is different than aligning the text within a control. Aligning the text within a control does not move the placement of the control on the form, only the contents of the control.
- The five sections of a form include Detail, Form Header, Form Footer, Page Header, and Page Footer sections.
- The Page Header section and Page Footer section can be seen in Print Preview or when the form is printed.
- When you select a label or any other object, selection handles appear around the object.
- When resizing and moving controls, you can use the gridline marks, vertical ruler, and horizontal ruler to position the edges of each control.
- The property settings of a control allow you to more precisely modify a control.
- A Picture Size Mode can be set to Clip, Stretch or Zoom modes.
- A label control is only associated with the major object to which it is attached.
- An unbound text box is the easiest control to change to a calculated control.
- A calculated control can contain an expression or a function.
- When printing a form, the Page Header section and Page Footer section will print on each vertical page.
- When printing a specific range of pages, you must enter a single page number, a list of page numbers separated by commas, or a page range including the first page through the last page.

- To print a single record, first you must select the record through the form. You cannot select to print a single record or range of records through the Options in the Print or Print Preview commands.
- The order in which multiple records will print depends on how the dynaset is sorted.

LESSON 7		Command Summary	
Feature	**Button**	**Path**	**Keyboard**
Controls, Date and Time		Design, Header/Footer, Date and Time	
Controls, Padding		Arrange, Position Control Padding	
Controls, Special Effects		Right-click control, Special Effects	
Controls, Tab Order		Design, Tools, Tab Order	
Controls, Text Box, Add		Design, Controls, Text Box	
Controls, Title		Design, Header/Footer, Title	
Fields, Background Color		Format, Font, Background Color	
Fields, Font Color		Format, Font, Font Color	
Fields, Remove One		Remove One	
Fields, Size to Fit		Right-click control, Size, To Fit	
Form View		Home, Views, Form View	
Form, Add New Column		Arrange, Rows & Columns, Insert Left or Insert Right	
Form, Add New Row		Arrange, Rows & Columns, Insert Above or Insert Below	
Form, Control Layout Selector		Arrange, Rows & Columns, Selector Layout	
Form, Create, Datasheet Form		Create, Forms, More Forms, Datasheet Form	
Form, Create, Multiple Form		Create, Forms, More Forms, Multiple Form	
Form, Create, Split Form		Create, Forms, More Forms, Split Form	

continues

LESSON 7		Command Summary	
Feature	**Button**	**Path**	**Keyboard**
Form, More Forms		Create, Forms, More Forms	
Form, Move control		Arrange, Move, Move Up or Move Down	
Form, Save As		File, Save As	
Form, View Page Header/Footer		Right-click section bar, Page Header/Footer	
Form, Wizard		Create, Forms, More Forms, Form Wizard	
Label, Add		Design, Controls, Label	
Layout, Merge Cells		Arrange, Merge/Split, Merge	
Layout, Select Row		Arrange, Rows & Columns, Select Row	
Layout, Split Horizontally		Arrange, Merge/Split, Split Horizontally	
Layout, Stacked		Arrange, Table, Stacked	
Print Preview, Two Pages		File, Print, Print Preview, Zoom, Two Pages	

Concepts Review

True/False Questions

Each of the following statements is either true or false. Indicate your choice by circling T or F.

T F 1. As you move controls on a form, the tab order adjusts so controls are always in left-to-right and top-to-bottom order.

T F 2. Every form contains a main section and a subsection.

T F 3. A Multiple Items Form shows multiple items in a datasheet, displaying one record per row.

T F 4. Control padding is the specified location of information inside a control.

T F 5. Aligning a control is the same as aligning the text within a control.

T F 6. The Page Header section of a form displays at the top of each printed page.

T F 7. The top left selection handle is known as the Moving handle and is used to move the object without resizing it.

T F 8. A label is associated with the data stored in the record source.

Short Answer Questions

Write the correct answer in the space provided.

1. What section on a form displays data for each record?

_____

2. What type of information might be displayed in the Form Header section?

_____

3. Which command do you use when adding a calculated control to a form?

_____

4. What opens when you click the Build button 🔲 in a form?

_____

5. What is the name of the Picture Size Mode setting that sizes an image to its original size?

_____

6. What determines where the insertion pointer moves when you press Tab in a form?

_____

7.   What command changes the text color in a label or a text box?

_____

8.   When you select a label, what appears around the object?

_____

Critical Thinking

Answer these questions on a separate page. There are no right or wrong answers. Support your answers with examples from your own experience, if possible.

1.   You can add, edit, delete, and search records through a datasheet of a table or query. When would it be more appropriate to use a form rather than a datasheet? When would it be more appropriate to use a datasheet?

2.   In this lesson, you were introduced to some ideas about designing forms. What design principles should be followed when creating forms? How would the design differ from printed reports? Would the form design be different based upon the database user's skill level and the confidentiality of the data?

Skills Review

Exercise 7-21

You have been asked to create a form that uses qryEmpDates to display, enter and edit employee information.

1.   Open a database by following these steps:
     a. Locate and open the **Lesson 07** folder.
     b. If you already have a copy of *[your initials]*-EcoMed-07, skip to step 1d.
     c. Make a copy of **EcoMed-07** and rename it *[your initials]*-EcoMed-07.
     d. Open and enable content for *[your initials]*-EcoMed-07.

2.   Create a multiple record form by following these steps:
     a. In the Navigation Pane, select **qryEmpDates**.
     b. From the Create tab, in the Forms group, click More Forms 🖺 and choose Multiple Items 🖼.
     c. From the Quick Access toolbar, click Save 🖫 to save the new form.
     d. Name the new form frmEmpDates.

3.   Format a form in Layout View by following these steps:
     a. From the Design tab, in the Header/Footer group, click Title 🖾.
     b. Replace the old title with EcoMed's Employee Dates.
     c. Click the first text box under the "Last Name" label.

d. Hover your mouse over the bottom edge of the text box until you see a double-arrow. Click and drag up until you have reduced the height of the control by half.

e. Click the **First Name** label.

f. From the Arrange tab, in the Rows & Columns group, click **Insert Right** .

g. Press Ctrl+S to save the changes to the form.

4. Select multiple records in a form by following these steps:

a. Switch to Form View.

b. Click the record selector for the first record and drag through the record for "Dyer." You should have 8 records selected.

TIP

If the Select records option is not available, you are trying to create a PDF from Print Preview. This feature only works from the Save & Publish, Save Object As method.

5. Save a form by following these steps:

a. Click the **File** tab and from the **Save & Publish** option, click **Save Object As** , then double-click **PDF or XPS** .

b. In the **Publish as PDF or XPS** dialog box, click the **Option** button. Select the **Select records** option and click **OK**.

c. Save the file as a PDF and name the file *[your initials]*-**07-21-A**.

d. Click **Publish**.

e. Save and close the form.

Assessment

- According to your classroom procedure, turn in your database only when you have completed all assigned exercises.

- Depending on your class procedures, print or turn in the PDF file.

-OR-

- Depending on your class procedures, print or turn in the PDF file.

07-21-A.pdf
1 Page

Exercise 7-22

Create a form to display, add, modify or delete employee job codes.

1. Create a single record form by following these steps:

a. Open and enable content for *[your initials]*-**EcoMed-07**.

b. In the Navigation Pane, select **tblJobCodes**.

c. From the Create tab, in the Forms group, click **Form** .

d. Press Ctrl+S. In the Save As dialog box, key **frmJobCodes**.

2. Modify the Title label by following these steps:

   a. Switch to **Design View**.

   b. From the **Design** tab, in the **Header/Footer** group, click **Title** ▣.

   c. Key **EcoMed's Job Codes** and press Enter.

   d. Right-click the Title label and select **Size**, then choose **To Fit** ▨.

3. Modify controls in **Design View** by following these steps:

   a. Click the **Job Code** text box. Drag the right edge to the 4-inch mark on the horizontal ruler.

   b. From the **Arrange** tab, in the **Merge/Split** group, click **Split Horizontally** ▦.

   c. From the **Arrange** tab, in the **Rows & Columns** group, click **Select Layout** ▦.

   d. Click and drag the layout up to the top of the **Detail** section.

   e. Drag the top of the **Form Footer** bar up until there is only one row of dots showing below the **JobTitle** text box.

   f. Move your mouse above the top part of the **JobCode** text box until you see a down arrow. Click to select only the text boxes.

   g. Right-click the selected controls, select **Special Effects** ▭, and choose Shadow effect (row 2, column 2).

4. Add a label by following these steps:

   a. Drag the bottom of the **Form Footer** bar down ½ inch.

   b. From the **Design** tab, in the **Controls** group, click Label **Aa**.

   c. Click in the **Form Footer** section.

   d. Key **Prepared by:** *[your full name]*. Press Enter.

   e. Drag the new label to the left part on the section.

   f. Press Ctrl+S to save the changes to the form.

TIP

Each section has its own vertical ruler that starts at 0 inches.

Assessment

- Close the form.
- According to your classroom procedure, turn in your database only when you have completed all assigned exercises.

-OR-

- Save a Form by following these steps:

   a. Click the **File** tab and from the **Print** option, click **Print Preview** ▣.

   b. From the **Print Preview** tab, in the **Data** group, click **PDF or XPS** ▤ to save the printout as a file.

   c. Save the file as a PDF and name the file *[your initials]*-07-22-A.

   d. Depending on your class procedures, print or turn in the PDF file.

   e. Close **Print Preview** and the form.

07-22-A.pdf
1 Page

Exercise 7-23

You have been asked to create a form based on qryVender that allows users to change vender information.

1. Create a single record form by following these steps:
   a. Open and enable content for *[your initials]*-EcoMed-07.
   b. In the Navigation Pane, select **qryVender**.
   c. From the Create tab, in the Forms group, click Form 🔲.
   d. Press Ctrl+S. In the Save As dialog box, key **frmVenInfo**.

2. Modify controls by following these steps:
   a. Press PageDown until you reach the record for **Vender ID** number "18." This is the longest vender name.
   b. Drag the right edge of the **Vender Name** text box to reduce its width to just fit the content of the field.
   c. Click the **City** text box. From the Arrange tab, in the Rows & Columns group, click Insert Right 🔳 twice.
   d. Click on the **State** text box and drag it to the right of the **City** text box.
   e. Click on the **Zip** text box and drag it to the right of the **State** text box.
   f. Click the label for the **City** control and press Delete.
   g. Click the label for the **State** control and press Delete.
   h. Click the label for the **Zip** control and press Delete.
   i. Click the blank cell above the **Phone Number** text box and press Delete.
   j. Select the **FAX** label. While pressing Ctrl, click the **FAX** text box.
   k. Drag the selected controls to the right of the **Phone Number** text box.
   l. Click the blank cell below the **FAX** text box and press Delete.
   m. Click the **FAX** text box and drag its right edge to the right until you can see of the FAX number.

3. Add a label to a form by following these steps:
   a. Switch to Design View.
   b. Drag the bottom edge of the **Form Footer** bar down to the ½-inch mark on the vertical ruler.
   c. From the Design tab, in the Controls group, click Label Aa.
   d. Click in the Form Footer section.
   e. Key **Prepared by:** *[your full name]* and press Enter.
   f. Drag the new label to the left part on the section.

4. Modify the Title label by following these steps:
   a. From the Design tab, in the Header/Footer group, click Title 🔲.
   b. Key **Vender Contact Information** and press Enter.
   c. Right-click the Title label and select Size, then choose To Fit 🔲.
   d. Save the form.

Assessment

- Close the form.
- According to your classroom procedure, turn in your database only when you have completed all assigned exercises.

-OR-

- Select a single record by following these steps:
  a. Switch to **Form View**.
  b. Press PageDown until you reach **Vender ID** number "4."
  c. Click the record selector.
- Save a single record by following these steps:

  07-23-A.pdf
  1 Page

  a. Click the **File** tab and from the **Save & Publish** option, click **Save Object As**, then double-click **PDF or XPS**.
  b. In the **Publish as PDF or XPS** dialog box, click the **Option** button. Select the **Select records** option and click **OK**.
  c. Save the file as a PDF and name the file *[your initials]*-**07-23-A**.
  d. Depending on your class procedures, print or turn in the PDF file.
  e. Close **Print Preview** and the form.

Exercise 7-24

Create a form to display employee names and their ages.

1. Create a form using a wizard by following these steps:
   a. Open and enable content for *[your initials]*-**EcoMed-07**.
   b. From the **Create** tab, in the **Forms** group, click **Form Wizard**.
   c. In the **Tables/Queries** drop-down box, choose **Table: tblEmployees**.
   d. In the **Available Fields** section, double-click **LastName**, **FirstName**, and **DOB**. Click **Next**.
   e. Select **Columnar**. Click **Next**.
   f. Name the form **frmEmpAge**. Click **Finish**.

2. Modify controls on a form by following these steps:
   a. Switch to **Design View**.
   b. Place your mouse pointer in the horizontal ruler at the 2-inch mark until it turns into a down arrow. Click to select the three text boxes in the **Detail** section.
   c. From the **Arrange** tab, in the **Table** group, click **Stacked**. Click the **Detail** to deselect the controls.
   d. Switch to **Layout View**.
   e. Click the **Last Name** text box. From the **Arrange** tab, in the **Rows & Columns** group, click **Insert Right** twice.

   f. Click the label for the **DOB** control. Press Ctrl and click the **DOB** text box.

   g. Drag the selected controls to the upper most right blank cell.

   h. Click the blank cell below the **First Name** label and press Delete.

3. Add a calculation to a form by following these steps:

   a. From the **Design** tab, in the **Controls** group, click Text Box ⓐ.

   b. Click below the **DOB** text box.

   c. Switch to **Design View**. Double-click the unbound text box. In the **Property Sheet**, click the **Data** tab.

   d. Click in the **Control Source** property and click the Build button ⊡.

   e. Key **(** (left parentheses).

   f. In the **Expression Elements** panel, click **Common Expressions**.

   g. In the **Expression Categories** panel, double-click **Current Date**. This action adds the function **Date()**, which returns the current date.

   h. In the top Expression window, key – (minus symbol).

TIP

The final value in the **Control Source** property is =(Date()-[DOB])/365.25.

   i. In the **Expression Elements** panel, click **frmEmpAge**.

   j. In the **Expression Categories** panel, click **<Field List>**.

   k. In the **Expression Values** panel, double-click **DOB**.

   l. In the top Expression window, key **) /365.25**.

   m. Click **OK**.

   n. In the **Property Sheet**, click the **Format** tab. In the **Format** property, choose **Fixed**.

   o. Change the **Decimal Places** property to **0**.

   p. Click the calculated control's label.

   q. In the **Property Sheet**, click the **Caption** property and key **Age**.

4. Modify labels in a form by following these steps:

   a. Drag the bottom edge of the **Form Footer** bar down to the ½-inch mark on the vertical ruler.

   b. From the **Design** tab, in the **Controls** group, click Label ⓐ.

   c. Click in the **Form Footer** section.

   d. Key **Prepared by:** *[your full name]* and press Enter.

   e. Drag the new label to the left part on the section.

   f. In the **Form Header**, click the label "frmEmpAge" and press Delete.

   g. From the **Design** tab, in the **Header/Footer** group, click Title ⓐ.

   h. Key **EcoMed's Employee Ages** and press Enter.

   i. Save the form.

Assessment

- Close the form.

- According to your classroom procedure, turn in your database only when you have completed all assigned exercises.

-OR-

- Select a single record by following these steps:

    a. Switch to Form View.

    b. Press [PageDown] until you find the record for "May Lee."

    c. Click the record selector.

- Save a single record by following these steps:

07-24-A.pdf
1 Page

    a. Click the File tab and from the Save & Publish option, double-click Save Object As , then double-click PDF or XPS.

    b. In the Publish as PDF or XPS dialog box, click the Option button. Select the Select records option and click OK.

    c. Save the file as a PDF and name the file *[your initials]*-07-24-A.

    d. Depending on your class procedures, print or turn in the PDF file.

    e. Close the form.

- Create a Database Documenter report by following these steps:

    a. From the Database Tools tab, in the Analyze group, click Database Documenter.

    b. From the Documenter dialog box, click **frmEmpAge** check box.

    c. Click Options.

    d. For Form, do not include any options.

    e. For Include for Sections and Controls, select Name and Properties.

    f. Click OK twice to go to Print Preview.

- Save a Database Documenter report by following these steps:

    a. From the Print Preview tab, in the Data group, click PDF or XPS to save the printout as a file.

    b. In the Publish as PDF or XPS dialog box, click the Option button. Select the Pages option. Print only page **10** and click OK.

    c. Save the file as a PDF and name the file *[your initials]*-07-24-B.

07-24-B.pdf
1 Page

    d. Depending on your class procedures, print or turn in the PDF file.

    e. Close Print Preview and the form.

Lesson Applications

Exercise 7-25

You have been asked to create a form to enter in the names and address of new interns.

1. Open and enable *[your initials]*-EcoMed-07.

2. Using the Form Wizard, create a Columnar form using the fields **LastName**, **FirstName**, **Street**, **City**, **State**, and **ZipCode** from **tblInterns**.

3. Save the form as frmInterAddress.

4. Delete the labels for **Street**, **City**, **State**, and **ZipCode**.

5. Move the **State** and **ZipCode** text boxes next to the **City** text box so that the address resembles the address on a mail label.

6. Delete the label that the wizard placed in the top of the form. Add a title control that reads EcoMed Intern's Address.

7. Add a label on the left section of the Form Footer. Key Prepared by: *[your full name]*.

8. Reduce the width of the **State** and **ZipCode** text box to fit the data. Reduce the width of the form to fit on one page.

9. Save the form as a PDF. Only show the record for intern "Ben Kyle." Name the file *[your initials]*-07-25-A.

07-25-A.pdf
1 Page

Assessment

- According to your class procedures, print or turn in the PDF file.
- According to your classroom procedure, turn in your database only when you have completed all assigned exercises.

-OR-

- According to your class procedures, print or turn in the PDF file.

Exercise 7-26

Create a form to display the names of the management companies for each facility. Include the state in which the facility is located.

1. Using *[your initials]*-EcoMed-07, create a Multiple Items form based on **qryManFac**.

2. Save the form as frmManFac.

3. Edit the title label to **EcoMed's Facilities by Management Corp.**. Size the label to fit the title.

4. Make the width of the **Manage Name** and **Facility Name** text boxes 3 inches and the **State** text box ½ inch.

5. Add Date and Time controls to the **Form Header**.

6. Add a label on the left section of the **Page Footer**. Key **Prepared by:** *[your full name]*.

Assessment

- According to your classroom procedure, turn in your database only when you have completed all assigned exercises.

-OR-

- Save the form as a PDF. Only show the records that have the Manage Name "Health Alliance." Name the file *[your initials]*-07-26-A.

- According to your class procedures, print or turn in the PDF file.

07-26-A.pdf
1 Page

Exercise 7-27

Create a form that displays the names and address of all medical facilities.

1. Create a new form for **tblFacilities** by using the Form command.

2. Name the form **frmFacData**.

3. Split the **City** text box into three cells. Move the **State** and **ZIP** text boxes to the blank cells next to the **City** text box.

4. Delete the labels for **City**, **State**, and **ZIP**. Remove the blank row of cells.

5. Widen the text boxes in the address so that all the data can be seen. Make sure that you do not make the **Address** text box wider than 3 inches.

6. Apply a shadowed effect to all the text boxes.

7. Delete both the **Region** text box and label.

TIP

You will need to use Print Preview to set the page orientation but must use the Backstage to save the form with a selected record.

8. By adding cells to the right of the control layout, create two new columns of cells. Move the labels and text boxes for **PhoneNum** through **ContactLastName** into the new cells. The controls for **FacilitiesID** and **PhoneNum** should be on the same row.

9. Delete all rows of blank cells in the form. Resize all labels and text boxes so that the data is visible without the form being wider than 10-inches.

10. Edit the title label and key **EcoMed's Facility Data**.

11. Add a label to the lower left section of the **Form Footer** and key **Prepared by:** *[your full name]*.

Assessment

- According to your classroom procedure, turn in your database only when you have completed all assigned exercises.

-OR-

- Save the form in landscape orientation as a PDF. Only show the records the Facilities ID "43." Name the file *[your initials]*-07-27-A.
- According to your class procedures, print or turn in the PDF file.

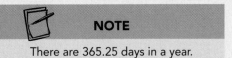

07-27-A.pdf
1 Page

Exercise 7-28 ◆ Challenge Yourself

Create a form that displays an employee's name, hire date, the date of his or her 5-year anniversary, the date of his or her 10-year anniversary, and the date of his or her 25-year anniversary.

1. Create a simple form based on **tblEmployees** and save it as **frmEmpAnniverDates**.

2. Delete all fields and labels except **Last Name**, **First Name**, and **Hire Date**.

3. Clean up the layout by deleting all blank rows.

4. Resize the width of the text boxes to **1.2** inches and their labels **.9** inches wide.

5. Add a new text box to the control layout, right of the **Hire Date** text box.

NOTE

There are 365.25 days in a year.

---

6. Change the label to read **5 Years**.

7. Set the **Control Source** property for the unbound text box to show a date five years after an employee's hire date.

8. Set the **Format** property for the **5 Years** text box to **Short Date**.

9. Repeat steps 5 through 8 but change the label and equation to represent 10 years. Place this new control to the right of the **5 Years** control.

10. Repeat steps 5 through 8 but change the label and equation to represent 25 years. Place this new control to the right of the **10 Years** control.

11. Edit the title to **EcoMed Employees' Anniversary Dates**.

12. Add a label to the lower left section of the **Page Footer** and key **Prepared by:** *[your full name]*.

13. Resize controls to fit the width of a portrait layout page.

Assessment

07-28-A.pdf
1 Page

- According to your classroom procedure, turn in your database only when you have completed all assigned exercises.

-OR-

07-28-B.pdf
4 Pages

- Save the form as a PDF. Only print the first page. Name the file *[your initials]*-07-28-A.
- According to your class procedures, print or turn in the PDF file.
- Create a **Database Documenter** report for **frmEmpAnniverDates** using the following settings:

  • Include for Form: Nothing
  • Include for Sections and Controls: **Names and Properties**

- Save pages 17 through 20 of the **Documenter** report as a PDF file named *[your initials]*-07-28-B.
- According to your class procedures, print or turn in the PDF file.
- Compact and close your database. Exit Access.

On Your Own

In these exercises, you work on your own, as you would in a real-life work environment. Use the skills you've learned to accomplish the task—and be creative.

Exercise 7-29

Using the Form Wizard, create a form for the main table of the database you modified in Exercise 6-32. Include all fields from the table in your form. On the form printout, sketch changes that will improve each form. Using the Form Wizard, create forms for each additional table in your database. Print a copy of each form. On each form printout, sketch changes that will improve each form. On each form, write your name and "Exercise 7-29." Continue to Exercise 7-30.

Exercise 7-30

Modify your forms to incorporate the improvements you sketched. In the Form Footer of each form, include your name and Exercise 7-30. In the Form Header, include the name of the form and the current date. Print the data contained in each of your tables. Print a copy of each form. Test your redesigned forms by having another person enter the data. On each form printout, sketch changes that will improve your form. Continue to Exercise 7-31.

Exercise 7-31

Modify your forms appropriately. Analyze your database design. Determine if any additional forms might be required for queries or recordsets. Create any additional forms you might need. On each form, include your name and Exercise 7-31 in the Form Footer. Print a copy of each form. Submit the copies of the forms you printed in Exercises 7-29 through 7-31 to your instructor. Keep a copy of the database you modified in this exercise. You will use it for the On Your Own exercises in subsequent lessons.

Lesson 8
Adding and Modifying Reports

OBJECTIVES *After completing this lesson, you will be able to:*

1. Generate reports quickly.

2. Modify controls in layout view.

3. Work with report sections.

4. Work with controls in a report.

5. Use Format Painter and Conditional Formatting.

6. Create a multicolumn report and labels.

Estimated Time: 2½ hours

In a previous lesson, you learned how to create and design effective and efficient forms. Forms are the best way to view data on your screen. On occasions when you only are printing a limited amount of information, you can use the form to create a printout. However, if you need to print large amounts of information, you should create an appropriate report. In a report you can:

- Show data in an attractive format that may include variations in fonts, colors, shading, and borders.
- Show certain fields or records rather than the entire table.
- Group and sort records with summaries and totals.
- Add images.
- Display fields from more than one table.

In this lesson, you learn how to create reports quickly using the Report Wizard. You also will work in Layout View and Design View to insert, delete, and modify the controls within a report. Finally, you will learn to control section and page breaks when designing reports that group information by sections.

Generating Reports Quickly

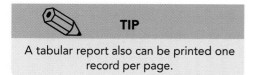

TIP

A tabular report also can be printed one record per page.

When you need to create a simple report that displays a limited number of fields per record, you can use the Report Wizard. The Report Wizard will allow you to select the source recordset and select simple format choices. A report usually has Report, Detail, and Page sections and can be either columnar or tabular.

Exercise 8-1 CREATE A REPORT WITH A WIZARD

You have been asked to create an inventory report that displays five fields, including an image field. Your manager recommends that you use the Report Wizard to design the report quickly.

1. Locate and open the **Lesson 08** folder.

2. Make a copy of **EcoMed-08** and rename it to *[your initials]*-EcoMed-08.

3. Open and enable content for *[your initials]*-**EcoMed-08**.

4. From the **Create** tab, in the **Reports** group, click **Report Wizard** 🔍.

5. In the **Tables/Queries** drop-down box, choose **Query: qryInvShort**.

6. The dialog box asks which fields to use on the form. Double-click the following fields to add them to the **Selected Fields** section.

   InvID
   ModelNum
   BulbShape
   Cost
   Image

Figure 8-1
Report Wizard dialog box
EcoMed-08.accdb

Report Wizard

Which fields do you want on your report?

You can choose from more than one table or query.

Tables/Queries

Query: qryInvShort

Available Fields:

Image.FileData
Image.FileFlags
Image.FileName
Image.FileTimeStamp
Image.FileType
Image.FileURL

Selected Fields:

InvID
ModelNum
BulbShape
Cost
Image

Cancel   < Back   Next >   Finish

7. Click **Next**. This part of the wizard asks to add groups. This skill will be covered later in this lesson. Click **Next**.

8. Click the first combo box drop-down arrow and select **ModelNum**. The report will be sorted by this field. Click **Next**.

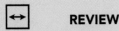

REVIEW

When creating a new report, you should use the Leszynski Naming Conventions. This rule means forms are preceded by the prefix "rpt," and the first letter of main words are capitalized with no spaces between words.

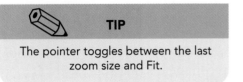

TIP

The pointer toggles between the last zoom size and Fit.

9. In the **Layout** section, select **Outline**, and in the **Orientation** section, select **Portrait**. Click **Next**.

10. Click **Next**. Modify the title to **rptInvShortOutline**.

11. You can choose to preview the report or modify the design. Select **Preview the report** and click **Finish**.

12. The report opens in **Print Preview**.

13. From the **Print Preview** tab, in the **Zoom** group, click **More Pages** 📖 and choose **Twelve Pages**. This report shows the three products of inventory per page.

14. From the **Print Preview** tab, in the **Close Preview** group, click **Close Print Preview** ⊠.

15. Close the report.

Exercise 8-2   GENERATE A REPORT WITH ONE CLICK

After reviewing the report you generated using the Report Wizard, your manager decides that perhaps you should create a simple report that displays more records per page. You will need to generate the report and then modify its controls and properties.

1. In the **Navigation Pane**, select **qryInvShort**.

2. From the **Create** tab, in the **Reports** group, click **Report** 📋. The new report is now in **Layout View** showing multiple records.

Figure 8-2
Report in Layout View
EcoMed-08.accdb
rptInvShortList

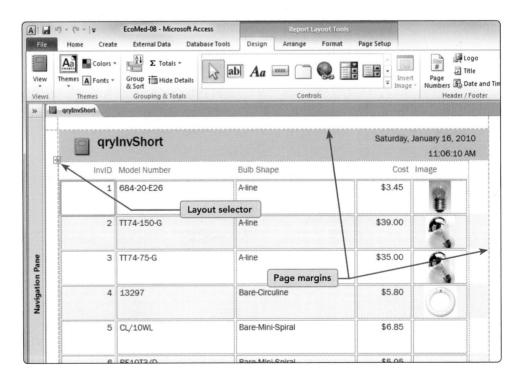

3. From the Quick Access toolbar, click **Save** 💾 to save the new report.

4. In the **Save As** dialog box, key **rptInvShortList** and click **OK**.

5. From the **Design** tab, in the **Views** group, click **Report View** 🖼.

6. Scroll down the report. Notice that there appears to be only one very long page. Only **Print Preview** will show horizontal page breaks.

7. Right-click the report's document tab and choose **Print Preview**.

8. From the **Print Preview** tab, in the **Zoom** group, click **Two Page** 🖽.

9. In the **Page** navigation tool, click **Last Page** ⧨. This report has 21 pages.

10. From the **Print Preview** tab, in the **Close Preview** group, click **Close Print Preview** ⊠.

Modifying Controls in Layout View

As with a form, you can modify an object's controls in Layout View. Layout View allows you to see not only the controls but also the actual data displayed for each record. Layout View allows you to modify the controls to effectively display all information for each record.

Exercise 8-3 FORMAT A REPORT IN LAYOUT VIEW

At EcoMed Services, each report must have a report title that identifies the report. The title should provide enough information to identify the source recordset and the purpose of the report. You should never use the same title for different reports. Your first tasks will be to add a title to the report and then add gridlines between records.

1. Switch to the **Layout View** for **rptInvShortList**.

2. From the **Design** tab, in the **Header/Footer** group, click **Title** 🗊.

3. Key **EcoMed's Inventory Quick Detail Report** and press [Enter]. The title has wrapped to a second row.

4. Drag the right edge of the title control to the right until the title fits on one line with about a ¼-inch space at the end. This action will also move the date and time control to the right.

5. Click the **Date** control.

6. Drag the right edge to the left until the control is inside of the margin dotted line.

7. Click the title control.

8. From the **Arrange** tab, in the **Position** group, click **Control Margins** 🄰 and choose **Wide** to add inside space between the text and the controls edge.

9. Click the **InvID** label. From the **Arrange** tab, in the **Rows & Columns** group, click **Select Row** 🖩.

10. From the **Format** tab, in the **Font** group, click **Center** ☰.

11. Click the **InvID** text box. From the **Arrange** tab, in the **Rows & Columns** group, click **Select Row** 🖩.

12. From the **Format** tab, in the **Control Formatting** group, click **Shape Outline** ☑ and choose **Transparent**.

13. Right-click the selected cells. From the menu, select **Gridlines** and choose **Horizontal** ▦.

14. Switch to **Report View**.

Figure 8-3
Formatting a report
in Layout View
**EcoMed-08.accdb
rptInvShortList**

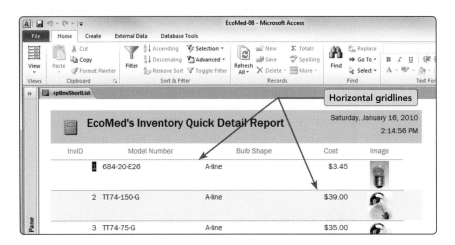

15. Save the report.

Exercise 8-4   ADD AND REARRANGE CONTROLS IN A REPORT

Your manager asks you to add vendor identification as the first column to the report you just created. You will need to use the Field List pane to select and insert the field. The Field List pane comprises of three sections. The top section displays the fields in the recordset. The middle section displays fields from tables that have a relationship to the recordset. Finally, the bottom section displays the fields from all tables in the database.

1. Switch to **Layout View** and click the column heading **Bulb Shape**.

2. From the **Arrange** tab, in the **Rows & Columns** group, click **Select Column** ▦.

3. Press [Delete]. The other fields in the control layout have moved over to the left.

4. From the **Design** tab, in the **Tools** group, click **Add Existing Fields** ▥. The **Field List** pane appears.

5. If the **Field List** only shows one section, click **Show all tables**.

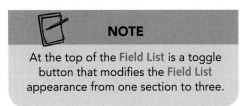

NOTE

At the top of the Field List is a toggle button that modifies the Field List appearance from one section to three.

6. From the **Field List**, in the **Fields available for this view:** section, drag the field **VenderID** to the left of **InvID** in the report until you see a vertical insertion bar.

Figure 8-4
Adding a field to a
report in Layout View
EcoMed-08.accdb
rptInvShortList

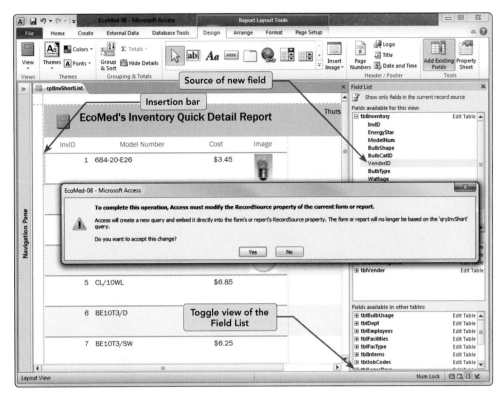

Figure 8-4
Adding a field to a
report in Layout View
EcoMed-08.accdb
rptInvShortList

NOTE

The Column Count property for the field Vender is 2, because this field is a lookup field from the table, so the first column is the VenderID and the second is the Vender Name. Only the Vender Name value is visible because of the Column Widths property.

7. The warning dialog box states that the recordset for this form must be modified to include the table and field just added. Click **Yes**.

8. From the **Design** tab, in the **Tools** group, click **Add Existing Fields** to remove the **Field List**.

9. Click the **Vender** text box. From the **Home** tab, in the **Sort & Filter** group, click **Ascending**.

10. Save the report.

Exercise 8-5 FORMAT A REPORT USING THE PROPERTY SHEET

The vendor name that displays as the first field will need to be modified to display only once. You will need to hide the duplicate values per section. This process is an effective way of displaying information, but only if the records are sorted by the vendor name. You also need to change the padding and margins. Just like with forms, the padding is the space between the gridlines, and the margin is distance between the edge of the control and the displayed information.

1. Click the column header **InvID** label.

2. From the **Design** tab, in the **Tools** group, click **Property Sheet**.

3. In the **Format** tab, click in the **Caption** property and edit the text to read "Inv ID."

4. On the **Format** tab, change the **Width** property to **.6**.

5. Click the **Inv ID** text box.

6. On the **Format** tab, in the **Text Align** property, click the drop-down arrow and choose **Center**.

7. Click the **Vender** text box.

8. On the **Format** tab, change the **Width** property to **2.3**.

9. In the **Hide Duplicates** property, click the drop-down arrow, and choose **Yes**.

10. Click the **Vender** text box. From the **Arrange** tab, in the **Rows & Columns** group, click **Select Row** 🔳.

11. While pressing Ctrl, click the **Image** control to remove it from the selection. Image controls have different properties than text boxes.

12. In the **Property Sheet**, on the **Format** tab, click in the **Top Margin** property and key **.15**.

13. Press ↓. The content of each control selected has moved down. Close the **Property Sheet**.

14. From the **Design** tab, in the **Views** group, click **Print Preview** 🔍.

15. From the **Print Preview** tab, in the **Zoom** group, click **Two Pages** 🔳.

Figure 8-5
Final report
EcoMed-08.accdb
rptInvShortList

16. Save and close the report.

Working with Report Sections

Reports can have numerous sections. A report has a Detail section which shows records. The Report Header/Footer is a section of a report that prints once at the beginning or the end of the report (first or last page). Headers and footers can contain main titles, summary calculations, design lines, and even images. The Page Header/Footer sections that print at the top/bottom of every page are often used for page numbers and the date. Reports may also have one or more Group Header/Footer sections. Group Header/Footer are sections of a report that print before or after each defined group.

TABLE 8-1 Sections of a Report

Name of Section	Purpose
Detail Section	Prints each record from the table or query.
Group Footer	Prints once at the end of each group. It may include a total or other calculation for the group.
Group Header	Prints once at the start of each group. It may display a group title.
Page Footer	Prints once at the bottom of every page. It may include page numbers or a date.
Page Header	Prints once at the top of every page. It may include column headings, page numbers, or a date.
Report Footer	Prints once at the bottom (last page). It may include summaries or totals.
Report Header	Prints once at the top (first page). It may include a title, a logo, or an image.

Exercise 8-6 CREATE A GROUPED REPORT USING A WIZARD

The facilities table includes a field that contains the reported annual revenue for each facility. The sales department has asked that you create a report to display the revenues broken down by region. You will use the facilities revenue query as the recordset, group the records by region, and sort the records by state. A report group organizes or categorizes a recordset by a particular field.

1. From the **Create** tab, in the **Reports** group, click **Report Wizard** 🔍.
2. In the **Tables/Queries** drop-down box, choose **Query: qryFacRev**.
3. Click the **Add All** button >>.
4. Click **Next**. The wizard has determined that this report could be grouped by the field **Region**. We will keep this setting. Click **Next**.
5. Click the first combo box drop-down arrow and select **State**. The report will be sorted by this field.

6. Click **Summary Options**. You can pick what type of aggregate functions to have added to the report.

7. Click the check box for **Sum**.

Figure 8-6
Summary Options in
the Report Wizard
EcoMed-08.accdb

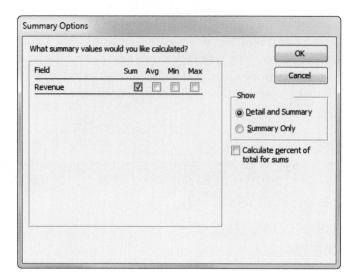

8. Click **OK** to close the **Summary Option** dialog box. Click **Next**.

9. In the **Layout** section, select **Stepped**, and in the **Orientation** section, select **Portrait**. Click **Next**.

10. Modify the title to **rptFacRevByRegion**.

11. Select **Preview the report** and click **Finish**.

12. Close **Print Preview** and switch to **Layout View**.

13. Adjust the width of the controls with "###" so that you can see all of the data without crossing the right margin (dotted line).

14. Scroll through the report. Notice the functions at the bottom of each **Region** grouping.

15. Switch to **Design View**. Notice that there are two new sections in the report: **Region Header** and **Region Footer**.

16. Save the report.

Exercise 8-7   ADD A GROUP SECTION IN DESIGN VIEW

You will need to sort the facility names. You first will need to add a state group and then select the state field as the sort value. To add a group, you add a Group Header/Footer to the report.

1. From the **Design** tab, in the **Grouping & Totals** group, click **Group & Sort** to open the **Group, Sort, and Total** pane. The wizard added one grouping and one sort.

Figure 8-7
Show Group, Sort, and Total pane
EcoMed-08.accdb
rptFacRevByRegion

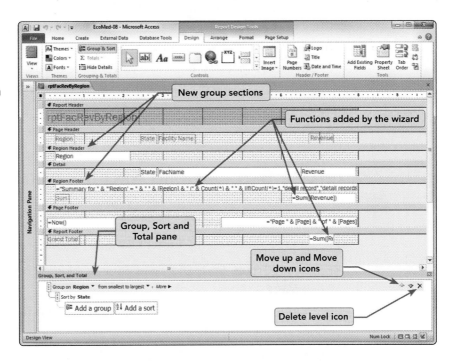

NOTE

You do not have to add a Sort level for fields that have a Group level because a sorting option is included in the Group level.

2. In **Group, Sort, and Total** pane, click the **Add a group** button and choose **State**. A new **State Header** section has been added.

3. At the right end of the **Group on State** row, click the **Move up** icon 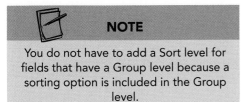 to move the **Group on State** above the **Sort by State**.

4. From the **Group, Sort, and Total** pane, in the **Sort by State** level, click the down arrow next to **State** and choose **FacName**.

Figure 8-8
Modifying a sort order in a report
EcoMed-08.accdb
rptFacRevByRegion

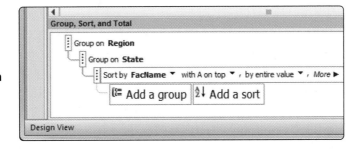

5. In the **Region Footer** section, select all controls and press ⌈Delete⌋.

6. In the **Report Footer** section, select all controls and press ⌈Delete⌋.

7. In the **Page Header** section, place your mouse in the vertical ruler until you see the right black arrow. Click and drag down through the **Detail** section to select all of the controls in the **Page Header**, **Region Header**, **State Header**, and **Detail** sections.

8. From the **Arrange** tab, in the **Table** group, click **Tabular** ▦ to add all the controls to a layout control.

9. Click in the **Report Header** to deselect the controls.

10. In the **Detail** section, click the **Revenue** label and drag it up into the **Page Header** section, above the **Revenue** text box.

11. Click in the blank cell to the left of the **Revenue** label and press [Delete]. This action removes the blank column from the layout.

12. Save the report.

Exercise 8-8   MODIFY GROUP OPTIONS

To make the report more versatile, you have been asked to print the average revenue values for each state and region and for all facilities. You will need to add calculated values to the footer sections of state, region, and report.

1. From the **Group, Sort, and Total** pane, click the **Group on Region** level. Click **More**.

2. Click **with no totals** drop-down arrow. Click the **Total On** drop-down arrow and choose **FacName**. For the **Type**, choose **Count Records**.

3. Click the check box **Show Grand Total** and **Show subtotal in group footer**. You now have added a control that will calculate the number of facilities in each region and a control to calculate the total number of facilities in the report.

Figure 8-9
Add an aggregate
function to a group
EcoMed-08.accdb
rptFacRevByRegion

4. Without closing the **Totals** window, in **Total On**, choose **Revenue** and **Average** for the **Type**.

5. Click the check boxes for **Show Grand Total** and **Show subtotal in group footer**. This action adds the **Avg** function to both the **Region Footer** and **Report Footer** sections. Notice that the name of the option in the **Region** group is no longer "with no totals" but reflects the fields that now have functions added to the report.

6. From the **Group, Sort, and Total** pane, in the **Group on State** level, click **More**.

7. Click **with FacName, Revenue totaled** drop-down arrow. For **Total On**, choose **State** and **Count Records** for the **Type**.

8. Click the check boxes for only **Show subtotal in group footer**.

9. Without closing the **Totals** window, in **Total On**, choose **Revenue** and **Average** for the **Type**.

10. The option for **Show Grand Total** is already checked, because this function was added by a previous step. Click the check box for **Show subtotal in group footer**.

11. Press ⎋Esc to close the **Total** window. There should be a **Count** and **Avg** function in the **State Footer**, **Region Footer**, and **Report Footer** sections. Notice that two functions are the same; the only difference is the section in which it appears.

12. You can see there are no controls in the **State Header** section. In the **Group, Sort, and Total** pane, for the **Group on State**, click the **with a header section** drop-down arrow and choose **without a header section** to remove this section from the report.

Figure 8-10
Functions in report
sections
**EcoMed-08.accdb
rptFacRevByRegion**

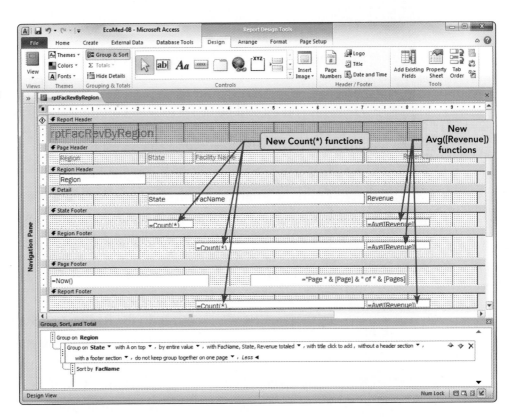

13. From the **Group, Sort, and Total** pane, in the **Group on Region** level, click **More**.

14. Click the **do not keep group together on one page** drop-down arrow and choose **keep header and first record together on one page**. This selection controls where page breaks are placed in the report.

Figure 8-11
Page break options
**EcoMed-08.accdb
rptFacRevByRegion**

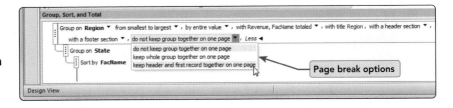

15. From the **Design** tab, in the **Grouping & Totals** group, click **Group & Sort** ⌷ to close **Group, Sort, and Total** pane.

16. Switch to **Report View** to see the new functions. We will be sizing these new controls in the next exercise.

17. Switch to **Design View** and save the report.

Working with Controls in a Report

Just like a form, reports have bound controls (text boxes), unbound controls (labels), and calculated controls. You can move, size, align, and format controls using the same techniques that you learned when creating and modifying forms. When moving and sizing controls in a report, you should periodically preview your report to ensure that all values are visible.

Exercise 8-9   MOVE AND RESIZE CONTROLS

Depending on the amount of changes you will need to make to a report, you may find that it will be faster to select multiple controls and then resize them together, rather than resizing them individually. You will now resize the three controls displaying the count value in each section.

1. In the **Page Header**, click the **Region** label.

2. From the **Arrange** tab, in the **Rows & Columns** group, click **Select Layout** ▦.

3. From the **Arrange** tab, in the **Sizing & Ordering** group, click **Size/Space** ⁜ and choose **To Tallest** ⬚. All the controls in the layout now have the same height values.

4. Click in the **Report Header** to deselect the layout.

5. In the **Page Header**, select both the **Region** and **State** labels.

6. From the **Arrange** tab, in the **Sizing & Ordering** group, click **Size/Space** ⁜ and choose **To Fit** ▥.

7. In the **Region Footer** section, click the "Count" text box.

8. From the **Arrange** tab, in the **Merge/Split** group, click **Split Horizontally** ▦.

9. Drag the selected "Count" text box to the blank cell to the right.

10. From the **Arrange** tab, in the **Merge/Split** group, click **Split Horizontally** ▦.

11. In the **State Footer**, click the blank cell to the right of the "Count" text box.

12. From the **Arrange** tab, in the **Merge/Split** group, click **Split Horizontally** ▦ twice.

13. In the **State Footer**, click the "Count" text box and drag it to the right until it is above the "Count" text box in the **Region Footer**.

14. In the **Report Footer**, click the "Count" text box.

15. From the **Arrange** tab, in the **Merge/Split** group, click **Split Horizontally** ▦ twice.

16. In the **Report Footer**, click the "Count" text box and drag it to the right until it is under the "Count" text box in the **Region Footer**.

17. From the Design tab, in the Tools group, click Property Sheet 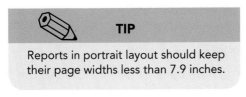.
18. In the Property Sheet, change the Width property to .35, which resizes the entire column.
19. In the Detail section, click the FacName text box.
20. In the Property Sheet, change the Width property to 5.
21. Close the Property Sheet.

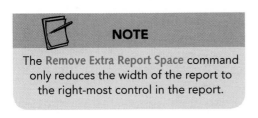

TIP

Reports in portrait layout should keep their page widths less than 7.9 inches.

NOTE

The Remove Extra Report Space command only reduces the width of the report to the right-most control in the report.

22. Right-click the report's tab and choose Print Preview. A dialog box opens to tell you that the width of the report is too wide. Click OK.
23. From the Print Preview tab, in the Zoom group, click Two Pages . The report's width needs to be reduced.
24. Close Print Preview. Notice that the Report Selector has a green triangle that indicates a possible error.
25. Click the Report Selector. Notice that a yellow diamond information icon appears.
26. Click the information icon and choose Remove Extra Report Space.

Figure 8-12
Adjusting report
width
**EcoMed-08.accdb
rptFacRevByRegion**

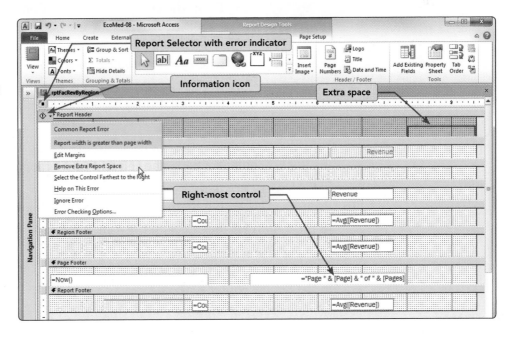

27. Switch to Print Preview. The report now fits within the page margins.
28. Close Print Preview and save the report.

Exercise 8-10 ADD AND MODIFY LABELS

When you add a value in a footer section, you should also add a label to identify the new control.

1. Switch to Layout View.

2. From the **Design** tab, in the **Controls** group, click Label . Move your mouse over the controls in the report. When you point over a blank cell, the cell turns orange.

3. Locate the blank cell to the left of the first "Count" function (in this view, the result of the first function is 3) and click to add the label.

4. Key **Count of Facilities by State** and press Enter.

5. From the **Design** tab, in the **Controls** group, click Label .

6. Click in the blank cell to the right of the count "3."

7. Key **State Average Revenue** and press Enter.

8. From the **Design** tab, in the **Controls** group, click Label . Click in the blank cell below the second appearance of the "Count of Facilities by State" label.

9. Key **Count of Facilities by Region** and press Enter.

10. From the **Design** tab, in the **Controls** group, click Label . Click in the blank cell below the second appearance of "State Average Revenue" label.

11. Key **Region Average Revenue** and press Enter.

12. Switch to **Design View**.

NOTE

In **Design View**, labels cannot be added directly to a control layout. Create the label in an open area of the report and then drag the label to a blank cell in the control layout.

---

13. From the **Design** tab, in the **Controls** group, click Label . Hover your mouse over the blank cell in the report. Notice that in this view, cells don't turn orange when your pointer is over them.

14. In the **Report Header**, click at the 4-inch mark on the horizontal ruler. Key **Total Number of Facilities** and press Enter.

15. Drag the new label to the blank cell to the left of the "Count" text box in the **Report Footer** section. The cell will turn orange when you are over a blank cell.

16. From the **Design** tab, in the **Controls** group, click Label .

17. In the **Report Header**, click at the 4-inch mark on the horizontal ruler. Key **Average of all Facilities** and press Enter.

18. Drag the new label to the blank cell to the right of the "Count" function in the **Report Footer** section.

19. Switch to **Layout View**. Scroll through the report to see all the new labels.

20. Press Ctrl+Home to return to the top of the report.

Exercise 8-11 FORMAT THE REPORT HEADER

Whenever you create a report through the Report Wizard, the report title is automatically created using the recordset name as the title. You now will need to delete the default title and add a new title.

1. Select the label at the top of the report and press Delete. With no controls in the **Report Header**, this section closes.

2. From the **Design** tab, in the **Header/Footer** group, click Title ⬚.

3. Key **EcoMed–Facility Annual Revenue**.

4. Press Ctrl+Enter to add a second line to the label. Key **Detailed Report** and press Enter.

5. From the **Design** tab, in the **Header/Footer** group, click **Date and Time** .

6. In the **Date and Time** dialog box, remove the checkmark for **Include Time** and click **OK**. The width of the **Title** control has been reduced.

7. From the **Design** tab, in the **Controls** group, click Label **Aa**. Click in the blank cell below the **Date** control.

8. Key **Prepared by:** *[your full name]* and press Enter. The new label shares the same font and size with the **Title** control.

9. From the **Format** tab, in the **Font** group, change the Font Size to **11**.

10. From the **Format** tab, in the **Font** group, click the **Align Text Right** .

11. Click the **Title** control. Drag the control's bottom border up until the extra space below the title is removed.

Figure 8-13
Formatted Report
Header
EcoMed-08.accdb
rptFacRevByRegion

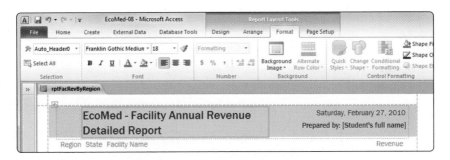

12. Save the report.

Exercise 8-12 ALIGN CONTROLS

There are two distinct activities when aligning controls. First, you can align the contents of a control. You can align a control to display its values left justified, centered, or right justified. Second, you can select multiple controls to align the outside edges of all the controls either to the left, right, top, or bottom. When you align the margins of multiple controls, the most extreme value will be used to set their positions. In other words, when aligning three controls to left alignment, the three controls will align even with the control farthest to the left. The same will occur for the three other alignments.

1. Click the **Region** text box that shows "1."

2. From the **Format** tab, in the **Font** group, click Center .

3. Click the **State** text box that shows "KS."

4. From the **Design** tab, in the **Tools** group, click **Property Sheet** .

5. Change the **Text Align** property to **Center**.

6. Click the **Region** label. From the **Arrange** tab, in the **Rows & Columns** group, click **Select Row** 🔲.

7. While pressing ⌃Ctrl, click the **Facility Name** label to deselect it from the others.

8. In the **Property Sheet**, change the **Text Align** property to **Center**.

9. Switch to **Design View** and close the **Property Sheet**.

10. In the **State Footer**, click the **Count of Facilities by State** label. While pressing ⌃Ctrl, click the other label in the section and the two labels in the **Region Footer** section.

11. From the **Format** tab, in the **Font** group, click Align Text Right 🔳.

12. In the **Page Footer**, click the "Now" function and press ⌃Delete. It is not needed because we added a **Date** function to the **Report Header**.

13. In the **Detail** section click the **FacName** text box. While pressing ⌃Ctrl, click the page numbering control in the **Page Footer** section.

14. From the **Arrange** tab, in the **Sizing & Ordering** group, click **Align** 🔳 and choose **Left** 🔳.

Figure 8-14
Aligning controls
EcoMed-08.accdb
rptFacRevByRegion

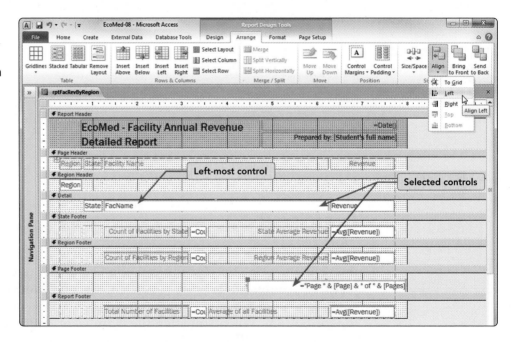

15. From the **Arrange** tab, in the **Sizing & Ordering** group, click **Size/Space** 🔳 and choose **To Widest** 🔳.

16. Click the **Page Footer** bar to deselect the two controls. Click just the page numbering control.

17. From the **Format** tab, in the **Font** group, click Center 🔳.

18. Switch to **Layout View** to see your changes. Save the report.

Exercise 8-13   ADD LINES AND GRIDLINES TO A REPORT

Many reports display a large amount of information. To improve the report's readability, you can add lines and gridlines. Lines and gridlines help the reader easily identify information.

1. Click the **Region** label. From the **Arrange** tab, in the **Rows & Columns** group, click **Select Row** .

2. Right-click the selected controls, select **Gridlines** and choose **Bottom** .

3. Click in the blank cell below "KS." There is a line at the top of the cell.

4. Right-click the selected control, select **Gridlines**, and choose **None** .

5. Switch to **Design View**. Deselect the controls. In the **State Footer**, click the "Avg" text box.

6. Right-click the selected text box, select **Special Effect** , and choose **Shadow** .

7. From the **Design** tab, in the **Controls** group, click the down arrow button to see the second row of controls. Click the Line control . Your mouse pointer is now a line and crosshair.

Figure 8-15
Controls in ribbon
EcoMed-08.accdb
rptFacRevByRegion

8. In the **Page Footer**, click in the far left of the section above the page numbering control and drag right, just shy of the 8-inch mark on the horizontal ruler. If your line is not straight, we will fix it.

9. Open the **Property Sheet**.

10. To create a straight horizontal line, its **Height** property must be **0**. Change the **Height** property to **0** if needed.

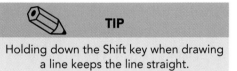
TIP

Holding down the Shift key when drawing a line keeps the line straight.

11. In the **Border Width** property, click the drop-down arrow and choose **2 pt**.

12. In the **Region Footer**, click the "Count of Facilities by Region" label.

13. In the **Property Sheet**, the property **Gridline Style Top** might be set to **Solid**. If so, change this value to **Transparent**.

14. Switch to **Print Preview**.

Figure 8-16
Report with lines
added
**EcoMed-08.accdb
rptFacRevByRegion**

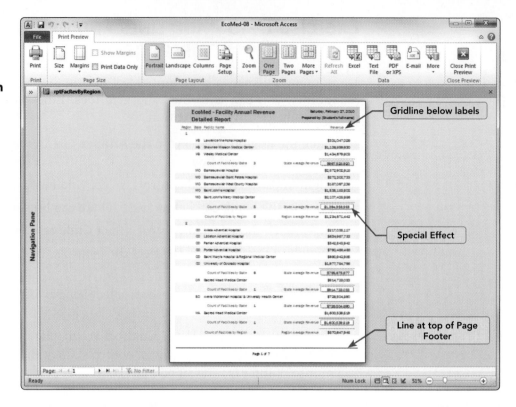

15. Save the report.

16. Close **Print Preview**.

Exercise 8-14   EDIT COMMON EXPRESSION CONTROLS

By default, the Page Header contains text boxes that use the common expression to display the current date. A common expression is a control with built-in commands to display dates, times, or page numbers. The Page Footer contains a text box that displays the current page number.

1. In the **Report Header** section, click the **=Date()**control. The **Property Sheet** shows that this is a text box.

2. In the **Property Sheet**, click the **Data** tab. The **Control Source** for this control is an Access common expression that displays the current date.

Figure 8-17
The =Date()
Property Sheet
**EcoMed-08.accdb
rptFacRevByRegion**

Property Sheet		✕
Selection type: Text Box		
Auto_Date	▼	

Format	**Data**	Event	Other	All

Control Source	=Date() ▼ ⋯
Text Format	Plain Text
Running Sum	No
Input Mask	
Enabled	No
Smart Tags	

3. Click the **Format** tab. Click the **Format** property drop-down arrow and choose **Medium Date**.

4. In the **Page Footer** section, click the page number control.

5. In the **Property Sheet**, on the **Data** tab, click the **Control Source** property. Click the **Build** button ▣. The **Expression Builder** shows the Access code for this control.

6. Close the **Expression Builder** and click the **Format** tab. Change the **Font Italic** property to **Yes**.

7. Close the **Property Sheet**.

8. Switch to **Print Preview** and review the report.

9. Switch to **Design View** and save the report.

Exercise 8-15   CREATE A SUMMARY REPORT

You have been asked to create a summary report. After asking your coworkers in the IT department, you have discovered that the easiest way to create the report is to first create a detailed report that displays all records and then remove the detail section. Follow these steps to create the report.

1. From the **Design** tab, in the **Grouping & Totals** group, click **Hide Details** ▤. Notice that the **Detail** section of the report is still visible.

2. Switch to **Report View**. The details of each facility and their revenue are now hidden, but so is the **State** text box.

3. From the **File** tab, click **Save Object As** ▣.

4. In the **Save As** dialog box, key **rptFacRevSummary** and click **OK**.

5. Click the **Home** tab. Switch to **Design View**, which is the **Design View** for the new report.

6. Open the **Group, Sort, and Total** pane, click **Group on State**, and then click **More**.

7. Click the **without a header section** drop-down arrow and choose **with a header section**. Close the **Group, Sort, and Total** pane.

8. In the **Detail** section, click the **State** text box.

9. From the **Arrange** tab, in the **Move** group, click **Move Up** ➡ to move the **State** text box into the **State Header** section.

10. While pressing [Ctrl], click the **Region** text box in the **Region Header** section to select both controls.

11. From the **Arrange** tab, in the **Sizing & Ordering** group, click **Size/ Space** ⊞ and choose **To Tallest** ▣.

12. In the **Report Header**, click the title label. Double-click the word "Detailed" and key **Summary**.

13. In the **Page Header**, click the **Facility Name** label and press [Delete].

14. Save and switch to **Report View**.

Figure 8-18
Finished summary
report
**EcoMed-08.accdb
rptFacRevSummary**

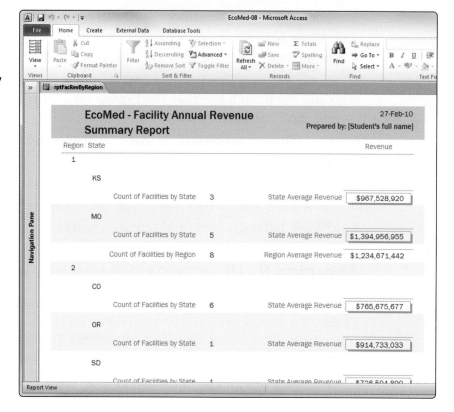

15. Close the report.

Working with Format Painter and Conditional Formatting

Access has a Format Painter like Word and Excel. The Format Painter is a tool that copies the font, size, color, and alignment from one control to another control. It saves you from having to set the individual properties for each control. To use the Format Painter, you first select the control that has the desired formatting, click the Format Painter button, and then click the control to be changed.

You can also apply conditional formatting. Conditional formatting is formatting that displays in certain conditions, such as a style, color, or other setting. For example, you can set conditional formatting to show values over $15,000 in a different color, bolded, and underlined.

Exercise 8-16   USE THE FORMAT PAINTER

The calculated control should have the same format as the other controls in the **Detail** section. Use the **Format Painter** to match the control characteristics.

1. Open **rptFacRevByRegion** in **Layout View**.

2. Select the **Count of Facilities by State** label.

3. From the **Format** tab, in the **Font** group, click Bold B .

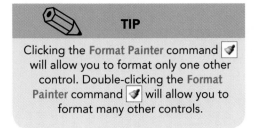

TIP

Clicking the Format Painter command will allow you to format only one other control. Double-clicking the Format Painter command will allow you to format many other controls.

4. From the **Format** tab, in the **Font** group, change the Font to **Calibri** and Font Size to **12**.

5. From the **Format** tab, in the **Font** group, double-click **Format Painter**. The pointer changes to an arrow with a paintbrush.

6. Click the **State Average Revenue** label. The formats are copied.

7. Click the **Count of Facilities by Region** label.

8. Click the **Region Average Revenue** label. Press Esc to cancel the **Format Painter**.

9. Save the report.

Exercise 8-17   USE CONDITIONAL FORMATTING

Many database designers use conditional formatting to call attention to records that are outside a specified parameter. Often managers use reports to track sales, production, and inventory levels. Conditional formatting helps quickly identify exceptional or abnormal information. You have been asked to modify the current report to highlight any facility with revenue greater than or equal to $2 billion.

1. Click the first number under the **Revenue** label.

2. From the **Format** tab, in the **Control Formatting** group, click **Conditional Formatting**.

3. In the **Conditional Formatting Rules Manager**, click **New Rule**.

4. In the **New Formatting Rule** dialog box, you have the option of two different rule types. Select **Check values in the current record or use an expression**.

5. Press Tab twice to move to the second combo box. Click the drop-down arrow and choose **greater than or equal to**.

6. Press Tab and key **2000000000** (9 zeros).

7. Click Bold **B**, click Font Color **A**, and choose Dark Red (seventh row, first column).

Figure 8-19
New Formatting Rule
dialog box
**EcoMed-08.accdb
rptFacRevByRegion**

New Formatting Rule

Select a rule type:

Check values in the current record or use an expression
Compare to other records

Edit the rule description:

Format only cells where the:

Field Value Is	greater than or equal to	2000000000	

Preview: AaBbCcYyZz   **B** *I* <u>U</u>

OK   Cancel

8. Click **OK**.

9. Click **New Rule**.

10. Select the **Compare to other records** rule type.

11. In the **Bar color** control, click the drop-down arrow and choose Yellow (seventh row, fourth column). Click **OK**.

Figure 8-20
Conditional
Formatting Rules
Manager
**EcoMed-08.accdb
rptFacRevByRegion**

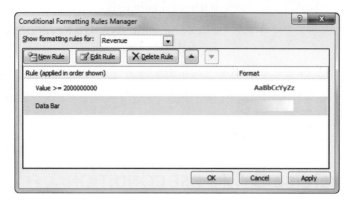

12. Click **OK**. Preview your report.

13. Save and close the report.

Creating a Multicolumn Report and Labels

In addition to columnar and tabular reports, you can format a report to show the data in more than one column. You can use Design View or the Report Wizard to organize fields in a single column, and then you can use the Page Setup command to set the number and width of the printed columns.

You can also create labels using the Label Wizard, which is an option in the New Report dialog box. The Label Wizard lists common label brands and sizes, including mailing labels, package labels, and even CD labels.

Exercise 8-18   CREATE A MULTICOLUMN REPORT FOR A QUERY

You will now create a multicolumn report to display inventory information using two columns per page.

1. In the **Navigation Pane**, select **qryInvShort**.

2. From the **Create** tab, in the **Reports** group, click **Report** ▤.

3. From the Quick Access toolbar, click **Save** 🖫. Key **rptInvMultiCol** and click **OK**.

4. Click the **Bulb Shape** label. From the **Arrange** tab, in the **Rows & Columns** group, click **Select Column** ▥. Press Delete .

5. Resize the **Model Number** control to just fit the data.

6. Resize the **Cost** control to just fit the data.

7. Resize the width of the **Image** control to make it square.

8. Switch to **Design View**. In the **Detail** section, resizing the InvID text box until the right edge of the **Picture** control at 4 inches on the horizontal ruler.

9. From the **Page Setup** tab, in the **Page Layout** group, click **Columns** 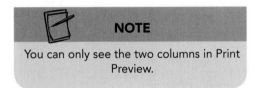.

10. Set the **Number of Columns** to **2** and the **Column Spacing** to **.1**.

11. Set the **Column Size Width** to **3.9**.

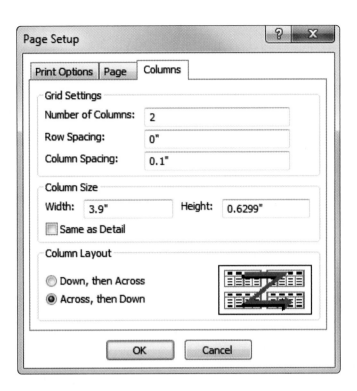

12. Click **OK**. Switch to **Print Preview** and view all 11 pages.

13. Close and save the report.

NOTE

You can only see the two columns in Print Preview.

Exercise 8-19   CREATE MAILING LABELS

The Label Wizard assists creating package labels. After you select a label type and size, the Label Wizard asks which fields to place on the label, which font to use, and how to sort the labels. You will now create a report to print mailing labels needed to mail information to our current vendors.

1. In the **Navigation Pane**, select **tblVender**.

2. From the **Create** tab, in the **Reports** group, click **Labels** .

3. In the **Label Wizard** dialog box, in the **Filter by manufacturer** section, choose **Avery**.

4. In the **Unit of Measure** section, choose **English** and in the **Label Type** section, choose **Sheet Feed**.

5. In the top list box, choose the **Product number** "5160." Click **Next**.

6. Set the **Font name** to **Times New Roman**, the **Font size** to **8**, the **Font weight** to **Normal**, and the **Text color** to black. Click **Next**.

7. In the **Available fields**, double-click **ContactName** and press Enter.

8. In the **Available fields**, double-click **VenderName** and press Enter.

9. In the Available fields, double-click **Address** and press [Enter].

10. In the Available fields, double-click **City**.

11. Key a comma and a space.

12. In the Available fields, double-click **State**.

13. Key two spaces.

14. In the Available fields, double-click **ZIP**.

Figure 8-22
Label Wizard
dialog box
EcoMed-08.accdb
rptVenderLabels

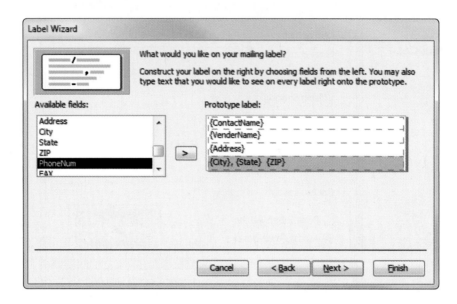

15. Click Next. In the next dialog box, double-click **VenderName** to add it to the Sort by section and click Next.

16. Edit the report name to rptVenderLabels. Select the option Modify the label design. Click Finish.

Figure 8-23
Design View for
mailing labels
EcoMed-08.accdb
rptVenderLabels

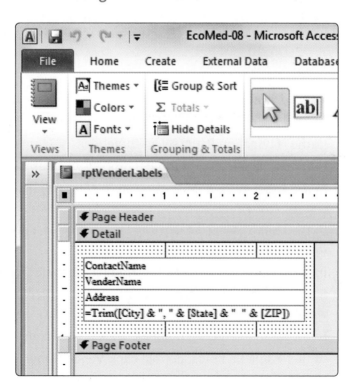

17. From the **Page Setup** tab, in the **Page Layout** group, click **Columns** 🔲. The **Number of Columns** is set to 3. Click **OK**.

18. Right-click the **rptVenderLabel** document's tab and choose **Print Preview**.

19. If an information dialog box appears, just click **OK**. All the labels fit on one page.

20. Close **Print Preview**. Close and save the report.

21. Compact and repair the database, and then close it.

Lesson 8   Summary

- Before printing a report, it is good practice to view the report in Print Preview.
- In Print Preview, you can change the zoom size.
- Columnar style reports are most commonly used when the length of the data is too wide to display properly in tabular format.
- The properties of controls can be modified.
- Simple reports can be created using the Report Wizard.
- Horizontal lines in a report can be created, moved, or resized, just as any other object.
- In a tabular report, each record displays on a separate line.
- Section properties can be viewed and modified in the Property Sheet.
- Group sections can organize and summarize information based on categories.
- Page breaks can be forced to occur before and after group sections.
- Fields can be added to a report through the Field List window.
- When adding or moving fields in a report, care should be given to align other controls in the header or footer to match the detail section.
- Controls should be sized and aligned to make the report easier to read.
- The date and the page number are common controls created by the Report Wizard.
- The Property Sheet for each object in a report lists all the characteristics or attributes for that object.
- Calculated controls display the results of a numeric expression based on one or more fields in a record.
- A summary report can be created by hiding the detail section of a standard report.
- The properties of multiple objects can be set simultaneously through the Format Painter.
- Conditional Formatting applies the property only when certain conditions are met.
- Records in a multicolumn report or label display in two or more columns.
- The Label Wizard can create non-standard package labels.

LESSON 8		Command Summary	
Feature	**Button**	**Menu**	**Keyboard**
Add Line control		Design, Controls	
Align controls		Arrange, Sizing & Ordering, Align	
Align text		Format, Font	
Apply Conditional Formatting		Format, Control Formatting	
Apply Format Painter		Format, Font	
Apply Sorting and Grouping		Design, Grouping & Totals, Group & Sort	
Create Labels		Create, Reports	
Create Multicolumn Report		Page Setup, Page Layout, Columns	
Create Report		Create, Reports	
Create Report, wizard		Create, Reports	
Format, Bold		Format, Font	
Format, Grid bottom			
Format, Grid Horizontal			
Format, Shape Outline		Format, Control Formatting	
Format, Size, Tallest		Arrange, Sizing & Ordering, Size/Space	
Format, Size, Widest		Arrange, Sizing & Ordering, Size/Space	
Hide Detail section		Design, Grouping & Totals	
Promote a grouping level			
Remove gridlines			
Select Column		Arrange, Rows & Columns	

Concepts Review

True/False Questions

Each of the following statements is either true or false. Indicate your choice by circling T or F.

T F 1. The Size/Space controls are only found in **Design View**.

T F 2. By default, the **Page Footer** contains a text box that displays the current date.

T F 3. Use the Text Box button to add a calculated control to a report.

T F 4. Conditional formatting depends on criteria that you enter in a formatting rule dialog box.

T F 5. The Bar color control can be applied to both numeric and text values.

T F 6. A **Report Header** prints at the top of every page.

T F 7. Common expressions include calculations such as =[HourlyRate]+[Bonus].

T F 8. You add a new section to a report when you group records.

Short Answer Questions

Write the correct answer in the space provided.

1. What section of a report displays the data from the records?

2. When adding a field to a report in **Layout View**, what displays allow you to select fields?

3. What is the quickest way to create a grouped report?

4. What is the name of the dialog box you use to select fields, common expressions, or arithmetic operators?

5. What does the expression =Now() do?

6. What control should you use to add a calculated control to a report?

7. Which line property changes the width of the line?

_____

8. What command copies the font and colors from one control to another?

_____

Critical Thinking Questions

Answer these questions on a separate page. There are no right or wrong answers. Support your answers with examples from your own experience, if possible.

1. You used the Line tool in this lesson to add a design element to a report. What other tools might improve the readability of a printed report?

2. In this lesson you learned how to change the size, position, and color of labels and text boxes using the Property Sheet. When changing these values, what are the advantages of using the Property Sheet instead of the mouse and toolbars?

Skills Review

Exercise 8-20

EcoMed Services employs numerous interns. To easily identify the interns, create a Label report that will allow name badges to be printed.

1. Open a database by following these steps:
    a. Locate and open the **Lesson 08** folder.
    b. If you already have a copy of *[your initials]*-**EcoMed-08**, skip to step 1d.
    c. Make a copy of **EcoMed-08** and rename it *[your initials]*-**EcoMed-08**.
    d. Open and enable content for *[your initials]*-**EcoMed-08**.

2. Create a label report by following these steps:
    a. In the Navigation Pane, select the table **qryInternBadge**.
    b. From the Create tab, in the Reports group, click Labels 🗐.
    c. In the Label Wizard dialog box, in the Filter by manufacturer section, choose Avery.
    d. In the Unit of Measure section, choose English, and in the Label Type section, choose Sheet Feed.
    e. In the top list box, choose the Product number "5392." Click Next.
    f. Set the Font name to Arial, the Font size to 16, the Font weight to Normal, and the Text color to black. Click Next.
    g. Press Enter to move the second line.
    h. In the Available fields section, double-click **FirstName**.
    i. Press Enter three times.

j. In the Available fields section, double-click **FirstName**.

k. Key a space and double-click **LastName**.

l. Press Enter twice.

m. In the Available fields section, double-click **Department**.

n. Click **Next**.

o. In the Available fields section, double-click **LastName** and **FirstName**. Click **Next**.

p. Name the report **rptInternBadge**.

q. Click **Finish**.

3. Modify controls by following these steps:

a. Switch to **Design View**.

b. Click each of the four text boxes that start with **=""** and press Delete.

c. Click the **FirstName** text box.

d. From the **Format** tab, in the **Font** group, click Center ▤.

e. From the **Format** tab, in the **Font** group, change the Font Size to **36**.

f. Right-click the selected text box, select **Size**, and choose **To Fit** ▧.

g. Select the next text box. While pressing Ctrl, click the third text box.

h. From the **Format** tab, in the **Font** group, click Center ▤.

i. From the Quick Access toolbar, click **Save** ▤.

Assessment

- According to your classroom procedure, turn in your database only when you have completed all assigned exercises.

-OR-

- Save the first page of a report by following these steps:

a. Click the **File** tab and from the **Print** option, click **Print Preview** ▨.

b. In the **Publish as PDF or XPS** dialog box, click the **Option** button. Select the **Page(s)** option to print only the first page and click **OK**.

c. Save the file as a PDF and name the file *[your initials]*-**08-20-A**.

d. Depending on your class procedures, print or turn in the PDF file.

e. Close **Print Preview**.

08-20-A.pdf
1 Page

Exercise 8-21

Create a report that lists all employees grouped by job title. Be certain to sort the records by employee names.

1. Create a report by following these steps:

a. Open and enable content for *[your initials]*-**EcoMed-08**.

b. In the **Navigation Pane**, select **qryEmpJobs**.

    c. From the **Create** tab, in the **Reports** group, click **Report** .

    d. From the Quick Access toolbar, click **Save** . Key **rptEmpJobs**.

2. Modify the control layout by following these steps:

    a. Click the **Job Title** label.

    b. From the **Arrange** tab, in the **Rows & Columns** group, click **Select Column** .

    c. Drag the selected controls to the left of the **First Name** controls.

    d. Click the **Job Title** text box.

    e. From the **Design** tab, in the **Tools** group, click **Property Sheet** .

    f. Change this control's **Hide Duplicates** property to **Yes**.

    g. From the **Arrange** tab, in the **Rows & Columns** group, click **Select Row** .

    h. In the **Property Sheet**, change this control's **Border Style** property to **Transparent**.

    i. While pressing Ctrl, click the **Job Title** text box to deselect it from the other controls.

    j. Change the control's **Gridline Style Bottom** property to **Solid**.

3. Modify the **Report Header** by following these steps:

    a. Click the title label and change its **Caption** property to **EcoMed– Employees by Job Title**.

    b. From the **Arrange** tab, in the **Position** group, click **Control Margins** and choose **Narrow**.

    c. Click the time control and press Delete.

    d. From the **Design** tab, in the **Controls** group, click Label **Aa**.

    e. Click where the time control once was.

    f. Key **Prepared by:** *[your full name].*

    g. From the **Design** tab, in the **Format** group, change the Font Size to **11**.

    h. From the **Design** tab, in the **Format** group, click **Align Text Right** .

    i. Click and drag the bottom of the label up to remove the blank space.

    j. Close the **Property Sheet**.

    k. Resize the new label so that it fits with in the margin dotted-line.

4. Sort the report by following these steps:

    a. From the **Design** tab, in the **Grouping & Totals** group, click **Group & Sort** .

    b. In the **Group, Sort, and Total** pane, click **Add a sort** and choose **JobTitle**.

    c. Save the report.

Assessment

 - According to your classroom procedure, turn in your database only when you have completed all assigned exercises.

-OR-

- Save a report by following these steps:

a. Click the File tab and from the Print option, click Print Preview.

b. From the Print Preview tab, in the Data group, click PDF or XPS to save the printout as a file.

c. Save the file as a PDF and name the file *[your initials]*-08-21-A.

d. Depending on your class procedures, print or turn in the PDF file.

e. Close Print Preview.

08-21-A.pdf
1 Page

Exercise 8-22

Each medical facility has a unique Medicare number. Create a report to display the name of the management company, the name of the facility, and the facility's Medicare number.

1. Create a report with the Report Wizard by following these steps:

   a. Open and enable content for *[your initials]*-EcoMed-08.

   b. In the Navigation Pane, select qryMedicareNum.

   c. From the Create tab, in the Reports group, click Report Wizard.

   d. Click the Add All button to add all the fields in the Available Fields area to the Selected Fields area.

   e. Click Next. View the data by tblManagment. Click Next.

   f. Double-click State to add a group. Click Next.

   g. Click the drop-down arrow for the first sort level. Choose FacName and click Next.

   h. For the Layout, choose Stepped. For the Orientation, choose Portrait. Click Next.

   i. Key rptMedicareList as the title for the report.

   j. Select the option to Preview the report. Click Finish.

   k. Close Print Preview.

2. Modify the size of controls by following these steps:

   a. Switch to Design View. Select of of the controls in the Page Header, ManageName Header, State Header, and Detail section.

   b. From the Arrange tab, in the Table group, click Tabular.

   c. In the ManageName Header section, double-click the ManageName text box.

   d. In the Property Sheet, change this control's Width property to 2.6.

   e. Change the Height property to .5.

   f. In the State Header section, click the State text box.

   g. Change this control's Width property to .4.

   h. In the Detail section, click the FacName text box.

   i. Change this control's Width property to 3.3.

   j. Change the Height property to .5.

k. In the **Detail** section, click the **MedicareNum** text box.

l. Change this control's **Width** property to **1.2**.

m. In the **Page Footer** section, click the page numbering text box.

n. Change this control's **Width** property to **3**.

o. Click the Report Selector.

p. Change the report's **Width** property to **7.9**.

3. Modify the **Report Header** by following these steps:

a. In the **Report Header**, click the label and press [Delete].

b. From the **Design** tab, in the **Header/Footer** group, click **Title** 🔳.

c. Key **EcoMed–Facility's Medicare Number Report** and press [Enter].

d. Right-click the title label, and select **Size** and choose **To Fit** 🔳.

e. Switch to **Layout View**.

f. From the **Design** tab, in the **Controls** group, click Label 🔠.

g. There are two blank cells to the right of the title; click the bottom cell.

h. Key **Prepared by:** *[your full name]*.

i. From the **Design** tab, in the **Format** group, change the Font Size to **11**.

j. Click and drag the right edge of the new label to the right until the text fits on one line but stays to the left of the margin line.

k. Click and drag the bottom of the label up to remove the blank space.

4. Add gridlines to controls by following these steps:

a. Click the **Manage Name** label.

b. In the **Property Sheet**, change this control's **Caption** property to **Management Company**.

c. From the **Arrange** tab, in the **Rows & Columns** group, click **Select Row** 🔳.

d. Right-click the selected labels, select **Gridlines**, and choose **Bottom** 🔳.

e. In the **Property Sheet**, change this control's **Gridline Width Bottom** property to **2 pt**.

f. Close the **Property Sheet**.

Assessment

- According to your classroom procedure, turn in your database only when you have completed all assigned exercises.

-OR-

- Save the first page of a report by following these steps:

a. Click the **File** tab and from the **Print** option, click **Print Preview** 🔍.

b. In the **Publish as PDF or XPS** dialog box, click the **Option** button. Select the **Page(s)** option to print only the first page and click **OK**.

c. Save the file as a PDF and name the file *[your initials]*-**08-22-A**.

d. Depending on your class procedures, print or turn in the PDF file.

e. Close **Print Preview**.

08-22-A.pdf
1 Page

Exercise 8-23

You have been asked to create a report to track the hire date of employees. Group the employees by the year that they were hired and count the total number of employees hired in each year.

1. Create a report by following these steps:
   a. Open and enable content for *[your initials]*-EcoMed-08.
   b. In the Navigation Pane, select **qryEmpHireDate**.
   c. From the Create tab, in the Reports group, click Report 🖼.
   d. In Layout View, click the **HireDate** label.
   e. From the Arrange tab, in the Rows & Columns group, click Select Column 🖼.
   f. Drag the selected controls to the left of the **Last Name** controls.
   g. Click the **Year** label.
   h. From the Arrange tab, in the Rows & Columns group, click Select Column 🖼.
   i. Drag the selected controls to the left of the **HireDate** controls.
   j. Click the **SSN** label. Click on the label's right margin and drag to the left until the control fits inside of the page's margin line.
   k. Save the report as rptEmpHireDate.

2. Add a group and sort to a report by following these steps:
   a. From the Design tab, in the Grouping & Totals group, click Group & Sort 📧.
   b. In the Group, Sort, and Total pane, click Add a group and choose **Year**.
   c. In the Group on Year level, click More. Click the from smallest to largest drop-down arrow and choose from largest to smallest.
   d. In the Group on Year level, click the without a footer section drop-down arrow and choose with a footer section.
   e. In the Group on Year level, click with LastName totaled drop-down arrow.
   f. In the Total On option, choose SSN.
   g. In the Type option, choose Count Records.
   h. Add a checkmark to Show subtotal in group footer.
   i. In the Group, Sort, and Total pane, click Add a sort and choose HireDate.

3. Modify controls in a report by following these steps:
   a. From the Design tab, in the Controls group, click Label 𝐀𝐚.
   b. Click in the blank cell under the **First Name** "Heidi" text box.
   c. Key Employee Count.
   d. Click the time control at the top of the report and press ⌴Delete⌴.
   e. From the Design tab, in the Controls group, click Label 𝐀𝐚.
   f. At the top of the report, click in the blank cell below the date control.

g. Key **Prepared by:** *[your full name].*

h. Click the date control. From the **Format** tab, in the **Font** group, click **Format Painter** and click the new label you just added.

i. Verify that the right edge of the date control is inside of the right margin line. If not, resize the control.

j. From the **Design** tab, in the **Header/Footer** group, click **Title** .

k. Key **EcoMed–Employee Hire Report**.

l. Click the **Year** label. From the **Format** tab, in the **Font** group, click **Center** .

m. Click the **HireDate** label. From the **Format** tab, in the **Font** group, click Center .

n. For the label **HireDate**, add a space between Hire and Date.

o. Switch to **Design View**.

p. Click the **Year** label. From the **Arrange** tab, in the **Rows & Columns** group, click **Select Layout** .

q. From the **Arrange** tab, in the **Sizing & Ordering** group, click **Size/ Space** and choose **To Tallest** .

r. In the **Page Footer**, click the page numbering control. Drag the control to the left until its right edge aligns with the other controls in the report.

REVIEW

The Report Selector is the small square in the upper left corner of the report.

s. Double-click the Report Selector. In the **Property Sheet**, change the **Width** property to **7.9**. If the report width can't be set to this size, resize the controls along the right edge of the report until you can make the width of the report 7.9 inches wide.

t. Save the report.

Assessment

- According to your classroom procedure, turn in your database only when you have completed all assigned exercises.

-OR-

- Save the first page of a report by following these steps:

a. Click the **File** tab and from the **Print** option, click **Print Preview** .

b. In the **Publish as PDF or XPS** dialog box, click the **Option** button. Select the **Page(s)** option to print only the first page and click **OK**.

c. Save the file as a PDF and name the file *[your initials]*-08-23-A.

d. Depending on your class procedures, print or turn in the PDF file.

e. Close **Print Preview**.

08-23-A.pdf
1 Page

Lesson Applications

Exercise 8-24

EcoMed Services has started a recycling program for its customers. Customers now can return light bulbs that contain heavy metals. Create a shipping label for vendors to use when returning their recyclable bulbs.

1. Open and enable content for *[your initials]*-**EcoMed-08**.

2. Create a label report based on the **qryFacAddress**.

3. Use the Avery 8389 labels. Make the font Arial 16, bold, and black text.

4. In the first three lines of the label, create a return address structure with the vender data.

5. Skip a row and then enter the following:

   EcoMed Services, Inc.
   attn: Recycling Department
   1111 West 46th Street # 29
   Kansas City, MO 64112

6. Sort by facility name.

7. Save the report as **rptReturnLabels**.

8. Change the width of the last four controls to 4 inches and place them in the lower right corner of the label.

Assessment

- According to your classroom procedure, turn in your database only when you have completed all assigned exercises.

-OR-

- Save the form as a PDF. Save only the first page of the report.
- Name the file *[your initials]*-**08-24-A**.
- According to your class procedures, print or turn in the PDF file.

08-24-A.pdf
1 Page

Exercise 8-25

EcoMed Services needs a current phone list for its employees. Create a two-column report to display the names and phone numbers of its employees sorted by the employee names.

1. Using *[your initials]*-**EcoMed-08,** create a simple report for **qryEmpPhone**.

2. Save the report as **rptEmpPhone**.

3. Delete the **Employee ID** column.

4. Resize the three controls in the Detail section so that the right edge of the **HomePhone** control is at the 3½-inch mark.

5. Remove the borders around the text boxes.

6. Make the bottom padding of the text boxes **.2**.

7. Select the three labels in the Page Header section and make a copy. Place the copied labels to the right of the originals, starting at the 4-inch mark.

8. Delete the page number control. In the Page Footer, add a label with the caption **Prepared by:** *[your full name]*.

9. Change the report to use **2** columns that are **3.5** inches wide, with a column spacing of **.45**. The columns should run down and then across. The report must fit one page.

10. Delete all controls in the Report Footer and make its height **0**.

11. Edit the label in the Report Header section to **EcoMed–Employee Phone List**.

12. Use the Group & Sort command to add a sort by **Last Name**.

Assessment

- According to your classroom procedure, turn in your database only when you have completed all assigned exercises.

-OR-

- Save the report as a PDF. Name the file *[your initials]*-**08-25-A**.
- According to your class procedures, print or turn in the PDF file.

08-25-A.pdf
1 Page

Exercise 8-26

You have been asked to create a report to display inventory by vendor that highlights any item that costs more than $100.

1. Use *[your initials]*-**EcoMed-08.accdb** to create a report using a wizard for **qryInvByCatVen**.

2. Use all fields. Group by **BulbCategory**, then **VenderName**. Use a stepped layout and portrait orientation. Name the report **rptInvByCatVen**.

3. Change the title label to **EcoMed–Bulb Costs by Category and Vender**.

4. Create a tabular layout for all controls that are not in the Report Header and Report Footer sections

5. Merge the **VenderName** text box with the blank cell to its right.

6. Resize the **VenderName** label to just fit the text.

7. Resize the **Cost** label to 1 inch and center its text.

8. In the **VenderName Footer**, add a sum function that will calculate the costs per vender. Make sure that the new text box is the same height as the other text boxes.

9. Make sure that each vender's group is kept together on one page.

10. Add a conditional format to the **Cost** text box that will format any bulb's **Cost** over $100 to have a red font and be italic.

11. Add a label to right side of the **Report Header** with the caption **Prepared by:** *[your full name].*

12. The data needs to be sorted by **Bulb Category** (ascending), **Vender Name** (descending), and **Cost** (ascending).

13. Make sure that report width is less than 8 inches.

Assessment

- According to your classroom procedure, turn in your database only when you have completed all assigned exercises.

-OR-

- Save the form as a PDF. Only save the first page of the report.
- Name the file *[your initials]*-**08-26-A**.
- According to your class procedures, print or turn in the PDF file.

08-26-A.pdf
1 Page

Exercise 8-27 ◆ Challenge Yourself

You have been asked to create a report to track annual leave and sick leave taken by employees. Group the information by job title and sort the records by the name of the employee.

1. Using *[your initials]*-**EcoMed-08, c**reate a report using the **Report Wizard**.

2. From **tblJobCodes**, select **JobTitle**. From **tblEmployees**, select **LastName** and **FirstName**. From **tblLeaveDays**, select **LeaveCategory** and **LeaveDate**.

3. Create three groups: **JobTitle**, **LastName** with **FirstName**, and **LeaveCategory**. The only field in the **Detail** section should be LeaveDate.

4. Name the report **rptEmpLeave**.

5. Resize the controls. Make certain that all data are visible and that the report is no wider than 7.9 inches.

6. In the **LeaveCategory Header** section, add a function that will count the number of leave dates.

7. Open the **EmployeeID Footer** and add a straight horizontal line under the **Last Name** through **Leave Date** controls.

8. Hide the details of the report.

9. Edit the title label to **Employee Leave Breakdown**.

10. Add a label in the far right of the **Report Header** section with the caption **Prepared by:** *[your full name]*.

11. Size the two labels in the **Report Header** to fit on one line.

12. Verify that the report fits on three pages.

Assessment

- According to your classroom procedure, turn in your database only when you have completed all assigned exercises.

-OR-

- Save the form as a PDF. Only save the first page the report.
- Name the file *[your initials]*-08-27-A.
- According to your class procedures, print or turn in the PDF file.
- Compact the database and close it.

08-27-A.pdf
1 Page

On Your Own

In these exercises, you work on your own, as you would in a real-life work environment. Use the skills you've learned to accomplish the task—and be creative.

Exercise 8-28

Review the design of the database that you modified in Exercise 7-31. On a sheet of paper, sketch three reports that will enhance the usability of this database. On each sketched report, describe who would use the report, the reason that the information on the report is valuable, and the frequency with which the report will be printed. Name each report and give it a title that best describes the purpose for the report. Write your name and Exercise 8-28 on each sketch. Continue to Exercise 8-29.

Exercise 8-29

Based on the sketches that you created in Exercise 8-28, create three reports. Select the style and layout most appropriate for each report. Arrange the controls as necessary. In the Page Footer, include your name and Exercise 8-29. In the Report Header, include the title of the report. Print a copy of each report. Continue to Exercise 8-30.

Exercise 8-30

Create a Group for your report. Depending on your design, you may need to add a field to a table and enter in appropriate data. Select the name, title, style, and layout most appropriate for the report. Arrange the controls as necessary. In the Page Footer, include your name and Exercise 8-30. Test your report in Print Preview. You may need to sort the records for the grouping to work appropriately. Print the report. Submit the copies of the sketches and reports that you printed in Exercises 8-28 through 8-30 to your instructor. Keep a copy of the database you modified in this exercise. You will use it for the On Your Own exercises in subsequent lessons.

Unit 2 Applications

Unit Application 2-1

You have been asked to create a relationship and lookup field. You have also been asked to add a subdatasheet to the department table.

1. From the **Unit 02** folder, copy the file **EcoMed-U2** and rename it *[your initials]*-EcoMed-U2. Open and enable the database.

2. Modify the one-to-many relationship between **tblInterns** and **tblDept**. Set the relationship to allow only departments found in the table **tblDept** to be entered in the table **tblInterns**.

3. In **tblInterns**, create a lookup field called School that will receive its data from **tblInstitutions**. Store the ID but show the name of the schools.

4. Create a subdatasheet in **tblDept** that will show the records from **tblInterns** using **DeptID** as the common field.

Assessment

- According to your classroom procedure, turn in your database only when you have completed all assigned exercises.

-OR-

- Create a Database Documenter report for **tblInterns** using the following settings:

  - Include for Table: Relationships
  - Include for Fields: Names, Data Types, Sizes, and Properties
  - Include for Indexes: Nothing

- Save pages 7 and 8 of the Documenter report as a PDF file.
- Name the report *[your initials]*-U2-01-A.
- According to your class procedures, print or turn in the PDF file.

U2-01-A.pdf
2 Pages

Unit Application 2-2

Create a query based on two tables that will calculate the years of service for each employee. After you have created the query, create a form that will display the date of each employee's 10-year service review.

1. Using *[your initials]*-EcoMed-U2, add a Memo field to **tblEmployees** and name it Review10.

2.   Create a query named **qryReview10** that includes the following fields:

tblEmployees:
   EmployeeID
   Review10
tblJobCodes:
   JobTitle

REVIEW

Most years have 365 days, but every fourth year, a leap year, has 366 days. Therefore, on average, a year has 365.25 days.

TIP

Depending on the date that you are completing this exercise, the number of records that meet this criteria will vary. The number of records will not affect your grade.

3.   Add a calculated field named **Full Name** that concatenates **LastName** and **FirstName** for **tblEmployees**. Include a comma and a space between the two fields.

4.   Add a calculated field named **Yr of Service** that will find the difference between today's date and the employee's hire date, which is found in **tblEmployees**.

5.   Set a criteria to **between 10 and 11** for the field **Yr of Service**.

6.   Create a form based on the **qryReview10** that is named **frmReview10**.

7.   Make the title **EcoMed Employees' 10 Year Service Review** and add a label with the caption **Prepared by:** *[your full name]* in the **Page Footer**. Close all unused form sections.

8.   The form should not be more than 8 inches wide. Align the controls so that they match the following layout. All controls should have their **Border Style** properties set to **Transparent**. You will not be including **Yr of Service** in this form.

Employee ID	*ID data*	Full Name	*Full Name data*
Review	*blank*	Job Title	*Job Title data*
Review10 data			

Assessment

- According to your classroom procedure, turn in your database only when you have completed all assigned exercises.

-OR-

- Create a Database Documenter report for **qryReview10** using the following settings:

  • Include for Query: **Properties, SQL**
  • Include for Fields: **Names, Data Types, and Sizes**
  • Include for Indexes: **Nothing**

- Save of the Documenter report as a PDF file named *[your initials]-*U2-02-A.

- Save **frmReview10** as a PDF. Only save the first record. Name the file *[your initials]*-U2-02-B.

- According to your class procedures, print or turn in the PDF file.

U2-02-A.pdf
1 Page

U2-02-B.pdf
1 Page

Unit Application 2-3

You have been asked to create a query that will calculate the line of credit for each facility based on its annual revenue.

1. Using *[your initials]*-**EcoMed-U2**, create a query named **qryCredit** that includes the following fields:

    tblManagement:
      MgtId
    tblFacilities:
      FacName
      State
      Revenue

REVIEW

Fields that are empty are NULL, but if a field stores a 0, it is not empty.

TIP

The values stored in the field **Revenue** are yearly totals. Therefore, before calculating the value of 10 percent, you will need to divide the revenue by 12.

2. Edit the query to show only records for "Mountain States Health Alliance" (**MgtID 38**) when its **Revenue** doesn't equal **0**.

3. Add a calculated field named **Line Of Credit** that will return 10 percent of the monthly revenue. Format the results as currency.

4. Create a report based on the **qryCredit** that is named **rptCredit**.

5. Make the title **Line of Credit Report for Mountain State Health Alliance** and add a label with the caption **Prepared by:** *[your full name]* in the **Report Footer**.

6. Delete the **Management ID** column. Group the report by **State** and sort by **FacName** in ascending order. Move the **State** control to the first column in the control group and move its text box to the **State Header** section. Resize the controls so that all of the data are visible and keep the report no wider than 7.9 inches. Delete the page control.

7. Remove the **Borders** around all the text boxes and add a bottom horizontal gridline to all the control in the **Detail** section. Format the **Line of Credit** data as currency with no decimals.

Assessment

- According to your classroom procedure, turn in your database only when you have completed all assigned exercises.

-OR-

U2-03-A.pdf
1 Page

- Create a Database Documenter report for **qryCredit** using the following settings:
  - Include for Query: Properties, SQL
  - Include for Fields: Nothing
  - Include for Indexes: Nothing
- Save of the Documenter report as a PDF file named *[your initials]*-U2-03-A.
- Save **rptCredit** as a PDF. Name the file *[your initials]*-U2-03-B.
- According to your class procedures, print or turn in the PDF file.

U2-03-B.pdf
1 Page

Unit Application 2-4 ◆ **Using the Internet**

EcoMed is planning to photograph more of its inventory. You will need to research digital cameras for the company's president. Begin this task by searching the Internet for office supply vendors that sell digital cameras priced between $200 and $1,000. Create a new table and form to enter the name of the camera manufacturer, the name/model of the camera, the store that sells the camera, the price of the camera, and an image of the camera. Using the form, enter data for at least four manufacturers and twelve cameras. Add your full name to the Form Header. Name the table tblCamera and the form frmCamera.

    Design a report on paper that displays the manufacturer, name/model of the camera, store, and price. Group the data by manufacturer and sort by price in ascending order. On the Page Footer of the report, add your name as a label. Name the report rptCamera.

Assessment

- According to your classroom procedure, turn in your database only when you have completed all assigned exercises.

-OR-

- Save the Datasheet View of the table as a PDF named *[your initials]*-U2-04-T.
- Save the first record of the form as a PDF named *[your initials]*-U2-04-F.
- Save the first page of the report as a PDF named *[your initials]*-U2-04-R.

Unit 3

INTEGRATING DATABASE OBJECTS

Building Links, Relationships, and Indexes

OBJECTIVES

After completing this lesson, you will be able to:

1. Link external objects.

2. Create relationships.

3. Work with linked tables.

4. Create and edit a join.

5. Use referential integrity and cascade options.

6. Work with indexes.

Estimated Time: 1½ hours

A major advantage of relational databases over flat databases is their ability to link records between tables. This ability to associate data makes it possible for the database to ensure the consistency of data among all tables. The associated or linked tables must share a common field. Although common fields do not need to have the same name, the common fields must have the same data type and size.

Access links information from different tables by applying certain rules. These rules can restrict how data are entered or deleted. These rules determine how the records between the associated tables relate to each other.

Another major advantage of an Access database is its ability to link data from an external source, such as another database or a spreadsheet. Up until now, you have been working with a single EcoMed database. You will now begin using two databases. The first database, EcoMed.accdb, will store inventory, customer, and sales data. The second database, HR.accdb, will store human resources, employee, and payroll data.

Figure 9-1
New database strategy

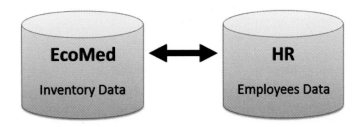

In this lesson, you learn to create, edit, and delete relationships between tables. You will also learn how to link tables between two databases.

Linking External Objects

An Access database can link external tables from another Access database or an Excel workbook. A *linked table* is a table that stores data outside the current database. In a linked table, you can add, delete, and edit records; however, you cannot modify the table's structure.

When linking a table, you use the Linked Table Manager to locate the external data source and link the appropriate table(s) or spreadsheet(s). The Linked Table Manager maintains a list of linked data files and where the files are located relative to the current database. If you move the current database or any of the external files, you must refresh the link for the data source to continue working properly.

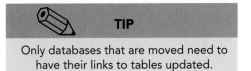

TIP

Only databases that are moved need to have their links to tables updated.

Access uses different icons to identify different types of data sources. Linked tables and spreadsheets are displayed in the current database's Navigation Pane. If you delete the icon for a linked table or spreadsheet, you only delete the link to the data source. Although the link is destroyed, the external data source and its contents are unaffected.

Exercise 9-1   LINK ACCESS TABLES

You can use a linked table similar to other tables in your database. You can add, delete, and modify data through the table. You also can create forms, reports, and queries based on a linked table. You will now link tables stored in the HR database to the EcoMed database.

1. Locate and open the **Lesson 09** folder.
2. Copy **EcoMed-09** and rename it *[your initials]*-EcoMed-09.
3. Open and enable content for *[your initials]*-EcoMed-09.
4. From the **External Data** tab, in the **Import & Link** group, click **Linked Table Manager** .

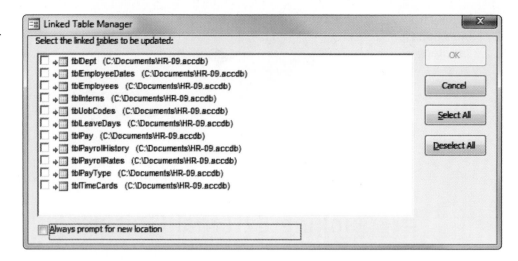

5. Click **Select All**, then **OK**. In the **Select New Location of tblDept** dialog box, locate the **HR-09** database, select and click **Open**. Because all the tables in the list are found in the same database, you will not be asked to find the matching database for each table.

6. Click **OK** to the message dialog box. Click **Close**.

7. In the **Navigation Pane**, expand the **Tables** section. The 11 tables linked to **HR-09** are displayed with right-pointing arrows before the object names. Place your pointer over each linked table. A ScreenTip shows the location of the table.

Exercise 9-2   LINK AN EXCEL TABLE

Sometimes data are stored in a spreadsheet. You can link data from an Excel workbook in the same way you link an Access table. You reference the data source in a spreadsheet either by the name of an entire worksheet or by using a range name in the workbook. The data in the spreadsheet must be stored in a tabular format to be successfully linked.

At EcoMed, sometimes sales information is stored in spreadsheets. For many employees, spreadsheets are easier to manipulate than databases. You now will link an Excel spreadsheet that stores sales data.

1. From the **External Data** tab, in the **Import & Link** group, click **Excel** .

2. Click the **Browse** button.

3. In the **File Open** dialog box, navigate to the location of the **Lesson 09** folder.

4. Select the worksheet **SaleRepReports** and click **Open**.

5. Select the **Link to the data source by creating a linked table**.

Figure 9-3
Get External Data
dialog box
EcoMed-09.accdb

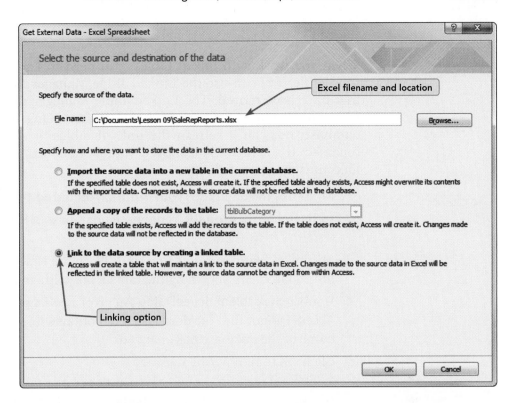

6. Click **OK**. An import spreadsheet wizard opens.

7. The **Link Spreadsheets Wizard** dialog box shows that this spreadsheet has three worksheets: **Projected Sales**, **Visit Notes**, and **Sheet3**. With **Projected Sales** selected, click **Next**.

8. The next dialog box lets you specify whether the first row of the range contains column headings. If the data contain column headings, Access uses the column headings as the field names.

9. Deselect **First Row Contains Column Headings**. The headings now look like data.

10. Select **First Row Contains Column Headings**. The column headings are again used as field names.

11. Click **Next**.

12. Key **tblProjectedSales** as the **Linked Table Name**.

13. Click **Finish** and then click **OK** to finish linking the new table.

14. In the **Navigation Pane**, you will see all the tables are organized by location: local tables, linked tables, and a linked spreadsheet.

15. Open **tblProjectedSales**. Notice that the **Datasheet View** of the linked Excel data looks the same as any other table.

16. Switch to **Design View**. The structure of a linked spreadsheet cannot be changed. Click **Yes** in response to the information dialog box.

17. Notice that each field has been given a Data Type. Close the linked table.

Exercise 9-3 USE THE LINKED TABLE MANAGER

When you work with linked tables, you need to know the location of the source file. You can use the Linked Table Manager to refresh links to files that have been moved. The Linked Table Manager cannot refresh links to files whose names have been changed after being linked to the current database, nor can it refresh the links if tables or source files have been renamed. If a source file is moved, a table renamed, or a file renamed, the links must be recreated.

1. Minimize the database *[your initials]*-EcoMed-09.

2. In the folder **Lesson 09**, rename the database **HR-09** to *[your initials]*-HR-09.

3. Maximize *[your initials]*-EcoMed-09. In the Navigation Pane, the linked tables are shown by the table icons with an arrow to the left.

4. Double-click **tblEmployeeDates**. An error message appears because Access cannot find the database that contains this table, because the name of the database has changed.

5. Click OK to remove the message.

TIP

By selecting all objects found in the same database, Access updates the links without prompting you for each individual object.

6. From the External Data tab, in the Import & Link group, click Linked Table Manager . The tables were originally in **HR09**, but you renamed that database to include your initials.

7. Click Select All. Click the check box for the Excel file **tblProjectedSales** to deselect it.

Figure 9-4
Linked Table Manager with Excel file **EcoMed-09.accdb**

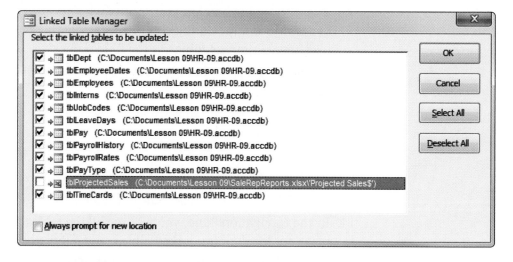

8. Click OK. The Select New Location dialog box enables you to find the correct database.

9. Choose *[your initials]*-HR-09 and click Open. The links have been refreshed. Close the message box and the Linked Table Manager .

NOTE

If the linked tables are in a different location or the database has been renamed, Access opens the Select New Location dialog box.

10. Double-click **tblDept**. The linked table's data are acceptable, just like a local table.

11. Close the table.

Creating Relationships

You create relationships in the Relationships window by dragging the common field name from one table to another. A Relationships dialog box allows you to define properties of the relationship.

The four types of relationships that can exist between tables in a relational database are One-to-One, One-to-Many, Many-to-Many, and Indeterminate. Each relationship is based upon the type of fields used for common fields. When the common field in each table is a primary key, the relationship is One-to-One. When the common field is a primary key in one table but not the other, then the relationship is One-to-Many. When the common field in each table is not a primary key, the relationship is Indeterminate. A Many-to-Many relationship is created by relating two tables through a multi-valued Lookup field in a third table. An Indeterminate relationship is created by relating two tables through two fields that are neither primary keys nor have unique index values.

Related tables allow for complex forms and reports to be created. With a One-to-Many relationship, the dynaset for a report can use data from the one side of the relationship to display information in the report header and then use data from the many side of the relationship to display information in the detail section of the report.

Figure 9-5
Structure of a
Shipping Manifest
EcoMed-09.accdb

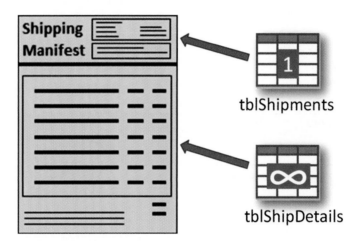

tblShipments

tblShipDetails

Exercise 9-4 CREATE A ONE-TO-MANY RELATIONSHIP

EcoMed Services uses One-to-Many relationships to create shipping manifests. The primary key for the Shipments table is ShipID. Each ShipID is unique and is the "one" side of the relationship.

The Shipment Details table also stores shipment information for each order. Each record includes a field for the ShipID. Details for each item shipped are stored as a separate line item record. The ShipID identifies the manifest to which each of the line items belongs. The shipment details table is the "many" side of the relationship.

1. Open *[your initials]*-**EcoMed-09**, if it is not already open.

2. From the **Database Tools** tab, in the **Relationships** group, click **Relationships** 📇.

3. From the **Navigation Pane**, drag **tblShipments** to the Relationships window.

4. From the **Design** tab, in the **Relationships** group, click **Direct Relationships** 📇. At this time, this table has no relationship with any other tables.

5. From the **Design** tab, in the **Relationships** group, click **Show Table** 📇.

6. In the **Show Table** dialog box, double-click **tblShipDetails** and click **Close**. Resize the borders of each Field List until you can see all the field names.

7. From **tblShipments**, drag the **ShipID** field to the **ShipID** field in **tblShipDetails**. You dragged the primary key field (key icon) to the foreign key field (no key icon). Release the mouse button.

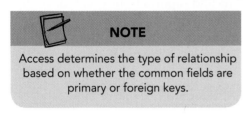

NOTE

Access determines the type of relationship based on whether the common fields are primary or foreign keys.

8. The **Edit Relationships** dialog box opens. The primary table is on the left; the related table is on the right. The **Relationship Type** is **One-To-Many**, shown near the bottom of the dialog box.

9. Add a checkmark for **Enforce Referential Integrity**.

Figure 9-6
Edit Relationships
dialog box
EcoMed-09.accdb

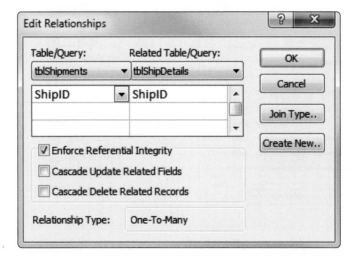

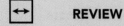

REVIEW

Referential integrity is a set of database rules for checking, validating, and keeping track of data entry changes in related tables.

10. Click **Create**. The join line appears in the window.

11. From the **Navigation Pane**, drag **tblInventory** to the Relationships window. Resize the border of the Field List until you can see all the field names.

12. From **tblShipDetails**, drag the **InvID** field to the **InvID** field in **tblInventory**. You dragged the foreign key to the primary key.

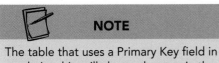

NOTE

The table that uses a Primary Key field in a relationship will always show up in the Edit Relationship dialog box on the left. There is no difference between dragging from Primary to Foreign Key or from Foreign to Primary Key.

13. In the **Edit Relationships** dialog box, notice that **tblInventory** is on the left.

14. Add a checkmark for **Enforce Referential Integrity** and click **Create**. Notice the **DetailID** in **tblShipDetails** is not being used in either relationship.

Figure 9-7
Two One-to-Many relationships
EcoMed-09.accdb

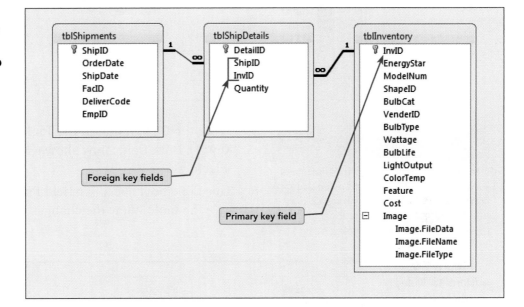

Exercise 9-5 CREATE A MANY-TO-MANY RELATIONSHIP

A Many-to-Many Relationship is created by joining two tables through a join table. A *join table* is a table that contains common fields that are not primary keys from two tables that contain common fields that are Primary keys. The join table is the many side of a One-to-Many relationship with the other two tables.

1. Open **tblShipDetails** in **Design View**. The Primary Key field for this table is **DetailID**.

2. Click the field selector for **DetailID** to select the entire row.

3. Press Delete to delete the field. Click **Yes** twice to verify the deletion.

4. Place the mouse pointer over the first field selector until a right-pointing arrow appears. Click and drag until the first two fields are selected.

Figure 9-8
Creating a two-field
primary key
EcoMed-09.accdb
tblShipDetails

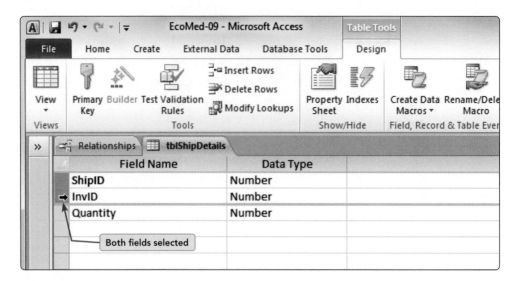

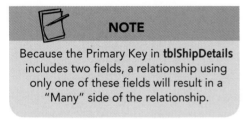

NOTE

Because the Primary Key in **tblShipDetails** includes two fields, a relationship using only one of these fields will result in a "Many" side of the relationship.

5. From the **Design** tab, in the **Tools** group, click **Primary Key**. Both fields now show a key icon in their field selectors.

6. This table now has a two field Primary Key. Close and save the table. View the changes to the relationships.

Figure 9-9
A Many-to-Many
relationship

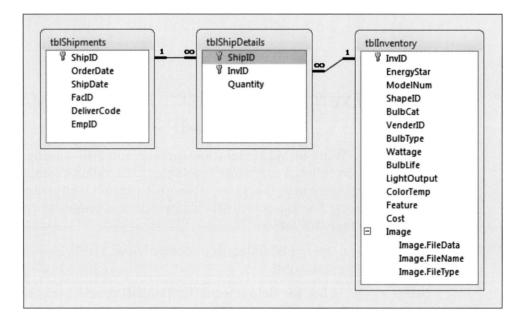

7. Close the Relationships window and save the layout.

Exercise 9-6 USE A MANY-TO-MANY RELATIONSHIP IN A QUERY

You used tblShipDetails to create the Many-to-Many relationship between tblShipments and tblInventory. All three tables must be added to a query to display the dynaset.

1. From the Create tab, in the Queries group, click **Query Design** 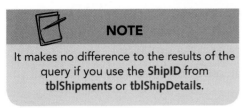.
2. From the Show Table dialog box, double-click **tblShipments**, **tblShipDetails**, and **tblInventory**.
3. Close the Show Table dialog box.

> **NOTE**
>
> It makes no difference to the results of the query if you use the **ShipID** from **tblShipments** or **tblShipDetails**.

4. Size the panes and Field Lists.
5. From **tblShipments**, double-click **ShipID** and **OrderDate**.
6. From **tblShipDetails**, double-click **Quantity**.
7. From **tblInventory**, add **ModelNum**.

Figure 9-10
Building a query for a Many-to-Many relationship
EcoMed-09.accdb qryShipQty

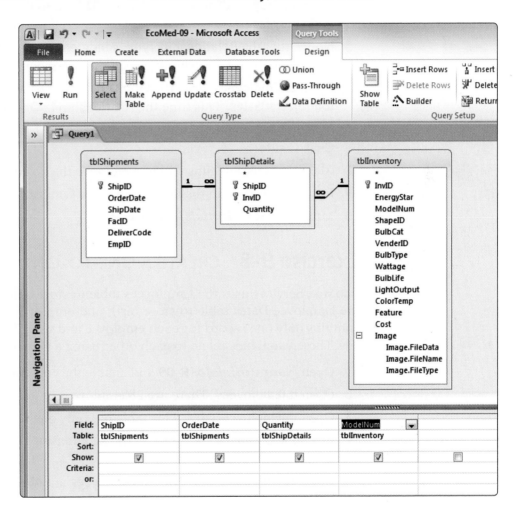

8. View the dynaset. Save the query as **qryShipQty** and close it.

Exercise 9-7 CREATE A RELATIONSHIP WITH EXCEL DATA

Unlike a data source from an Access database, the data source from an Excel spreadsheet cannot have a primary key. When linking two tables through fields that neither are primary keys nor have unique index values, you create an Indeterminate relationship. You cannot set referential integrity when you have an Indeterminate relationship.

1. From the **Database Tools** tab, in the **Relationships** group, click **Relationships** .
2. From the **Design** tab, in the **Tools** group, click **Clear Layout** ✗ and click **Yes**.
3. From the **Navigation Pane**, drag **tblEmployees** and **tblProjectedSales** to the Relationships window. Resize the borders of each Field List until you can see all the field names.
4. From **tblProjectedSales**, drag the **EmpID** field to the **EmpID** field in **tblEmployees**.
5. Notice that the **Relationship Type** is **Indeterminate**. Access cannot determine the relationship between the two recordsets. Click **Cancel**.
6. From **tblEmployees**, drag the **EmpID** field to the **EmpID** field in **tblProjectedSales**. This time the relationship is **One-To-Many**.
7. Notice that you cannot set referential integrity for this relationship. Click **Create**.
8. Close the Relationships window and save the layout.
9. From the **File** tab, in the **Info** group, click **Compact & Repair Database** .
10. Minimize *[your initials]*-**EcoMed-09**.

Exercise 9-8   CREATE A ONE-TO-ONE RELATIONSHIP

EcoMed Services uses the Employees table to store employee addresses and the Employee Dates table to store birth and employment dates. Each table contains only one record for each employee and uses EmpID as the primary key. These two tables relate to each other using a One-to-One relationship.

1. Open *[your initials]*-**HR-09** and enable the content.
2. Open **tblEmployees**. There are 28 employees in this table.
3. Open **tblEmployeeDates**. This table has only one record per employee.
4. From the **Database Tools** tab, in the **Relationships** group, click **Relationships** .
5. In the **Navigation Pane**, drag **tblEmployees** and **tblEmployeeDates** to the Relationships window.
6. Resize each Field List until you can see all the field names.
7. From **tblEmployees**, drag the **EmpID** field to the **EmpID** field in **tblEmployeeDates**. You dragged the primary key from the first table to the primary key in the second table.
8. The **Edit Relationships** dialog box opens. The **Relationship Type** is **One-To-One**, shown near the bottom of the dialog box.
9. Click **Create**. The join line appears in the window.
10. Close both tables and the Relationships window. Save the changes to the layout.
11. Switch to the database *[your initials]*-**EcoMed-09**.

12. From the **Database Tools** tab, in the **Relationships** group, click **Relationships** 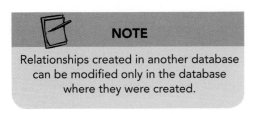.

13. From the **Design** tab, in the **Tools** group, click **Clear Layout** ☒. Click **Yes**.

14. In the **Navigation Pane**, drag **tblEmployees** and **tblEmployeeDates** to the Relationships window.

15. Double-click the sloping portion of the join line. Notice that no changes are allowed to this relationship.

Figure 9-11
Edit Relationships
dialog box of
external relationship
EcoMed-09.accdb

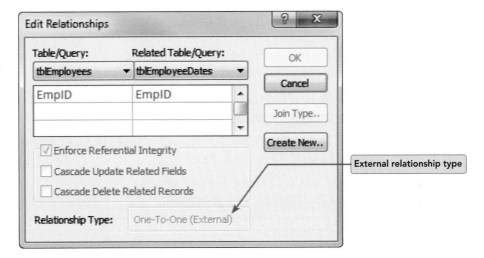

16. Click **Cancel**. Close the Relationships window and save the layout.

Working with Linked Tables

When a company uses two or more databases to store related data, often the tables in one database are linked to tables in another database. Organizations use separate databases to prevent duplication of data and to secure important or private data.

With both databases and spreadsheets, you use the Linked Table Manager to view paths and refresh links to the database or spreadsheet. You will need to refresh the links when the path for a linked data source has changed.

Exercise 9-9   EDIT DATA IN A LINKED TABLE

You can edit data in a linked table in the same way as you would edit data in any other table in the database. Changes to data in the current database will replicate immediately in the source file. You will now change an employee's last name. Although you will make the changes in the EcoMed database, the changes will be stored in the HR database.

1. Open *[your initials]*-**EcoMed-09**, if it is not already open.

2. Open **tblEmployees** in **Datasheet View**.

3. For employee #103, change the **Last Name** from "Lee" to Williams.

4. Close the table.

5. Switch to *[your initials]*-**HR-09**.

6. Open **tblEmployees**. Employee #103 has a new last name.

7. Close the table.

8. Minimize *[your initials]*-**HR-09**.

Exercise 9-10   MODIFY THE STRUCTURE OF A TABLE

You cannot change the structure of a linked table. Changes can only be made in the source file. You cannot change the structure of the employee table while you are in the EcoMed database. You can only make changes to the employee table while you are in the HR database.

1. Switch to *[your initials]*-**EcoMed-09** and open **tblEmployees** in **Design View**.

2. The message dialog box states that the structure of a linked table cannot be modified. Click **Yes**.

Figure 9-12
Modify a link table
warning message
EcoMed-09.accdb
tblEmployees

3. In the **Field Properties**, the help window in the lower right corner states no properties can be changed. Close the table.

4. Switch to *[your initials]*-**HR-09**.

5. Open **tblEmployees** in **Design View**.

6. Click the **PostalCode** field and press F6 to change the properties of this field.

7. Change the **Caption** property to **ZIP Code**.

8. Close the table and save the changes.

9. Switch to *[your initials]*-**EcoMed-09**.

10. Open **tblEmployees**. The **PostalCode** column heading is now **Zip Code**.

11. Close the table.

Exercise 9-11   CREATE LINKED TABLE RELATIONSHIPS

You can create a relationship between two linked tables. The relationship will exist in the current database; however, the relationship will not be reflected for the tables in the source database. When creating a relationship for linked tables, you should always create the relationships in the source database.

1. From the Database Tools tab, in the Relationships group, click Relationships ▣.
2. From the Design tab, in the Relationships group, click Show Table ▣.
3. Double-click **tblPay** and click Close.
4. From **tblEmployees**, drag the **EmpID** field to the **EmpID** field in **tblPay**.
5. The Relationship Type is One-To-One. Click Create.
6. Switch to *[your initials]*-**HR-09**.
7. From the Database Tools tab, in the Relationships group, click Relationships ▣.
8. From the Design tab, in the Relationships group, click Show Table ▣.
9. Double-click **tblPay** and click Close. No join line appears between the two tables. The relationship between **tblPay** and **tblEmployees** is only located in the other database.
10. Switch to *[your initials]*-**EcoMed-09**.

Exercise 9-12 RELOCATE A RELATIONSHIP

Whenever possible, you should move all relationships to the source database rather than creating relationships for linked tables. Relocating a relationship is a two-step process. First, you must delete the relationship in the database with the linked tables. Second, you must create the same relationship in the source database.

1. Right-click the join line between **tblEmployees** and **tblPay.**
2. From the menu, choose Delete. A confirmation message box appears.
3. Click Yes to delete the relationship.
4. Close the Relationships window and save the changes to the layout.
5. Switch to *[your initials]*-**HR-09**.
6. In the relationship window, drag the **EmpID** field from **tblEmployees** to the **EmpID** field in **tblPay**.
7. In the Edit Relationships dialog box, add a checkmark to Enforce Referential Integrity.
8. Click Create.
9. Close the Relationships window and save the changes.
10. Close *[your initials]*-**HR-09**.
11. Switch to *[your initials]*-**EcoMed-09**.
12. From the Database Tools tab, in the Relationships group, click Relationships ▣.

Figure 9-13
Relationships of
linked tables
EcoMed-09.accdb

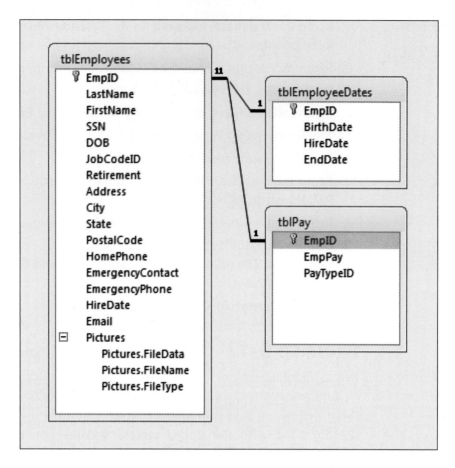

13. Close the Relationships window and save the layout changes.

Creating and Editing Joins

A join is a link between two recordsets. The first (known as the left) recordset is joined by a common field to the second (known as the right) recordset. Left and Right Joins are determined by the SQL statement. In Design View, a displayed arrow points from one table to the other—the join includes all records from the source table (from where the line originates) and the records that match in the destination table (to where the arrow points).

In a query, the join is a temporary link that does not affect relationships outside the query. There a three types of joins:

- An inner join displays records that have the same value in the common field. This default is the most common type of join.

- A left outer join shows all records from the first (left) recordset and fields from the second (right) recordset where the common fields are equal. All records from the left recordset are displayed even if there are no matching values in the right recordset.

- A right outer join shows all records from the second (right) recordset and fields from the first (left) recordset where the common fields are equal. All records from the right recordset are displayed even if there are no matching values in the left recordset.

Figure 9-14
Join types
EcoMed-09.accdb

Join Properties

Left Table Name	Right Table Name
tblBulbShapes	tblInventory

Left Column Name	Right Column Name
ShapeID	ShapeID

◉ **1:** Only include rows where the joined fields from both tables are equal.

○ **2:** Include ALL records from 'tblBulbShapes' and only those records from 'tblInventory' where the joined fields are equal.

○ **3:** Include ALL records from 'tblInventory' and only those records from 'tblBulbShapes' where the joined fields are equal.

[OK]   [Cancel]   [New]

Exercise 9-13   CREATE AND EDIT JOINS IN A QUERY

In a query, when using two tables that already have a defined global join, Access automatically displays the relationship. A *global join* is a relationship created through the Relationships window. When a global join has not been defined, you can create a local join. A *local join* is a relationship created within a query. A local join is available only for the query in which it is created.

When two tables used in a query are not joined to each other, Access cannot accurately join records from one table to another table. Using non-related tables causes Access to display a Cartesian product. A *Cartesian product* is the combination of all possible ordered pairs within the joined components. In the case of a query joining a table with 10 records to a table with 5 records, the Cartesian product would display 50 (10 × 5) combinations.

NOTE

In queries, Access will always try to find a common field between tables that have the same name and data types.

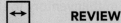

REVIEW

Because the two tables do not have a defined relationship, the dynaset is a Cartesian product. Every combination between the 310 records in **tblInventory** and the 16 records in **tblBulbShapes** is shown (310 × 16 = 4960).

1. Open *[your initials]*-**EcoMed-09**, if it is not already open.

2. From the **Create** tab, in the **Queries** group, click **Query Design** 📄.

3. In the **Show Table** dialog box, double-click **tblInventory** and **tblBulbShapes**. Click **Close**. There is no global relationship between these two tables, but Access has still added a join line.

4. Right-click the sloping part of the join line and choose **Delete** to delete the relationship between these two tables.

5. From **tblInventory**, double-click **ModelNum**. From **tblBulbShapes**, double-click **BulbShape**.

6. View the dynaset. 4960 records are displayed. This is a Cartesian recordset.

Figure 9-15
Cartesian results
EcoMed-09.accdb
qryInvByShape

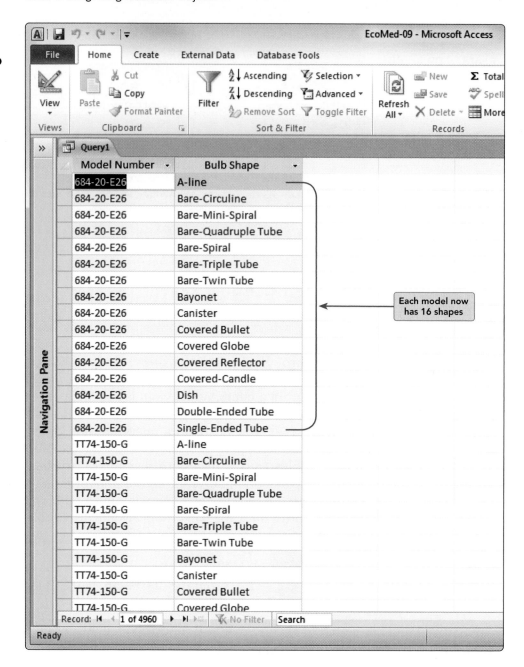

7. Switch to Design View. Drag the **ShapeID** field from **tblInventory** to the **ShapeID** field in **tblBulbShapes**.

8. View the dynaset. 310 records are displayed, one record for every model in the inventory. Switch to Design View.

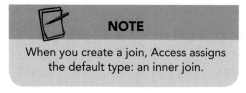

NOTE

When you create a join, Access assigns the default type: an inner join.

9. Double-click the slope of the join line between the two tables.

10. In the Join Properties dialog box, select join type 3.

11. Click **OK**. Notice that the join line now has an arrow pointing at **tblInventory**.

12. View the dynaset. There are now 311 records.

13. At the bottom of the screen, in the search tool, key **Bayonet**. Notice that there are no bulbs in the inventory that have the bulb shape "Bare-Twin Tube."

14. From the **Home** tab, in the **Views** group, click the bottom half of the View ↙ and choose **SQL View** ᴷ. This SQL statement shows a Right Join type.

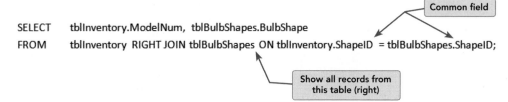

Figure 9-16
SQL statement with
Right Join type
EcoMed-09.accdb
qryInvByShape

SELECT   tblInventory.ModelNum, tblBulbShapes.BulbShape
FROM   tblInventory RIGHT JOIN tblBulbShapes ON tblInventory.ShapeID = tblBulbShapes.ShapeID;

Common field

Show all records from
this table (right)

15. Save the query as **qryInvByShape**.

16. Close the query.

Exercise 9-14 CREATE AND EDIT A GLOBAL JOIN

Global joins help maintain database normalization by preventing certain errors. A global join can create rules that local joins cannot. These rules can prevent incorrect additions or deletions of data.

1. From the **Database Tools** tab, in the **Relationships** group, click **Relationships** ᴹ.

2. From the **Design** tab, in the **Tools** group, click **Clear Layout** ✗ and click **Yes**.

3. In the **Navigation Pane**, drag **tblShipDetails** and **tblInventory** to the Relationships window. These tables have a relationship, created earlier in this lesson.

4. Resize the Field Lists.

5. Double-click the join line between the two tables.

6. In the **Edit Relationships** dialog box, click **Join Type**.

7. Select join type **2**. Click **OK**.

8. In the **Edit Properties** dialog box, click **OK**. The join line now has an arrow.

Figure 9-17
Global join type
EcoMed-09.accdb

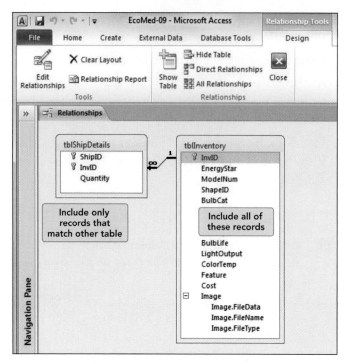

9. Close the Relationships window and save the layout.

10. From the **Create** tab, in the **Queries** group, click **Query Design** .

11. In the **Show Table** dialog box, double-click **tblInventory** and **tblShipDetails**. Click **Close**. The query inherits the relationship you created in the Relationships window.

12. From **tblInventory**, double-click **ModelNum**. From **tblShipDetails**, double-click **Quantity**.

13. View the dynaset. Scroll down the results. Notice that bulb models have been sold many times, but others have never been sold.

14. Close the query and name it **qrySalesQty**.

Using Referential Integrity and Cascade Options

Certain database properties, such as referential integrity, reduce data entry errors. These properties enforce the relationship structure between two tables. You can enable referential integrity for two tables if:

*   The common fields have the same type of data.
*   The tables are in the same database.
*   The common field in the primary table is the primary key for that table.

You can modify the referential integrity rules by enabling Cascade Update Related Fields. With this option enabled, changes in one table automatically invoke changes in all related records in the corresponding table. Most business applications will require you to enable the Cascade Update Related Fields rule. However, on a few occasions, you will not.

For example, when a customer changes his or her shipping address, you would not want to update the records for previous shipment manifests. If you did, then whenever you would re-print a shipment record, the address re-printed would not match the address to where the shipment was actually shipped.

Another option is Cascade Delete Related Records. With this option enabled, deleting one record deletes all linked records in the corresponding tables.

Exercise 9-15   ENFORCE AND TEST REFERENTIAL INTEGRITY

For EcoMed Services, you will want to enable referential integrity to prevent someone from creating a shipment manifest for a nonexistent facility. For all shipment records, the facility must already exist in tblFacilities (the primary table) before a related record can be created in tblShipments.

Enabling referential integrity also prevents someone from deleting a facility record in the tblFacilities if the facility has one or more associated records in tblShipments. Without this restriction, you might accidentally delete a facility that has current or historical shipments. Referential integrity will also prevent someone from indiscriminately changing a facility's ID.

REVIEW

Clearing the layout in the Relationships window does not destroy the relationships but just hides them.

1. Open *[your initials]*-**EcoMed-09**, if necessary.

2. From the **Database Tools** tab, in the **Relationships** group, click **Relationships** ▣.

3. From the **Design** tab, in the **Tools** group, click **Clear Layout** ☒ and click **Yes**.

4. From the **Design** tab, in the **Relationships** group, click **Show Table** ▣.

5. In the **Show Table** dialog box, double-click **tblShipments** and **tblFacilities**. Click **Close**. Resize the borders of each Field List until you can see all the field names.

6. Drag the **FacID** field from **tblShipments** to the **FacID** field in **tblFacilities**.

7. In the **Edit Relationships** dialog box, check the **Enforce Referential Integrity** box and click **Create**.

8. The relationship line shows a "1" on the "one" side (**tblFacilities**) and an infinity sign (∞) on the "many" side (**tblShipments**).

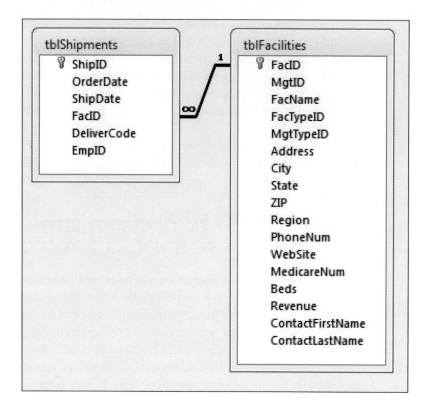

9. Close the Relationships window and save the layout.

10. Open **tblFacilities**. Notice that the facilities' IDs are 1 through 175. Close the table.

11. Open **tblShipments**.

12. From the **Home** tab, in the **Records** group, click **New** ▣. Enter the following record.

Ship ID:	*Press* Tab
Order Date:	*Press* Ctrl + ;
Ship Date:	*Press* Tab
Facility ID:	200

13. Press ↑ to leave the new record. There is no facility ID 200. You cannot complete the record until you fix the problem. Click **OK** in the error box.

Figure 9-19
Error message for
violation of
referential integrity
EcoMed-09.accdb
tblShipments

14. Change the **Facility ID** to **150**.

15. Press ⬆ to move away from the new record. The record is now added to the table. Close the table.

Exercise 9-16 ENABLE CASCADE UPDATE RELATED FIELDS

Referential integrity prevents you from changing common field values in just one table. However, with Cascade Update enabled, you can change the IDs in the Facilities table, and Access simultaneously will update values in all corresponding tables.

1. From the Database Tools tab, in the Relationships group, click Relationships ⬚.

2. Double-click the relationship between **tblShipments** and **tblFacilities**.

NOTE

If a table has more than one relationship using referential integrity, an error can occur when all referential integrity rules are not the same.

3. Click the Cascade Update Related Fields box to turn on the option. Click OK.

4. Open **tblFacilities** and **tblShipments**.

5. In Datasheet View of **tblShipments** , click in the **Facility ID** field. Facility "57" last ordered on 2/22/2011 and had two deliveries.

6. In **tblFacilities**, edit the **Facilities ID** "57" to **500**. Press ⬆ to save the changes.

7. Switch to **tblShipments**. The first two records now show the **Facilities ID** "500."

8. Close both tables.

Exercise 9-17 ENABLE CASCADE DELETE RELATED RECORDS

Deleting a customer record from only the Facilities table might strand related information in other tables. To ensure that all facilities data will be deleted, you must enable the Cascade Delete Related Records option. With this option enforced, deleting a customer record in the facilities table automatically deletes all linked records in related tables.

1. In the Relationships window, double-click the slope of the join line between **tblFacilities** and **tblShipments**.

NOTE

The tables must be closed to change the relationship to Cascade Delete.

2. In the Edit Relationships dialog box, select the Cascade Delete Related Records option. Click OK.

3. Open **tblShipments** and **tblFacilities**.

4. Switch to **tblShipments** and click in the **Facility ID** field.

5. From the Home tab, in the Sort & Filter group, click Ascending ⬚. There is one shipment to **Facility ID** "1."

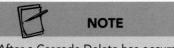

NOTE

After a Cascade Delete has occurred, you cannot use the Undo command.

6. Switch to **tblFacilities** and click the record selector for **Facilities ID** "1."

7. From the Home tab, in the Records group, click Delete ✕. A warning message box appears. Click Yes.

8. Switch to **tblShipments**. The shipment to facility "1" has now been deleted.

9. The records in **tblShipments** are marked #Deleted. When you close or refresh the table, the indicator and record will be removed.

10. From the Home tab, in the Records group, click Refresh All ⬚.

11. Close both tables and save the changes.

12. Save and close the Relationships window.

Working with Indexes

Most modern databases use indexes. An *index* is a sort order used to identify records in a table. Access uses an index to quickly match and locate records based upon a specific criterion. Indexes can be based on one or more fields.

When Access searches a dynaset for specific information, it first looks to the index. If no index match is located, Access then redirects its search to the entire dynaset.

When creating indexes, you should use fields that you often use when searching or sorting the recordset. You can create indexes for a field with a Data Type of Text, Number, Currency, or Date/Time.

Exercise 9-18   ANALYZE PERFORMANCE

In addition to identifying redundant data, the Analyzer can identify data that can be converted to more efficient data types. Often the recommendations involve converting text data types to numeric values.

1. From the Database Tools tab, in the Analyze group, click Analyze Performance ⬚.

2. In the Performance Analyzer dialog box, on the All Object Types tab, and click Select All. Click OK.

3. In the Analysis Results section, you will see a collection of recommendations, suggestions, and ideas.

4. Scroll down until you see a recommendation (red exclamation mark). This point refers to a missing index for **FacName** in **tblFacilities**.

5. Click the recommendation and read the comments in the Analysis Notes section.

6. Click Optimize. The red exclamation mark has turned into a checkmark.

Figure 9-20
Performance
Analyzer
EcoMed-09.accdb

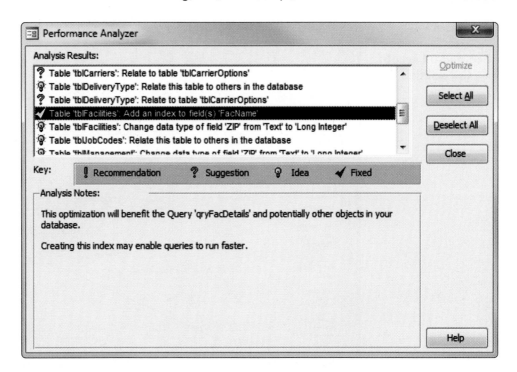

Figure 9-20
Performance
Analyzer
EcoMed-09.accdb

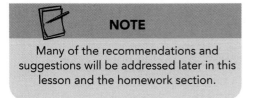

NOTE

Many of the recommendations and suggestions will be addressed later in this lesson and the homework section.

7. The other suggestions and ideas listed refer to the fact that information stored as a number takes up less space than Text fields. Click on the Idea (yellow light bulb) that suggests changing the field "ZIP" from "Text" to "Long Integer." Read the Analysis Notes.

8. This database needs this field to stay Text. Click Close.

Exercise 9-19 DELETE INDEXES

An index for a table can be compared to an index in a book. An index improves the speed when locating information, but only if the proper subjects are indexed. Too many indexes can slow down the process of editing records. Every time you make a change to an indexed field, Access must update the indexes to include the new information. Based upon your information needs, you might discover changing or delete an index would improve the performance of your searches.

1. Open **tblFacilities** in Design View.

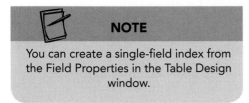

NOTE

You can create a single-field index from the Field Properties in the Table Design window.

2. Click the field name **ZIP**. Press F6. Locate the Indexed property; it is set to Yes (Duplicates OK) .

3. From the Design tab, in the Show/Hide group, click Indexes. The Indexes dialog box opens, listing five existing indexes.

4. Click the row selector for the Index Name **ZIP**.

Figure 9-21
Indexes dialog box
**EcoMed-09.accdb
tblFacilities**

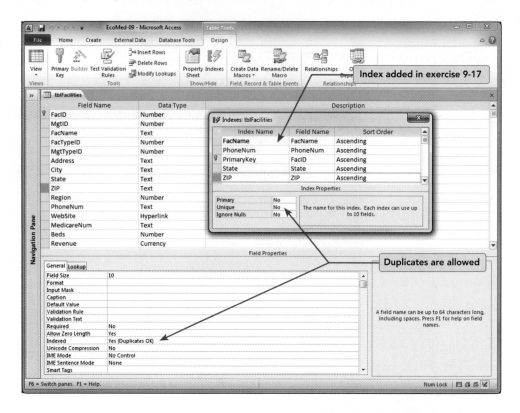

5. With the row selected, press Delete. Notice that in table's properties, the **Indexed** property for the **ZIP** field has changed to **No**.

6. Click the row selector for **PhoneNum** to select the whole row. Press Delete.

Exercise 9-20 CREATE A TWO-FIELD INDEX

Often a search requires two or more fields, such as using the last name and first name of a person to search for a telephone number in a phone book. In Access, you can use two or more fields to create a unique index.

1. Click the third row in the **Index Name** column. Replace "State" with **FullAddress** and press Tab.

2. Click the drop-down arrow and choose **Address**. Press ↓.

3. Click the drop-down arrow and choose **City**. Press ↓.

4. Click the drop-down arrow and choose **State**. Press ↓.

5. Click the drop-down arrow and choose **ZIP**. Press ↓.

6. Click the **FullAddress** in the **Index Name** column.

7. In the **Index Properties** section, change **Ignore Nulls** property to **Yes**.

Figure 9-22
Indexes dialog box
**EcoMed-09.accdb
tblFacilities**

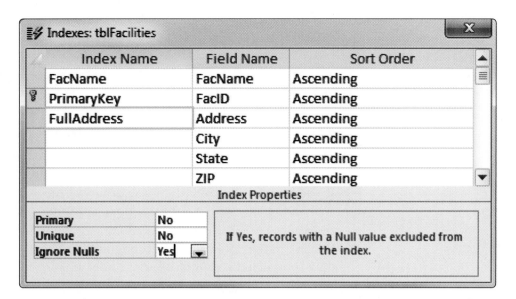

Index Name	Field Name	Sort Order
FacName	FacName	Ascending
PrimaryKey	FacID	Ascending
FullAddress	Address	Ascending
	City	Ascending
	State	Ascending
	ZIP	Ascending

Index Properties

Primary	No
Unique	No
Ignore Nulls	Yes

If Yes, records with a Null value excluded from the index.

REVIEW

You can see a Help message in the Index Properties pane as you click each property.

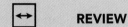
REVIEW

A null value in a database means "blank," "nothing," or "empty." It is not the same as zero (0).

8. Click the **FacName** in the **Index Name** column.

9. In the **Index Properties** section, change **Ignore Nulls** to **Yes**.

10. Close the **Indexes** dialog box.

11. Close the table and save the design changes.

12. From the **Database Tools** tab, in the **Analyze** group, click **Database Documenter** 📑.

13. From the **Tables** tab, select **tblFacilities**. Click the **Options** button.

14. From the **Include for Table** section, choose only **Properties**.

15. From the **Include for Fields** section, choose **Nothing**.

16. From the **Include for Indexes** section, choose **Names and Fields**. Click **OK** to close the **Print Table Definition** dialog box.

17. Click **OK**. Review the report to see the changes that you made to the table's indexes. Based on your classroom procedure, you can print this report like any other report.

18. Close the report.

19. Compact and close the database.

Lesson 9   Summary

- A major advantage of relational databases over flat databases is their ability to connect data from two or more tables.

- You can add, delete, and modify data through linked tables. Linked tables can originate from an Access database or Excel spreadsheet.

- The Linked Table Manager maintains a list of linked data files and where the files are located relative to the current database.

- If you move the current database or any of the external files, you must refresh the link for the data source to continue working properly.

- If you delete the icon for a linked table or spreadsheet, you only delete the link to the data source. Although the link is destroyed, the external data source and its contents are unaffected.

- The Linked Table Manager cannot refresh links to files whose names have been changed after being linked to the current database, nor can it refresh the links if tables or source files have been renamed.

- The four types of relationships that can exist between tables in a relational database are One-to-One, One-to-Many, Many-to-Many, and Indeterminate.

- When you create a Many-to-Many Relationship, the term "Many-to-Many" does not appear in the Relationships dialog box.

- You can edit data in a linked table in the same way as any other table in the database.

- You cannot change the structure of a linked table. Changes can only be made in the source file.

- Through the Relationships window, you can create relationships using linked tables.

- A join is a link between two recordsets. Join types include inner join, left outer join, and right outer join

- Using non-related tables in a query causes Access to display the combination of all possible ordered pairs within the joined components.

- Global joins help maintain database normalization by preventing certain errors.

- Referential integrity is a set of database rules used to reduce human error, such as accidental deletions.

- Referential integrity prevents you from changing common field values in just one table.

- With the Cascade Delete Related Records option enforced, deleting a record in the one-side table automatically deletes all linked records in related tables.

- An index is a sort order used to identify records in a table. Every time you make a change to an indexed field, Access must update the indexes to include the new information.

- In Access, you can use two or more fields to create a unique index.

Command Summary

Feature	Button	Task Path	Keyboard
Analyze Performance		Database Tools, Analyze, Analyze Performance	
Indexes		Design, Show/Hide, Indexes	
Link Table Manager		External Data, Import & Link, Link Table Manager	
Relationships, Direct		Database Tools, Relationships, Design, Relationships, Direct Relationships	
Compact and repair database		File, Info, Compact & Repair	

Concepts Review

True/False Questions

Each of the following statements is either true or false. Indicate your choice by circling T or F.

T F 1. When you clear the Relationships window, you also delete the relationships.

T F 2. The most common type of relationship is One-to-One.

T F 3. You can use the Cascade Delete Related Records option when you enforce referential integrity.

T F 4. When the common field is a primary key in one table, but not the other, the relationship is One-to-Many.

T F 5. A local join created in a query is available for use in all other queries.

T F 6. Common fields must have the same data type.

T F 7. Data stored in a linked table cannot be modified.

T F 8. Two fields can be used to create a unique index.

Short Answer Questions

Write the correct answer in the space provided.

1. In a One-to-Many relationship, what do you call the common field on the One side?

_____

2. What is the name of the set of Access rules governing relationships?

_____

3. Name three types of joins.

_____

4. Where can you see what relationships already exist among tables?

_____

5. With referential integrity, what option enables you to simultaneously change all records in related tables?

_____

6. In a One-to-Many relationship with referential integrity, how can you identify the table on the "Many" side of the relationship?

_____

7. In the Relationships window, how can you identify the primary field in a Field List?

_____

8. What is the purpose of an index?

_____

Critical Thinking

Answer these questions on a separate page. There are no right or wrong answers. Support your answers with examples from your own experience, if possible.

1. Why do companies use relational databases? Why are data broken down into subsections? Why don't companies place all their data in one large table?

2. Discuss how referential integrity would be helpful in managing a database. What problems or issues are connected with using referential integrity?

Skills Review

Exercise 9-21

You have been requested to modify the database so a One-to-Many relationship exists between tables tblInterns and tblDept.

1. Open a database by following these steps:
   a. Locate and open the **Lesson 09** folder.
   b. If you already have a copy of *[your initials]*-**HR-09**, skip to step 1d.
   c. Make a copy of **HR-09** and rename it *[your initials]*-**HR-09**.
   d. Open and enable content for *[your initials]*-**HR-09**.

2. Create a One-to-One relationship by following these steps:
   a. From the Database Tools tab, in the Relationships group, click Relationships 🗗.
   b. In the Navigation Pane, drag **tblInterns** and **tblDept** into the Relationships window.
   c. From **tblInterns**, drag the **DeptID** field to the **DeptID** field in **tblDept**.
   d. Click Enforce Referential Integrity and then Cascade Update Related Fields.
   e. Click Create.
   f. Close the Relationships window and save the changes to the layout.

UNIT 3 LESSON 9

Assessment

- Turn in your **HR-09** database only when all assigned exercises have been completed, according to your classroom procedure.

-OR-

- Create a **Database Documenter** report by following these steps:

    a. From the **Database Tools** tab, in the **Analyze** group, click **Database Documenter** 🖶.

    b. On the **Tables** tab, select **tblDept**.

    c. Click **Options**. From the **Include for Tables** section, only include **Properties** and **Relationships**.

    d. From the **Include for Fields** section, choose **Nothing**.

    e. From the **Include for Indexes** section, choose **Nothing**.

    f. Click **OK** twice.

- Save a **Database Documenter** report by following these steps:

    a. From the **Print Preview** tab, in the **Data** group, click **PDF or XPS** 🖳 to save the printout as a file.

    b. Save the file as a PDF and name the file *[your initials]*-09-21-A.

    c. Depending on your class procedures, print or turn in the PDF file.

    d. Close **Print Preview**.

09-21-A.pdf
1 Page

Exercise 9-22

The employees table has two fields that do not need to be indexed. Open the table and delete the indexes.

1. Delete indexes by following these steps:

    a. Open and enable content for *[your initials]*-**HR-09**.

    b. Open **tblEmployees** in **Design View**.

    c. From the **Design** tab, in the **Show/Hide** group, click **Indexes** 📝.

    d. Click the field selector for **EmployeeID1** and press Delete.

    e. Click the field selector for **LastName** and press Delete.

2. Create a multiple field index by following these steps:

    a. Click in the first open row in the **Index Name**.

    b. Key **FullName** and press Tab.

    c. Click the drop-down arrow and choose **LastName**. Click ⬇.

    d. Click the drop-down arrow and choose **FirstName**. Click ⬇.

    e. Close the **Indexes** dialog box.

    f. Close and save the table.

Assessment

- Turn in your **HR-09** database only when all assigned exercises have been completed, according to your classroom procedure.

-OR-

- Create a Database Documenter report by following these steps:

  a. From the Database Tools tab, in the Analyze group, click Database Documenter.

  b. On the Tables tab, select **tblEmployees**.

  c. Click Options. From the Include for Tables section, only include Properties.

  d. For Include for Fields, select Nothing.

  e. For Include for Indexes, select Names and Fields.

  f. Click OK twice.

- Save a Database Documenter report by following these steps:

  a. From the Print Preview tab, in the Data group, click PDF or XPS to save the printout as a file.

  b. Save the file as a PDF and name the file *[your initials]*-09-22-A.

  c. Depending on your class procedures, print or turn in the PDF file.

  d. Close Print Preview.

09-22-A.pdf
1 Page

Exercise 9-23

You have been instructed to improve the efficiency of the database. First, link the pension fund table. Second, in the carrier options table, make the shipment option ID field a primary key. Third, create a Many-to-Many relationship between two tables.

1. Update linked tables by following these steps:

   a. Open and enable content for *[your initials]*-EcoMed-09.

   b. From the External Data tab, in the Import & Link group, click Linked Table Manager.

   c. In the Linked Table Manager dialog box, click Select All.

   d. Remove the checkmark next to the Excel spreadsheet **tblProjectedSales**. Click OK.

   e. Locate the database *[your initials]*-**HR-09** and click Open.

   f. Click OK and then close the Linked Table Manager dialog box.

2. Create a multiple field Primary Key by following these steps:

   a. Open **tblCarrierOptions** in Design View.

   b. Select the field selector for **ShipOptionID**.

   c. From the Design tab, in the Tools group, click Delete Rows.

    d. Click **Yes** to both warning messages.

    e. Select both remaining fields.

    f. From the **Design** tab, in the **Tools** group, click **Primary Key** .

    g. Save and close the table.

3.   Create a Many-to-Many relationship by following these steps:

    a. From the **Database Tools** tab, in the **Relationships** group, click **Relationships** .

    b. In the **Navigation Pane**, drag **tblCarriers**, **tblCarrierOptions**, and **tblDeliveryType**.

    c. From **tblCarriers**, drag the **CarrierID** field to the **CarrierID** field in **tblCarrierOptions**.

    d. In the **Edit Relationship** dialog box, click **Enforce Referential Integrity**, and click **Create**.

    e. From **tblDeliveryType**, drag the **DeliveryID** field to the **DeliveryID** field in **tblCarrierOptions**.

    f. In the **Edit Relationship** dialog box, click **Enforce Referential Integrity** and click **Create**.

    g. Close the Relationships window and save the changes.

Assessment

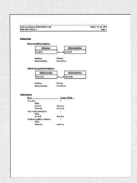

09-23-A.pdf
1 Page

DB - Turn in your **EcoMed-09** database only when all assigned exercises have been completed, according to your classroom procedure.

-OR-

PDF - Create a **Database Documenter** report by following these steps:

    a. From the **Database Tools** tab, in the **Analyze** group, click **Database Documenter** .

    b. On the **Tables** tab, select **tblCarrierOptions**.

    c. Click **Options**. From the **Include for Tables** section, choose only **Relationships**.

    d. From the **Include for Fields** section, choose **Nothing**.

    e. From the **Include for Indexes** section, choose **Names and Fields**.

    f. Click **OK** twice.

- Save a **Database Documenter** report by following these steps:

    a. From the **Print Preview** tab, in the **Data** group, click **PDF or XPS** to save the printout as a file.

    b. Save the file as a PDF and name the file *[your initials]*-**09-23-A**.

    c. Depending on your class procedures, print or turn in the PDF file.

    d. Close **Print Preview**.

Exercise 9-24

After reviewing the database structure, your boss instructs you to create a One-to-Many relationship and refresh a linked table.

1. Create a One-to-Many relationship by following these steps:

    a. Open and enable content for *[your initials]*-**HR-09**.

    b. From the Database Tools tab, in the Relationships group, click Relationships �lq.

    c. In the Navigation Pane, drag **tblEmployees** and **tblJobCodes**.

    d. From **tblEmployees**, drag the **JobCodeID** field to the **JobCodeID** field in **tblJobCodes**.

    e. Click Enforce Referential Integrity and then Cascade Update Related Fields.

    f. In the Edit Relationship dialog box, click Join Type.

    g. Select join type **2** and click OK.

    h. Click Create.

    i. Close the Relationships window and save the changes.

    j. Close *[your initials]*-**HR-09**.

2. Open a database and refresh linked tables by following these steps:

    a. Open and enable content for *[your initials]*-EcoMed-09.

    b. From the External Data tab, in the Import & Link group, click Link Table Manager 🔲.

    c. Click Select All. Remove the checkmark for **tblProjectedSales**.

    d. Locate the database *[your initials]*-**HR-09** and click Open.

    e. Click OK and then close the Linked Table Manager dialog box.

Assessment

- Turn in your **EcoMed-09** and **HR-09** databases only when all assigned exercises have been completed, according to your classroom procedure.
- Close both databases.

-OR-

- Create a Database Documenter report by following these steps:

    a. From the Database Tools tab, in the Analyze group, click Database Documenter 📄.

    b. On the Tables tab, select **tblJobCodes**.

    c. Click Options. From the Include for Tables section, only include Properties and Relationships.

    d. From the Include for Fields section, choose Nothing.

09-24-A.pdf
1 Page

e. From the **Include for Indexes** section, choose **Nothing**.

f. Click **OK** twice.

- Save a **Database Documenter** report by following these steps:

a. From the **Print Preview** tab, in the **Data** group, click **PDF or XPS** 🔽 to save the printout as a file.

b. Save the file as a PDF and name the file *[your initials]*-09-24-A.

c. Depending on your class procedures, print or turn in the PDF file.

d. Close **Print Preview**.

e. Close both databases.

Lesson Applications

Exercise 9-25

You have been informed that the time card table needs to be related to the employee table. Create the appropriate relationship and enforce referential integrity.

1. Open and enable content for *[your initials]*-**HR-09**.

2. Create a One-to-Many relationship for **tblEmployees** and **tblTimeCards**.

3. Enforce referential integrity.

Assessment

- Turn in your **HR-09** database only when all assigned exercises have been completed, according to your classroom procedure.

-OR-

- Create a Database Documenter report for **tblTimeCards** using the following settings:
  - Include for Table: Properties and Relationships only
  - Include for Fields: Nothing
  - Include for Indexes: Nothing
- Save the Documenter report as a PDF file named *[your initials]*-**09-25-A**.
- Depending on your class procedures, print or turn in the PDF file.

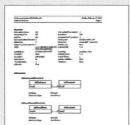

09-25-A.pdf
1 Page

Exercise 9-26

You have been instructed to create a query to display a list of employees who have not taken any annual leave. You will need to create a relationship between the employee and leave day tables. You will then need to create a query using the appropriate criterion.

1. Using *[your initials]*-**HR-09**, create a global One-to-Many relationship for **tblEmployees** and **tblLeaveDays**.

2. Apply a join type 2 and enforce referential integrity.

3. Create a query using both tables that displays the **FirstName**, **LastName**, and **LeaveDate** fields.

4. For the **LeaveDate** field, add criteria to display only "Null" values.

5. Save the query as qryEmpNoLeave.

Assessment

- Turn in your **HR-09** database only when all assigned exercises have been completed, according to your classroom procedure.

-OR-

- Create a **Database Documenter** report for **qryEmpNoLeave** using the following settings:
  - Include for Query: **Properties, SQL only**
  - Include for Fields: **Nothing**
  - Include for Indexes: **Nothing**
- Save the **Documenter** report as a PDF file named *[your initials]*-09-26-A.
- Depending on your class procedures, print or turn in the PDF file.

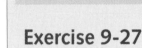

09-26-A.pdf
1 Page

Exercise 9-27

The Intern table needs to be modified to make the overall database design more efficient for mailing documents. Create an appropriate multifield index and primary key.

1. Using *[your initials]*-**HR-09**, in **tblInterns**, create a two-field index called **FullName** using **LastName** and **FirstName**.

2. Create a multifield index called **FullAddress**, using **Street**, **City**. and **State**.

3. Make the field **InternID** the **Primary Key**.

Assessment

- Turn in your **HR-09** database only when all assigned exercises have been completed, according to your classroom procedure.

-OR-

- Create a **Database Documenter** report for **tblInterns** using the following settings:
  - Include for Table: **Properties**
  - Include for Fields: **Nothing**
  - Include for Indexes: **Names and Fields**
- Save the **Documenter** report as a PDF file named *[your initials]*-09-27-A.
- Depending on your class procedures, print or turn in the PDF file.

09-27-A.pdf
1 Page

Exercise 9-28 ◆ Challenge Yourself

You have been asked to create a query to display the site visit notes written by sales representatives whenever they visit a facilty. The notes are stored in a spreadsheet.

1. Open *[your initials]*-EcoMed-09 and refresh the linked tables.

2. Link **Visit Notes** data from the spreadsheet **SalesRepReports** into *[your initials]*-EcoMed-09.

3. Name the table **tblFacNotes**.

4. Create a **One-To-Many** relationship between **tblEmployees** and **tblFacNotes**.

5. Create a **One-To-Many** relationship between **tblFacilities** and **tblFacNotes**.

6. Using these tables, create a query that displays the **FirstName** and **LastName** of the sales representatives in addition to the **FacName**, **Date**, and **SiteNotes** fields.

7. Only show records from the sales representative "Herberling."

8. Save the query as **qryHerberlingNotes**.

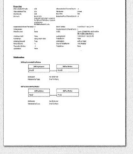

09-28-A.pdf
1 Page

Assessment

- Turn in your **EcoMed-09** database only when all assigned exercises have been completed, according to your classroom procedure.

-OR-

- Create a **Database Documenter** report for **tblFacNotes**.
  - Include for Table: **Properties** and **Relationships**
  - Include for Fields: **Nothing**
  - Include for Indexes: **Nothing**
- Save the **Documenter** report as a PDF file named *[your initials]*-09-28-A.
- Create a **Database Documenter** report for **qryHerberlingNotes**.
  - Include for Query: **Properties** and **SQL**
  - Include for Fields: **Nothing**
  - Include for Indexes: **Nothing**
- Save the **Documenter** report as a PDF file named *[your initials]*-09-28-B.
- Depending on your class procedures, print or turn in the PDF file.

09-28-B.pdf
1 Page

On Your Own

In these exercises you work on your own, as you would in a real-life work environment. Use the skills you've learned to accomplish the task—and be creative.

Exercise 9-29

Review the design of the database you created and modified in Exercises 8-27 through 8-29. Identify at least two additional tables requiring referential integrity that will enhance your database design. Consider adding tables that will keep cumulative or historical information. On a sheet of paper, list the fields that will be stored in each table. Draw the relationships among all the tables in your database. Identify the type of integrity and cascade options to be used for each relationship. On each sheet, write your name, the date, your class, and the exercise number. Continue to the next exercise.

Exercise 9-30

Create each table you designed in Exercise 9-29. Create the relationships and enforce the proper integrity and cascade options. Enter at least five records into each new table. Test the integrity and cascade options for each relationship. Identify any errors in your design and make the appropriate corrections. Continue to the next exercise.

Exercise 9-31

On separate printouts, print each relationship between all tables. For each relationship printout, write the type of referential integrity used and the cascade option applied. Print the Relationships window, showing all relationships for the entire database. On each printout, write your name, the date, your class, and the exercise number. Submit to your instructor the sheets from Exercise 9-29 and the printouts from Exercise 9-31. Keep a copy of the database you modified in this exercise. You will use it for the On Your Own exercises in subsequent lessons.

Lesson 10
Designing Advanced Queries

OBJECTIVES *After completing this lesson, you will be able to:*

1. Create and use select queries.

2. Create and use summary queries.

3. Work with summary query options.

4. Create and use a parameter query.

5. Create and use action queries.

Estimated Time: 1½ hours

Most database users consider tables to be the foundation of databases. However, queries, rather than tables, most often are used to view, modify, and analyze information in a database. Queries provide the power to accomplish most business tasks, such as combining data, calculating totals, updating records, copying groups of records, deleting inactive records, and even creating new tables.

In Access, queries can be categorized as follows:

- Select query: A query that displays data from one or more tables.

- Summary query: A query that shows aggregate values for a recordset.

- Parameter query: A query that prompts a user for criteria when executed.

- Action query: A query that performs an action such as append, update, delete, or make table.

Creating Select Queries

In the EcoMed Services database, forms and reports most often use a select query as its record source. A *select query* is a query that displays data from one or more tables. A select query can display all or a subset of the fields and records stored in the source table(s). A select query can also display the dynaset in a predefined sorted order.

Exercise 10-1 CREATE A QUERY FROM A FILTER

Just like a select query, a filter limits the number of records displayed in a dynaset based on the criterion set in the filter. You will now use a filter to create a query to display bulbs used in outdoor fixtures.

1. Locate and open the **Lesson 10** folder.

2. Copy **EcoMed-10** and rename it *[your initials]*-EcoMed-10. Copy **HR-10** and rename it *[your initials]*-HR-10.

3. Open, enable content, and refresh the linked tables for *[your initials]*-**EcoMed-10**.

4. Open **tblInventory** in Datasheet View.

5. From the Home tab, in the Sort & Filter group, click Advanced 🔽 and choose Filter By Form.

6. In the **Bulb Category** field, choose "Outdoor."

7. From the Home tab, in the Sort & Filter group, click Toggle Filter 🔽. The number of records has been reduced from 310 to 70.

8. From the Home tab, in the Sort & Filter group, click Advanced 🔽 and choose Filter By Form.

9. From the Home tab, in the Sort & Filter group, click Advanced 🔽 and choose Save As Query 🔖.

Figure 10-1
Save a filter as a query
EcoMed-10.accdb

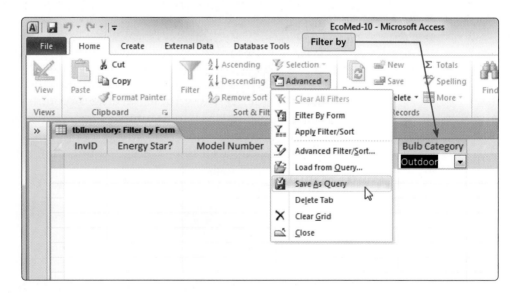

10. Save the query as **qryOutdoorBulbs**.

11. From the Home tab, in the Sort & Filter group, click Toggle Filter 🔽.

12. Close the table without saving the changes.

13. Open **qryOutdoorBulbs**. Only records with the bulb category of "Outdoor" are in this dynaset.

14. Close the query.

Exercise 10-2 CREATE A SUBQUERY

Each query creates a unique dynaset. When you use a query within a query, you create a subquery. Depending on the structure of your database and the number of records and fields in your record source, a subquery may improve the speed with which a dynaset displays. Using the query that you just created, you will now create a subquery that will display the cost of each outdoor bulb.

1. From the **Create** tab, in the **Queries** group, click **Query Design** .

2. In the **Show Table** dialog box, double-click **tblBulbShapes**.

3. Click the **Queries** tab and double-click **qryOutdoorBulbs**.

4. Click **Close**.

5. From **tblBulbShapes**, double-click **BulbShape**. From **qryOutdoorBulbs**, double-click **ModelNum**, **VenderID** and **Cost**.

6. View the 70 records in the dynaset. Since **qryOutdoorBulbs** already had the criterion "Outdoor," there was no need to repeat it in this query.

7. Close and save the query as qryOutdoorCost.

Creating and Using a Summary Query

So far, the queries you have created and been using are select queries. A *select query* is a query that retrieves information from one or more tables and displays the results in a datasheet. A *summary query* is a select query that displays summarized rather than individualized data.

Summary queries show totals, averages, counts, minimums, or maximums for grouped records. In a summary query, each field is used for grouping or in an aggregate function. An *aggregate function* is a mathematical equation that calculates a sum, average, count, minimum, or maximum for a specific group of records.

> **TIP**
>
> To produce a practical summary query, do not include fields that are not being used for grouping, criteria, or calculations.

Exercise 10-3   CREATE A SUMMARY QUERY BY USING A WIZARD

Business activities often must analyze data. Minimum values, maximum values, and averages can be displayed and analyzed. Using the inventory table, you now will create a query to analyze summarized inventory values.

For each field summarized, Access creates a caption based on the function and the name of the field. For example, when applying the Avg function to the field Cost, Access creates the caption "Avg of Cost." When you apply the Min function to the field Wattage, the caption becomes "Min of Wattage."

REVIEW

Tables precede queries in the Tables/ Queries list.

1. From the **Create** tab, in the **Queries** group, click **Query Wizard**.

2. In the **New Query** dialog box, choose **Simple Query Wizard** and click **OK**.

3. In the **Table/Queries** list, choose **Table: tblInventory**. Add **ShapeID**, **Wattage**, and **Cost** to the **Selected Fields** list. Click **Next**.

4. Click the **Summary** option button. Click **Summary Options**. From the fields you selected in the previous step, Access lists all numeric fields.

5. For the field **Wattage**, add checkmarks to **Min** and **Max**.

6. For the field **Cost**, add a checkmark to **Avg**.

Figure 10-2
Summary options
EcoMed-10.accdb

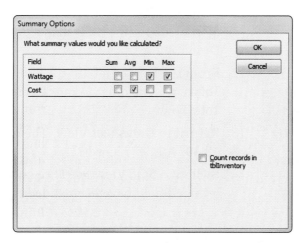

7. Click **OK**. Click **Next**. Key qryBulbShapeStats as the title and then click **Finish**. The dynaset shows the maximum and minimum wattage and the average of the cost for each bulb shape.

8. Switch to **Design View**. The design grid shows a **Total** row below the **Table** row in the lower pane. This query groups the records by **ShapeID** and uses aggregate functions on the fields **Wattage** and **Cost**.

Figure 10-3
Design grid for
summary query
EcoMed-10.accdb
qryBulbShapeStats

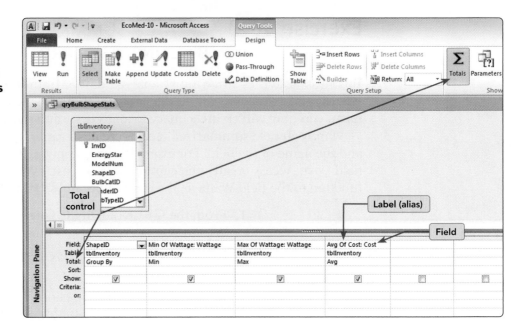

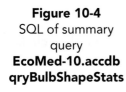

NOTE

The Totals button Σ toggles the Total row off and on.

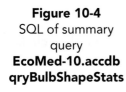

NOTE

In summary queries, you cannot modify data because you are not looking at individual records but at summaries of records.

9. Set the query to sort in ascending order by **ShapeID**.

10. From the **Design** tab, in the **Show/Hide** group, click **Totals** Σ. This action removes the **Total** row from the design grid which changes the Summary query to a Select query.

11. Switch to **Datasheet View**. Notice that there are 30 records for the bulb shape "A-line." Return to **Design View**.

12. From the **Design** tab, in the **Show/Hide** group, click **Totals** Σ. The query remembered the settings in the **Total** row.

13. Return to **Datasheet View**. The query has combined all 30 "A-line" records.

14. Switch to **SQL View** ᴄᴏᴸ. Three functions and the grouped field have been added to the SQL statement.

Figure 10-4
SQL of summary
query
EcoMed-10.accdb
qryBulbShapeStats

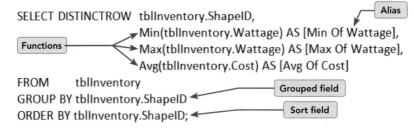

```
SELECT DISTINCTROW  tblInventory.ShapeID,
                    Min(tblInventory.Wattage) AS [Min Of Wattage],
                    Max(tblInventory.Wattage) AS [Max Of Wattage],
                    Avg(tblInventory.Cost) AS [Avg Of Cost]
FROM      tblInventory
GROUP BY tblInventory.ShapeID
ORDER BY tblInventory.ShapeID;
```

15. Save and close the query.

Exercise 10-4 CREATE A SUMMARY QUERY IN DESIGN VIEW

To create a summary query, you add the Total row to the design grid of a select query. All fields are initially set to Group By. Each field to be summarized then can be set to display an aggregate function. Using Design View, you now will count the total number of bulbs.

1. From the **Create** tab, in the **Queries** group, click **Query Design** [icon].
2. From the **Show Table** dialog box, double-click **tblInventory** and click **Close**.
3. Size the panes and the Field Lists.
4. From **tblInventory**, add **VenderID**, **BulbCatID**, and **ModelNum** to the design grid.
5. Add **Ascending** sort orders to both **VenderID** and **BulbCatID**.
6. Switch to **Datasheet View**. At this point, you have a simple select query.
7. Return to **Design View**.
8. From the **Design** tab, in the **Show/Hide** group, click **Totals** Σ. The **Total** row appears below the **Table** row in the design grid.
9. Click the **Total** row for the **ModelNum** field. Choose **Count** from the drop-down list. Your query now counts the **ModelNum** field and groups records by **VenderID** and **BulbCatID**.

Figure 10-5
Grouping and counting
**EcoMed-10.accdb
qryVenBulbCount**

Field:	VenderID	BulbCatID	ModelNum	
Table:	tblInventory	tblInventory	tblInventory	
Total:	Group By	Group By	Count ▾	
Sort:	Ascending	Ascending		
Show:	☑	☑	☑	
Criteria:				
or:				

10. Switch to **Datasheet View**. The first vender only supplies us with 4 kinds of indoor bulbs.
11. Save the query as **qryVenBulbCount**.
12. Switch to **SQL View** [icon].

Figure 10-6
SQL statement with multiple grouped fields
**EcoMed-10.accdb
qryVenBulbCount**

```
SELECT    tblInventory.VenderID,
          tblInventory.BulbCatID,
          Count(tblInventory.ModelNum) AS CountOfModelNum
FROM      tblInventory
GROUP BY tblInventory.VenderID, tblInventory.BulbCatID
ORDER BY tblInventory.VenderID, tblInventory.BulbCatID;
```

Multiple grouped fields

13. Close the query.

Working with Summary Query Options

Aggregate functions summarize large or complex data. Many businesses rely on summarized rather than detailed data to forecast trends. Often management reports are based on queries that use aggregate functions. Summary queries display data based on criteria that include, exclude, or hide individual records.

Exercise 10-5 USE AGGREGATE FUNCTIONS IN A QUERY

You have been directed to create a query to display sales statistics for the six sales regions. You will display the total and average of retail sales made in each region.

1. Open **qryShipDetails** in **Design View**.
2. This query shows all of the bulbs sold, their quantity sold, their cost, and the extended retail price (quantity sold × bulb cost × 48 percent markup). Close the query.
3. From the **Create** tab, in the **Queries** group, click **Query Design** .
4. From the **Show Table** dialog box, double-click **tblFacilities** and **tblShipments**.
5. From the **Show Table** dialog box, click the **Queries** tab and double-click **qryShipDetails**. Close the dialog box.
6. Resize and align the Field Lists.
7. From the **tblFacilities** Field List, double-click **Region**.
8. From the **qryShipDetails** Field List, double-click **ExtRetail** twice.
9. In the design grid for **Region**, in the **Sort** row, click the drop-down arrow and choose **Descending**.
10. Switch to **Datasheet View**. There are 1662 records. Notice that there are 14 orders in region 9. Return to **Design View**.
11. Save the query as **qryRegionSaleStats**.
12. From the **Design** tab, in the **Show/Hide** group, click **Totals** Σ .
13. In the design grid for the first **ExtRetail**, in the **Total** row, click the drop-down arrow, and choose **Sum**.
14. In the design grid for the second **ExtRetail**, in the **Total** row, click the drop-down arrow, and choose **Avg**.
15. In the design grid for the first **ExtRetail**, in the **Field** row, click and press Home . Key **Total Retail:**.
16. In the design grid for the second **ExtRetail**, in the **Field** row, click and press Home . Key **Average Retail:**.
17. From the **Design** tab, in the **Show/Hide** group, click **Property Sheet** .
18. In the **Property Sheet**, click the **Format** property and choose **Currency**.

19. Click anywhere in the "Total Retail" column in the design grid. Set the **Format** property for this field to **Currency**.

Figure 10-7
Setting properties in a query
EcoMed-10.accdb
qryRegionSaleStats

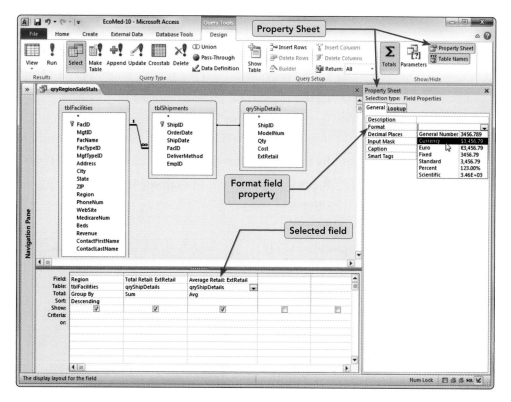

20. Close the **Property Sheet** and switch to **Datasheet View**. The 14 orders in region 9 have been grouped into one summarized record. Resize each column to all of the data.

21. Close and save the query.

Exercise 10-6 USE THE MONTH FUNCTION IN A QUERY

Often summary queries display information based on dates. In a summary query, a date/time value can be used to display years, months, days, hours, minutes, or seconds. Depending on the type of information needed, you can create queries for specific date ranges, such as fiscal years, quarters, or months.

The Month Function extracts the numeric value of the month from a date/time value. Dates between January 1, 2011, and January 31, 2011, would return the numeric value of 1. Dates between April 1, 2012, and April 30, 2012, would return the numeric value of 4.

You have been asked to create a query to calculate the average length of time it takes to ship an item. You will begin this task by displaying the month of the order date as a numeric value.

1. From the **Create** tab, in the **Queries** group, click **Query Design**.

2. From the **Show Table** dialog box, double-click **tblShipments** and click **Close**.

3. Resize the Field List. In the design grid, in the first column, click in the **Field** row.

4. Save the query as **qryAvgShipTime**.

5. From the **Design** tab, in the **Query Setup** group, click **Builder** 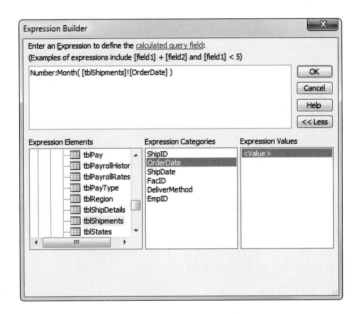.

6. In the **Expression Elements** panel, double-click the **Functions** folder and click **Built-In Functions**.

7. In the **Expression Categories** panel, click **Date/Time**.

8. In the **Expression Values** panel, double-click **Month**.

9. In the top panel, click <<date>>.

10. In the **Expression Elements** panel, double-click **EcoMed-10.accdb** and double-click the **Tables** folder. Scroll down and click **tblShipments**.

11. In the **Expression Categories** panel, double-click **OrderDate**.

12. Press Home to move the cursor to the beginning of the expression in the top panel. Key **Number:**.

Figure 10-8
Month function
**EcoMed-10.accdb
qryAvgShipTime**

13. Click **OK**. Widen the column so that you can see the whole expression.

14. Switch to **Datasheet View**. This function returns the number of each month. Return to **Design View**.

15. Save the query.

Exercise 10-7   USE THE MONTHNAME FUNCTION IN A QUERY

Now that you have created an expression that extracted the month from the shipping date value, you will create an express to display the name of the month rather than just its numeric value.

1. Click in the second field column's **Field** row.

2. From the **Design** tab, in the **Query Setup** group, click **Builder** .

3. In the **Expression Elements** panel, double-click the **Functions** folder and click the **Built-In Functions** folder.

4. In the **Expression Categories** panel, click **Date/Time**.

5. In the **Expression Values** panel, double-click **MonthName**.

6. In the top panel, click **<<abbreviate>>**. This parameter of the function can be used to tell the function if you want the results to be abbreviated.

7. Press ⌈Delete⌉ and press ⌈Backspace⌉ until you delete the comma.

8. Click **<<month>>**.

9. In the **Expression Values** panel, double-click **Month**.

10. In the top panel, click **<<date>>**.

11. In the **Expression Elements** panel, double-click the **EcoMed-10.accdb** folder and double-click the **Tables** folder. Click **tblShipments**.

12. In the **Expression Categories** panel, double-click **OrderDate**.

13. In the top panel, click on the expression and press ⌈Home⌉. Key **Month:**, which will be the calculated field's alias.

Figure 10-9
MonthName function
EcoMed-10.accdb
qryAvgShipTime

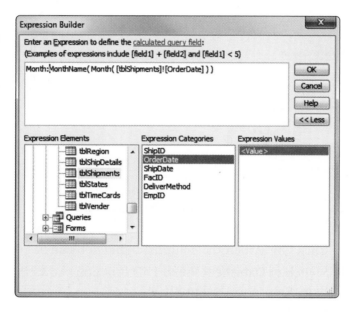

14. Click **OK**. Widen the column so that you can see the whole expression.

15. Switch to **Datasheet View**. This function spells out the name of each month. Return to **Design View**.

16. Save the query.

Exercise 10-8   USE THE YEAR FUNCTION IN A QUERY

The Year Function extracts the numeric value of the year from a date/time value. Dates between January 1, 2010, and December 31, 2010, would return the numeric value of 2010. Dates between July 1, 2011, and December 31, 2011, would return the numeric value of 2011.

1. Click in the third field column's **Field** row.

2. From the **Design** tab, in the **Query Setup** group, click **Builder** ⬈.

3. In the **Expression Elements** panel, double-click the **Functions** folder and click the **Built-In Functions** folder.

4. In the **Expression Categories** panel, click **Date/Time**.

5. In the **Expression Values** panel, double-click **Year**.

6. Click <<date>>.

7. In the **Expression Elements** panel, double-click the **EcoMed-10.accdb** folder and double-click the **Tables** folder. Click **tblShipments**.

8. In the **Expression Categories** panel, double-click **OrderDate**.

9. In the top panel, click on the expression and press Home. Key **Year:**.

Figure 10-10
Year function
EcoMed-10.accdb
qryAvgShipTime

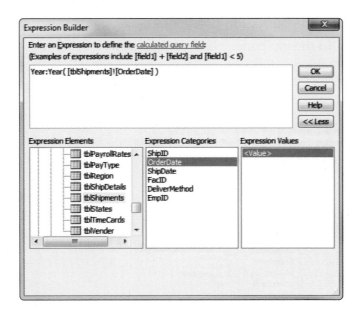

10. Click **OK**. Widen the column so that you can see the whole expression.

11. Switch to **Datasheet View**. This function shows the year of the order date. Return to **Design View**.

12. Save the query.

Exercise 10-9   ENTER A CALCULATION IN A QUERY

Date/time values display as dates and time. However, in reality, date/time values are numeric values with special display properties. Most application software, such as Access, begins incrementing numeric values starting January 1, 1900. Each day equals the number one.

The numeric values of two dates can be subtracted to display a numeric value. Assume that EcoMed Services receives an order on February 11, 2011, and ships it on February 15, 2011. Access calculates the time it takes to fulfill the order by subtracting the ship date from the order date.

Access stores the order date as 40585 and the ship date as 40589. Subtracting the order date from the ship date would return a value of 4 days.

1. Click in the fourth field column's **Field** row.

2. From the **Design** tab, in the **Query Setup** group, click **Builder** 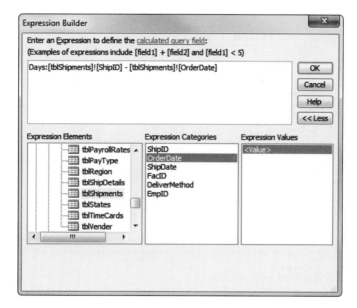.

3. In the **Expression Elements** panel, double-click the **EcoMed-10.accdb** folder and double-click the **Tables** folder. Click **tblShipments**.

4. In the **Expression Categories** panel, double-click **ShipDate**.

5. Press ⌷.

6. In the **Expression Categories** panel, double-click **OrderDate**.

7. In the top panel, click on the expression and press ⌷Home⌷. Key **Days:**.

Figure 10-11
Data calculation
EcoMed-10.accdb
qryAvgShipTime

8. Click **OK**. Widen the column so that you can see the whole expression.

9. Switch to **Datasheet View**. This calculation shows the number of days between the order date and the ship date.

10. Return to **Design View**.

11. Save the query.

Exercise 10-10   CREATE A SUMMARY QUERY

You will now create a summary query that will display the average number of days it's **Field** row takes EcoMed Services to ship an order. For each order you will calculate the difference between the order date and the shipping date.

Rather than sort by the alpahabetic name of the month, you will sort by the numeric value of the month. If you sorted by the alphabetic name, the months would appear alphabetically starting with April then August and ending with October then September.

1. In the design grid for **Number**, in the **Sort** row, click the drop-down arrow and choose **Ascending**.

2. For the **Number** field, remove the **Show** checkmark.

3. From the **Design** tab, in the **Show/Hide** group, click **Property Sheet** 📰.

4. For the calculated field **Days**, set the **Format** property to **Standard**.

5. Set the **Decimal Places** property to **2**. Close the **Property Sheet**.

6. From the **Design** tab, in the **Show/Hide** group, click **Totals** Σ.

7. For the **Year** field, in the **Total** row, change **Group By** to **Where**. The **Show** checkmark has automatically been removed.

8. For the **Year** field, in the **Criteria** row, key **2011**.

9. For the **Days** field, in the **Total** row, change **Group By** to **Avg**.

Figure 10-12
Final
qryAvgShipTime
EcoMed-10.accdb
qryAvgShipTime

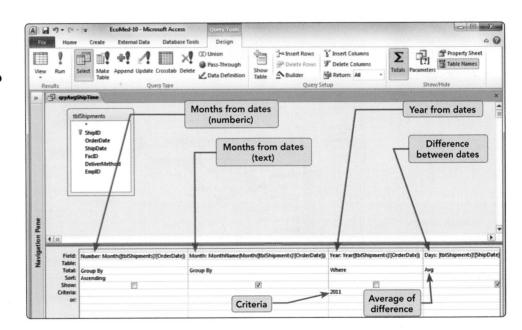

10. Switch to **Datasheet View**. The query now shows the average days between the order and shipping dates by months in 2011.

11. Switch to **SQL View** 🗒. Notice that the **Year** function only appears as a criterion and not after the **Select** keyword. Only fields with a **Show** checkmark are listed after the **Select** keyword.

Figure 10-13
qryAvgShipTime SQL
statement
EcoMed-10.accdb
qryAvgShipTime

Nested functions   Alias

SELECT   MonthName(Month([tblShipments]![OrderDate])) AS [Month],
         Avg([tblShipments]![ShipDate]-[tblShipments]![OrderDate]) AS Days
FROM   tblShipments   Criteria
WHERE   (((Year([tblShipments]![OrderDate]))=2011))
GROUP BY MonthName(Month([tblShipments]![OrderDate])),
         Month([tblShipments]![OrderDate])
ORDER BY Month([tblShipments]![OrderDate]);

12. Save and close the query.

Creating and Using a Parameter Query

Some queries use dynamic criteria to create a dynaset. A parameter query prompts the user for criteria each time it runs. Using a parameter query makes databases more flexible and powerful. Rather than creating unique queries for each possible value, you can run a single query that displays a dialog box, prompting you for a criterion.

Exercise 10-11   RUN A PARAMETER QUERY

EcoMed Services has unique job codes for its employees. Employees with a job code beginning with MF are part of the manufacturing/warehouse operations. Employees with a job code beginning with OF are part of the office/administrative operations.

If you wanted to display employees for each job code, and you used common select queries, you would need to create and save a different query for each job code. A more efficient way is to display this information is to use a parameter query that prompts the user for the job code each time the query runs. To see how this works, run the employee by job code query.

1. In the **Navigation Pane**, double-click the query **qryEmpByJobCode**.

2. The **Enter Parameter Value** dialog box opens as the query runs.

3. Key **mf04** in the dialog box.

Figure 10-14
Enter Parameter
Value dialog box
EcoMed-10.accdb
qryEmpByJobCode

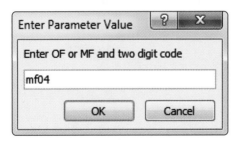

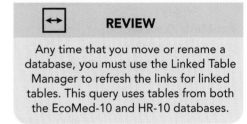

REVIEW

Any time that you move or rename a database, you must use the Linked Table Manager to refresh the links for linked tables. This query uses tables from both the EcoMed-10 and HR-10 databases.

4. Press Enter or click **OK**. The dynaset shows employees who work as Inspectors (job code MF04).

5. Switch to **Design View**.

6. Click the **Criteria** row for the **JobCode** field.

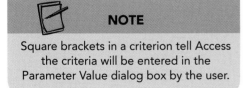

NOTE

Square brackets in a criterion tell Access the criteria will be entered in the Parameter Value dialog box by the user.

7. Press Shift+F2 to open the **Zoom** dialog box. The prompt is enclosed in square brackets. Click **Cancel**.

8. From the **Design** tab, in the **Results** group, click **Datasheet View**. The query runs and again displays the **Enter Parameter Value** dialog box.

9. Key **mf03** and click **OK**. This dynaset shows the stock managers (job code MF03) who work at EcoMed.

10. Close the query.

Exercise 10-12 CREATE A PARAMETER QUERY

You have been asked to create a parameter query that will display the name of the facility, the city, the state, and the order date. When you create a parameter query, you must first choose the field or fields in which comparisons will be made. For this example, you will compare the state and order date.

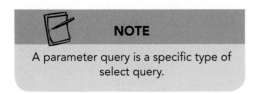

NOTE

A parameter query is a specific type of select query.

1. From the **Create** tab, in the **Queries** group, click **Query Design**.

2. Add the tables **tblFacilities** and **tblShipments**. You should see the join line with referential integrity for the **FacID** field.

3. Size the panes and the Field Lists.

4. Save the query as **qryFac-ShipByState**.

5. From **tblFacilities**, double-click these field names in the order shown: **FacName**, **City**, and **State**.

6. From **tblShipments**, add the field **OrderDate**.

7. Click the **Criteria** row for the **State** field.

8. Key **[Enter a State]** (include the square brackets).

Figure 10-15
Create a parameter criteria
EcoMed-10.accdb
qryFac-ShipByState

Field:	FacName	City	State	OrderDate	
Table:	tblFacilities	tblFacilities	tblFacilities	tblShipments	
Sort:					
Show:	☑	☑	☑	☑	
Criteria:			[Enter a State]		
or:					

9. Switch to **Datasheet View**. Key **oh** and click **OK**. These are the facilities in Ohio that placed recent orders.

10. From the **Home** tab, in the **Records** group, click **Refresh All** 🔄.

11. Key **ca** and press Enter. Only facilities in California that placed recent orders are now shown.

12. Return to **Design View**.

Exercise 10-13 SET DATA TYPES IN A PARAMETER QUERY

You can also add or change parameters through the Query Parameters dialog box. Open the dialog box and examine the parameter that you just created.

1. Click in the **Criteria** row for the field **State**. Press F2 to select the prompt. Press Ctrl+C to copy the prompt to the Office Clipboard.

2. From the **Design** tab, in the **Show/Hide** group, click **Parameters** .

3. Press Ctrl+V to paste the text from the Clipboard.

4. Click in the **Data Type** column and select **Text**.

Figure 10-16
Setting a parameter
data type
**EcoMed-10.accdb
qryCust&Orders**

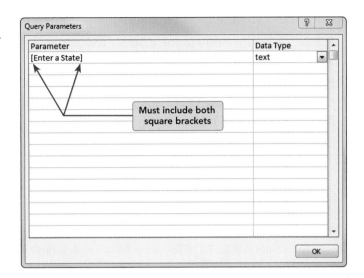

5. Click **OK** to close the **Query Parameters** dialog box.

Exercise 10-14 USE MULTIPLE CRITERIA IN A PARAMETER QUERY

Similar to creating a single-parameter query, you can create a query using multiple parameters. If you place two parameters on the same Criteria row, both criteria must match for the record to be included in the dynaset. If you place parameters on separate rows, either criterion must match for the record to be included in the dynaset.

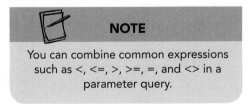

NOTE

You can combine common expressions such as <, <=, >, >=, =, and <> in a parameter query.

1. From the **Design** tab, in the **Show/Hide** group, click **Parameters** .

2. Click into the second row and key **[Enter Date]**.

3. In the **Data Type** column, choose **Date/Time**.

4. Click **OK** to close the **Query Parameters** dialog box.

5. Click in the first criteria row for **OrderDate** to create an "AND" criteria.

6. Key **>[e**. A list of Explicit Parameters appears.

Figure 10-17
Add a parameter to
a query
**EcoMed-10.accdb
qryFac-ShipByState**

Field:	FacName	City	State	OrderDate	
Table:	tblFacilities	tblFacilities	tblFacilities	tblShipments	
Sort:					
Show:	✓	✓	✓	✓	☐
Criteria:			[Enter a State]	>[e	
or:					

[?] Enter a State
[?] Enter Date   Explicit Parameter

7. From the list, double-click "Enter Date."

8. Switch to **Datasheet View**. Key **oh** and click **OK**. Key **3/1/11** and click **OK**. Three facilities in Ohio ordered since March 1, 2011.

9. Return to **Design View**.

10. Click the parameter **>[Enter Date]** and press F2. Press Ctrl+X to cut it.

11. Press ↓ to move down one criteria row. Press Ctrl+V to paste. This action creates an "OR" criteria.

12. Switch to **Datasheet View**. Key **oh** and click **OK**. Key **3/1/11** and click **OK**. These are all the Ohio customers or any facilities that ordered after March 1, 2011 (37 records).

13. Switch to **SQL View** SQL.

Parameters defined

Figure 10-18
Parameter in an SQL
statement
**EcoMed-10.accdb
qryFac-ShipByState**

PARAMETERS [Enter a State] Text (255), [Enter Date] DateTime;
SELECT   tblFacilities.FacName, tblFacilities.City, tblFacilities.State, tblShipments.OrderDate
FROM   tblFacilities INNER JOIN tblShipments ON tblFacilities.FacID = tblShipments.FacID
WHERE   (((tblFacilities.State)=[Enter a State])) OR (((tblShipments.OrderDate)>[Enter Date]));

Parameters in criteria

14. Save and close the query.

Exercise 10-15   USE A PARAMETER QUERY WITH WILDCARDS

Sometimes wildcards cannot be used in a parameter. Access assumes that the values you enter in a parameter are the exact characters that you mean to use. You can use wildcards when you only know a portion of the criterion or when you want to find values that follow specific patterns. Wildcards can be used with text and numeric fields.

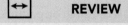

REVIEW

Valid wildcards include an asterisk (*) to represent any number of characters, a question mark (?) to represent a single character, and a number sign (#) to represent a single numeric character.

REVIEW

The criterion used to list all job codes that start with the letter m is "m*". When using a wildcard in criteria, you must precede the criteria with the keyword "Like."

1. Double-click **qryEmpByJobCode**. The **Enter Parameter Value** dialog box opens.

2. Key **m*** and press Enter. No records are shown because the query does not regard the asterisk as a wildcard.

3. Return to **Design View**.

4. Click in the **Criteria** row for **JobCodeID**. Press Shift+F2 to open the **Zoom** dialog box. Click anywhere in the **Zoom** dialog box and then press Home. Key **like** and click **OK**.

Figure 10-19
Criteria using a
keyword and a
parameter
**EcoMed-10.accdb
qryEmpByJobCode**

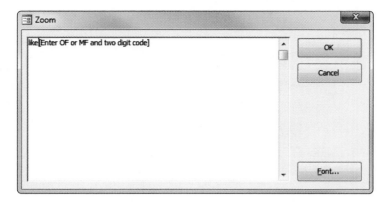

5. Switch to **Datasheet View**. In the **Enter Parameter Value** dialog box, key **m*** and press Enter to display all employees with a job code starting with "M."

6. From the **Home** tab, in the **Records** group, click **Refresh All** ▣.

7. In the **Enter Parameter Value** dialog box, key **o*** and press Enter to display all the employees with a job code starting with "O."

8. Save and close the query.

Exercise 10-16 USE A PARAMETER QUERY WITH A REPORT

The EcoMed Services inventory is categorized by bulb wattage. To create a separate report for each product group, you would need a matching select query and report for each wattage size. Rather than create separate queries and reports, you can create a single parameter query that lets you apply criteria each time you execute the report.

1. Open **qryBulbDetails** in **Design View**.

2. From the **Design** tab, in the **Show/Hide** group, click **Parameters** ▦.

3. Key **[Enter Bulb Wattage]**.

4. Press Tab. In the **Data Type** column, choose **Integer**.

5. Click **OK** to close the **Query Parameters** dialog box.

6. Click the **Criteria** row for the **Wattage** field.

7. Key **[e**. In the **Explicit Parameter** list, double-click **[Enter Bulb Wattage]**.

8. Switch to **Datasheet View**. In the **Enter Parameter Value** dialog box, key **20** and press Enter to display all bulbs that are 20 watts.

9. Save and close the query.

10. Open the report **rptBulbDetails**.

11. In the **Enter Parameter Value** dialog box, key **30** and press Enter.

12. Switch to **Design View**.

Figure 10-20
Report in Design
View
**EcoMed-10.accdb
rptBulbDetails**

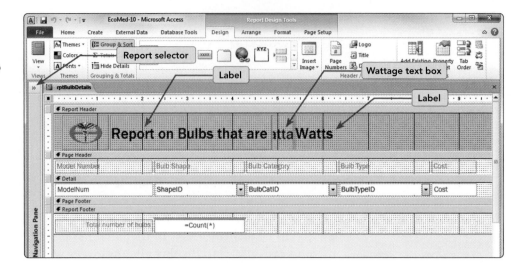

13. Double-click the Report Selector to open the Report's **Property Sheet**.

14. Click the **Data** tab. The query **qryBulbDetails** is the **Record Source** for this report. Close the **Property Sheet**.

15. From the **Design** tab, in the **Views** group, click **Report View**.

16. In the **Enter Parameter Value** dialog box, key **25** and press [Enter].

17. From the **Design** tab, in the **Records** group, click **Refresh All** 🗎.

18. In the **Enter Parameter Value** dialog box, key **10** and press [Enter].

19. Press [F5]. In the **Enter Parameter Value** dialog box, key **15** and press [Enter].

20. Close the report.

Creating and Using Action Queries

Select queries do not automatically change data. When you use a select query, you must key the necessary changes. When you use an action query, changes to records are completed automatically.

Action queries carry out commands you choose. An action query might change the sales representative for all customers in a particular state, delete all bulbs made by a certain supplier, add records from one table to another table, or make a new table.

A *make-table query* is an action query that creates a new table from all or part of the data in one or more tables. In this type of query, you can select fields for the new table and enter criteria to select only certain records. For example, you might create a historical table for sales from last year. After creating the new table with last year's sales, you can delete the records from the current sales table.

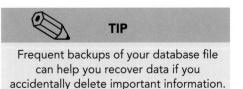

TIP

Frequent backups of your database file can help you recover data if you accidentally delete important information.

A *delete query* is an action query that deletes a group of records from one or more tables. For example, you might delete all the customers from a particular state when they are assigned to a new distributor. You also might delete a group of light fixtures when you stop manufacturing a specific category. You need to be cautious with delete queries if you have created relationships with referential integrity.

An *append query* is an action query that adds a group of records from one or more tables to the end of a table. When you build an append query, you use a single Append To table as your target table. The records in the table(s) from which you appended are copied into the target table but also remain in the original tables. Appended records are added at the end of the target table.

Exercise 10-17 CREATE AN UPDATE QUERY

An *update query* is an action query that makes global changes to a group of records in one or more tables. You can use an update query when one or more fields must be changed in a group of records. For example, you can use an update query to change the pay rate for all hourly employees.

NOTE

It is a best practice to back up your database before changing a large amount of information.

1. From the **Create** tab, in the **Queries** group, click **Query Design** .
2. Add the tables **tblPay** and **tblPayType**.
3. Size the panes and the Field Lists.
4. From **tblPay**, double-click **EmpID** and **EmpPay** to add it to the grid. Sort by **EmpID** in **Ascending** order.
5. From **tblPayType**, double-click **PayType** to add it to the grid.
6. Switch to **Datasheet View**. The dynaset is showing both hourly and salaried employees.
7. Switch to **Design View**. Click the **Criteria** row for the **PayType** field and key **hourly**.
8. Switch to **Datasheet View**. The dynaset is now showing only hourly employees. Switch to **Design View**.
9. Save the query as **qryHrPayUpdate**.

NOTE

Although the criteria row is not case sensitive, the Update To row is case sensitive. Exactly what you key will appear in the record.

10. From the **Design** tab, in the **Query Type** group, click **Update** . The **Update To** row appears below the **Table** row in the design grid.
11. Click in the **Update To** row for **EmpPay**.
12. From the **Design** tab, in the **Query Setup** group, click **Builder** .
13. In the **Expression Elements** panel, double-click the **EcoMed-10.accdb** folder and double-click the **Tables** folder. Click **tblPay**.
14. In the **Expression Categories** panel, double-click **EmpPay**.
15. Key *** 1.15**, which will increase the pay by 15 percent. Click **OK**.

Figure 10-21
Increase pay
**EcoMed-10.accdb
qryHrPayUpdate**

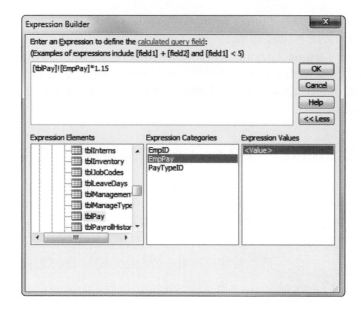

16. From the **Design** tab, in the **Results** group, click **Datasheet View**. The dynaset shows the fields from the records that will be changed; they have not yet been updated. Twelve records will be updated. Return to **Design View**.

17. From the **Design** tab, in the **Results** group, click **Run** 🔲. A warning box tells you that 12 records will be changed. Click **Yes**.

18. Switch to **SQL View** 🔲.

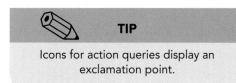

TIP

Icons for action queries display an exclamation point.

Figure 10-22
Update query SQL
statement
**EcoMed-10.accdb
qryHrPayUpdate**

UPDATE   tblPayType INNER JOIN tblPay ON tblPayType.PayTypeID = tblPay.PayTypeID
SET   tblPay.EmpPay = [tblPay]![EmpPay]*1.15 ← Field to be updated and new value
WHERE   (((tblPayType.PayType)="hourly"));

19. Save and close the query. The update query displays a pencil and an exclamation point as a reminder that it is an action query.

20. Double-click **qryHrPayUpdate**. A dialog box reminds you that this query will modify data.

21. Because you have already updated the records, we don't want to increase the pay again. Click **No**.

Exercise 10-18 CREATE AN UPDATE QUERY WITH A FUNCTION

Update queries are frequently created to make a one-time change to a table. For example, you might create an update query to change the cost of an inventory. Because this type of change would occur only once, you would not want to save the query. Other times, such as when you make routine changes, you would save the query. In the following example, you will create a query that changes the area code for employees living in a certain city.

1. From the Create tab, in the Queries group, click Query Design.

2. Add **tblEmployees**.

3. Size the panes and the Field List.

4. From **tblEmployees**, double-click **City** and **HomePhone** to add them to the grid.

5. Click the Criteria row for the **City** field and key **raytown**.

6. Switch to Datasheet View. The dynaset shows three employees who live in Raytown.

7. Switch to Design View.

8. Save the query as **qryPhoneUpdate**.

9. From the Design tab, in the Query Type group, click Update.

10. Click in the Update To row for **HomePhone**.

11. From the Design tab, in the Query Setup group, click Builder.

12. In the top panel, key **"(816)"**.

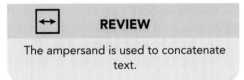

> **REVIEW**
>
> The ampersand is used to concatenate text.

13. In the Expression Elements panel, click the Operators folder. In the Expression Values panel, double-click **&**.

14. In the Expression Elements panel, double-click the Functions folder. Click Built-In Functions.

15. In the Expression Categories panel, click Text.

16. In the Expression Values panel, double-click Right.

17. In the top panel, click <<string>>.

18. In the Expression Elements panel, double-click the EcoMed-10.accdb folder and double-click the Tables folder. Click **tblEmployees**.

19. In the Expression Categories panel, double-click **HomePhone**.

20. In the top panel, click <<length>> and key **9**. This function will return the right-most 9 characters (space, ###-####) in the **HomePhone** field. Click OK.

Figure 10-23
Function in Update To row
EcoMed-10.accdb qryPhoneUpdate

21. From the **Design** tab, in the **Results** group, click **Run** 📍. A warning box tells you that three records will be changed. Click **Yes**.

22. Save the query.

23. From the **Design** tab, in the **Query Type** group, click **Select** 📭. The **Update To** row has been removed.

24. Switch to **Datasheet View** to see the changes to the phone numbers.

25. Switch to **Design View**.

26. From the **Design** tab, in the **Query Type** group, click **Update** 📄. Access will remember the values in the **Update To** row until the query is closed.

27. Save and close the query.

Exercise 10-19   CREATE A MAKE-TABLE QUERY

As databases grow, information that originally is stored in a single table should be moved into separate tables. EcoMed Services stores payroll information for hourly and salaried employees in a single table. However, salaried employees are paid differently than hourly employees. Therefore, separating salaried and hourly employees would be advantageous. You now will create a query to copy salaried employees' data and create a new table in which to store those data.

1. From the **Create** tab, in the **Queries** group, click **Query Design** 📭.

2. Add the tables **tblPay** and **tblPayType**.

3. Size the design grid and the Field List.

4. From **tblPay**, add the fields **EmpID**, **EmpPay**, and **PayTypeID**.

5. From **tblPayType**, add **PayTypeID** to the design grid.

6. Switch to **Datasheet View**. The last two fields store the same numeric data, but the **PayTypeID** from **tblPay** is using a lookup so it shows text instead. Notice that pay type "1" equals hourly and pay type "2" equals salary.

7. Switch to **Design View** and save the query as **qrySalaryMakeTbl**.

8. Click the Field List for **tblPayType** and press Delete to remove it from the query.

9. In the **Criteria** row for **PayTypeID**, key **2**.

10. From the **Design** tab, in the **Query Type** group, click **Make Table** 📭. The **Make Table** dialog box opens.

11. In the **Table Name** box, key **tblSalaried**. Choose **Current Database**.

Figure 10-24
Naming the new
table
**EcoMed-10.accdb
qrySalaryMakeTbl**

12. Click **OK**.

13. From the **Design** tab, in the **Results** group, click **Datasheet View** to preview the records for the new table. The new table is not created until you click the **Run** button 🔔.

14. Switch to **SQL View** 🔲.

Figure 10-25
Make table SQL
statement
**EcoMed-10.accdb
qrySalaryMakeTbl**

SELECT	tblPay.EmpID, tblPay.EmpPay, tblPay.PayTypeID
INTO	tblSalaried
FROM	tblPay
WHERE	(((tblPay.PayTypeID)=2));

Destination table

15. Switch to **Design View**.

16. From the **Design** tab, in the **Results** group, click **Run** 🔔. Click **Yes**, when the warning dialog box opens.

17. Open **tblSalaried**. Switch to **Design View**. The fields do not inherit the field properties (captions, input masks, and so on), and the primary key is not copied.

18. Save and close all major objects.

Exercise 10-20 CREATE A DELETE QUERY

Now that you have a new table that stores the data for salaried employees, you need to delete the original information still stored in the pay table.

1. From the **Create** tab, in the **Queries** group, click **Query Design** 🗔.

2. Add **tblPay**.

3. Size the design grid and the Field List.

4. Double-click the asterisk in the Field List to add all the fields without needing to add each field.

5. Double-click **PayTypeID** to add it to the second column. You need this field for your criteria.

6. In the **Criteria** row for **PayTypeID**, key **2**.

7. Save the query as **qrySalaryDel**.

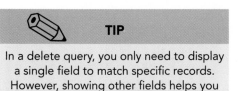

TIP

In a delete query, you only need to display a single field to match specific records. However, showing other fields helps you identify which records will be deleted.

8. From the **Design** tab, in the **Query Type** group, click **Delete** 📍. The **Delete** row appears in the grid below the **Table** row. The first column shows "From" in the **Delete** row to show from where you are deleting records. The **PayTypeID** column shows "Where." Access is building an expression similar to this one: "Delete all records from **tblPay** where the **PayTypeID** =2."

Figure 10-26
Delete query with criteria
EcoMed-10.accdb
qrySalaryDel

Field:	tblPay.*	PayTypeID	
Table:	tblPay	tblPay	
Delete:	From	Where	
Criteria:		2	
or:			

9. From the **Design** tab, in the **Results** group, click **Datasheet View**. These are the same records you just made into a new table.
10. Switch to **Design View**.
11. From the **Design** tab, in the **Results** group, click **Run** ❗. Click **Yes** when the warning dialog box opens.
12. Save and close the query.
13. Open **tblPay**. The salaried workers have been deleted. Close the table.

Exercise 10-21 CREATE AN APPEND QUERY

When two tables use the same structure, you can combine the data into a single table. The pay table and the salaried table both have the same structure. Create an append query and test that you can combine the two tables together.

1. From the **Create** tab, in the **Queries** group, click **Query Design** 📊.
2. Add the table **tblSalaried**.
3. Add each field from the Field List to the design grid.
4. Save the query as **qrySalaryApp**.
5. From the **Design** tab, in the **Query Type** group, click **Append** 📍. The **Append** dialog box opens.
6. Click the **Table Name** drop-down arrow and choose **tblPay**.
7. You can append records from a table in the current or another database. Choose **Current Database**.

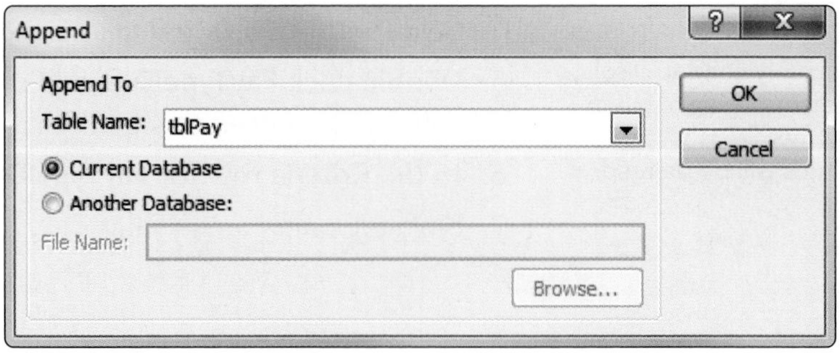

Figure 10-27
Append dialog box
EcoMed-10.accdb
qrySalaryApp

NOTE

The field names are the same in both tables, so they match up automatically. If the table that you are appending has different field names but the same type of data, you can set the fields in the Append To row by hand.

8. Click **OK**. An **Append To** row appears in the grid.
9. From the **Design** tab, in the **Results** group, click **Datasheet View**. All records in **tblSalaried** will be appended to **tblPay**.
10. Switch to **Design View**.
11. From the **Design** tab, in the **Results** group, click **Run** [!]. Click **Yes** when the warning dialog box opens.
12. Open **tblPay** to see that it includes all employees again.
13. Save and close the query and table.
14. From the **Navigation Pane**, right-click **tblSalaried** and choose **Delete**. Choose **Yes**.

Lesson 10   Summary

- Queries can be categorized as select queries, summary queries, parameter queries, and action queries.
- A select query displays data from one or more tables and displays the dynaset in a defined order.
- A summary query shows aggregate values for a recordset.
- A parameter query prompts a user for criteria when executed.
- An action query performs an action such as append, update, delete, or make table.
- A filter can be used to create a select query.
- When you use a query within a query, you create a subquery.
- For each summarized field in a query, Access creates a caption based on the function and the name of the field.
- Aggregate functions are mathematical equations that calculate results for numeric values.
- The Month function extracts the numeric value of the month from a date/time value.
- The MonthName function extracts the name of the month from a date/time value.
- The Year function extracts the numeric value of the year from a date/time value.
- The numeric values of two dates can be subtracted to display a numeric value.
- A parameter query prompts the user for criteria each time it runs. When you create a parameter query, you must first choose the field or fields in which comparisons are to be made.
- When you create a parameter, Access sets the format to the default data type of variant.
- If you place two parameters on the same Criteria row, both criteria must match for the record to be included in the dynaset.

- If you place parameters on separate rows, either criterion must match for the record to be included in the dynaset.
- Wildcards can only be used with text and numeric fields.
- A make-table query is an action query that creates a new table.
- A delete query is an action query that deletes a group of records.
- An append query is an action query that adds a group of records to the end of a table.
- An update query is an action query that makes global changes to a group of records.

LESSON 10		Command Summary	
Feature	**Button**	**Task Path**	**Keyboard**
Filter Saved as a Query		Home, Sort & Filter, Advanced	
Query, Append, Create		Design, Query Type, Append	
Query, Delete, Create		Design, Query Type, Delete	
Query, Make Table, Create		Design, Query Type, Make Table	
Query, Parameters		Design, Show/Hide, Parameters	
Query, Select		Design, Query Type, Select	
Query, Update, Create		Design, Query Type, Update	

Concepts Review

True/False Questions

Each of the following statements is either true or false. Indicate your choice by circling T or F.

T F 1. You can use an append query to edit multiple records at one time.

T F 2. A summary query can be based on two or more dates.

T F 3. A make-table query is an action query that creates a new table from one or more tables.

T F 4. In **Design View** of a query, you can select all fields in a Field List by double-clicking the primary key.

T F 5. **Count** and **Sum** are examples of aggregate functions.

T F 6. A summary query shows each record for a predefined group.

T F 7. In a parameter query, you make changes to the **Criteria** row each time you need to run the query.

T F 8. You use an update query to add records from one table to another table.

Short Answer Questions

Write the correct answer in the space provided.

1. What kind of action query would you use to remove records from a table?

2. How do you enter parameters in **Design View** of a query?

3. What is the fastest way to add all the fields to the design grid?

4. What row might show "Group By" or "Count" in the **Design View** of a query?

5. What happens when you run a parameter query?

6. What button do you click to preview the records that will be changed in an update query?

7. What symbol appears as part of the icon for all action queries in the **Navigation Pane**?

_____

8. What two types of queries copy records from one table to another table?

_____

Critical Thinking

Answer these questions on a separate page. There are no right or wrong answers. Support your answers with examples from your own experience, if possible.

1. Think about the database your school uses to maintain student records. Discuss when you might use an update query, a delete query, or an append query to manage the student information.

2. An aggregate function shows a sum, count, or average. Using the database that your school uses, describe the types of summary queries that might be useful.

Skills Review

Exercise 10-22

You have been asked to create a query to display the total number of shipments that were sent during the month of February in 2011. For the same time period, also display the total number of facilities that received shipments.

1. Open a database by following these steps:
    a. Locate and open the **Lesson 10** folder.
    b. If you already have a copy of *[your initials]*-**EcoMed-10**, skip to step 1d.
    c. Make a copy of **EcoMed-10** and rename it *[your initials]*-EcoMed-10.
    d. Open and enable content for *[your initials]*-**EcoMed-10**.
    e. Refresh the links with *[your initials]*-**HR-10**.

2. Create a summary query using a Wizard by following these steps:
    a. From the Create tab, in the Queries group, click Query Wizard 📰.
    b. In the New Query dialog box, choose Simple Query Wizard and click OK.
    c. In the Table/Queries list, choose Table: tblFacilities. Add **FacName** to the Selected Fields list.
    d. In the Table/Queries list, choose Table: tblShipments. Add **ShipID** to the Selected Fields list. Click Next.

e. Click the **Summary** option. Click **Summary Options**.

f. Click the **Count records in tblShipments** check box and click **OK**. Click **Next**.

g. Key **qryFac-Ship-Sum** as the title and then click **Finish**.

3. Modify the query by following these steps:

a. Switch to **Design View**.

b. Delete the second field in the design grid.

c. Resize the column for the second field so that you can see all content of the **Field** row.

d. Replace the text "Count Of tblShipments" with **Number of Orders**. Make sure that you do not delete the colon between the alias and function.

e. Click in the **Sort** row for this field and choose **Descending**.

f. Switch to **Datasheet View**.

g. Resize the columns so that you can see all of the data.

4. Add a criteria to a query by following these steps:

a. Switch to **Design View**.

b. From the **tblShipments** Field List, double-click **OrderDate**.

c. For the **OrderDate**, in the **Total** row, change **Group By** to **Where**.

d. For the **OrderDate**, in the **Criteria** row, key **between 2/1/2011 and 2/28/2011**.

e. Switch to **Datasheet View**.

f. Save and close the query.

Assessment

 - Turn in your database only when all assigned exercises have been completed, according to your classroom procedure.

-OR-

 - Create a **Database Documenter** report by following these steps:

a. From the **Database Tools** tab, in the **Analyze** group, click **Database Documenter** 📄.

b. On the **Queries** tab, select **qryFac-Ship-Sum**.

c. Click **Options**. From the **Include for Query** section, choose **Properties** and **SQL**.

d. For the **Include for Fields** section, choose **Nothing**.

e. For the **Include for Indexes** section, choose **Nothing**.

f. Click **OK** twice.

- Save a **Database Documenter** report by following these steps:

a. From the **Print Preview** tab, in the **Data** group, click **PDF or XPS** 📄 to save the printout as a file.

b. Save the file as a PDF and name the file *[your initials]*-**10-22-A**.

c. Depending on your class procedures, print or turn in the PDF file.

d. Close **Print Preview**.

10-22-A.pdf
1 Page

Exercise 10-23

You have been asked to create query data from the history shipment table based on a variable range of dates.

1. The database *[your initials]*-**EcoMed-10** is required to complete this exercise.

   a. Open, enable, and update links for *[your initials]*-**EcoMed-10**.

2. Create a query by following these steps:

   a. From the Create tab, in the Queries group, click Query Design 📇.

   b. From the Show Table dialog box, double-click **tblHistoryShipments**. Click Close.

   c. Double-click the asterisk to add all fields to the grid.

   d. Double-click **OrderDate** to add the field to the second column.

   e. Click the Show check box for **OrderDate** field to turn off the display of this column.

   f. Save the query as **qryHistoryShipByDate**.

3. Add parameters to a query by following these steps:

   a. From the Design tab, in the Show/Hide group, click Parameter 📇.

   b. For the first parameter, key **[Enter beginning date]**.

   c. Press Tab, click the drop-down arrows, and choose Date/Time.

   d. For the second parameter, key **[Enter ending date]**.

   e. Press Tab, click the drop-down arrows, and choose Date/Time. Click OK to close the Query Parameters dialog box.

   f. Click the Criteria row for **OrderDate** and key >=[e. Double click [Enter beginning date] from the list.

   g. Key **and** <=[e. Double click [Enter ending date] from the list.

   h. At this time, the table **tblHistoryShipments** only includes October 2010 data. Test the query with 10/7/2010 as both parameters (26 records).

   i. Save and close the query.

Assessment

- Turn in your database only when all assigned exercises have been completed, according to your classroom procedure.

-OR-

- Create a Database Documenter report by following these steps:

   a. From the Database Tools tab, in the Analyze group, click Database Documenter 📇.

   b. On the Queries tab, select **qryHistoryShipByDate**.

   c. Click Options. From the Include for Query section, choose Properties and SQL.

10-23-A.pdf
1 Page

d. For the Include for Fields section, choose Nothing.

e. For the Include for Indexes section, choose Nothing.

f. Click OK twice.

- Save a Database Documenter report by following these steps:

a. From the Print Preview tab, in the Data group, click PDF or XPS to save the printout as a file.

b. Save the file as a PDF and name the file *[your initials]*-**10-23-A**.

c. Depending on your class procedures, print or turn in the PDF file.

d. Close Print Preview.

Exercise 10-24

You have been directed to increase the cost of all halogen bulbs by ten percent.

1. The database *[your initials]*-**EcoMed-10** is required to complete this exercise.

   a. Open, enable, and update links for *[your initials]*-**EcoMed-10**.

2. Create an update query by following these steps:

   a. From the Create tab, in the Queries group, click Query Design .

   b. From the Show Table dialog box, double-click **tblInventory**. Click Close.

   c. Double-click **ModelNum**, **Cost**, and **BulbTypeID** to add them to the design grid.

   d. Save the query as **qryInv-ModifyCost**.

   e. From the Design tab, in the Query Type group, click Update 🅰.

   f. On the Update To row for **Cost**, key **[cost]*1.1** to increase the price by 10 percent.

   g. On the Criteria row for **BulbTypeID**, key **2** to apply this price increase to the halogen bulbs.

   h. From the Design tab, in the Results group, click the Run command ❗. Twenty-two records will be updated. Click Yes.

   i. Save and close the query.

Assessment

 - Turn in your database only when all assigned exercises have been completed, according to your classroom procedure.

-OR-

- Create a Database Documenter report by following these steps:

    a. From the Database Tools tab, in the Analyze group, click Database Documenter .

    b. On the Queries tab, select **qryInv-ModifyCost**.

    c. Click Options. From the Include for Query section, choose Properties and SQL.

    d. For the Include for Fields section, choose Nothing.

    e. For the Include for Indexes section, choose Nothing.

    f. Click OK twice.

- Save a Database Documenter report by following these steps:

    a. From the Print Preview tab, in the Data group, click PDF or XPS 🔙 to save the printout as a file.

    b. Save the file as a PDF and name the file *[your initials]*-10-24-A.

    c. Depending on your class procedures, print or turn in the PDF file.

    d. Close Print Preview.

10-24-A.pdf
1 Page

Exercise 10-25

You have been asked to create a query to display summarized shipment data. The query should allow the user to select which month to summarize.

1. The database *[your initials]*-EcoMed-10 is required to complete this exercise.

    a. Open, enable, and update links for *[your initials]*-EcoMed-10.

2. Create a query by following these steps:

    a. From the Create tab, in the Queries group, click Query Design 📧.

    b. From the Show Table dialog box, double-click **tblFacilities** and **tblShipments**.

    c. Click the Queries tab. Double-click **qryShipDetails**. Click Close.

    d. From the **tblFacilities** Field List, double-click **FacName**.

    e. From the **qryShipDetails** Field List, double-click **ExtRetail**.

    f. Click in the **ExtRetail** field in the design grid.

    g. From the Design tab, in the Show/Hide group, click Property Sheet 📝.

    h. Change the Format property to Currency.

3. Add a calculated field by following these steps:

    a. Click in the third column in the design grid.

    b. From the Design tab, in the Query Setup group, click Builder 📐.

    c. In the Expression Elements panel, double-click Functions. Click Built-In Functions.

    d. In the Expression Categories panel, click Date/Time.

    e. In the Expression Values panel, double-click Month.

    f. In the top panel, click in <<date>>.

    g. In the **Expression Elements** panel, double-click the **EcoMed-10.accdb** folder. Double-click **Tables** folder. Click **tblShipments**.

    h. In the **Expression Categories** panel, double-click **OrderDate**.

    i. Press ⏎Home⏎ and key **Month:**. Click **OK**.

    j. Save the query as **qryShipByMonth**.

4.   Change a summary query by following these steps:

    a. From the **Design** tab, in the **Show/Hide** group, click **Totals** Σ .

    b. For the **ExtRetail**, in the **Total** row, change **Group By** to **Sum**.

    c. For the calculated field **Month**, in the **Total** row, change **Group By** to **Where**.

5.   Add a parameter to a query by following these steps:

    a. From the **Design** tab, in the **Show/Hide** group, click **Parameter** .

    b. For the first parameter, key **[Enter a month #, 1-12]**.

    c. Press ⏎Tab⏎, click the drop-down arrows, and choose **Integer**. Click **OK**.

    d. For the calculated field **Month**, in the **Criteria** row, key [e. Double-click **[Enter a month #, 1-12]** from the list.

    e. From the **Design** tab, in the **Results** group, click **Run** .

    f. Key **2** and click **OK**.

    g. Resize the columns. There are 27 facilities that ordered in February.

    h. Save and close the query.

Assessment

- Turn in your database only when all assigned exercises have been completed, according to your classroom procedure.

-OR-

- Create a **Database Documenter** report by following these steps:

    a. From the **Database Tools** tab, in the **Analyze** group, click **Database Documenter** .

    b. On the **Queries** tab, select **qryShipByMonth**.

    c. Click **Options**. From the **Include for Query** section, choose **Properties** and **SQL**.

    d. For the **Include for Fields** section, choose **Nothing**.

    e. For the **Include for Indexes** section, choose **Nothing**.

    f. Click **OK** twice.

- Save a **Database Documenter** report by following these steps:

10-25-A.pdf
1 Page

    a. From the **Print Preview** tab, in the **Data** group, click **PDF or XPS** to save the printout as a file.

    b. Save the file as a PDF and name the file *[your initials]*-**10-25-A**.

    c. Depending on your class procedures, print or turn in the PDF file.

    d. Close **Print Preview**.

Lesson Applications

Exercise 10-26

You have been directed to create a query that will the display the last date when a shipment has been sent to each facility.

1. Open, enable, and update links for *[your initials]*-EcoMed-10.
2. Create a query using **tblShipments**, **tblFacilities**, and **tblRegion**.
3. Add the fields **Region**, **FacName**, and **OrderDate**.
4. Change the query to a summary query that finds the newest order (hint: Last or Max).
5. Create a new caption for the **OrderDate** field to Last Order Date:.
6. Sort by **Region** in descending order. Result is 95 records.
7. Save the query as qryLastOrder.

Assessment

- Turn in your database only when all assigned exercises have been completed, according to your classroom procedure.

-OR-

- Create a Database Documenter Report for **qryLastOrder**.
  - Include for Query: Properties, SQL only
  - Include for Fields: Nothing
  - Include for Indexes: Nothing
- Save the Documenter report as a PDF file named *[your initials]*-10-26-A.
- Depending on your class procedures, print or turn in the PDF file.

10-26-A.pdf
1 Page

Exercise 10-27

The AnyBulb company has raised the prices of its bulbs by 15 percent. Create a query to update the item prices for any item sold by that vender.

1. Open, enable, and update links for *[your initials]*-EcoMed-10.
2. Create an Update query using **tblVender** and **tblInventory**.
3. Add the fields **ModelNum**, **Cost**, and **VenderID**.
4. The vender AnyBulb (Vender ID 4) has raised the price of all its bulbs 15 percent. Make the appropriate changes to the query to increase the appropriate prices. There are 30 records for vender ID 4.
5. Save the query as qryUpdateCost.

Assessment

- Turn in your database only when all assigned exercises have been completed, according to your classroom procedure.

-OR-

- Create a Database Documenter Report for **qryUpdateCost**.
  - Include for Query: Properties, SQL only
  - Include for Fields: Nothing
  - Include for Indexes: Nothing
- Save the Documenter report as a PDF file named *[your initials]*-10-27-A.
- Depending on your class procedures, print or turn in the PDF file.

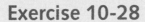

10-27-A.pdf
1 Page

Exercise 10-28

EcoMed Services periodically archives shipment data to a historical table. You have been instructed to create a query that will allow the sales manager to select a range of records to archive based on the shipment date.

1. Open, enable, and update links for *[your initials]*-EcoMed-10.

2. Record the fields that are in **tblHistoryShipments** since this will be the target table.

3. Create an Append query using **tblShipments**, **tblShipDetails**, **tblInventory**, and **tblFacilities**.

4. The destination table will be **tblHistoryShipments**.

5. Add only fields that are found in the destination table. Each field in the destination table must be used.

6. Add two parameters to prompt the user for both the start and end order dates to be archived.

7. Set both prompts to the data type Date/Time.

8. Save the query as **qryArchiveShip**.

9. Run the query and archive records between **12/1/2010** and **12/31/2010**. There are 352 records in December.

Assessment

- Turn in your database only when all assigned exercises have been completed, according to your classroom procedure.

-OR-

- Create a **Database Documenter Report** for **qryArchiveShip**.
  • Include for Query: **Properties**, **SQL** only
  • Include for Fields: **Nothing**
  • Include for Indexes: **Nothing**
- Save the **Documenter** report as a PDF file named *[your initials]*-**10-28-A**.
- Depending on your class procedures, print or turn in the PDF file.

10-28-A.pdf
1 Page

Exercise 10-29 ◆ Challenge Yourself

You have been directed to create a query that allows a database operator to display shipment information based on the month the shipment was made.

1. Open, enable, and update links for *[your initials]*-**EcoMed-10**.

2. Create a query using **tblShipments**.

3. Include the field **ShipID**.

4. Add a calculated field to retrieve the month from the field **OrderDate** with the alias **MonthNum**.

5. Create a parameter to ask the user to enter a month. Use this parameter to only show order dates that match the users input.

6. Name the query **qryShipByMonthNum**.

REVIEW

All Field Lists must have relationships with the other Field List to avoid a Cartesian effect.

7. Create a new summary query using **qryShipByMonthNum**, **tblShipDetails**, **tblShipments**, and **tblFacilities**.

8. Include the fields **FacName** and **Qty**.

9. Use the aggregate function **Sum** for the **Qty** field.

10. Add **Bulbs Sold** as the alias for the field **Qty**.

11. Sort by **FacName** in ascending order.

12. Name the query **qryFacQtySold**.

13. Run **qryFacQtySold** and enter **1**. There should be 22 records in which the facility Advocate Lutheran General Hospital bought 1,060 bulbs.

Assessment

- Turn in your database only when all assigned exercises have been completed, according to your classroom procedure.

10-29-A.pdf
1 Page

-OR-

- Create a Database Documenter Report for **qryShipByMonthNum**.
  - Include for Query: Properties, SQL only
  - Include for Fields: Nothing
  - Include for Indexes: Nothing
- Save the Documenter report as a PDF file named *[your initials]*-10-29-A.
- Create a Database Documenter Report for **qryFacQtySold**.

  - Include for Query: Properties, SQL only
  - Include for Fields: Nothing
  - Include for Indexes: Nothing
- Save the Documenter report as a PDF file named *[your initials]*-10-29-B.
- Depending on your class procedures, print or turn in the PDF file.

10-29-B.pdf
1 Page

On Your Own

**In these exercises you work on your own, as you would in a real-life work
environment. Use the skills you've learned to accomplish the task—and be
creative.**

Exercise 10-30

Review the design of the database you created and modified in Exercises 9-29
through 9-31. Identify at least two summary queries and two parameter
queries that will enhance your database design. Identify either a make-table
query or an append query that will enhance your database design. For each
query, write the name of the query on a sheet of paper, describe its purpose,
and list the fields that will be used in the query. On each sheet of paper,
write your name, class information, and "Exercise 10-30." Continue to the
next exercise.

Exercise 10-31

Design and create each query you identified in Exercise 10-30. Before
testing the queries, create a backup copy of your database. Modify your
designs appropriately. Continue to the next exercise.

Exercise 10-32

Print the Object Definitions reports for each query you created in Exercise 10-31.
Print the SQL properties for each summary query and parameter query you
created. On the printouts, write your name, class information, and "Exercise
10-32." Submit these printouts to your instructor. Keep a copy of the database
you modified in this lesson. You will use it for the On Your Own exercises in
subsequent lessons.

Lesson 11
Building Advanced Forms

OBJECTIVES *After completing this lesson, you will be able to:*

1. Create a form in Design View.

2. Add command buttons.

3. Work with image controls.

4. Use a wizard to create a form with a subform.

5. Use subforms.

6. Create calculated controls.

Estimated Time: 2½ hours

Microsoft Access provides numerous tools to create complex forms. Some of these features, such as command buttons, can enhance the performance of any form. Other features, including imbedding a form inside another form, should be used only for specific purposes.

When designing a form, you should always consider the needs of the user. Some users need summary information, while other users need detailed information. The needs of the user should determine the design of the form.

Creating a Form in Design View

Most database designers create forms by first using the Form Wizard and then modifying the controls on the form. However, on occasion, designers need to create a form so unique that using the Form Wizard is impractical. This situation might be the case if you were trying to reproduce a printed form already in use by the company.

Exercise 11-1 CREATE A FORM IN DESIGN VIEW

When you create a form in Design View, you start with a blank form that contains only a Detail section. To complete the form, you insert fields, labels, and additional design elements. The default name for a form will be the name of the source recordset. Rather than use the default name for the form, you always should use a meaningful name that follows the Leszynski Naming Conventions.

To be an efficient and effective database designer, you need to learn how to design a useful form. There are many techniques that you can use to select and organize the many controls located within a form. You will start to learn these techniques by creating a form based upon the pension fund table.

1. Locate and open the **Lesson 11** folder.

2. Copy **EcoMed-11** and rename it *[your initials]*-EcoMed-11. Copy **HR-11** and rename it *[your initials]*-HR-11.

3. Open and enable content for *[your initials]*-**HR-11**.

4. From the **Create** tab, in the **Forms** group, click **Form Design** 🖼.

5. From the **Design** tab, in the **Tools** group, click **Add Existing Fields** 🔠.

6. In the **Field List**, click **Show all tables** if needed to see all of the tables. Click the Expand button ⊞ for the table **tblPensionFund**.

7. From the **Field List**, double-click the field **CompanyName** to add the field to the **Detail** section of the new form.

8. From the **Arrange** tab, in the **Table** group, click **Tabular** ▦.

9. From the **Field List**, drag the field **Symbol** to the right of the **CompanyName** control until you see a yellow "I" bar. This action will add the new field to the control layout.

10. From the **Field List**, drag the field **Percent** to the right of the **Symbol** control to add it to the control layout.

11. Save the form as **frmPensionFund**.

12. Select all the labels in the **Form Header** by placing your mouse pointer in the vertical ruler until you see a right pointing arrow, then click.

Figure 11-1
Selecting an entire row of controls
HR-11.accdb
frmPensionFund

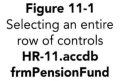

13. From the **Arrange** tab, in the **Move** group, click **Move Down** ⤓ to move the label to the **Detail** section of the form.

14. From the **Arrange** tab, in the **Rows & Columns** group, click **Select Layout** ▦. Drag the controls to the 1/4-inch mark on the vertical ruler and the 1/2-inch mark on the horizontal ruler.

15. From the **Field List**, click the field **Contact**. While pressing Ctrl, click the fields **Phone** and **Fax**. All three fields are now selected.

16. Drag the three fields from the **Field List** to the **Detail** section of the form around the 1-inch mark on the vertical ruler and 2-inch mark on the horizontal ruler.

17. From the **Arrange** tab, in the **Table** group, click **Stacked** ▦.

18. Close the **Field List** pane.

19. Click the **Symbol** text box. From the **Arrange** tab, in the **Rows & Columns** group, click **Insert Left** ▦.

20. Click the **Percent** text box. From the **Arrange** tab, in the **Rows & Columns** group, click **Insert Left** ▦.

Figure 11-2
Placement of six fields
HR-11.accdb
frmPensionFund

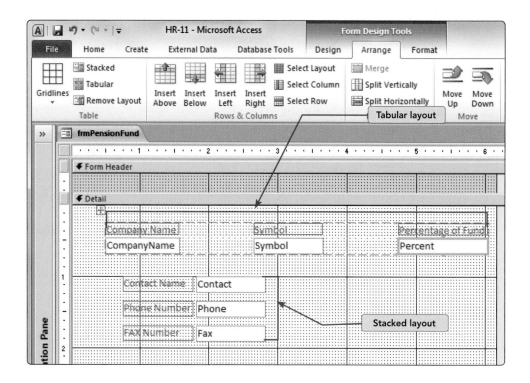

21. Save the form.

Exercise 11-2 MODIFY CONTROL PROPERTIES

You can adjust the size and position of controls by selecting the control and moving the sizing handles to resize or move the control. An alternative is to open the property sheet of a control and change the specific properties that set its position, height, or width.

1. From the **Design** tab, in the **Tools** group, click **Property Sheet** ☞.

2. In the **Detail** section, click the **Symbol** control's label.

3. In the **Property Sheet**, on the **Format** tab, click in the **Height** property and key .25.

4. In the second column of the layout, click a blank cell. Press Ctrl and click one of the blank cells in the fourth column to select both controls.

5. In the **Property Sheet**, on the **Format** tab, click in the **Width** property and key .5.

6. Click the **CompanyName** text box. In the **Property Sheet**, on the **Format** tab, click in the **Width** property and key 1.8.

7. Click the **Percent** text box. In the **Property Sheet**, on the **Format** tab, click in the **Width** property and key 1.5.

8. Click the **Contact Name** label. In the **Property Sheet**, on the **Format** tab, click in the **Top** property and key 1.25.

9. In the **Property Sheet**, on the **Format** tab, click in the **Left** property and key .75.

10. Click the **Contact** text box. In the **Property Sheet**, on the **Format** tab, click in the **Width** property and key 1.4.

11. From the **Arrange** tab, in the **Rows & Columns** group, click **Select Column** ▦.

12. In the **Property Sheet**, on the **Format** tab, click in the **Left Margin** property and key .1.

13. Click the **Company Name** label. From the **Arrange** tab, in the **Rows & Columns** group, click **Select Row** ▦.

14. From the **Arrange** tab, in the **Position** group, click **Control Margins** ▣ and choose **Medium** to change all four margins around the data to .03 inches.

15. Click the **Detail** section bar. In the **Property Sheet**, on the **Format** tab, click in the **Height** property and key 2.5.

16. From the **Design** tab, in the **Header/Footer** group, click **Title** ▣. Key **EcoMed - Pension Information** and press Enter.

17. Click the **Title** label. From the **Format** tab, in the **Font** group, change the font to **20-point Rockwell**.

18. Close the **Property Sheet** and switch to **Form View**.

Figure 11-3
Controls after
formatting
**HR-11.accdb
frmPensionFund**

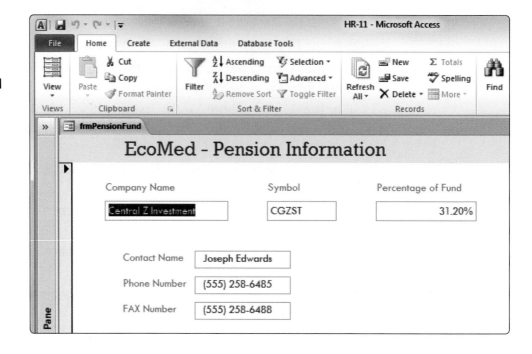

19. Save the form.

Exercise 11-3   FORMAT USING THEMES

Access provides standard themes that can be applied to forms. An Access theme defines the fonts and colors that will be used throughout the form. Formatting a form with a theme is a quick way to make a form look professional. To see how a theme affects a form, apply the Thatch theme to the pension fund form.

1. Switch to **Design View**.
2. From the **Navigation Pane**, open **frmEmpShort**. Notice the similar color of the **Form Header**.
3. Return to **frmPensionFund**.
4. Click the Form Selector ▣.
5. From the **Design** tab, in the **Themes** group, click **Themes** 🖼. Hover your mouse over each of the themes and notice how the live preview affects the form's color and fonts.
6. Scroll down the **Theme** gallery until you reach the bottom of the list. Select the theme **Thatch** (right-column in the next to last row).

Figure 11-4
Theme gallery
HR-11.accdb
frmPensionFund

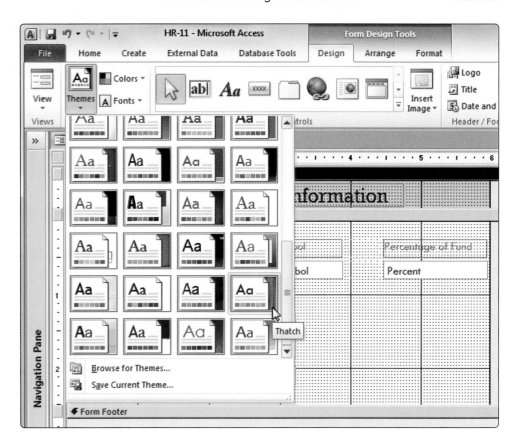

7. The background color of the Form Header is now a light blue.

8. Click the document tab for **frmEmpShort**. The theme has affected all the forms and reports in the database. Close the form. Even though the color of the Form Header changed, you were not asked to save the changes.

9. Save the form.

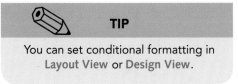

NOTE

Custom Themes are stored on your computer, not in the database file.

Exercise 11-4   SET CONDITIONAL FORMATTING FOCUS

One method for improving the speed and accuracy of data entry is to highlight the control that has the focus. *Focus* is the status of a control that occurs when the control has the ability to receive user input through mouse or keyboard actions. Only one control can have the focus at any time. A control that has the focus is also known as the active control.

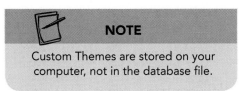

TIP

You can set conditional formatting in Layout View or Design View.

You can highlight a control by changing its color. Changing the color of the active control allows the data entry operator to identify where data can be entered or changed. You can change the color of the active control by adding conditional formatting to the fields in the form.

1. In Design View, click the **Contact** text box.

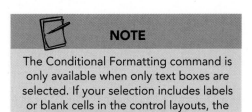

NOTE

The Conditional Formatting command is only available when only text boxes are selected. If your selection includes labels or blank cells in the control layouts, the command will not be available.

2. From the **Arrange** tab, in the **Rows & Columns** group, click **Select Column** ▦.

3. Press Ctrl and click the **CompanyName**, **Symbol**, and **Percent** text boxes. All text boxes are now selected.

4. From the **Format** tab, in the **Control Formatting** group, click **Conditional Formatting** 🗐.

5. In the **Conditional Formatting Rules Manager** dialog box, click **New Rule** 🗐 to open the **New Formatting Rule** dialog box.

6. In the **Edit the rule description**, click the first drop-down box and choose **Field Has Focus**.

7. Click the drop-down arrow for the Background Color button 🖉 and choose **Dark Blue 1** (column 4, row 2). Click **OK**.

Figure 11-5
New conditional
format rule
**HR-11.accdb
frmPensionFund**

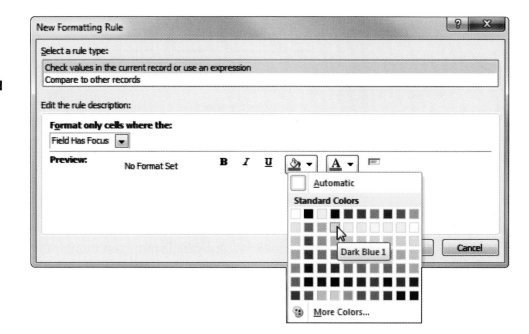

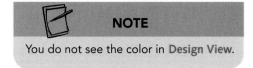

NOTE

You do not see the color in **Design View**.

8. Click **OK** to close the **Conditional Formatting Rules Manager** dialog box. Click in an unused part of the form to deselect the controls.

9. Switch to **Form View**. Press Tab to move the focus from one control to another.

Figure 11-6
Text box with focus
**HR-11.accdb
frmPensionFund**

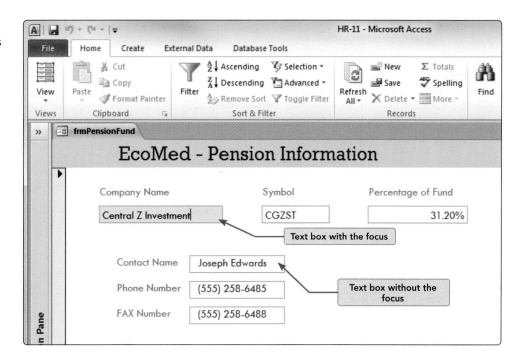

10. Save the form.

Exercise 11-5   INSERT A SMART TAG

Access provides three ready-to-use Smart Tags. A Smart Tag delivers data to another application and performs specific actions. For example, the name of a person or the date of a shipment can be assigned a Smart Tag.

The three ready-to-use Smart Tags in Access are as follows:

- Person Name Smart Tag launches Microsoft Outlook to edit the contact information, send an e-mail message, schedule an appointment, or add the name to the list of contacts.

- Financial Symbol Smart Tag launches Internet Explorer to look up information regarding a financial symbol or obtain a stock quote, financial report, or recent news about a company.

- Date Smart Tag launches Microsoft Outlook to schedule an appointment or display a calendar.

1. Switch to Design View.
2. Double-click the **Symbol** text box to open its Property Sheet.
3. On the Data tab, click the Smart Tags property. Click Build [...] to open the Actions Tags dialog box.
4. In the Available Action Tags list, choose Financial Symbol and click OK.

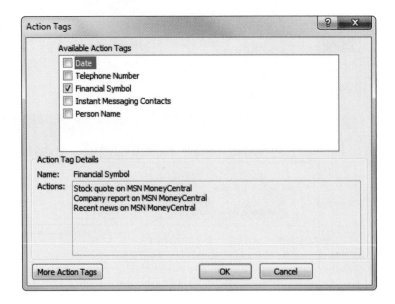

5. Close the **Property Sheet**. Return to **Form View**. Tab over to the **Symbol** text box.

6. A Smart Tag Actions button 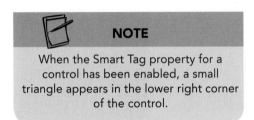 appears to the right of the text box. Point and click the **Smart Tag** and choose **Stock quote on MSN MoneyCentral**.

7. Access launches a Web browser and displays a Web page for the symbol found in the text box. Close the Web browser.

8. Save and close the form.

> **NOTE**
>
> When the Smart Tag property for a control has been enabled, a small triangle appears in the lower right corner of the control.

Exercise 11-6 CREATE A DATA ENTRY FORM

Depending on the purpose of the form, you can change how the form behaves. A form can be set to only allow new records to be entered, not allow new records to be entered, not allow records to be deleted, or not allow records to be edited. You now will create a form that only can be used to enter new records into the pension fund table.

TABLE 11-1 Form Behavior Properties

Data Entry	Whether, when opened, a form displays only a blank (new) record.
Allow Additions	Whether new records can be added through the form.
Allow Deletions	Whether records can be deleted through the form.
Allow Edits	Whether changes to saved records can be made through the form.

1. In the Navigation Pane, right-click **frmPensionFund** and choose Copy.

2. Anywhere in the Navigation Pane, right-click and choose Paste.

3. In the Paste As dialog box, key **frmPensionFundNew**. Click OK.

4. Open **frmPensionFundNew** in Design View.

5. Double-click the Form Selector ▣ to open the form's property sheet.

6. In the Property Sheet, on the Data tab, change the Data Entry property to Yes.

7. Edit the Title label to EcoMed – Enter New Pension Information.

8. Switch to Form View. This form can only be used to enter new records.

Figure 11-8
Changing the
Default View
**HR-11.accdb
frmPensionFundNew**

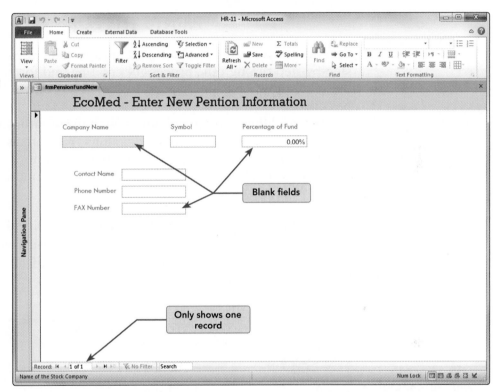

9. Enter the following data:

Company:	Acme
Symbol:	TEST
Percentage of Fund:	5%
Contact Name:	*[your full name]*
Phone Number:	(555) 258-9797
FAX Number:	(555) 258-9799

10. Press Tab after entering all the data. Notice that the form is cleared and ready to have you enter a new fund.

11. Save and close the form.

Adding Command Buttons

The most common way to add a command button to a form is though a wizard. A *command button* is a control that when clicked executes an action or series of actions. The wizard prompts you for information and then creates the command button based on your answers.

Standardized command buttons allow a user to perform more than 30 specific actions, such as print a record, preview a report, find a specific record, run a query, or close the form. Each command button can display an icon, text, or both.

Exercise 11-7   ADD A COMMAND BUTTON THAT PRINTS THE FORM

Certain controls such as command buttons have wizards that can take you step-by-step through the process of creating and formatting the control. To use a wizard when creating a control, the Use Control Wizards feature must be active.

When adding a command button with the wizard, you can select from six categories of commands or related actions. You can also specify whether the button will display an icon, text, or both. You now will add a command button to print all the records in the pension fund table.

1. Open **frmPensionFund** in **Design View**.

2. From the **Design** tab, in the **Controls** group, click the More button to expand the **Controls** gallery. By default, the **Use Control Wizards** should be active. If this control is not automatically selected, click to activate the control.

Figure 11-9
Control Wizard
option
HR-11.accdb
frmPensionFund

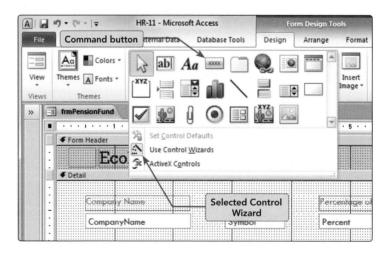

3. From the **Design** tab, in the **Controls** group, click Button.

4. Just below the **Form Footer** section bar, click at the 5-inch mark. The **Form Footer** opens, and the **Command Button Wizard** launches.

5. In the **Categories** section, click **Form Operations**.

6. In the **Actions** section, click **Print Current Form**. Click **Next**.

7. A sample of the command button is on the left. Click **Next**.

8. Name this control **cmdPrintAll** and click **Finish**.

TABLE 11-2 Prefixes for Control Objects*

Prefix	Control Type	Example
cbo	Combo box	cboPaymentMethod
chk	Check box	chkCollate
cmd	Command button	cmdPrint
grp	Option group	grpOrientation
img	Image	imgEmployee
lbl	Label	lblEmployeeID
lst	List box	lstDepartments
opt	Option button	optOrientation
txt	Text box	txtEmployeeID

*For a comprehensive list, see Appendix B-2.

9. Double-click **cmdPrintAll** to open its **Property Sheet**. On the **Format** tab, change the **Caption** property to **All Records**.

10. Change the **Picture Caption Arrangement** property to **Bottom**.

11. In the **Form Footer**, double-click the upper-right corner of the **cmdPrintAll** control to resize it.

12. In the **Property Sheet** for **cmdPrintAll**, on the **Other** tab, change the **ControlTip Text** property to **Click to print all records**.

13. Save the form and switch to **Form View**.

14. Place your pointer over the new button and read the ScreenTip. Based on your classroom procedure, test the new button.

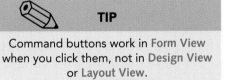

TIP

Command buttons work in Form View when you click them, not in Design View or Layout View.

Exercise 11-8 ADD A COMMAND BUTTON THAT PRINTS THE CURRENT RECORD

Creating a command button to print the current records is useful when the database operator is not familiar with the manual process of printing a single record or when the form does not have the record selector visible. You now will add a command button to print the current record displayed in the form.

1. Switch to **Design View**.

2. From the **Design** tab, in the **Controls** group, click Button.

3. In the **Form Footer**, click at the 6-inch mark.

4. In the **Categories** section, click **Record Operations**.

5. In the **Actions** section, click **Print Record**. Click **Finish**.

6. In the **Property Sheet** of the new command button, on the **Other** tab, change the **Name** property to **cmdPrintOne**.

7. Change the **ControlTip Text** property to **Click to print the current record**.

8. On the **Format** tab, change the **Caption** property to **Current Record**.

9. Change the **Picture Caption Arrangement** property to **Bottom**.

10. In the **Form Footer**, double-click the upper-right corner of the **cmdPrintOne** control to resize it.

11. Select both command button controls.

12. From the **Arrange** tab, in the **Table** group, click **Tabular**.

13. From the **Arrange** tab, in the **Sizing & Ordering** group, click **Size/Space**, and choose **To Widest**.

14. In the **Property Sheet** for the two buttons, on the **Format** tab, change the **Height** property to **.5**.

15. Save the form and switch to **Form View**.

16. Place your pointer over the new button and read the ScreenTip. Based on your classroom procedure, test the new button.

Figure 11-10
Command buttons in
Form View
HR-11.accdb
frmPensionFund

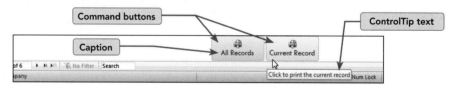

Exercise 11-9   ADD A COMMAND BUTTON THAT CLOSES THE FORM

If you choose to use command buttons to assist the database operator to perform basic record operations, you should also add a command button to close the form. Even though the user can close the form by clicking the close icon on the title bar of the form, adding a command button to close the form keeps a consistent functionality to the form.

1. Switch to **Design View**.

2. From the **Design** tab, in the **Controls** group, click Button.

3. In the **Form Footer** section, click at the 4-inch mark.

4. In the **Categories** section, click **Form Operations**.

5. In the **Actions** section, click **Close Form**. Click **Next**.

6. With **Picture** selected, click **Next**.

7. Name the control **cmdClose**. Click **Finish**.

8. Drag **cmdClose** to the right until you see a yellow "I" bar next to the **cmdPrintAll** control. All three command buttons are in the same control layout.

9. In the **Property Sheet** of **cmdClose**, on the **Format** tab, change the **Caption** property to **Close**.

10. Change the **Picture Caption Arrangement** property to **Bottom**.

11. Change the **Width** property to **.6**.

12. On the **Other** tab, change the **ControlTip Text** property to **Click to close the form**.

13. From the **Arrange** tab, in the **Rows & Columns** group, click **Select Layout** ▦.

14. Drag the selected control to the left until the left edge of the control layout is at the 4-inch mark.

Figure 11-11
Moving all command buttons
HR-11.accdb
frmPensionFund

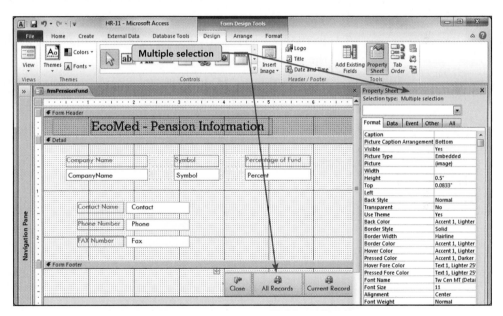

15. Save the form and switch to **Form View**.

16. Click the command button **Close** to close the form.

Working with Image Controls

Companies often include a standardized image, such as a corporate logo, to identify the source and purpose of a document or form. File types used for images can be icons, bitmaps, metafiles, and graphics files.

When creating forms in Access, you can include an image control or the logo control. The *logo control* is an image control assigned to a specific control named Auto_Logo0. Any image file can be assigned to the logo control. After an image file has been assigned to the logo control, a copy of the image is stored in the database. The image file and the logo control are not dynamically linked. Therefore, changes made to the source file will not be reflected to the copy of the image stored in the logo control.

Exercise 11-10 ADD A LOGO

When selecting the logo control, an image is added to the form header. The logo can be repositioned within the same section or moved to another section. You will now assign an image file to the logo control and position the image in the header of the form.

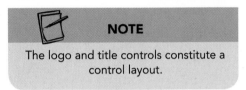

NOTE

The logo and title controls constitute a control layout.

1. Open **frmPensionFund** in Design View.
2. From the **Design** tab, in the **Header/Footer** group, click **Logo** to open the **Insert Picture** dialog box.
3. Locate the **Lesson 11** folder and select **Logo_sm.gif**.
4. Click **OK**.
5. In the logo's **Property Sheet**, on the **Format** tab, in the **Picture** property, the name of the file appears.
6. Change the **Width** property to .8 and the **Height** property to .5.
7. Save and switch to **Form View**.

Figure 11-12
Form with a Logo
HR-11.accdb
frmPensionFund

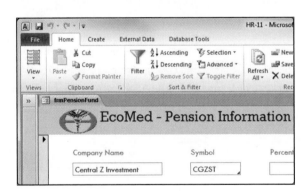

Exercise 11-11 ADD IMAGE CONTROL

In addition to the logo control, you can add image files as controls within a form. You can add an image such as a digital photograph, computer graphic, or scanned art to a form.

1. Switch to **Design View** for **frmPensionFund**.

2. From the **Design** tab, in the **Controls** group, click the More button and choose the Image control 🖼.

3. In **Form Header**, click at the top of the section at the 5½-inch mark.

4. Locate the **Lesson 11** folder and select **Stock Chart**.

5. Click **Open**.

6. In the **Property Sheet** for the new image, on the **Format** tab, change the **Width** property to **.5** and the **Height** property to **.5**.

7. Click the **Form Header** section bar. In the section's **Property Sheet**, on the **Format** tab, change the **Height** property to **.83**.

8. Save the form and switch to **Form View**.

Exercise 11-12   ADD A BACKGROUND PICTURE

You can add a background image to a form to help a database operator quickly distinguish the form from other forms in your database. A *background image* is an image control that prints behind the controls on an object.

You will now add a background image to the pension fund form. The image will be aligned with the top left so that it appears only in the header. The property of the image will be set to Stretch Horizontally, to ensure that the image will expand to the entire width of the form regardless of the size of the form.

1. Switch to **Design View** for **frmPensionFund**.

2. Select the **Form Selector**. In the form's **Property Sheet**, on the **Format** tab, click in the **Picture** property.

3. Click Build 🔲.

4. In the **Insert Picture** dialog box, locate the **Lesson 11** folder and choose **Office**. Click **OK**. The image is now in the center of the **Detail** section. This image is a small image that transition between two colors.

5. In the form's **Property Sheet**, on the **Format** tab, change the **Picture Alignment** property to **Top Left**.

6. Change the **Picture Size Mode** property to **Stretch Horizontal**.

7. Close the **Property Sheet**.

8. Save the form and switch to **Form View**.

Figure 11-13
Stretched image in
Form Header
**HR-11.accdb
frmPensionFund**

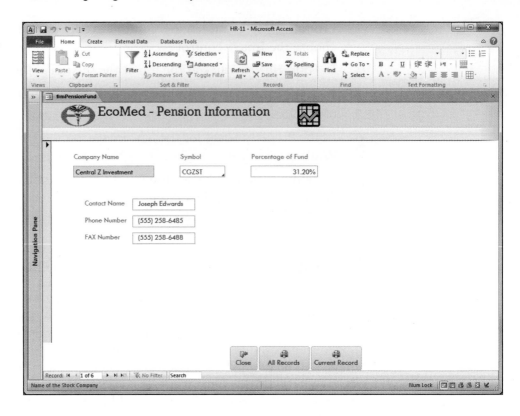

9. Close the database.

Using a Wizard to Create a Form with a Subform

Forms can present information in a hierarchical format by using main forms and subforms. A *main form* is a form that contains a subform control. A *subform* is a form that is embedded in another form. Subforms show data from tables or queries that have a One-To-Many relationship. A form/subform combination is sometimes referred to as a hierarchical form, a master/detail form, or a parent/child form.

A simple way to create a main form with a subform is to use the Form Wizard. The wizard lets you identify the source tables or queries for each form. You also are allowed to select the appropriate fields to include.

Exercise 11-13   CREATE A FORM AND SUBFORM

A simple way to create a main form with a subform is to use the Form Wizard. The Form Wizard will work only when a relationship exists between the two tables used in the form. Most often the relationship will be One-To-Many.

1. Open, enable content, and refresh links for *[your initials]*-EcoMed-11.

2. From the **Create** tab, in the **Forms** group, click **Form Wizard** 🖼.

3. In the **Tables/Queries** drop-down box choose **Table: tblVender**.

4. From the **Available Fields** section, double-click **VenderID, VenderName, PhoneNum,** and **FAX** to add them to the **Selected Fields** section.

5. In the Tables/Queries drop-down box, choose Table: tblInventory.

6. From the Available Fields section, double-click **InvID**, **ModelNum**, and **Cost** to add them to the Selected Fields section.

7. Click Next. The default settings have the data being viewed by tblVender and with Form with subform(s) selected.

Figure 11-14
Setting the main
form in the wizard
EcoMed-11.accdb

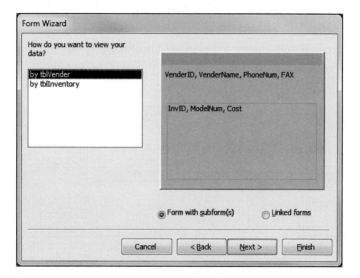

8. Click Next. Choose a Tabular layout. Click Next.

9. Edit the name for the Form to **frmVenInv-Main**. Edit the Subform name to **frmVenInv-Sub**. Choose Open the form to view or enter information, and click Finish.

10. In Form View, press PageDown a few times to move from one record to another. Notice that inventory data changes each time you move to a different vender.

11. Save the form.

12. From the Navigation Pane, open **frmInvVender-Sub**. You only see three fields in a tabular layout. This form has 310 records. The total numbers refer to all bulb models in inventory. Close the form.

Exercise 11-14   MODIFY A FORM WITH A SUBFORM

The main form and subform are individual main objects. Each form possesses individual properties. Changes made to the main form do not appear in the subform, nor do the changes made to the subform appear in the main form.

The subform control has its own properties, including Source Object. When resizing a subform in a main form, you are resizing the subform control for the main form, not the actual major object used as the subform control.

1. Switch to Design View.

2. Select the text boxes for **VenderID**, **VenderName**, **PhoneNum**, and **FAX**.

3. From the **Arrange** tab, in the **Table** group, click **Stacked**.

4. Deselect the control layout and then click just the **Phone Number** label.

5. From the **Arrange** tab, in the **Sizing & Ordering** group, click **Size/Space** and choose **To Fit**.

6. Click the label for the subform (frmVenInv-Sub) and press Delete.

7. Open the **Property Sheet** and click the **Data** tab.

8. Click the subform control. The **Property Sheet** shows the **Selection type** as **Subform/Subreport**.

Figure 11-15
Selected subform
EcoMed-11.accdb
frmVenInv-Main

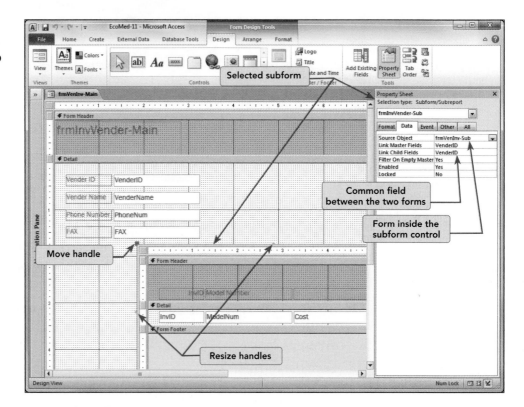

9. In the **Property Sheet**, on the **Format** tab, change the **Width** property to **5.2** and the **Height** property to **4.5**.

10. On the **Format** tab, change the **Top** property to **.25** and the **Left** property to **3.5**.

11. Click the subform's Form Selector. The **Property Sheet** shows the **Selection type** is now **Form**.

12. Change the **Default View** property to **Datasheet**. The subform will not change appearance in **Design View**.

13. Change the **Record Selectors** property to **No**.

14. On the **Data** tab, change the **Allow Additions** to **No**.

15. Switch to **Layout View** and delete the label in the **Form Header**.

16. From the **Design** tab, in the **Header/Footer** group, click **Title**.

17. Key **EcoMed – Bulb Inventory by Vender**.

18. Save and switch to **Form View**. Navigate through several records and see the corresponding data appear in the subform.

Figure 11-16
Final Form with
subform
**EcoMed-11.accdb
frmVenInv-Main**

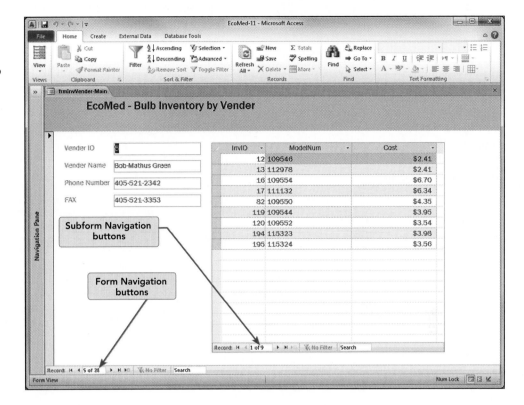

19. Close the form.

Using Subforms

To create a main form/subform, the dynaset for the main form and the dynaset for the subform must be linked by a relationship. If Access cannot determine how to link the subform to the main form, you must set these properties for the Link Child Field and Link Master Field.

Exercise 11-15 ADD A PIVOTTABLE TO A FORM

The individual view properties of a form can be changed to allow or not allow a user's ability to display data in Form View, Datasheet View, PivotTable View, PivotChart View, and Layout View.

Pivot tables can quickly and dynamically arrange information without creating specialized queries. For example, you can create a pivot table to summarize raw sales data and easily rearrange the table elements so that the table summarizes the data based on sales region or state or inventory item. With a pivot table, you can analyze the same information in many different ways to identify patterns and trends important trends.

1. Open **frmSalesByMan-Sub** in **Design View**.

2. In the form's **Property Sheet** on the **Format** tab, change the **Default View** property to **PivotTable**.

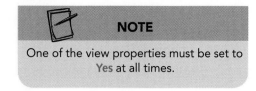

NOTE

One of the view properties must be set to Yes at all times.

3. Change the Allow PivotTable View property to Yes.

4. Change the Allow Form View property to No.

5. From the Design tab, in the Views group, click PivotTable View. The PivotTable design has already been done for you.

6. Right-click the column control button (**Month**) and choose Subtotal. This removes the Grand Total column from the PivotTable.

Figure 11-17
Modify a PivotTable
EcoMed-11.accdb
frmSalesByMan-Sub

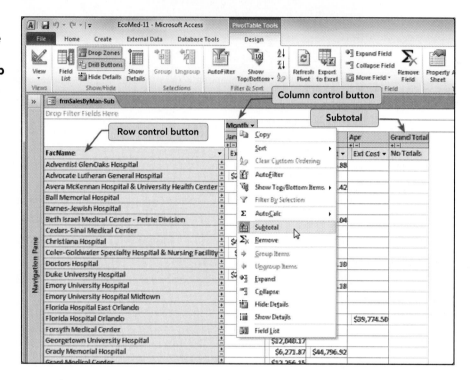

7. Right-click the row control button (**FacName**) and choose Subtotal. This removes the Grand Total row from the bottom of the PivotTable.

8. Save and close the form.

9. Open **frmSalesByMan-Main** in Design View.

10. From the Design tab, in the Controls group, click Subform/Subreport (next to the radio button control).

11. In the Detail section, click under the **Management ID** label.

12. In the SubForm Wizard dialog box, in the Use an existing form section, choose **frmSalesByMan-Sub**. Click Next.

13. Choose Choose from a list. Notice that the choice selected has the common field as **MgtID**.

Figure 11-18
SubForm Wizard
**EcoMed-11.accdb
frmSalesByMan-Sub**

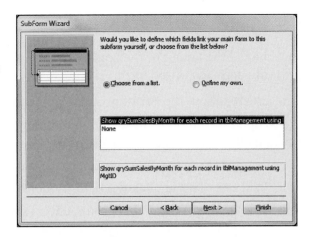

14. Click **Next**. Keep the name and click **Finish**.

15. The subform shows the **Form View** while in the main form's **Design View**. Switch to **Layout View**.

16. Delete the subform's label.

17. Using PageDown, navigate through the records in the main form. The data in the subform is related to the management data in the main form.

Figure 11-19
PivotTable in a form
**EcoMed-11.accdb
frmSalesByMan-Main**

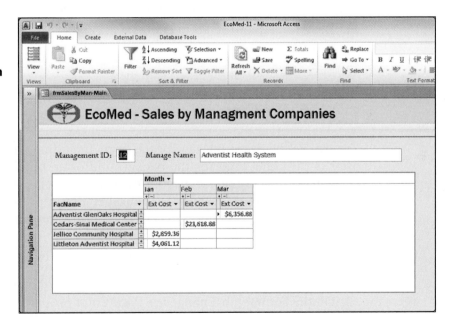

18. Save and close the form.

Exercise 11-16   CREATE A SUBFORM IN DESIGN VIEW

You will now change the layout of the controls in the subform. You will align the controls to the left side of the form.

1. From the Create tab, in the Forms group, click Form Design 🖼.
2. Press F4 to open the Property Sheet. On the Data tab, in the Record Source property and click the drop-down arrow and choose **qryShipment-Sub**.
3. From the Design tab, in the Tools group, click Add Existing Fields 🖼.
4. From the Field List, double-click the field **ModelNum**.
5. From the Arrange tab, in the Table group, click Tabular 🖼.
6. From the Field List, click the field **Qty**. Press Ctrl and click the fields **Unit Price**, and **Ext Cost**.
7. Drag the fields to the right edge of the text box **ModelNum** until you see the yellow "I" bar, so that the three fields will be added to the control layout.
8. From the Arrange tab, in the Rows & Columns group, click Select Layout 🖼. Drag the control layout to the far left of the form.
9. Drag the top of the Form Header section bar up to the bottom of the labels. Deselect the control layout.
10. In the Detail section, select all the text boxes. Drag them up to the top of the Detail section. Deselect the control layout.
11. Drag the top of the Form Footer section bar up to the bottom of the text boxes.
12. Save the form as frmShipment-Sub.

Exercise 11-17   MODIFY A SUBFORM APPEARANCE

You can define the properties for the form, including the back color. The *back color* is the color used for the background of an object. You can select the color from a palette or create your own custom color. A custom color can be defined by a unique hexadecimal number that represents a corresponding RGB (red, green, and blue) or HSL (hue, saturation, and luminance) color.

You will now change the properties of a subform, including the color, scroll bars, and record selector features.

1. Double-click the Form Header section bar to open its Property Sheet.
2. On the Format tab, change the Back Color property to #EFF2F7.
3. Click the Detail section bar. In the section's Property Sheet, on the Format tab, change the Back Color property to #EFF2F7.
4. Click the Form Footer section bar. In the section's Property Sheet, on the Format tab, change the Back Color property to #EFF2F7.
5. In the Form Header, select all the labels and change their Font to Perpetua, 12-pt, Bold with black Font Color.
6. In the Detail section, select the text boxes for **Qty**, **Unit Price**, and **Ext Cost**. From the Format tab, in the Font group, click Right 🖼.

7. Click the **ModelNum** text box. In the Property Sheet, on the Format tab, change the Width property to **1.8**.

8. Click the Form Selector. In the form's Property Sheet, on the Format tab, change the Default View property to Continuous Forms.

9. Change the Record Selectors property to No.

10. Change the Navigation Buttons property to No.

11. Change the Scroll Bar property to Vertical Only.

12. On the Data tab, change the Allow Additions property to No.

13. Close the Property Sheet and switch to Layout View.

14. Click the **Ext Cost** label. From the Home tab, in the Sort & Filter group, click Descending ⤓.

15. Resize the **Ext Cost** text box so that all of the data can be seen.

16. Save the form and switch to Form View.

Figure 11-20
Subform in Form
View
EcoMed-11.accdb
frmShipment-Sub

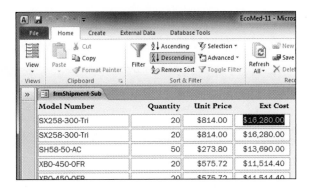

17. Close the form.

Exercise 11-18 ADD A SUBFORM CONTROL

In Access, you can add a subform to a main form by inserting a subform control. The subform will display the fields that you placed on the form and can be viewed as a single form, continuous form, or datasheet.

1. Open **frmShipment-Main** in Design View.

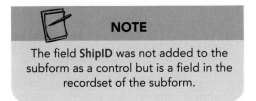

NOTE

The field **ShipID** was not added to the subform as a control but is a field in the recordset of the subform.

2. From the Design tab, in the Controls group, click Subform/Subreport ▦.

3. In the Detail section, click to the right of the other controls.

4. In the SubForm Wizard dialog box, in the Use an existing form section, choose **frmShipment-Sub**. Click Next.

5. Choose **Define my own**. In the **Form/report fields**, click the drop-down arrow and choose **ShipID**.

6. In the **Subform/Subreport fields**, click the drop-down arrow and choose **ShipID**.

7. Click **Next**. Keep the name and click **Finish**.

8. Click the subform's label and press Delete.

9. Drag the subform's upper-left corner level with the gridline of the other controls while leaving two columns of dots between the controls.

10. Drag the bottom of the subform so it is the same height as the other controls.

11. Press F4 to open the **Property Sheet**. On the **Format** tab, in the **Border Color** property, click the drop-down arrow and choose **Text Black**.

12. On the **Data** tab, notice that the **Link Master Fields** and **Link Child Fields** properties are set to the common field between the main and subform (**ShipID**).

13. Switch to **Layout View**. Click the subform and drag its right edge to the left to better fit the controls. Switch to **Form View**.

Figure 11-21
Form with a subForm
EcoMed-11.accdb
frmShipment-Main

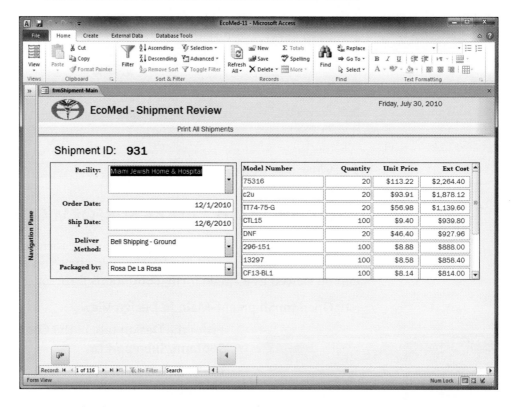

14. Save the form.

Creating Calculated Controls

A calculated control can be any combination of mathematical operations, logical operators, constants, functions, and fields. A calculated control evaluates an expression and displays a single value. Expressions can perform calculations, manipulate characters, or test data.

Exercise 11-19   ADD A CALCULATED CONTROL TO THE SUBFORM

Although any control that has a Control Source property can be used to create a calculated control, the easiest control to use is a text box.

1. Open **frmShipment-Sub** in **Layout View**.

2. Click the first **Ext Cost** text box.

3. From the **Arrange** tab, in the **Rows & Columns** group, click **Insert Below** ⊞.

4. From the **Design** tab, in the **Controls** group, click **Text Box** [abl].

5. Click in the blank cell below the first **Ext Cost** text box.

6. From the **Arrange** tab, in the **Move** group, click **Move Down** ⬇. The new text box has been moved from the **Detail** section to the **Form Footer** but is still part of the control layout.

7. Switch to **Design View** and select the new text box in the **Form Footer**.

8. From the **Arrange** tab, in the **Sizing & Ordering** group, click **Size/Space** ▦ and choose **To Fit** ▦.

9. In the new text box's **Property Sheet**, on the **Other** tab, change the **Name** property to **txtSubtotal**.

10. On the **Format** tab, change the **Format** property to **Currency**.

11. In the **Form Footer**, click the label.

12. In the label's **Property Sheet**, on the **Format** tab, change the **Caption** property to **Subtotal**.

13. Select **txtSubtotal** and its label.

14. From the **Arrange** tab, in the **Table** group, click **Gridlines** ⊞ and choose **Top**.

15. Drag the **Form Footer** section bar's top edge up to the base of the controls in the **Detail** section.

16. Click **txtSubtotal**. In the text box's **Property Sheet**, on the **Data** tab, click the **Control Source** property and then the Build button ▣.

17. In the **Expression Elements** panel, double-click the **Functions** folder and click **Built-In Functions**.

18. In the **Expression Categories** panel, click **SQL Aggregate**.

19. In the **Expression Values** panel, double-click **Sum**.

20. In the Expression box, click **<<expression>>**.

21. In the **Expression Elements** panel, click the **frmShipment-Sub**.

22. In the **Expression Categories** panel, double-click **Ext Cost**.

23. Click **OK**. Close the **Property Sheet**.

Figure 11-22
Calculation in a
subForm
**EcoMed-11.accdb
frmShipment-Sub**

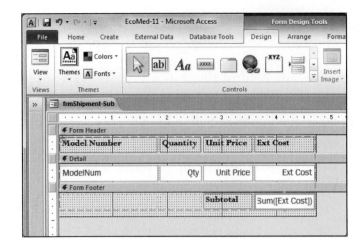

24. Save and close the form.

Exercise 11-20   ADD CALCULATED CONTROLS TO THE MAIN FORM

An easy way to create new calculated controls on a form is to copy an existing control and modify the properties for the new control.

1. Open **frmShipment-Main** in **Form View**. The changes to the subform are visible in the main form.

2. Switch to **Design View**.

3. Drag the bottom of the **Form Footer** section bar down 1/2 inch.

4. In the subform, select **txtSubtotal** and its label. Press Ctrl+C to copy the control.

5. Click under the subform and press Ctrl+V to paste. The pasted control is placed in the upper left corner of the **Detail** section.

6. Drag the new controls under the subform. Press F4 to open the **Property Sheet**.

7. Select only the new label. On the **Format** tab, change the **Caption** property to **Discount**.

8. Click the new text box. On the **Other** tab, change the **Name** property to **txtDiscount**.

9. On the **Data** tab, delete the value in the **Control Source** property. Click the Build button ⬚.

10. In the **Expression Elements** panel, double-click the **frmShipment-Main** folder. The subform appears. Click **frmShipmenting-Sub**.

11. In the **Expression Categories** panel, double-click **txtSubtotal**.

12. Press *.

13. In the **Expression Elements** panel, click the **frmShipment-Main** folder.

14. In the **Expression Categories** panel, click <Field List>.

15. In the **Expression Values** panel, double-click **Discount**.

Figure 11-23
Calculate the
Discount
EcoMed-11.accdb
frmShipment-Main

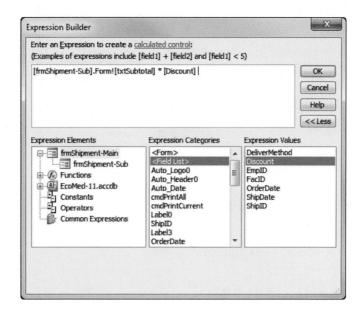

16. Click **OK**.

17. Select **txtDiscount** and its label. Press Ctrl+C and then Ctrl+V. This time, the paste occurs under the original.

18. In the new label's **Property Sheet**, on the **Format** tab, change the **Caption** property to **Total**.

19. In the new text box's **Property Sheet**, on the **Other** tab, change the **Name** property to **txtTotal**.

20. On the **Data** tab, delete the value in the **Control Source** property. Click the Build button ⊡.

21. In the **Expression Elements** panel, click the Expand button ⊞ to the left of the **frmShipment-Main** folder. Click the **frmShipment-Sub** folder.

22. In the **Expression Categories** panel, double-click **txtSubTotal**.

23. Press ⊡.

24. In the **Expression Elements** panel, click the **frmShipment-Main** folder.

25. In the **Expression Categories** panel, double-click **txtDiscount**.

26. Click **OK**.

Figure 11-24
Calculate the Total
EcoMed-11.accdb
frmShipment-Main

27. Save and view the form.

Exercise 11-21 ADD COMMAND BUTTONS TO THE MAIN FORM

A command button is a control that, when clicked, executes an action or series of actions. Standardized command buttons allow users to perform more than 30 actions, such as printing a record, previewing a report, running a query, or closing a form.

1. Switch to **Layout View**.

2. From the **Design** tab, in the **Controls** group, click Button ⊡. Hover your pointer to the right on the navigation command button at the bottom of the form until you see a yellow box. Click to start the **Command Button Wizard**.

3. In the **Actions** section, choose **Go To Next Record**. Click **Next**.

4. With the **Picture** option **Go To Next** selected, click **Next**.

5. Name the command button **cmdNextRec** and click **Finish**.

6. From the **Design** tab, in the **Controls** group, click Button ⊡. Hover your pointer to the right of the "Print All Shipments" command button in the **Form Header**, until you see a yellow box. Click to start the **Command Button Wizard**.

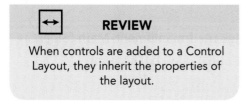

REVIEW

When controls are added to a Control Layout, they inherit the properties of the layout.

7. In the **Categories** section, choose **Form Operations**, and in the **Actions** section, choose **Print Current Form**. Click **Next**.

8. Click **Text** and edit the text to read **Print Current Record**, then click **Next**.

9. Name the command button cmdPrintCurrent and click **Finish**.

10. Resize **cmdPrintCurrent** so that all of the text is visible.

11. With **cmdPrintCurrent** selected, press F4. Notice that the Back Style property is set to Transparent.

12. Switch to Form View. Use the navigation command buttons to view Shipment ID "935."

Figure 11-25
Completed form
EcoMed-11.accdb
frmShipment-Main

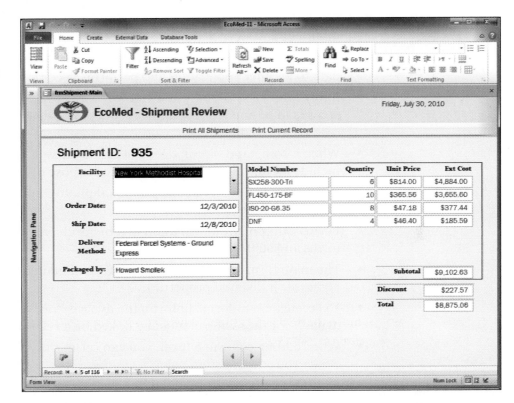

13. Save and close the form.

14. Compact and close your database.

Lesson 11   Summary

- Whenever designing a form, you should always consider the needs of the user.
- The default name for a form will be the name of the source recordset.
- Most database designers create forms by first using the Form Wizard and then modifying the controls on the form.

- When you create a form in Design View, you start with a blank form that contains only a Detail section. To complete the form, you insert fields, labels, and additional design elements.

- You can adjust the size and position of controls by selecting the control or through the property sheet of a control.

- A form can contain special controls such as the Title control, the Page Number control, and the Date & Time control.

- One method for improving the speed and accuracy of data entry is to highlight the control that has the ability to receive user input through mouse or keyboard actions.

- Access provides three ready-to-use Smart Tags. A Smart Tag delivers data to another application and performs specific actions.

- A form can be set to only allow new records to be entered, not allow new records to be entered, not allow records to be deleted, or not allow records to be edited.

- When a command button does not display text, it is a good idea to include a ControlTip that explains the purpose of the control.

- You can add an image such as a digital photograph, computer graphic, or scanned art to a form.

- Forms can present information in a hierarchical format by using main forms and subforms.

- The main form and subform are individual main objects. Each form possesses individual properties.

- To create a main form/subform, the dynaset for the main form and the dynaset for the subform must be linked by a relationship.

- When adding color to a form, you can select the color from a palette or create your own custom color.

- A custom color can be defined by a unique hexadecimal number that represents a corresponding RGB (red, green, and blue) or HSL (hue, saturation, and luminance) color.

- A calculated control can be any combination of mathematical operations, logical operators, constants, functions, and fields.

- Although any control that has a Control Source property can be used to create a calculated control, the easiest control to use is a text box.

- A command button is a control that, when clicked, executes an action or series of actions.

LESSON 11		Command Summary	
Feature	**Button**	**Task Path**	**Keyboard**
Controls, Command Button, Create		Design, Controls, Button	
Controls, Control Wizards		Design, Controls, Use Control Wizards	
Controls, Size, Tallest		Arrange, Sizing & Ordering, Size/Space, Size to Tallest	
Controls, Tabular Layout		Arrange, Table, Tabular	
Form Selector		Design View, Form Selector	
Form, Create		Create, Forms, Form Design	
Gridlines		Arrange, Table, Gridlines	
Image, Insert		Design, Controls, Image	
Insert, Column to Left		Arrange, Rows & Columns, Insert Left	
Logo, Insert		Design, Header/Footer, Logo	
Move, Control Down		Arrange, Move, Move Down	
Smart Tag		Property Sheet, Data, Smart Tags	
Subform/Subreport, Create		Design, Controls, Subform/Subreport	
Themes, Apply		Design, Themes, Themes	
Themes, Colors		Design, Themes, Colors	

Concepts Review

True/False Questions

Each of the following statements is either true or false. Indicate your choice by circling T or F.

T F 1. A Smart Tag can launch another application such as Microsoft Outlook or Microsoft Internet Explorer.

T F 2. A command button can display a **ControlTip** that describes the purpose of the button.

T F 3. A control can be resized through its property sheet.

T F 4. The Title control can be an image, such as a digital photograph.

T F 5. The **Allow Deletions** property of a main form prevents a user from accidentally deleting a subform control.

T F 6. You can change the back color of a form based on the control that has the focus.

T F 7. Each command button can display either an icon or text, but not both.

T F 8. Standardized command buttons allow users to perform more than 30 actions, such as printing a record, previewing a report, and running a query.

Short Answer Questions

Write the correct answer in the space provided.

1. What property must a control have so it can have a calculated control?

_____

2. What is an active control?

_____

3. Which Smart Tag launches Internet Explorer?

_____

4. Which form property determines whether changes to a saved record can be made through the form?

_____

5. To use a wizard when adding a control to a form, what feature must first be active?

_____

6. What type of image shows or prints behind the controls on an object?

_____

7. What control executes an action or series of actions when clicked?

_____

8. When following the Leszynski Naming Conventions, what three lettered prefix should be used for an image?

_____

Critical Thinking

Answer these questions on a separate page. There are no right or wrong answers. Support your answers with examples from your own experience, if possible.

1. Designing a good-looking, professional form can be tedious. Explain how creating and saving task-specific forms can increase productivity for a company.

2. Databases include employee records in addition to tables containing activities such as upcoming events. Explain how using Smart Tags can be useful for scheduling meetings.

Skills Review

Exercise 11-22

You have been directed to create a form to add new records to the management table. This form will not allow records to be edited, only added.

1. Open a database by following these steps:
    a. Locate and open the **Lesson 11** folder.
    b. If you already have a copy of *[your initials]*-**EcoMed-11**, skip to step 1d.
    c. Make a copy of **EcoMed-11** and rename it *[your initials]*-EcoMed-11.
    d. Open and enable content for *[your initials]*-**EcoMed-11**.
    e. Refresh the links with *[your initials]*-**HR-11**.

2. Copy a form by following these steps:
    a. In the Navigation Pane, select **frmMasterForm**.
    b. From the File tab, click Save Object As 🖫.
    c. In the Save As dialog box, name the new form **frmAddMan**.
    d. Open the form and switch to Design View.

3. Add fields to a control layout by following these steps:
    a. From the Design tab, in the Tools group, click Add Existing Fields 🔢.
    b. In the Field List, click Show all tables. Click the Expand button ⊞ for the table **tblManagement**.

c. From the Field List, double-click the field **MgtID**.

d. From the Arrange tab, in the Table group, click Tabular ▦.

e. From the Field List, click the field **ManageName**. Press Ctrl and click the field **ContractEnds**.

f. Drag both fields to the right edge of the text box **MgtID** until you see the yellow "I" bar, so that the two fields will be added to the control layout.

g. In the From Header, click the **Management ID** label.

h. From the Arrange tab, in the Rows & Columns group, click Select Row ▦.

i. From the Arrange tab, in the Move group, click Move Down ➥.

j. From the Arrange tab, in the Rows & Columns group, click Select Layout ▦.

k. From the Arrange tab, in the Sizing & Ordering group, click Size/ Space ▦ and choose To Tallest ▣.

l. Click and drag the control layout to the upper left corner of the Detail section. Leave two rows of dots above the labels and 4 columns of dots to the left of the controls.

4. Add fields to two more control layouts by following these steps:

a. From the Field List, click the field **Address**. Press Ctrl and click the fields **City**, **State**, and **ZIP**.

b. Drag the selected fields about 1/2 inch below the other control layout.

c. From the Arrange tab, in the Table group, click Stacked ▥.

d. From the Field List, click the field **PhoneNum**. Press Ctrl and click the fields **ContactFirstName** and **ContactLastName**.

e. Drag the selected fields to the right of the other control layout.

f. From the Arrange tab, in the Table group, click Stacked ▥.

5. Align and move control layouts by following these steps:

a. In the Detail section, click the **ManageName** text box.

b. Press F4. In the Property Sheet, on the Format tab, change the Width property to **4.5**.

c. Switch to Layout View.

d. Click the **Address** text box and drag its right edge to the right until you can see all of the data.

e. From the Arrange tab, in the Rows & Columns group, click Select Layout ▦.

f. Drag the control layout so that the left edge of the **Address** text box aligns with the left edge of the **Manage Name** controls.

g. Click the **Phone Number** text box and drag its right edge to the right until you can see all of the data.

h. Click the **Phone Number** label and drag its right edge to the right until you can see every label in the control layout.

i. From the Arrange tab, in the Rows & Columns group, click Select Layout ▦.

j. Drag the control layout so that its right edge aligns with the right edge of the **Contract Ends** controls.

k. Switch to **Design View**.

l. Select both stacked control layouts.

m. From the **Arrange** tab, in the **Sizing & Ordering** group, click **Align** and choose **Top**.

n. Make sure the two selected control layouts are no more than 1/4 inch below the **Tabular** layout.

6. Modify the **Form Header** by following these steps:

a. Edit the Title to **EcoMed – New Management Company**.

b. From the **Design** tab, in the **Controls** group, click Label $\boxed{Aa}$.

c. Click in the **Form Header** section below the title control and key **Prepared by:***[your full name]*.

d. Align the new label with the right edge of the right edges of the control in the **Detail** section.

7. Modify form properties by following these steps:

a. Click the Form Selector $\boxed{\blacksquare}$.

b. In the **Property Sheet**, on the **Format** tab, change the **Record Selector** property to **No**.

c. Change the **Navigation Buttons** property to **No**.

d. On the **Data** tab, change the **Data Entry** property to **Yes**.

Assessment

 - Turn in your database only when all assigned exercises have been completed, according to your classroom procedure.

-OR-

- Save a form by following these steps:

a. Switch to **Form** view. Press Tab and in the **Manage Name** text box key your full name. Do not finish the form.

b. Click the **File** tab and from the **Print** option, click **Print Preview** $\boxed{\text{Q}}$.

c. From the **Print Preview** tab, in the **Data** group, click **PDF or XPS** $\boxed{\text{T}}$ to save the printout as a file.

d. Save the file as a PDF and name the file *[your initials]***-11-22-A**.

e. Depending on your class procedures, print or turn in the PDF file.

11-22-A.pdf
1 Page

Exercise 11-23

You have been directed to create a professional-looking master form with subform to enter and edit management company data.

1. Create a form using a wizard by following these steps:

a. Open, enable content, and refresh links for *[your initials]***-EcoMed-11**.

b. From the **Create** tab, in the **Forms** group, click **Form Wizard** $\boxed{\text{图}}$.

c. In the Tables/Queries drop-down box, choose Table: tblManagement.

d. From the Available Fields section, double-click ManageName and PhoneNum to add them to the Selected Fields section.

e. In the Tables/Queries drop-down box, choose Table: tblFacilities.

f. From the Available Fields section, double-click FacName, State, and PhoneNum to add them to the Selected Fields section. Click Next.

g. With the data being viewed by tblManagement and with Form with subform(s) selected. Click Next.

h. Select the layout of the subform to be Tabular. Click Next.

i. Edit the name for the Form to frmCust-Main. Edit the Subform name to frmCust-Sub. Choose Open the form to view or enter information, and click Finish.

2. Arrange controls in a form by following these steps:

a. Switch to Design View.

b. In the Form Header, delete the label.

c. Select the label and text box for both ManageName and PhoneNum.

d. From the Arrange tab, in the Table group, click Tabular 🖿.

e. In the Form Header, select both labels.

f. From the Arrange tab, in the Move group, click Move Down ➡.

g. From the Arrange tab, in the Rows & Columns group, click Select Layout 🖿.

h. Press F4. In the Property Sheet, on the Format tab, change the Height property to .24.

i. Click and drag the control layout to the upper left corner of the Detail section. Leave two rows of dots above the labels and 4 columns of dots to the left of the controls.

j. Select the subform's label and press Delete.

k. Drag the subform control under the ManageName text box leaving two rows of dots between them and aligned to the left edge.

3. Format a form by following these steps:

a. Click the main form's Form Selector 🔳.

b. In the form's Property Sheet, on the Format tab, click in the Picture property.

c. Click the Ellipse button 🔳.

d. In the Insert Picture dialog box, locate the Lesson 11 folder and choose Office. Click OK.

e. Change the Picture Alignment property to Top Left.

f. Change the Picture Size Mode property to Stretch Horizontal.

g. Select the Detail section bar. In the section's Property Sheet, on the Format tab, change the Back Color property to #EFF2F7.

4. Format the Form Header by following these steps:

a. From the Design tab, in the Header/Footer group, click Logo 🖾.

b. Locate the Lesson 11 folder and choose Logo_sm.

c. In the logo's Property Sheet, change the Width property to .8 and the Height property to .55.

d. From the Design tab, in the Header/Footer group, click Title 🔳.

    e. Key **EcoMed – Customer Listing**.

    f. From the **Design** tab, in the **Controls** group, click Label .

    g. Click in the **Form Header** section below the title control and key **Prepared by:***[your full name]*.

    h. Move the label to the right edge of the form.

5. Format a subform by following these steps:

    a. In the subform's **Form Header**, select all the labels and drag them to the top of the section.

    b. Drag the top of the **Detail** section bar up to the bottom of the labels.

    c. Select the text boxes in the **Detail** section.

    d. From the **Arrange** tab, in the **Sizing & Ordering** group, click **Size/ Space** and choose **To Shortest**.

    e. Drag the top of the **Form Footer** section bar up to the bottom of the text boxes. Leave one row of dots below the text boxes.

    f. Select the **Form Header** section bar. In the section's **Property Sheet**, on the **Format** tab, change the **Back Color** property to **#EFF2F7**.

    g. Select the **Detail** section bar. In the section's **Property Sheet**, on the **Format** tab, change the **Back Color** property to **#EFF2F7**.

    h. Select the subform's Form Selector. In the subform's **Property Sheet**, on the **Format** tab, change the **Record Selector** property to **No**.

    i. Change the **Navigation Buttons** property to **No**.

    j. On the **Data** tab, change the **Allow Additions** property to **No**.

6. Resize control on a form by following these steps:

    a. Switch the **Layout View**.

    b. In the subform, resize the PhoneNum text box until yo can see all the data.

    c. Select the **Manage Name** text box. Drag its right edge to the right until the **Phone Number** text box's right edge is aligned with the right edge of the subform.

Assessment

- Turn in your database only when all assigned exercises have been completed, according to your classroom procedure.

-OR-

11-23-A.pdf
1 Page

- Save a form by following these steps:

    a. Click the **File** tab and from the **Print** option, click **Print Preview** .

    b. From the **Print Preview** tab, in the **Data** group, click **PDF or XPS** to save the printout as a file.

    c. In the **Publish as PDF or XPS** dialog box, click the **Option** button. Select the **Pages** option. Print only page **1** and click **OK**.

    d. Save the file as a PDF and name the file *[your initials]*-11-23-A.

    e. Depending on your class procedures, print or turn in the PDF file.

Exercise 11-24

You have been asked to create a form to assist sales personnel locate information regarding the bulbs that are in stock. Create a master form and subform that will aid a database operator to locate and display this information.

1. Create forms by following these steps:

   a. Open, enable content, and refresh links for *[your initials]*-EcoMed-11.

   b. In the Navigation Pane, select frmMasterForm.

   c. From the File tab, click Save Object As 🖪.

   d. In the Save As dialog box, name the new form frmBulbFinder-Main.

   e. From the Create tab, in the Forms group, click Form Design 🖳.

   f. Save the new form as frmBulbFinder-Sub.

2. Format a subform by following these steps:

   a. Press F4 to open the Property Sheet for the form.

   b. On the Format tab, change the Default View property to Datasheet.

   c. On the Data tab, in the Record Source property, click the drop-down arrow and choose tblInventory.

3. Add and Align controls in a subform by following these steps:

   a. From the Design tab, in the Tools group, click Add Existing Fields 🖽.

   b. From the Field List, double-click the field ModelNum, ShapeID, and Cost.

   c. Select all the controls in the Detail sections.

   d. From the Arrange tab, in the Table group, click Tabular 🎛.

   e. Save and close the form.

4. Format a main form by following these steps:

   a. Open frmBulbFinder-Main in Design View.

   b. In the form's Property Sheet, on the Data tab, in the Record Source property, click the drop-down arrow and choose tblBulbType.

   c. From the Design tab, in the Tools group, click Add Existing Fields 🖽.

   d. From the Field List, double-click BulbType.

   e. Drag the control up to the upper left corner of the Detail section. Drag the left margin of the BulbType text box to the left until it meets the label.

   f. From the Design tab, in the Header/Footer group, click Title 🗉 and key EcoMed – Bulb Finder by Bulb Type.

   g. From the Design tab, in the Controls group, click Label 𝐀𝐚.

   h. Click in the Form Header section below the Title to the right and key Prepared by:*[your full name]*.

5. Add command buttons to a form by following these steps:

   a. From the Design tab, in the Controls group, click Button ▭. Click in the middle of the Detail section.

   b. In the Command Button Wizard, in the Categories section, choose Form Operations and as an Action, choose Close Form. Click Next.

c. Choose the **Picture** option and click **Finish**.

d. From the **Arrange** tab, in the **Table** group, click **Stacked** .

e. From the **Arrange** tab, in the **Rows & Columns** group, click **Insert Right** twice to add two blank cells.

f. Switch to **Layout View**.

g. From the **Design** tab, in the **Controls** group, click Button . Click in the blank cell to the right of the close button.

h. In the **Command Button Wizard**, in the **Categories** section, choose **Record Navigation**, and as an **Action**, choose **Go To Previous Record**. Click **Finish**.

i. From the **Design** tab, in the **Controls** group, click Button . Click in the blank cell to the right of the other buttons.

j. In the **Command Button Wizard**, in the **Categories** section, choose **Record Navigation**, and as an **Action**, choose **Go To Next Record**. Click **Finish**.

k. Switch to **Design View**.

l. Click the Close command button. From the **Arrange** tab, in the **Rows & Columns** group, click **Insert Right** to add a blank cell between the close and navigation buttons.

m. From the **Arrange** tab, in the **Rows & Columns** group, click **Select Layout** .

n. In the **Property Sheet**, on the **Format** tab, change the **Width** property to **.5** and the **Height** property to **.23**.

o. Drag all the buttons to the bottom of the **Form Header** under the **Logo** without joining it to the **Logo's** control layout.

6. Add a subform to a form by following these steps:

a. From the **Design** tab, in the **Controls** group, click **Subform/ Subreport** .

b. Click to the right of the **BulbType** text box.

c. From the **SubForm Wizard**, select the existing form **frmBulbFinder-Sub** and click **Next**.

d. The wizard found the common field was **BulbType**. Click **Finish**.

e. Select the subform label and press Delete .

f. Resize the subform so that its right side does not extend past the 8-inch mark.

g. Resize the form so that it is not wider than 8-inches.

Assessment

 - Turn in your database only when all assigned exercises have been completed, according to your classroom procedure.

-OR-

 - Save a form by following these steps:

a. Use the navigation buttons to find the bulb type "Mercury." Click the record selector.

11-24-A.pdf
1 Page

b. Click the **File** tab and from the **Save & Publish** option, click **Save Object As** 🖾, then double-click **PDF or XPS** 🖺.

c. In the **Publish as PDF or XPS** dialog box, click the **Option** button. Select the **Select records** option and click **OK**.

d. Save the file as a PDF and name the file *[your initials]*-**11-24-A**.

e. Depending on your class procedures, print or turn in the PDF file.

Exercise 11-25

You have been directed to create a form that displays sales information based on region. On the form, include a map of the United States, separated by sales region.

1. Create forms by following these steps:

    a. Open, enable content, and refresh links for *[your initials]*-**EcoMed-11**.

    b. In the **Navigation Pane**, select **frmMasterForm**.

    c. From the **File** tab, click **Save Object As** 🖾.

    d. In the **Save As** dialog box, name the new form **frmRegionSales-Main**.

    e. In the **Navigation Pane**, select **frmMasterForm**.

    f. From the **File** tab, click **Save Object As** 🖾.

    g. In the **Save As** dialog box, name the new form **frmRegionSales-Sub**.

2. Format a subform by following these steps:

    a. Open **frmRegionSales-Sub** in **Design View**.

    b. Delete the **Title** and **Logo** controls from the **Form Header**.

    c. Click the Form Selector 🔳.

    d. In the form's **Property Sheet**, on the **Format** tab, delete the value in the **Picture** property. Press Enter and click **Yes** to confirm the deletion.

    e. On the **Data** tab, in the **Record Source** property, click the drop-down arrow and choose **qryRegionShip**.

    f. On the **Format** tab, change the **Default View** property to **Continuous Forms**.

    g. Change the **Record Selector** property to **No**.

    h. Change the **Navigation Buttons** property to **No**.

    i. Select the **Form Header** section bar. In the section's **Property Sheet**, on the **Format** tab, change the **Back Color** property to **#EFF2F7**.

3. Add controls to the subform by following these steps:

    a. From the **Design** tab, in the **Tools** group, click **Add Existing Fields** 🎟.

    b. From the **Field List**, double-click the fields **FacName** and **Total Billed**.

    c. Select all controls in the **Detail** section.

    d. From the **Arrange** tab, in the **Table** group, click **Tabular** 🎞.

    e. Drag the control layout to the far left of the form.

    f. Drag the top of the **Detail** section bar up to the bottom of the labels. Deselect the control layout.

g. In the Detail section, select both text boxes. Drag them up to the top of the Detail section.

h. Drag the top of the Form Footer section bar up to the bottom of the text boxes, leaving one row of dots below the text boxes.

i. Select **FacName** text box. In the Property Sheet, on the Format tab, change the value in the Width property to **3.7**.

j. Select **Total Billed** text box. In the Property Sheet, on the Format tab, change the value in the Width property to **1.15**.

k. Drag the right edge of the form as far to the left as you can.

4. Add calculations to the subform by following these steps:

a. From the Design tab, in the Controls group, click Text Box [abl].

b. Click below the **Total Billed** text box and the Form Footer section.

c. Change the Caption of the new label to **Region Total**. Resize the label.

d. Click the unbound text box. In the Property Sheet, on the Format tab, change the Format property to Currency.

e. Change the Width property to **1.15**.

f. In the Data tab, click in the Control Source property. Click the Build button [⊡] to open the Expression Builder.

g. In the Expression Elements panel, double-click the Functions folder and click Built-In Functions.

h. In the Expression Categories panel, click SQL Aggregate.

i. In the Expression Values panel, double-click Sum.

j. In the Expresson box, click <<expression>>.

k. In the Expression Elements panel, click the **frmRegionSales-Sub**.

l. In the Expression Categories panel, double-click **Total Billed**. Click OK.

m. On the Other tab, change the Name property to **txtTotal**.

n. Align **txtTotal** under the **Total Billed** text box.

o. Save and close the form.

5. Format the main form by following these steps:

a. Open **frmRegionSales-Main** in Design View. From the Design tab, in the Tools group, click Add Existing Fields [▥].

b. In the Field List, click Show all tables. Click the Expand button [⊞] for the table **tblRegion**.

c. Double-click the field **Region**.

d. Drag the **Region** text box closer to its label and resize the text box to show only the field name.

e. Drag both controls to the upper left corner of the Detail section.

f. From the Design tab, in the Controls group, click the More button and choose the Image control [▦].

g. Click in the middle of the Detail section.

h. Locate the **Lesson 11** folder and select **RegionCodes.jpg**. Click Open.

i. In the Property Sheet, on the Format tab, change the Width property to **3**.

j. Change the Height property to **1.8**.

k. Drag the image under the **Region** controls.

6. Add labels to the form by following these steps:

   a. From the **Design** tab, in the **Header/Footer** group, click **Title** and key **EcoMed – Year to Date Sales by Region**.

   b. From the **Design** tab, in the **Controls** group, click Label **Aa**.

   c. Click in the **Form Header** section below the **Title** to the right and key **Prepared by:***[your full name]*.

7. Add a subform to a form by following these steps:

   a. From the **Design** tab, in the **Controls** group, click **Subform/Subreport** ▦.

   b. Click to the right of the image.

   c. From the **SubForm Wizard**, select the existing form **frmRegionSales-Sub** and click **Next**.

   d. The wizard found the common field was **Region**. Click **Finish**.

   e. Select the subform label and press ⌨Delete.

   f. Drag the subform control to the top of the **Detail** section and touching the right edge of the image control.

   g. Drag the bottom of the subform control down to the 4-inch mark on the vertical ruler.

8. Add a calculation to the main form by following these steps:

   a. From the **Design** tab, in the **Controls** group, click **Text Box** abl.

   b. Click to the right of the **Region** control and above the image control.

   c. Edit the label to **Profit**. Move the label to the right of the **Region** text box.

   d. Drag the left edge of the new text box closer to its label.

   e. In the **Property Sheet**, on the **Format** tab, change the **Format** property to **Currency**.

   f. In the **Data** tab, click in the **Control Source** property. Click the Build button ⊡ to open the **Expression Builder**.

   g. In the **Expression Elements** panel, double-click the **frmRegionSales-Main** folder and click **frmRegionSales-Sub**.

   h. In the **Expression Categories** panel, double-click **txtTotal**.

   i. Press ⎄.

   j. In the **Expression Categories** panel, double-click **txtTotal**.

   k. Key **/1.48**. Click **OK**.

   l. Review and save the form.

Assessment

🗄 **DB**   - Turn in your database only when all assigned exercises have been completed, according to your classroom procedure.

-OR-

- Save a form by following these steps:

a. Click the **File** tab and from the **Print** option, click **Print Preview** .

b. From the **Print Preview** tab, in the **Page Layout** group, click **Landscape** .

c. From the **Print Preview** tab, in the **Data** group, click **PDF or XPS** to save the printout as a file.

d. In the **Publish as PDF or XPS** dialog box, click the **Option** button. Select the **Pages** option. Print only page **1** and click **OK**.

e. Save the file as a PDF and name the file *[your initials]*-**11-25-A**.

f. Depending on your class procedures, print or turn in the PDF file.

11-25-A.pdf
1 Page

Lesson Applications

Exercise 11-26

The director of human resources has asked you to create a form that can be used to edit employee information, including a picture of the employee.

REVIEW

To make a copy of an object you can use Copy and Paste, or from the File tab, click Save Object As.

1. Using *[your initials]*-**HR-11**, make a copy of **frmMasterForm** and name the copy frmEmpInfo.

2. Add a title with the caption Employee Information.

3. Add the following fields to the Detail section of the form.
   - **tblEmployees**: **EmpID**, **FirstName**, and **LastName**.

4. Arrange these controls in a Tabular layout in the order above.

5. Place all three text boxes and their labels in the upper left corner of the Detail section with medium Control Padding.

6. Add the following fields to the Detail section of the form.
   - **tblEmployees**: **SSN**, **DOB**, **HireDate**, and **JobCodeID**.

7. Arrange these controls in a Stacked layout in the order above.

8. Place all four text boxes and their labels below the **EmpID** text box with medium Control Padding.

9. From **tblEmployees**, add the **Pictures** field to the Detail section to the right of the **LastName** text box.

10. Delete the **Pictures** control's label and resize the attachment control to 2.5 inches square. Align this control with the top of the **LastName** label. Make sure that this control does not join any of the control layouts in the Detail section.

11. Add the Date to the Form Header without the Time. Align to the right.

12. Below the Date control, add a label to the Form Header with the caption Prepared by: *[your full name]*. Align to the right.

13. Resize all controls so that all data can be seen and the form is no wider than 7.9 inches.

11-26-A.pdf
1 Page

Assessment

- Turn in your database only when all assigned exercises have been completed, according to your classroom procedure.

-OR-

- Save the form as a PDF. Only show the record for employee #111, Maria Floria. Name the file *[your initials]*-11-26-A.
- According to your class procedures, print or turn in the PDF file.

Exercise 11-27

The director of human resources has asked you to create another form that will display employee job titles.

1. Using *[your initials]*-**HR-11**, create a main form with subform using a wizard.

2. From **tblJobCodes**, select **JobTitle**. From **tblEmployees**, select **FirstName** and **LastName**.

3. Have the layout for the subform be Tabular.

4. Name the Form frmEmpByJob-Main and the Subform frmEmpByJob-Sub.

5. Change the form's title to **EcoMed - Employees by Job Category**.

6. Add the Logo **Logo_sm**.

7. In the Form Header section, to the right of the Title, add a label with the caption **Prepared by:** *[your full name]*.

8. Format the main form to include the following:

    *   Do not allow this form to add additional records.
    *   Add the Picture **HROffice**.
        *   Set the picture to the Top Left and Stretch Horizontally.
    *   Resize the Form Header to a height of **.92**.
    *   For the Detail section, change the Back Color to **#F7F9F1**.
    *   Size the form to be no wider than 7.9 inches wide.

9. Format the subform to include the following:

    *   Delete the subform label.
    *   Do not allow this form to add additional records.
    *   Do not show Record Selectors.
    *   Do not show Navigations Buttons.
    *   In the Form Header, move the labels as far up in the section as you can and resize the section as small as possible.
    *   For the Form Header and Detail section, change the Back Color to **#F7F9F1**.
    *   Align text boxes under their labels.
    *   Size the subform to be no wider than 3.5 inches wide.

11-27-A.pdf
1 Page

Assessment

- Turn in your database only when all assigned exercises have been completed, according to your classroom procedure.

-OR-

- Save the form as a PDF. Only show the record for sales representatives. Name the file *[your initials]*-**11-27-A**.

According to your class procedures, print or turn in the PDF file.

Exercise 11-28

The human resource department needs your assistance to create a form to display historical payroll information.

1. Using *[your initials]*-**HR-11**, make a copy of **frmMasterForm** and name the copy frmEmpPayHistory-Main.

2. In the main form, use **tblEmployees** to add the fields **EmpID**, **FirstName**, **LastName**, and **SSN**.

3. Create a Tabular layout for the three controls. Place the labels under the Logo (in the dark green bar). In the Detail section, place the text boxes so that there are only two rows of dots above the controls. Arrange the text boxes in the same order as in step 2. Change the Font Color of the labels to black.

4. Add a title of EcoMed - Employee Payroll History.

5. In the Form Header section, aligned to the right margin, add a label and key Prepared by: *[your full name]*. Align the text to the right. Change the Font Color of the labels to black.

6. Create a subform that includes from **tblPayrollHistory** the fields **EmpID**, **ChkDate**, **ChkNum**, **RegHr**, and **OvrHr**. Name the form frmEmpPayHistory-Sub.

7. Remove the navigation controls and the ability of the form to add additional records. Set the form to only Allow Datasheet View.

8. Add the subform to the main form under the **Employee ID** control. The two forms need to be joined by the field **EmpID**.

9. Delete the **EmpID** text box from the subform. Make the subform 3.5 inches tall and 3.28 inches wide. Delete the subform's label.

10. Close the main form's Form Footer.

11. In Detail section of the main form, below the subform control, add five command buttons that will have the following actions: close form, first record, previous record, next record, and last record. Only show icons in the command buttons. Resize and align them in one row to make them look professional.

11-28-A.pdf
1 Page

Assessment

- Turn in your database only when all assigned exercises have been completed, according to your classroom procedure.

-OR-

- Save the form as a PDF. Only show the record for Jamel Abdone. Name the file *[your initials]*-11-28-A.

- According to your class procedures, print or turn in the PDF file.

Exercise 11-29 ◆ Challenge Yourself

The president of the company has asked all department supervisors to monitor the leave activity of their employees. You have been directed by your boss to create a new form to assist the other supervisors.

1. Using *[your initials]*-**HR-11**, make a copy of **frmMasterForm** and name the copy **frmLeave-Main**.

2. Include the title **EcoMed - Employee Leave Summary**.

3. In the main form, use **tblEmployees** to add the fields **EmpID**, **FirstName**, and **LastName**.

4. Create a **Tabular** layout for the three controls. Place the labels under the **Logo**. In the **Detail** section, place the text boxes so that there are only two rows of dots above the controls.

5. Add a label in the far right of the **Form Header** section and key **Prepared by:** *[your full name]*.

6. Create a **Multiple Items** subform for **qryVacDays** and name it **frmLeaveVac-Sub**.

7. Delete the **Logo** and **Title** controls and reduce the height of the **Form Header** to just fit the text boxes labels. Delete the controls for **EmpID** and **LeaveCategory**. Remove the blank columns in the control layout, leaving only the **Leave Date** text box and label.

8. Add a calculated field to the **Form Footer** that displays a count of records displayed in the form. Edit the label's **Caption** to **Total Vacation Days**. Name the text box **txtVacCount**.

9. Align the **Leave Date** controls above **txtVacCount**.

10. Remove the **Navigation Buttons**, **Record Selector**, and **Scroll Bars**. Set it so that this subform will not **Allow Additions**. Change the **Back Color** of all sections to **#F7F9F1**. Make the subform as small as possible but still make sure you can see all the data.

11. Make a copy of **frmLeaveVac-Sub** and name the copy **frmLeaveSick-Sub**.

12. In **frmLeaveSick-Sub**, edit the label in the **Form Footer** to read **Total Sick Days**. Change the calculated text box **Name** to **txtSickCount**. Change the subform's **Control Source** to **qrySickDays**.

13. In the **Detail** section of the main form, under the other controls, add the two subforms side by side. Both subforms should use **EmpID** to link to the main form. Delete the labels from both subforms. Make each subform **3.5** inches tall.

14. In the main form, add a calculated field to the control layout right of the **Last Name** text box that adds the total leave days from each subform. Edit the label to **Total Leave Days**.

15. In the **Form Header**, change the **Font Color** of the labels to black. Make sure that the form has a width less than 8 inches.

Assessment

- Turn in your database only when all assigned exercises have been completed, according to your classroom procedure.

-OR-

- Save the form as a PDF. Only show the record for Kathy Fernandez. Name the file *[your initials]*-11-29-A.
- According to your class procedures, print or turn in the PDF file.

On Your Own

11-29-A.pdf
1 Page

In these exercises you work on your own, as you would in a real-life work environment. Use the skills you've learned to accomplish the task—and be creative.

Exercise 11-30

Review the design of the database that you modified in Exercise 10-32. On a sheet of paper, sketch two new forms based on the queries that you created in Lesson 10. One of the forms must include a new image field currently not in your database. The other form must include a Subform control. Name each form and give each a title that best describes the purpose for the form. Write your name, class information, and Exercise 11-30 on each sketch. Continue to Exercise 11-31.

Exercise 11-31

Add the image field to the appropriate table for the form you designed in Exercise 11-30. Locate and attach at least five images to your database. Based on the sketches that you created in Exercise 11-30, create the two forms. Select the style and layout most appropriate for each form. Arrange the controls as necessary. In the Form Footer, include your name and Exercise 11-31. In the Form Header, include the title of the form. Continue to Exercise 11-32.

Exercise 11-32

Remove the navigation controls from each form that you created in Exercise 11-31. Add appropriate command buttons to replace the navigation controls. Add a control to close the form and another control to print the current record. Print a copy of each form. Submit copies of the sketches and forms that you printed to your instructor. Keep a copy of the database you modified in this lesson. You will use it for the On Your Own exercises in subsequent lessons.

Lesson 12
Building Advanced Reports

OBJECTIVES   *After completing this lesson, you will be able to:*

1. Create a report using a wizard.
2. Create a report with a subreport.
3. Add expressions to a report.
4. Add PivotCharts to a report.
5. Work with image controls.

Estimated Time: 3 hours

Reports are management tools that communicate information in a concise, logical manner. Effective reports display the essential information necessary to make effective business decisions.

Although business reports can be created to display a wide range of data, most often a report is designed to display information for a specific purpose or specific audience. Adding images, alternating colors, and including a cover page often improve the functionality of a report.

Creating a Report Using a Wizard

As with forms, you can create a report using the Report Wizard. However, most often a wizard will not be able to create a complete report. You will need to rearrange, resize, and reformat most controls and sections. As you work with reports, you will discover that using the Report Wizard often is the fastest way to create a basic report that can be modified later.

Exercise 12-1 CREATE A REPORT USING A WIZARD

Using the Report Wizard is often the easiest way to create a simple report. The report that you create can be based upon any recordset, such as a table or query. You now will now use the Report Wizard to create a report based upon the employees table.

1. Locate and open the **Lesson 12** folder.
2. Copy **EcoMed-12** and rename it *[your initials]*-EcoMed-12. Copy **HR-12** and rename it *[your initials]*-HR-12.
3. Open *[your initials]*-**HR-12**.
4. From the Create tab, in the Reports group, click Report Wizard 🔍.
5. In the Tables/Queries drop-down box, choose Table: tblEmployees. Add **LastName**, **FirstName**, **HomePhone**, and **EmergencyPhone** to the Selected Fields section. Click Next.
6. In the Do you want to add any grouping levels? section, double-click **LastName**.
7. Click Grouping Options. Click the Grouping intervals drop-down arrow and choose 1st Letter. Click OK.

Figure 12-1
Setting grouping options in the wizard
EcoMed-12.accdb rptEmpPhone

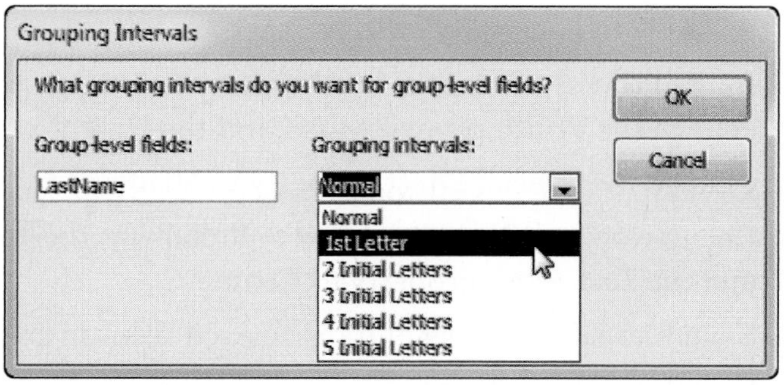

8. Click Next. Click the first drop-down arrow and choose **LastName**. Click Next.
9. With the Layout being Stepped and the Orientation being Portrait, click Next.
10. Name the report rptEmpPhone and click Finish.
11. View both pages of the report, and then close Print Preview.

Exercise 12-2 FORMAT CONTROLS

Creating professional-looking reports often requires significant effort to include formatted controls. Because the reports you create will be printed and seen by many other people, you should make certain that all controls are properly formatted. You now will format and modify the controls in the report.

1. In the Report Header, delete the label.
2. From the Design tab, in the Header/Footer group, click Logo 🖼 and choose the file **Logo_sm.gif**.

3. From the **Design** tab, in the **Header/Footer** group, click **Title** 📄 and key **EcoMed - Employee's Phone List**.

4. In the **Page Header**, click the **LastName by 1st Letter** label and press ⌦Delete.

5. In the **Page Header**, select all the labels. While pressing ⌃Ctrl, click each of the text boxes in the **Detail** section.

6. From the **Arrange** tab, in the **Table** group, click **Tabular** ▦.

7. Drag the control layout to the right so that the left edge of the **LastName** text box is at 1-inch on the horizontal ruler.

8. From the **Design** tab, in the **Grouping & Totals** group, click **Group & Sort** 🗐. This report has two **Sort by LastName** levels.

9. In the **Group, Sort, and Total** section, click the second **Sort by LastName** and click the drop-down arrow next to **LastName** and choose **FirstName**.

10. From the **Design** tab, in the **Grouping & Totals** group, click **Group & Sort** 🗐 to close the tool.

11. In the **LastName Header** section, click the text box. The **Control Source** of this text box uses the **LEFT$** function. In this case, the function finds the first letter in the field **LastName**.

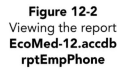

NOTE:

The **Group on LastName** will sort the control in the **LastName Header**. The **Sort by LastName** and **Sort by FirstName** will sort the data in the **Detail** section.

12. Press ⎇F4 to open the **Property Sheet**.

13. In the **Property Sheet** for **LastName by 1st Letter**, on the **Format** tab, change the **Width** property to **.5** and the **Height** property to **.4**.

14. Change the **Special Effect** property to **Shadowed**.

15. Change the **Font Name** property to **Broadway**, the **Font Size** property to **20**, and the **Text Align** property to **Center**.

16. Switch to **Layout View** and resize each column so all data can be seen.

17. Switch to **Report View**.

Figure 12-2
Viewing the report
EcoMed-12.accdb
rptEmpPhone

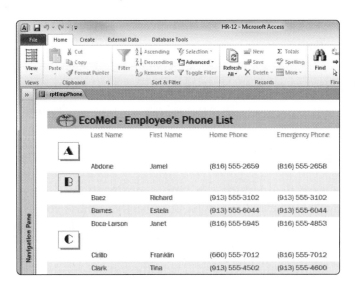

18. Save the report.

Exercise 12-3 ADD GRIDLINES

You can add gridlines to visually help you place and separate the controls. The gridlines will appear on the report in Design View but will not appear in Report View or Layout View.

1. Switch to **Design View**.

2. In the **Page Header**, select all the labels.

3. From the **Arrange** tab, in the **Table** group, click **Gridlines** ⊞ and choose **Bottom**.

4. From the **Arrange** tab, in the **Table** group, click **Gridlines** ⊞, and then click **Width** ☰ and choose **4 pt** (fifth on the list).

Figure 12-3
Adding Gridlines
EcoMed-12.accdb
rptEmpPhone

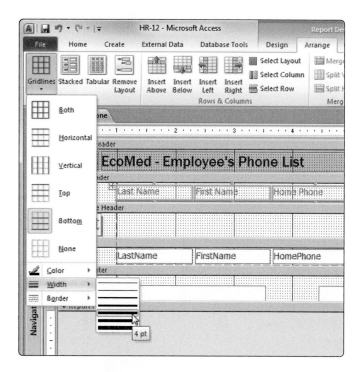

5. In the **Detail** section, select all the text boxes.

6. From the **Arrange** tab, in the **Table** group, click **Gridlines** ⊞ and choose **Bottom**.

7. Switch to **Report View**.

Exercise 12-4 ADD CUSTOM COLORS

Certain control properties can contain a predefined color or a custom color. You can create a custom color through the Color Builder. The *Color Builder* is an Access tool for selecting colors from a palette or for creating custom colors.

A custom color is defined by six settings: Red, Green, Blue, Hue, Sat, and Lum. For the Red, Green, or Blue settings, you can enter a number from 0 through 255. For the Sat (saturation) and Lum (luminosity) settings, you can enter a number between 0 and 240. For the Hue setting, you can enter a number between 0 and 239.

The combination of these settings creates one of 16.8 million unique colors expressed as a unique hexadecimal number. A hexadecimal number is a numerical expression based upon a system (base) of 16 characters written using the symbols 0–9 and A–F.

1. Switch to **Design View** and click the **LastName by 1st Letter** text box.

2. In the **Property Sheet** for **LastName by 1st Letter**, on the **Format** tab, click in the **Fore Color** property.

3. Click the Build button 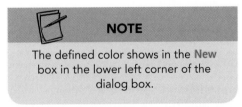 and click **More Color**. On the **Standard** tab, you can select from 127 different colors, plus a gray scale.

4. Click the **Custom** tab.

5. In the **Colors** box, drag the cross-hair around to see the changes in the **New** box.

Figure 12-4
Define a custom color
EcoMed-12.accdb rptEmpPhone

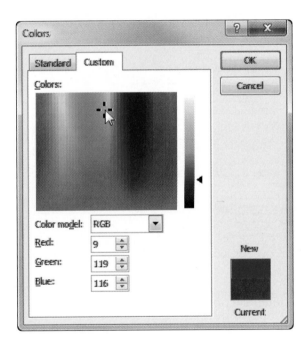

6. In the **Red** control, key **192**. For **Green**, key **80**, and for **Blue**, key **77**.

7. Click **OK**. The custom color is expressed as a hexadecimal number (**#C0504D**).

8. Press ⬆ to see the changes in the report.

9. In the **Fore Color** property, press F2 and press Ctrl+C to copy the number.

10. In the **Page Header**, select all the labels.

11. Click in the **Gridline Color** property, press F2 and press Ctrl+V to paste the color from the text box. Press ↑.

12. Click the **Page Header** section bar. In the section's **Property Sheet**, click in the **Back Color** property and press F2. Key **#f3f8ff** and press ↑. The section is now a light blue.

13. Select the hexadecimal code in the **Back Color** property and press Ctrl+C.

14. In the **LastName Header** section, click the **LastName by 1st Letter** text box.

15. In the **Property Sheet**, on the **Format** tab, select the **Back Color** property value and press Ctrl+V.

16. Click the **LastName Header** section bar. In the section's **Property Sheet**, on the **Format** tab, click in the **Back Color** property and press F2, then Ctrl+C to copy the **Background 1** color.

17. Press ↓. In the **Alternate Back Color** property, click Ctrl+V.

18. Click the **Detail** section bar. In the section's **Property Sheet**, on the **Format** tab, click in the **Alternate Back Color** property.

19. Press F2 and then Ctrl+V. Close the **Property Sheet**.

20. Switch to **Print Preview**.

Figure 12-5
Finished report
**EcoMed-12.accdb
rptEmpPhone**

21. Close **Print Preview**. Save and close the report.

22. Close database **HR-12**.

Creating a Report with a Subreport

Some business operations require information to be displayed in a hierarchal structure. *Hierarchal structure* is a method of classifying items or information according to criteria that places the items or information in successive levels or layers.

A common method of organizing hierarchal information in a report is to include a subreport. A *subreport* is a report that is embedded in another report. The report in which the subreport is located is known as the main report. The main report contains the highest level of information while the subreport contains the subordinate or lower level of information.

The main report and subreport must share a common field, most often in a One-to-Many relationship. The "One" side of the relationship is in the main report, and the "Many" side is in the subreport. The subreport displays only data that are related to the record displayed in the main report.

Figure 12-6
Sample shipping
manifest
EcoMed-12.accdb

Exercise 12-5   CREATE A SUBREPORT

A subreport can be created similar to any normal report. You can design the report in Design View or through the Report Wizard. You now will create a report that will be used as a shipping manifest for EcoMed Services.

1. Open *[your initials]*-**EcoMed-12**, Enable content, and refresh the linked tables for *[your initials]*-**HR-12.**

2. In the Navigation Pane, select **qryShipDetails-Sub**.

3. From the Create tab, in the Reports group, click Report. Switch to Design View.

4. In the Report Header, delete all the controls.

5. In the Page Footer, delete the page control.

6. In the Page Header, select all the labels.

7. From the Arrange tab, in the Move group, click Move Up.

8. From the Arrange tab, in the Rows & Columns group, click Select Layout.

9. From the Arrange tab, in the Sizing & Ordering group, click Size/Space and choose To Tallest.

10. Close both the Page Header and Page Footer sections.

11. Deselect the control layout.

12. In the Report Footer, click the text box and press Delete.

13. In the Report Footer, select all blank cells.

14. From the Arrange tab, in the Table group, click Gridlines ⊞ and choose None.

15. In the Detail section, select all of the text boxes.

16. Press F4 to open the Property Sheet. On the Format tab, change the Border Style property to Transparent.

17. Click the Report Header section bar.

18. In the section's Property Sheet, on the Format tab, click in the Back Color property. Click the Build button … and choose Automatic.

19. In the Report Header, select all the labels.

20. From the Arrange tab, in the Table group, click Gridlines ⊞ and choose Bottom.

21. Save the report as rptShipDetails-Sub.

Exercise 12-6 ADD A CALCULATION TO A SUBREPORT

As you learned in Lesson 6, you can create and use calculated fields in queries. You can also create and use calculated fields in reports. Just like in a query, the displayed value in these calculated fields is dynamically assigned each time the report is displayed. In the shipping manifest report, the extended cost for each item is generated by multiplying the quantity by the unit cost.

1. Switch to Layout View. Scroll down to the bottom of the report.

2. From the Design tab, in the Controls group, click Text Box ⎁ and click in the blank cell below the farthest right column (sixth column).

3. Double-click the new label and key Subtotal.

4. Switch to Design View.

5. In the horizontal ruler above the **Shipment ID** label, with the black down arrow visible, click to select the entire column. Press Delete to remove the **Shipment ID** controls from the subreport.

6. Drag the right edge of the report to the left, to the right edge of the controls.

7. Click the unbound text box.

8. From the Arrange tab, in the Table group, click Gridlines ⊞ and choose Top.

9. From the Arrange tab, in the Table group, click Gridlines ⊞ and choose Width ☰, and then choose 3 pt.

10. Press F4. In the Property Sheet, on the Data tab, click the Control Source property.

11. Click the Build button 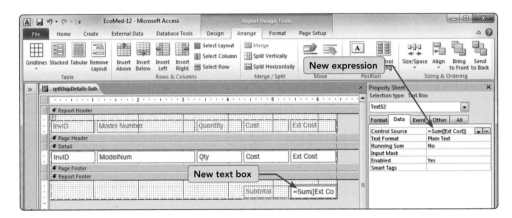.

12. In the **Expression Elements** panel, double-click the **Functions** folder and click **Built-In Functions**.

13. In the **Expression Categories** panel, click **SQL Aggregate**.

14. In the **Expression Values** panel, double-click **Sum**.

15. In the Expression box, click <<expression>>.

16. In the **Expression Elements** panel, click the **rptShipDetails-Sub**.

17. In the **Expression Categories** panel, click <Field List>.

18. In the **Expression Values** panel, double-click **Ext Cost**.

19. Click **OK**.

Figure 12-7
Calculation in a subreport
**EcoMed-12.accdb
rptShipDetails-Sub**

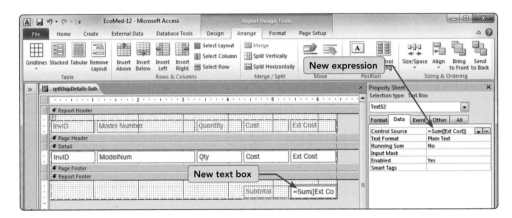

20. On the **Other** tab, change the **Name** property to **txtSubtotal**.

21. Save and close the report.

Exercise 12-7   PREPARE A MAIN REPORT

The main report determines the data that will display on the top (or main part) of the report. You must create the main report before you can add the subreport to it.

1. Open **rptShipDetails-Main**. The report has already been started.

2. Switch to **Design View**.

3. In the report's **Property Sheet**, on the **Data** tab, click in the **Record Source** property. This report is based on a **qryShipDetails-Main**.

4. Click the Build button . The query opens in a new document tab.

5. From the **Design** tab, in the **Results** group, click **Run** to view the shipment records. With 116 shipment records, there is too much data to show on one report.

6. Switch to **Design View** for the query.

7. From the **Design** tab, in the **Show/Hide** group, click **Parameters** .

8. Key [**Enter a Shipping ID**]. Press Tab and choose Integer as the Data Type. Click OK.

9. In the design grid, for the **ShipID** field, click the Criteria row and key [e. From the pop-up list, choose the parameter you created in the previous step.

Figure 12-8
Editing a query from
a report
EcoMed-12.accdb
rptShipDetails-Main

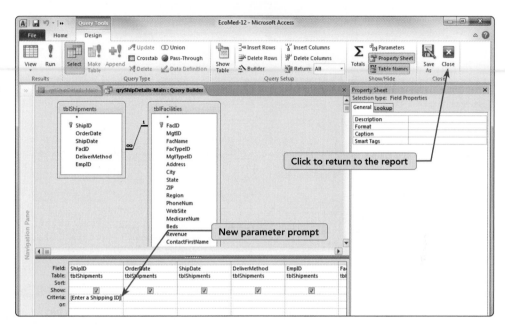

Figure 12-8
Editing a query from a report
EcoMed-12.accdb
rptShipDetails-Main

10. From the Design tab, in the Close group, click Close ☒.

11. Click Yes to the dialog box so that your changes are saved. You return to the Design View of the report.

12. Switch to Report View. At the prompt, key 947 and click OK. Only one manifest is now shown. Return to Design View.

13. Save the report.

Exercise 12-8   ADD A SUBREPORT CONTROL

A subreport is a control inserted into a main report. When you insert a subreport control, Access automatically creates a label for the control. In the same way that you can insert a subform control in a main form, you can insert a subreport control in a main report.

1. From the Navigation Pane, drag **rptShipDetails-Sub** to the Detail section positioned at the 1-inch mark on the horizontal ruler and the 2-inch mark on the vertical ruler.

2. From the Arrange tab, in the Control Layout group, click Stacked ▦. Deselect the subreport.

3. Click the subreport's label and press Delete.

Figure 12-9
Placing a subreport
EcoMed-12.accdb
rptShipDetails-Main

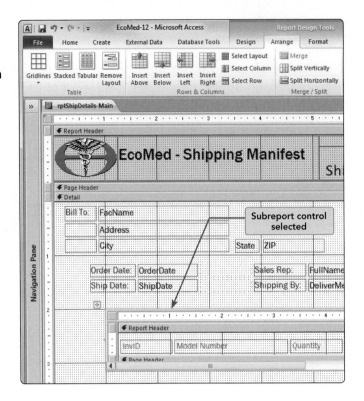

4. Resize the width of the report to less than 7 3/4 inches on the ruler.

5. Switch to **Report View**. Key **947** and click **OK**.

6. The top of the invoice shows the right information, but the subform is showing details of all 116 manifests. Return to **Design View**.

7. Click the subreport and open its **Property Sheet**.

8. On the **Data** tab, you will see that the **Link Master Fields** and **Link Child Fields** properties are empty.

9. Click in the **Link Master Fields** property and click the Build button ⊡.

Figure 12-10
Creating a link
between the two
reports
EcoMed-12.accdb
rptShipDetails-Main

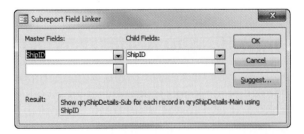

10. Access has determined that the field **ShipID** is the common field. Click **OK**.

11. Switch to **Report View**. Key **947** and click **OK**.

12. Notice that the subreport's gridline color is different than in the main report. Return to **Layout View**.

Exercise 12-9   MODIFY A SUBREPORT

The main report and subreport should be formatted to appear as a single unified report. Often after inserting a subreport, either the subreport or the main report will need to be modified to match in color and appearance.

1. In the **Report Header** of the main report, click the **Shipment ID** label.

2. In the label's **Property Sheet**, on the **Format** tab, click the **Gridline Color** property. Press F2 to select **#CF7B79** and then Ctrl+C.

3. In the subreport control, click the **Inv ID** label.

4. From the **Arrange** tab, in the **Rows & Columns** group, click **Select Row** ▦.

5. In the selected label's **Property Sheet**, on the **Format** tab, click the **Gridline Color** property. Press F2 and then Ctrl+V to paste **#CF7B79**.

6. Click the **Fore Color** property and click the Build button ⋯. Click **Automatic**. The font color is now black.

7. In the main report, click the **Ship Date** label.

8. In the **Property Sheet**, click the drop-down arrow (object selector) at the top for **Label12**. This list includes all of the objects on the main report.

9. From the drop-down list, choose **rptShipDetails-Sub** to select the subreport control.

Figure 12-11
Select an object from the Property Sheet.
**EcoMed-12.accdb
rptShipDetails-Main**

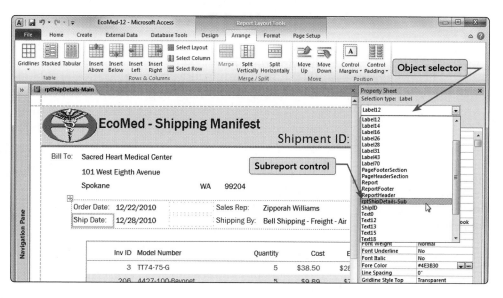

10. On the **Format** tab, change the **Border Style** property to **Transparent**.

11. On the **Format** tab, change the **Gridline Style Top** property to **Solid**.

12. On the **Format** tab, change the **Gridline Style Bottom** property to **Solid**.

13. On the **Format** tab, change the **Gridline Color** property to **#CF7B79**.

14. On the **Format** tab, change the **Gridline Width Top** property to **2 pt**.

15. On the **Format** tab, change the **Gridline Width Bottom** property to **2 pt**.

16. In the subreport, click **txtSubtotal** (text box to the right of the **Subtotal** label).

17. In the **Property Sheet**, on the **Format** tab, change the **Format** property to **Currency**.

18. On the **Format** tab, change the **Border Style** property to **Transparent**.

19. On the **Format** tab, change the **Gridline Color** property to **#CF7B79**.

20. Save and switch to **Report View**. Key **1300** and press Enter. It is not a valid **Shipment ID**.

21. Press F5. Key **1010** and press Enter. Notice that the subreport grows to fit the number of records.

Adding Expressions to a Report

Expressions allow you to create or use values that are not included in your data. For example, you might need to calculate the total value of a sales order. You can calculate new values by creating expressions.

To create an expression, you must use proper syntax. *Syntax* is the set of rules by which the words and symbols in an expression are correctly combined.

Exercise 12-10 CREATE A CONCATENATED EXPRESSION

Using the Expression Builder, you can concatenate multiple fields with values that vary into a single field expression. A *concatenated expression* is a text expression that joins two or more fields so that they appear to be one field. The most common fields used in concatenated expressions are names and addresses.

1. In the **Design View** of **rptShipDetails-Main**, in the **Detail** section, click the **City** text box.

2. In the text box's **Property Sheet**, on the **Other** tab, change the **Name** property to **txtAddress2**.

3. On the **Data** tab, clear the **Control Source** property and press ↓. The control is now unbound.

4. Click in the **Control Source** property and click the Build button .

5. In the **Expression Builder** dialog box, in the top panel, key **c**. Scroll down the list to all the different elements that can be added to an expression.

Figure 12-12
Build an expression
EcoMed-12.accdb
rptShipDetails-Main

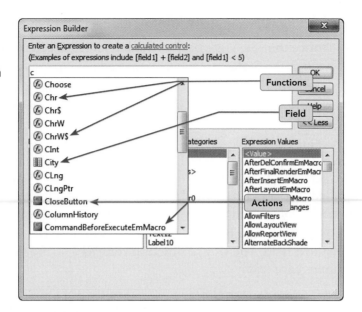

TIP

Only use this method of creating a calculation when you are sure of the names of all the elements to be used.

6. Key **it** and press ⟦Tab⟧ to add the **City** field to the equation. Notice that the square brackets were added for you.

7. Key **&** " **,** " (quotation mark, comma, a space, quotation mark) and key **&**.

8. Key **st** and then ⟦Tab⟧ to add the **State** field.

9. Key **&** " " (quotation mark, two spaces, quotation mark), and key **&**.

10. Key **z** and then press ⟦Tab⟧ to add the **ZIP** field.

Figure 12-13
Concatenated
expression
EcoMed-12.accdb
rptShipDetails-Main

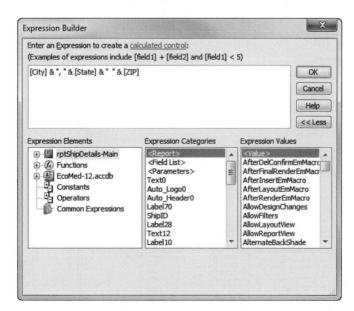

11. Click **OK**.

12. Save the report and switch to **Report View**. Key **988** and press ⟦Enter⟧.

13. The **City**, **State**, and **ZIP** information is now in one text box.

14. Notice that the state part of the **txtAddress2** control is lower case, even though the **State** control is formatted as upper case in the table.

Exercise 12-11 ADD A UCASE FUNCTION

Text values in a table can be stored as upper and lower case characters. If the Format property of a text field uses the greater than symbol, >, then all characters in that field will display as upper case characters. The format is applied to the entire content of the field for each record. Similarly, the less than symbol, <, will display all text characters as lower case characters.

The UCase function can be used to capitalize the first letter of each word in the text field. The UCase function returns a string that has been converted to upper case text.

1. Switch to **Design View**.

2. Select **txtAddress2** text box. In its **Property Sheet**, on the **Data** tab, click the **Control Source** property and click the Build button 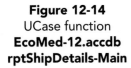.

3. In the **Expression Builder** dialog box, in the upper panel, double-click **[State]** and press ⌈Delete⌉.

4. In the **Expression Elements** panel, double-click the **Functions** folder and click the **Build-In Functions** folder.

5. In the **Expression Categories** panel, click **Text**.

6. In the **Expression Values** panel, double-click **UCase** to add the function to the expression.

7. In the Expression box, click **<<string>>**.

8. In the **Expression Elements** panel, click **rptShipDetails-Main**.

9. In the **Expression Categories** panel, click **<Field List>**.

10. In the **Expression Values** panel, double-click **State** to add the field to the expression.

Figure 12-14
UCase function
EcoMed-12.accdb
rptShipDetails-Main

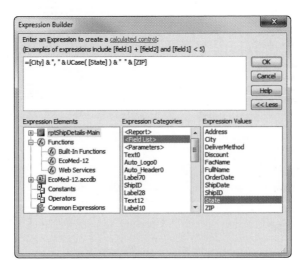

11. Click **OK** and switch to **Report View**. Key **1000** and press Enter. The state data are now upper case.

12. Return to **Design View**. In the **Detail** section, delete the **State** and **ZIP** text boxes.

13. Save the report.

Exercise 12-12 ADD TEXT BOXES

To complete the shipping manifest, we need to add both a discount value and a total shipment value. You now will add text boxes to display these values.

1. From the **Design** tab, in the **Controls** group, click Text Box [abl].

2. Click in the right side of the **Report Footer**. Edit the label's caption to **Discount:**.

3. In the new unbound text box's **Property Sheet**, on the **Other** tab, change the **Name** property to **txtDiscount**.

4. In the **Detail** section of the main report, click any text box. From the **Format** tab, in the **Font** group, click Format Painter [✔]. Click the **txtDiscount** text box.

5. Click the label **Discount**. Drag its right edge over to the left edge of **txtDiscount**.

6. In the **Property Sheet** for **txtDiscount**, on the **Format** tab, change the **Format** property to **Currency**.

7. On the **Format** tab, change the **Text Align** property to **Right**.

8. Switch to **Layout View**. Key **1000**. Click **txtDiscount**.

9. From the **Arrange** tab, in the **Table** group, click **Stacked** [▦].

10. From the **Arrange** tab, in the **Rows & Columns** group, click **Insert Below** [▦].

11. From the **Design** tab, in the **Controls** group, click Text Box [abl].

12. In the **Report Footer**, click in the right-most blank cell below **txtDiscount**. Change the label's caption to **Shipment Total:**.

13. In the new unbound text box's **Property Sheet**, on the **Other** tab, change the **Name** property to **txtTotal**.

14. On the **Format** tab, change the **Format** property to **Currency**.

15. On the **Format** tab, change the **Text Align** property to **Right**.

16. Save the report.

Exercise 12-13 ADD AN IIF FUNCTION

At EcoMed Services, some customers get discounts; others do not. If a customer is entitled to a discount, you should display the discount value. If a customer is not entitled to a discount, you can create an expression to show the word "None" instead of just displaying a zero.

To determine which condition to display, you need to use an IIF function An IIF function evaluates a "true/false" expression and then performs one of two choices. The three parts of an IIF are separated by commas. The first part of the expression is the Boolean (true/false) condition. The second part of the expression is the action performed if a true condition exists. The third part of the expression is the action performed if the false condition exists.

1. Switch to **Design View** and select **txtDiscount**.

2. On the **Data** tab, click the **Control Source** property and click the Build button ⬚.

3. In the **Expression Elements** panel, double-click the **Functions** folder and click the **Built-In Functions** folder.

4. In the **Expression Categories** panel, click **Program Flow**.

5. In the **Expression Values** panel, double-click **IIF** to add the function to the top panel.

6. In the Expression box, click **<<expression>>**.

7. In the **Expression Elements** panel, click the **rptShipDetails-Main** folder.

8. In the **Expression Categories** panel, click **<Field List>**.

9. In the **Expression Values** panel, double-click **Discount** and key **=0**.

10. In the Expression box, click **<<truepart>>** and key **"None"**.

11. In the top panel, click **<<falsepart>>**.

12. In the **Expression Values** panel, double-click **Discount** and press ⬚.

13. Key **txt**. Only the text boxes from the main report are shown, but we need a text box from the subreport. Press Backspace three times.

14. In the **Expression Elements** panel, double-click the **rptShipDetails-Main** folder and click the **rptShipDetails-Sub** folder.

15. In the **Expression Categories** panel, double-click **txtSubtotal** to add the text box value to the expression. Click **OK**.

Figure 12-15
IIF function
EcoMed-12.accdb
rptShipDetails-Main

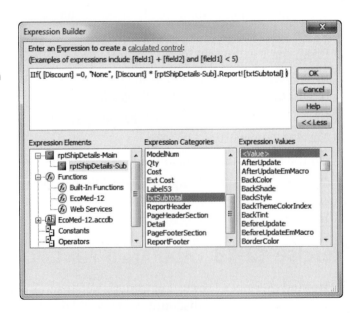

16. Save and switch to **Report View**. Key **1000** and press Enter. The discount is calculated.

17. From the **Home** tab, in the **Records** group, click **Refresh All** 🗐.
18. Key **977** and press Enter. This invoice has no discount.

Exercise 12-14   ADD AN ISNUMERIC FUNCTION

Functions that require numeric values to perform calculations cannot use text values for input. To avoid an error, you can use the IsNumeric Function. The IsNumeric Function returns a Boolean (true/false) value indicating whether an expression can be evaluated as a number.

TABLE 12-1 Inspection Functions

Function Name	Function Purpose
Is Date	If the expression is a date, it returns TRUE, otherwise FALSE.
IsError	If the expression is an error, it returns TRUE, otherwise FALSE.
IsNull	If the expression is NULL, it returns TRUE, otherwise FALSE.
IsNumeric	If the expression is a number, it returns TRUE, otherwise FALSE.

1. Switch to **Design View** and select **txtTotal**.
2. On the **Data** tab, click the **Control Source** property and click the Build button ⊡.
3. In the **Expression Elements** panel, double-click the **Functions** folder and click the **Built-In Functions** folder.
4. In the **Expression Categories** panel, click **Program Flow**.
5. In the **Expression Values** panel, double-click **IIf** to add the function to the top panel.
6. In the Expression box, click <<expression>>.
7. In the **Expression Categories** panel, click **Inspection**.
8. In the **Expression Values** panel, double-click **IsNumeric** to add the function to the top panel.
9. In the Expression box, click <<expression>>.
10. Key **txt**. From the pop-up list, double-click **txtDiscount**.
11. In the Expression box, click <<truepart>>.
12. In the **Expression Elements** panel, double-click the **rptShipDetails-Main** folder and click the **rptShipDetails-Sub** folder.
13. In the **Expression Categories** panel, double-click **txtSubtotal** and press ⊡.
14. In the **Expression Elements** panel, click the **rptShipDetails-Main** folder.
15. In the **Expression Categories** panel, double-click **txtDiscount**.
16. In the top panel, click <<falsepart>>.
17. In the **Expression Elements** panel, click the **rptShipDetails-Sub** folder.
18. In the **Expression Categories** panel, double-click **txtSubtotal**. Click **OK**.

Figure 12-16
IIf and IsNumeric
function
**EcoMed-12.accdb
rptShipDetails-Main**

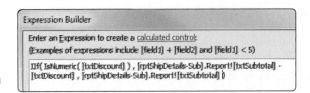

19. Switch to **Report View**. Key **960** and press Enter.

20. From the **Home** tab, in the **Records** group, click **Refresh All** 🖹.

21. Key **977** and press Enter. Even without a discount the **Shipment Total** calculation works.

22. Save the report.

Exercise 12-15   FORMAT THE REPORT

Reports that display numeric values should be formatted to follow standardized accounting standards. All numeric values used in calculations should be aligned vertically and right justified. Decimal spaces should be consistent throughout the entire report.

1. Switch to **Design View** and select the **Bill To** label.

2. From the **Arrange** tab, in the **Rows & Columns** group, click **Select Row** 🖽.

3. From the **Arrange** tab, in the **Table** group, click **Gridlines** 🖽 and **Top**.

4. Select **txtAddress2** (control with the concatenated expression).

5. From the **Arrange** tab, in the **Rows & Columns** group, click **Select Row** 🖽.

6. From the **Arrange** tab, in the **Table** group, click **Gridlines** 🖽 and **Bottom**.

7. Select the **Bill To** label.

8. From the **Arrange** tab, in the **Rows & Columns** group, click **Select Column** 🖽.

9. In the label's **Property Sheet**, on the **Format** tab, change the **Gridline Style Left** property to **Solid**.

10. Select the **FacName** text box.

11. From the **Arrange** tab, in the **Rows & Columns** group, click **Select Column** 🖽.

12. In the label's **Property Sheet**, on the **Format** tab, change the **Gridline Style Right** property to **Solid**.

13. Select the **Order Date** label. While pressing Ctrl, click the **Order Date** text box, both **Sales Rep** controls, both the **Ship Date** controls, the **Shipping By** label, and the **DeliverMethod** text box.

14. From the **Arrange** tab, in the **Table** group, click **Gridlines** 🖽 and **Bottom**.

15. Drag the top of the **Page Footer** up until you only have two rows of dots below the subreport.

16. Click the **Discount** label.

17. From the Arrange tab, in the Rows & Columns group, click Select Layout 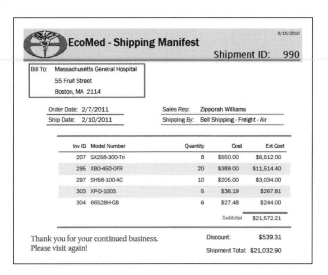.

18. Drag the control layout so its text boxes are under the subreport's **Ext Cost** column.

19. Switch to Report View and key 990 and press Enter.

20. Switch to Print Preview.

Figure 12-17
Final Invoice report
**EcoMed-12.accdb
rptShipDetails-Main**

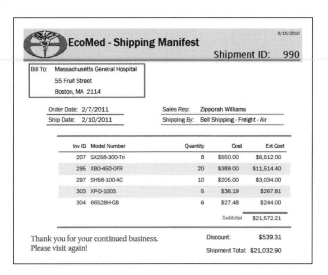

21. Close Print Preview. Close and save the report.

Adding PivotCharts to a Report

PivotCharts are a special types of images used in Microsoft Office applications such as Microsoft Excel and Microsoft Access. A PivotChart, similar to a PivotTable, summarizes information from selected fields in a data source.

A PivotChart dynamically changes as the record source changes. A Pivot-Chart includes aggregate functions, or calculations involving aggregate functions.

Exercise 12-16   CREATE A PIVOTCHART

Because reports do not include a PivotChart View, you must use a form. A form can be used as a subreport control in a report. When adding a PivotChart to a report, you must insert a subform into the main report.

1. Open **qryProfitTrend**. This query has 1662 records. Close the query.

2. From the Create tab, in the Forms group, click Form.

3. Save the form as **frmQ1ProfitTrend**.

4. Switch to Design View. Open the form's Property Sheet. On the Format tab, click the Default View property.

5. Click the drop-down arrow and choose PivotChart.

6. Change the Allow PivotChart View property to Yes.

7. Change the Allow Form View property to No.

8. From the Design tab, in the Views group, click PivotChart 📊.

9. If the Chart Field List is not visible, click the Field List in the Show/Hide group. From the Chart Field List, drag the **BulbCat** field to the Drop Series Fields Here drop zone (to the right of the chart).

10. Click the Expand icon ⊞ for **OrderDate By Month**.

11. Drag **Quarters** to the Drop Category Fields Here drop zone (below the chart).

12. Drag **Months** to the right of the **Quarters** field control at the bottom of the chart to create a two-level X-axis.

13. Drag **Profit** to the middle of the chart. Close the Chart Field List.

14. Click the Plot Area (gray background) of the chart.

15. From the Design tab, in the Type group, click Change Chart Type 📊. In the Properties dialog box, choose SmoothLine and the first subtype (top left icon).

Figure 12-18
Selecting a chart type
EcoMed-12.accdb
frmQ1ProfitTrend

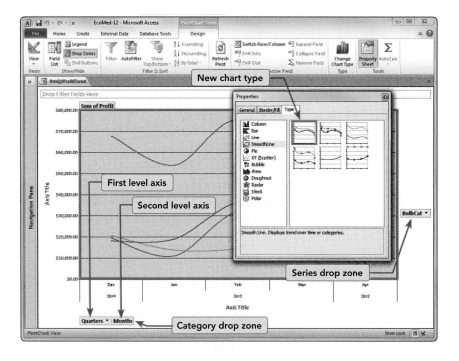

16. Click the X-axis's Axis Title (below the chart). In the Properties dialog box, on the Format tab, change the Caption property to Months and the Font Size property to 20.

17. Click the Y-axis's Axis Title (left of chart). In the Properties dialog box, on the Format tab, change the Caption property to Net Profit and the Font Size property to 20.

18. Close the Properties dialog box.

Figure 12-19
Filtering data in a
PivotChart
EcoMed-12.accdb
frmQ1ProfitTrend

19. In the **Quarters** field control (bottom of chart), click the drop-down arrow.

20. In the pop-up window, expand both year controls. Remove the checkmarks from every quarter except **Qtr1** of 2011. Click **OK**. The PivotChart will now only show data from the first quarter of 2011.

21. From the **Design** tab, in the **Show/Hide** group, click **Drop Zones** 🖬 to remove them from the PivotChart.

22. From the **Design** tab, in the **Show/Hide** group, click **Legend** 🖩 to add the legend to right side of the PivotChart.

23. Save and close the form.

Exercise 12-17   CREATE A REPORT USING REPORT DESIGN

When using a PivotChart, it is not necessary to make an elaborate main report. Most information will be presented through the PivotChart.

1. From the **Create** tab, in the **Reports** group, click **Report Design** 🖼.

2. From the **Design** tab, in the **Tools** group, click **Add Existing Fields** 🛅.

3. Click **Show all tables**.

4. Expand the table **tblBulbCategory**. Double-click **BulbCatID** and **BulbCat** to add them to the **Detail** section.

5. Delete the control labels.

6. Delete the **BulbCatID** text box. By adding the field to the report, you have added it to the recordset of the report. There is no need to show this information.

7. From the **Design** tab, in the **Grouping & Totals** group, click **Group & Sort** 🗒.

8. In the **Group, Sort, and Total** pane, click **Add a group** and choose **BulbCat**.

9. Close the **Group, Sort, and Total** pane.

10. Drag the **BulbCat** text box into the left part of the **BulbCat Header**.

11. Change the **BulbCat** text box Font to **Elephant** with a Font Size of **26**.

12. In the text box's **Property Sheet**, on the **Format** tab, change the **Border Style** property to **Transparent**.

13. Resize the text box to 1/2 inch tall and 5 inches wide.

14. Click the **Page Header** section bar. In the section's **Property Sheet**, on the **Format** tab, change the **Back Color** property to **#E6EDD7**.

15. From the **Design** tab, in the **Header/Footer** group, click **Title** ⊞ and key EcoMed - Q1 Profit Trends by Bulb Category. Press Enter.

16. From the **Arrange** tab, in the **Rows & Columns** group, click **Select Layout** ▦.

17. From the **Arrange** tab, in the **Move** group, click **Move Down** ⤓ to move the control layout to the **Page Header**.

18. Save the report as rptQ1ProfitTrend.

Exercise 12-18 ADD PIVOTCHARTS TO A REPORT

A PivotChart is added to a report as a subreport control. Even though the PivotChart is created as a form, it can be used as a control within a report.

1. From the **Navigation Pane**, drag **frmQ1ProfitTrend** to the **Detail** section of the report.

2. Delete the subform's label.

3. In the subform's **Property Sheet**, in the **Format** tab, change the **Width** property to **7.5** and the **Height** property to **5**.

4. On the **Format** tab, change the **Top** property to **.1** and the **Left** property to **.1**.

5. On the **Data** tab, click the **Link Master Fields** property and click the Build button ⊡. Access has determined that the common field is **BulbCatID**.

Figure 12-20
Subreport Field
Linker dialog box
EcoMed-12.accdb
rptQ1ProfitTrend

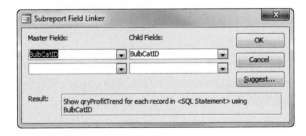

6. Click **OK**.

7. Switch to **Report View**. A PivotChart displays for each product group.

8. Return to **Design View**.

9. From the **Navigation Pane**, drag **frmQ1ProfitTrend** to the **Report Footer** section of the report.

10. Delete the subform's label.

11. In the second subform's **Property Sheet**, in the **Format** tab, change the **Width** property to **7.5** and the **Height** property to **5**.

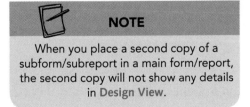

NOTE

When you place a second copy of a subform/subreport in a main form/report, the second copy will not show any details in Design View.

12. On the **Format** tab, change the **Top** property to **1.0** and the **Left** property to **.1**.

13. Click the **Report Selector**. The report is too wide. Click the information tag and choose **Remove Extra Report Space**.

14. Save the report and switch to **Report View**.

15. The PivotChart on the last page of the report shows all bulb categories. This PivotChart is not bound to the recordset.

Exercise 12-19   MODIFY SECTIONS

The information displayed in a PivotChart depends on the section in which it is placed. Each section will need to be formatted to display the subreport control appropriately.

1. Switch to **Design View**.

2. In the **Report Header** section's **Property Sheet**, on the **Format** tab, click the **Back Color** property.

3. Click the Build button 🔲 and choose **Automatic**.

4. Change the **Force New Page** property to **After Section** and create a blank first page (cover page).

5. In the **BulbCat Header** section's **Property Sheet**, on the **Format** tab, click the **Alternate Back Color** property.

6. Click the Build button 🔲 and choose **No Color**.

7. In the **Detail** section's **Property Sheet**, on the **Format** tab, change the **Force New Page** property to **After Section**, which creates a new page for each product line.

8. From the **Design** tab, in the **Controls** group, click Label 🔠.

9. In the **Report Footer**, click above the PivotChart and key **Summary**.

10. In the **BulbCat Header**, click the **BulbCat** text box.

11. From the **Format** tab, in the **Font** group, click Format Painter 🖌 and click the label in the **Report Footer**.

12. Drag the new label to the upper left corner of the **Report Footer** section. Resize the label.

13. Drag the top of **BulbCat Header** section bar down until the **Page Header** is .75 inches tall.

14. In the **Page Header** section, click the Title label and press Ctrl+C.

15. Click the **Report Header** section bar and press Ctrl+V.

16. Change the new label's Font to **Georgia** and Font Size to **24**.

17. Drag the right edge of the label to the 7.5 inch mark and center the text.

18. From the **Design** tab, in the **Header/Footer** group, click **Page Numbers** 🔢.

19. Set the **Format** to **Page N of M**, centered at the **Bottom of the Page**. Remove the check box for **Show Number on First Page**.

Figure 12-21
Add a Page control
EcoMed-12.accdb
rptQ1ProfitTrend

20. Click **OK**. Save the report and switch to **Report View**. The changes to the sections cannot be seen in this view.

21. Switch to **Print Preview** to view the changes to the sections. The report is now 6 pages.

22. Close **Print Preview**.

Working with Image Controls

Adding Image controls to a report can improve the appearance. An *image control* is a photograph, picture, or graphic attached to a form or report. For example, you could include an image control for a watermark or logo on an Invoice report.

A *watermark* is an image control that displays in the background of a page on a form or report. Unlike a watermark, a logo displays only in the section on which it is placed.

An image control has different picture size modes. *Clip mode* shows the image at the size in which it was originally drawn or scanned. If the image is bigger than the control, the excess portion of the image is cut off. *Stretch mode* sizes the image to fit the frame. Stretch mode can distort the image by changing the height-to-width proportions. *Zoom mode* sizes the image to fill either the height or width of the control. Zoom mode does not change image proportions.

Exercise 12-20   ADD AN WATERMARK

Watermarks often distort the text displayed on a page. For this reason, many reports only use a watermark on the first page of the report but not on subsequent pages.

1. Switch to the **Design View** for **rptQ1ProfitTrend**.

2. In the report's **Property Sheet**, on the **Format** tab, click the **Picture** property, click the Build button 🔲, and choose **Logo_lite**.

3. On the **Format** tab, change the **Picture Size Mode** property to **Zoom**.

4. Change the **Picture Pages** property to **First Page**.

5. In the **Report Header**, click the label. On the **Format** tab, change the **Top** property to **2**.

6. Save the report and switch to **Report View** to view the changes. The watermark does not display correctly in **Report View**.

Figure 12-22
Report in Report
View
**EcoMed-12.accdb
rptQ1ProfitTrend**

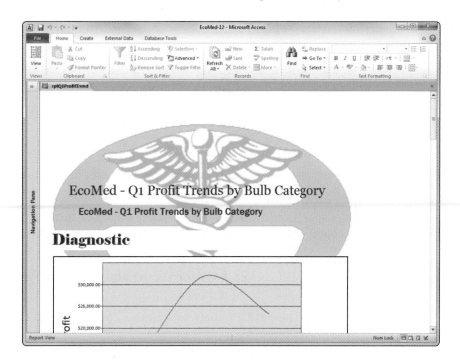

7. Switch to Print Preview. From the Print Preview tab, in the Zoom group, click More Pages ▦ and choose Eight Pages.

8. Close Print Preview.

Exercise 12-21 ADD A LOGO

Standardized reports for a company often include a company logo. Depending on whether the report will be printed in color or black and white, the image used for the logo may change.

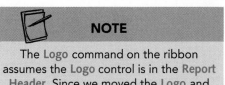

NOTE

The Logo command on the ribbon assumes the Logo control is in the Report Header. Since we moved the Logo and Title control layout to the Page Header, using the Logo command will add a second Logo control in the Report Header.

1. Switch to Layout View.

2. From the Design tab, in the Controls group, click Image (last control in the list).

3. Click the blank cell to the left of the second Title label.

4. Locate the **Lesson 12** folder and double-click **Logo_sm**.

5. In the control's Property Sheet, on the Format tab, change the Back Style property to Transparent. Save the report.

Exercise 12-22 ADD AN IMAGE CONTROL

After adding an image control, you should format it to fit the report.

1. Switch to the Design View. From the Design tab, in the Controls group, click Insert Image 🖼 and choose Browse.

2. From the Insert Picture dialog box, click the Web-Ready Image Files control and choose All Files. Double-click **GreenBulb**.

3. In the **Report Footer**, below the subform control, in the gray area, click to add the image.

4. In the image's **Property Sheet**, on the **Format** tab, the **Size Mode** property should be **Zoom** and the **Picture Alignment** should be **Center**.

5. On the **Format** tab, change the **Width** property to **2** and the **Height** property to **2.7**.

6. Change the **Top** property to **6.1** and the **Left** property to **2.75**.

TIP

To remove unused space in a report, just enter a small number. The report will automatically adjust to the minimum size required. The width for this report should change to around 7.7 inches.

7. In the report's **Property Sheet**, on the **Format** tab, change the **Width** property to **5**.

8. In the **Property Sheet** of the **Report Footer**, on the **Format** tab, change the **Height** property to **5**. The height should change to around 8.8 inches.

9. Save the report and switch to **Print Preview** to view the changes.

10. From the **Print Preview** tab, in the **Zoom** group, click **More Pages** and choose **Eight Pages**.

Figure 12-23
Final report
EcoMed-12.accdb
rptQ1ProfitTrend

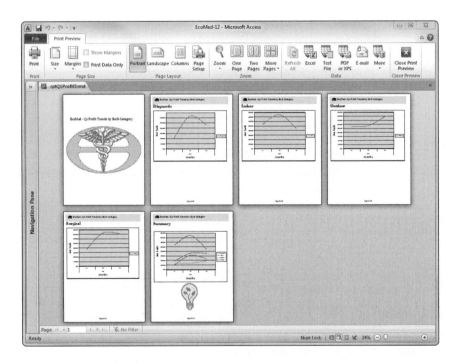

11. Close **Print Preview** and the report.

12. Compact and close your database.

Lesson 12   Summary

- Reports are the database object most often seen by people inside or outside the company.
- Using the Report Wizard is often the easiest way to create a simple report.
- Creating professional-looking reports requires efforts to properly format all controls and sections.
- When controls are part of a control layout, you can add gridlines to visually separate the control with borderlines.
- The Color Builder is an Access tool for selecting colors from a palette or for creating custom colors.
- A common method of organizing hierarchical information in a report is to include a subreport.
- A subreport is a control inserted into a main report.
- The main report and subreport should be formatted to appear as a single unified report.
- Expressions allow you to create or use values that are not included in your data.
- The UCase function returns a string that has been converted to uppercase text.
- An IIF function evaluates a "true/false" expression and then performs one of two choices.
- Functions that require numeric values to perform calculations cannot use text values for input.
- Reports that display numeric values should be formatted to follow standardized accounting standards.
- A PivotChart, similar to a PivotTable, summarizes information from selected fields in a data source.
- A PivotChart is added to a report as a subreport control.
- The information displayed in a PivotChart depends on the section in which it is placed.
- A watermark is an image control that displays in the background of a page on a form or report.

Command Summary			
Feature	**Button**	**Task Path**	**Keyboard**
Report Design		Create, Reports, Report Design	
Page Number, Inserts		Design, Header/Footer, Page Numbers	
Image, Insert		Design, Controls, Insert Image	

Concepts Review

True/False Questions

Each of the following statements is either true or false. Indicate your choice by circling T or F.

T F 1. Gridlines can be added to controls outside of a control layout.

T F 2. A hexadecimal number is a numerical expression based upon a system (base) of 16 characters.

T F 3. A subform can be attached to a main report.

T F 4. The UCase Function is the only method of converting lower case text to upper case text.

T F 5. PivotCharts show graphical summaries of a recordset.

T F 6. Address fields cannot be concatenated into a single expression.

T F 7. The first part of an IIF expression is the true condition.

T F 8. The IsNumeric function evaluates numeric and text expressions.

Short Answer Questions

Write the correct answer in the space provided.

1. For a main report and subreport to work properly, what must be used to link them?

2. What term describes an expression that causes multiple fields to display as one field?

3. What dialog box allows you to create expressions?

4. What function should be used to determine if an expression can be evaluated as a number?

5. A Boolean condition is also known as what type of condition?

6. A custom color can be displayed as what type of number?

7. In what type of object can a PivotChart be displayed?

_____

8. What image control displays in the background of a page on a form or report?

_____

Critical Thinking

Answer these questions on a separate page. There are no right or wrong answers. Support your answers with examples from your own experience, if possible.

1. Designing a professional, good-looking report or form can be tedious. Explain how creating and saving a weekly report can increase your productivity.

2. An image has three size modes: Clip, Stretch, and Zoom. In what situation would Clip be best? What about Stretch and Zoom? When might Stretch be a poor choice?

Skills Review

Exercise 12-23

Your supervisor has requested that you create a report to display information regarding facilities including facility type and Medicare number. Include appropriate header and footer values.

1. Open a database by following these steps:
   a. Locate and open the **Lesson 12** folder.
   b. If you already have a copy of *[your initials]*-EcoMed-12, skip to step 1d.
   c. Make a copy of **EcoMed-12** and rename it *[your initials]*-EcoMed-12.
   d. Open and enable content for *[your initials]*-EcoMed-12.
   e. Refresh the links with *[your initials]*-HR-12.

2. Create a subreport by following these steps:
   a. From the Create tab, in the Reports group, click Report Design 🖼.
   b. From the Design tab, in the Tools group, click Add Existing Fields 🖽.
   c. In the Field List, click Show all tables.
   d. Expand **tblFacilities**. Double-click **FacID**, **FacName**, **MedicareNum**, and **FacTypeID**.
   e. Select all of the controls.
   f. From the Arrange tab, in the Table group, click Tabular 🖽.
   g. Save the subreport as **rptFacType-Sub**.

3. Arrange controls in a subreport by following these steps:

   a. Select all of the controls.

   b. Drag the control layout to the far left.

   c. In the Detail section, select only the text boxes.

   d. Drag the selected control to the top of the Detail section.

   e. From the Design tab, in the Header/Footer group, click Title 🔲. This action will open the Report Header section.

   f. Delete the controls in the Report Header.

   g. In the Page Header, select all of the labels. From the Arrange tab, in the Move group, click Move Up 🔼.

   h. From the Arrange tab, in the Rows & Columns group, click Select Layout 🔲.

   i. From the Arrange tab, in the Sizing & Ordering group, click Size/Space 🔲 and choose To Tallest 🔲.

   j. Select only the **FacTypeID** controls and press ⌑Delete⌑.

   k. Select the **FacName** text box. In the text box's Property Sheet, on the Form tab, change the Width property to **4**.

   l. Click the Report Header section bar. In the section's Property Sheet, on the Format tab, click the Back Color property. Click the Build button 🔲 and choose Automatic.

4. Format a subreport by following these steps:

   a. Switch to Layout View.

   b. Select the **Facilities ID** label. Double-click the label's right edge to resize the label.

   c. Select the **Medicare Number** label. Double-click the label's right edge to resize the label.

   d. Click the **Facilities ID** text box.

   e. From the Arrange tab, in the Rows & Columns group, click Select Row 🔲.

   f. In the selected text box's Property Sheet, on the Format tab, change the Border Style property to Transparent.

   g. Click the **Facility Name** label. From the Arrange tab, in the Rows & Columns group, click Select Row 🔲.

   h. From the Arrange tab, in the Table group, click Gridline 🔲 and choose Bottom.

   i. From the Arrange tab, in the Table group, click Gridline 🔲 and click Width and choose **3 pt**.

   j. In Design View, drag the right side of the report as far to the left as possible and drag the Page Footer up to the bottom of the text boxes. Close the Page Header and Page Footer sections.

   k. Save and close the subreport.

5. Create a report by following these steps:

   a. In the Navigation Pane, select **tblFacType**.

   b. From the Create tab, in the Reports group, click Report 🔲.

   c. From the Design tab, in the Header/Footer group, click Logo 🔲 and choose **Logo_sm**. Double-click the right edge to resize the image.

  d. From the Design tab, in the Header/Footer group, click Title and key EcoMed – Facilities by Facility Type.

  e. Delete the Time control.

  f. In the blank cell below the Date control, add a label and key Prepared by: *[your full name]*.

  g. Click the Date control. From the Format tab, in the Font group, click the Format Painter and click the label with your name.

  h. Size the controls in the Report Header so that all controls fit the width of the page.

  i. Click the **Facility Type ID** label. From the Arrange tab, in the Rows & Columns group, click Select Column ▦ and press ⌷Delete⌷.

  j. Click the **Facility Type** text box. In the Property Sheet, on the Format tab, change the Border Style property to Transparent.

  k. Save the report as rptFacType-Main.

6. Add a subreport to a report by following these steps:

  a. Switch to Design View.

  b. Delete the control and blank cells in the Report Footer and close the section.

  c. Size the Detail section to 1.5-inches tall.

  d. In the Navigation Pane, drag **rptFacType-Sub** to the Detail section below the text box.

  e. Delete the subreport control's label.

  f. In the subreport's Property Sheet, on the Data tab, verify that the Link Master Field and Link Child Fields is **FacTypeID**.

  g. Click the Detail section bar, in the section's Property Sheet, on the Format tab, click the Alternate Back Color property. Click the Build button ⋯ and choose No Color.

  h. Save and view the report.

Assessment

- Turn in your database only when all assigned exercises have been completed, according to your classroom procedure.

- OR -

- Save a report by following these steps:

  a. Click the File tab and from the Print option, click Print Preview ▣.

  b. From the Print Preview tab, in the Data group, click PDF or XPS ▧ to save the printout as a file.

  c. In the Publish as PDF or XPS dialog box, click the Option button. Select the Pages option. Print only page 1 and click OK.

  d. Save the file as a PDF and name the file *[your initials]-12-23-A*.

  e. Depending on your class procedures, print or turn in the PDF file.

12-23-A.pdf
1 Page

EXERCISE 12-24

You have been directed to modify the facility contacts report to concantinate the contact names and apply the UCase to the State field. You will also need to add an IIF function to check if the facility has an associated phone number.

1. Copy a report by following these steps:

    a. Open, enable content, and refresh links for *[your initials]-EcoMed-12*.

    b. Open **rptFacContacts** in Design View.

2. Concatenate two fields by following these steps:

    a. Select the **ContactLastName** text box press Delete.

    b. Click the **ContactFirstName** text box.

    c. In the text box's Property Sheet, on the Other tab, change the Name property to **txtFullName**.

    d. On the Data tab, in the Control Source property, press Delete and then click the Build button ⟐.

    e. Key **con** and press Tab to add the **ContactFirstName** field.

    f. Key **&" "&** (ampersand, double quote, space, double quote, ampersand).

    g. Key **con**. From the pop-up list, double-click **ContactLastName**.

    h. Click OK.

3. Modify a function by following these steps:

    a. Click the calculated control below the **Address** text box.

    b. In the text box's Property Sheet, on the Data tab, in the Control Source property, click the Build button ⟐.

    c. In the Expression box, in the equation, double-click **[State]** and press Delete.

    d. In the Expression Elements panel, double-click the Functions folder and click the Built-In Functions folder.

    e. In the Expression Categories panel, click Text.

    f. In the Expression Values panel, double-click UCase.

    g. In the Expression box, click <<string>>.

    h. In the Expression Elements panel, click the **rptFacContacts** folder.

    i. In the Expression Categories panel, click <Field List>.

    j. In the Expression Values panel, double-click **State**.

    k. Click OK.

4. Add a function to a text box by following these steps:

   a. Select the **PhoneNum** text box.

   b. In the text box's **Property Sheet**, on the **Other** tab, change the **Name** property to **txtPhone**.

   c. On the **Data** tab, in the **Control Source** property, press Delete , and then click the Build button ⊡.

   d. In the **Expression Elements** panel, double-click the **Functions** folder and click the **Built-In Functions** folder.

   e. In the **Expression Categories** panel, click **Program Flow**.

   f. In the **Expression Values** panel, double-click IIf.

   g. In the Expression box, click <<expression>>.

   h. In the **Expression Categories** panel, click **Inspection**.

   i. In the **Expression Values** panel, double-click IsNull.

   j. In the Expression box, click <<expression>>.

   k. In the **Expression Elements** panel, click the **rptFacContacts** folder.

   l. In the **Expression Categories** panel, click <Field List>.

   m. In the **Expression Values** panel, double-click **PhoneNum**.

   n. In the Expression box, click <<truepart>> and key "No Number Given".

   o. In the Expression box, click <<falsepart>>.

   p. In the **Expression Values** panel, double-click **PhoneNum**.

   q. Click **OK**.

5. Add a label and format the report by following these steps:

   a. Switch to **Layout View**.

   b. From the **Design** tab, in the **Controls** group, click Label Aα.

   c. In the **Report Header**, below the **Date** control, click in the blank cell and key **Prepared by:** *[your full name]*.

   d. Click the **Date** control.

   e. From the **Format** tab, in the **Font** group, click the Format Painter ✒ and click the label with your name.

   f. Size the controls in the **Report Header** so that all controls fit the width of the page.

Assessment

- Turn in your database only when all assigned exercises have been completed, according to your classroom procedure.

- OR -

12-24-A.pdf
1 Page

- Save a report by following these steps:

a. Click the File tab and from the Print option, click Print Preview.

b. From the Print Preview tab, in the Data group, click PDF or XPS to save the printout as a file.

c. In the Publish as PDF or XPS dialog box, click the Option button. Select the Pages option. Print only page 1 and click OK.

d. Save the file as a PDF and name the file *[your initials]*-12-24-A.

e. Depending on your class procedures, print or turn in the PDF file.

EXERCISE 12-25

The director of the human resources department has asked you to create a phone list to display the contact information for the student interns.

1. Create a report using a wizard by following these steps:

   a. Open, enable content, and refresh links for *[your initials]*-EcoMed-12.

   b. From the Create tab, in the Reports group, click Report Wizard.

   c. In the Tables/Queries drop-down box, choose Table: tblInterns.

   d. Add **LastName** and **Phone** to the Selected Fields section. Click Next.

   e. In the Do you want to add any grouping levels? section, double-click **LastName.**

   f. Click Grouping Options. Click the Grouping intervals drop-down arrow and choose 1st Letter. Click OK.

   g. Click Next twice.

   h. With the Layout being Stepped and the Orientation being Portrait, click Next.

   i. Name the report rptInternPhone and click Finish.

   j. View the report, and then close Print Preview.

2. Format the report by following these steps:

   a. In Design View, delete the label in the Report Header.

   b. From the Design tab, in the Header/Footer group, click Title and key EcoMed - Intern Phone List.

   c. Click the Report Header section bar. In the section's Property Sheet, on the Format tab, click the Back Color property. Click the Build button and choose Automatic.

   d. Click the Page Header section bar. In the section's Property Sheet, on the Format tab, change the Back Color property to #E6EDD7.

   e. Click the LastName Header section bar. In the section's Property Sheet, on the Format tab, click the Alternate Back Color property. Click the Build button and choose No Color.

f. Click the Detail section bar. In the section's Property Sheet, on the Format tab, click the Alternate Back Color property. Click the Build button ⊡ and choose No Color.

g. Select all the controls in the Page Header, LastName Header, and Detail sections.

h. From the Arrange tab, in the Table group, click Tabular ⊞. Deselect the control layout.

i. In the Page Header, click in the LastName by 1st Letter label and press [Delete].

j. In the LastName Header, change the text box's Font to Wide Latin and its Font Size to 22.

k. Select all of the controls on the report. From the Arrange tab, in the Sizing & Ordering group, click Size/Space ⊠ and choose To Fit.

l. In the Page Footer, delete both controls and close the section.

3. Add a text box by following these steps:

a. Switch to Layout View. In the Detail section, select the LastName text box.

b. From the Arrange tab, in the Rows & Columns group, click Insert Left ⊞.

c. From the Design tab, in the Controls group, click Text Box ⊡. Click in the blank cell to the left of the last name.

d. Select the new label that was added with the text box and drag it to the blank cell to the left of the Last Name label. Change the label's Caption to Name.

e. Select the Last Name label and text box and press [Delete].

f. Switch to Design View. In the Detail section, click the Unbound text box. In the control's Property Sheet, on the Other tab, change the Name property to txtFullName.

g. From the Arrange tab, in the Rows & Columns group, click Select Layout ⊞. In the control's Property Sheet, on the Format tab, change the Back Style property to Transparent.

h. Select both text boxes in the Detail section. Change the controls Font Size to 12 and apply Bold effect.

4. Add a concatenation expression by following these steps:

a. In the Property Sheet for txtFullName, on the Data tab, in the Control Source property and click the Build button ⊡.

b. In the Expression box, key las and then press [Tab] to add the LastName field.

c. Key &", "& (ampersand, quotation mark, comma, space, quotation mark, ampersand).

d. Key fir and then press [Tab] to add the FirstName field.

e. Click OK.

5. Add images by following these steps:

a. In form's **Property Sheet**, on the **Format** tab, in the **Picture** property, click the Build button and choose **Logo_lite**.

b. On the **Format** tab, change the **Picture Alignment** property to **Center**.

c. Change the **Picture Size Mode** property to **Zoom**.

d. From the **Design** tab, in the **Header/Footer** group, click **Logo** and choose **Logo_sm**.

e. Change the **Width** property to **.67**.

6. Finish the report by following these steps:

a. In the **Page Header**, select all the labels. From the **Format** tab, in the **Font** group, click Font Color **A** and choose **Automatic**.

b. Change the label's Font Size to **16**.

c. From the **Design** tab, in the **Controls** group, click Label **Aa**.

d. In the **Report Header** to the right of the title control, click and key **Prepared by:***[your full name]*. Change the label's Font Size to **12**.

e. Resize each control so all labels and data can be seen on one page.

f. Save and view your report.

Assessment

- Turn in your database only when all assigned exercises have been completed, according to your classroom procedure.

- OR -

- Save a report by following these steps:

a. Click the **File** tab and from the **Print** option, click **Print Preview** 🔍.

b. From the **Print Preview** tab, in the **Data** group, click **PDF or XPS** 🗔 to save the printout as a file.

c. Save the file as a PDF and name the file *[your initials]*-**12-25-A**.

d. Depending on your class procedures, print or turn in the PDF file.

12-25-A.pdf
1 Page

EXERCISE 12-26

The sales department has asked that you create a report to display a breakdown of bulbs sold, organized by shape and region.

1. Create a **PivotChart** by following these steps:

a. Open, enable content, and refresh links for *[your initials]*-**EcoMed-12**.

b. In the **Navigation Pane**, select **qrySalesByRegion**.

c. From the **Create** tab, in the **Forms** group, click **Form** 🖼.

d. Switch to **Design View**.

e. In the form's Property Sheet, on the Format tab, change the Default View property to PivotChart.

f. On the Format tab, change the Allow PivotChart View property to Yes.

g. On the Format tab, change the Allow Form View property to No.

h. From the Design tab, in the Views group, click PivotChart 📊.

i. Save the form as **frmSalesByRegion**.

2. Format a PivotChart by following these steps:

a. Click the Plot Area (gray area).

b. From the Design tab, in the Type group, click Change Chart Type 📊.

c. In the Properties dialog box, click the Bar chart and then choose the Clustered Bar subtype (row 1, column 1). Close the dialog box.

d. From the Chart Field List, drag BulbShape to the Drop Zone Drop Category Fields Here (left side of the window).

e. From the Chart Field List, drag SumofQty to the Drop Zone Drop Data Fields Here (center of the chart).

f. From the Design tab, in the Show/Hide group, click Drop Zone 📇.

g. From the Design tab, in the Show/Hide group, click Field List 🗇 to hide the Field List.

h. Save and close the form.

3. Create a report by following these steps:

a. In the Navigation Pane, select **tblRegion**.

b. From the Create tab, in the Reports group, click Report 📄.

c. Switch to Design View.

d. Click the Report Header section bar. In the section's Property Sheet, on the Format tab, click the Back Color property. Click the Build button 🔲 and choose Automatic.

e. Click the Detail section bar. In the section's Property Sheet, on the Format tab, click the Alternate Back Color property. Click the Build button 🔲 and choose No Color.

f. In the Report Footer, delete the calculated control and the blank cells.

g. Save the report as **rptSalesByRegion**.

4. Add and modify controls in a report by following these steps:

a. From the Design tab, in the Header/Footer group, click Logo 🖼 and choose **logo_sm**.

b. From the Design tab, in the Header/Footer group, click Title 🔲.

c. Key EcoMed - Shift + Enter Units Sold by Shape per Region. This title is now on two rows.

d. Resize the Logo and Title so they can clearly be seen.

e. Delete the Time control and replace it with a new label. Key **Prepared by:** *[your full name]*.

f. Use the Format Painter to make the new label the same format as the Date control.

g. In the Detail section, click the **Region** text box.

h. From the Arrange tab, in the Rows & Columns group, click Insert Below 🔲.

   i. Drag the **States** text box to the blank cell below the **Region** text box.

   j. Delete the label **States** and column of blank cells that remain when you delete the label.

5. Add a subform to a report by following these steps:

   a. From the Navigation Pane, drag the form **frmSalesByRegion** to the Detail section of the report.

   b. Delete the subform's label. Move the subform to the top of the Detail section and up close to the **Region** text box.

   c. In the subform's Property Sheet, on the Format tab, change the Width property to **6.7**.

   d. On the Format tab, change the Height property to **4**.

6. Add an image to a report by following these steps:

   a. Click the Report Header section bar. In the section's Property Sheet, on the Format tab, change the Height property to **2**.

   b. From the Design tab, in the Controls group, click Insert Image and click Browse.

   c. From the **Lesson 12** folder, double-click **RegionCodes**.

   d. Click below the Title control in the Report Header.

   e. Align the image to the subform in the Detail section.

   f. Adjust controls as needed to make the report no wider than 7.9 inches.

   g. Save and switch to Print Preview.

Assessment

- Turn in your database only when all assigned exercises have been completed, according to your classroom procedure.

- OR -

- Save a report by following these steps:

   a. From the Print Preview tab, in the Data group, click PDF or XPS to save the printout as a file.

   b. In the Publish as PDF or XPS dialog box, click the Option button. Select the Pages option. Print only page **1** and click OK.

   c. Save the file as a PDF and name the file *[your initials]*-**12-26-A**.

   d. Depending on your class procedures, print or turn in the PDF file.

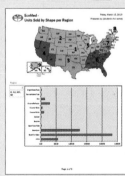

12-26-A.pdf
1 Page

Lesson Applications

Exercise 12-27

The sales department needs for you to create a phone list to display contact information for all management companies.

1. Open, enable, and update links for *[your initials]*-EcoMed-12.

2. Create a report based on **tblManagement** that groups the company names by their first letter.

3. Include the fields **ManageName** and **PhoneNum**.

4. Name the report **rptManContacts**.

5. Make the report title **Management Contact Numbers**.

6. Select all of the controls in the Page Header, ManageName Header, and Detail sections. Apply a tabular control layout.

7. To the left of the **PhoneNum** control, add a column to the layout. Add a text box to show the contacts first and last name concatenated. Modify the new label to read **Contact Name**.

8. Delete the label in the first column of the control layout. Format single letter text box to Font Size 12 and Bold.

9. Add a label to the Report Header with the caption **Prepared by:***[your full name]*.

10. Add the logo image **Logo_sm** to the Report Header.

11. Arrange the controls so that the report looks professional and fits on four pages.

Assessment

- Turn in your database only when all assigned exercises have been completed, according to your classroom procedure.

-OR-

12-27-A.pdf
1 Page

- Save the report as a PDF. Only save the first page of the report. Name the file *[your initials]*-12-27-A.

- According to your class procedures, print or turn in the PDF file.

Exercise 12-28

The director of the human resource department needs you to create a report to display the sick days each employee has taken and indicate if they have never taken a sick day. The report will determine if the employee is eligible to donate unused days to the company sick bank.

1. Open, enable, and update links for *[your initials]*-**EcoMed-12**.

2. Create a report based from **qryEmpSickCount**. Name the report rptEmpSickCount.

3. Add the **logo Logo_sm** and make the report title Sick Days Taken Year-to-Date. Resize the logo so that you can see the entire image.

4. In the Report Header, replace the Time control with a label with the caption **Prepared by:** *[your full name]*.

5. Delete the **LastName** and **FirstName** fields. Add a new text box that uses a concatenated expression joining the **LastName** and **FirstName** fields, separated by a comma. Change the label to Employee Name.

6. Add a new text box to the right of the **Days** control. Change the label to Sick Bank. Create a Control Source expression using an IIF function to display Eligible for employees that have no sick days. For the false part of the expression, key " ".

7. Center the labels and data for the **Days** and **Sick Bank** columns.

8. Delete any controls in the Page Footer and Report Footer. Close the sections.

9. Format the report so that it fits on one page.

Assessment

- Turn in your database only when all assigned exercises have been completed, according to your classroom procedure.

-OR-

- Save the report as a PDF. Name the file *[your initials]*-**12-28-A**.
- According to your class procedures, print or turn in the PDF file.

12-28-A.pdf
1 Page

Exercise 12-29

Your supervisor had directed you to create a report to display details of each facility, along with a sales summary for the facility.

1. Open, enable, and update links for *[your initials]*-**EcoMed-12**.

2. Make a copy of **rptFacDetails**. Save the copy as **rptFacSales-Main**, which will be your main report.

3. Make a copy of **rptShipSummary**. Save the copy as **rptFacSales-Sub**. which will be your subreport.

4. In **rptFacSales-Sub**, remove the title for the report.

5. In the **Page Footer**, delete all controls and close the section.

6. Move the remaining labels in the **Report Header** to the top of the section. Resize the **Report Header** to just fit the labels.

7. Reduce the width of the report as much as possible.

8. Make the **Border Style** of all controls in the report **Transparent**.

9. In the **Report Header**, add a **3 pt** gridline to the bottom of the labels

10. In the **Report Footer**, add a **3 pt** gridline to the top of only the text box.

11. In **rptFacSales-Main**, add **rptFacSales-Sub** to the right of the controls in the **Details** section. Delete the subreport label. The common field between the report and the subreport is **FacID**.

12. Resize the subreport so all information is showing. Hide the control's borders.

13. In the **Report Header**, under the **Date** control, add a label to with the caption **Prepared by: *[your full name]***.

14. Make sure the report is no wider than 7.75 inches.

12-29-A.pdf
1 Page

Assessment

- Turn in your database only when all assigned exercises have been completed, according to your classroom procedure.

-OR-

- Save the report as a PDF. Only save the first page of the report. Name the file *[your initials]*-**12-29-A**.
- According to your class procedures, print or turn in the PDF file.

Exercise 12-30 ◆ Challenge Yourself

You have been asked to create a report that will display the total number of shipments by shipping company and region.

1. Open, enable, and update links for *[your initials]*-**EcoMed-12**.

2. Create a new form based on **qryDelByRegion**. Save the form as **frmDelByRegion**.

3. Set this form to only be viewed in **PivotChart View**.

4. Add the **Years** and **Months** fields to the **Category** drop zone. Add the **Carrier** field to the **Series** drop zone.

5. Add the **ShipID** to the **Data** drop zone. Right-click the **Sum of ShipID** button and select **AutoCalc**, then choose **Count**.

6. Change the **PivotChart** type to **Smooth Line**.

7. Change the **Caption** of the bottom **Axis Title** to **Prepared by:***[your full name]* and change the **Caption** of the left **Axis Title** to **Number of Shipments**.

8. Hide the **Drop Zones** and show the **Legend**.

9. Create a query named qryRegion based on **tblRegion** that only includes the **Region** field. Add an integer parameter with the prompt **[Enter a Region number (1-9)]** that will only show one region's number at a time.

10. Make a copy of **rptMasterReport**. Save the copy as rptDelByRegion. Modify the title to read EcoMed – Deliveries by Region.

11. Make the new report's **Record Source** qryRegion. Place the field **Region** in the report so that the label is in the **Page Header** and the text box in the **Detail** section.

12. Add the image **RegionCodes** to the top of the **Page Header** to the right of the **Region** label. Move the label to the bottom of the section.

13. Add the form **frmDelByRegion** to the **Detail** section. Delete the subreport label. The subform and the main report should be linked by the field **Region**. Make the subform's width the same as the images in the **Page Header** and a height of 4 inches.

14. Modify the report so that the report does not exceed the page width of 7.9 inches.

Assessment

- Turn in your database only when all assigned exercises have been completed, according to your classroom procedure.

-OR-

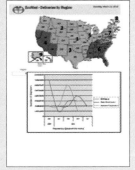

- Save the report as a PDF. Save the report that shows the data for region 6. Name the file *[your initials]*-12-30-A.
- According to your class procedures, print or turn in the PDF file.

12-30-A.pdf
1 Page

On Your Own

In these exercises, you work on your own, as you would in a real-life work environment. Use the skills you've learned to accomplish the task—and be creative.

Exercise 12-31

Review the design of the database you modified in Exercise 11-32. On a sheet of paper, sketch two new reports. One of the reports must include a logo and an expression. The other report must include a subreport control. Name each report with a title that best describes the purpose of the report. Write your name, class information, and "Exercise 12-31" on each sketch. Continue to the next exercise.

Exercise 12-32

Based on the sketches that you created in Exercise 12-31, create the two reports. Select the style and layout most appropriate for each form. Arrange the controls as necessary. In the Report Footer, include your name, class information and "Exercise 12-32." In the Report Header, include the title of the report. Continue to the next exercise.

Exercise 12-33

Create a report containing a PivotChart. Print a copy of each new report. Submit copies of the report sketches and printed reports to your instructor. Keep a copy of the database you modified in this lesson. You will use it for the On Your Own exercise in subsequent lessons.

Unit 3 Applications

Unit Application 3-1

The sales department would like to know which facilities placed orders for the first quarter of 2011. You will need to create a report based on a new query. You will also need to create a relationship between the new table and the facilities table.

1. From the **Unit 03** folder, copy the file **EcoMed-U3** and rename it *[your initials]*-EcoMed-U3. Copy the file **HR-U3** and rename it *[your initials]*-HR-U3.

2. Open *[your initials]*-**EcoMed-U3**, enable content, and refresh the linked tables for *[your initials]*-**HR-U3**.

3. Create a query for **tblFacilities** and **tblShipments**. Include the fields **FacID**, **FacName**, **OrderDate**, and **ShipDate**. Add a calculated field called Contact that concatenates the **ContactFirstName** and **ContactLastName** fields.

4. Move the calculated field after the **FacName** field. Modify the query to only show shipments in the first quarter of 2011 and sort in ascending order by **FacName**. Query has 89 records.

5. Change the query to a make-table query. Name the query qryShipQ1-2011. Run the query to create tblShipQ1-2011.

6. Create a relationship with enforced referential integrity between **tblShipQ1-2011** and the **tblFacilities** table.

7. Create a simple report based on **tblShipQ1-2011** and save it as rptShipQ1-2011.

8. Make the title Facilities 1st Quarter Shipments. Include the logo **Logo_sm**. Delete and replace the Time control in the Report Header with a label with the caption Prepared by: *[your full name]*. Format the new label to match the Date control. Modify the **FacName** label to read Facility Name.

9. Add spaces to the two date labels to improve their readability. Change the Report Header section Back Color to 230 Red, 237 Green, and 215 Blue.

10. Make the Border Style of all text boxes in the Detail section Transparent. Place a 3 pt gridline below the labels in the Page Header.

Assessment

- According to your classroom procedure, turn in your database only when you have completed all assigned exercises.

- OR -

- Create a Database Documenter report for **tblShipQ1-2011** using the following settings:

  • Include for Table: **Relationships**
  • Include for Fields: **Names, Data Types, and Sizes**
  • Include for Indexes: **Nothing**

- Save the Documenter report as a PDF file named *[your initials]*-**U3-01-A**.
- Save **rptShipQ1-2011** as a PDF. Only save the first page. Name the file *[your initials]*-**U3-01-B**.
- According to your class procedures, print or turn in the PDF files.

U3-01-A.pdf
1 Page

U3-01-B.pdf
1 Page

Unit Application 3-2

Management is looking for ways to reduce shipping costs. They have asked you to create a summary query to count the number of deliveries for each carrier and carrier type, display the information as a PivotChart, and print the chart as a report.

1. Using *[your initials]*-**EcoMed-U3**, create a summary query using **tblShipments**.

2. Show the **DeliverMethod**, **ShipID**, and **OrderDate** fields. Count the **ShipID** field and use **OrderDate** (Where) to only show shipments in 2011. The result should be 8 records.

3. Save the query as **qryDelSum**.

4. Create a form based on **qryDelSum** named **frmDelSum**.

5. Change the form to only be seen in PivotChart View.

6. Use **DeliverMethod** as the Series Area and **CountOfShipID** as the Data Area.

7. Add Delivery By and Number of Shipments as Axis Titles.

8. Hide the Drop Zones and show the Legend.

9. Create a Report based on **tblCarriers** named **rptDelSum**.

10. Make the title EcoMed - Carrier Report Year to Date. Include the logo **Logo_sm**. Delete and replace the Time control in the Report Header with a label with the caption Prepared by: *[your full name]*. Format the new label to match the Date control.

11. Delete the **Rates** text box and label. Delete the page controls in the **Page Footer** and close the section.

12. In the **Report Footer**, delete all controls and blank cells. Add the form **frmDelSum**. Delete the subform's label. Make the subform **5** inches tall. Move subform to the upper left of the **Detail** section. This subform will not change because it is not linked to the main report.

13. Make sure that this report fits on one page.

Assessment

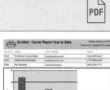

- According to your classroom procedure, turn in your database only when you have completed all assigned exercises.

- OR -

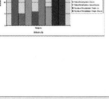

U3-02-A.pdf
1 Page

- Save **rptDelSum** as a PDF. Name the file *[your initials]*-U3-02-A.
- According to your class procedures, print or turn in the PDF file.

Unit Application 3-3

The sales department has been developing a schedule of trade shows that EcoMed Services will attend. The information is stored in an Excel spreadsheet. You have been instructed to link the data, create a query that concatenates the employee names, create a form to display the data, add an image to the form, and add a function to capitalize the state.

1. Using *[your initials]*-EcoMed-U3, link the Excel file **TradeShows** and create a new table. Use **TradeShowID** as the primary key. Name the table **tblTradeShows**.

2. Create a one-to-many relationship between **tblEmployees** and **tblTradeShows**.

3. Create a query using **tblTradeShows** and **tblEmployees**. Save it as **qryTradeShows**.

4. Show all trade show fields and the employee first and last name in a single field called **Full Name**.

5. Create a form to display all the information from **qryTradeShows**. Include a label in the **Form Header** with the caption **Prepared by:** *[your full name]*.

6. Make the title **Trade Shows**. Include the logo **Logo_sm**.

7. Add the picture **Office** to the form. Format the picture so that it is stretched along the entire **Form Header**.

8. Resize the controls to use only the left half of the form. In the **Detail** section, add **GreenBulb** to the right of the controls. Size the new image 2.5 inches wide and 4 inches tall.

9. Make the form no wider than 7.5 inches. Display only one record per page.

10. Change the **Name** of the **State** text box to **txtState** and add a function to the **State** text box to capitalize the data.

11. Save the form as **frmTradeShows**.

Assessment

- According to your classroom procedure, turn in your database only when you have completed all assigned exercises.

- OR -

- Create a **Database Documenter** report for **tblTradeShows** using the following settings:

  • Include for Table: **Properties, Relationships**

  • Include for Fields: **Names, Data Types, and Sizes**

  • Include for Indexes: **Nothing**

- Save the **Documenter** report as a PDF file named *[your initials]*-**U3-03-A**.

- Save **frmTradeShows** as a PDF. Only save the first record. Name the file *[your initials]*-**U3-03-B**.

- According to your class procedures, print or turn in the PDF files.

U3-03-A.pdf
1 Page

U3-03-B.pdf
1 Page

Unit Application 3-4 ◆ Using the Internet

You have been temporarily assigned to the sales department and directed to find two additional trade shows and assign an employee to attend. Create an appropriate report.

1. Using *[your initials]*-**EcoMed-U3**, locate two additional tradeshows listed on the Internet. Using the information you located on the Internet, modify **tblTradeShows** to include the Web site from which you located the information, the beginning date of the show, and the ending date of the show. Add the appropriate fields to **tblTradeShows**. Assign employee **117** to the new tradeshows. Create a report, named **rptTradeShows**, which shows all information for the tradeshows. Add an EcoMed logo. Add your name to the page header. Format the report to look appealing. Print the report pages that show the two new tradeshows.

2. Add a group level for **EmpID**. Move the employee name to the header section of the **EmpID** group. Format the page to look appealing.

Assessment

 - According to your classroom procedure, turn in your database only when you have completed all assigned exercises.

- OR -

 - Save the **Datasheet View** of **tblTradeShows** as a PDF named *[your initials]*-U2-04-T.

- Save the first page of the report as a PDF named *[your initials]*-U2-04-R.

Unit 4

USING ADVANCED FEATURES

Lesson 13
Advanced Database Features

OBJECTIVES   *After completing this lesson, you will be able to:*

1. Convert databases.
2. Manage import specifications.
3. Manage export specifications.
4. Use Mail Merge.
5. Use advanced navigation techniques.
6. Use security tools.

Estimated Time: 1½ hours

Database administrators are responsible not only for designing a database but also for ensuring the accuracy and security of its data. A skilled database administrator must understand the principles of converting, importing, exporting, securing, and sharing data.

For shared data to be useful, both the sender and the receiver must to be able to use the data. The data must be in a format that both the sender and receiver can use. It is equally important that the shared data remain confidential. In this lesson, you learn different methods of sharing and protecting a database.

Converting Databases

Access databases are upwardly but not downwardly compatible. That means you can open an Access 2003 database in Access 2010, but you cannot open an Access 2010 database in Access 2003. Access 2007 and Access 2010 use the new file format ACCDB. Previous versions of Access used the MDB format.

Advanced database features available in either Access 2007 or Access 2010 include:

- Complex data (multi-valued data types)
- Attachment date type
- Append only memo fields
- Compressed image storage
- E-mail database as attachment
- Linked tables to files in ACCDB format
- Encrypt with database password

Advanced database features available in only Access 2010 include:

- Table layout for control layouts
- Navigation forms

Exercise 13-1 OPEN PREVIOUS VERSION OF ACCESS

When using Microsoft Access 2010 to open a database created in a previous version, you do not need to convert the database to the 2010 format. You can open these databases in Office Access 2010. When using Access 2010 to open a previous database file format, not all features may be available to use. Some advanced features are available only for Access 2010 databases. The supported database file formats for Access 2010 are Access 2000, Access 2002-2003, Access 2007, and Access 2010.

1. Locate and open the **Lesson 13** folder.
2. Copy the database **Assets-2000** and rename it *[your initials]*-Assets-2000.
3. Open and enable *[your initials]***-Assets-2000**. The title bar of Access shows the file format.

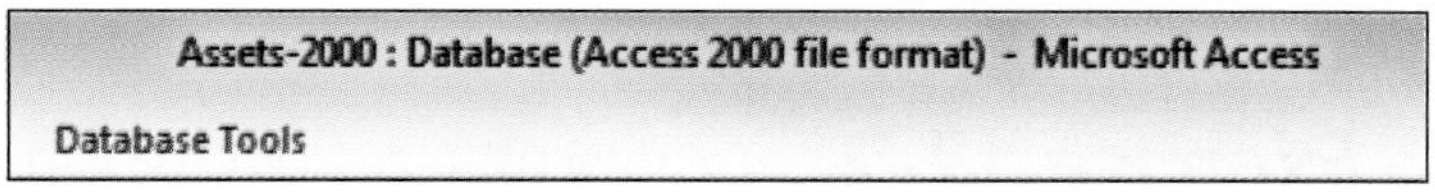

Figure 13-1
Access 2000 file opened in Access 2010
Assets-2000.mdb

Assets-2000 : Database (Access 2000 file format) - Microsoft Access

Database Tools

4. From the Navigation Pane, open the table **Asset Categories**. The table is opened into its window inside of Access instead of a document tab.
5. From the Navigation Pane, open the table **Assets**. The second table has covered the first.
6. From the Home tab, in the Window group, click Switch Windows and choose Tile Horizontally.

7. From the **Home** tab, in the **Window** group, click **Switch Windows** and choose **Cascade**.

8. From the **File** tab, click **Options** .

9. In the **Access Options** dialog box, on the left, click **Current Database**. In the **Application Options** section, select the option **Tabbed Documents**.

10. Click **OK** to close the **Access Options** dialog box.

Figure 13-2
Overlapping
windows
**Assets-2000.mdb
Assets**

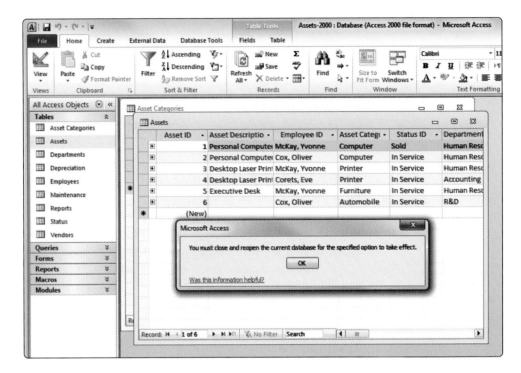

11. Click **OK** and close the database.

12. Open the *[your initials]*-**Assets-2000** again.

13. From the **Navigation Pane**, open the table **Assets**. The table now has a tab.

14. Close the table.

Exercise 13-2   CONVERT A DATABASE TO ACCESS 2010

Access 2010 provides a conversion tool to allow you to change an Access 2000, Access 2002-2003, or Access 2007 file format to Access 2010. Access 97 or earlier format databases are converted into Access 2002-2003 format by default and then can be converted to Access 2010. The database file format is shown next to the file name in the title bar of the database window.

Access 2010 uses the same file format as Access 2007, which not mean that all 2010 databases are compatible in Access 2007. New features that are found only in Access 2010 will not open in Access 2007 even though they share the same file format.

1. From the **File** tab, click the **Save & Publish** tab. In the **Save Database As** section, click **Access Database**. Click the **Save As** button 🔲.

2. In the **Save As** dialog box, verify the folder where the database will be saved. Key *[your initials]*-Assets-2010 and click **Save**.

3. Read the information given in the dialog box and click **OK**.

4. In the **Security Warning** bar, click **Enable Content**.

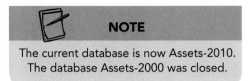

NOTE

The current database is now Assets-2010. The database Assets-2000 was closed.

Exercise 13-3   CONVERT DATABASE AS A PREVIOUS VERSION

Access allows you to convert a 2010 database format to a previous version format. When you convert a 2010 database to a previous version file format, the database loses the ability to use the advanced features available only in Access 2010.

1. From the **File** tab, click the **Save & Publish** tab. Under the **Save Database As** option, click **Access 2002-2003 Database**.

2. Click the **Save As** button 🔲.

3. In the **Save As** dialog box, verify the folder where the database will be saved. Key *[your initials]*-Assets-2003 and click **Save**.

4. Click the **File** tab and click **Close Database** 🗁.

EXERCISE 13-4   CREATE A DATABASE TEMPLATE

Access allows you to customize certain application options. For example, you can select an image to use as an icon for major objects. We can create a template database so that other departments of EcoMed do not have to start from scratch when creating their databases. Templates are stored on workstations. The file extension for a template is .ACCDT.

1. From the **File** tab and click the **New** option. Select the **Blank database**.

2. In the lower-right corner of the window, next to the **File Name** control, click the Browse icon 🗁.

3. In the **File New Database** dialog box, if needed navigate to the **Lesson 13** folder. Key *[your initials]*-EcoMed-Master and click **OK**.

4. Click the **Create** button 🗋.

5. Close the table. The template database will not be including any tables.

6. From the **External Data** tab, in the **Import & Link** group, click **Access** 🗗.

7. In the **Get External Data** dialog box, click **Browse**.

8. In the **File Open** dialog box, in the **Lesson 13** folder, choose **EcoMed-13**. Click **Open**.

9. Select the option to **Import tables, queries, forms, reports, macros, and modules into the current database**. Click **OK**.

10. From the **Import Objects** dialog box, click the **Forms** tab and select **frmMasterForm**.

11. Click the **Reports** tab and select **rptMasterReport**. Click **OK**, then **Close**. The new database now has two objects.

12. From the **File** tab, click **Options** 🗎.

13. On the left, click **Current Database**. In the **Application Title**, key **EcoMed**.

14. For the **Application Icon** option, click **Browse**. Locate the **Lesson 13** folder and choose **LighBulb**.

15. Click the check box for **Use as Form and Report Icon**.

16. Click the check box for **Compact on Close**.

17. Click **OK**. The message dialog box states that the database needs to be restarted. Click **OK**.

18. From the **File** tab, click the **Save & Publish** tab. In the **Save Database As** section, double-click **Template**.

19. For the **Name**, key **EcoMed Startup Template**.

Figure 13-3
Template options
EcoMed.accdt

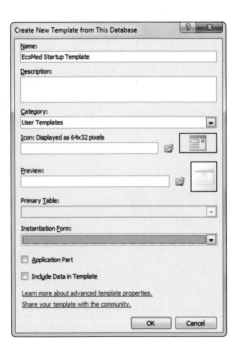

20. Click **OK**. The dialog box shows the location of the new template. Click **OK**.

21. Click the **File** tab and click **Close Database** 🗁.

22. From the New option, select My templates. The template that you just created is now located here.

23. Close Access.

Managing Import Specifications

When you run the Access 2010 Import or Export Wizard, you can save the specifications and easily repeat the operation at any time. A saved specification contains all the information Access needs to repeat the import or export operation. For example, you can save a specification that imports data from a Microsoft Office Excel 2010 workbook. The specification saves the name of the source Excel file, the name of the destination database, and details to either append data into an existing table or create a new table.

After saving the specifications, you change detail parameters such as the name of the source or destination file. You can create a single specification and modify it for use with different source or destination files.

Exercise 13-5 SAVING IMPORT SPECIFICATIONS

Whenever you routinely import data from similarly structured files, you can save the import specifications. One of the most common file formats used for importing and exporting is a text file. A *text file* is a file that only contains unformatted textual characters. Text files are delimited or fixed-width.

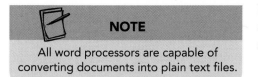

NOTE

All word processors are capable of converting documents into plain text files.

A *delimited file* is a file in which all fields are separated by an identifiable character, such as a tab, semicolon, or comma. A *fixed-width file* is a file in which each field starts at the same character position for each record.

Plain text files are sometimes referred to as ASCII or ANSI files. In a text file, there is no easy way to tell which fields are numbers, text, dates, or currency.

1. Copy the database **EcoMed-13** and rename it *[your initials]-* **EcoMed-13**. Copy the **HR-13** database and rename it *[your initials]-* **HR-13**.

2. Copy the text file **R3mgt.txt** and rename the copy NewMgt.txt.

3. Open *[your initials]*-**EcoMed-13** and enable and refresh all the linked tables.

4. From the External Data tab, in the Import & Link group, click Text File 📄.

5. In the Get External Data dialog box, click Browse.

6. In the File Open dialog box, in the **Lesson 13** folder, choose **NewMgt**. Click Open.

7. Select the option to Append a copy of the records to the table: , and from the drop-down list, choose **tblManagement**.

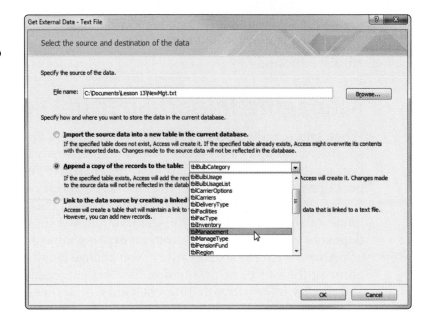

8. Click **OK**.

9. The **Import Text Wizard** starts and correctly determines that the fields are **Delimited**.

10. Click **Next**. Common delimiters are listed across the top.

11. Choose **Comma**. The commas in the description are being interpreted as delimiters.

12. For the control **Text Qualifier**, click the drop-down arrow and choose " (double quotation mark.) The quotation marks are removed from around the data, and all the data are now aligned.

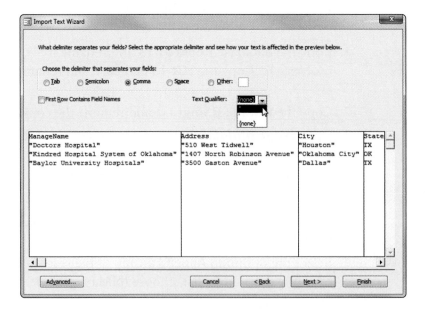

13. Click the check box for **First Row Contains Field Names**.

14. In the lower left corner, click **Advanced**.

15. The setting for **File Format**, **Field Delimiter**, and **Text Qualifier** are shown here. Click **Save As** and key **NewMgt**. Click **OK**.

16. Click **Specs**. The specifications for the text file are now stored at the bottom of the list. Click **Cancel**.

17. Click **OK**. Click **Finish**.

18. In the **Get External Data** dialog box, click the check box for **Save import steps**.

19. Click **Save Import**.

20. Open **tblManagement** in **Datasheet View** and sort the table by **Management ID** in descending order. The three new records do not have **Contract Ends** data.

21. Close the table and save the change.

Exercise 13-6   RUN A SAVED IMPORT TASK

You can run saved specifications for import and export tasks. Each time you launch an import or export operation, you can save additional specifications for future use.

1. Minimize the database. In the folder **Lesson 13**, delete the text file **NewMgt**.

2. Copy the text file **R5mgt** and rename it **NewMgt**.

3. From the **External Data** tab, in the **Import & Link** group, click **Saved Imports** 📇.

Figure 13-7
Manage Data Tasks
EcoMed-13.accdb

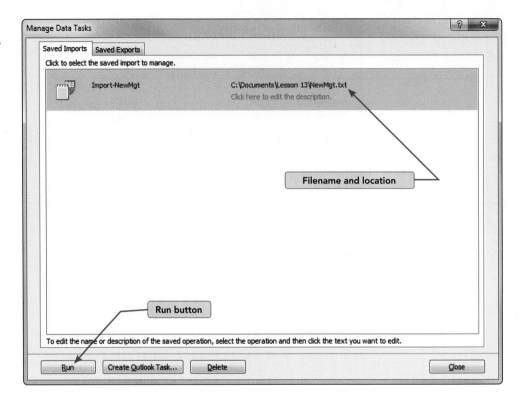

4. You have one saved Import. Click **Import-NewMgt** and click **Run**.

5. When all the objects (records) are copied, click **OK**.

6. Click **Close** to close the **Manage Data Tasks** dialog box.

7. Open **tblManagement** in **Datasheet View**. Notice the 2 new records for a total of 5 new management companies.

8. Close the table.

Exercise 13-7   IMPORT TEXT DATA INTO A NEW TABLE

You now will import a text file into a new table. The text file contains OSHA regulations and hyperlinks to the OSHA Web site.

1. From the **External Data** tab, in the **Import & Link** group, click **Text File** 📄.

2. In the **Get External Data** dialog box, click **Browse**.

3. In the **File Open** dialog box, in the **Lesson 13** folder, choose **OSHA.txt**. Click **Open**.

4. Select the option to **Import the source data into a new table in the current database**. Click **OK**.

5. The **Import Text Wizard** starts and correctly determines that the fields are **Delimited**. Click **Next**.

6. Choose **Comma** as the delimiter.

7. For the control **Text Qualifier**, click the drop-down arrow and choose " (double quotation mark).

8. Click the check box for **First Row Contains Field Names**. Click **Next**. Click **Next**.

9. Each imported field can have its **Field Name**, **Data Type**, and **Indexed** properties changed in this step. Click each field. The wizard has correctly identified the fields data types as **Text**, **Data/Time**, and **Hyperlink**. Click **Next**.

10. Since a title is a poor primary key, we will allow the wizard to create a primary key for us. Notice that we can't name this field. Click **Next**.

11. Name the new table **tblText** so that we know that the data came from a text file. Click **Finish**.

12. We don't plan to import this data on a regular basis, so we do not need to save the import steps. Click **Close**.

13. Open **tblText** to review the nine new records. Close the table.

Exercise 13-8   IMPORT XML DATA INTO A NEW TABLE

Another common file format used for import and export tasks is XML. An *XML file* is an Extensible Markup Language text file that can store table names, field names, field properties, data types, and data. You now will import an XML file into a new table. The data in this file are the same as in the OSHA text file.

1. From the **External Data** tab, in the **Import & Link** group, click **XML File** 📲.

2. In the **Get External Data** dialog box, click **Browse**.

3. Select **OSHA.xml** and click **Open**. Click **OK**. In the **Import XML** dialog box, one table in the file is called **OSHA**. Expand the **OSHA** table to see the fields that are included in this file.

Figure 13-8
Tables and fields stored in the XML file **EcoMed-13.accdb tblXML**

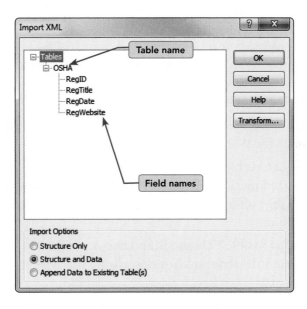

4. Three **Import Options** appear at the bottom of the dialog box. Because we want to compare these data with the previous exercise, select **Structure and Data**. Click **OK**.

5. The file is imported. We do not need to save the import steps. Click **Close**.

6. Open **tblText** in **Design View** and review the properties for each field.

7. Open **OSHA** in **Design View** and review the properties for each field. A summary of the differences between the two tables is listed in Table 13-1.

TABLE 13-1 Import Comparison

Object	Text File	XML File
RegID field	Can't import an Autonumber field	Imports an Autonumber field
RegTitle field	Field Size set to default 255	Field Size is 50
RegDate field	No Format property setting	Format property set to Short Date
All fields	No Field Description or Caption text	Field Description or Caption text
Table	Can name the table in import wizard	Can only rename table after import is completed

8. Close both tables. Delete the table **tblText**.

9. Rename the table **OSHA** to **tblOSHA_Reg**.

Managing Export Specifications

When sharing data from an Access database to other applications, often you will need export data to standardized formats. Just as you can manage import specifications, you can save export tasks. Saved specifications can be launched at any time.

Data interchange file formats include:

- HTML—Hypertext Markup Language. The standard formatting language for Web documents.

- XML—Extensible Markup Language. A condensed form of standard generalized markup language (SGML) that enables developers to create custom tags offering flexibility when organizing and presenting information.

- XSD—Extensible Scheme Standard. An approved W3C standard design as a basic infrastructure for describing the type and structure of XML documents.

- XSL—Extensible Stylesheet Language. Used to describe how files encoded in the XML standard are to be formatted or transformed.

Exercise 13-9 EXPORT DATA AS AN XML FILE

An advantage of using a XML file format for exporting data is the ease in transferring the data to different applications such as Word, Excel, or non-Access databases. You now will create a query to find all of the new management companies that were added to tblManagement. You then will export these records to an XML file.

1. From the Create tab, in the Queries group, click Query Design 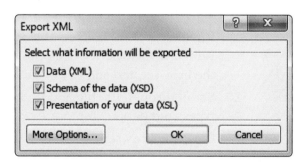.
2. Add **tblManagement** to the query.
3. From the Field List, double-click the asterisk.
4. Add the field **ContractEnds** to the design grid and set its criteria to is null.
5. Remove the Show checkmark for the **ContractEnds** field.
6. Run the query. Only companies with which we do not have contracts are listed.
7. Close and save the query as qryNewMgt.
8. In the Navigation Pane, select **qryNewMgt**.
9. From the External Data tab, in the Export group, click XML File .
10. Click the Browse button. Locate the **Lesson 13** folder and modify the Filename to PossibleNewMgt. Click Save.
11. Click OK. The Export XML dialog box opens. Select all three choices.

Figure 13-9
Save data to an
XML file
**EcoMed-13.accdb
qryNewMgt**

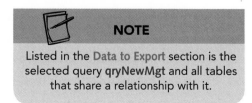

12. Click More Options. On the Data tab is a list of Data to Export.
13. Click the Schema tab. In the Export Location section, select Embed schema in exported XML data document to place the field's properties (XSD) inside the data (XML) file.

> **NOTE**
>
> Listed in the Data to Export section is the selected query qryNewMgt and all tables that share a relationship with it.

Figure 13-10
Modify XML Export
structure
**EcoMed-13.accdb
qryNewMgt**

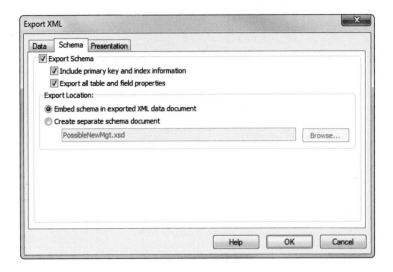

14. Click the **Presentation** tab. The presentation will have an HTML file type and use the information stored in the XSL file.

15. Click **OK** to finish the export.

16. In the **Export** dialog box, click the **Save export steps** check box. Click **Save Export**. Three files are created.

17. Locate where you saved the exported file. Right-click **PossibleNewMgt. htm** and choose **Open With** and **Internet Explorer**.

18. Click the security message and choose **Allow Blocked Content**. Click **Yes** in response to the second security message. The content of **PossibleNewMgt. htm** is now visible in the browser. There are five records.

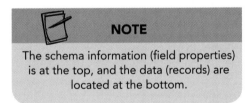

NOTE

The schema information (field properties) is at the top, and the data (records) are located at the bottom.

19. Right-click **PossibleNewMgt.xml** and choose **Open With** and **XML Editor**. This choice opens the data in the browser and shows the data and XML tags.

20. Scroll through the file and find the field names, field types, and data.

21. Close the browser.

Exercise 13-10   RUN A SAVED EXPORT TASK

When exporting data to an existing file, you must either rename or replace the original file. Exporting does not allow you to append data to an existing file. You now will delete two of the new management companies and run the export steps a second time.

1. Open **tblManagement** in **Datasheet View**.

2. Delete the record for management companies Mercy Health Partners and Doctors Hospital. Close the table.

3. From the **External Data** tab, in the **Export** group, click **Saved Exports** 🖼.

4. In the **Manage Data Tasks** dialog box, on the **Saved Exports** tab, you see that there is only one saved export task.

5. Click **Run**. The file **PossibleNewMgt.xml** already exists. Click **Yes** to save the latest data to the file.

6. Click **OK** to the confirmation message.

7. Click **Close**.

8. Open **PossibleNewMgt.htm** in Internet Explorer. There are now only three records in the exported files. Close the browser.

Exercise 13-11　EXPORT A TEXT FILE

You can export a recordset from a table or query. You now will export all the surgical bulbs in the inventory table to a text file. You will need to create a query to display only surgical bulbs.

1. From the **Create** tab, in the **Queries** group, click **Query Design** 🗔.

2. Add **tblInventory** to the query.

3. From the Field List, double-click the asterisk.

4. Add the field **BulbCatID** to the design grid and set its criteria to **4**.

5. Remove the **Show** checkmark for the **BulbCatID** field.

6. Run the query. Only bulbs with the category of "Surgical" are listed.

7. Close and save the query as **qrySurgicalData**.

8. In the **Navigation Pane**, select **qrySurgicalData**.

9. From the **External Data** tab, in the **Export** group, click **Text File** 🗔.

10. Click the **Browse** button. Locate the **Lesson 13** folder and modify the **Filename** to SurgicalData.txt with a .txt filename extension. Click **Save**.

11. For the **Specify export options**, click the **Export data with formatting and layout** check box.

12. Add a checkmark to the **Open the destination file after the export operation is complete** option.

13. Click **OK**.

14. The default encoding is **Windows**. Click **OK**.

Figure 13-11
Record exported
with text layout
**EcoMed-13.accdb
qrySurgicalData**

Inv ID	Energy Star?	Model Number	Bulb Shape	Bulb Category	ven
2	No	TT74-150-G	A-line	Surgical	Unio Lighting
3	No	TT74-75-G	A-line	Surgical	Unio Lighting
207	No	SX258-300-Tri	Canister	Surgical	Unio Lighting
208	No	002854-150-Tri	Canister	Surgical	Unio Lighting
209	No	CL259-300-BF	Canister	Surgical	Unio Lighting
210	No	CL259-500-BF	Canister	Surgical	Unio Lighting
211	No	FL450-175-BF	Canister	Surgical	Unio Lighting
212	No	FL450-300-BF	Canister	Surgical	Unio Lighting
290	No	DNF	Dish	Surgical	Unio Lighting
291	No	EFP	Dish	Surgical	Unio Lighting
298	No	BBL-7400	Single-Ended Tube	Surgical	AnyBulb
302	No	SK-D-220	Single-Ended Tube	Surgical	AnyBulb
303	No	XP-D-100S	Single-Ended Tube	Surgical	AnyBulb
304	No	66528H-G8	Single-Ended Tube	Surgical	AnyBulb
305	No	A4366-40-E11	Single-Ended Tube	Surgical	AnyBulb
306	No	A4366-60-E11	Single-Ended Tube	Surgical	AnyBulb
307	No	A4366-60-E10	Single-Ended Tube	Surgical	AnyBulb
308	No	5588-Bi-Pin	Single-Ended Tube	Surgical	AnyBulb
309	No	HIP-1452-GX7.9	Single-Ended Tube	Surgical	Unio Lighting

15. This data look nice but can't be imported to different applications. Close the text file. Close the **Export – Text File** dialog box.

16. From the **External Data** tab, in the **Export** group, click **Text File** 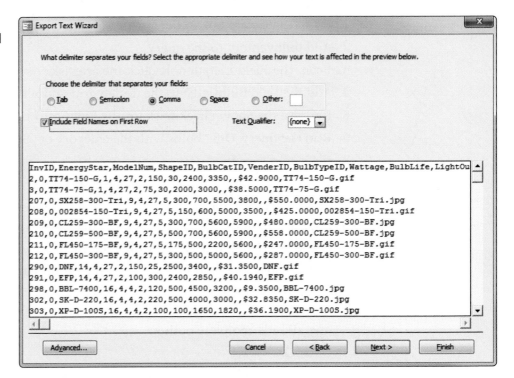.

17. Modify the name to **SurgicalData.txt**. Click **OK**.

18. Click **Yes** to overwrite the old file.

19. The **Export Text Wizard** defaults to **Delimited** format. Click **Next**.

20. Because none of the data has commas, click the **Text Qualifier** drop-down arrow and choose **{None}**. This choice removes the quotes for the text data.

21. Click the **Include Field Names on First Row** check box.

22. Both the path and filenames are the same as you saw earlier. Click **Finish**, and then click **Close**.

23. Locate and open **SurgicalData.txt** to view the data. Each row is a different record.

24. Close the text file.

Exercise 13-12   EXPORT AN HTML DOCUMENT

When exporting to certain applications such as word processors, you may select the HTML (HyperText Markup Language) format. HTML is the predominant markup language for the creation of Web pages. HTML provides the structure of text-based information in a document.

1. In the **Navigation Pane**, right-click **qrySurgicalData** and choose **Export**, then **HTML Document**.

2. Set the appropriate location for the file and modify the filename to **SurgicalData.html**.

3. For the **Specify export options**, click both **Export data with formatting and layout** and **Open the destination file after the export operation is complete** check box.

4. Click **OK**.

5. In the **HTML Output Options** dialog box, click **OK**.

6. The table and its data are shown in a browser. Close the browser.

7. In the **Export – HTML Document** dialog box, click **Close**.

Using Mail Merge

One of the many benefits of using a database system is that records from the database can be used to create Mail Merge documents. *Mail Merge* is a word processing feature that creates a merged document by combining a source document and a record source from an external file. The external file can be a database, spreadsheet, text file, or XML file.

In a merged document, the text and graphics contained in the source document are identical for all merged documents; however, field information from each record source, such as names and addresses, changes for each merged document. When Mail Merge is executed, the application creates a merged document for each corresponding row in the database using the fixed text, exactly as it appears in the source document.

Exercise 13-13   CREATE A MAIL MERGE LETTER

You now will use the Mail Merge function of Access to send a letter to all facilities in the state of California. The letter informs them of the California regulations for shipments of toxic substances.

1. Select **qryFac-CA**.

2. From the **External Data** tab, in the **Export** group, click **Word Merge** [icon].

3. The wizard asks if you want to link to an already created Word file or if you need to create it now. Click **Link your data to an existing Microsoft Word document**. Click **OK**.

4. In the folder **Lesson 13**, select the Word file **CA Dept of Toxic Substance Control** and click **Open**.

5. The **Mail Merge** task pane should be on the right side of the screen. This letter has place holders for the database data.

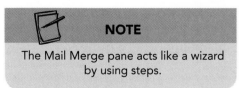

NOTE

The Mail Merge pane acts like a wizard by using steps.

6. The middle area of the task pane shows that you are using table **[qryFac-CA] in EcoMed-13.accdb**. Click **Next: Write your letter**.

7. In the letter, select **<Date>**.

8. From the **Insert** tab, in the **Text** group, click **Date & Time** 🔟.

9. Choose the third option (month spelled out, the day, and a four-digit year). Click to select **Update automatically**. Click **OK**.

10. Press Enter. Select **<Address Block>** and press Delete.

11. From the **Mail Merge** task pane, click **Address block**. With all four check boxes selected, the standard address block will include the recipient's name, the company name, and the postal address.

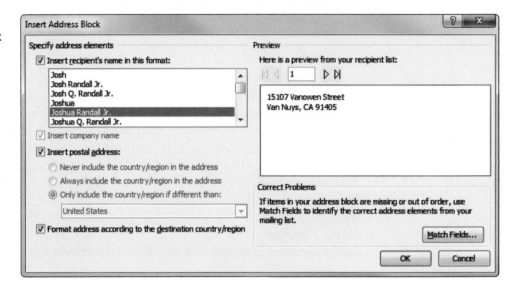

Figure 13-13
Insert Address Block
EcoMed-13.accdb

12. The contact name and facility name is missing. Click **Match Fields**. Word tries to match specific information with the fields from the merged recordset. You only need to change the field names if they do not match.

13. For the **First Name** option, click the drop-down arrow and choose **ContactFirstName**.

14. For the **Last Name** option, click the drop-down arrow and choose **ContactLastName**.

15. For the **Company** option, click the drop-down arrow and choose **FacName**. Click **OK**.

16. Click **OK** to close the **Insert Address Block** dialog box. Word inserts a field that marks where the address information will be inserted.

17. In the letter, select **<Contact First Name>**.

18. In the task pane, click **More items**.

19. Double-click **ContactFirstName**. The field **ContactFirstName** is inserted. Click **Close**.

20. Press Spacebar and select **<Contact Last Name>**.

21. From the **Mailings** tab, in the **Write & Insert Fields** group, click the bottom half of the **Insert Merge Field** and choose **ContactLastName**.

Figure 13-14
Form letter
EcoMed-13.accdb

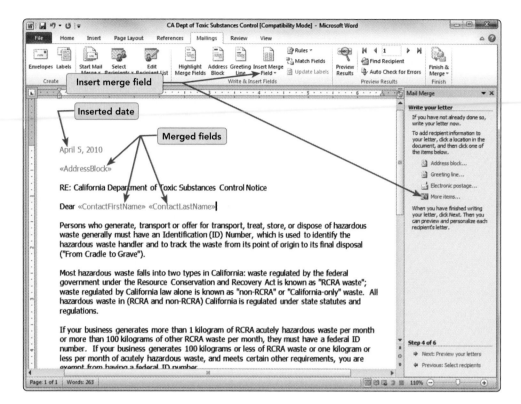

22. In the letter, scroll down to the bottom and select **<Employee Name>**.

23. From the **Mailings** tab, in the **Write & Insert Fields** group, click the bottom half of the **Insert Merge Field** and choose **EmpName**.

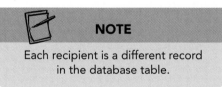

NOTE

Each recipient is a different record in the database table.

24. In the task pane, click **Next: Preview your letters**. The first letter is displayed.

25. From the **Mailings** tab, in the **Preview Results** group, use the record navigation buttons to view each of the letters.

26. The place holders are still a different color than the rest of the letter. Click in the letter and press Ctrl+A to select all of the text. From the **Home** tab, in the **Font** group, change the font color to black.

27. Click **Next: Complete the merge**. You can send the completed letters directly to the printer or edit them on the screen.

28. Click **Edit individual letters**. Choose **All** and click **OK**. A document is created containing one letter (page) for each person in **qryFac-CA**.

29. In the folder **Lesson 13**, save the merged document as **CA_letters** and save the changes to the original Word file. Exit both Word files.

Using Advanced Navigation Techniques

TIP

Typically, designing a database involves planning table structures, identifying fields, establishing relationships, designing forms and reports, and creating macros and modules.

Two techniques to assist users to navigate database objects are a custom navigation pane and navigation forms. A *custom navigation pane* is a method of organizing major database objects along common activities and tasks. A *navigation form* is a form that contains menus and command buttons, allowing a user to navigate around major database objects.

Custom navigation panes and navigation forms are simple methods to add low-level security to your database by displaying or hiding major objects.

EXERCISE 13-14   CUSTOM NAVIGATION PANE

To limit the groups and objects viewed in the Navigation Pane by a user, you can create custom categories and groups. A custom category is visible only in the database in which it was created.

Objects that are placed in Custom groups are hidden, and a shortcut is placed in the Group. Not all objects need to be added the custom groups.

1. In the **Navigation Pane**, click the **All Access Objects** and choose **Custom**.

2. Click the **Custom Group 1**. This group is empty; all major objects are located in the **Unassigned Objects** group.

3. Right-click the **Custom Group 1** bar, and choose **Rename**.

4. Key **Sales** and press Enter.

5. Drag **tblShipments** up to the **Sales** bar to add the table to the group.

6. Drag **tblShipDetails** to the **Sales** group.

7. Scroll down the list of objects until you reach the queries.

8. While pressing Ctrl, click the following queries:

   qryCarrierOptions
   qrySalesByRegion
   qryShipByMonthNum
   qryShipDetails-Main
   qryShipDetails-Sub

9. Right-click the selected queries. From the pop-up menu, select **Add to group** and choose **Sales**.

10. Scroll down to the bottom of the **Navigation Pane**. Select **rptShipDetails-Main**, **rptShipDetails-Sub**, and **rptShipSummary**.

11. Right-click the selected queries. From the pop-up menu, select **Add to group** and choose **Sales**.

12. From the **File** tab, click **Options** 📄.

13. In the left pane, click **Current Database**. Click the **Navigation Options** button.

14. In the **Navigation Options** dialog box, in the **Categories** panel, click **Custom**. The custom group **Sales** now appears in the right panel.

15. Click **Add Group** button and key **Inventory**.

16. Click the Move Up button to move the **Inventory** group above **Sales**.

Figure 13-15
Custom group
EcoMed-13.accdb

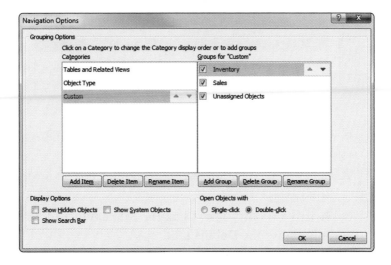

17. In the **Navigation Options** dialog box, click **Add Group** button and key **Customers**. Click **OK**.

18. In the **Access Option** dialog box, click **OK**. The two new groups are ready to have objects added to them.

Exercise 13-15   CREATE A NAVIGATION FORM

You now will create a navigation form that can be used for people to select specific forms and reports to view and print. You will use two tabs. The first tab will have objects related to management companies. The second tab will have objects related to facilities.

1. From the **Create** tab, in the **Forms** group, click **Navigation** 🖾 and choose **Horizontal Tabs, 2 Levels**.

2. The form has two levels of controls. Click the top (level 1) **[Add New]** placeholder tab and key **Management**. Press **Enter**. A new tab appears on level 1.

3. On level 2, click the **[Add New]** placeholder tab and key **Details**.

4. Click the second **[Add New]** placeholder tab on level 1 and key **Facility**. Press ⌈Enter⌉. Notice that the second level only has one placeholder tab. Each level 1 tab has its own level 2 tabs.

5. Click the **[Add New]** placeholder tab on the level 2 and key **Details**. Press ⌈Enter⌉.

Figure 13-16
Navigation Form tabs
EcoMed-13.accdb

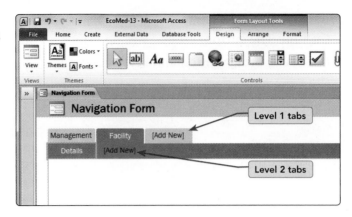

6. Click the next **[Add New]** placeholder tab on level 2 and key **Contacts**. Press Enter.

7. Click the next **[Add New]** placeholder tab on level 2 and key **Sales**. Press Enter.

8. Switch to **Form View**. Click the **Management** tab. Notice that level 2 only shows the **Details** tab.

9. Click the **Facility** tab. Notice that level 2 only shows three tabs.

10. Switch to **Layout View**.

11. Click the **Details** tab under the **Management** tab. Press F4 to open the **Property Sheet** for the navigation controls.

12. On the **Data** tab, in the property **Navigation Target Name**, click the drop-down arrow. A list of all the forms and reports in the database are listed.

13. Choose **Form.frmManagement**. The form has been added to the navigation form.

14. Save the form as **frmNav-Customers**.

15. Switch to **Form View**. Notice that there are logos in both **frmNav-Customers** and **frmManagement**.

16. Close the form.

Exercise 13-16   MODIFY A NAVIGATION FORM

You will now modify the navigation form that you created. The forms that will be used in the navigation form should not have a header or footer since the navigation form already has these sections. For forms that show only one record at a time, you should also include command buttons to move through the records.

1. Open **frmManagement** in **Design View**.

2. In the **Form Header**, click the **Logo** control. Press Delete.

3. In the **Title** control, remove "EcoMed -" from the title and press Enter.

4. Open **frmFacContacts** in **Design View**. There are four command buttons in this form.

5. In the **Detail** section, select all four command buttons and press Ctrl+C.

6. Switch to the **Design View** of **frmManagement**. Click the **Detail** section bar and press Ctrl+V. The command buttons have been added to the top of the **Detail** section.

7. Drag the command buttons under the **ContractEnds** text box without adding them to the control layout.

8. Save and close both forms.

9. Open **frmNav-Customers**. The navigation form now shows the new **frmManagement**.

10. Switch to **Layout View**.

11. In the form, click the **Facility** tab. Now click the **Details** tab.

12. In the controls **Property Sheet**, on the **Data** tab, in the property **Navigation Target Name**, choose **Form.frmFacilities**.

13. In the form, click the **Contacts** tab.

14. On the **Data** tab, in the property **Navigation Target Name**, choose **Form.frmFacContacts**.

15. In the form, click the **Sales** tab.

16. On the **Data** tab, in the property **Navigation Target Name**, choose **Report.rptFacSales-Main**.

17. Switch to **Form View**.

18. Test each of the tabs.

Figure 13-17
Two-level navigation form
EcoMed-13.accdb

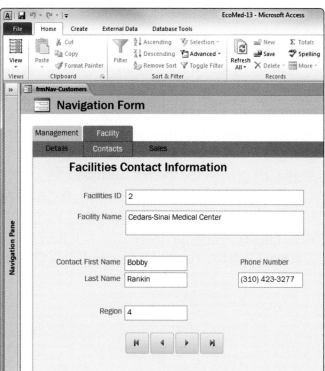

19. Close and save the form.

Using Security Tools

Access 2010 provides several tools to help make your data and workstation more secure. For example, you can trust a database temporarily or permanently. You also can add a password and encrypt a database.

You can trust the database permanently by placing the database in a trusted location. A *trusted location* is a local or network folder on a workstation that a user marks as trusted. When you move a database to a trusted location, the security warning in the Message Bar no longer displays.

Adding a password to your database helps keep unauthorized people from opening your database. Be cautious when creating and assigning passwords. If you forget the password, there is no method by which it can be retrieved. You can lock yourself permanently out of your own database.

Encrypting is the process of obscuring information to make it virtually unreadable. The encryption tool in Office Access 2010 forces a database user to enter a password before deciphering the database. Encryption is a safeguard for information transported across the Internet.

Exercise 13-17   USING THE TRUST CENTER

The Trust Center is a dialog box that provides a single location to set security options for Access 2010. You use the Trust Center to set security options or change trusted locations. The Trust Center settings affect how new and existing databases behave.

The Trust Center also contains logic for evaluating the components in a database and determining whether the database is safe to open or whether the Trust Center should let you decide to enable a database's contents. Since you are using a workstation that is used by other students, you will be directed to delete the Trusted folder at the end of this exercise. Leaving the Trusted folder could provide a method for files that have malicious code to be enabled.

1. From the **File** tab, click **Options** 🖹.
2. In the left pane, click **Trust Center**. In the **Microsoft Office Access Trust Center** section, click **Trust Center Settings**.
3. In the left pane, click **Trusted Locations**.
4. Click **Add new location**. In the **Microsoft Office Trusted Location** dialog box, click **Browse**.
5. Select the **Documents** folder and click **New Folder**. Name the folder **Trusted**. Click the **Trusted** folder and click **OK**.

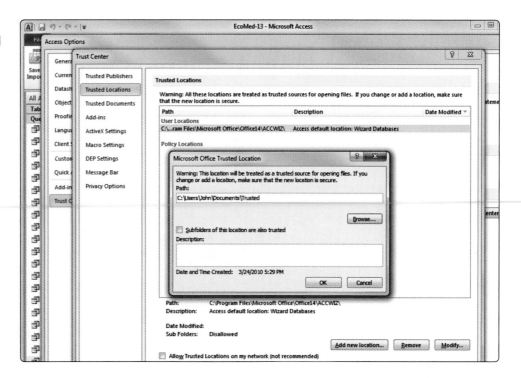

6. Click **OK**. The **Trusted** folder is now a Trusted Location. Click **OK** twice.

7. Close the database. Copy the database *[your initials]*-**EcoMed-13** and paste a copy in the folder **Trusted**.

8. Open the database located in the **Trusted** folder. Access did not ask you to enable the content of the database.

9. From the File tab, click **Options** 📄.

10. In the left pane, click Trust Center. In the Microsoft Office Access Trust Center section, click Trust Center Settings.

11. In the left pane, click Trusted Locations.

12. In the User Locations section, click **. . . Documents\Trusted** and click Remove. This action removes the folder as a Trusted Location.

13. Click **OK** twice. Close the database.

14. Delete the folder **Trusted** and the database inside.

Exercise 13-18   USE THE DATABASE SPLITTER

Access has a utility that will split a database into a front-end and a back-end database. A *front-end database* is a database interface that integrates data stored in another database. A *back-end database* is a database that contains data utilized by other applications.

A front-end database contains major objects such as queries, forms, and reports, but no tables. A back-end database contains tables and standardized major objects that structure the data used by one or more front-end applications.

Splitting a database protects record source data structure while allowing front-end users to develop independent forms, reports, and queries. Multiple unique front-end designs can be linked to a single standardized back-end database.

Figure 13-19
Front-end database sharing back-end data

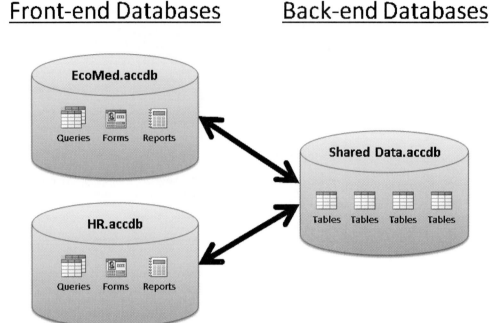

1. In the **Lesson 13** folder, make a copy of *[your initials]*-**EcoMed-13** and name the copy *[your initials]*-EcoMed-Front.

2. Open and enable *[your initials]*-**EcoMed-Front**.

3. Notice the title bar is still showing **EcoMed-13**. From the File tab, click **Options** 🖪.

4. In the left pane, click Current Database. Delete the content of the Application Title.

5. Click OK. The current name of the database is now shown.

6. From the Database Tools tab, in the Move Data group, click Access Database 🗃.

7. Read the Database Splitter dialog box and click Split Database.

8. Change the filename to Shared Data and click Split. The message box tells you that the database has been split.

9. Click OK. The tables in this database are now linked to **Shared Data** and **HR-13**.

10. Open the table **tblCarriers**. Data can still be added but changes to the table's structure must be done in the **Shared Data** database.

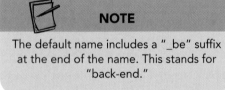

NOTE

The default name includes a "_be" suffix at the end of the name. This stands for "back-end."

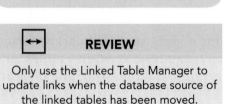

REVIEW

Only use the Linked Table Manager to update links when the database source of the linked tables has been moved.

11. Close the table.

12. From the **File** tab, click **Close Database** 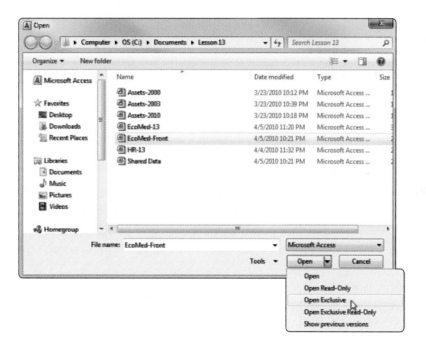.

Exercise 13-19   ENCRYPT AND DECRYPT A DATABASE

To encrypt a database, the original file must be closed. A new database must be created. When another person opens the encrypted database, Access decodes each object as it is opened. This function slows performance but adds security.

To assign a password, you must open the database for exclusive use. This status means that in a multi-user environment, no one else can open the database while you are using it. To change or remove the password, you also must open it exclusively.

1. From the **File** tab, click **Open**.

2. In the **Open** dialog box, locate the **Lesson 13** folder, and select *[your initials]*-**EcoMed-Front**. Click the **Open** drop-down arrow. Choose **Open Exclusive**.

Figure 13-20
Opening a database
for exclusive use

3. Enable the content of the database.

4. From the **File** tab, on the **Info** tab, click **Encrypt with Password**.

5. In the **Password** text box, key **123**. Press Tab.

6. In the **Verify** text box, key **123**. Click **OK** twice.

7. From the **File** tab, click **Close Database**.

8. From the **File** tab, click **Open**, select **EcoMed-Front**.

9. Click the **Open** drop-down arrow. Choose **Open Exclusive**.

10. In the **Password Required** dialog box, key **123**. Click **OK**.

11. From the **File** tab, on the **Info** tab, click **Decrypt Database** 🗐.

12. In the **Unset Database Password** dialog box, key **123**. Click **OK**. The database no longer is encrypted or has a password.

13. Close the database and Access.

Lesson 13   Summary

- Access databases are upwardly but not downwardly compatible. That means you can open an Access 2003 database in Access 2010, but you cannot open an Access 2010 database in Access 2003.

- When using Office Access 2010, you do not need to convert Access 2000 or 2002-2003 databases.

- Access 97 or earlier format databases are converted into Access 2002-2003 format by default and then can be converted to Access 2010.

- When you convert a 2010 database to a previous version file format, the database loses the ability to use the advanced features available only in Access 2007 or 2010.

- Whenever you routinely import data from similarly structured files, you can save the import specifications.

- Each time you launch an import or export operation, you can save additional specifications for future use.

- An advantage of using an XML file format over a text file is the ease in transforming the data to different applications such as Word, Excel, or non-Access databases.

- An HTML file format provides a means for describing the structure of text-based information in a document.

- Mail Merge is a word processing feature that creates a merged document by combining a source document and a record source from an external file.

- Two techniques to assist users navigate database objects are a custom navigation pane and a navigation form.

- Access 2010 provides several tools to help make your data and workstation more secure, such as trusting a database, adding a password, and encrypting a database.

- Trust Center allows a user to set security options or change trusted locations.

- Splitting a database into a front-end and a back-end database provides a level of security.

- To assign a password, you must open the database for exclusive use.

Command Summary

Feature	Button	Task Path	Keyboard
Create, Navigation Form		Create, Forms, Navigation	
Database, Decrypt		File, Info, Decrypt Database	
Database, Encrypt		File, Info, Encrypt with Password	
Database, Split		Database Tools, Move Data, Access Database	
Export, Mail Merge		External Data, Export, Word Merge	
Export, Saved Exports		External Data, Export, Saved Exports	
Export, Text File		External Data, Export, Text File	
Import, Saved Imports		External Data, Import & Link, Saved Imports	
Import, Text File		External Data, Import & Link, Text File	
Import, XML File		External Data, Import & Link, XML File	
Switch Windows		Home, Window, Switch Windows	

Concepts Review

True/False Questions

Each of the following statements is either true or false. Indicate your choice by circling T or F.

T F 1. An Access 2010 database uses the same file format as an Access 2003 database.

T F 2. A text file contains unformatted textual characters.

T F 3. An XLS file is a text file that stores table names, field names, field properties, and data.

T F 4. An advantage of using a text file format for exporting data is the ease in transforming the data into different applications.

T F 5. Custom categories and groups can limit the objects viewed in the **Navigation Pane**.

T F 6. You permanently can trust a database by placing it in a trusted location.

T F 7. The **Database Splitter** creates an exact copy of a database.

T F 8. Encrypting a database affects only the data in a database, but not the major objects.

Short Answer Questions

Write the correct answer in the space provided.

1. How can XML files be viewed?

_____

2. Name three common delimiters used in a text file.

_____

3. In the **Navigation Pane**, when the **Custom** view is being used, what is the default location of all major objects?

_____

4. What no longer displays when you place a database in a trusted location?

_____

5. What two major objects can a navigation form show?

_____

6. What is the most common use for a Mail Merge document?

_____

7. In a multi-user environment, how must you open a database before assigning a password?

_____

8. How can you protect a record source data structure while allowing front-end users to develop independent forms, reports, and queries?

_____

Critical Thinking

Answer these questions on a separate page. There are no right or wrong answers. Support your answers with examples from your own experience, if possible.

1. What are the reasons for converting a database from Access 2010 to an older version? What are the reasons for not converting?

2. Discuss the reasons for adding a password to a database.

Skills Review

Exercise 13-20

You have been asked to convert a database that has hotel information to Access 2010 and password protect the database.

1. Convert a database by following these steps:
   a. Locate and open the **Lesson 13** folder.
   b. Open and enable the database **Hotels**.
   c. From the File tab, on the Save & Publish tab, select Access Database as the new file type and click the Save As button.
   d. Locate the **Lesson 13** folder and name the file *[your initials]* -Hotels-2010.
   e. Enable the content for the new database.

2. Export data as a HTML file by following these steps:
   a. Open the table **Hotels** and add your full name as a new hotel name. Close the table.
   b. In the Navigation Pane, right-click the table **Hotels** and select Export, then choose HTML Document.
   c. Add a check mark to the Export data with formatting and layout option.
   d. Save the file in the **Lesson 13** folder and name it 13-20-A.
   e. In the Export – HTML Document dialog box, click OK. In the HTML Output Options dialog box, click OK then Close.

13-20-A.html
2 Pages

3. Encrypt with password a database by following these steps:

    a. From the **File** tab, click **Close Database**.

    b. From the **File** tab, click **Open**.

    c. In the **Lesson 13** folder, select *[your initials]*-**Hotels-2010**.

    d. Click the drop-down arrow next to the **Open** button and choose **Open Exclusive**.

    e. From the **File** tab, on the **Info** tab, click **Encrypt with Password**.

    f. Key **123** for the **Password** and again in the **Verify** control. Click **OK**.

    g. Close the database.

Assessment

- Turn in the database *[your initials]*-**Hotels-2010.accdb** only when all assigned exercises have been completed, according to your classroom procedure.
- According to your class procedures, print or turn in the HTML file **13-20-A.html**.

- OR -

- According to your class procedures, print or turn in the HTML file **13-20-A.html**.

Exercise 13-21

EcoMed Services will be purchasing shirts for all its employees. You have been asked to import the text file listing the employees and their shirt preferences.

1. Open a database by following these steps:

    a. Locate and open the **Lesson 13** folder.

    b. If you already have a copy of *[your initials]*-**HR-13**, skip to step 1d.

    c. Make a copy of **HR-13** and rename it to *[your initials]*-**HR-13**.

    d. Open and enable content for *[your initials]*-**HR-13**.

2. Import data from a text file by following these steps:

    a. From the **External Data** tab, in the **Import & Link** group, click **Text File** ▣.

    b. In the **Get External Data** dialog box, click the **Browse** button.

    c. In the **Lesson 13** folder, double-click the text file **Shirts**.

    d. Select the option **Import the source data into a new table in the current database** and click **OK**.

e. In the Import Text Wizard, you can see that the data is delimited, so click Next.

f. Add a checkmark to First Row Contains Field Names and click Next.

g. Change the **Employee ID** field's Indexed property to Yes (No Duplicates). Click Next.

h. Select Choose my own primary key. **Employee ID** should appear in the combo box. Click Next.

i. Name the table tblEmpShirts. Click Finish.

j. In the Get External Data dialog box, click Close.

3. Modify a table by following these steps:

a. Open **tblEmpShirts** in Design View.

b. For the field **Style**, change the **Field Size** to 30.

c. For the field **Size**, change the **Field Size** to 10.

d. For the field **Color**, change the **Field Size** to 20.

e. Save the table. Click Yes to the warning dialog box.

f. Close the table.

Assessment

- Turn in the database only when all assigned exercises have been completed, according to your classroom procedure.

- OR -

- Create a Database Documenter report by following these steps:

a. From the Database Tools tab, in the Analyze group, click Database Documenter 📄.

b. On the Tables tab, select **tblEmpShirts**.

c. Click Options.

d. For Table, include only Properties.

e. From the Include for Fields section, choose Names, Data Types, and Sizes.

f. From the Include for Indexes section, choose Nothing.

g. Click OK twice to go to Print Preview.

- Save a Database Documenter report by following these steps:

a. From the Print Preview tab, in the Data group, click PDF or XPS 📥 to save the printout as a file.

b. Save the file as a PDF and name the file *[your initials]*-13-21-A.

c. Depending on your class procedures, print or turn in the PDF file.

13-21-A.pdf
1 Page

Exercise 13-22

You have been asked by your supervisor to create a navigation form to assist the human resources department to manage employee information.

1.   Modify a form by following these steps:
   a. Open and enable content for *[your initials]*-**HR13**.
   b. Open **frmEmpAge** in **Design View**.
   c. Select the **Logo** control and press [Delete].
   d. Open **frmEmpAnniverDates** in **Design View**.
   e. Copy all four command buttons.
   f. Switch to **frmEmpAge** and paste the controls into the **Design View**.
   g. Move the command buttons below the other controls in the section.
   h. Save and close both forms.

2.   Create a navigation form by following these steps:
   a. From the **Create** tab, in the **Forms** group, click **Navigation** 🔲 and choose **Horizontal Tabs, 2 Levels**.
   b. Click the level 1 **[Add New]** placeholder tab and key **Employees**.
   c. Click the level 2 **[Add New]** placeholder tab and key **Ages**.
   d. Click the next level 2 **[Add New]** placeholder tab and key **Anniversaries**.
   e. From the **Design** tab, in the **Header/Footer** group, click **Logo** 🖼. Locate the **Lesson 13** folder and double-click **Logo_sm**. Resize the **Logo** so it fits the header.
   f. Modify the **Title** control to **EcoMed – Employee Information**.
   g. From the **Design** tab, in the **Controls** group, click Label 🔤, then click to the right of the **Title** control in the **Form Header**.
   h. Key **Prepared by:** *[your full name]*.
   i. Save the form as **frmNav-Emp**.

3.   Assign objects to the navigation form by following these steps:
   a. Click the **Ages** tab under the **Employees** tab. Press [F4] to open the **Property Sheet** for the navigation controls.
   b. On the **Data** tab, in the property **Navigation Target Name**, click the drop-down arrow and choose **frmEmpAge**.
   c. Click the **Anniversaries** tab.
   d. On the **Data** tab, in the property **Navigation Target Name**, click the drop-down arrow and choose **frmEmpAnniverDates**.
   e. Save the form.

Assessment

- Turn in your database only when all assigned exercises have been completed, according to your classroom procedure.

- OR -

13-22-A.pdf
1 Page

13-22-B.pdf
1 Page

- Save a form by following these steps:

   a. In **frmNav-Emp**, click the **Ages** tab.
   b. Click the **File** tab and from the **Print** option, click **Print Preview** .
   c. From the **Print Preview** tab, in the **Data** group, click **PDF or XPS** to save the printout as a file.
   d. In the **Publish as PDF or XPS** dialog box, click the **Option** button. Select the **Pages** option. Print only page **1** and click **OK**.
   e. Save the file as a PDF and name the file *[your initials]*-**13-22-A**.

- Save a form by following these steps:

   a. In **frmNav-Emp**, click the **Anniversaries** tab.
   b. Click the **File** tab and from the **Print** option, click **Print Preview** .
   c. From the **Print Preview** tab, in the **Data** group, click **PDF or XPS** to save the printout as a file.
   d. In the **Publish as PDF or XPS** dialog box, click the **Option** button. Select the **Pages** option. Print only page **1** and click **OK**.
   e. Save the file as a PDF and name the file *[your initials]*-**13-22-B**.
   e. Depending on your class procedures, print or turn in both PDF files.

Exercise 13-23

You have been asked to merge and print a letter that will go out to all management companies in Wisconsin.

1. Start a Mail Merge letter by following these steps:
   a. Open, enable, and update links for *[your initials]*-**EcoMed-13**.
   b. Select **qryMgt-WI**. There is only one record in this query.
   c. From the **External Data** tab, in the **Export** group, click **Word Merge** .
   d. Select **Link your data to as existing Microsoft Word document** and click **OK**.
   e. Locate the **Lesson 13** folder and choose **WECC letter**. Click **Open**.

2. Add a date and address block to a letter by following these steps:
   a. In the letter, select **<Date>**.
   b. Form the **Insert** tab, in the **Text** group, click **Date & Time** .
   c. Select the third option in the list.
   d. Add a checkmark to **Update automatically**. Click **OK**.

e. Press [Enter] and delete "<Address Block>".

f. In the **Mail Merge** pane, click **Next: Write your letter**.

g. In step 4 of the **Mail Merge**, click **Address block**.

h. Click **Match Fields**.

i. For the **First Name** field, click the drop-down arrow and choose **ContactFirstName**.

j. For the **Last Name** field, click the drop-down arrow and choose **ContactLastName**.

k. For the **Company** field, click the drop-down arrow and choose **ManageName**. Click **OK**.

l. Click **OK** to finish the **Address block**.

3. Add fields to a letter by following these steps:

a. In the letter, select "<Contact First Name>".

b. From the **Mailings** tab, in the **Write & Insert Fields** group, click the bottom half of the **Insert Merge Field** button and choose **ContactFirstName**.

c. Select "<Contact Last Name>".

d. From the **Mailings** tab, in the **Write & Insert Fields** group, click the bottom of the **Insert Merge Field** button and choose **ContactLastName**.

e. Near the bottom of the letter, select <Manage Name>.

f. From the **Mailings** tab, in the **Write & Insert Fields** group, click the bottom of the **Insert Merge Field** button and choose **ManageName**.

4. Finalize a merged letter by following these steps:

a. In the **Mail Merge** pane, click **Next: Preview your letters**.

b. Press [Ctrl]+[A] to select all of the text.

c. From the **Home** tab, in the **Font** group, change the font color to black.

d. After the last line in the letter, press [Enter] three times and key **Prepared by:** *[your full name]*.

e. In the **Mail Merge** pane, click **Next: Complete the merge** and then click **Edit individual letters**.

f. Click **OK** in the **Merge to New Document** dialog box Merge all the letters into one file.

g. Save the new Word document as **13-23-A**.

h. Save and close both Word files.

13-23-A.docx
1 Page

Assessment

- Depending on your class procedures, print or turn in the Word file **13-23-A**.

- OR -

- Depending on your class procedures, print or turn in the Word file **13-23-A**.

Lesson Applications

Exercise 13-24

You have been asked to convert a database that has hotel information to Access 2010 and export information to an XML file.

1. Open and convert the database **CarRentals** to a 2007 format.

2. Save the new database as *[your initials]*-CarRentals-2010.

3. In the table **USCarRentalCompanies**, add your full name as a new car company.

4. Export the table **USCarRentalCompanies** as an XML file. Embed the schema data inside the XML file. Do not export any presentation data. Name the file **13-24-A**.

5. Encrypt the database and set the password to **123**.

13-24-A.xml
2 Pages

Assessment

- Turn in the database **CarRentals-2010-*[your initials]*** only when all assigned exercises have been completed, according to your classroom procedures.
- According to your class procedures, print or turn in the XML file.

- OR -

- Open **CarRentals-2010-*[your initials]*.**
- Create a **Database Documenter** report for the **Current Database** including only the **Properties**.
- Save the report as a PDF. Name the file *[your initials]*-13-24-B.
- According to your class procedures, print or turn in the XML and PDF files.

13-24-B.pdf
1 Page

Exercise 13-25

You have been asked by your supervisor to import car rental data a text file. Both files will be imported into the same table.

1. Open and enable *[your initials]*-**CarRentals-2010.accdb**, which you created in Exercise 13-24.

2. Import the data from the file **CarRental-Abroad** to create a new table called **tblCarRental-Abroad**.

3. The data contain field names and will need the wizard to add a primary key.

4. Change the primary key field to **RentalID**.

5. Change the field **Company**'s Field Size to 40.

6. Change the field **Phone Number**'s Field Size to 10.

7. Save and close the table.

Assessment

- Turn in your database only when all assigned exercises have been completed, according to your classroom procedure.

- OR -

- Create a Database Documenter report for **tblCarRental-Abroad** using the following settings:

  • Include for Table: Properties only

  • Include for Fields: Names, Data Types, and Sizes

  • Include for Indexes – Nothing

- Save the report as a PDF. Name the file *[your initials]*-13-25-A.

- According to your class procedures, print or turn in the PDF file.

13-25-A.pdf
1 Page

Exercise 13-26

You have been asked to create a navigation form that will show vender and inventory data. You will need to modify the associated forms before they are assigned to the navigation form.

1. Open, enable, and update the links for *[your initials]*-**EcoMed-13**.

2. Remove the Logo, Date, and Time controls from **frmVender**.

3. In the **Detail** section, add four command buttons to navigate through the records in this form.

4. Create a new two-level, horizontal tabbed navigation form.

5. Add the EcoMed logo and modify the title to read *EcoMed – Inventory information*. Make the color of the **Form Header** #EFF2F7.

6. Add a label to the **Form Header** with the caption **Prepared by:** *[your full name]*.

7. The level one tab should be **Inventory**.

8. The level two tabs should be **Details** and **Vender**.

9. Assign to the **Details** tab the form **rptInvDetails**.

10. Assign to the **Vender** tab the form **frmVender**.

11. Save the navigation form as **frmNav-Inv**.

Assessment

- Turn in your database only when all assigned exercises have been completed, according to your classroom procedures.

- OR -

- In **frmNav-Inv**, select the tab **Inventory** and then **Details**.
- Save **frmNav-Inv** as a PDF. Save only the first page of the form. Name the file *[your initials]*-13-26-A.
- In **frmNav-Inv**, select the tab **Inventory** and then **Vender**.
- Save **frmNav-Inv** as a PDF. Save only the first page of the form. Name the file *[your initials]*-13-26-B.
- According to your class procedures, print or turn in both PDF files.

13-26-A.pdf
1 Page

13-26-B.pdf
1 Page

Exercise 13-27 ◆ Challenge Yourself

You have been asked to send a letter to facility number 22. You will need to create a query and merge the records with a Word file.

1. Open, enable, and update links for *[your initials]*-EcoMed-13.

2. Create a query using the data from **tblFacilities**. Include the name of the facility, contact names, number of beds, and mailing address information. Create a criterion to show only the **Facilities ID** "22".

13-27-A.docx
1 Page

3. The data in the **State** field are lower case. Modify the query to change these data to all capital letters and use the alias **St**. Save the query as **qryFac-Best**.

4. Merge the record in **qryFac-Best** with the Word document **Best hospital letter**. Replace the place holders in the letter with data from Access. The address block should include the name of the contact person and the facility's name.

5. Insert a date that will update each time the letter is printed. At the bottom of the letter, key **Prepared by:***[your full name]*. All of the text in the letter should be black.

6. Save the individual letter as **13-27-A**.

Assessment

- Depending on your class procedures, print or turn in the Word file **13-27-A**.

- OR -

- Depending on your class procedures, print or turn in the Word file **13-27-A**.

On Your Own

In these exercises you work on your own, as you would in a real-life work environment. Use the skills you've learned to accomplish the task—and be creative.

Exercise 13-28

Review the design of the database you modified in Exercise 12-33. Using the Documenter, print the structure of your database. Include the properties, relationships, and permissions for your tables and queries. Include the names, data types, and field sizes. Include the names and field names for the indexes. On each printout, write your name and "Exercise 13-28a." Split your database. Verify your links. Print the structure of the split databases. On each printout, write your name and "Exercise 13-28b." Continue to the next exercise.

Exercise 13-29

Create a navigation form for your primary database. Add your forms, reports, and queries to the navigation form. Print/save the navigation form. Continue to the next exercise.

Exercise 13-30

Encrypt your primary database. Print/save each form of your navigation form. Submit to your instructor printouts from Exercise 13-28 through 13-30. Keep a copy of the database you modified in this lesson. You will use it for the On Your Own exercises in subsequent lessons.

Lesson 14

Using Special Controls and Tools

OBJECTIVES   *After completing this lesson, you will be able to:*

1. Add and format an option group.

2. Change control types.

3. Use list and combo boxes.

4. Use tab controls in a form.

5. Create and modify charts.

6. Add hyperlinks.

Estimated Time: 1½ hours

Access provides advanced controls and tools that can be used to improve the accuracy and efficiency of data entry. If you need to control the accuracy of data entered, you can use several of these controls to restrict or limit the manner by which a user can enter data. For example, rather than allowing a user to key data directly to a text field, you can add these specialized controls to display a list from which a user can select.

Not all controls are appropriate for use with every form. Some controls are appropriate for text values. Other controls are appropriate for only Yes/No fields. Most likely you are familiar with these types of controls.

If you have ever been at a restaurant and completed a customer satisfaction survey, the choices for a question asking about the service that you received might be: very good, good, poor, and very poor. This question would allow for you to select only one answer. Another single-answer question might ask a Yes/No question such as, "Will you return to this restaurant?" Other questions might have the option of more than one possible answer such as, "At what other restaurants do you eat?" That question would allow for more than one answer.

Adding and Formatting an Option Group

Whenever a field has a limited number of possible answers, you can use an option group. An *option group* is a control object bound to a single field containing a set of controls representing choices. An option group allows a user to view all valid choices but limits the user to select one or more choices from the list. Choices in an option group can be represented as check boxes, toggle buttons, or option buttons.

Exercise 14-1   ADD A NEW FIELD TO A TABLE

You have been asked to add an option group to assign interns to specific departments. Before creating an option group on a form, you must modify the underlying table structure to accept the new format. The value selected by an option group is stored in a numeric field. Whenever a user selects a choice in the option group, only the numeric value is stored.

1. Copy **EcoMed-14**, **HR-14**, and **Shared Data-14**. Add your initials to the beginning of each copied file.

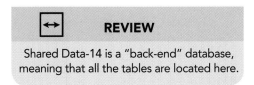

REVIEW

Shared Data-14 is a "back-end" database, meaning that all the tables are located here.

2. Open and enable *[your initials]*-**Shared Data-14** database.

3. Open **tblInterns** in Datasheet View. The **Department** field contains each department's name. Switch to Design View.

4. Click the Field Name **Department**. It is a Text field.

5. From the Design tab, in the Tools group, click Insert Rows.

6. Name the new field DeptID and press Tab.

7. Click the drop-down arrow and choose Number. This field will contain integers.

8. Save and switch to Datasheet View.

9. Right-click in the **Department** column and choose Sort A to Z.

10. Click in the field **DeptID** for the first record and key **1**. The ID "1" will stand for "Administrative."

11. Finish entering the values for the field **DeptID** using the following information.

DeptID	Department
1	Administrative
2	Human Resources
3	Marketing
4	Sales
5	Shipping
6	Stocking

Figure 14-1
Populating a new field
**Shared Data-14.
accdb
tblInterns**

te ▾	DeptID ▾	Department ⊣
2/2010	1	Administrative
7/2010	1	Administrative
5/2010	2	Human Resources
5/2010	3	Marketing
5/2010	4	Sales
8/2010	4	Sales
9/2010	4	Sales
9/2010	5	Shipping
5/2010	5	Shipping
5/2010	5	Shipping
9/2010	6	Stocking
8/2010	6	Stocking

12. Click the **Department** column header to select the entire column.

13. From the Home tab, in the Records group, click Delete ☒. Click Yes to the message box.

14. Save the changes and close the table.

15. Click the File tab, and click Close Database 🗗 to close the database without closing Access.

Exercise 14-2 CREATE AN OPTION GROUP

Now that you have created and populated the numeric department field, you can add the option group to the intern form.

1. On the File tab, click Open 🖼. Locate the database *[your initials]-***HR-14** and click Open.

2. Enable the content and update the links with *[your initials]-***Shared Data-14**.

3. Open **frmInterns**. The **Department** control is broken because we deleted the field to which it was bound.

4. Switch to Design View. Click the **Department** text box and click the Error indicator. Read that the field no longer exists.

5. From the Error indicator, choose Edit the Control's Control Source Property.

6. Click the Control Source property's drop-down arrow and choose **DeptID**. Switch to Form View.

7. Navigate through a few records. The **DeptID** control only shows a number. Return to Design View.

8. Delete the **DeptID** control.

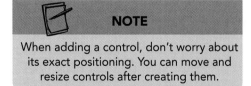
NOTE

When adding a control, don't worry about its exact positioning. You can move and resize controls after creating them.

9. From the Design tab, in the Controls group, click Option Group 🖂 and then click under the **Intern ID** control.

10. In the Option Group Wizard, key **Administrative**. Press Tab to move to the next row.

11. Key **Human Resources**, **Marketing**, **Sales**, **Shipping**, and **Stocking** in the other rows.

Figure 14-2
Entering labels for
the option buttons
HR-14.accdb
frmInterns

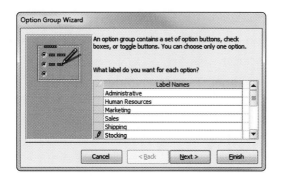

12. Click **Next**. Click the option for **No, I don't want a default**. Click **Next**.

13. In the next dialog box, the wizard assigns each department a numeric value. These values, not the label names, are stored in **tblInterns**, the underlying recordset for the form.

Figure 14-3
Each label is
assigned a value.
HR-14.accdb
frmInterns

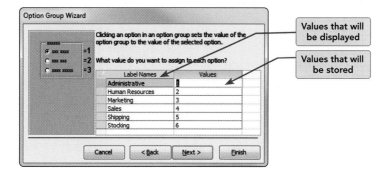

14. Click **Next**. Click the option for **Store the value in this field**. Click the drop-down arrow and choose **DeptID** from the list. Click **Next**.

15. In the next dialog box, click each of the different controls that can be part of the option group control. Choose **Option buttons** for the type of control and **Sunken** for the style. Click **Next**.

16. Edit the default caption to **Department**. Click **Finish**.

17. Move the option group control so that it fits inside of the white box. Save the form.

Exercise 14-3 MODIFY AND USE THE OPTION GROUP

You will now change the appearance of the option group. The visual appearance of the option group should identify the purpose and values for the field.

An option group consists of four elements that can be formatted separately. The four option group elements are:

• Option group frame: Possesses an independent property sheet that includes settings for the frame and the option group as a whole.

- Option group label: Title for the frame.
- Option button: Boolean image that allows the user to choose a predefined option.
- Option button label: Text describing option value.

Figure 14-4
Parts of an option group
HR-14.accdb
frmInterns

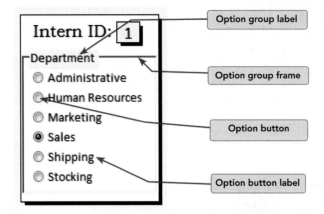

1. Switch to **Form View**. Scroll through a few records. The selected option changes to match the **DeptID** in the recordset.
2. Return to **Design View**. Click any part of the option frame except the label. Check the **Property Sheet** to be sure it shows the **Selection type** is **Option Group**.
3. On the **Other** tab, in the **Name** property, key **grpDept**.

Figure 14-5
Option group
Property Sheet
HR-14.accdb
frmInterns

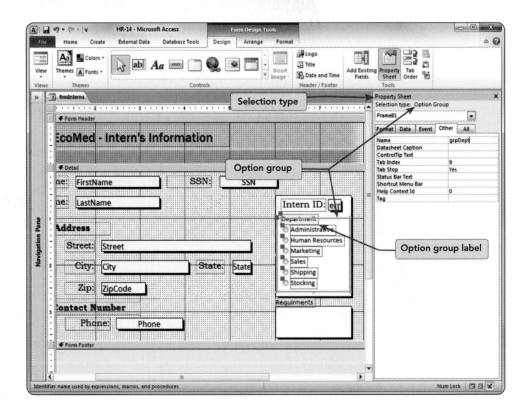

4. Press the down arrow. The object name updates. If you do not rename objects, they have names like "Frame14" that do not clearly identify them.

5. On the **Format** tab, click in the **Special Effect** property, choose **Etched**.

6. Click the label for **grpDept** control. In the control's **Property Sheet**, on the **Format** tab, click in the **Back Color** property. Click the Build button ▣ and choose **Automatic**.

7. In the **Font Weight** property, choose **Bold**.

8. Click the option group frame.

9. Select the first option button label (Administrative). On the **Format** tab, in the **Font Italic** property, choose **Yes**.

10. Repeat this step for the other five option button labels.

11. Click the first option button. On the **Format** tab, in the **Special Effect** property, choose **Raised**.

12. Repeat this step for the other five option button.

13. Click the first option button. Click the **Data** tab and check its **Option Value** property. This value will be stored if this option is selected.

14. Save the form and switch to **Form View**. For Intern #1, click the **Marketing** option button. The change to **DeptID** is stored in **tblInterns**.

TABLE 14-1 Standard Uses of Some Control Objects

Object	Usage
Check Box	Each check box is a Yes/No field. Used when all, some, or none of the choices can be selected. Used alone or in a group.
Option Button	Each button represents a unique value. Used with a limited number of values. Frequently embedded in an option group.
Option Group	Often used to limit selection to only one choice. Objects in group share a common subject or purpose.

Changing Control Types

When designing a form, you should select control types to match the form's purpose. Keep in mind that you want to improve the accuracy of the data entry as well as the speed by which the data can be entered. Depending on the data type of a field, you can change a control from one type to another. For example, because a check box is used for a Yes/No field, the check box can be changed to an option button or a toggle button.

Exercise 14-4   CHANGE A CHECK BOX TO AN OPTION BUTTON

Although the default control for a Yes/No field is a check box, a Yes/No field can be displayed as either a check box or option button. You have been asked to change the field that indicated whether or not an intern has received CPR training from a check box to an option button.

1. In **frmInterns**, switch to Design View.

2. From the Design tab, in the Controls group, click the Option Button 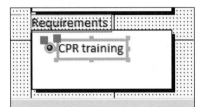 and click in the **Requirements** rectangle.

3. In the option button's Property Sheet, on the Data tab, in the Control Source property, choose CPR.

4. Click the option button's label. In its Property Sheet, on the Format tab, in the Caption property, key CPR training.

5. Widen the label so the caption is visible.

Figure 14-6
Format an Option
Button control
HR-14.accdb
frmInterns

6. Right-click the option button and choose Change To, then Check Box.

7. Switch to Form View and scroll through several records to find an intern that has not taken his or her CPR training.

8. Save the form.

Exercise 14-5   CHANGE A CHECK BOX TO A TOGGLE BUTTON

In addition to a check box or option button, you can use a toggle button for a Yes/No field. A *toggle button* is a control that acts as an on/off button in a form or report. A toggle button can display either text or an image. When using a toggle button, it is very important to format the toggle button control so that the user can tell what value the control is displaying.

1. Switch to Design View.

2. From the Design tab, in the Tools group, click Add Existing Fields 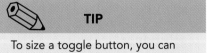.

3. From the Field List, drag the field **Safety** to the form under the **CPR** check box control.

4. The field appears as a check box. Delete the check box's label.

5. Right-click the **Safety** check box and choose Change To, then Toggle Button.

TIP

To size a toggle button, you can double-click a handle to fit its caption.

6. In the toggle button's Property Sheet, on the Format tab, in the Caption property, key Safety training?.

7. Size the button so you see the label.

8. Move the toggle button so that it is centered under the **CPR** control.

9. Switch to **Form View** and scroll through the records. The background and font (fore) color change depending on if the control is showing "Yes" or a "No" value.

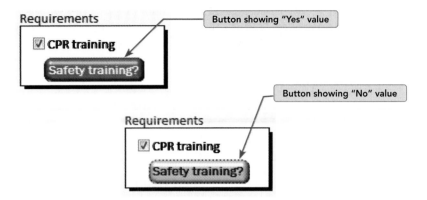

10. Switch to **Design View**. Click the **Safety** control.

11. From the **Design** tab, in the **Themes** group, click **Colors** and choose **Office**. This theme includes a green color option.

12. From the **Format** tab, in the **Control Formatting** group, click **Quick Style** and choose **Intense Effect – Olive Green, Accent 3** (row 6, column 4).

13. In the toggle button's **Property Sheet**, notice that the **Back Color**, **Border Color**, and **Fore Color** properties show **Quick Style**. Other properties like **Hover Color**, **Pressed Color**, **Hover Fore Color**, and **Pressed Fore Color** are also changed by the **Quick Style** command.

14. On the **Format** tab, click the **Pressed Fore Color** property. Click the Build button, and in the **Theme Colors** section, choose **Black, Text 1** (row 1, column 2).

15. From the **Format** tab, in the **Control Formatting** group, click **Shape Effect** and choose **Shadow** then **No Shadow**.

16. Switch to **Form View** and scroll through the records. The font (fore) color is black if the control is showing "Yes" or white when the value is "No."

17. Save and close the form.

Using List and Combo Boxes

Improving the design of a form often requires knowing which type of control best improves the speed and accuracy of data entry. List boxes and combo boxes allow the user to enter data by selecting a value from a list rather than keying an entry. A *list box* is a control showing choices in a box. If more choices are available than can be visible in the box, the control displays a vertical scroll bar.

When you need to display more possible values than can be viewed easily through an option group, you should use a list box. List boxes ensure that only appropriate values are entered. Since the user is limited to the choices given in the list box, it is not possible to key inappropriate values.

Exercise 14-6   ADD A LIST BOX CONTROL

You will now add a list box control to the current employee form. You will use the list box wizard to create a list box control for employee job titles.

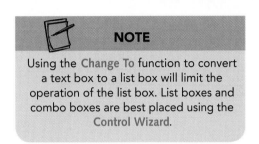

NOTE

Using the Change To function to convert a text box to a list box will limit the operation of the list box. List boxes and combo boxes are best placed using the Control Wizard.

1. Open **frmCurrentEmp** in Form View and scroll through several records to see how the form behaves. Switch to Design View.

2. Right-click the **JobCodeID** text box and choose Change To, then List Box.

3. Switch to Form View. The **JobCodeID** list box is empty because a list box has different data requirements than a text box.

4. Return to Design View.

5. Delete the **JobCodeID** control and its label.

6. From the Design tab, in the Controls group, click List Box 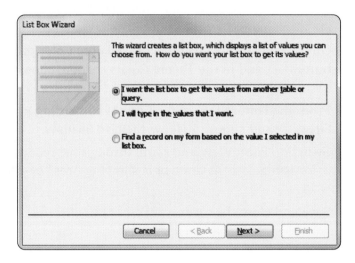 and click on the 5-inch mark on the horizontal ruler.

7. With the option I want the list box to get the values from another table or query selected, click Next.

Figure 14-8
List Box Wizard
dialog box
HR-14.accdb
frmCurrrentEmp

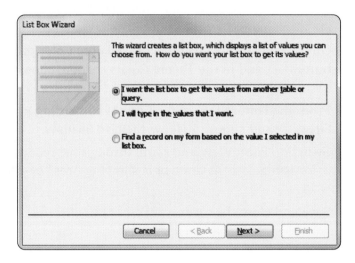

8. Choose Table: tblJobCodes and click Next.

9. In the Available Fields section, double-click **JobTitle** and click Next.

10. Choose **JobTitle** to be sorted in Ascending order and click Next.

11. Adjust the column width in the next dialog box so you can see all the job titles.

12. Click the **Hide key column** check box to deselect it. Both fields are shown. The values in the left column will be stored, and the values in the right column will be displayed in the list box.

Figure 14-9
List Box values
HR-14.accdb
frmCurrrentEmp

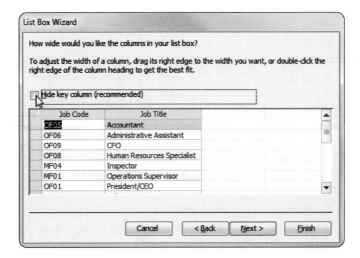

13. Click the **Hide key column** check box to select it. Click **Next**.

14. Click the option for **Store that value in this field**. Select the **JobCodeID** field and click **Next**.

15. Key **Job Title** for the label. Click **Finish**.

16. In the control's **Property Sheet**, on the **Other** tab, in the **Name** property, key **lstJobCode**.

17. Move the **Job Title** label closer to the list box.

18. Select all the controls in the **Detail** section. From the **Arrange** tab, in the **Sizing & Ordering** group, click **Align** and choose **Top**.

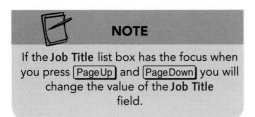

NOTE

If the **Job Title** list box has the focus when you press [PageUp] and [PageDown] you will change the value of the **Job Title** field.

19. Switch to **Layout View**. Drag the bottom of the **Job Title** list box until the scroll bar disappears. Widen the control so that you can see all of the job titles.

20. Switch to **Form View** and click in the **Full Name** text box. Scroll through several records. The employee's **Job Title** is selected in the list.

21. Save the form.

Exercise 14-7 ADD A COMBO BOX CONTROL

A combo box control provides a compact method of displaying a list of choices. In a combo box, the list of values is hidden until you click the drop-down arrow. You can set a combo box to limit users to select from the list, or you can set it to allow a user to enter a new value not included in the original list.

1. Switch to **Design View**.

2. From the **Design** tab, in the **Controls** group, click Combo Box 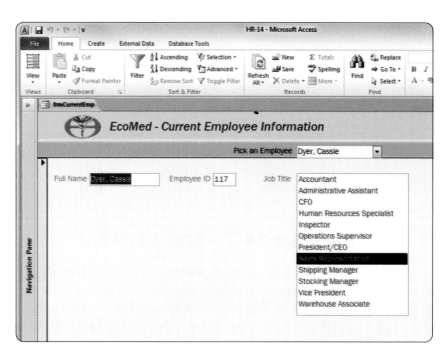 and click in the dark green area below the title label in the **Form Header** at the 5-inch mark on the horizontal ruler.

3. Click the button for **Find a record on my form based on the value I selected in my combo box**. Click **Next**.

4. From the **Available Fields** section, double-click **EmpID** and **FullName**. Click **Next**.

5. Drag the right edge of the first column to the left until the column disappears. Only the **FullName** field is now visible. Click **Next**.

NOTE

The combo box control still shows "Unbound" because the Row Source property is being used instead of the Control Source property.

6. Key **Pick an Employee** for the label. Click **Finish**.

7. In the combo box's **Property Sheet**, on the **Data** tab, notice that the **Row Source** property is an SQL statement.

8. On the **Format** tab, notice that the **Column Width** property has two numbers. The first should be 0" (**EmpID**). Change the second number to **1.1**.

9. Change the **Width** property to **1.7**.

10. On the **Other** tab, in the **Name** property, key **cboEmp**.

11. Click the combo box's label. On the **Format** tab, click the **Fore Color** property. Click the Build button and choose **Automatic**.

12. Switch to **Form View**. Click the combo box and choose "Dyer, Cassie." The form now shows employee #117's information.

Figure 14-10
Added Combo box
HR-14.accdb
frmCurrrentEmp

13. Save the form.

Exercise 14-8 CHANGE LIST AND COMBO BOX CONTROLS

A list box usually is sized to display several rows of values. If the list has more rows than can be displayed, the control displays a vertical scroll bar. You will now change the job code field from a list box to a combo box.

1. Switch to **Design View**.

2. Right-click the combo box **cboEmp** and choose **Change To**, then **List Box**.

3. Switch to **Form View**. The same information is shown in the list box as in the combo box.

4. Return to **Design View** and click the Undo button ⟲.

5. Right-click the list box **lstJobCode** and choose **Change To**, then **Combo Box**.

6. Switch to **Form View**. Use the combo box in the **Form Header** to navigate through a few employees.

7. Save the form.

Using Tab Controls in a Form

Most often, a form allows a user to view one record at a time. However, some records have too many fields to display on a single screen. One solution to this problem is to create a form larger than the screen. When you do this, the form will be either too wide or too long to display. A database user would need to scroll vertically or horizontally to see all the fields. A more practical solution is to use tab controls.

A *tab control* is a control that defines a layered space on a form. Each tab can contain unique controls. The layered space on a tab control is referred to as a page. Therefore, each tab is considered a separate page on the form. You can move to individual pages by clicking the page's corresponding tab.

Exercise 14-9 ADD A TAB CONTROL

When adding a tab control to a form, it is best to start in Design View, add and size the tab controls, and then add the appropriate controls to each page. When printing the form, only the active page will print. You will now add two tabs (pages) to the current employee form. The first tab will have employee information fields. The second tab will have the pictures of the employees.

1. In **frmCurrentEmp**, switch to **Design View**.

REVIEW

By default, a new control name is a text description followed by a sequential number.

2. From the **Design** tab, in the **Controls** group, click Tab Control ▦ and click below the **Full Name** label in the **Detail** section. The tab control inserts a two-page object.

3. You can select the entire object or each "page" separately. Click each tab to select the page. Click the unused tab area across the top edge of the object to select the entire control.

Figure 14-11
Tab control in a form
HR-14.accdb
frmCurrrentEmp

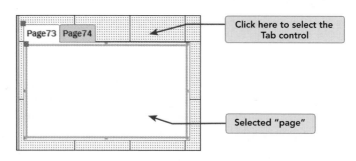

4. Click the first tab. In the control's Property Sheet, on the Other tab, in the Name property, key **tabContact**.

5. On the Format tab, in the Caption property, key **Contact Info**.

6. Click the second tab. In the control's Property Sheet, on the Other tab, in the Name property, key **tabPicture**.

7. On the Format tab, in the Caption property, key **Picture**.

8. Click the **Contact Info** tab. From the Design tab, in the Tools group, click Add Existing Fields .

9. From the Field List, drag the field **Address** to the middle of the **tabContact** control.

10. From the Arrange tab, in the Control Layout group, click Stacked 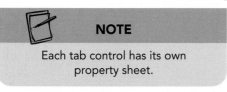.

> **NOTE**
>
> Each tab control has its own property sheet.

> **TIP**
>
> Access changes a tab control to black when you are going to add the new control or field to the "page" instead of placing the control in front of or behind the tab control.

11. Drag the text box up to the upper left corner of the tab control.

12. From the Field List, drag the field **Address2** under the **Address** control. Drag the **Address2** control up until it joins the control layout.

13. Drag **HomePhone** and **EmergencyPhone** fields under the **Address2** control so that they are added to the control layout.

Figure 14-12
Add a field to a tab control
HR-14.accdb
frmCurrrentEmp

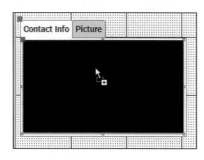

14. Select just the **Address** text box and drag the right edge to the 4-inch mark. The tab control adjusts to fit the text box.

15. Delete the **Address2** label.

16. Select the **Emergency Phone** label. Double-click the label's right edge to resize the label.

17. Switch to **Form View**. Navigate through several records.

18. Click the **Picture** tab. The contact information is no longer visible.

19. Save the form.

Exercise 14-10   ADD AN IMAGE TO A TAB CONTROL

When adding an image control to a form, you can add a default picture. A *default picture* is an image that displays on a form whenever an image is not attached to a record. The image that you select will display on the form whenever an image is not attached to a record.

1. Switch to **Design View**.

2. Click the **tabPicture** control. From the **Field List**, drag the field **Pictures** to the middle of the tab control.

3. Delete the **Pictures** label.

4. Size the **Pictures** control a little smaller than the tab control itself.

5. In the control's **Property Sheet**, on the **Format** tab, change the **Border Style** property to **Transparent**.

6. In the **Default Picture** property, click the Build button ⬜.

7. Locate the **Lesson 14** folder and choose **Photo_Default**.

8. Switch to **Form View**. Navigate through several records. Employees without a picture now will show the default image.

9. Save the form.

Exercise 14-11   USE THE INSERT PAGE CONTROL

Once a tab control has been defined on a form, you can add a new page by selecting the Page Control. The Page Control will add a new page (tab) behind the last page in the tab control. You will now add a new tab to display birth date, age, hire date, and tenure fields.

1. Switch to **Design View**. Click the blank space to the right of the **Picture** tab control to select the entire tab control.

2. From the **Design** tab, in the **Controls** group, click Insert Page 🗔.

3. In the new tab's **Property Sheet**, on the **Other** tab, in the **Name** property, key **tabDates**.

4. On the **Format** tab, in the **Caption** property, key **Dates**.

5. In the **Page Index** property, key **1**. The tab **tabDates** is now the second tab.

6. From the **Design** tab, in the **Tools** group, click **Add Existing Fields** 📭.

7. From the **Field List**, drag the field **BirthDate** to the unused part of the form to the right of the tab control.

8. Drag the **BirthDate** control over the tab control. Notice that the tab control did not turn black.

9. Switch to **Form View**. Click each of the tabs. The date can be seen on each tab because the text box was not added to the tab control but placed behind it.

10. Return to **Design View**. Delete the **BirthDate** control.

11. From the **Field List**, click the field **BirthDate**. While pressing Ctrl, click **Age**, **HireDate**, and **Tenure**. Drag the fields to the center of the tab control.

12. From the **Arrange** tab, in the **Table** group, click **Stacked** 📰.

13. Move the control layout to the left side of the tab control.

14. Switch to **Layout View**. Resize the controls so the dates can be seen.

15. Switch to **Form View**. Using the combo box in the **Form Header**, select "Floria, Maria." Click the **Dates** tab.

Figure 14-14
Modify controls
HR-14.accdb.accdb
frmCurrrentEmp

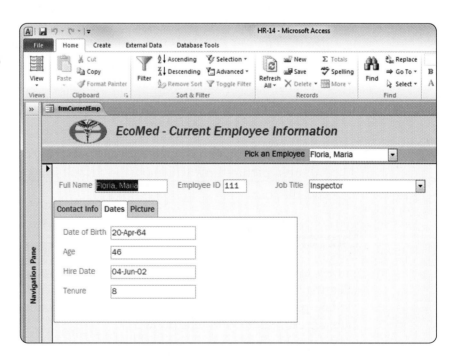

16. Save and close the form.

Creating and Modifying Charts

In Access, a chart can be linked to an object or designed as stand-alone images. Access regenerates a chart each time someone views the form on which that chart is placed. Each time the form refreshes the record source data, the image on the chart is overwritten.

A professionally designed chart displays comparisons, patterns, and trends in data. For many businesses such as EcoMed Services, use of charts assists managers evaluate and make operational adjustments quickly. For example, if a sales chart indicates that certain items are being sold in large quantities, then the inventory manager may place a special order to ensure that the company does not run out of that item.

Exercise 14-12   INSERT A CHART CONTROL

A chart created using the Chart Wizard can be a global chart or a record-bound chart. A *global chart* is a chart control that displays fields from more than one record. A *record-bound chart* is a chart control that displays data from only the current record. You will now add a chart to display the sick and vacation days that an employee has taken.

1. From the **Create** tab, in the **Forms** group, click **Form Design** .

2. From the **Design** tab, in the **Controls** group, click **Chart** . Click in the **Detail** section of the form.

3. Choose **Table: tblLeaveDays** and click **Next**.

4. Double-click **LeaveCategory** and **LeaveDate**. Click **Next**.

5. Click the **3-D Column Chart** (first row, second column) and **Next**.

6. There are three areas that data can be dropped. Two of these areas have been filled. On the left, under the chart, drag the **LeaveCategory** field to the right and out of the box.

7. Do the same to **LeaveDate by month**.

Figure 14-15
Drop Zones in Chart
Wizard
HR-14.accdb
frmLeaveDays

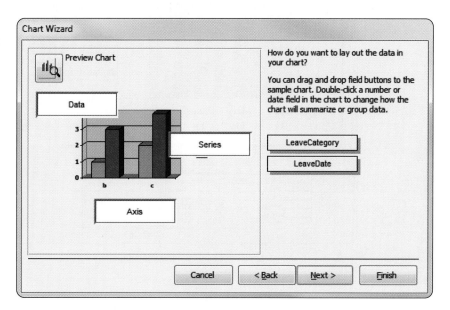

8. From the right, drag and drop the **LeaveDate** button to the **Axis** area on the left.

9. Double-click **LeaveDate by month** to open the **Group** dialog box. Here you can change the way dates are organized. Click **Cancel**.

10. From the right, drag and drop the **LeaveCategory** button to the **Series** area on the left.

11. From the right, drag and drop the **LeaveDate** button to the **Data** area on the left.

12. The Wizard will count the leave days in the **Data** area. Click **Next**.

13. Click the option **Yes, display a legend**.

14. Click **Finish**. Switch to **Form View** to see the chart. Return to **Design View**.

15. Drag the chart control to the very upper left corner of the **Detail** section.

16. In the chart's **Property Sheet**, on the **Format** tab, in the **Width** property, key **6**.

17. In the **Height** property, key **4**.

18. Double-click the chart to open it in chart edit mode. From the drop-down menu **Chart**, choose **Chart Options**.

19. In the **Chart Options** dialog box, edit the **Chart title** to **Leave Days this Year**. Click **OK** to close the dialog box.

Figure 14-16
Edit chart properties
HR-14.accdb
frmLeaveDays

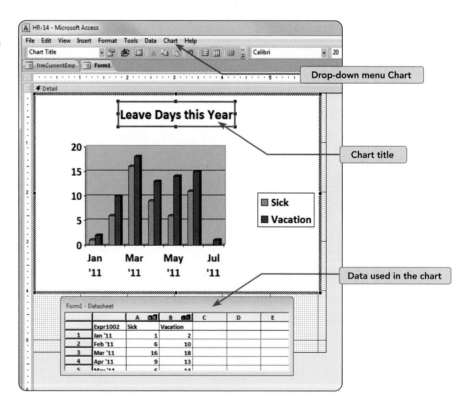

20. Click away from the chart to return to the normal Design View.
21. Save the form as frmLeaveDays.

Exercise 14-13   CONVERT A CHART TO AN IMAGE

A chart is dynamically linked to its source data. When you convert a chart to a static image, the links are removed, and you can no longer edit or update the chart. The chart becomes a static image that cannot change as the recordset refreshes. One advantage of a static image is that it takes up less space than a dynamic chart.

1. Right-click the chart control and choose Change To, then Image.
2. Access displays a warning message. Read and then click Yes.
3. Another warning message appears referencing the chart size. Click OK.
4. Notice the chart's Property Sheet. It now shows the control is an Image.
5. Save the form.

Exercise 14-14   FORMAT A FORM AS A DIALOG BOX

Forms can be formatted as a dialog box. When you format a form as a dialog box, it becomes a pop-up form. A pop-up form stays on top of other opened database objects, even when the other object is active. A pop-up form can display information or prompt a user for data.

1. Click the Form Selector.
2. Change the following properties in the form's Property Sheet on the Format tab.

Property	Value
Caption	EcoMed
Width	6
Auto Center	Yes
Border Style	Dialog
Record Selectors	No
Navigation Buttons	No
Scroll Bars	Neither
Control Box	No
Close Button	No
Min Max Buttons	None

3. On the Other tab, change the Pop Up property to Yes.
4. Change the Modal property to Yes.
5. From the Design tab, in the Controls group, click Command Button and click under the chart control.
6. In the Command Button Wizard, in the Category section, choose Form Operations.
7. In the Actions section, choose Close Form. Click Next.
8. Choose the Picture and select Exit Doorway. Click Next.

9. Name the button **cmdClose** and click **Finish**.

10. From the **Format** tab, in the **Control Formatting** group, click **Quick Styles** 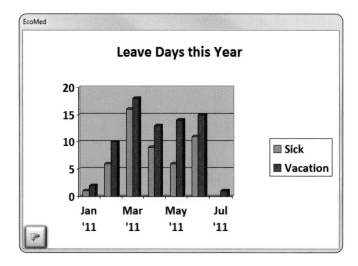 and choose **Subtle Effect – Olive Green, Accent 3** (row four, column four).

11. From the **Format** tab, in the **Control Formatting** group, click **Shape Effects** , and in the **Bevel** section, choose **Circle** (row one, column one).

12. Drag the command button on top of the chart image in the lower left corner.

13. Drag the bottom of the **Detail** section up as far as it will go.

14. Save and switch to **Form View**.

Figure 14-17
Dialog box form
HR-14.accdb
frmLeaveDays

Figure 14-17
Dialog box form
HR-14.accdb
frmLeaveDays

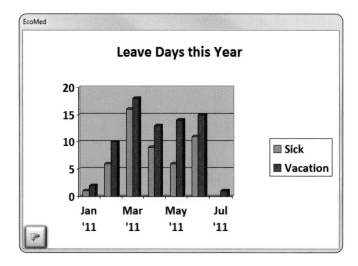

15. Click the close button.

Adding Hyperlinks

You probably are already familiar with hyperlinks. A *hyperlink* is a navigation element pointer, referencing an object from an external source. A hyperlink acts as an active connection from one application to another. A hyperlink connects to a Web page, image, e-mail address, or electronic file. A hyperlink can be displayed as text or an image.

Whenever you frequently reference or look up information stored in another application, in Access you can create a hyperlink to launch the application quickly. Selecting a hyperlink automatically launches an appropriate application and displays the referred object.

Exercise 14-15   ADD A HYPERLINK TO OPEN A FILE

Adding a hyperlink to open a file requires that you know the location and name of the file that needs to be linked. The file can be stored locally or online. If the file is stored locally, then the path to the file must be fully defined. If the file is stored online, then an active network or Internet connection must be available.

By default, the caption of a hyperlink displays the name of the referenced file. You can change the name by changing the Caption property for the hyperlink control. The caption should describe the purpose of the hyperlink.

1. Open **frmCurrentEmp** in Design View.
2. From the Design tab, in the Controls group, click Hyperlink 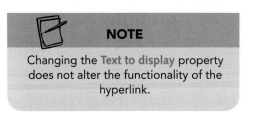.

3. In the Insert Hyperlink dialog box, in the Link to section, choose Existing File or Web Page.
4. In the Look in control, locate the **Lesson 14** folder and choose the file **Notice of Confidentiality**.
5. In the Text to display control, key Click to view Confidentiality letter.

> **NOTE**
>
> Changing the Text to display property does not alter the functionality of the hyperlink.

Figure 14-18
Insert Hyperlink
dialog box
HR-14.accdb
frmCurrrentEmp

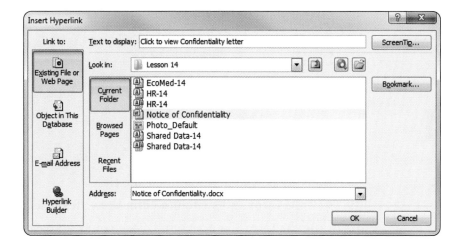

6. Click OK. The hyperlink is added to the upper left corner of the Detail section.
7. Drag the hyperlink under the **JobCodeID** control.
8. Change the Font Size to 12. Resize the label so you can see all of the text.
9. Switch to Form View and test the hyperlink. A Security Notice appears.
10. Read and click Yes. Exit Word and return to Access.

Exercise 14-16   ADD A HYPERLINK TO OPEN A FORM

Clicking on a hyperlink launches the linked object. The new object becomes the active window. You will now add a hyperlink to open a form in the current database.

1. Switch to Design View.
2. From the Design tab, in the Controls group, click Hyperlink 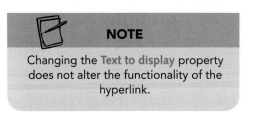.

3. In the **Insert Hyperlink** dialog box, in the **Link to** section, choose **Object in This Database**.

4. Expand the forms and choose **frmLeaveDays**.

5. In the **Text to display** control, key **Click to view Leave to Date Chart**.

Figure 14-19
Hyperlink to a
database object
**HR-14.accdb
frmCurrrentEmp**

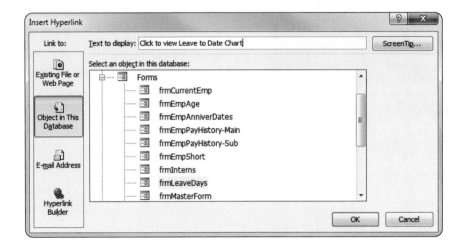

6. Click **OK**.

7. Change the Font Size to **12**.

8. Align the new hyperlink under the first.

9. Save the form and switch to **Form View**. Test the new hyperlink.

10. Close the form. Compact and close your database.

Lesson 14   Summary

- An option group is a control object bound to a single field containing a set of controls representing choices.
- An option group consists of four components that can be formatted separately.
- A Yes/No field can be displayed as either a check box or toggle button.
- A toggle button is a control that acts as an on/off button in a form or report.
- A combo box control provides a compact method of displaying a list of choices.
- A combo box can allow a user to enter a new value not included in the original list.
- If the combo box list contains more rows than can be seen at one time, the control displays a vertical scroll bar.

- A tab control is a control that defines a layered space on a form.
- A default picture is an image displayed on a form whenever an image is not attached to a record.
- A global chart is a chart control that shows all fields. A record-bound chart is a chart control that shows only the data in the current record.
- When you convert a chart to a static image, the links to its source data are removed.
- A pop-up form stays on top of other open database objects, even when another object is active.
- A hyperlink is a navigation element pointer referencing an object from an external source.

Command Summary			
Feature	**Button**	**Task Path**	**Keyboard**
Chart, Insert		Design, Controls, Chart	
Controls, Combo Box		Design, Controls, Combo Box	
Controls, List Box		Design, Controls, List Box	
Controls, Option Button		Design, Controls, Option Button	
Controls, Option Group		Design, Controls, Option Group	
Controls, Page, Insert		Design, Controls, Insert Page	
Controls, Tab Control		Design, Controls, Tab Control	
Format object, Quick Styles		Format, Control Formatting, Quick Styles	
Hyperlink, Insert		Design, Controls, Hyperlink	
Shape Effects		Format, Control Formatting, Shape Effects	

Concepts Review

True/False Questions

Each of the following statements is either true or false. Indicate your choice by circling T or F.

T F 1. An option button can control two or more option groups.

T F 2. An option button allows a user to choose a predefined option.

T F 3. An option group frame is the title for the option group.

T F 4. Usually a list box occupies less space than a combo box.

T F 5. A combo box control can have one value shown in the control but a different value stored in the control's bound field.

T F 6. The layered space on a tab control is sometimes referred to as a page.

T F 7. An object referenced in a hyperlink can be stored locally or online.

T F 8. In a database, a static image takes up more space than a dynamic chart.

Short Answer Questions

Write the correct answer in the space provided.

1. What control should be used when all, some, or none of the choices can be selected?

   _____

2. Option groups should contain how many choices?

   _____

3. What types of controls might you use for Yes/No fields?

   _____

4. What control creates multiple pages in a form?

   _____

5. What type of chart control shows only the data from the current record?

   _____

6. What two controls allow a user to select from a list rather than keying an entry?

   _____

7. What command can convert a check box to an option button?

8. How do you know when a tab control is ready to except the placement of a control?

Critical Thinking

Answer these questions on a separate page. There are no right or wrong answers. Support your answers with examples from your own experience, if possible.

1. What are the advantages of check boxes, combo boxes, and list boxes? How can you decide which is the best to use?

2. What kind of information might be used as a hyperlink? What information would be inappropriate to use for a hyperlink?

Skills Review

Exercise 14-17

You have been directed to add the vender list report as a hyperlink in the vender form. You also will add a second hyperlink to display the United States Postal Service Web site that allows you to look up zip codes for known addresses.

1. Open a database by following these steps:
    a. Locate and open the **Lesson 14** folder.
    b. If you already have a copy of *[your initials]*-**EcoMed-14**, skip to step 1d.
    c. Make a copy of **EcoMed-14** and rename it to *[your initials]*-EcoMed-14.
    d. Open and enable content for *[your initials]*-**EcoMed-14**.
    e. Refresh the links with *[your initials]*-**Shared Data-14**.

2. Add a hyperlink to a form by following these steps:
    a. Open **frmVender** in Layout View.
    b. From the Design tab, in the Controls group, click Hyperlink 🔍.
    c. In the last column of the control layout, click in the first blank cell.
    d. In the Insert Hyperlink dialog box, in the Link to section, choose Object in This Database.

e. Expand the Reports and choose **rptVenderList**.

f. In the Text to display control, key List of Venders and click OK.

3. Add a second hyperlink to a form by following these steps:

a. From the Design tab, in the Controls group, click Hyperlink .

b. Click in the blank cell above the **ZIP** text box.

c. In the Insert Hyperlink dialog box, in the Link to section, choose Existing File or Web Page.

d. In the Address control, key http://zip4.usps.com.

e. In the Text to display control, key Lookup +4 ZIP codes.

f. Click OK.

4. Add a label to a form by following these steps:

a. From the Design tab, in the Controls group, click Label , then click in the blank cell under the Date control.

b. Key Prepared by: *[your full name]*.

c. Format the label to match the Date control.

d. Save the form and test each hyperlink.

Assessment

- Turn in your database only when all assigned exercises have been completed, according to your classroom procedure.

-OR-

- Save a form by following these steps:

a. Click the File tab and from the Print option, click Print Preview.

b. From the Print Preview tab, in the Data group, click PDF or XPS to save the printout as a file.

c. In the Publish as PDF or XPS dialog box, click the Option button. Select the Pages option. Print only page **1** and click OK.

d. Save the file as a PDF and name the file *[your initials]*-14-17-A.

e. Depending on your class procedures, print or turn in the PDF file.

14-17-A.pdf
1 Page

Exercise 14-18

You have been asked by the inventory department to add a chart to the January shipping details form. You will need to format the chart appropriately.

1. Add a chart to a form by following these steps:

a. Using *[your initials]*-**EcoMed-14** open **frmShipDetail-Jan** in Design View.

b. From the Design tab, in the Controls group, click Chart.

c. Click in the **Form Footer**.

d. Choose **Query: qryShipDetail-Jan** and click **Next**.

e. Use both fields. Click **Next**.

f. Choose the **3-D Pie Chart** (row 4, column 2) and click **Next**.

g. The fields are properly placed. Click **Next**.

h. The wizard wants to link this chart with the main form. From the **Form Fields** control, choose <No Field>.

i. From the **Chart Fields** control, choose <No Field>. Click **Next**.

j. Change the title to **January Total Sales by Region**.

k. Click **Finish**.

l. Switch to **Form View** to see the chart. Switch to **Design View**.

2. Format a chart and change it to an image by following these steps:

a. Drag the chart to the top of the **Form Footer**.

b. In the chart's **Property Sheet**, change the **Width** property to **4.5** and the **Height** property to **2**.

c. Center the chart under the controls in the **Detail** section.

d. Right-click the chart and choose **Change To**, then **Image**.

e. Click **Yes** to the first message and **OK** to the second.

3. Add a label by following these steps:

a. From the **Design** tab, in the **Controls** group, click Label **Aa**, then click in the **Form Header**.

b. Key **Prepared by:** *[your full name]*.

c. Save the form.

Assessment

- Turn in your database only when all assigned exercises have been completed, according to your classroom procedure.

-OR-

- Save a form by following these steps:

a. Click the **File** tab and from the **Print** option, click **Print Preview** .

b. From the **Print Preview** tab, in the **Data** group, click **PDF or XPS** to save the printout as a file.

c. In the **Publish as PDF or XPS** dialog box, click the **Option** button. Select the **Pages** option. Print only page **1** and click **OK**.

d. Save the file as a PDF and name the file *[your initials]*-**14-18-A**.

e. Depending on your class procedures, print or turn in the PDF file.

14-18-A.pdf
1 Page

Exercise 14-19

You have been directed to add an option group to select the sales regions in the facilities contact form.

1. Remove a control by following these steps:
   a. Open, enable, and update the links for *[your initials]*-EcoMed-14.
   b. Open **frmFacContacts** in Design View.
   c. Delete the **Region** text box and its label.
   d. Delete the two rows of blank cells below the **Contact Name** text box.

2. Add an option group control by following these steps:
   a. From the Design tab, in the Controls group, click Option Group, and then click under the **Contact Name** text box.
   b. Key the number 1 in the first row of Label Names and press [Tab].
   c. In the second row, key 2.
   d. Continue adding the numbers 3 through 9 on different rows.
   e. Click Next. Choose the option **No, I don't want a default** and click Next.
   f. The values should match the label names. Click Next.
   g. Choose the option **Store the value in this field** and then choose **Region**. Click Next.
   h. Choose the **Option buttons** control type and the style **Shadowed**. Click Next.
   i. Edit the default caption to **Sales Regions**. Click Finish.

3. Format an option group control by following these steps:
   a. Widen the option group control to 4 inches.
   b. Select the option button for sales region 2. Drag the option button to the right of sales region 1. Leave two columns of dots between option 2's button and option 1's label.
   c. Arrange the option buttons and the option group borders to match Figure 14-20.

Figure 14-20
Option Group layout

   d. Select all of the options buttons and their labels.
   e. From the Arrange tab, in the Sizing & Ordering group, click Align, and then choose Top.
   f. Drag the whole option group control so that its left edge aligns with the left edge of the **Contact Name** controls.
   g. Resize the Detail section to be 4 inches tall.

4.   Add a label and print the form by following these steps:

   a. From the **Design** tab, in the **Controls** group, click Label , then click to the right of the **Title** control in the **Form Header**.

   b. Key **Prepared by:** *[your full name]*.

   c. Resize the label so that it fits on one line.

   d. Move the new label to the white bar in the **Form Header** with the label's right edge at the 7.5-inch mark on the horizontal ruler.

   e. Save the form.

Assessment

- Turn in your database only when all assigned exercises have been completed, according to your classroom procedure.

-OR-

- Save a form by following these steps:

   a. Click the **File** tab and from the **Print** option, click **Print Preview**.

   b. From the **Print Preview** tab, in the **Data** group, click **PDF or XPS** to save the printout as a file.

   c. In the **Publish as PDF or XPS** dialog box, click the **Option** button. Select the **Pages** option. Print only page **1** and click **OK**.

   d. Save the file as a PDF and name the file *[your initials]*-**14-19-A**.

   e. Depending on your class procedures, print or turn in the PDF file.

14-19-A.pdf
1 Page

Exercise 14-20

The inventory department manager has asked you to make changes to the main form that is used to find appropriate bulbs for customers. After reviewing the form with your supervisor, you have decided to add a combo box control and tabs.

1.   Add a combo box to a form by following these steps:

   a. Open, enable, and update the links for *[your initials]*-**EcoMed-14**.

   b. Open **frmBulbFinder-Main** in **Design View**.

   c. Delete the **BulbType** text box and label.

   d. From the **Design** tab, in the **Controls** group, click Combo Box and click in the **Form Header** under the **Title** control at the 6-inch mark on the horizontal ruler.

   e. Click the button for **Find a record on my form based on the value I selected in my combo box**. Click **Next**.

   f. From the **Available Fields** section, double-click **BulbTypeID** and **BulbType**. Click **Next**.

g. Double-click the right edge of the **BulbType** column to resize it. Click Next.

h. Key Pick a Bulb Type for the label. Click Finish.

i. Select the combo box and its label. Change the Font Size to 12 and Bold the controls. Resize as needed but don't add the combo box control to the Title layout control.

2. Add a tab control to a form by following these steps:

a. In the Detail section, delete the subform control so the whole section is empty.

b. From the Design tab, in the Controls group, click Tab Control 🔲 and click in the Detail section.

c. In the tab control's Property Sheet, on the Format tab, set the Width property to 6 and the Height property to 4.

d. Set the Top and Left properties to .125.

e. Click the first tab. In the control's Property Sheet, on the Format tab, in the Caption property, key Bulbs by Shape.

f. Click the second tab. On the Format tab, in the Caption property, key Bulbs by Category.

3. Add content to the tab pages by following these steps:

a. Click the **Bulbs by Shape** tab control.

b. From the Navigation Pane, drag **frmBulbFinder-Sub** to the tab control.

c. Delete the subform's label. Select the subform.

d. In the subform's Property Sheet, on the Format tab, set the Top property to .5 and the Left property to .25.

e. Set the Width property to 4.8 and the Height property to 3.

f. Click the **Bulbs by Category** tab control.

g. From the Navigation Pane, drag **frmBulbCat** to the tab control.

h. Delete the subform's label. Select the subform.

i. In the subform's Property Sheet, on the Format tab, set the Top property to .5 and the Left properties to .25.

j. Set the Width property to 4.8 and the Height property to 3.

k. Resize the tab control to remove the white space.

4. Add a label to the form by following these steps:

a. From the Design tab, in the Controls group, click Label 𝐀𝐚, then click under the Title control in the Form Header.

b. Key Prepared by: *[your full name]*.

c. Save the form and switch to Form View.

Assessment

- Turn in your database only when all assigned exercises have been completed, according to your classroom procedure.

-OR-

- Using the combo box, select **CFL** and click the **Bulbs by Shape** tab.
- Save a form by following these steps:

   a. Click the File tab and from the Print option, click Print Preview 🔍.

   b. From the Print Preview tab, in the Data group, click PDF or XPS 📄 to save the printout as a file.

   c. In the Publish as PDF or XPS dialog box, click the Option button. Select the Pages option. Print only page 1 and click OK.

   d. Save the file as a PDF and name the file *[your initials]*-14-20-A.

- Using the combo box, select **CFL** and click the **Bulbs by Category** tab.
- Save a form by following these steps:

   a. Click the File tab and from the Print option, click Print Preview 🔍.

   b. From the Print Preview tab, in the Data group, click PDF or XPS 📄 to save the printout as a file.

   c. In the Publish as PDF or XPS dialog box, click the Option button. Select the Pages option. Print only page 1 and click OK.

   d. Save the file as a PDF and name the file *[your initials]*-14-20-B.

   e. Depending on your class procedures print or turn in the PDF files.

14-20-A.pdf
1 Page

14-20-B.pdf
1 Page

Lesson Applications

Exercise 14-21

You have been directed by your supervisor to modify the management information form. You will need to add a hyperlink to the Web site for the American Hospital Association.

1. Open, enable, and update the links for *[your initials]*-EcoMed-14.

2. In **frmMgtInfo**, add a hyperlink that will open the **rptMgtUniv**.

3. Change the hyperlink's caption to University Management Companies.

4. Place the hyperlink under the **txtAddress2** control the first column of the control layout.

5. Add another hyperlink to the form. Have this control open the Web site http://aha.org with the caption American Hospital Association.

6. Place the hyperlink below the other hyperlink the first column of the control layout.

7. Add a label to the Form Header to the right of the title label, with the caption **Prepared by:** *[your full name]*.

8. Resize controls to make the form no wider than 7.9 inches.

Assessment

- Turn in your database only when all assigned exercises have been completed, according to your classroom procedure.

-OR-

- Save the form as a PDF. Only save the first page of the form. Name the file *[your initials]*-14-21-A.

- According to your class procedures, print or turn in the PDF file.

14-21-A.pdf
1 Page

Exercise 14-22

The inventory details form needs to be modified to include a combo box for the bulb type. Review the form and make the appropriate changes.

1. Open, enable, and update the links for *[your initials]*-EcoMed-14.

2. In **frmInvDetails**, delete the **BulbTypeID** text box and replace it with a combo box control.

TIP

You will need to close the form and reopen the form to see the text in a new combo box.

3. Base the combo box on both fields in **tblBulbType**. Sort the combo box data by **BulbType** and store the data in the field **BulbTypeID**.

4. Set the caption to Bulb Type.

5. Delete the **BulbCatID** text box and label.

6. Centered under the **Image** control, add an option group control with the following data and without a default value.

   Diagnostic
   Indoor
   Outdoor
   Surgical

7. Store the value of the option group in the field **BulbCatID**.

8. Use Option buttons and Shadowed style.

9. Set the caption to Bulb Categories. Set the option group's Back Color of #EFF2F7.

10. Add a label to the Form Header with the caption Prepared by: *[your full name]*.

Assessment

DB

- Turn in your database only when all assigned exercises have been completed, according to your classroom procedure.

-OR-

PDF

- Save the form as a PDF. Only save the first page of the form. Name the file *[your initials]*-14-22-A.
- According to your class procedures, print or turn in the PDF file.

14-22-A.pdf
1 Page

Exercise 14-23

The manager of the inventory department has asked you to modify the ship by state form to include a chart.

1. Open, enable, and update the links for *[your initials]*-EcoMed-14.

2. In **frmShipByState**, add a label to the Form Header below the title label, with the caption Prepared by: *[your full name]*.

3. Insert a chart control into the Detail section.

4. The chart will use the fields **OrderDate**, **Orders**, and **State** from **qryShipByState**. The query has a parameter criteria for the **Region** field.

5. Use a 3-D Column Chart where **OrderDate** is in the Axis, **Orders** is the Data, and **State** is the Series. **OrderDate** should be organized by Month.

6. Make the title of the chart Sales to Date by State.

7. Display a legend.

8. Move the chart to the upper left corner of the **Detail** section of the form. Resize the chart to **7.5** inches wide and **4** inches tall.

Assessment

- Turn in your database only when all assigned exercises have been completed, according to your classroom procedure.

-OR-

- Save the form as a PDF. In the prompt, enter Region **5**. Name the file *[your initials]*-**14-23-A**.

- According to your class procedures, print or turn in the PDF file.

14-23-A.pdf
1 Page

Exercise 14-24 ◆ Challenge Yourself

Your supervisor has asked you to improve the functionality of the main form that displays sales by region. You have been instructed to add tabs to the form.

1. Open, enable, and update the links for *[your initials]*-**EcoMed-14**.

2. In **frmRegionSales-Main**, add a combo box control to the **Form Header** under the **Title** control. This control needs to show only region numbers and will find a record based on the value selected.

3. The value of this combo box needs to be stored in the field **Region** with a caption **Pick a Region**.

4. In the **Detail** section, delete the **Region** text box, the image, and the subform. Move the calculated control **Profit** to the right, until the left edge of the text box is at the 4-inch mark on the horizontal ruler.

5. Add a tab control to the **Detail** section of the form under the **Profit** controls and to the far left.

6. Name the first tab **Facility Billing** and the second **Region Map**.

7. Add the form **frmRegionSales-Sub** to the **Facility Billing** tab. Delete the subform's label and resize the subform to **5** inches wide by **4** inches tall. Place the subform in the upper left corner of the tab control.

8. You will need to use the field **Region** to link the subform with the main form.

9. Add an image control to the **Region Map** tab and select the file **RegionCode**. Resize the image to a width of **5** inches wide.

10. Size the tab control to just fit the subform and image.

11. Add a label to the **Form Header** with the caption **Prepared by:** *[your full name]*.

12. Make the form **7.9** inches wide and the **Detail** section **5** inches tall.

14-24-A.pdf
1 Page

Assessment

- Turn in your database only when all assigned exercises have been completed, according to your classroom procedure.

-OR-

- Using the combo box, select **Region** 1 and click the **Facility Billing** tab.
- Save the form as a PDF. Only save the first page of the form. Name the file *[your initials]*-14-24-A.
- Using the combo box, select **Region** 1 and click the **Region Map** tab.
- Save the form as a PDF. Only save the first page of the form. Name the file *[your initials]*-14-24-B.
- According to your class procedures, print or turn in the PDF files.

14-24-B.pdf
1 Page

On Your Own

In these exercises you work on your own, as you would in a real-life work environment. Use the skills you've learned to accomplish the task—and be creative.

Exercise 14-25

Review the designs of the databases you modified in Exercise 13-30. Select two existing forms to modify by changing a control to an option group, combo box, or list box. Print the forms and sketch your changes on the printouts. You may modify your table structures to better accommodate your designs. On each printout, write your name and "Exercise 14-25." Continue to the next exercise.

Exercise 14-26

Based on the sketches you created in Exercise 14-25, make the modifications to your forms. For both forms, include your name and "Exercise 14-26" in the footer. Include the title of the form in the header. Print a copy of each form. Continue to the next exercise.

Exercise 14-27

Sketch a new form that includes either a dynamic chart or a tab control. Create the form. Include your name and "Exercise 14-27" in the footer of the form. Print/Save As one record from your form. Keep a copy of the database you modified in this lesson. You will use it for the On Your Own exercises in the next lesson.

Working with Macros and Modules

OBJECTIVES **After completing this lesson, you will be able to:**

1. Create and edit macros.

2. Create submacros.

3. Create a macro with conditions.

4. Create a module and a Visual Basic routine.

5. Modify a form module routine.

Estimated Time: 2 hours

In your work in other software applications such as Excel or Word, you may have created a macro. A *macro* is an object that completes an action or set of actions. In this final lesson, you will create, name, and run simple macros; add conditions in macros; and create submacros.

In addition to macros, you will create and edit modules. A *module* is a collection of Visual Basic declarations and procedures that are stored together as a unit. Visual Basic for Applications (VBA) is an object-oriented programming language used to enhance Office applications. VBA code follows the same syntax as Visual Basic programs.

The main difference between a macro and a module is the level of complexity. Generally, macros are simple procedures with a limited number of steps. Modules, in contrast, are involved procedures used to build user interfaces.

Because both macros and modules are multistep activities, it is important that you plan the sequence of these activities. A good programmer plans, develops, and then writes the macro or the module. Proper planning helps avoid time-consuming corrections and costly modifications.

Creating and Editing Macros

A macro consists of individual macro actions. Most actions require one or more arguments. Access provides a large number of actions from which to choose, enabling a wide variety of commands. For example, some of the more commonly used actions open a report, find a record, display a message box, or apply a filter to a form or report.

There are two types of macros, stand-alone and embedded. A *stand-alone macro* is a global macro that you can assign to numerous objects. An *embedded macro* is an object macro occurring on a specific control in a form or report. Only stand-alone macros are visible as major objects in the module section of the Navigation Pane. An embedded macro only is visible when the Build button is clicked. Access, unlike Word or Excel, has no macro recorder.

Exercise 15-1 RUN A MACRO FROM A COMMAND BUTTON

You can identify the macro assigned to a command button by viewing the command button's property sheet. Typically a macro attached to a command button is assigned to the On Click event. The macro executes each time the command button is clicked.

Macros must be written in the Macro Design window. The Macro Design window has two panes. The top pane shows Actions, which are selected from a list. The lower pane shows Action Arguments.

1. Copy the databases **EcoMed-15**, **HR-15**, and **Shared Data-15** from your student disk. Add your initials to the beginning of each copied file.

2. Open *[your initials]*-**HR-15** database, enable it, and refresh its links to *[your initials]*-**Shared Data-15**.

3. Open **frmInterns** in **Form View**. This form has a command button that runs a macro.

4. Click the **Preview Report** button. The report **rptInternInfo** opens in the **Print Preview** window. Close the **Print Preview** window.

5. Switch to **Design View**. Open the **Property Sheet** for the command button.

6. Click the **Event** tab and find the **On Click** property. This property has an **Embedded Macro**.

Figure 15-1
Property Sheet for a command button
HR-15.accdb
frmInterns

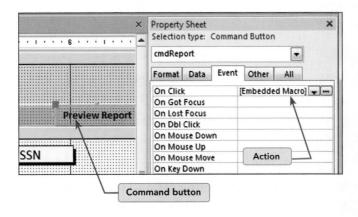

NOTE

The On Click event triggers the actions when you click an object in Form View. The event does not trigger the actions in Design View.

7. For the **On Click** property, click the Build button. Place your mouse over the **OpenReport** action and read the ScreenTip.

8. Click just under the action **OpenReport**. The five arguments can be edited. Click **OpenReport**. Place your mouse over the values of each argument to read its ScreenTip.

Figure 15-2
Macro Design
window
HR-15.accdb
frmInterns

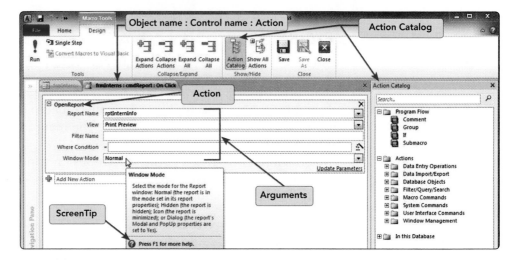

NOTE

The Document tab shows the major object, the control, and the Event to which this macro will be assigned.

9. This action will open the report **rptInternInfo** in **Print Preview**.

10. From the **Design** tab, in the **Close** group, click **Close** to return to the form.

Exercise 15-2   CREATE A MACRO USING A WIZARD

When creating a macro, you select actions from the Action Catalog and then complete required information for each argument. Macros allow you to add actions to forms, reports, and controls.

For simple actions, you can use the Control Wizard. The Control Wizard can build a macro with actions. For more complex actions, you can use the Macro Builder to build the list of actions.

1. From the **Design** tab, in the **Controls** group, click the Build button and click in the lower right corner of the **Detail** section.

2. In the **Command Button Wizard**, in the **Categories** section, choose **Form Operations**.

3. In the **Actions** section, choose **Open Form** and click **Next**.

4. Choose **frmInternOfficeData** and click **Next**.

5. Choose the **Open the form and find specific data to display** option and click **Next**.

6. In the **frmInterns** field list, choose **InternID**. In the **frmInternOfficeData** field list, choose **InternID**.

7. Click the Match button ⬌.

Figure 15-3
Set matching data
HR-15.accdb
frmInterns

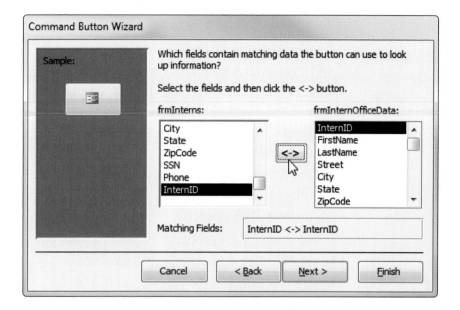

8. Click **Next**. Add a checkmark in the **Show all Pictures** check box. From the list of pictures, choose **Magnifying Glass**. Click **Next**.

9. Name the button **cmdOfficeData**. Click **Finish**.

10. On the **Event** tab, in the **On Click** property, click the Build button ⋯ to open the **Macro Designer** window.

11. The wizard stored the actions for the command button in an embedded macro. From the **Design** tab, in the **Close** group, click **Close** ☒.

12. In **Property Sheet** for **cmdOfficeData**, on the **Format** tab, in the **Caption** property, key **Office Use Only**.

13. In the **Picture Caption Arrangement** property, choose **Bottom**.

14. Resize the button to display the text on one line.

15. Save the form and switch to **Form View**.

16. Press PageDown to navigate to the record for "Nancy Boone" and click the **Office Use Only** button. Only Boone's data appears in the pop-up window. Click **OK**.

17. Press PageDown to navigate to the record for "Albert Avila" and click the **Office Use Only** button. Click **OK**.

18. Close the form.

Exercise 15-3 ADD A COMMAND BUTTON TO A FORM

Macros must be assigned to an event on an object or control. Many macros are assigned to a command button on forms and reports. In the employee data form, you will add a command button to preview the hourly pay report.

1. Open **frmEmpData** in **Design View**.
2. Add a command button to the **Form Header** under the title label, in the darker colored bar. Because the **Use Control Wizards** is active by default, the **Command Button Wizard** starts. Click **Cancel**.
3. In the new control's **Property Sheet**, on the **Other** tab, change the **Name** property to **cmdHrRpt**.
4. On the **Format** tab, change the **Caption** property to **Preview Hourly Pay Report**.
5. In the **Back Style** property, choose **Transparent**.
6. In the **Border Style** property, choose **Transparent**.
7. In the **Fore Color**, choose **Text Black**.
8. Resize **cmdHrRpt** so the text fits on one row.
9. Save the form. At this time the command button has no action when pressed.

Exercise 15-4 CREATE AN EMBEDDED MACRO

When creating an embedded macro, you must use the Macro Builder to build the list of actions and arguments. When you first open the Macro Builder, the Action column, the Arguments column, and the Comment column display. The actions that will be assigned to the event can be written using the Expression Builder, Macro Builder, or Code Builder (VBA).

1. With the **Property Sheet** for **cmdHrRpt** open, click the **Event** tab, and click in the **On Click** property.
2. Click the Build button [...]. The **Choose Builder** dialog box opens. You can start the **Expression Builder**, the **Macro Builder**, or the **Code Builder**.

Figure 15-4
Choose Builder
dialog box
HR-15.accdb
frmEmpData

3. Choose Macro Builder and click OK. The Macro Design window opens.

4. In the Action Catalog pane, you will find all of the actions organized by subject. In the main body of the Macro Builder, click the drop-down arrow for the Add New Action control.

5. Choose OpenReport as the first action. This action has five arguments.

6. In the Report Name argument, choose **rptHrPayInfo**.

7. In the View argument, choose Print Preview.

8. In the Action Catalog pane, under User Interface Commands, double-click MessageBox. A second action is added to the Marco Builder window.

9. In the Message argument, key the following:

   This is the Hourly Pay Report for the week. Click OK to close this message box. Then click either Print or Close.

10. In the Type argument, choose Information.

TABLE 15-1 Message Box Types

Icon	Macro Name	VB Name	Description
⊗	Critical	vbCritical	Display Critical Message icon
❓	Warning?	vbQuestion	Display Question icon
⚠	Warning!	vbExclamation	Display Warning Message icon
ⓘ	Information	vbInformation	Display Information Message icon

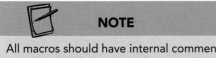

NOTE

All macros should have internal comments above each action so that you (the designer) and others can be reminded of the inner workings of the macro.

11. In the Title argument, key Helpful Information.

12. In the Action Catalog pane, under Program Flow, double-click Comment. At the right of the comment box is a green up-arrow. Click it twice to move the comment above the OpenReport action.

13. Key This action opens the Hourly Payroll Report.

14. Click in the OpenReport action.

15. In the Action Catalog pane, under Program Flow, double-click Comment. Key This action displays a custom message box.

16. Right-click the frmEmpData : cmdHrRpt : On Click tab and choose Save.

Figure 15-5
Finished macro
HR-15.accdb
frmEmpData

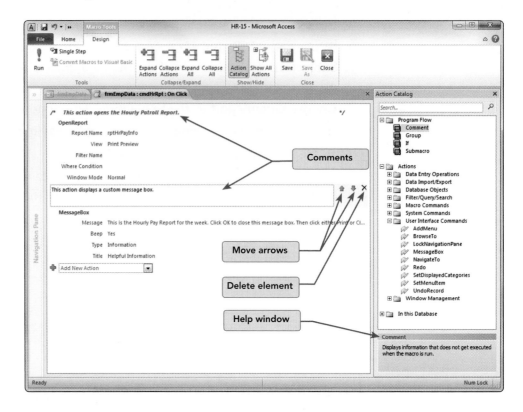

Figure 15-5
Finished macro
HR-15.accdb
frmEmpData

17. From the **Design** tab, in the **Close** group, click **Close** ⊠.

18. Switch to **Form View** and click the new command button to test it.

19. Click **OK** to close the message box. Close the **Print Preview**.

20. Save and close the form.

Exercise 15-5   CREATE A STAND-ALONE MACRO

A stand-alone macro can be applied to numerous controls and objects. A common use for a macro is to display a message as a formatted message box that can be used on more than one form.

A message box contains three sections of text. The first section of text displays as a bold heading. The second section displays as plain text beneath that heading. The third section displays as plain text beneath the second section. A blank line displays between each section. The @ symbol is used to distinguish each section.

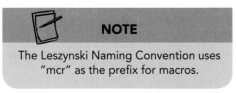

NOTE

The Leszynski Naming Convention uses "mcr" as the prefix for macros.

1. From the **Create** tab, in the **Macros & Code** group, click **Macro** 📄.

2. Save the macro as **mcrMsgCopyright**.

3. Click in the **Add New Action** control and key me. The **MessageBox** appears in the control. Press Tab.

4. In the **Message** argument, key the following:

   Attention @All information and images are protected by copyright laws. @Reproduction is prohibited without prior written consent.

5. In the Type argument, choose **Critical**.

6. In the Title argument, key **Copyright Notice**.

7. Save and close the macro.

8. Open **frmEmpData** in **Design View**.

9. In the form's **Property Sheet**, on the **Event** tab, in the **On Load** property, click the drop-down arrow and choose **mcrMsgCopyright**.

10. Save and close the form.

11. Open **frmEmpData** in **Form View**. The macro runs before the form is loaded.

Figure 15-6
Custom message box
HR-15.accdb
frmEmpData

12. Click **OK**. The form now opens.

13. Close the form.

Using a Submacro

A method of increasing the flexibility of a macro is to create a macro group. A *submacro* is a macro that contains two or more actions. A macro group displays in the Navigation Pane as a single macro object. The name of each submacro displays in the Macro Name column.

Using submacros can help you organize the steps or sequence of actions. For database designers that have programming experience, submacros can be an effective method of developing macros.

Exercise 15-6 RUN A MACRO WITH SUBMACROS

Individual macros contained in a macro group can be executed individually or as part of the macro group. Open the form that displays interns by department and run the submacros associated with that form.

1. Open **frmInternByDept** in **Form View**. This form is formatted to be a pop-up form. Notice that there are 12 interns in the database.

2. Click the **Marketing** button. Navigate through the records to see that there are only two interns that work in the **Marketing** department.

3. Click the **Show All** button. The filter has been removed so all 12 intern records are now visible.

4. Click the **Sales** button. Nothing happens. This button has not been assigned a macro yet.

5. Close the form and reopen it in **Design View**.

6. In the **Marketing** button's (**cmdShwMarket**) **Property Sheet**, on the **Event** tab, and click in the **On Click** property. Click the Build button 🔲. In the **Macro Builder** window opens.

7. From the **Design** tab, in the **Collapse/Expand** group, click **Collapse All** 🔳.

8. This macro contains four submacros, each with its own name. Click **ShwMarket**. Click the submacro's expand button ⊞.

9. From the **Design** tab, in the **Collapse/Expand** group, click **Expand Actions** 🔳. This submacro sets the form's filter to "[DeptID]=1".

Figure 15-7
Submacros in the
Macro Builder
HR-15.accdb
mcrShwDept

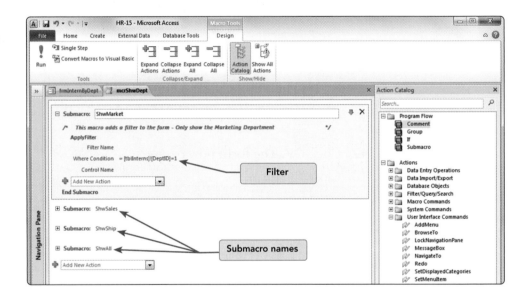

10. Expand each of the submacros to see the differences in the filters.

11. Close the macro. Since we changed the appearance of the macro, click **Yes** to save the macro.

Exercise 15-7   EDIT A SUBMACRO

Each submacro is an independent macro that can be modified individually. A submacro can be added, edited, or deleted from the main macro.

1. Click the **Sales** button. In its **Property Sheet**, on the **Event** tab, in the **On Click** property, choose **mcrShwDept.ShwSales**.

2. Switch to **Form View**. Test the **Sales** button. There are five interns in the sales department.

3. Right-click the title bar of the form and choose **Design View**.

4. From the Navigation Pane, right-click **mcrShwDept** and choose Design View.

5. From the Design tab, in the Collapse/Expand group, click Collapse All 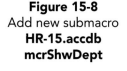.

6. From the Action Catalog pane, under Program Flow, double-click Submacro and key ShwStocking.

7. Click the Add New Action control that is within the submacro **ShwStocking**. Click the drop-down arrow, choose ApplyFilter, and press [Tab].

8. In the Where Condition argument, key tbli and press [Tab] to add the table **tblInterns** to the expression.

9. Key .d and press [Tab] to add the field **DeptID** to the expression.

10. Key =4. The final expression is **[tblInterns].[DeptID]=4**.

11. Click the submacro **ShwStocking**. Both the submacro and action have a move and delete control. Click the submacro's green up arrow to move the submacro above **ShwAll**.

12. In the Action Catalog pane, under Program Flow, double-click Comment. Key This macro adds a filter to the form – Only show the Stocking Department.

13. Click the comment's green up arrow to move the comment above **ApplyFilter**.

14. From the Design tab, in the Collapse/Expand group, click Collapse All 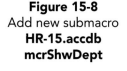.

15. Click the **ShwStocking** submacro's expand button ⊞.

Figure 15-8
Add new submacro
**HR-15.accdb
mcrShwDept**

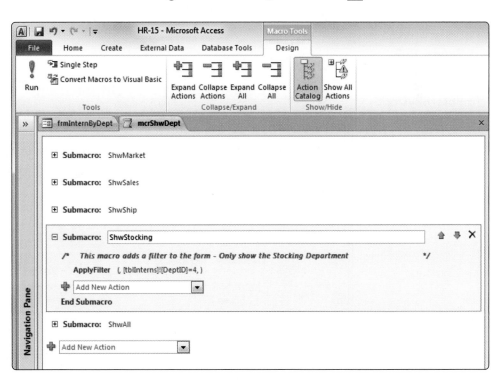

16. Save and close the macro.

Exercise 15-8 ADD A COMMAND BUTTON WITH MACRO

Some wizards, like the Command Button Wizard, allow you to assign macros while in the wizard. You will now use the Command Button Wizard to assign a macro to a command button in the Intern by Department form.

1. Return to the Design View of **frmInternByDept**.

2. From the Design tab, in the Controls group, click the Build button ▦, then click below the title in the Form Header.

3. In the Command Button Wizard, in the Category section, choose Miscellaneous. In the Actions section, choose Run Macro. Click Next.

4. From the list of macros, choose **mcrShwDept.ShwStocking**. Click Next.

5. Select the Text option and key Stocking. Click Next.

6. Name the control **cmdShwStock** and click Finish.

7. Drag the command button **cmdShwStock** between the **Shipping** and **Show All** command buttons.

8. Click the **Shipping** command button. From the Format tab, in the Font group, click Format Painter ✈. Now click the command button **cmdShwStock**.

9. In Property Sheet for **cmdShwStock**, on the Form tab, change the Height property to **.25**.

10. Save the form and switch to Form View and test the **Stocking** button. There are two interns in the stocking department.

Figure 15-9
Completed form
HR-15.accdb
frmInternByDept

11. Close the form.

Creating Macros with Conditions

Some macros can have conditions. A *macro condition* is a macro property that specifies criteria that must be met before an action executes. A macro condition can contain any combination of mathematical or logical operators, constants, functions, and fields. Expressions in a macro condition can perform calculations, manipulate characters, or test data.

Exercise 15-9 CREATE MACRO CONDITIONS

If you are a programmer, you are familiar with IF statements. An IF statement is a common macro condition. You now will create an IF statement to determine the pay classification of each employee. At EcoMed Services, employees are classified as monthly or hourly. For monthly employees, the value of the PayTypeID field is set to 1. For hourly employees, the value of the PayTypeID field is set to 2.

The macro condition can be evaluated as either true or false. In Lesson 3, you worked with criteria in queries. The true and false values in a macro are the same as in a query. True values are stored as –1 and false values are stored as 0. Therefore, if the field is checked, it is equal to –1; if the field is not checked, it is equal to 0.

REVIEW

The Yes/No data type stores the value 0 for unchecked check box and –1 for checked.

1. Open **frmEmpData** in Design View.
2. Click the label of the **EmpPay** control under the employee photo.
3. In the label's Property Sheet, on the Other tab, change the Name property to **lblEmpPay**.
4. Click the Form Selector. In the form's Property Sheet, on the Event tab, in the On Current property, click the Build button .

NOTE

Access uses exclamation marks (!) between object categories, major objects, and fields. Periods (.) are used between controls and their properties.

5. In the Choose Builder dialog box, choose Macro Builder and click OK.
6. From the Action Catalog pane, under the Program Flow, double-click If.
7. The data that we need to check are on the form. Key **forms** and press Tab.

8. Next we need to pick which form to look at. Key **!frm** and double-click **frmEmpData** from the list.
9. Next we need to look at the field in the form. Key **!p** and press Tab to add the field **PayTypeID**.
10. We now need to compare the field to a value. Key **=1**. The final expression should be: **[Forms]![frmEmpData]![PayTypeID]=1**.
11. Click the Add New Action control below the If control and choose SetProperty.

12. Next we need to identify the control whose properties need to be changed. In the **Control Name** argument, key **lbl** and press ⎋Tab⎋ to add the control **lblEmpPay**.

13. In the **Property** argument, key **c** and press ⎋Tab⎋ to add the property **Caption**.

14. In the **Value** argument, key **Hourly Pay**.

15. Click on the **If** control. Select all of the text in the control and press ⎋Ctrl⎋+⎋C⎋.

16. On the right side of the **Macro Builder** window, click the **Add Else If** link. This location is where we will check to see if **PayTypeID** equals two.

17. In the **Else If** control, press ⎋Ctrl⎋+⎋V⎋. Change the last number from a 1 to a **2**.

18. Click in the **Add New Action** control under the **Else If** control. Key **setp** and press ⎋Tab⎋ to add the action **SetProperty**.

19. In the **Control Name** argument, key **lbl** and press ⎋Tab⎋ to add the control **lblEmpPay**.

20. In the **Property** argument, choose **Caption**.

21. In the **Value** argument, key **Monthly Pay**.

22. From the **Design** tab, in the **Collapse/Expand** group, click **Expand All** ⊞.

Figure 15-10
If Else statement in a macro
HR-15.accdb
frmEmpData

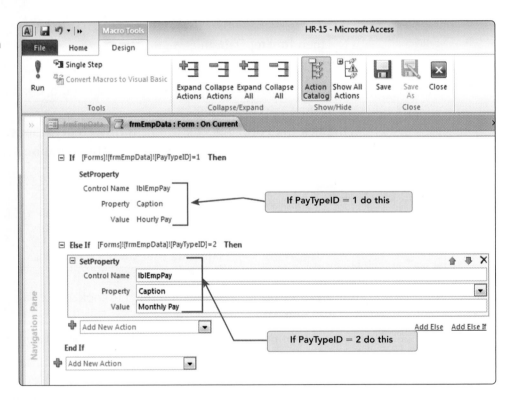

23. From the **Design** tab, in the **Close** group, click **Close** ⊠ and save the changes.

24. Switch **frmEmpData** to **Form View** and navigate through several records to see the label change for hourly and monthly employees.

Exercise 15-10 TRAP INVALID DATA IN A MACRO

The macro that we just created will work as long as the value of PayTypeID is either 1 or 2. It will not work if the value is another number or if the field is left empty (null). We will add an error trap to tell us if any other value is present in this field. In this case, a null value is considered invalid data.

You will improve the macro by adding an error trap. An *error trap* is a procedure that tests for an error condition and provides a corresponding procedure to recover from the error.

1. Switch to Design View.

2. In the form's Property Sheet, on the Event tab, in the On Current property, click the Build button ⊡.

3. Click the Else If control.

4. On the right side of the Macro Builder window, click the Add Else link. This location is where we can place an error message.

5. We need to add a message box. Key me and press Tab.

6. In the Message argument, key The field PayTypeID contains invalid data. This field should only store the values 1 or 2.

7. In the Type argument, choose Critical.

8. In the Title argument, key Invalid Data.

Figure 15-11
Error trapped macro
**HR-15.accdb
frmEmpData**

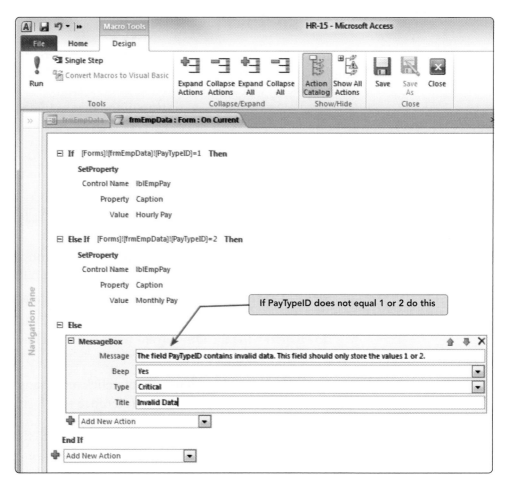

9. Save and close the macro.

10. From the Navigation Pane, double-click **tblPay**. Locate the record for **EmployeeID** "101." Delete this record's **PayTypeID**. This action creates a NULL value in this field.

11. Switch **frmEmpData** to Form View.

12. Press PageDown to move to employee 101.

Figure 15-12
Error message
HR-15.accdb
frmEmpData

13. Click OK.

14. In **tblPay**, change **EmployeeID** "101" **PayTypeID** to **Salary**. Close the table.

15. In **frmEmpData**, press PageUp and then PageDown. The error message does not appear.

16. Save the form.

Exercise 15-11 TRAP MISUSE OF A MACRO

The macro that you created is a stand-alone macro. It can only be used in the employee data form. If you try to run the macro anywhere else, a standard error message will appear.

You now will add an error trap in the macro to display more information than the standard error message.

1. Switch to Design View.

2. In the form's Property Sheet, on the Event tab, in the On Current property, click the Build button ⊡.

3. Press Ctrl+A to select all of the macro. Press Ctrl+C to copy the macro. Close the macro.

4. From the Create tab, in the Macros & Code group, click Macro ⊠. Press Ctrl+V to paste the embedded macro into the stand-alone macro.

5. Save the macro as mcrChangeLabel. Close the macro.

6. In the Property Sheet for **frmEmpData**, on the Event tab, click the drop-down arrow for the On Current property and choose **mcrChangeLabel**.

7. Close and save the form.

8. From the Navigation Pane, double-click **mcrChangeLabel**. An error message appears stating that a reference to a form is missing. A more detailed message is needed.

9. Click OK. The macro failed, so click Stop All Marcos.

10. From the Navigation Pane, right-click **mcrChangeLabel** and choose Design View.

11. From the Action Catalog pane, under the Program Flow, double-click Submacro. Key **ErrorMsg** as the new name of the submacro.

12. From the Action Catalog pane, under Actions, expand the User Interface Commands folder.

13. Double-click the action MessageBox.

14. In the Message argument, key **This macro is intended to only be used by the form frmEmpData and can't be used by any other object.**

15. In the Type argument, choose Critical.

16. In the Title argument, key **Usage Error.**

17. From the Design tab, in the Collapse/Expand group, click Collapse All ⬛.

18. From the Action Catalog pane, under Actions, expand the Macro Commands folder. Drag the action OnError above the If control. The OnError action needs to be the first action in the macro.

19. In the Go to argument, choose Macro Name.

20. In the Macro Name argument, key **ErrorMsg.**

Figure 15-13
Error trap
HR-15.accdb
mcrChangeLabel

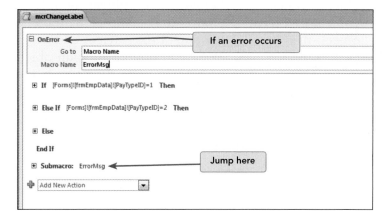

21. Save and close the macro.

22. From the Navigation Pane, double-click **mcrChangeLabel**. Our custom error message now appears. Click OK.

Exercise 15-12 PRINT MACRO DEFINITIONS

Because a macro is a major object, you can print its definition using the Database Documenter.

1. From the Database Tools tab, in the Analyze group, click Database Documenter 📄.

2. On the Macros tab and select **mcrChangeLabel.**

3. Click **Options**.

4. Only include **Actions and Arguments**. Click **OK**.

5. Click **OK** again. View the report. Each line of the macro is displayed.

6. Close the report.

Creating a Module and a Visual Basic Routine

When automating procedures, many database professionals prefer to create modules rather than macros. Modules use the Visual Basic for Applications language. To truly use the power of modules, you need to become knowledgeable in Visual Basic syntax, coding techniques, and control structures.

Exercise 15-13   EXPLORE VISUAL BASIC EDITOR

The Visual Basic Editor defaults to display three docked panes. On the left are the Project and Properties panes. On the right is the Code pane. Listed in the Project pane are the modules associated with the current database.

You will work with two types of modules: stand-alone and embedded. A *stand-alone module* is a global module that you can assign to numerous objects. An *embedded module* is an object module occurring on a specific control in a form or report. Only stand-alone modules are visible as major objects in the module section of the Navigation Pane.

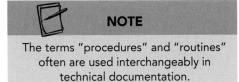

NOTE

The terms "procedures" and "routines" often are used interchangeably in technical documentation.

When you double-click an object in the Project pane, the associated code displays in the Code pane. Code is divided into procedures. A *procedure* is a series of commands and properties that performs a specific task. When a module has multiple procedures, horizontal lines separate each procedure.

1. From the **Database Tools** tab, in the **Macro** group, click **Visual Basic**. A new window opens called **Microsoft Visual Basic for Applications** (VBA).

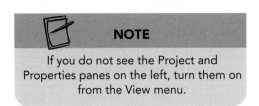

NOTE

If you do not see the Project and Properties panes on the left, turn them on from the View menu.

2. If the database **EcoMed (HR-15)** is not already expanded, click Expand ⊞ in the **Project** pane.

3. If needed, click Expand ⊞ by the **Microsoft Access Class Objects** folder.

4. Double-click the form **Form_frmEmpConfidential**. The code that is stored in the module is now viewable in the Code pane.

Figure 15-14
Visual Basic Editor
HR-15.accdb
frmEmpConfidential

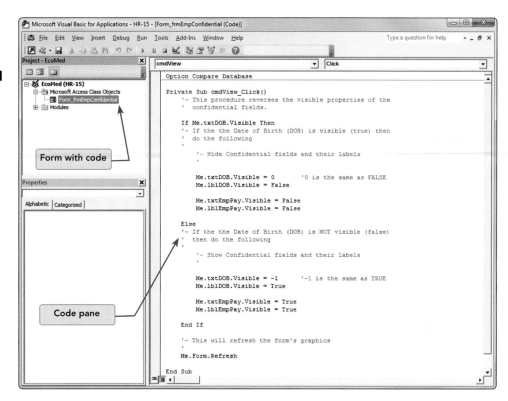

5. Click **View Microsoft Access** to return to Access without closing VBA.

Exercise 15-14 CREATE A MODULE AND VISUAL BASIC ROUTINE

Creating a Visual Basic routine often requires you to use special characters and system functions. The special characters and system functions for this lesson are listed in the following table.

Table 15-2 Common Visual Basic Symbols and Functions

Special Character/System Function	Description
&	Concatenates two strings (must have a space before and after it)
_ (underscore)	Joins two lines (must have a space before it)
Chr(13)	Inserts a hard return
Date	Returns current date
Time	Returns current time

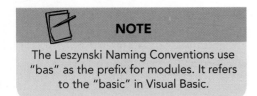

1. From the **Create** tab, in the **Macros & Code** group, click **Module** ⚛. This action will reopen the VBA Editor and create a new module within the **Modules** folder named **Module1** by default.

2. Click **Module1**. From the button bar, click Save 🖫 and key **basMsg**. Click **OK**.

Figure 15-15
Saving a module
HR-15.accdb
frmEmpConfidential

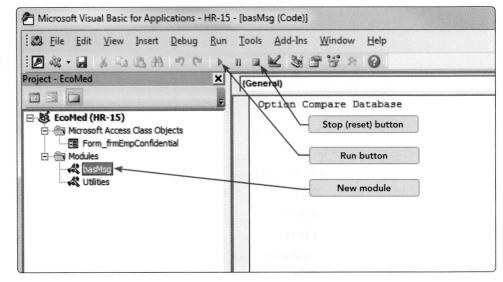

3. Click in the Code pane. From the **Insert** menu, choose **Procedure** to open the **Add Procedure** dialog box.

4. In the **Name** control, key **ShowDateTime**. Click **OK**. The VBA Editor adds the first and last line of the new procedure for you.

5. Press Tab. Key the text shown in Figure 15-16, including a space and underscore at the end of the first line.

Figure 15-16
Parts of the MsgBox statement
HR-15.accdb
frmEmpConfidential

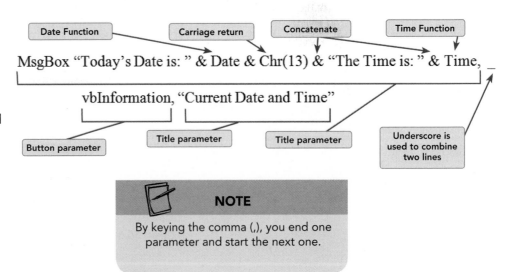

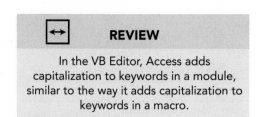

6. Press `PageDown` to see the completed message box statement.

7. Click on the first line of the procedure. Click Save 💾.

8. Click Run ▶ to test your message box. Click **OK**.

Figure 15-17
Current Date and Time dialog box
HR-15.accdb
frmEmpConfidential

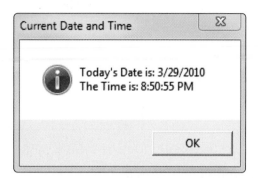

9. Click **View Microsoft Access** 📷 to return to Access.

Exercise 15-15 ASSIGN A PROCEDURE TO AN EVENT

As you know, a procedure is a series of commands and properties that perform a task. After writing a procedure, you must assign it to an event on an object. Assigning a procedure to an event provides a means to execute the procedure.

1. Open **frmEmpData** in **Design View**.

2. In the **Form Header**, add a command button to the left of the other button. Cancel the wizard.

3. In the command button's **Property Sheet**, on the **Other** tab, change the **Name** property to **cmdDateTime**.

4. On the **Format** tab, change the **Caption** property to **Show Date and Time**.

5. On the **Event** tab, in the **On Click** property, click the Build button 🔳.

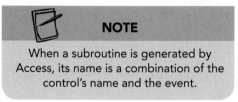

6. From the **Choose Builder** dialog box, choose **Code Builder** and click **OK**. The VBA Editor opens, and a new procedure has been added.

7. Press `Tab`. Key the following (including the period): **basMsg.**

8. After you type the period, the names of all procedures in the module **basMsg** appear. Key **s** and then press `Tab` to complete the statement. Press `↓`.

Figure 15-18
Use the procedure
ShowDateTime.
**HR-15.accdb
frmEmpData**

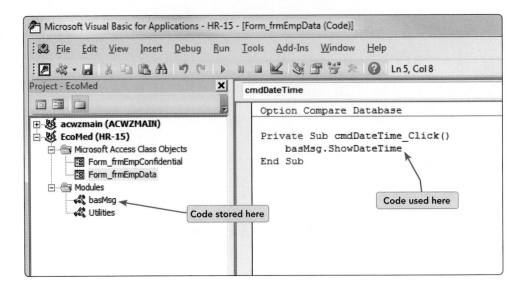

9. Save the procedure and return to Access.

10. Use the Format Painter to format the new button like the other command button in the **Form Header**. Resize the button so all text is visible.

11. In **Form View**, test the **Show Date and Time** button.

12. Save and close the form.

Modifying a Form Module Routine

Form modules often contain event procedures. An event procedure automatically executes in response to an action initiated by a user, program code, or system-triggered event. You can use event procedures to control the behavior of a form or report.

Exercise 15-16 MODIFY A TEXT BOX AND LABEL PROPERTY

You now will create a procedure that displays or hides confidential information when a command button is clicked. Even when the confidential information is not visible, the controls are still part of the form. You will create a routine to hide the social security number of each employee.

1. Open **frmEmpConfidential** in **Form View**. Click the **Confidential Information** button. The last two fields are removed from the form. Click the button again, and the fields reappear.

2. Switch to **Design View**.

3. With the Property Sheet open, click the drop-down arrow for the Object box. Notice that most of the controls in this form have been named using the Leszynski Naming Conventions.

4. In the Form Header section, click the **Confidential Information** command button. In the Property Sheet, on the Format tab, notice the Caption shows the text on the button. The name for this control is **cmdView**.

5. Click the Event tab and click in the On Click property. This control has an Event Procedure (VBA Code.) Click the Build button ⊡.

Figure 15-19
cmdView_Click
subroutine
HR-15.accdb
frmEmpConfidential

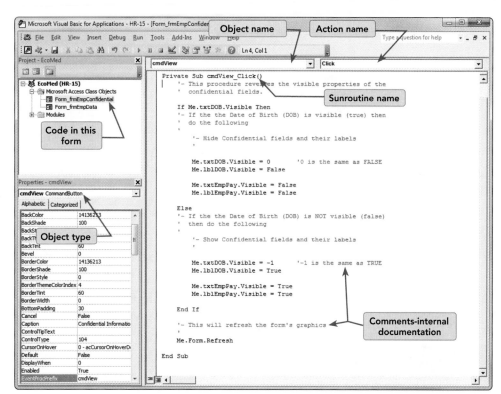

6. Click in the row right above the "Else" statement. Press Tab twice. Key **me**.

7. Key a period. A list box appears with all the object and actions that are part of the form. Key **txt**. All the text boxes are grouped together on the list.

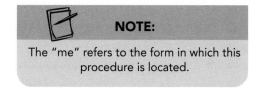

NOTE:

The "me" refers to the form in which this procedure is located.

Figure 15-20
List with properties
and actions
HR-15.accdb
frmEmpConfidential

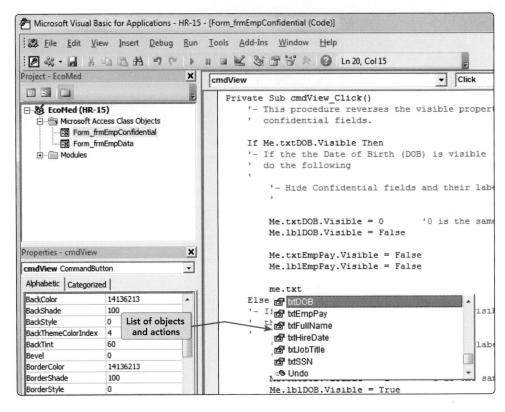

8. Key **s** and press Tab to add **txtSSN** to the expression.

9. Key a period. A list box appears with all the properties for the text box control that you would see in the control's **Property Sheet**. Key **vi**. Press Tab to add the property **Visible** to the expression.

10. Key **=**.

11. This property has two possible settings: **True** and **False**. Key **f**.

12. To complete the expression, press Enter. This expression will make the control **txtSSN** invisible.

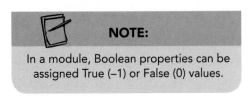

NOTE:

In a module, Boolean properties can be assigned True (–1) or False (0) values.

Figure 15-21
New VBA expression
HR-15.accdb
frmEmpConfidential

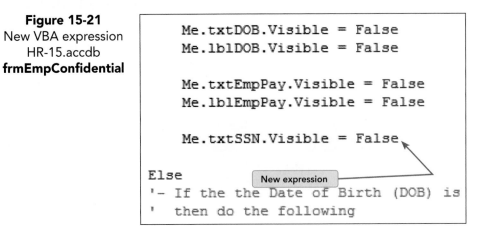

```
    Me.txtDOB.Visible = False
    Me.lblDOB.Visible = False

    Me.txtEmpPay.Visible = False
    Me.lblEmpPay.Visible = False

    Me.txtSSN.Visible = False

Else                     New expression
'-  If the the Date of Birth (DOB) is
'   then do the following
```

13. Key the following statement, using the same steps as above:

    Me.lblSSN.Visible = False

14. Copy the two statements that you have created and paste them above the "End If" statement.

15. Change the copied statements, so that instead of ending with "False," they are True.

Figure 15-22
Change a text box
and label property
HR-15.accdb
frmEmpConfidential

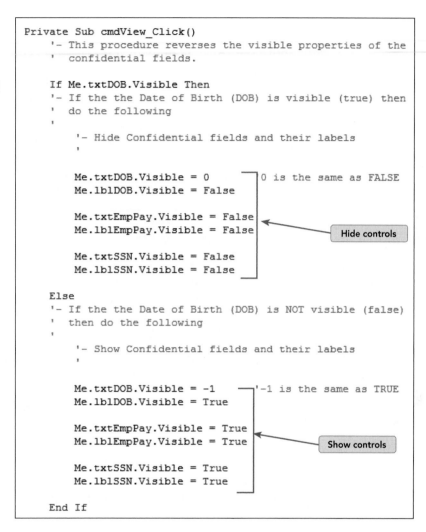

```
Private Sub cmdView_Click()
    '- This procedure reverses the visible properties of the
    ' confidential fields.

    If Me.txtDOB.Visible Then
    '- If the the Date of Birth (DOB) is visible (true) then
    ' do the following
    '

        '- Hide Confidential fields and their labels
        '

        Me.txtDOB.Visible = 0          0 is the same as FALSE
        Me.lblDOB.Visible = False

        Me.txtEmpPay.Visible = False
        Me.lblEmpPay.Visible = False   ← Hide controls

        Me.txtSSN.Visible = False
        Me.lblSSN.Visible = False

    Else
    '- If the the Date of Birth (DOB) is NOT visible (false)
    ' then do the following
    '

        '- Show Confidential fields and their labels
        '

        Me.txtDOB.Visible = -1         '-1 is the same as TRUE
        Me.lblDOB.Visible = True

        Me.txtEmpPay.Visible = True
        Me.lblEmpPay.Visible = True    ← Show controls

        Me.txtSSN.Visible = True
        Me.lblSSN.Visible = True

    End If
```

16. Click Save 🖫 and then View Microsoft Access 🔲. The form reappears.

17. Switch to **Form View** and test the **Confidential Information** button. The button now hides and displays the last three columns.

18. Save the form.

Exercise 15-17 MODIFY A COMMAND BUTTON PROPERTY

After creating a command button, you can modify its properties. You should always change the visible properties of the button to inform the user of the purpose of the button.

1. From the **Database Tools** tab, in the **Macro** group, click **Visual Basic**. You return to the VBA Editor.

2. In the Code pane for the procedure **cmdView_Click**, click in the row right above the "Else" statement. Press Enter.

3. Press Tab and key **me**, then a period.

4. Key **cmd** and press Tab to add the command button to the expression. Key a period.

5. Key **cap** and press Tab to add the **Caption** property to the expression.

6. Key = "**Show Confidential Information**" and press Enter.

Figure 15-23
Change a command
button property
HR-15.accdb
frmEmpConfidential

```
      Me.txtDOB.Visible = False
      Me.lblDOB.Visible = False

      Me.txtEmpPay.Visible = False
      Me.lblEmpPay.Visible = False

      Me.txtSSN.Visible = False
      Me.lblSSN.Visible = False

      Me.cmdView.Caption = "Show Confidential Information"

Else
'- If the the Date of Birth (DOB) is NOT visible (false)
'  then do the following
'
```

7. Click in the row right above the "End If" statement. Press Enter.

8. Key the following statement, using the same steps as above:
   Me.cmdView.Caption = "Hide Confidential Information"

9. Press Enter.

TIP

Indenting makes the code easier to
read but has no effect on the function
of the code.

Figure 15-24
Completed
procedure
**HR-15.accdb
frmEmpConfidential**

```
Private Sub cmdView_Click()
    '- This procedure reverses the visible properties of the
    ' confidential fields.

    If Me.txtDOB.Visible Then
    '- If the the Date of Birth (DOB) is visible (true) then
    ' do the following
    '
        '- Hide Confidential fields and their labels
        '

        Me.txtDOB.Visible = 0          '0 is the same as FALSE
        Me.lblDOB.Visible = False

        Me.txtEmpPay.Visible = False
        Me.lblEmpPay.Visible = False

        Me.txtSSN.Visible = False
        Me.lblSSN.Visible = False

        Me.cmdView.Caption = "Show Confidential Information"

    Else
    '- If the the Date of Birth (DOB) is NOT visible (false)
    ' then do the following
    '
        '- Show Confidential fields and their labels
        '

        Me.txtDOB.Visible = -1         '-1 is the same as TRUE
        Me.lblDOB.Visible = True

        Me.txtEmpPay.Visible = True
        Me.lblEmpPay.Visible = True

        Me.txtSSN.Visible = True
        Me.lblSSN.Visible = True

        Me.cmdView.Caption = "Hide Confidential Information"

    End If

    '- This will refresh the form's graphics
    '
    Me.Form.Refresh

End Sub
```

10. Click Save ⊞. Close the VBA Editor.

11. Return to the form. Test the button. The caption changes with each click.

12. Close the form.

Exercise 15-18 PRINT VISUAL BASIC CODE

Through VBA, you can print standard, form, and report modules. Code that is stored in an object like a form must be printed using the Documenter on the form. Code that is created in the VBA Editor is stored in Modules.

Printing this code requires the Documenter to look at the Module object. Printing a module's code provides external documentation for developing code and error trapping.

1. From the Database Tools tab, in the Analyze group, click Database Documenter ▣.
2. On the Modules tab, select **basMsg**.
3. Click Options.
4. Only include Code. Click OK.
5. Click OK again. View the report.
6. Close the report.
7. From the Database Tools tab, in the Analyze group, click Database Documenter ▣.
8. On the Forms tab and select **frmEmpConfidential**.
9. Click Options.
10. In the Include for Form section, include only Code.
11. In the Include for Sections and Controls section, select Nothing. Click OK.
12. Click OK again. View the report.
13. Close Print Preview.

Exercise 15-19   CREATE AN ACCDE FILE

In an ACCDE file, the Visual Basic code continues to run, but it can no longer be viewed or modified. Because all source code is removed, ACCDE databases are typically smaller than ACCDB databases.

In an ACCDE database, you cannot make changes to its forms, reports, or modules. Therefore, it is very important that you always safeguard the original file and its source code.

1. From the File tab, in the Save & Publish option, double-click Make ACCDE ▣.
2. Name the file **HR-exe** and click Save. Close the database.
3. Compare the size of the files *[your initials]*-**HR-15** and **HR-exe**. Is there a difference?
4. Open the database **HR-exe**.
5. Click Open in the security notice.
6. From the Database Tools tab, in the Macro group, click Visual Basic ▣.
7. Expand the folders in the Project pane until you find **Form_frmEmpData**. Double-click it. All the code is locked.
8. Click OK. Close both the VBA Editor and the database.

Lesson 15   Summary

- A macro is an object that completes an action or set of actions.
- A module is a collection of Visual Basic declarations and procedures that are stored together as a unit.
- The main difference between a macro and a module is the level of complexity. Generally, macros are simple procedures with a limited number of steps. Modules, in contrast, are involved procedures used to build user interfaces.
- A macro consists of individual macro actions. Most actions require one or more arguments.
- A stand-alone macro is a global macro that you can assign to numerous objects.
- An embedded macro is an object macro occurring on a specific control in a form or report.
- Typically a macro attached to a command button is assigned the On Click event.
- When you open the Macro Builder, Access displays the Action column, the Arguments column, and the Comment column.
- To be executed, a macro should be assigned to an event on an object or control.
- A stand-alone module is a global module that you can assign to numerous objects. An embedded module is an object module occurring on a specific control in a form or report.
- To print stand-alone code, you must use the documenter on the module object. To print embedded code, you must use the documenter on the source object.
- A macro condition is a macro property that specifies criteria that must be met before an action executes.
- An error trap is a procedure that tests for an error condition and provides a corresponding procedure to recover from the error.
- The Visual Basic Editor defaults to display three docked panes.
- A stand-alone module is a global module that you can assign to numerous objects.
- An embedded module is an object module occurring on a specific control in a form or report.
- A procedure is a series of commands and properties that perform a specific task.
- Converting a database to an ACCDE file compiles modules, removes comments, removes source code, and compacts the destination database.
- In an ACCDE database, you cannot make changes to its forms, reports, or modules.

Command Summary			
Feature	**Button**	**Task Path**	**Keyboard**
Macro, Create		Create, Macros & Code, Macro	
Macros, Expand Action		Design View, Collapse/Expand, Expand Action	
Macro, Collapse All		Design View, Collapse/Expand, Collapse All	
Visual Basic		Database Tools, Macro, Visual Basic	Alt + F11
VBA, Access, View		View, Microsoft Access	Alt + F11
Module, Create		Create, Macros & Code, Module	
Visual Basic, Run		Run, Run Macro	F5

Concepts Review

True/False Questions

Each of the following statements is either true or false. Indicate your choice by circling T or F.

T F 1. Macros are involved procedures used to build Visual Basic interfaces.

T F 2. Modules run faster than macros.

T F 3. In Access, macros are recorded similar to the way macros are recorded in Word and Excel.

T F 4. You can test a macro by running it from the Macro Design window.

T F 5. A procedure is a series of commands and properties that perform a specific task.

T F 6. You can insert, but not delete, Action rows in a macro.

T F 7. Standard modules can be used by only one form or report.

T F 8. In an ACCDE file, you can view the Visual Basic code in each module.

Short Answer Questions

Write the correct answer in the space provided.

1. Typically, a macro attached to a command button is assigned to what event?

   _____

2. In the Design View of a macro, what two columns always display?

   _____

3. What are the names of the two arguments in a SetProperty action?

   _____

4. In the Navigation Pane, what types of modules are listed?

   _____

5. What property hides or shows a control?

   _____

6. In the VBA Editor, what is displayed in the Code pane when you double-click an object in the Project pane?

   _____

7. What are the VBA names of the four icons you can display in a message box?

_____

8. What does the function Chr(13) represent in a VBA module?

_____

Critical Thinking

Answer these questions on a separate page. There are no right or wrong answers. Support your answers with examples from your own experience, if possible.

1. Discuss the similarities and differences between using a macro and a Visual Basic module.

2. Open the Property Sheet for a command button in one of your forms and look at the Help screen for several events. Develop ideas for macros or modules that might be appropriate for three new events.

Skills Review

Exercise 15-20

You have been asked to modify the inventory details form with VBA code to hide the picture on the form when the form is printed. Hiding the picture will reduce the amount of toner needed to print the record.

1. Open a database by following these steps:
   a. Locate and open the **Lesson 15** folder.
   b. If you already have a copy of *[your initials]*-**EcoMed-15**, skip to step 1d.
   c. Make a copy of **EcoMed-15** and rename it to *[your initials]*-EcoMed-15.
   d. Open and enable content for *[your initials]*-**EcoMed-15**.
   e. Refresh the links with *[your initials]*-**Shared Data-15**.

2. Add a command button to a form by following these steps:
   a. Open **frmInvDetails** in Design View.
   b. From the Design tab, in the Controls group, click Button ▭ and click to the left side of the **Picture OFF** button. Click Cancel to close the wizard.
   c. Use Format Painter 🖌 to copy the format from the **Picture OFF** button to the new command button.

d. In the new command button's Property Sheet, on the Format tab, change the Caption property to Picture ON.

e. On the Other tab, change the Name property to cmdPicOn.

3. Create a procedure by following these steps:

a. On the Event tab, click the On Click property, then click the Build button and choose Code Builder. Click OK.

b. In the VBA Editor, press Tab and then ' (apostrophe) and key Created by: *[your full name]*.

c. Press Enter twice.

d. Key me.imgpic.visible=true.

e. Press Enter.

f. Save the procedure and click View Microsoft Access to return to Access.

g. Test both command buttons.

h. Save and close the form.

Assessment

> - Turn in your database only when all assigned exercises have been completed, according to your classroom procedure.

- OR -

15-20-A.pdf
1 Page

> - Create a Database Documenter report by following these steps:
>
> a. From the Database Tools tab, in the Analyze group, click Database Documenter 📑.
>
> b. On the Forms tab, select **frmInvDetails**.
>
> c. Click Options. From the Include for Form section, choose only Code.
>
> d. For the Include for Sections and Controls section, choose Nothing.
>
> e. Click OK twice.
>
> - Save a Database Documenter report by following these steps:
>
> a. From the Print Preview tab, in the Data group, click PDF or XPS 🗔 to save the printout as a file.
>
> b. Save the file as a PDF and name the file *[your initials]*-15-20-A.
>
> c. Depending on your class procedures, print or turn in the PDF file.

Exercise 15-21

Your supervisor has asked you to add a notice of confidential information that can be added to more than one form.

1. Create a standard module by following these steps:

a. Open, enable, and update the links for *[your initials]*-EcoMed-15.

b. From the Create tab, in the Macros & Code group, click Module .

c. Click Save 🖫 and key basMsg.

2. Create a procedure by following these steps:

a. Click in the code area. From the Insert menu, click Procedure. Name the new procedure LegalNotice. Click OK.

b. Press [Tab] and then ['] (apostrophe) and key Created by: *[your full name]*.

c. Press [Enter] twice and key msgbox.

d. Finish the statement to match Figure 15-25. Remember to always key a space before and after using the & (ampersand) symbol.

Figure 15-25
MsgBox Statement

```
msgbox    "CONFIDENTIALTY STATEMENT" & chr(13) & chr(13) & _

          "This database contains information that is confidential. " & _

          "Dissemination, distribution, copying, or use of this " & _

          "information by anyone other than current employees of " & _

          "EcoMed is prohibited. " , vbcritical, "Legal Notice"
```

NOTE

If the statement turns red, a typographical error has occurred. Correct the error and click away from the message box statement to see if you were able to fix the expression.

e. Press [Enter]. If you keyed the statement correctly, Access will add capitalization to keywords.

f. Save the procedure and click View Microsoft Access 🖺 to return to Access.

3. Assign a procedure to an event by following these steps:

a. Open frmShipment-Main in Design View.

b. In the form's Property Sheet, on the Event tab, in the On Open property, click the Build button 📖 and choose Code Builder. Click OK.

c. Press [Tab] and then ['] (apostrophe) and key Created by: *[your full name]*.

d. Press [Enter] twice and key basmsg.legalnotice.

e. Press [Enter]. Save and click View Microsoft Access 🖺 to return to Access.

f. Switch to Form View. Click OK in the Legal Notice dialog box.

g. Save and close the form and then reopen it. Click OK.

h. Close the form.

Assessment

- Turn in your database only when all assigned exercises have been completed, according to your classroom procedure.

- OR -

- Create a Database Documenter report by following these steps:

  a. From the Database Tools tab, in the Analyze group, click Database Documenter.

  b. On the Modules tab, select **basMsg**.

  c. Click Options. From the Include for Module section, choose only Code.

  d. Click OK twice.

- Save a Database Documenter report by following these steps:

  a. From the Print Preview tab, in the Data group, click PDF or XPS to save the printout as a file.

  b. Save the file as a PDF and name the file *[your initials]*-15-21-A.

15-21-A.pdf
1 Page

- Create a Database Documenter report by following these steps:

  a. From the Database Tools tab, in the Analyze group, click Database Documenter.

  b. On the Forms tab, select **frmShipment-Main**.

  c. Click Options. From the Include for Form section, choose only Code.

  d. For the Include for Sections and Controls section, choose Nothing.

  e. Click OK twice.

- Save a Database Documenter report by following these steps:

  a. From the Print Preview tab, in the Data group, click PDF or XPS to save the printout as a file.

  b. Save the file as a PDF and name the file *[your initials]*-15-21-B.

  c. Depending on your class procedures, print or turn in both PDF files.

15-21-B.pdf
1 Page

Exercise 15-22

The sales department has noticed that not all facilities have a Medicare number. You have been asked to add a flag to facilities' contact form to display a notice whenever a facility does not have a Medicare number.

1. Add a label to a form by following these steps:

  a. Open, enable, and update the links for *[your initials]*-EcoMed-15.

  b. Open **frmFacContacts** in Design View.

  c. From the Design tab, in the Controls group, click Label and click in the Form Header below the title label.

  d. Key No Medicare Number Stored and press Enter.

  e. In the label's Property Sheet, on the Format tab, change the Visible property to No.

  f. Change the Font Weight property to Bold and the Fore Color property to #ED1C24.

  g. On the Other tab, change the Name property to lblMedicare.

h. Resize the label so that all of the text is visible.

i. Save the form.

2. Create an embedded macro by following these steps:

   a. In the form's **Property Sheet**, on the **Event** tab, in the **On Current** property, click the Build button ⬚.

   b. In the **Choose Builder** dialog box, choose **Macro Builder** and click **OK**.

   c. From the **Action Catalog**, under **Program Flow**, double-click **If**.

   d. On the right of the **If** expression, click the Build button ⬚.

   e. In the **Expression Builder**, in the **Expression Elements** panel, double-click the **Functions** folder. Click **Built-In Functions**.

   f. In the **Expression Categories** panel, click **Inspection**.

   g. In the **Expression Values** panel, double-click **IsNull**.

   h. In the top panel, click **<<expression>>**.

   i. In the **Expression Elements** panel, click the **frmFacContacts** folder.

   j. In the **Expression Categories** panel, click **<Field List>**.

   k. In the **Expression Values** panel, double-click **MedicareNum**. Click **OK**.

REVIEW

The results of the **IsNull** function is either True or False.

3. Add an action to a macro by following these steps:

   a. Under the **If** expression, click **Add New Action** and key **setp** and press ⟨Tab⟩ to add the **SetProperty** action.

   b. In the **Control Name** argument, key **lb** and then press ⟨Tab⟩ to add the label **lblMedicare**.

   c. In the **Property** argument, choose **Visible**.

   d. In the **Value** argument, key **−1**. Read the ToolTip for the **Value** argument. −1 = True and 0 = False.

   e. On the right side of the window, click **Add Else**.

   f. Key **setp** and press ⟨Tab⟩ to add the **SetProperty** action.

   g. In the **Control Name** argument, key **lb** and then press ⟨Tab⟩ to add the label **lblMedicare**.

   h. In the **Property** argument, choose **Visible**.

   i. In the **Value** argument, key **0**. This sets the visible property to false which hides the label.

4. Add a comment to a macro by following these steps:

   a. From the **Design** tab, on the **Collapse/Expand** group, click **Collapse All** ⬚.

   b. From the **Action Catalog**, under **Program Flow**, double-click **Comment**.

   c. Key **Created by:** *[your full name]*.

   d. Click the comment's green up arrow until the comment is above the **If** expression.

5. Save the macro as a stand-alone macro by following these steps:

   a. Click in the **If** expression. Press ⟨Ctrl⟩+⟨A⟩ to select all of the macro.

   b. Press ⟨Ctrl⟩+⟨C⟩ to copy the macro.

c. From the Design tab, in the Close group, click Close ☒. Click Yes to save the changes.

d. From the Create tab, in the Macros & Code group, click Macro .

e. Press Ctrl+V to paste the macro.

f. Press Ctrl+S and save the macro as mcrChkMed.

g. Close mcrChkMed.

h. In the Property Sheet for frmFacContacts, on the Event tab, click the drop-down arrow for the On Current property and choose mcrChkMed.

i. Save the form and switch to Form View.

j. Test your macro. Press PageDown to move through the records. Facility IDs 6, 7, and 9 don't have Medicare numbers.

k. Close the form.

Assessment

- Turn in your database only when all assigned exercises have been completed, according to your classroom procedure.

- OR -

15-22-A.pdf
2 Pages

- Create a Database Documenter report by following these steps:

a. From the Database Tools tab, in the Analyze group, click Database Documenter .

b. On the Macro tab, select mcrChkMed.

c. Click Options. From the Include for Macro section, choose only Actions and Arguments.

d. Click OK twice.

- Save a Database Documenter report by following these steps:

a. From the Print Preview tab, in the Data group, click PDF or XPS 🖫 to save the printout as a file.

b. Save the file as a PDF and name the file *[your initials]*-15-22-A.

c. Depending on your class procedures, print or turn in the PDF file.

d. Close Print Preview.

Exercise 15-23

Because there are so many items in the inventory, you have been asked to find a way to show only one bulb category at a time without creating four different forms.

1. Create a macro by following these steps:

a. Open, enable, and update the links for *[your initials]*-EcoMed-15.

b. Open **frmInvList**. This form has four command buttons that need to filter the form by bulb categories.

c. From the Create tab, in the Macros & Code group, click Macro ▨.

d. From the Action Catalog, under Program Flow, double-click Comment and key **Created by:** *[your full name]*.

e. Press Ctrl+S and name the macro **mcrBulbFilter**.

2. Add submacros to a macro by following these steps:

a. From the Action Catalog, under Program Flow, double-click Submacro and key **Diagnostic**.

b. Press Tab to move to the first Add New Action. Key **ap** and press Tab to add **ApplyFilter** action to the expression.

c. Press Tab. In the Where Condition argument, key **tbli** and press Tab to add the table **tblInventory** to the expression.

d. Key a period and press Tab to add the field **BulbCatID** to the expression.

e. Key **=1**, which is the **BulbCatID** for diagnostic bulbs.

f. Repeat step 2a through 2e to create submacros for the following categories.

Subform Name	BulbCatID
Indoor	2
Outdoor	3
Surgical	4

g. Save and close the macro.

3. Assign macros to command buttons by following these steps:

a. Open **frmInvList** in Design View.

b. In the **Diagnostic** command button's Property Sheet, on the Event tab, in the On Click property, choose **mcrBulbFilter.Diagnostic**.

c. In the **Indoor** command button's Property Sheet, on the Event tab, in the On Click property, choose **mcrBulbFilter.Indoor**.

d. In the **Outdoor** command button's Property Sheet, on the Event tab, in the On Click property, choose **mcrBulbFilter.Outdoor**.

e. In the **Surgical** command button's Property Sheet, on the Event tab, in the On Click property, choose **mcrBulbFilter.Surgical**.

4. Test the buttons by following these steps:

a. Switch to Form View and click each button.

b. The first diagnostic bulb's ID is 206. The first indoor bulb's ID is 1. The first outdoor bulb's ID is 55. The first surgical bulb's ID is 2.

c. Save and close the form.

Assessment

- Turn in your database only when all assigned exercises have been completed, according to your classroom procedure.

- OR -

15-23-A.pdf
2 Pages

- Create a Database Documenter report by following these steps:

    a. From the Database Tools tab, in the Analyze group, click Database Documenter 📄.

    b. On the Macro tab, select **mcrBulbFilter**.

    c. Click Options. From the Include for Macro section, choose only Actions and Arguments.

    d. Click OK twice.

- Save a Database Documenter report by following these steps:

    a. From the Print Preview tab, in the Data group, click PDF or XPS 📄 to save the printout as a file.

    b. Save the file as a PDF and name the file *[your initials]*-15-23-A.

15-23-B.pdf
2 Pages

- Save a form by following these steps:

    a. Click the **Diagnostic** command button.

    b. Click the File tab and from the Print option, click Print Preview 📄.

    c. From the Print Preview tab, in the Data group, click PDF or XPS 📄 to save the printout as a file.

    d. Save the file as a PDF and name the file *[your initials]*-15-23-B.

    e. Depending on your class procedures, print or turn in both PDF files.

Lesson Applications

Exercise 15-24

As part of a company-wide initiative to focus employees on core company values, the company president has asked you to create a method to display the company's Value Statement.

1. Open, enable, and update the links for *[your initials]*-EcoMed-15.

2. Create a new module called **basAbout**.

3. Create a new procedure called **ValueStatement**.

4. Add your name as a comment in the code.

5. Have the procedure display a message box with the text found in Figure 15-26.

Figure 15-26
Value Statement

```
EcoMed Services, Inc., is a forward-looking company that
believes energy efficiency is a fundamental factor in
progress toward sustainable energy usage. As a global
partner seeking to assist companies reduce their lighting
energy consumption, EcoMed Services, Inc., values pursuing
economical approaches to lighting effectiveness and
efficiency as a sustainable and environmentally friendly
service to consumers around the world.
```

6. The message box icon should be the **vbInformation**.

7. The message box title should be **Value Statement**.

8. In **frmJanShipStats**, add a command button under the logo control that when pressed will run the procedure **ValueStatment**.

9. Name the button **cmdValue**, with the caption **Value Statement**. Format the button so that both the **Back Style** and **Border Style** properties are transparent.

10. Test the new command button. Save and close the form.

Assessment

 - Turn in your database only when all assigned exercises have been completed, according to your classroom procedure.

- OR -

- Create a Database Documenter Report for **frmJanShipStats**.

  • Include for Form: Code only

  • Include for Sections and Controls: Nothing

- Save the Documenter report as a PDF file named *[your initials]*-15-24-A.

- Create a Database Documenter Report for **basAbout**.

  • Include for Module: Code only

- Save the Documenter report as a PDF file named *[your initials]*-15-24-B.

Depending on your class procedures, print or turn in both PDF files.

15-24-A.pdf
1 Page

15-24-B.pdf
1 Page

Exercise 15-25

Facilities are located in one of nine possible shipping regions. You have been directed to create nine submacros to filter the facilities to display only one region at a time.

1. Open, enable, and update the links for *[your initials]*-**EcoMed-15**.

2. Create a macro that will contain nine submacros, each filtering the list of facilities by regions.

3. Name the macro **mcrRegionFilter**.

4. Add the following comment Created by: *[your full name]* to the macro.

5. Use the following filters:

Submacro Name	Where Conditions
R1	[tblFacilities]![Region] = 1
R2	[tblFacilities]![Region] = 2
R3	[tblFacilities]![Region] = 3
R4	[tblFacilities]![Region] = 4
R5	[tblFacilities]![Region] = 5
R6	[tblFacilities]![Region] = 6
R7	[tblFacilities]![Region] = 7
R8	[tblFacilities]![Region] = 8
R9	[tblFacilities]![Region] = 9

6. In **frmFacList**, you will find nine command button. Assign each macro the appropriate command button. Test each command buttons. Region 2 has nine records and region 7 has 35 records.

7. Save and close the form.

Assessment

- Turn in your database only when all assigned exercises have been completed, according to your classroom procedure.

- OR -

15-25-A.pdf
4 Pages

- Create a Database Documenter Report for **mcrRegionFilter**.

  • Include for Query: Properties, SQL only
  • Include for Fields: Nothing
  • Include for Indexes: Nothing

- Save the Documenter report as a PDF file named *[your initials]*-15-25-A.

- Save **frmFacList** in Landscape and only showing **Region** 8 as a PDF file named *[your initials]*-15-25-B.

- Depending on your class procedures, print or turn in both PDF files.

15-25-B.pdf
1 Page

Exercise 15-26

You have been asked to modify the inventory specifications form to add a command button to hide or display the picture of the inventory item.

1. Open, enable, and update the links for *[your initials]*-EcoMed-15.

2. The form **frmInvSpecs** has two image controls, **imgPic** and **sbfIcon**, that need to be hidden in the form.

3. The form has command button called **cmdOnOff** under the title.

4. Modify the embedded module for the event **On Click** for **cmdOnOff**.

5. The module will perform the following actions:

   If the picture (**imgPic**) is visible, then
   • Set **imgPic** Visible property to **False**.
   • Set **sbfIcon** Visible property to **False**.
   • Change the **cmdOnOff's** Caption to Show Images.

   If Else (the picture is not visible)
   • Set **imgPic** Visible property to **True**.
   • Set **sbfIcon** Visible property to **True**.
   • Change the **cmdOnOff's** Caption to Hide Images.

6. Add a comment in the code, indicating **Created by:** *[your full name]*.

7. Test the button on different records.

Assessment

- Turn in your database only when all assigned exercises have been completed, according to your classroom procedure.

- OR -

- Create a Database Documenter Report for **frmInvSpecs**.
  - Include for Form: Code only
  - Include for Sections and Controls: Nothing
- Save the Documenter report as a PDF file named *[your initials]-* **15-26-A**.
- Depending on your class procedures, print or turn in the PDF file.

15-26-A.pdf
1 Page

Exercise 15-27 ◆ Challenge Yourself

Your supervisor has asked you to modify the vender form to change its properties to allow only data entry or editing of data.

1. Open, enable, and update the links for *[your initials]*-EcoMed-15.

2. In **frmVender**, there is a command button **cmdNewRecord** that has a module assigned to its **On Click** event. Change the caption of this button to **Add Vender**.

3. Modify the procedure to perform the following routine when clicked:

   If Data Entry for the form is equal to True, then
   - Set the Data Entry property to False.
   - Change the command button's Caption to Add Vender.
   - Change the form title's Caption to EcoMed – Venders Contact Information.

   If Else (the form is viewing all Vender records)
   - Set the Data Entry property to True.
   - Change the command button's Caption to View Venders.
   - Change the form title's Caption to EcoMed – Enter New Vender.

4. Add a comment to the code that includes your name.

5. Text your new code. When the form's Data Entry property is set to True will show "(New)" in the first field.

6. Save and close the form.

Assessment

- Turn in your database only when all assigned exercises have been completed, according to your classroom procedure.

- OR -

15-27-A.pdf
1 Page

- Create a **Database Documenter Report** for **frmVender.**

- Include for Form: **Code** only

- Include for Sections and Controls: **Nothing**

- Save the **Documenter** report as a PDF file named *[your initials]-*
  15-27-A.

- Depending on your class procedures, print or turn in the PDF file.

On Your Own

In these exercises you work on your own, as you would in a real-life work environment. Use the skills you've learned to accomplish the task—and be creative.

Exercise 15-28

Review the designs of the databases you modified in Exercise 14-27. Sketch a combination of three macros or Visual Basic modules that will enhance your design. You can modify your table structures to better accommodate your needs. For each sketch, write the name of the macro or module, describe its purpose, list the source dynaset(s), and list all object(s) with which the macro or module will be associated. Below each macro, write one to two paragraphs explaining why using a macro is more appropriate than using a module. Below each module, write one to two paragraphs explaining why using a module is more appropriate than using a macro. On each printout, write your name and "Exercise 15-28." Continue to the next exercise.

Exercise 15-29

Based on the sketches you created in Exercise 15-28, create the macros and modules. Associate each macro or module to the appropriate objects. Test each macro or module and all associated object(s). Print documentation for each macro or module. On each printout, write your name and "Exercise 15-29." Continue to the next exercise.

EXERCISE 15-30

Document your databases by providing printouts of the databases' structures and printouts of all your objects. Organize the printouts in an organized and logical manner. Include a cover page with your name, class information, and current date. Immediately behind the cover page, write at least three pages describing the most significant or important skills you learned and how you might approach designing a similar database differently in the future. Submit sketches and printouts from Exercises 15-28 through 15-30 to your instructor.

Unit 4 Applications

Unit Application 4-1

As part of the classroom requirements for your internship at EcoMed Services, Inc., you are required to demonstrate the skills that you have learned. The information at EcoMed Services contains proprietary information, such as item costs and employee information; therefore, you have decided to create a new database that can be used at your school. You will start by creating the tables and structures.

1. Create a blank database named *[your initials]*-School to track students, courses, and instructors for a school similar to yours.

2. Create a new table named tblStudents. Use the following fields: StudentID, LastName, FirstName, MiddleInitial, Address, City, State, ZIP, and Phone. Determine the best data type and size (other than 255) for each field. Use StudentID as the primary key.

3. Create a new table named tblInstructors. Use these fields: InstructorID, LastName, and FirstName. Determine the best data type and size for each field. Use InstructorID as the primary key.

4. Create a new table named tblCourses. Use these fields: CourseID, CourseNum, Title, Days , StartTime, EndTime, Room, and InstructorID. Assume that courses are listed in the format "MATH 110 Freshman Algebra" with "MATH 110" as the course number, and "Freshman Algebra" as the course title. Determine the best data type and size for each field. Use CourseID as the primary key.

5. Create a new table named tblEnrollment. Use these fields: EnrollID, Yr, Semester, StudentID, and CourseID. Determine the best data type and size for each field. Use EnrollID as the primary key. Make CourseID a lookup field that will display the CourseNum from tblCourses and stores only the CourseID.

6. Show all tables in the Relationships window. Establish the appropriate relationships between tables. Enforce referential integrity and cascade update.

Assessment

- Continue to the next exercise.

- OR -

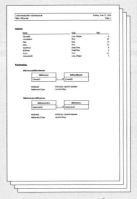

U4-01-A.pdf
4 Pages

- Create one **Database Documenter** report for all tables using the following settings:
  - Select all of the tables in the database
  - Include for Table: **Relationships**
  - Include for Fields: **Names, Data Types, and Sizes**
  - Include for Indexes: **Nothing**
- Save the **Documenter** report as a PDF file named *[your initials]-U4-01-A*.
- Continue to the next exercise.

Unit Application 4-2

Using the tables and relationships you made, create appropriate forms to display and enter data.

1. Create three forms named **frmStudents**, **frmInstructors**, and **frmCourses** that are based on tables of the same names. Each form should show only one record at a time, with the controls organized in a professional and functional layout.

2. Using the forms you created, add ten students, five instructors, and ten courses. Use data that are relevant to your school.

3. Create a main/subform for **tblStudents** and **tblEnrollment**. Name the forms **frmEnrollStudent** and **frmEnrollStudentSub**. The form should allow a student to enroll in multiple courses.

NOTE

Create appropriate queries when necessary.

4. Create a concatenated expression for the **City**, **State** and **ZIP** code data. Name the control **txtAddress2**. Organize the controls in a professional and functional layout.

5. Using **frmEnrollStudent**, enroll each student in at least two courses.

Assessment

- Continue to the next exercise.

- OR -

- Continue to the next exercise.

Unit Application 4-3

The next step is to create reports to support the needs of the school. The reports will need to be professionally designed, using groups. Command buttons will be added to forms to open these reports. Finally, create a navigation form to show the other forms in the database.

1. Create a grouped report showing all courses and all enrolled students enrolled in each course. Sort the courses and students in ascending order. Organize the controls in a professional and functional layout. Name the report **rptEnroll**.

2. Create a grouped report listing all instructors and the courses that they are scheduled to teach. Sort both courses and instructors in ascending order. Organize the controls in a professional and functional layout. Name the report **rptInstSchedule**.

3. Write a stand-alone macro that will open **rptEnroll** in Print Preview. Name the macro **mcrOpenRptEnroll**.

4. Write a stand-alone macro that will open **rptInstSchedule** in Print Preview. Name the macro **mcrOpenRptInstSchedule**.

5. Create a command button in **frmEnrollStudent** that will run **mcrOpenRptEnroll** when clicked. Create a command button in **frmInstructors** that will run **mcrOpenRptInstSchedule** when clicked.

6. Create a navigation form for your database. Name the form **frmNav**. Include a selection for each form. Set the navigation form to display automatically when the database opens.

Assessment

 - Continue to the next exercise.

- OR -

 - Continue to the next exercise.

Unit Application 4-4 ◆ Using the Web

Customize your database for your school by adding an image or logo of your school and a hyperlink to your school's Web site.

1. Locate your school's Web site. Download an image of your school or your school's logo.

NOTE

If your school does not have a Web site, inform students that they can substitute another school's site.

2. Insert your school's logo into the headers for each form and report in your database.

3. Add your name to the header for each form and report in your database.

4. Add a hyperlink to your school's Web site in the footer of **frmNav**.

Assessment

- According to your classroom procedure, turn in your database only when you have completed all assigned exercises.

- OR -

- Save the first page of each of the following forms:
  - **frmCourses** - Save as a PDF file named *[your initials]*-U4-04-A.
  - **frmEnrollStudent** - Save as a PDF file named *[your initials]*-U4-04-B.
  - **frmInstructors** - Save as a PDF file named *[your initials]*-U4-04-C.
  - **frmStudents** - Save as a PDF file named *[your initials]*-U4-04-D.
- Save the first page of **frmNav** with **frmCourses** showing as a PDF file named *[your initials]*-U3-01-E.
- Save the first page of **rptEnroll** as a PDF file named *[your initials]*-U3-01-F.
- Save the first page of **rptInstSchedule** as a PDF file named *[your initials]*-U3-01-G.
- Create a **Database Documenter** report for the macros using the following settings:
  - Select both macros for this one report
  - Include for Macro: **Actions and Arguments**
- Save the **Documenter** report as a PDF file named *[your initials]*-U3-01-H.

APPENDICES

Microsoft Certification Application Specialist

Lesson	Code	Activity
01	AC07 6.1.2	Back up databases
01	AC07 6.2.2	Configure database options
01	AC07 6.1.3	Compact and repair databases
01	AC07 3.2	Navigate among records
01	AC07 5.5	Save database objects as other file types
01	AC07 5.6	Print database objects
02	AC07 3.1	Enter, edit, and delete records
02	AC07 3.2	Navigate among records
02	AC07 3.4	Attach documents to and detach from records
02	AC07 5.5	Save database objects as other file types
02	AC07 5.6	Print database objects
03	AC07 5.1.1	Sort data within tables
03	AC07 5.2.1	Filter data within tables
03	AC07 5.1.2	Sort data within queries
03	AC07 5.2.2	Filter data within queries
03	AC07 5.1.3	Sort data within reports
03	AC07 5.2.3	Filter data within reports
03	AC07 5.1.4	Sort data within forms
03	AC07 5.2.4	Filter data within forms
03	AC07 2.3.5	Summarize table data adding a Total row
03	AC07 5.2.5	Remove filters
03	AC07 6.2.5	Print database information using the Database Documenter
03	AC07 3.3	Find and replace data
03	AC07 5.5	Save database objects as other file types
04	AC07 1.1.1	Define table fields
04	AC07 1.3.1	Define and modify primary keys
04	AC07 2.1.1	Create databases using templates
04	AC07 2.2.1	Create custom tables in Design View
04	AC07 2.3.1	Modify table properties
04	AC07 2.4.1	Create commonly used fields
04	AC07 3.5.1	Import data from a specific source

Lesson	Code	Activity
04	AC07 5.4.1	Export data from tables
04	AC07 1.1.2	Define appropriate table field data types for fields in each table
04	AC07 2.1.2	Create blank databases
04	AC07 2.2.2	Create tables by copying the structure of other tables
04	AC07 2.4.2	Modify field properties
04	AC07 5.4.2	Export data from queries
04	AC07 1.1.3	Define tables in databases
04	AC07 2.2.3	Create tables from templates
04	AC07 2.3.3	Rename tables
04	AC07 6.2.3	Set database properties
04	AC07 2.3.4	Delete tables
04	AC07 2.4.4	Create and modify attachment fields
05	AC07 1.2.1	Create relationships
05	AC07 1.2.2	Modify relationships
05	AC07 2.3.2	Evaluate table design using the Table Analyzer
05	AC07 1.2.3	Print table relationships
05	AC07 2.4.3	Create and modify multivalued fields
05	AC07 6.2.4	Identify object dependencies
06	AC07 4.1.1	Create queries based on single tables
06	AC07 4.2.1	Add tables to and remove tables from queries
06	AC07 4.1.2	Create queries based on more than one table
06	AC07 4.2.2	Add criteria to queries
06	AC07 4.1.4	Create crosstab queries
06	AC07 4.2.4	Create calculated fields in queries
06	AC07 4.2.5	Add aliases to query fields
06	AC07 4.2.6	Create sum, average, min, max, and count queries
07	AC07 2.7.1	Add controls
07	AC07 2.5.2	Create datasheet forms
07	AC07 2.7.2	Bind controls to fields
07	AC07 2.5.3	Create multiple item forms
07	AC07 2.7.3	Define the tab order of controls
07	AC07 2.5.4	Create split forms
07	AC07 2.7.4	Format controls

Lesson	Code	Activity
07	AC07 2.7.5	Arrange controls
07	AC07 5.5	Save database objects as other file types
07	AC07 5.6	Print database objects
07	AC07 2.5.7	Create forms using Layout View
07	AC07 2.7.7	Apply AutoFormats to forms and reports
07	AC07 2.5.8	Create simple forms
08	AC07 2.6.1	Create reports as a simple report
08	AC07 2.7.1	Add controls
08	AC07 2.6.2	Create reports using the Report Wizard
08	AC07 2.6.4	Define group headers
08	AC07 2.7.4	Format controls
08	AC07 2.6.5	Create aggregate fields
08	AC07 2.7.5	Arrange controls
08	AC07 2.6.6	Set the print layout
08	AC07 2.7.6	Apply and change conditional formatting on controls
08	AC07 2.6.7	Create labels using the Label Wizard
08	AC07 2.7.7	Apply AutoFormats to forms and reports
09	AC07 1.2.1	Create relationships
09	AC07 2.3.1	Modify table properties
09	AC07 1.2.2	Modify relationships
09	AC07 1.3.2	Define and modify multi-field primary keys
09	AC07 3.5.2	Link to external data sources
09	AC07 4.2.3	Create joins
09	AC07 6.2.6	Reset or refresh table links using the Linked Table Manager
09	AC07 3.1	Enter, edit, and delete records
10	AC07 4.1.1	Create queries based on single tables
10	AC07 4.2.1	Add tables to and remove tables from queries
10	AC07 4.1.2	Create queries based on more than one table
10	AC07 4.2.2	Add criteria to queries
10	AC07 4.1.3	Create action queries
10	AC07 4.2.4	Create calculated fields in queries
10	AC07 4.1.5	Create subqueries
10	AC07 4.1.6	Save filters as queries

Lesson	Code	Activity
10	AC07 4.2.6	Create sum, average, min, max, and count queries
11	AC07 2.5.1	Create forms by using Design View
11	AC07 2.7.1	Add controls
11	AC07 2.7.4	Format controls
11	AC07 2.5.5	Create subforms
11	AC07 2.7.5	Arrange controls
11	AC07 2.5.6	Create PivotTable forms
12	AC07 2.6.1	Create reports as a simple report
12	AC07 2.7.1	Add controls
12	AC07 2.6.2	Create reports using the Report Wizard
12	AC07 2.7.2	Bind controls to fields
12	AC07 2.6.3	Create reports using Design View
12	AC07 2.7.4	Format controls
12	AC07 2.5.5	Create subforms
12	AC07 2.6.6	Set the print layout
12	AC07 2.7.7	Apply AutoFormats to forms and reports
13	AC07 3.5.1	Import data from a specific source
13	AC07 5.4.1	Export data from tables
13	AC07 6.1.1	Open databases
13	AC07 6.2.1	Encrypt databases using passwords
13	AC07 5.4.2	Export data from queries
13	AC07 6.2.2	Configure database options
13	AC07 3.5.3	Save and run import specifications
13	AC07 5.4.3	Save and run export specifications
13	AC07 6.2.3	Set database properties
13	AC07 6.1.4	Save databases as a previous version
13	AC07 1.4	Split databases
14	AC07 2.7.1	Add controls
14	AC07 5.3.1	Create charts
14	AC07 5.3.2	Format charts
14	AC07 5.3.3	Change chart types
14	AC07 2.7.4	Format controls
14	AC07 2.7.5	Arrange controls
15	NONE	

Leszynski Naming Conventions

TABLE B-1 Prefixes for Major Objects – Leszynski Naming Conventions

Prefix	Object Type	Example
tbl	Table	tblEmployees
qry	Query	qrySuppliers
frm	Form	frmPayroll
rpt	Report	rptInventoryValue
mcr	Macro	mcrPreviewReport
bas	Module	basMyProgram

TABLE B-2 Prefixes for Control Objects – Leszynski Naming Conventions

Prefix	Object Type	Example
bof	Bound Object Frame	bofPhotos
cbo	Combo box	cboPaymentMethod
chk	Check box	chkCollate
cmd	Command button	cmdPrint
img	Image	imgEmployee
lbl	Label	lblEmployeeID
lin	Lines	linTitle
lst	List box	lstDepartments
opb	Option button	opbOrientation
opg	Option group	opgOrientation
pgb	Page Break	pgbNewPage
rct	Rectangles	rctBox
sbf	Sub Forms	sbfLineItems
sbr	Sub Reports	sbrSales
tgb	Toggle	tgbCollated
txt	Text box	txtEmployeeID
uof	Unbound Object Frame	uofLogo

TABLE B-3 Variable Names – Microsoft Standards

Prefix	Object Type	Example
bln	Boolean	blnContinue
cur	Currency	curSalary
dat	Date	datHire
dbl	Double	dblCompanySales
err	Error	errReport
int	Integer	intItemNumber
ing	Long	ingPopulation
rst	Recordset	rstEmployees
sng	Single	sngRoomSize
str	String	strName

TABLE B-4 Custom Input Masks

Symbol	Description
0	Digit (0 to 9, entry required)
9	Digit or space (entry optional)
#	Digit or space (entry optional; spaces are displayed as blanks while in Edit mode, but blanks are removed when data is saved)
L	Letter (A to Z, entry required)
?	Letter (A to Z, entry optional)
A	Letter or digit (A to Z, entry required)
a	Letter or digit (A to Z, entry optional)
&	Any character or a space (entry required)
C	Any character or a space (entry optional)
<	Causes all characters to be converted to lowercase
>	Causes all characters to be converted to uppercase
!	Causes the input mask to display from right to left, rather than from left to right
\	Causes the character that follows to be displayed as the literal character
"abc"	Displays exactly what is between the quotation marks
.,:; - /	Placeholders (decimal, thousand, date and time separators)
Password	Any character typed in the control is stored as the character but is displayed as an asterisk (*)

TABLE B-5 Custom Formats – Numbers and Currency

Symbol	Description
.(period)	Decimal separator
,(comma)	Thousand separator
"(double quotation)	Surrounds any text that you want users to see
0	Digit placeholder. Display a digit or 0
#	Digit placeholder. Display a digit or nothing
$	Display the literal character "$"
!	Forces left alignment
%	Percentage. The value is multiplied by 100 and a percent sign is appended
E− or e+	Scientific notation with a minus sign next to negative exponents and nothing next to positive exponents.
E− or e+	Scientific notation with a minus sign next to negative exponents and a plus sign next to positive exponents.

TABLE B-6 Custom Formats – Date and Time

Symbol	Description
:	Time separator
/	Date separator
c	Same as the General Date predefined format
d	Day of the month in one or two digits (1 to 31)
dd	Day of the month in two digits (01 to 31)
ddd	First three letters of the weekday (Sun to Sat)
dddd	Full name of the weekday (Sunday to Saturday)
ddddd	Same as the Short Date predefined format
dddddd	Same as the Long Date predefined format
w	Day of the week (1 to 7)
ww	Week of the year (1 to 53)
m	Month of the year in one or two digits (1 to 12)
mm	Month of the year in two digits (01 to 12)
mmm	First three letters of the month (Jan to Dec)
mmmm	Full name of the month (January to December)
q	Date displayed as quarter of the year (1 to 4)
y	Number of the day of the year (1 to 366)

continued

Symbol	Description
yy	Last two digits of the year (01 to 99)
yyyy	Full year (0100 to 9999)
h	Hour in one or two digits (0 to 23)
hh	Hours in two digits (00 to 23)
n	Minute in one or two digits (0 to 59)
nn	Minute in two digits (00 to 59)
s	Second in one or two digits (0 to 59)
ss	Second in two digits (00 to 59)
tttt	Same as the Long Time predefined format
AM/PM	Twelve-hour clock with the uppercase letters "AM" or "PM"
am/pm	Twelve-hour clock with the lowercase letters "am" or "pm"
A/P	Twelve-hour clock with the uppercase letters "A" or "P"
a/p	Twelve-hour clock with the lowercase letters "a" or "p"
[ ]	Stops resetting of seconds, minutes, hours, or days

TABLE B-7 Custom Formats – Text and Memo

Symbol	Description
@	Text character (either a character or a space) is required
&	Text character is not required
<	Force all characters to lowercase
>	Force all characters to uppercase

TABLE B-8 Number Field Size Settings

Setting	Stores Number From	Decimal Precision	Storage Size
Byte	0 to 255	(None)	1 byte
Integer	$-32,768$ to $+32,767$	(None)	2 bytes
Long Integer	$-2,147,483,648$ to $+2,147,483,647$	(None)	4 bytes
Single	-3.40×10^{38} to $+3.40 \times 10^{38}$	7	4 bytes
Double	-1.79×10^{308} to $+1.79 \times 10^{308}$	15	8 bytes
Decimal	-10^{28} to $+10^{28}$	28	12 bytes

TABLE B-9 Access 2007 Database Specifications

Attribute	Maximum
Access database (.accdb) file size	2 gigabytes
Number of objects in a database	32,768
Number of modules (including forms and reports modules)	1,000
Number of characters in an object name	64
Number of concurrent users	255

Best Practices for Designing a Database

Whenever you design a database, you should structure your activities. Most database designers follow the Systems Development Life Cycle (SDLC) method. Depending on the version of the SDLC used, a developer will complete five to seven phases beginning with an analysis phase and ending with a maintenance phase. At the conclusion of each phase, the developer will document findings, suggest possible solutions, estimate costs, meet with the client, and get written approval to continue to the next phase.

Regardless of the number of phases taken, documentation is crucial. In highly formalized business settings, the documentation follows prescribed formats that include authorization to continue to the next phase. For less formal settings, the documentation may be simplified.

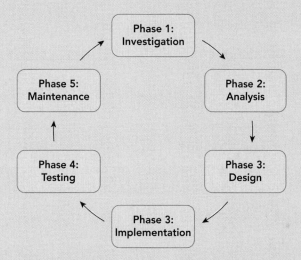

Phase 1: Investigation

Step 1: Meet with key personnel who use the system including data entry operators to management end users. Identify overall goals of project.

Step 2: If an automated system exists, review the internal and external documentation including user manuals, table structures, relationships, forms, reports and queries.

Step 3: If an automated system does not exist, review the procedures for the manual process.

Step 4: Document all findings. Estimate the time and cost it will take to develop a new system. Include costs for hardware and software, if necessary.

Step 5: Obtain authorization to continue to the analysis phase.

Phase 2: Analysis

Step 1: Interview system users to identify deficiencies in current system. Most often concerns will be noted in data entry procedures or report layouts.

Step 2: Interview key personnel to refine overall goals of project. Determine operational and fiscal limitations.

Step 3: Based upon interviews create report and input screen mockups of input screens and reports for the new system.

Step 4: Document all findings.

Step 5: Meet with decision maker(s) to review findings and mockups.

Step 6: Redesign reports and input screen mockups if necessary.

Step 7: Estimate the time and cost it will take to develop a new system.

Step 8: Obtain authorization to continue to the design phase.

Phase 3: Design

Step 1: Base upon mockups, create table structures.

Step 2: Create relationships and queries as necessary.

Step 3: Create operational and exception reports.

Step 4: Create input forms.

Step 5: Document database structure. If required, create user manual(s).

Step 6: Enter test data and verify that the new system is working properly.

Step 6: Meet with decision maker(s) to review prototype system.

Step 7: Obtain authorization to continue to the implementation phase.

Phase 4: Implementation

Step 1: Install hardware and software.

Step 2: Train end-user on use of new system.

Step 3: Document any changes that users may request.

Step 4: Meet with decision maker(s) to review requested changes.

Step 5: Obtain authorization to make changes and continue to the testing phase.

Phase 5: Testing

Step 1: Complete a full business cycle including, data input and report generation.

Step 2: Verify all input data are accurate. Verify that all information displayed on reports and forms are accurate.

Step 3: Interview system users and key personnel to identify inaccuracies.

Step 4: Document any changes that users may request.

Step 5: Meet with decision maker(s) to review requested changes.

Step 6: Obtain authorization to make changes and continue to the maintenance phase.

Phase 6: Maintenance

Step 1: Periodically interview system users and key personnel to identify desired changes or improvements to system.

Step 2: Estimate the time and cost it will take to develop a new system.

Step 3: Meet with decision maker(s) to review requested changes.

Step 4: Obtain authorization to make changes.

action query A query that performs an action such as append, update, delete or make a table. (10)

aggregate function A dynamic mathematical calculation that displays a single value for a specific field. (3) (6)

append query An action query that adds a group of records from one or more tables to the end of a table. (10)

argument A reference in a function assigned as a single variable. (6)

arithmetic operator A word or symbol that calculates a value from two or more numbers. (6)

AutoCorrect An application feature that automatically corrects commonly misspelled words. (2)

back color The color used for the background of an object. (11)

back-end database A database that contains data utilized by other applications. (13)

background image An image control that prints behind the controls of an object. (11)

bound control A control whose source of data is a field in a table or query. (7)

calculated control A control whose source of data is an expression, rather than a field. (7)

calculated field A field that uses an expression or formula as its data source. (6)

Cartesian product The combination of all possible ordered pairs from two components. (9)

clip mode An image view that shows the image at the size in which it was originally drawn or scanned. If the image is bigger than the control, the excess portion of the image is cut off. (12)

color builder An Access tool for selecting colors from a palette or creating custom colors. (12)

command button A control that when clicked executes an action or series of actions. (11)

command group A collection of logically organized commands. (1)

comparison operator A symbol or combination of symbols that specifies a comparison between two values. (6)

concatenate The operation of joining two or more character strings end to end. (6)

concatenated expression A text expression that joins two or more fields so that they appear to be one field. (12)

concatenation operator A symbol, word, group of symbols, or group of words used to combine two text values into a single text value. (6)

control A database object that displays data, performs actions, and lets you view and work with information that enhances the user interface, such as labels and images. (7)

control margin The specified location of information inside a control. (7)

control padding The space between the gridline of the form and the control. (7)

criterion A rule or test placed on a field. (3)

custom navigation pane A method of organizing major database objects along common activities and tasks. (13)

data integrity The condition through which data can be assumed to be accurate. (4)

database A logically organized collection of data. (1)

Database Documenter An Access tool used to display the indexes, properties, relationships, parameters, and permissions of major database objects. (3)

database template A ready-to-use database containing all the tables, queries, forms, and reports needed to perform a specific task. (4)

Datasheet View A screen view used to display data in rows and columns, similar to a spreadsheet. (1)

default picture An image that displays on a form whenever an image is not attached to a record. (14)

delete query An action query that deletes a group of records from one or more tables. (10)

delimited file A file in which all fields are separated by an identifiable character, such as a tab, semicolon, or comma. (13)

Design View A screen view used to modify the structure of a major object. (1)

dynaset A dynamic recordset that automatically reflects changes to its underlying data source. (6)

Edit Mode The mode in which changes to the content of a field can be made and the insertion point is visible. (1)

electronic data interchange The transfer of electronic data from one computer system to another. (4)

embedded macro A object macro occurring on a specific control in a form or report. (15)

error trap A procedure that tests for an error condition and provides a corresponding procedure to recover from the error. (15)

Expression Builder An interface used to create a function, calculation, or expression. (6)

field The smallest storage element that contains an individual data element within a record. (1)

filter A database feature that limits the number of records displayed. (3)

Filter by Selection A filter applied to a single field. (3)

fixed-width file A file in which each field starts at the same character position for each record. (13)

focus The status of a control that occurs when the control has the ability to receive user input through mouse or keyboard actions. (11)

foreign key A field that links to a primary key field in the related table. (5)

front-end database A database interface that integrates data stored in another database. (13)

function A procedure used in an expression. (6)

global chart A chart control that shows fields from more than one record. (14)

global join A relationship created through the Relationships window. (9)

hierarchal structure A method of classifying items or information according to criteria that place the items or information in successive levels or layers. (12)

hyperlink A navigation element pointer referencing an object from an external source. (14)

image control A photograph, picture, or graphic attached to a form or report. (12)

indeterminate relationship A relationship that occurs when Access does not have enough information to determine the relationship between the two tables. (5)

index A sort order used to identify records in a table. (9)

join table A table that contains common fields that are not primary keys from two tables that contain common fields that are primary keys. (9)

linked table A table that is stored outside the current database. (9)

list box A control showing choices in a box. (14)

local join A relationship created within a query. (9)

logical operator A symbol, word, group of symbols, or group of words used to construct an expression with multiple conditions. (6)

logo control An image control assigned to a specific control named Auto_Logo0. (11)

lookup field A field property that displays input choices from another table and allows these choices to be selected from a list. (5)

macro An object that completes an action or set of actions. (15)

macro condition A macro property that specifies criteria that must be met before an action executes. (15)

mail merge A word processing feature that creates a merged document by combining a source document and a record source from an external file. (13)

main form A form that contains a subform control. (11)

make-table query An action query that creates a new table from all or part of the data in one or more tables. (10)

module A collection of Visual Basic declarations and procedures stored together as a unit. (15)

navigation form A form that contains menus and command buttons, allowing a user to navigate around major database objects. (13)

Navigation Mode The mode in which an entire field is selected and the insertion point is not visible. (1)

normalization The process of restructuring a relational database for the purposes of organizing data efficiently, eliminating field redundancy, and improving data consistency. (5)

object dependency A condition in which an object requires the existence of another object. (5)

One-to-Many relationship A relationship that occurs when the common field is a primary key in the first table and not a primary key field in the second. (5)

One-To-One relationship A relationship that occurs when the common field is a primary key in the first table and a primary key field in the second. (5)

operator A word or symbol that indicates a specific arithmetic or logical relationship between the elements of an expression. (6)

option button A control identifying one choice. (14)

option group A control object bound to a single field containing of a set of controls representing choices. (14)

parameter query A query that prompts a user for a criterion when executed. (10)

PDF The file extension used by a Portable Document Format (PDF) for document exchange, originally created by Adobe Systems in 1993 and released as an open standard in 2008. (1)

PivotChart An interactive graphical representation of data displayed in a PivotTable. (6)

PivotTable An interactive table that combines and compares data in a summarized view. (6)

primary key A field or set of fields in a table that provides a unique identifier for every record. (4)

Print Preview A method for displaying on the screen how an object will appear if printed on paper. (2)

procedure A series of commands and properties that perform a specific task. (15)

record A complete set of related data about one entity or activity. (1)

record navigation button An icon that moves the pointer within a recordset to the next, previous, first, or last record. (1)

record-bound chart A chart control that shows data only from the current record. (14)

referential integrity A set of database rules for checking, validating, and keeping track of data entry changes in related tables. (5)

relationship A link or connection of a common field between two tables, two queries, or a table and a query. (5)

Relationship Report A graphical report showing related tables. Each created Relationship Report can be saved. (5)

Relationships window A visual interface that displays, creates, destroys, or documents relationships between tables, queries, or both. (5)

ScreenTip The name of or information regarding a specific object. (1)

select query A query that locates data from one or more tables. (10)

special operator   A symbol, word, group of symbols, or group of words used to express a relationship between two values. (6)

SQL (Structured Query Language)   A computer language designed to manipulate data in relational databases. (6)

stand-alone macro   A global macro that can be assigned to numerous objects. (15)

Stretch mode   An image view that sizes the image to fit the frame. (12)

subdatasheet   A datasheet linked within another datasheet. (5)

Subform   A form that is embedded in another form. (11)

submacro   A macro that contains two or more actions. (15)

subreport   A report that is embedded in another report. (12)

summary query   A query that shows aggregate values for a recordset. (10)

syntax   The set of rules by which the words and symbols in an expression are correctly combined. (12)

tab control   A control that defines a layered space on a form. (14)

table   A major database object that stores all data in a subject-based list of rows and columns. (1)

text file   A file that only contains unformatted textual characters. (13)

theme   A set of unified design elements and color schemes for bullets, fonts, horizontal lines, background images, and other elements of a database object. (7)

toggle button   A control that acts as an on/off button in a form or report. (14)

Trust Center   A dialog box that provides a single location to set security options for Access 2010. (13)

trusted location   A local or network folder on a workstation that a user marks as trusted. (13)

unbound control   A control without a source of data. (7)

update query   An action query that makes global changes to a group of records in one or more tables. (10)

Validation Rule   A condition specifying criteria for entering data into an individual field. (4)

Validation Text   An error message that appears when a value prohibited by the validation rule is entered. (4)

watermark   An image control that displays in the background of a page on a form or report. (12)

wildcard   A character or group of characters used to represent one or more alphabetical or numerical characters. (3)

XML file   An Extensible Markup Language text file that can store table names, field names, field properties, data types, and data. (13)

XPS   The file extension used by an XML Paper Specification (XPS) file format that preserves document formatting and enables file sharing of printable documents. (1)

zoom mode   An image view that sizes the image to fill either the height or width of the control. (12)